A THOMAS MERTON READER

Edited by THOMAS P. MC DONNELL

A Thomas Merton Reader

HARCOURT, BRACE & WORLD, INC., NEW YORK

M
248
ᵐᵉᵀ

This Book Is Dedicated to All My Friends

To the Old Ones and the New Ones

To Those Who Are Near and Those Who Are Far Away

To Those on Earth and Those in Heaven

To Those I Know and Those I Have Never Met

To Those Who Agree and Those Who Disagree

To Those I Have Never Heard of

In the Hope That We May All Meet in the One Light

THOMAS MERTON

FIRST AND LAST THOUGHTS: *An Author's Preface*

THIS BOOK is a selection from roughly twenty-five years of writing, most of which was done in a contemplative monastery. The texts, arranged as they are by Mr. Thomas P. McDonnell, the editor, in his carefully thought-out plan, cannot help but explain themselves. I have had the satisfaction of sharing to some extent in the selection, cutting, and correcting here and there, and even adding a few lines on occasion, in order to help this book to be in some sense a summing up of twenty-five years of thought.

In the course of this task I have naturally reflected on the implications of such a collection, and have attempted to take stock of the past purposes, the attempted articulations, the changes of perspective which it contains. It is doubtless fitting that the book ends, as it begins, with an excerpt from *The Seven Storey Mountain*. This is the early work which is now, as I hear, inflicted on school children and is therefore apparently considered most representative of its author. Doubtless it must be so.

Much that is spelled out in later books and articles is already implied in *The Seven Storey Mountain*. But it cannot really be seen until it is found in more articulate statements—or perhaps more cryptic ones, like *Atlas and the Fat Man*. There are essays and prose poems, for instance "Prometheus," "The Wisdom of the Desert," "Herakleitos," and "The Good Samaritan," which seem to me to be maturer efforts at saying what I mean.

Then, too, a long string of selections from *The Sign of Jonas* communicates something that could never be said in any other way. Texts on poetry, war, love, art, the psalms, monastic life and contemplation fill in the whole picture.

Not everything I would have liked to see in a *Reader* has finally succeeded in getting there. Unavoidable limitations have prevented this. But on the whole the book seems to me to be representative, and I am indebted to all those whose kind co-operation has made it possible.

Well, what is it that I have been trying to say? Certainly it would be a gross oversimplification to reduce it to the proposition that happiness is to be found (at least by some men) in the contemplative life: or that the contemplative life is vitally necessary, and that it has been unduly neglected in the modern world. This I would agree to, but to consider this my total message would be a misapprehension. And it would be a still greater misapprehension to say I am simply trying to prove that the contemplative life is "better than the active life," and that contemplative prayer is within the easy reach of everybody. Not only am I not trying to prove these propositions, but stated in this bald and unqualified manner, I do not even hold them. It is true that fifteen years ago I was able to get excited about such theses, but I have come to see that controversy about speculative matters of this sort is not only a waste of time but is seriously misleading. We are all too prone to believe in our own programs and to follow the echo of our own slogans into a realm of illusion and unreality.

Therefore I have lately tried to avoid writing simply as a propagandist for a particular cause or for a limited program. I am not merely a spokesman for a contemplative or monastic movement, and I am not purely and simply a "spiritual writer."

The earliest pieces of writing in this book are two book reviews done for the New York *Herald Tribune Books* in May of 1938. These were written when I was a graduate student at Columbia, about six months before my baptism into the Catholic Church. About three years later I entered the novitiate of the Cistercian Abbey of Gethsemani to become what is popularly called a "Trappist" Monk. There are a few poems here written when I was living in Greenwich Village and later when I was teaching English at St. Bonaventure College. But the vast majority of these pages were written at Gethsemani, and of these a very fair proportion represents work done in the last six years.

I would say that my life at Gethsemani has fallen roughly into four periods. First, the novitiate. I was a novice in 1942-1944. Those were hard years, before the days when radiators were much in favor during the winter, when the hours of communal prayer were much longer, when the fasts were much stricter. It was a period of training, and a happy, austere one, during which I wrote little. The best Gethsemani poems belong to this period.

At the end of the novitiate my health broke down and I was appointed to write and do translations of French books and articles. I was also studying philosophy and theology in preparation for ordination to the priesthood. This second period extends from 1944, my first vows, to ordination in 1949. At first the writing done was very bad. Two books were written which are *not* represented here, although they were unfortunately published. In 1946 I wrote *The Seven Storey Mountain,* in 1947 *Seeds of Contemplation,* and in 1948 *The Waters of Siloe.* After ordination, in 1949, there was another brief period of poor health and nervous exhaustion. I was almost incapable of writing for at least a year and a half after I became a priest. Then after a rest period in the hospital, I wrote *The Ascent to Truth* and *Bread in the Wilderness* (both about 1951) and finished *The Sign of Jonas,* 1952. In 1951 I was appointed the Master of the Scholastics, that is, of the young monks studying for ordination in the monastery. This entailed a fair amount of work preparing conferences and classes. Books like *The Living Bread* and particularly *No Man Is an Island* and *The Silent Life* belong to the end of this period.

Finally, a fourth stage. In 1955 I was made Master of the Choir Novices. This is an office involving considerable work and responsibility. No writing of any account was done in 1956, but after that it was possible to produce short books or collections of essays, and some poetry. *Disputed Questions, The Wisdom of the Desert, The Behavior of Titans,* and *New Seeds of Contemplation* belong to this last period. So too do more recent essays on nuclear war, on Chinese thought, on liturgy, and on solitude.

The books of the second period are the ones most widely known and read. The books and articles of the fourth period are, perhaps naturally, the ones that seem most significant to me. Maybe one reason for this is that, to me at least, they represent a successful attempt to escape the limitations that I inevitably created for myself with *The Seven Storey Mountain,* a refusal to be content with the artificial public image which this autobiography created.

I have had to accept the fact that my life is almost totally paradoxical. I have also had to learn gradually to get along without apologizing for the fact, even to myself. And perhaps this preface is an indication that I have not yet completely learned. No matter. It is in the paradox itself, the paradox which was and still is a source of insecurity, that I have come to find the greatest security. I have become convinced that the very contradictions in my life are in some ways signs of God's mercy to me:

if only because someone so complicated and so prone to confusion and self-defeat could hardly survive for long without special mercy. And since this in no way depends on the approval of others, the awareness of it is a kind of liberation.

Consequently I think I can accept the situation with simplicity. Paradoxically, I have found peace because I have always been dissatisfied. My moments of depression and despair turn out to be renewals, new beginnings. If I were once to settle down and be satisfied with the surface of life, with its divisions and its clichés, it would be time to call in the undertaker, except that in the monastery we do without the ministrations of an embalmer. So, then, this dissatisfaction which sometimes used to worry me and has certainly, I know, worried others, has helped me in fact to move freely and even gaily with the stream of life. My unspoken (or spoken) protests have kept me from clinging to what was already done with. When a thought is done with, let go of it. When something has been written, publish it, and go on to something else. You may say the same thing again, some day, on a deeper level. No one need have a compulsion to be utterly and perfectly "original" in every word he writes. All that matters is that the old be recovered on a new plane and be, itself, a new reality. This, too, gets away from you. So let it get away.

In other words, I have tried to learn in my writing a monastic lesson I could probably not have learned otherwise: to let go of my idea of myself, to take myself with more than one grain of salt. If the monastic life is a life of hardship and sacrifice, I would say that for me most of the hardship has come in connection with writing. It is possible to doubt whether I have become a monk (a doubt I have to live with), but it is not possible to doubt that I am a writer, that I was born one and will most probably die as one. Disconcerting, disedifying as it is, this seems to be my lot and my vocation. It is what God has given me in order that I might give it back to Him.

In religious terms, this is simply a matter of accepting life, and everything in life as a gift, and clinging to none of it, as far as you are able. You give some of it to others, if you can. Yet one should be able to share things with others without bothering too much about how they like it, either, or how they accept it. Assume they will accept it, if they need it. And if they don't need it, why should they accept it? That is their business. Let me accept what is mine and give them all their share, and go my way.

All life tends to grow like this, in mystery inscaped with paradox and contradiction, yet centered, in its very heart, on the divine mercy. Such is my philosophy, and it is more than philosophy—because it consists not in statements about a truth that cannot adequately be stated, but in grace, mercy, and the realization of the "new life" that is in us who believe, by the gift of the Holy Spirit. Without this gift we would have no philosophy, for we could never experience such simplicity in the midst of contradiction. Without the grace of God there could be no unity, no simplicity in our lives: only contradiction. We can overlay the contradiction with statements and explanations, we can produce an illusory coherence, we can impose on life our intellectual systems and we can enforce upon our minds a certain strained and artificial peace. But this is not peace.

Out of the false peace that is imposed by means of an arbitrary system comes nothing but further conflict, resentment, hatred, war. We live on the brink of disaster because we do not know how to let life alone. We do not respect the living and fruitful contradictions and paradoxes of which true life is full. We destroy them, or try to destroy them, with our obsessive and absurd systematizations. Whether we do this in the name of matter or in the name of spirit makes little difference in the end. There are atheists who fight God and atheists who claim to believe in Him: what they both have in common is the hatred of life, the fear of the unpredictable, the dread of grace, and the refusal of every spiritual gift.

Nor can I complacently say "they" and blame others as if I were not to blame. The evil is in us all. It is the blindness of a world that wants to end itself. It is the blindness from which we must pray with tears and anguish that we may be delivered. It is the blindness with which we must never cease to struggle as long as we are in the world. Those who give up the struggle are themselves in turmoil, and impose their turmoil on the whole human race. Those who continue to struggle are at peace. If God wills, they can pacify the world. For he who accepts the struggle in the name of Christ is delivered from its power by the victory of Christ.

My first and last words in this book are, then, to summarize whatever "witness" these pages may contain. When a man enters a monastery he has to stand before the community, and formally responds to a ritual question: *Quid petis?* "What do you ask?" His answer is not that he seeks a happy life, or escape from anxiety, or freedom from sin, or moral perfection, or the summit of contemplation. The answer is that he seeks *mercy.* "The mercy of God and of the Order." Whatever else it may do, this book should bear witness to the fact that I have found what I sought and continue to find it. The Order has been patient with me, God has been merciful to me, and more, countless readers have given me a gift of friendship and of love which is to me precious beyond estimation.

These readers sometimes write to me, and generally I am not able to reply. But here at least let me assure them of my gratitude, my love, and my prayers. They are in my silence, in my Mass, and in my solitude. I hope we will be together in Paradise.

CONTENTS

PART ONE

The
Unreal
City

What negligence, what delay is this?
  Run to the mountain and get rid of the slough
  which keeps you from seeing God.

One: PRISONER'S BASE

On THE LAST DAY OF JANUARY 1915, under the sign of the Water Bearer, in a year of a great war, and down in the shadow of some French mountains on the borders of Spain, I came into the world. Free by nature, in the image of God, I was nevertheless the prisoner of my own violence and my own selfishness, in the image of the world into which I was born. That world was the picture of hell, full of men like myself, loving God and yet hating Him; born to love Him, living instead in fear and hopeless self-contradictory hungers.

Not many hundreds of miles away from the house where I was born, they were picking up the men who rotted in the rainy ditches among the dead horses and the ruined seventy-fives, in a forest of trees without branches along the river Marne.

My father and mother were captives in that world, knowing they did not belong with it or in it, and yet unable to get away from it. They were in the world and not of it—not because they were saints, but in a different way: because they were artists. The integrity of an artist lifts a man above the level of the world without delivering him from it.

My father painted like Cézanne and understood the southern French landscape the way Cézanne did. His vision of the world was sane, full of balance, full of veneration for structure, for the relations of masses and for all the circumstances that impress an individual identity on each created thing. His vision was religious and clean, and therefore his paintings were without decoration or superfluous comment, since a religious man respects the power of God's creation to bear witness for itself. My father was a very good artist.

I inherited from my father his way of looking at things and some of his integrity and from my mother some of her dissatisfaction with the mess the world is in, and some of her versatility. From both I got capacities for work and vision and enjoyment and expression that ought to have made me some kind of a king, if the standards the world lives by were the real ones. Not that we ever had any money: but any fool knows that you don't need money to get enjoyment out of life.

If what most people take for granted were really true—if all you needed to be happy was to grab everything and see everything and investigate every experience and then talk about it, I should have been a very happy person, a spiritual millionaire, from the cradle even until now.

If happiness were merely a matter of natural gifts, I would never have entered a Trappist monastery when I came to the age of a man.

II

MY FATHER AND MOTHER came from the ends of the earth, to Prades, and though they came to stay, they stayed there barely long enough for me to be born and get on my small feet, and then they left again. And they continued and I began a somewhat long journey: for all three of us, one way and another, it is now ended.

And though my father came from the other side of the earth, beyond many oceans, all the pictures of Christchurch, New Zealand, where he was born, look like the suburbs of London, but perhaps a little cleaner. There is more sunlight in New Zealand, and I think the people are healthier.

My father's name was Owen Merton. Owen because his mother's family had lived for a generation or two in Wales, though I believe they were originally Lowland Scotch. And my father's father was a music master, and a pious man, who taught at Christ's College, Christchurch, on the South Island.

My father had a lot of energy and independence. He told me how it was in the hill country and in the mountains of the South Island, out on the sheep farms and in the forests where he had been, and once, when one of the Antarctic expeditions came that way, my father nearly joined it, to go to the South Pole. He would have been frozen to death along with all the others, for that was the one from which no one returned.

When he wanted to study art, there were many difficulties in his way, and it was not easy for him to convince his people that that was really his vocation. But eventually he went to London, and then to Paris, and in Paris he met my mother, and married her, and never went back to New Zealand.

My mother was an American. I have seen a picture of her as a rather slight, thin, sober little person with a serious and somewhat anxious and very sensitive face. And this corresponds with my memory of her—worried, precise, quick, critical of me, her son. Yet in the family she has always been spoken of as gay and very lighthearted. My grandmother kept great locks of Mother's red hair, after she died, and Mother's happy laughter as a boarding-school girl was what never ceased to echo in my grandmother's memory.

It seems to me, now, that Mother must have been a person full of insatiable dreams and of great ambition after perfection: perfection in art, in interior decoration, in dancing, in housekeeping, in raising children. Maybe that is why I remember her mostly as worried, since the imperfection of myself, her first son, had been a great deception.

III

MY FATHER CAME TO THE PYRENEES because of a dream of his own: more single, more concrete and more practical than Mother's numerous and haunting ideals of perfection. Father wanted to get some place where he could settle in France, and raise a family, and paint, and live on practically nothing, because we had practically nothing to live on.

Father and Mother had many friends at Prades, and when they had moved there, and had their furniture in their flat, and the canvasses piled up in the corner, and the whole place smelling of fresh oil paints and water color and cheap pipe tobacco and cooking, more friends came down from Paris. And Mother would paint in the hills, under a large canvas parasol, and Father would paint in the sun, and the friends would drink red wine and gaze out over the valley at Canigou, and at the monastery on the slopes of the mountain.

There were many ruined monasteries in those mountains. My mind goes back with great reverence to the thought of those clean, ancient stone cloisters, those low and mighty rounded arches hewn and set in place by monks who have perhaps prayed me where I now am. St. Martin and St. Michael the Archangel, the great patron of monks, had churches in those mountains. Saint Martin-du-Canigou; Saint Michel-de-Cuxa. Is it any wonder I should have a friendly feeling about those places?

One of them, stone by stone, followed me across the Atlantic a score of years later, and got itself set up within convenient reach of me when I most needed to see what a cloister looked like, and what kind of place a man might live in, to live according to his rational nature, and not like a stray dog. St. Michel-de-Cuxa is all fixed up in a special and considerably tidy little museum in an uptown park, in New York, overlooking the Hudson River, in such a way that you don't recall what kind of a city you are in. It is called The Cloisters. Synthetic as it is, it still preserves enough of its own reality to be a reproach to everything else around it, except the trees and the Palisades.

But when the friends of my father and mother came to Prades, they brought the newspapers, rolled up in their coat pockets, and they had many postcards carrying patriotic cartoons, representing the Allies overcoming the Germans. My grandparents—that is, my mother's father and mother in America—were worried about her being in a land at war, and it was evident that we could not stay much longer at Prades.

IV

THEN IN NOVEMBER 1918, about a week before the Armistice of that particular world war, my younger brother was born. He was a child with a much serener nature than mine, with not so many obscure drives and impulses. I remember that everyone was impressed by his constant and unruffled happiness. In the long evenings, when he was put to bed before the sun went down, instead of protesting and fighting, as I did when I had to go to bed, he would lie upstairs in his crib, and we would hear him singing a little tune. Every evening it was the same tune, very simple, very primitive; a nice little tune, very suitable for the time of day and for the season. Downstairs, we would all fall more or less silent, lulled by the singing of the child in the crib, and we would see the sunrays slanting across the fields and through the windows as the day ended.

I had an imaginary friend, called Jack, who had an imaginary dog, called Doolittle. The chief reason why I had an imaginary friend was that there were no other children to play with, and my brother John Paul was still a baby. When I tried to seek diversion watching the gentlemen who played pool at Mr. Duggan's saloon, I got into much trouble. On the other hand, I could go and play at Burroughs' place, in their garden and in the room full of old lumber over the studio. Betty Burroughs knew how to join in games in a way that did not imply patronage, though she was practically grown up. But for friends of my own age, I had to fall back on my imagination, and it was perhaps not a good thing.

Mother did not mind the company I kept in my imagination, at least to begin with, but once I went shopping with her, and refused to cross

Main Street, Flushing, for fear that the imaginary dog, Doolittle, might get run over by real cars. This I later learned from her record of the affair in her diary.

By 1920 I could read and write and draw. I drew a picture of the house, and everybody sitting under the pine trees, on a blanket, on the grass, and sent it to Pop in the mail. He lived at Douglaston, which was about five miles away. But most of the time I drew pictures of boats. Ocean liners with many funnels and hundreds of portholes, and waves all around as jagged as a saw, and the air full of "v's" for the sea gulls.

It seems strange that Father and Mother, who were concerned almost to the point of scrupulosity about keeping the minds of their sons uncontaminated by error and mediocrity and ugliness and sham, had not bothered to give us any formal religious training. The only explanation I have is the guess that Mother must have had strong views on the subject. Possibly she considered any organized religion below the standard of intellectual perfection she demanded of any child of hers. We never went to church in Flushing.

In fact, I remember having an intense desire to go to church one day, but we did not go. It was Sunday. Perhaps it was an Easter Sunday, probably in 1920. From across the fields, and beyond the red farmhouse of our neighbor, I could see the spire of St. George's church, above the trees. The sound of the churchbells came to us across the bright fields. I was playing in front of the house, and stopped to listen. Suddenly, all the birds began to sing in the trees above my head, and the sound of birds singing and churchbells ringing lifted up my heart with joy. I cried out to my father:

"Father, all the birds are in their church."

And then I said: "Why don't we go to church?"

My father looked up and said: "We will."

"Now?" said I.

"No, it is too late. But we will go some other Sunday."

And yet Mother did go somewhere, sometimes, on Sunday mornings, to worship God. I doubt that Father went with her; he probably stayed at home to take care of me and John Paul, for we never went. But anyway, Mother went to the Quakers, and sat with them in their ancient meeting house. This was the only kind of religion for which she had any use, and I suppose it was taken for granted that, when we grew older, we might be allowed to tend in that direction too. Probably no influence would have been brought to bear on us to do so. We would have been left to work it out more or less for ourselves.

Meanwhile, at home, my education was progressing along the lines laid down by some progressive method that Mother had read about in one of those magazines. She answered an advertisement that carried an oval portrait of some bearded scholar with a pince-nez, and received from Baltimore a set of books and some charts and even a small desk and blackboard. The idea was that the smart modern child was to be turned loose amid this apparatus, and allowed to develop spontaneously into a midget university before reaching the age of ten.

The ghost of John Stuart Mill must have glided up and down the room with a sigh of gratification as I opened the desk and began. I forget what came of it all, except that one night I was sent to bed early for stubbornly spelling "which" without the first "h": "w-i-c-h." I remember brooding about this as an injustice. "What do they think I am, anyway?" After all, I was still only five years old.

Still, I retain no grudge against the fancy method or the desk that went with it. Maybe that was where my geography book came from— the favorite book of my childhood. I was so fond of playing prisoner's base all over those maps that I wanted to become a sailor. I was only too eager for the kind of footloose and unstable life I was soon to get into.

My second best book confirmed me in this desire. This was a collection of stories called the *Greek Heroes*. It was more than I could do to read the Victorian version of these Greek myths for myself, but Father read them aloud, and I learned of Theseus and the Minotaur, of the Medusa, of Perseus and Andromeda. Jason sailed to a far land, after the Golden Fleece. Theseus returned victorious, but forgot to change the black sails, and the King of Athens threw himself down from the rock, believing that his son was dead. In those days I learned the name Hesperides, and it was from these things that I unconsciously built up the vague fragments of a religion and of a philosophy, which remained hidden and implicit in my acts, and which, in due time, were to assert themselves in a deep and all-embracing attachment to my own judgment and my own will and a constant turning away from subjection, towards the freedom of my own ever-changing horizons.

In a sense, this was intended as the fruit of my early training. Mother wanted me to be independent, and not to run with the herd. I was to be original, individual, I was to have a definite character and ideals of my own. I was not to be an article thrown together, on the common bourgeois pattern, on everybody else's assembly line.

If we had continued as we had begun, and if John Paul and I had grown up in that house, probably this Victorian-Greek complex would have built itself up gradually, and we would have turned into good-mannered and earnest skeptics, polite, intelligent, and perhaps even in some sense useful. We might have become successful authors, or editors of magazines, professors at small and progressive colleges. The way would have been all smooth and perhaps I would never have ended up as a monk.

V

MOTHER'S DEATH had made one thing evident: Father now did not have to do anything but paint. He was not tied down to any one place. He could go wherever he needed to go, to find subjects and get ideas, and I was old enough to go with him.

And so, after I had been a few months in the local school at Douglaston, and had already been moved up to the second grade, in the evil-smelling gray annex on top of the hill, Father came back to New York and announced that he and I were going somewhere new.

It was with a kind of feeling of triumph that I watched the East River widen into Long Island Sound, and waited for the moment when the Fall River boat, in all her pride, would go sweeping past the mouth of Bayside Bay and I would view Douglaston, as I thought, from the superiority of the open water and pass it by, heading for a new horizon called Fall River and Cape Cod and Provincetown.

We could not afford a cabin, but slept down below decks in the crowded steerage, if you could call it that, among the loud Italian families and the colored boys who spent the night shooting craps under the dim light, while the waters spoke loudly to us, above our heads, proclaiming that we were well below the waterline.

And in the morning we got off the boat at Fall River, and walked up the street beside the textile mills, and found a lunch wagon crowded with men getting something to eat on the way to work; and we sat at the counter and ate ham and eggs.

All day long after that we were in a train. Just before we crossed the great black drawbridge over the Cape Cod Canal, Father got off at a station and went to a store across the street and bought me a bar of Baker's chocolate, with a blue wrapper and a picture of a lady in an old-fashioned cap and apron, serving cups of chocolate. I was almost completely overwhelmed with surprise and awe at the fact of such tremendous largesse. Candy had always been strictly rationed.

Then came the long, long journey through the sand dunes, stopping at every station, while I sat, weary and entranced, with the taste of chocolate thick and stale in my mouth, turning over and over in my mind the names of places where we were going: Sandwich, Falmouth, Truro, Provincetown. The name Truro especially fascinated me. I could not get it out of my mind: Truro. Truro. It was a name as lonely as the edge of the sea.

That summer was full of low sand dunes, and coarse grasses as sharp as wires, growing from the white sand. And the wind blew across the sand. And I saw the breakers of the gray sea come marching in towards the land, and I looked out at the ocean. Geography had begun to become a reality.

Bermuda in those days had no big hotels and no golf courses to speak of. It was not famous for anything. It was simply a curious island, two or three days out of New York, in the Gulf Stream, where the British had a small naval base and where there were no automobiles and not much of anything else either.

We took a small boat called the *Fort Victoria,* with a red and black funnel, and surprisingly soon after we had left New York Harbor, the flying fishes began to leap out of the foam before her bows and skid along over the surface of the warm waves. And although I was very eager for my first sight of the island, it came upon us suddenly before I was aware, and stood up before us in the purple waters, green and white. You could already see the small white houses, made of coral, cleaner than sugar, shining in the sun, and all around us the waters paled over the shallows and became the color of emeralds where there was sand, or lavender where there were rocks below the surface. We threaded our way in a zigzag between the buoys that marked the path through the labyrinthine reefs.

The H.M.S. *Calcutta* lay at anchor off Ireland Island dockyard, and Father pointed to Somerset where, among the dark green cedars, was the place where we would live. Yet it was evening before we finally got there. How quiet and empty it was, in Somerset, in the gathering dusk! Our feet padded softly in the creamy dust of the deserted road. No wind stirred the paper leaves of the banana trees, or in the oleanders. Our voices seemed loud, as we spoke. It was a very friendly island. Those who occasionally came by saluted us as if we were old acquaintances.

The boardinghouse had a green verandah and many rocking chairs. The dark green paint needed renewing. The British officers, or whatever they were who lived in the place, sat and smoked their pipes, and talked, if they talked at all, about matters extremely profane. And here Father put down our bags. They were expecting us. In the shadows, we sat down to dinner. I quickly adjusted myself to the thought that this was home.

It is almost impossible to make much sense out of the continual rearrangement of our lives and our plans from month to month in my childhood. Yet every new development came to me as a reasonable and worthy change. Sometimes I had to go to school, sometimes I did not. Sometimes Father and I were living together, sometimes I was with strangers and only saw him from time to time. People came into our lives and went out of our lives. We had now one set of friends, now another. Things were always changing. I accepted it all. Why should it ever have occurred to me that nobody else lived like that? To me, it seemed as natural as the variations of the weather and the seasons. And one thing I knew: for days on end I could run where I pleased, and do whatever I liked, and life was very pleasant.

When Father left the boardinghouse, I remained there, and continued to live in it, because it was near the school. He was living in some other part of Somerset, with some people he had met, and he spent his days at work, painting landscapes. In fact, after that winter in Bermuda he had finished enough work to have an exhibition, and this made him enough money to go back to Europe. But meanwhile, I was going to the local school for white children, which was next to a large public cricket field, and I was constantly being punished for my complete inability to grasp the principles of multiplication and division.

It must have been very difficult for Father to try to make all these decisions. He wanted me to go to school, and he wanted me to be with him. When both these things ceased to be possible at the same time, he first decided in favor of the school: but then, after considering at length the nature of the place where I had to live, and the kind of talk I heard there, all day long, with my wide-open and impassive understanding, he took me out of the school, and brought me to live where he was. And I was very glad, because I was relieved of the burden of learning multiplication and long division.

The only worry was that my former teacher passed along that road on her bicycle on her way home, and if I was playing by the road, I had to get out of sight for fear that she would send the truant officer around and make me come back to school. One evening I did not see her coming, and I was a little late in diving into the bushes that filled a deserted quarry and, as I peeked out between the branches, I could see her looking back over her shoulder as she slowly pedaled up the white hill.

Day after day the sun shone on the blue waters of the sea, and on the islands in the bay, and on the white sand at the head of the bay, and on the little white houses strung along the hillside. I remember one day looking up into the sky, and taking it into my head to worship one of the clouds, which was shaped at one end like the head of Minerva with a helmet—like the head of the armed lady on the big British pennies.

VI

FATHER HELD his most successful exhibition at the Leicester Galleries early in 1925. When he returned to New York, in the early summer of that year, he came in a kind of triumph. He was beginning to be a successful artist. Long ago he had been elected to one of those more or less meaningless British societies, so that he could write F.R.B.A. after his name—which he never did—and I think he was already in *Who's Who*, although that was the kind of thing for which he had supreme contempt.

But now, what was far more useful to an artist, he had gained the attention and respect of such an important and venerable critic as Roger Fry, and the admiration of people who not only knew what a good painting was, but had some money with which to buy one.

As he landed in New York, he was a very different person—more different than I realized—from the man who had taken me to Bermuda two years before. All I noticed, at the moment, was the fact that he had a beard, to which I strenuously objected, being filled with the provincial snobbery so strong in children and adolescents.

"Are you going to shave it off now, or later?" I inquired, when we got to the house in Douglaston.

"I am not going to shave it off at all," said my father.

"That's crazy," I said. But he was not disturbed. He did shave it off, a couple of years later, by which time I had got used to it.

However, he had something to tell me that upset my complacency far more than the beard. For by now, having become more or less acclimatized in Douglaston, after the unusual experience of remaining some two years in the same place, I was glad to be there, and liked my friends, and liked to go swimming in the bay. I had been given a small camera with which I took pictures, which my uncle caused to be developed for me at the Pennsylvania Drug Store, in the city. I possessed a baseball bat with the word "Spalding" burnt on it in large letters. I thought maybe I would like to become a boy scout and, indeed, I had seen a great competition of boy scouts in the Flushing Armory, just next door to the Quaker meeting house where I had once got a glimpse of Dan Beard, with his beard.

My father said: "We are going to France."

"France!" I said, in astonishment. Why should anybody want to go to France? I thought, which shows that I was a very stupid and ignorant child. But he persuaded me that he meant what he said. And when all my objections were useless, I burst into tears. Father was not at all unsympathetic about it. He kindly told me that I would be glad to be in France, when I got there, and gave me many reasons why it was a good idea. And finally he admitted that we would not start right away.

With this compromise I was temporarily comforted, thinking perhaps the plan would be dropped after a while. But fortunately it was not. And on August the twenty-fifth of that year the game of Prisoner's Base began again, and we sailed for France. Although I did not know it, and it would not have interested me then, it was the Feast of St. Louis of France.

THE SEVEN STOREY MOUNTAIN

Two: OUR LADY OF THE MUSEUMS

I was tired, and fell asleep long before we got to Paris. I woke up long enough to be impressed by the welter of lights in the wet streets, and the dark sweep of the Seine, as we crossed one of the countless bridges, while far away the fires on the Eiffel tower spelled "C-I-T-R-O-Ë-N."

The words Montparnasse, Rue des Saint Pères, Gare d'Orléans filled my mind with their unmeaning, and spelled me no certitude concerning the tall gray houses, and the wide shady awnings of the cafés, and the trees, and the people, and the churches, and the flying taxis, and the green and white buses full of noise.

I did not have time, at the age of ten, to make anything out of this city, but already I knew I was going to like France: and then, once more, we were on a train.

That day, on that express, going into the south, into the Midi, I discovered France. I discovered that land which is really, as far as I can tell, the one to which I do belong, if I belong to any at all, by no documentary title but by geographical birth.

We flew over the brown Loire, by a long, long bridge at Orléans, and from then on I was home, although I had never seen it before, and shall never see it again. It was there, too, that Father told me about Joan of Arc, and I suppose the thought of her was with me, at least in the back of my mind, all the day long. Maybe the thought of her, acting as a kind of implicit prayer by the veneration and love it kindled in me, won me her intercession in heaven, so that through her I was able to get some sort of actual grace out of the sacrament of her land, and to contemplate God without realizing it in all the poplars along those streams, in all the low-roofed houses gathered about the village churches, in the woods and the farms and the bridged rivers. We passed a place called Châteaudun. When the land became rockier, we came to Limoges, with a labyrinth of tunnels, ending in a burst of light and a high bridge and a panorama of the city crowding up the side of a steep hill to the feet of the plain-towered cathedral. And all the time we were getting deeper and deeper into Aquitaine: toward the old provinces of Quercy and Rouergue, where, although we were not sure yet of our destination, I was to live and drink from the fountains of the Middle Ages.

In the evening we came to a station called Brive. Brive-la-Gaillarde. The dusk was gathering. The country was hilly, and full of trees, yet rocky, and you knew that the uplands were bare and wild. In the valleys were castles. It was too dark for us to see Cahors.

And then: Montauban.

What a dead town! What darkness and silence, after the train. We came out of the station into an empty, dusty square, full of shadows, and a dim light, here and there. The hoofs of a cabhorse clopped away along the empty street, taking some of the other people who had descended from the express off into the mysterious town. We picked up our bags and crossed the square to a hotel that was there, one of those low, undefined, gray little hotels, with a dim bulb burning in a downstairs window, illuminating a small café, with a lot of iron tables and a few calendars covered with fly specks and the big volumes of the Bottin crowding the rickety desk of the sour-faced lady in black who presided over the four customers.

And yet, instead of being dreary, it was pleasant. And although I had no conscious memory of anything like this, it was familiar, and I felt at home. Father threw open the wooden shutters of the room, and looked out into the quiet night, without stars, and said:

"Do you smell the woodsmoke in the air? That is the smell of the Midi."

II

WHEN WE WOKE UP in the morning, and looked out into the bright sunlit air, and saw the low tiled roofs, we realized that we had come upon a scene different from the last kind of landscape we had seen by the light of the previous evening in the train.

We were at the borders of Languedoc. Everything was red. The town was built of brick. It stood on a low bluff, over the clay-colored eddies of the river Tarn. We might almost have been in Spain. But oh! It was dead, that town!

Why were we there? It was not only that Father wanted to continue painting in the south of France. He had come back to us that year with more than a beard. Whether it was his sickness or what, I do not know, but something had made him certain that he could not leave the training and care of his sons to other people, and that he had a responsibility to make some kind of a home, somewhere, where he could at the same time carry on his work and have us living with him, growing up under his supervision. And, what is more, he had become definitely aware of certain religious obligations for us as well as for himself.

I am sure he had never ceased to be a religious man: but now—a thing which I did not remember from my earlier years—he told me to pray, to ask God to help us, to help him paint, to help him have a successful exhibition, to find us a place to live.

After the first day, it became clear that Montauban was no place for us. There was really nothing there worth painting. It was a good enough town, but it was dull. The only thing that interested Father was the Musée Ingres, filled with meticulous drawings by that painter, who had been born in Montauban: and that collection of cold and careful sketches was not enough to keep anyone at a high pitch of inspiration for much more than fifteen minutes. More characteristic of the town was a nightmarish bronze monument by Bourdelle, outside the museum, which seemed to represent a group of cliff dwellers battling in a mass of molten chocolate.

However, when we happened to inquire at the Syndicat d'Initiative about places to live, we saw photographs of some little towns which, as we were told, were in a valley of a river called the Aveyron not very far away to the northeast of the city.

The afternoon we took the peculiar, antiquated train out of Montauban into the country, we felt something like the three Magi after leaving Herod and Jerusalem when they caught sight once again of their star.

The locomotive had big wheels and a low, squat boiler, and an inordinately high smokestack, so that it seemed to have escaped from the museum, except that it was very sturdy and did its work well. And the three or four little coaches sped us quickly into a territory that was certainly sacramental.

The last town that had a brick campanile to its church, after the manner of all Languedoc, was Montricoux. Then the train entered the

Aveyron valley. After that, we were more or less in Rouergue. And then we began to see something.

I did not realize what we were getting into until the train swept around a big curve of the shallow river, and came to stop under the sunny plane trees along the platform of a tiny station, and we looked out the window, and saw that we had just passed along the bottom of a sheer cliff one or two hundred feet high, with a thirteenth-century castle on the top of it. That was Bruniquel. All around us, the steep hills were thick with woods, small gnarled oaks, clinging to the rock. Along the river, the slender poplars rippled with the light of late afternoon, and green waters danced on the stones. The people who got on and off the train were peasants with black smocks, and on the roads we saw men walking beside teams of oxen, drawing their two-wheeled carts: and they guided the placid beasts with their long sticks. Father told me that the people were all talking, not French, but the old patois, *langue d'oc.*

The next place was Penne. At the meeting of two valleys, a thin escarpment of rock soared up boldly over the river, bent and sharply rising, like an open wing. On the top were the ruins of another castle. Further down, straggling along the ridge, went the houses of the village and somewhere among them the small square tower of a church, an open iron belfry on top, with a visible bell.

The valley seemed to get narrower and deeper as the train followed its narrow single track between the river and the rocks. Sometimes there was enough space between us and the river to contain a small hayfield. Occasionally a deserted dirt road or cattle track would cross our way, and there would be a house and a crossing gate and one of those furious French bells, throwing the sudden scare of its clangor through the windows of the carriage as we passed by.

The valley widened a little to contain the village of Cazals, hanging on to the foot of the hill across the river, and then we were back in the gorge. If you went to the window and looked up, you could see the gray and yellow cliffs towering up so high they almost blocked out the sky. And now we could begin to distinguish caves high up on the rock. Later I would climb up there and visit some of them. Passing through tunnel after tunnel, and over many bridges, through bursts of light and greenery followed by deep shadow, we came at last to the town of our destination.

It was an old, old town. Its history went back to the Roman days— which were the times of the martyred saint, its patron. Antoninus had brought Christianity to the Roman colony in this valley, and later he had been martyred in another place, Pamiers, down in the foothills of the Pyrenees, near Prades, where I was born.

Even in 1925, St. Antonin preserved the shape of a round, walled *bourg*: only the walls themselves were gone, and were replaced on three sides by a wide circular street lined with trees and spacious enough to be called a Boulevard, although you hardly ever saw anything on it but oxcarts and chickens. The town itself was a labyrinth of narrow streets, lined by old thirteenth-century houses, mostly falling into ruins. Nevertheless, the medieval town was there, but for the fact that the streets were no longer crowded and busy, and the houses and shops were no longer occupied by prosperous merchants and artisans, and there was nothing left of the color and gaiety and noise of the Middle Ages. Nevertheless, to walk through those streets was to be in the Middle Ages: for nothing had been touched by man, only by ruin and by the passage of time.

It seems that one of the busiest guilds of the town had been that of the tanners and the old tanneries were still there, along a narrow foul-smelling sewer of a stream that ran through a certain section of the town. But in those old days the whole place had been filled with the activity of all the work belonging to a free and prosperous commune.

And as I say, the center of it all was the church.

Unfortunately, the very importance of the ancient shrine of St. Antonin had drawn down violence upon it in the days of the religious wars. The church that now stood on the ruins was entirely modern, and we could not judge what the old one had been like, or see, reflected in its work and construction, the attitude of the citizens who had built it. Even now, however, the church dominated the town, and each morning, noon, and evening sent forth the Angelus bells over the brown, ancient tiled roofs reminding people of the Mother of God who watched over them.

And even now, although I never thought of it and was, indeed, incapable of doing so, since I had no understanding of the concept of Mass, even now, several times each morning, under those high arches, on the altar over the relics of the martyr, took place that tremendous, secret, and obvious immolation, so secret that it will never be thoroughly understood by a created intellect, and yet so obvious that its very obviousness blinds us by excess of clarity: the unbloody Sacrifice of God under the species of bread and wine.

Here, in this amazing, ancient town, the very pattern of the place, of the houses and streets and of nature itself, the circling hills, the cliffs and trees, all focused my attention upon the one, important central fact of the church and what it contained. Here, everywhere I went, I was forced, by the disposition of everything around me, to be always at least virtually conscious of the church. Every street pointed more or less inward to the center of the town, to the church. Every view of the town, from the exterior hills, centered upon the long gray building with its high spire.

The church had been fitted into the landscape in such a way as to become the keystone of its intelligibility. Its presence imparted a special form, a particular significance to everything else that the eye beheld, to the hills, the forests, the fields, the white cliff of the Rocher d'Anglars and to the red bastion of the Roc Rouge, to the winding river, and the green valley of the Bonnette, the town and the bridge, and even to the white stucco villas of the modern bourgeois that dotted the fields and orchards outside the precinct of the vanished ramparts: and the significance that was thus imparted was a supernatural one.

The whole landscape, unified by the church and its heavenward spire, seemed to say: this is the meaning of all created things: we have been made for no other purpose than that men may use us in raising themselves to God, and in proclaiming the glory of God. We have been fashioned, in all our perfection, each according to his own nature, and all our natures ordered and harmonized together, that man's reason and his love might fit in this one last element, this God-given key to the meaning of the whole.

III

IN THOSE DAYS the whole south of France was infected with a furious and violent passion for rugby football, and played it with a bloodthirsty energy that sometimes ended in mortal injuries. In the really important games, the referee usually had to be escorted from the grounds afterward by a special bodyguard, and not infrequently had to make his escape over the fence and through the fields. The only sport that raised a more universal and more intense excitement than rugby, was long-distance bicycle racing. St. Antonin was off the circuit of the big road races, but occasionally there would be a race that came through our hills, and we would stand at the end of the long climb to the top of Rocher d'Anglars, and watch them coming slowly up the hill, with their noses almost scraping the front wheels of their bikes as they bent far down and toiled, with all their muscles clenched into tremendous knots. And the veins stood out on their foreheads.

One of the members of the rugby team was a small, rabbitlike man, the son of the local hay and feed dealer, who owned a car and drove most of the team back and forth from the games. One night he nearly killed himself and about six of us when a rabbit got into the lights on the road ahead of us and kept running in front of the car. Immediately, this wild Frenchman jammed his foot down on the gas and started after the rabbit. The white tail bobbed up and down in the light, always just a few feet ahead of the wheels, and whipping from one side of the road to the other, to throw the auto off his scent: only the auto didn't hunt that way. It just kept roaring after the rabbit, zigzagging from one side of the road to the other and nearly spilling us all into the ditch.

Those of us who were piled up in the back seat began to get a little nervous, especially when we observed that we were coming to the top of the long steep hill that went winding down into the valley where St. Antonin was. If we kept after that rabbit, we would surely go over the bank, and then we wouldn't stop turning over until we landed in the river, a couple of hundred feet below.

Somebody growled a modest complaint:

"*C'est assez, hein? Tu ne l'attraperas pas!*"

The son of the hay and feed dealer said nothing. He bent over the wheel with his eyes popping at the road, and the white tail in front of us kept darting away from the wheels of the car, zigzagging from the high bank on one side to the ditch on the other.

And then we came over the hill. The darkness and emptiness of the valley was before us. The road began to descend.

The complaints in the back seat increased, became a chorus. But the driver stepped on the gas even harder. The car careened wildly across the road; we had nearly caught the rabbit. But not quite. He was out there ahead of us again.

"We'll get him on the hill," exclaimed the driver. "Rabbits can't run downhill, their hind legs are too long."

The rabbit ahead of us was doing a fine job of running downhill, just about five feet ahead of our front wheels.

Then somebody began to yell: "Look out, look out!"

We were coming to a fork in the road. The main road went on to the left, and an older road sloped off at a steeper incline to the right.

In between them was a wall. And the rabbit headed straight for the wall.

"Stop! Stop!" we implored. Nobody could tell which way the rabbit was going to go: and the wall was flying straight at us.

"Hold on!" somebody shouted.

The car gave a wild lurch, and if there had been any room in the back we would all have fallen on the floor. But we were not dead. The car was still on the main road, roaring down into the valley and, to our immense relief, there was no rabbit, out there in the lights.

"Did you catch him?" I asked hopefully. "Maybe you caught him back there?"

"Oh, no," replied the driver sadly, "he took the other road."

Our friend the teamster Pierrot was a huge, powerful man, but he did not play on the football team. He was too lazy and too dignified, although he would have been a decorative addition to the outfit. There were three or four others like him, big men with huge black mustaches and bristling eyebrows, as wild as the traditional representations of Gog and Magog. One of them used to play whole games wearing a gray, peaked streetcap. I suppose if we had ever played on a really hot day he would have come out on the field with a straw hat on. Anyway, this element of the team would have made a fine subject for Douanier-Rousseau, and Pierrot would have fitted in admirably. Only his sport was sitting at the table of a café imbibing cognac. Sometimes, too, he made excursions to Toulouse, and once, while we were standing on the bridge, he gave me a blood-curdling description of a fight he had had with an Arab, with a knife, in the big city.

THE SEVEN STOREY MOUNTAIN

Three: AT SCHOOL IN ENGLAND

✧ OAKHAM

Oakham, oakham! The gray murk of the winter evenings in that garret where seven or eight of us moiled around in the gaslight, among the tuckboxes, noisy, greedy, foul-mouthed, fighting and shouting! There was one who had a ukulele which he did not know how to play. And Pop used to send me the brown rotogravure sections of the New York Sunday papers, and we would cut out the pictures of the actresses and paste them up on the walls.

I toiled with Greek verbs. And we drank raisin wine and ate potato chips until we fell silent and sat apart, stupefied and nauseated. And under the gaslight I would write letters to Father in the hospital, letters on cream-colored notepaper, stamped with the school crest in blue.

After three months it was better. I was moved up into the Upper Fifth, and changed to a new study downstairs, with more light, though just as crowded and just as much of a mess. And we had Cicero and European history—all about the nineteenth century, with a certain amount of cold scorn poured on Pio Nono. In the English class we read *The Tempest* and the *Nun's Priest's Tale* and the *Pardoner's Tale,* and the school chaplain tried to teach us trigonometry. With me, he failed. Sometimes he would try to teach us something about religion. But in this he also failed.

As long as I was among the fourteen- and fifteen-year-olds in Hodge Wing, I had to mind my behavior with the lords of the school, or at least in their presence. We were disciplined by the constant fear of one of those pompous and ceremonious sessions of bullying, arranged with ritualistic formality, when a dozen or so culprits were summoned into one of the hollows around Brooke hill, or up the Braunston road, and beaten with sticks, and made to sing foolish songs and to hear themselves upbraided for their moral and social defects.

When I got into the sixth form, which I did after a year, I came more directly under the influence and guidance of the new headmaster, F. C. Doherty. He was a young man for a headmaster, about forty, tall, with a great head of black hair, a tremendous smoker of cigarettes and a lover of Plato. Because of the cigarettes, he used to like to give his class in his own study, when he decently could, for there he could smoke one after another, while in the classrooms he could not smoke at all.

He was a broad-minded man, and I never realized how much I owed to him until I left Oakham. If it had not been for him, I would probably have spent years in the fifth form trying to pass the School Certificate in mathematics. He saw that I could far easier pass the Higher Certificate, specializing in French and Latin where, although the examination in these subjects would be very hard, there would be no maths. And the Higher Certificate meant far more than the other. It was he who began, from the start, to prepare me for the university, getting me to aim at a Cambridge scholarship. And it was he who let me follow the bent of my own mind, for modern languages and literature, although that meant that I spent much of my time studying alone in the library, since there was no real "modern" course at Oakham at that time.

I had several different masters in the one hour a week devoted to religious instruction (outside of the daily chapel). The first one just plodded through the third Book of Kings. The second, a tough little Yorkshireman, who had the virtue of being very definite and outspoken in everything he said, once exposed to us Descartes' proof of his own and God's existence. He told us that as far as he was concerned, that was the foundation of what religion meant to him. I accepted the *Cogito ergo sum* with less reserve than I should have, although I might have had enough sense to realize that any proof of what is self-evident must necessarily be illusory. If there are no self-evident first principles, as a foundation for reasoning to conclusions that are not immediately apparent, how can you construct any kind of a philosophy? If you have to prove even the basic axioms of your metaphysics, you will never have a metaphysics, because you will never have any strict proof of anything, for your first proof will involve you in an infinite regress, proving that you are proving what you are proving and so on, into the exterior dark-

ness where there is wailing and gnashing of teeth. If Descartes thought
it was necessary to prove his own existence, by the fact that he was
thinking, and that his thought therefore existed in some subject, how
did he prove that he was thinking in the first place? But as to the second step, that God must exist because Descartes had a clear idea of
him—that never convinced me, then or at any other time, or now either.

II

I WAS NOW A HOUSE PREFECT in Hodge Wing with a great big study
and a lot of slightly lopsided wicker armchairs full of cushions. On the
walls I hung Medici prints of Manet and some other impressionists and
photographs of various Greco-Roman Venuses from museums in Rome.
And my bookshelf was full of a wide variety of strange bright-colored
novels and pamphlets, all of which were so inflammatory that there
would never be any special need for the Church to put them on the
Index, for they would all be damned *ipso jure*—most of them by the
natural law itself. I will not name the ones I remember, because some
fool might immediately go and read them all: but I might mention that
one of the pamphlets was Marx's *Communist Manifesto*—not because
I was seriously exercised about the injustices done to the working class,
which were and are very real, but were too serious for my empty-headed
vanity—but simply because I thought it fitted in nicely with the *décor*
in which I now moved in all my imaginings.

For it had become evident to me that I was a great rebel. I fancied
that I had suddenly risen above all the errors and stupidities and mistakes of modern society—there are enough of them to rise above, I admit
—and that I had taken my place in the ranks of those who held up
their heads and squared their shoulders and marched into the future.
In the modern world, people are always holding up their heads and
marching into the future, although they haven't the slightest idea what
they think the "future" is or could possibly mean. The only future we
seem to walk into, in actual fact, is full of bigger and more terrible wars,
wars well calculated to knock our upraised heads off those squared
shoulders.

Here in this study I edited the school magazine which had fallen
into my hands that autumn, and read T. S. Eliot, and even tried to
write a poem myself about Elpenor, in Homer, getting drunk and falling off the roof of a palace. And his soul fled into the shades of hell.
And the rest of the time I played Duke Ellington's records or got into
arguments about politics and religion.

All those vain and absurd arguments! My advice to an ordinary religious man, supposing anyone were to desire my advice on this point, would be to avoid all arguments about religion, and especially about the existence of God. However, to those who know some philosophy I would recommend the study of Duns Scotus' proofs for the actual existence of an Infinite Being, which are given in the Second Distinction of the First Book of the *Opus Oxoniense*—in Latin that is hard enough to give you many headaches. It is getting to be rather generally admitted that, for accuracy and depth and scope, this is the most perfect and complete and thorough proof for the existence of God that has ever been worked out by any man.

I doubt if it would have done much good to bring these considerations before me in those days, when I was just turning seventeen, and thought I knew all about philosophy without ever having learned any. However, I did have a desire to learn. I was attracted to philosophy. It was an attraction the headmaster had worked hard to implant in our souls: but there was, and could be, no course in philosophy at Oakham. I was left to my own devices.

I remember once mentioning all this to Tom, my guardian. We were walking out of his front door, into Harley Street, and I told him of my desire to study philosophy, and to know the philosophers.

He, being a doctor, told me to leave philosophy alone: there were few things, he told me, that were a greater waste of time.

Fortunately, this was one of the matters in which I decided to ignore his advice. Anyway, I went ahead and tried to read some philosophy. I never got very far with it. It was too difficult for me to master all by myself. People who are immersed in sensual appetites and desires are not very well prepared to handle abstract ideas. Even in the purely natural order, a certain amount of purity of heart is required before an intellect can get sufficiently detached and clear to work out the problems of metaphysics. I say a certain amount, however, because I am sure that no one needs to be a saint to be a clever metaphysician. I dare say there are plenty of metaphysicians in hell.

However, the philosophers to whom I was attracted were not the best. For the most part, I used to take their books out of libraries, and return them without ever having opened them. It was just as well. Nevertheless, during the Easter vacation, when I was seventeen, I earnestly and zealously set about trying to figure out Spinoza.

I had gone to Germany, by myself as usual, for the vacation. In Cologne I had bought a big rucksack and slung it over my shoulders and started up the Rhine Valley on foot, in a blue jersey and an old pair of flannel bags, so that people in the inns along the road asked me if I was a Dutch sailor off one of the river barges. In the rucksack, which was already heavy enough, I had a couple of immoral novels and the Everyman Library edition of Spinoza. Spinoza and the Rhine Valley! I certainly had a fine sense of appropriateness. The two go very well together. However I was about eighty years too late. And the only thing that was lacking was that I was not an English or American student at Heidelberg: then the mixture would have been perfect in all its mid-nineteenth-century ingredients.

I picked up more, on this journey, than a few intellectual errors, half understood. Before I got to Koblenz, I had trouble in one foot. Some kind of an infection seemed to be developing under one of the toenails. But it was not especially painful, and I ignored it. However, it made walking unpleasant, and so, after going on as far as St. Goar, I gave up in disgust. Besides, the weather had turned bad, and I had got lost in the forest, trying to follow the imaginary hiker's trail called the Rhein-höhenweg.

I went back to Koblenz, and sat in a room over a big beer hall called the Neuer Franziskaner and continued my desultory study of Spinoza and my modern novelists. Since I understood the latter much better than the philosopher, I soon gave him up and concentrated on the novels.

◈ CAMBRIDGE

ANDREW WAS THE SON of a country parson in the Isle of Wight and he had been cricket captain at Oakham. He wore horn-rimmed spectacles and had a great chin that he held up in the air, and a lock of black hair fell down over his forehead, and he was one of the school intellectuals. He and I used to work, or rather sit, in the library at Oakham, with many books open before us, but talking about impertinent matters and drinking a foul purple concoction called Vimto out of bottles which we concealed under the table or behind the volumes of the Dictionary of National Biography.

He had discovered a black book called, as I think, *The Outline of Modern Knowledge,* which was something that had just come to the library and was full of information about psychoanalysis. Indeed, it went into some details of psychoanalytical fortunetelling by the inspection of feces which I never ran into anywhere else, and which I still preserved enough sense to laugh at, at that time. But later, at Cambridge, psychoanalysis was to provide me with a kind of philosophy of life and even a sort of pseudo-religion which was nearly the end of me altogether. By that time, Andrew himself had lost interest in it.

When we went up to the university, to sit for the scholarship exam, in the dank heavy-hanging mists of December, I spent most of the time between papers devouring D. H. Lawrence's *Fantasia of the Unconscious*, which, even as psychoanalysis, is completely irresponsible and, just as it says, a fantasia. Lawrence picked up a lot of terms like "lumbar ganglion" and threw them all together and stewed them up with his own worship of the sex instinct to produce the weird mixture which I read as reverently as if it were some kind of sacred revelation, sitting in the rooms of an undergraduate who liked Picasso, but who had gone down for the Christmas vacation. Andrew, for his part, was at St. Catherine's, terrified of a tutor who had a reputation for being a very ferocious person. All that week I sat under the high, silent rafters of the Hall, at Trinity College, and covered long sheets of foolscap with my opinions concerning Molière and Racine and Balzac and Victor Hugo and Goethe and Schiller and all the rest, and a few days after it was all over, we looked in the *Times* and this time both Andrew and I had succeeded. We were exhibitioners, he at St. Catherine's and I at Clare, while his studymate, Dickens, who was the only other person at Oakham besides myself who liked hot records, had another exhibition at St. John's.

THE SEVEN STOREY MOUNTAIN

Four: PASSAGE

THE EUROPE I FINALLY LEFT for good, in the late November of 1934, was a sad and unquiet continent, full of forebodings.

Of course, there were plenty of people who said: "There will not be a war. . . ." But Hitler had now held power in Germany for some time, and that summer all the New York evening papers had been suddenly filled with the news of Dollfuss' murder in Austria, and the massing of Italian troops on the Austrian borders. It was one of the nights when I was down at Coney Island, with Reginald Marsh, and I walked in the whirl of lights and noise and drank glasses of thin, icy beer, and ate hotdogs full of mustard, and wondered if I would soon be in some army or other, or perhaps dead.

It was the first time I had felt the cold steel of the war scare in my vitals. There was a lot more to come. It was only 1934.

And now, in November, when I was leaving England forever—the ship sailed quietly out of Southampton Water by night—the land I left behind me seemed silent with the silence before a storm. It was a land all shut up and muffled in layers of fog and darkness, and all the people were in the rooms behind the thick walls of their houses, waiting for the first growl of thunder as the Nazis began to warm up the motors of a hundred thousand planes.

Perhaps they did not know they were waiting for all this. Perhaps they thought they had nothing better to occupy their minds than the wedding of Prince George and Princess Marina which had taken place the day before. Even I myself was more concerned with the thought of some people I was leaving than with the political atmosphere at that precise moment. And yet that atmosphere was something that would not allow itself to be altogether ignored.

I had seen enough of the things, the acts and appetites, that were to justify and to bring down upon the world the tons of bombs that would someday begin to fall in millions. Did I know that my own sins were enough to have destroyed the whole of England and Germany? There has never yet been a bomb invented that is half so powerful as one mortal sin—and yet there is no positive power in sin, only negation, only annihilation: and perhaps that is why it is so destructive, it is a nothingness, and where it is, there is nothing left—a blank, a moral vacuum.

It is only the infinite mercy and love of God that has prevented us from tearing ourselves to pieces and destroying His entire creation long ago. People seem to think that it is in some way a proof that no merciful God exists, if we have so many wars. On the contrary, consider how in spite of centuries of sin and greed and lust and cruelty and hatred and avarice and oppression and injustice, spawned and bred by the free wills of men, the human race can still recover, each time, and can still produce men and women who overcome evil with good, hatred with love, greed with charity, lust and cruelty with sanctity. How could all this be possible without the merciful love of God, pouring out His grace upon us? Can there be any doubt where wars come from and where peace comes from, when the children of this world, excluding God from their peace conferences, only manage to bring about greater and greater wars the more they talk about peace?

We have only to open our eyes and look about us to see what our sins are doing to the world, and have done. But we cannot see. We are the ones to whom it is said by the prophets of God: "Hearing hear, and understand not; and see the vision, and know it not."

There is not a flower that opens, not a seed that falls into the ground, and not an ear of wheat that nods on the end of its stalk in the wind that does not preach and proclaim the greatness and the mercy of God to the whole world.

There is not an act of kindness or generosity, not an act of sacrifice done, or a word of peace and gentleness spoken, not a child's prayer uttered, that does not sing hymns to God before His throne, and in the eyes of men, and before their faces.

How does it happen that in the thousands of generations of murderers since Cain, our dark bloodthirsty ancestor, that some of us can still be saints? The quietness and hiddenness and placidity of the truly good people in the world all proclaim the glory of God.

All these things, all creatures, every graceful movement, every ordered act of the human will, all are sent to us as prophets from God. But because of our stubbornness they come to us only to blind us further.

"Blind the heart of this people and make their ears heavy, and shut their eyes: lest they see with their eyes, and hear with their ears and understand with their heart and be converted, and I heal them."

We refuse to hear the million different voices through which God speaks to us, and every refusal hardens us more and more against His grace—and yet He continues to speak to us: and we say He is without mercy!

"But the Lord dealeth patiently for your sake, not willing that any should perish, but that all should return to penance."

Mother of God, how often in the last centuries have you not come down to us, speaking to us in our mountains and groves and hills, and telling us what was to come upon us, and we have not heard you. How long shall we continue to be deaf to your voice, and run our heads into the jaws of the hell that abhors us?

Lady, when on that night I left the island that was once your England, your love went with me, although I could not know it, and could not make myself aware of it. And it was your love, your intercession for me, before God, that was preparing the seas before my ship, laying open the way for me to another country.

I was not sure where I was going, and I could not see what I would do when I got to New York. But you saw further and clearer than I, and you opened the seas before my ship, whose track led me across the waters to a place I had never dreamed of, and which you were even then preparing for me to be my rescue and my shelter and my home. And when I thought there was no God and no love and no mercy, you were leading me all the while into the midst of His love and His mercy, and taking me, without my knowing anything about it, to the house that would hide me in the secret of His Face.

Glorious Mother of God, shall I ever again distrust you, or your God, before Whose throne you are irresistible in your intercession? Shall I ever turn my eyes from your hands and from your face and from your eyes? Shall I ever look anywhere else but in the face of your love, to find out true counsel, and to know my way, in all the days and all the moments of my life?

As you have dealt with me, Lady, deal also with all my millions of brothers who live in the same misery that I knew then: lead them in spite of themselves and guide them by your tremendous influence, O

Holy Queen of souls and refuge of sinners, and bring them to your Christ the way you brought me. *Illos tuos misericordes oculos ad nos converte, et Jesum, benedictum fructum ventris tui, nobis ostende.* Show us your Christ, Lady, after this our exile, yes: but show Him to us also now, show Him to us here, while we are still wanderers.

THE SEVEN STOREY MOUNTAIN

Five: POEMS

LANDSCAPE: BEAST

Yonder, by the eastward sea
Where smoke melts in a saucer of extinguished cities,
The last men stand, in delegations,
Waiting to see the seven-headed business
Promised us, from those unpublished deeps:
Waiting to see those horns and diadems
And hear the seven voices of the final blasphemy.

And westward, where the other waters are as slick as silk
And slide, in the gray evening, with uncertain lights,
(Screened by the smoke of the extinguished studios)
The last men wait to see the seven-headed thing.
They stand around the radios
Wearing their regalia on their thin excited breasts,
Waving the signals of their masonry.
What will happen, when they see those heads, those horns
Dishevel the flickering sea?

How will they bare their foreheads and put forth their hands
And wince with the last indelible brand,
And wear the dolor of that animal's number,
And evermore be burned with her disgusting name?

Inland, in the lazy distance, where a dozen planes still play
As loud as horseflies, round the ruins of an average town,
A blue-green medium dragon, swimming in the river,
Emerges from the muddy waters, comes to romp awhile upon the land.

She rises on the pathless shore,
And goes to roll in the ashes of the ravaged country.
But no man turns to see and be surprised
Where those gray flanks flash palely in the sun.
Who shall gather to see an ordinary dragon, in this day of anger,
Or wonder at those scales as usual as sin?

Meanwhile, upon the broken mountains of the south
No one observes the angels passing to and fro:
And no one sees the fire that shoots beneath the hoofs
Of all the white, impatient horses.

And no one hears or fears the music of those blazing swords.

(Northward, northward, what lies there to see?
Who shall recount the terror of those ruined streets?

And who shall dare to look where all the birds with golden beaks
Stab at the blue eyes of the murdered saints?)

FIGURES FOR AN APOCALYPSE

SONG
from Crossportion's Pastoral

The bottom of the sea has come
And builded in my noiseless room
The fishes' and the mermaids' home,

Whose it is most, most hell to be
Out of the heavy-hanging sea
And in the thin, thin changeable air

Or unroom sleep some other where;
But play their coral violins
Where waters most lock music in:

The bottom of my room, the sea.
Full of voiceless curtaindeep
There mermaid somnambules come sleep
Where fluted half lights show the way,

And there, there lost orchestras play
And down the many quarterlights come
To the dim mirth of my aquadrome:
The bottom of my sea, the room.

A MAN IN THE DIVIDED SEA

LENT IN A YEAR OF WAR

One of you is a major, made of cord and catskin,

But never dreams his eyes may come to life and thread
The needle light of famine in a waterglass.

One of you is the paper Jack of Sprites
And will not cast his sentinel voice
Spiraling up the dark ears of the wind
Where the prisoner's yell is lost.

> "What if it was our thumbs put out the sun
> When the Lance and Cross made their mistake?
> You'll never rob us our Eden of drumskin shelters,
> You, with the bite of John the Baptist's halter,
> Getting away in the basket of Paul,
> Loving the answer of death, the mother of Lent!"

Thus, in the evening of their sinless murders,
Jack and the Major, sifting the stars for a sign
See the north-south horizon parting like a string!

A MAN IN THE DIVIDED SEA

THE FLIGHT INTO EGYPT

Through every precinct of the wintry city
Squadroned iron resounds upon the streets;
Herod's police
Makes shudder the dark steps of the tenements
At the business about to be done.

Neither look back upon Thy starry country,
Nor hear what rumors crowd across the dark
Where blood runs down those holy walls,
Nor frame a childish blessing with Thy hand
Toward that fiery spiral of exulting souls!

Go, Child of God, upon the singing desert,
Where, with eyes of flame,
The roaming lion keeps thy road from harm.

A MAN IN THE DIVIDED SEA

THE NIGHT TRAIN

In the unreason of a rainy midnight
France blooms along the windows
Of my sleepy bathysphere,
And runs to seed in a luxuriance of curious lights.

Escape is drawn straight through my dream
And shines to Paris, clean as a violin string,
While spring tides of commotion,
(The third-class pianos of the Orient Express)
Fill the hollow barrels of my ears.

Cities that stood, by day, as gay as lancers
Are lost, in the night, like old men dying.
At a point where polished rails branch off forever
The steels lament, like crazy ladies.
We wake, and weep the deaths of the cathedrals
That we have never seen,
Because we hear the jugulars of the country
Fly in the wind, and vanish with a cry.

At once the diplomats start up, as white as bread,
Buckle the careless cases of their minds
That just fell open in the sleeper:

For, by the rockets of imaginary sieges
They see to read big, terrible print,
Each in the other's face,

That spells the undecoded names
Of the assassins they will recognize too late:
The ones that seem to be secret police,
Now all in place, all armed, in the obvious ambush.

A MAN IN THE DIVIDED SEA

AUBADE: LAKE ERIE

When sun, light-handed, sows this Indian water
With a crop of cockles,
The vines arrange their tender shadows
In the sweet leafage of an artificial France.

Awake, in the frames of windows, innocent children,
Loving the blue, sprayed leaves of childish life,
Applaud the bearded corn, the bleeding grape,
And cry:

"Here is the hay-colored sun, our marvelous cousin,
Walking in the barley,
Turning the harrowed earth to growing bread,
And splicing the sweet, wounded vine.

Lift up your hitchhiking heads
And no more fear the fever,
You fugitives, and sleepers in the fields,
Here is the hay-colored sun!"

And when their shining voices, clean as summer,
Play, like churchbells over the field,
A hundred dusty Luthers rise from the dead, unheeding,
Search the horizon for the gap-toothed grin of factories,
And grope, in the green wheat,
Toward the wood winds of the western freight.

A MAN IN THE DIVIDED SEA

ASH WEDNESDAY

The naked traveler,
Stretching, against the iron dawn, the bowstrings of his eyes,
Starves on the mad sierra.

But the sleepers,
Prisoners in a lovely world of weeds,
Make a small, red cry,
And change their dreams.

Proud as the mane of the whinnying air,
Yet humble as the flakes of water
Or the chips of the stone sun, the traveler
Is nailed to the hill by the light of March's razor;

And when the desert barks, in a rage of love
For the noon of the eclipse,
He lies with his throat cut, in a frozen crater.
Then the sleepers,

Prisoners of a moonward power of tides,
Slain by the stillness of their own reflections,
Sit up, in their graves, with a white cry,
And die of terror at the traveler's murder.

A MAN IN THE DIVIDED SEA

AN ELEGY FOR ERNEST HEMINGWAY

Now for the first time on the night of your death
your name is mentioned in convents, *ne cadas in obscurum.*

Now with a true bell your story becomes final. Now men
in monasteries, men of requiems, familiar with the dead,
include you in their offices.

You stand anonymous among thousands, waiting in the dark
at great stations on the edge of countries known to
prayer alone, where fires are not merciless, we hope,
and not without end.

You pass briefly through our midst. Your books and
writings have not been consulted. Our prayers are
pro defuncto N.

Yet some look up, as though among a crowd of prisoners
or displaced persons, they recognized a friend once
known in a far country. For these the sun also rose
after a forgotten war upon an idiom you made great. They
have not forgotten you. In their silence you are still
famous, no ritual shade.

How slowly this bell tolls in a monastery tower for a
whole age, and for the quick death of an unready dynasty,
and for that brave illusion: the adventurous self!

For with one shot the whole hunt is ended.

Commonweal

LANDSCAPE

I

A Personage is seen
Leaning upon a cushion
Printed with cornflowers.

A Child appears
Holding up a pencil.

"This is a picture
(Says the Child to the Personage)
Of the vortex."

"Draw it your own way,"
Says the Personage.

(Music is heard
Pure in the island windows,
Sea music on the Child's
Interminable shore, his coral home.)

Behind a blue mountain
Covered with chickenfoot trees,
The molten sun appears,
A heavy, painted flower.

A personage is seen
Leaning upon the mountain
With the sun in one hand
And a pencil in the other.

"This is a picture
(Says the Personage to the Child)
Of the beginning of the world."

"Or of its end!" cries the Child
Hiding himself in the cushions.

2

A Woman appears
Leaning upon the Child's shoulder.
He looks up again.

"This is my Mother
(Says the Child to the Personage)
Older than the moon."

(Grecian horses are heard
Returning from the foam
Of the pure island's windows,
And the Child's horizons.)

"My Mother is a world
(Says the Child to the Personage)
Printed with gillyflowers."

"Paint her your own way"
(Says the Personage to the Child).
And, lifting up his pencil,
He crosses out the sun.

THE STRANGE ISLANDS

Six: CHILDREN IN THE MARKET PLACE

Pᴇʀʜᴀᴘs ᴛʜᴇ sᴛʏx, being only a river, does not seem so terribly wide. It is not its width that makes it difficult to cross, especially when you are trying to get out of hell, and not in. And so, this time, even though I got out of Europe, I still remained in hell. But it was not for want of trying.

It was a stormy crossing. When it was possible, I walked on the wide, empty decks that streamed with spray. Or I would get up forward where I could see the bows blast their way headfirst into the mountains of water that bore down upon us. And I would hang on to the rail while the ship reeled and soared into the wet sky, riding the sea that swept under us while every stanchion and bulkhead groaned and complained.

When we got on to the Grand Banks, the seas calmed and there was a fall of snow, and the snow lay on the quiet decks, and made them white in the darkness of the evening. And because of the peacefulness of the snow, I imagined that my new ideas were breeding within me an interior peace.

The truth is, I was in the thick of a conversion. It was not the right conversion, but it was a conversion. Perhaps it was a lesser evil. I do not doubt much that it was. But it was not, for all that, much of a good. I was becoming a Communist.

Stated like that, it sounds pretty much the same as if I said: "I was growing a mustache." As a matter of fact, I was still unable to grow a mustache. Or I did not dare to try. And, I suppose, my Communism was about as mature as my face—as the sour, perplexed, English face in the photo on my quota card. However, as far as I know, this was about as sincere and complete a step to moral conversion as I was then able to make with my own lights and desires, such as they then were.

It was some four years since I had first read the *Communist Manifesto,* and I had never entirely forgotten about it. One of those Christmas vacations at Strasbourg I had read some books about Soviet Russia, how all the factories were working overtime, and all the ex-moujiks wore great big smiles on their faces, welcoming Russian aviators on their return from Polar flights, bearing the boughs of trees in their hands. Then I often went to Russian movies, which were pretty good from the technical point of view, although probably not as good as I thought they were, in my great anxiety to approve of them.

Finally, I had in my mind the myth that Soviet Russia was the friend of all the arts, and the only place where true art could find a refuge in a world of bourgeois ugliness. Where I ever got that idea is hard to find out, and how I managed to cling to it for so long is harder still, when you consider all the photographs there were, for everyone to see, showing the Red Square with gigantic pictures of Stalin hanging on the walls of the world's ugliest buildings—not to mention the views of the projected monster monument to Lenin, like a huge mountain of soap sculpture, and the Little Father of Communism standing on top of it, and sticking out one of his hands. Then, when I went to New York in the summer, I found the *New Masses* lying around the studios of my friends and, as a matter of fact, a lot of the people I met were either party members or close to being so.

So now, when the time came for me to take spiritual stock of myself, it was natural that I should do so by projecting my whole spiritual condition into the sphere of economic history and the class struggle. In other words, the conclusion I came to was that it was not so much I myself that was to blame for my unhappiness, but the society in which I lived.

I considered the person that I now was, the person that I had been at Cambridge, and that I had made of myself, and I saw clearly enough that I was the product of my times, my society and my class. I was something that had been spawned by the selfishness and irresponsibility of the materialistic century in which I lived. However, what I did not see was that my own age and class only had an accidental part to play in this. They gave my egoism and pride and my other sins a peculiar character of weak and supercilious flippancy proper to this particular century: but that was only on the surface. Underneath, it was the same old story of greed and lust and self-love, of the three concupiscences bred in the rich, rotted undergrowth of what is technically called "the world," in every age, in every class.

It is true that the materialistic society, the so-called culture that has evolved under the tender mercies of capitalism, has produced what seems to be the ultimate limit of this worldliness. And nowhere, except perhaps in the analogous society of pagan Rome, has there ever been such a flowering of cheap and petty and disgusting lusts and vanities as in the world of capitalism, where there is no evil that is not fostered and encouraged for the sake of making money. We live in a society whose whole policy is to excite every nerve in the human body and keep it at the highest pitch of artificial tension, to strain every human desire to the limit and to create as many new desires and synthetic passions as possible, in order to cater to them with the products of our factories and printing presses and movie studios and all the rest.

Being the son of an artist, I was born the sworn enemy of everything that could obviously be called bourgeois, and now I only had to dress up that aversion in economic terms and extend it to cover more ground than it had covered before—namely, to include anything that could be classified as semifascist, like D. H. Lawrence and many of the artists who thought they were rebels without really being so—and I had my new religion all ready for immediate use.

It was an easy and handy religion—too easy in fact. It told me that all the evils in the world were the product of capitalism. Therefore, all that had to be done to get rid of the evils of the world was to get rid of capitalism. This would not be very hard, for capitalism contained the seeds of its own decay (and that indeed is a very obvious truth which nobody would trouble to deny, even some of the most stupid defenders of the system now in force: for our wars are altogether too eloquent in what they have to say on the subject). An active and enlightened minority—and this minority was understood to be made up of the most intelligent and vital elements of society, was to have the twofold task of making the oppressed class, the proletariat, conscious of their own power and destiny as future owners of all the means of production, and to "bore from within" in order to gain control of power by every possible means. Some violence, no doubt, would probably be necessary, but only because of the inevitable reaction of capitalism by the use of fascist methods to keep the proletariat in subjection.

It was capitalism that was to blame for everything unpleasant, even the violence of the revolution itself. Now, of course, the revolution had already taken the first successful step in Russia. The Dictatorship of the Proletariat was already set up there. It would have to spread through the rest of the world before it could be said that the revolution had

really been a success. But once it had, once capitalism had been completely overthrown, the semistate, or Dictatorship of the Proletariat,
would itself only be a temporary matter. It would be a kind of guardian
of the revolution, a tutor of the new classless society, during its minority. But as soon as the citizens of the new, classless world had had
all the greed educated out of them by enlightened methods, the last
vestiges of the "state" would wither away, and there would be a new
world, a new golden age, in which all property would be held in common, at least all capital goods, all the land, means of production and
so on, and nobody would desire to seize them for himself: and so there
would be no more poverty, no more wars, no more misery, no more
starvation, no more violence. Everybody would be happy. Nobody would
be overworked. They would all amicably exchange wives whenever they
felt like it, and their offspring would be brought up in big shiny incu-
bators, not by the state because there wouldn't be any state, but by that
great, beautiful surd, the lovely, delicious unknown quantity of the new
"Classless Society."

I don't think that even I was gullible enough to swallow all the business about the ultimate bliss that would follow the withering away of
the state—a legend far more naïve and far more oversimplified than the
happy hunting ground of the most primitive Indian. But I simply assumed that things would be worked out by the right men at the right
time. For the moment, what was needed was to get rid of capitalism.

The thing that made Communism seem so plausible to me was my
own lack of logic which failed to distinguish between the reality of the
evils which Communism was trying to overcome and the validity of its
diagnosis and the chosen cure.

For there can be no doubt that modern society is in a terrible condition, and that its wars and depressions and its slums and all its other
evils are principally the fruits of an unjust social system, a system that
must be reformed and purified or else replaced. However, if you are
wrong, does that make me right? If you are bad, does that prove that I
am good? The chief weakness of Communism is that it is, itself, only
another breed of the same materialism which is the source and root of
all the evils which it so clearly sees, and it is evidently nothing but another product of the breakdown of the capitalist system. Indeed, it seems
to be pieced together out of the ruins of the same ideology that once
went into the vast, amorphous, intellectual structure underlying capitalism in the nineteenth century.

However, as I say, perhaps the hopefulness that suddenly began to

swell in my breast as I stood on the deck of this ten-day liner going to
New York, via Halifax, was largely subjective and imaginary. The
chance association, in my mind, with fresh air and the sea and a healthy
feeling and a lot of good resolutions, coinciding with a few superficial
notions of Marxism, had made me—like so many others—a Communist
in my own fancy.

Added to this was my own personal conviction, the result of the uncertain and misdirected striving for moral reform, that I must now devote myself to the good of society, and apply my mind, at least to some
extent, to the tremendous problems of my time.

I don't know how much good there was in this: but I think there
was some. It was, I suppose, my acknowledgment of my selfishness, and
my desire to make reparation for it by developing some kind of social
and political consciousness. And at the time, in my first fervor, I felt
myself willing to make sacrifices for this end. I wanted to devote myself to the causes of peace and justice in the world. I wanted to do
something positive to interrupt and divert the gathering momentum
that was dragging the whole world into another war—and I felt there
was something I could do, not alone, but as the member of an active
and vocal group.

It was a bright, icy-cold afternoon when, having passed Nantucket
Light, we first saw the long, low, yellow shoreline of Long Island shining palely in the December sun. But when we entered New York Harbor the lights were already coming on, glittering like jewels in the hard,
clear buildings. The great, debonair city that was both young and old,
and wise and innocent, shouted in the winter night as we passed the
Battery and started up the North River. And I was glad, very glad to be
an immigrant once again.

I came down on to the dock with a great feeling of confidence and
possessiveness. "New York, you are mine! I love you!" It is the glad
embrace she gives her lovers, the big, wild city: but I guess ultimately
it is for their ruin. It certainly did not prove to be any good for me.

With my mind in the ferment in which it was, I thought for a moment of registering for courses at the New School for Social Research,
in the shiny, black building on Twelfth Street, but I was easily persuaded that I had better finish out a regular university course and get
a degree. And therefore I entered upon all the complicated preambles
to admission to Columbia.

❖ FRIENDS AND COMRADES

MY ACTIVE PART in the world revolution was not very momentous. It lasted, in all, about three months. I picketed the Casa Italiana, I went to the Peace Strike, and I think I made some kind of a speech in the big classroom on the second floor of the Business School, where the N.S.L. had their meetings. Maybe it was a speech on Communism in England—a topic about which I knew absolutely nothing; in that case, I was loyally living up to the tradition of Red oratory. I sold some pamphlets and magazines. I don't know what was in them, but I could gather their contents from the big black cartoons of capitalists drinking the blood of workers.

Finally, the Reds had a party. And, of all places, in a Park Avenue apartment. This irony was the only amusing thing about it. And after all it was not so ironical. It was the home of some Barnard girl who belonged to the Young Communist League and her parents had gone away for the weekend. I could get a fair picture of them from the way the furniture looked, and from the volumes of Nietzsche and Schopenhauer and Oscar Wilde and Ibsen that filled the bookcases. And there was a big grand piano on which someone played Beethoven while the Reds sat around on the floor. Later we had a sort of boy-scout campfire group in the living room, singing heavy Communist songs, including that delicate antireligious classic, "There'll be pie in the sky when you die."

One little fellow with buck teeth and horn-rimmed glasses pointed to two windows in a corner of one of the rooms. They commanded a whole sweep of Park Avenue in one direction and the crosstown street in another. "What a place for a machine-gun nest," he observed. The statement came from a middle-class adolescent. It was made in a Park Avenue apartment. He had evidently never even seen a machine gun, except in the movies. If there had been a revolution going on at the time, he would have probably been among the first to get his head knocked off by the revolutionists. And in any case he, like all the rest of us, had just finished making the famous Oxford Pledge that he would not fight in any war whatever. . . .

One reason why I found the party so dull was that nobody was very enthusiastic about getting something to drink except me. Finally one of the girls encouraged me, in a businesslike sort of a way, to go out and buy bottles of rye at a liquor store around the corner on Third Avenue, and when I had drunk some of the contents she invited me into a room and signed me up as a prospective member of the Young Communist League. I took the party name of Frank Swift. When I looked up from the paper the girl had vanished like a not too inspiring dream, and I went home on the Long Island Railroad with the secret of a name which I have been too ashamed to reveal to anyone until this moment when I am beyond humiliation.

I only went to one meeting of the Young Communist League, in the apartment of one of the students. It was a long discussion as to why Comrade So-and-so did not come to any of the meetings. The answer was that his father was too bourgeois to allow it. So after that, I walked out into the empty street, and let the meeting end however it would.

It was good to be in the fresh air. My footsteps rang out on the dark stones. At the end of the street, the pale amber light of a barroom beckoned lovingly to me from under the steel girders of the elevated. The place was empty. I got a glass of beer and lit a cigarette and tasted the first sweet moment of silence and relief.

And that was the end of my days as a great revolutionary.

II

MAY CAME, and all the trees on Long Island were green, and when the train from the city got past Bayside and started across the meadows to Douglaston, you could see the pale, soft haze of summer beginning to hang over the bay, and count the boats that had been set afloat again after the winter, and were riding jauntily at their moorings off the end of the little dock. And now in the lengthening evenings the dining room was still light with the rays of the sun when Pop came home for dinner, slamming the front door and whooping at the dog and smacking the surface of the hall table with the evening paper to let everybody know that he had arrived.

Soon John Paul was home from his school in Pennsylvania, and my exams were over, and we had nothing to do but go swimming and hang around the house playing hot records. And in the evening we would wander off to some appalling movie where we nearly died of boredom. We did not have a car, and my uncle would not let us touch the family Buick. It would not have done me any good anyway, because I never learned to drive. So most of the time, we would get a ride to Great Neck and then walk back the two or three miles along the wide road when the show was over.

Why did we ever go to all those movies? That is another mystery.

But I think John Paul and I and our various friends must have seen all the movies that were produced, without exception, from 1934 to 1937. And most of them were simply awful. What is more, they got worse from week to week and from month to month, and day after day we hated them more. My ears are ringing with the false, gay music that used to announce the Fox movietone and the Paramount newsreels with the turning camera that slowly veered its aim right at your face. My mind still echoes with the tones of Pete Smith and Fitzpatrick of the Travel-talks saying, "And now farewell to beautiful New South Wales."

And yet I confess a secret loyalty to the memory of my great heroes: Chaplin, W. C. Fields, Harpo Marx, and many others whose names I have forgotten. But their pictures were rare, and for the rest, we found ourselves perversely admiring the villains and detesting the heroes. The truth is that the villains were almost always the better actors. We were delighted with everything they did. We were almost always in danger of being thrown out of the theater for our uproarious laughter at scenes that were supposed to be most affecting, tender, and appealing to the finer elements in the human soul—the tears of Jackie Cooper, the brave smile of Alice Faye behind the bars of a jail.

The movies soon turned into a kind of hell for me and my brother and indeed for all my closest friends. We could not keep away from them. We were hypnotized by those yellow flickering lights and the big posters of Don Ameche. Yet as soon as we got inside, the suffering of having to sit and look at such colossal stupidities became so acute that we sometimes actually felt physically sick. In the end, it got so that I could hardly sit through a show. It was like lighting cigarettes and taking a few puffs and throwing them away, appalled by the vile taste in one's mouth.

In 1935 and 1936, without my realizing it, life was slowly, once more, becoming almost intolerable.

❖ COLUMBIA

OCTOBER IS A FINE AND DANGEROUS SEASON in America. It is dry and cool and the land is wild with red and gold and crimson, and all the lassitudes of August have seeped out of your blood, and you are full of ambition. It is a wonderful time to begin anything at all. You go to college, and every course in the catalogue looks wonderful. The names of the subjects all seem to lay open the way to a new world. Your arms are full of new, clean notebooks, waiting to be filled. You pass through the doors of the library, and the smell of thousands of well-kept books makes your head swim with a clean and subtle pleasure. You have a new hat, a new sweater perhaps, or a whole new suit. Even the nickels and the quarters in your pocket feel new, and the buildings shine in the glorious sun.

In this season of resolutions and ambitions, in 1935, I signed up for courses in Spanish and German and Geology and constitutional law and French Renaissance literature and I forget what else besides. And I started to work for *The Spectator* and the yearbook and *The Review* and I continued to work for *Jester* as I had already done the spring before. And I found myself pledging one of the fraternities.

The energy of that golden October and the stimulation of the cold, bright winter days when the wind swept down as sharp as knives from the shining Palisades kept driving me through the year in what seemed to be fine condition. I had never done so many different things at the same time or with such apparent success. I had discovered in myself something of a capacity for work and for activity and for enjoyment that I had never dreamed of. And everything began to come easy, as the saying goes.

It was not that I was really studying hard or working hard: but all of a sudden I had fallen into a kind of a mysterious knack of keeping a hundred different interests going in the air at the same time. It was a kind of a stupendous juggling act, a tour de force, and what surprised me most was that I managed to keep it up without collapsing. In the first place, I was carrying about eighteen points in my courses—the average amount. I had found out the simplest way of fulfilling the minimum requirements for each one.

II

THEN THERE WAS THE "FOURTH FLOOR." The fourth floor of John Jay Hall was the place where all the offices of the student publications and the Glee Club and the Student Board and all the rest were to be found. It was the noisiest and most agitated part of the campus. It was not gay, exactly. And I hardly ever saw, anywhere, antipathies and contentions and jealousies at once so petty, so open, and so sharp. The whole floor was constantly seething with the exchange of insults from office to office. Constantly, all day long, from morning to night, people were writing articles and drawing cartoons calling each other fascists. Or else they were calling one another on the phone and assuring one another in the coarsest terms of their undying hatred. It was all intellectual and verbal, as vicious as it could be, but it never became concrete, never descended into physical rage. For this reason, I think that it was all more or less of a game which everybody played for purposes that were remotely esthetic.

The campus was supposed to be, in that year, in a state of "intellectual ferment." Everybody felt and even said that there were an unusual number of brilliant and original minds in the college. I think that it was to some extent true. Ad Reinhardt was certainly the best artist that had ever drawn for *Jester*, perhaps for any other college magazine. His issues of *Jester* were real magazines. I think that in cover designs and layouts he could have given lessons to some of the art editors downtown. Everything he put out was original, and it was also funny, because for the first time in years *Jester* had some real writers contributing to it, and was not just an anthology of the same stale and obscene jokes that have been circulating through the sluggish system of American college magazines for two generations. By now Reinhardt had graduated, and so had the editor of the 1935 *Spectator*, Jim Wechsler.

My first approach to the Fourth Floor had been rather circumspect, after the manner of Cambridge. I went to my adviser, Professor McKee, and asked him how to go about it, and he gave me a letter of introduction to Leonard Robinson who was editor of *The Columbia Review*, the literary magazine. I don't know what Robinson would have made of a letter of introduction. Anyway, I never got to meeting him after all. When I went to the *Review* office I gave the note to Bob Giroux, an associate editor, and he looked at it and scratched his head some bit and told me to write something if I got an idea.

By 1936 Leonard Robinson had vanished. I always heard a lot about Robinson, and it all adds up to nothing very clear, so that I have always had the impression that he somehow lives in the trees. I pray that he may go to heaven.

As for *Review*, Robert Paul Smith and Robert Giroux were both editing it together, and it was good. I don't know whether you would use the term "ferment" in their case, but Smith and Giroux were both good writers. Also, Giroux was a Catholic and a person strangely placid for the Fourth Floor. He had no part in its feuds and, as a matter of fact, you did not see him around there very much. John Berryman was more or less the star on *Review* that year. He was the most earnest-looking man on the campus.

The place where I was busiest was the *Jester* office. Nobody really

worked there, they just congregated about noontime and beat violently
with the palms of their hands on the big empty filing cabinets, making
a thunderous sound that echoed up and down the corridor, and was
sometimes answered from the *Review* office across the hall. There I usually came and drew forth from the bulging leather bag of books that I
carried, copy and drawings which I put into the editor's hand. The
editor that year was Herb Jacobson, and he printed all my worst cartoons very large in the most prominent parts of the magazine.

I thought I had something to be proud of when I became art editor
of *Jester* at the end of that year. Robert Lax was to be editor and Ralph
Toledano managing editor, and we got along well together. The next
year *Jester* was well put together because of Toledano and well written
because of Lax and sometimes popular with the masses because of me.
When it was really funny, it was not popular at all. The only really
funny issues were mostly the work of Lax and Bob Gibney, the fruit
of ideas that came to them at four o'clock in the morning in their room
on the top floor of Furnald Hall.

The chief advantage of *Jester* was that it paid most of our bills for
tuition. We were happy about it all, and wandered around the campus
with little golden crowns dangling on our watch chains. Indeed, that
was the only reason why I had a watch chain. I did not have a watch.

III

I ALSO HANDED IN MY NAME for the Cross Country team. The fact that
the coach was not sorry to get me is sufficient indication of one reason
why we were the worst college Cross Country team in the East that
year. And so, in my afternoons, I would run around and around South
Field on the cinder path. And when winter came, I would go round
and round the board track until I had blisters all over the soles of my
feet and was so lame I could hardly walk. Occasionally I would go up to
Van Cortlandt Park and run along the sandy and rocky paths through
the woods. When we raced any other college, I was never absolutely
the last one home—there were always two or three other Columbia
men behind me. I was one of those who never came in until the crowd
had lost interest and had begun to disperse. Perhaps I would have been
more of a success as a long-distance runner if I had gone into training,
and given up smoking and drinking, and kept regular hours.

But no. Three or four nights a week my fraternity brothers and I
would go flying down in the black and roaring subway to 52nd Street,
where we would crawl around the tiny, noisy, and expensive nightclubs

that had flowered on the sites of the old speakeasies in the cellars of those dirty brownstone houses. There we would sit, for hours, packed in those dark rooms, shoulder to shoulder with a lot of surly strangers and their girls, while the whole place rocked and surged with storms of jazz. There was no room to dance. We just huddled there between the blue walls, shoulder to shoulder and elbow to elbow, crouching and deafened and taciturn. If you moved your arm to get your drink you nearly knocked the next man off his stool. And the waiters fought their way back and forth through the sea of unfriendly heads, taking away the money of all the people.

It was not that we got drunk. No, it was this strange business of sitting in a room full of people and drinking without much speech, and letting yourself be deafened by the jazz that throbbed through the whole sea of bodies binding them all together in a kind of fluid medium. It was a strange, animal travesty of mysticism, sitting in those booming rooms, with the noise pouring through you, and the rhythm jumping and throbbing in the marrow of your bones. You couldn't call any of that, *per se*, a mortal sin. We just sat there, that was all. If we got hangovers the next day, it was more because of the smoking and nervous exhaustion than anything else.

How often, after a night of this, I missed all the trains home to Long Island and went and slept on a couch somewhere, at the Fraternity House, or in the apartment of somebody I knew around town. What was worst of all was going home on the subway, on the chance that one might catch a bus at Flushing! There is nothing so dismal as the Flushing bus station, in the gray, silent hour just before the coming of dawn. There were always at least one or two of those same characters whose prototypes I had seen dead in the morgue. And perhaps there would be a pair of drunken soldiers trying to get back to Fort Totten. Among all these I stood, weary and ready to fall, lighting the fortieth or fiftieth cigarette of the day—the one that took the last shreds of lining off my throat.

The thing that depressed me most of all was the shame and despair that invaded my whole nature when the sun came up, and all the laborers were going to work: men healthy and awake and quiet, with their eyes clear, and some rational purpose before them. This humiliation and sense of my own misery and of the fruitlessness of what I had done was the nearest I could get to contrition. It was the reaction of nature. It proved nothing except that I was still, at least, morally alive: or rather that I had still some faint capacity for moral life in me. The term "morally alive" might obscure the fact that I was spiritually dead. I had been that long since!

I had at last become a true child of the modern world, completely tangled up in petty and useless concerns with myself, and almost incapable of even considering or understanding anything that was really important to my own true interests.

THE SEVEN STOREY MOUNTAIN

Seven: HELL AS HATRED

Hᴇʟʟ is where no one has anything in common with anybody else except the fact that they all hate one another and cannot get away from one another and from themselves.

They are all thrown together in their fire and each one tries to thrust the others away from him with a huge, impotent hatred. And the reason why they want to be free of one another is not so much that they hate what they see in others, as that they know others hate what they see in them: and all recognize in one another what they detest in themselves, selfishness and impotence, agony, terror, and despair.

The tree is known by its fruits. If you want to understand the social and political history of modern man, study hell.

And yet the world, with all its wars, is not yet hell. And history, however terrible, has another and a deeper meaning. For it is not the evil of history that is its significance and it is not by the evil of our time that our time can be understood. In the furnace of war and hatred, the City of those who love one another is drawn and fused together in the heroism of charity under suffering, while the city of those who hate everything is scattered and dispersed and its citizens are cast out in every direction, like sparks, smoke, and flame.

ᴏᴜʀ ɢᴏᴅ also is a consuming fire. And if we, by love, become transformed into Him and burn as He burns, His fire will be our everlasting joy. But if we refuse His love and remain in the coldness of sin and opposition to Him and to other men then will His fire (by our own choice rather than His) become our everlasting enemy, and Love, instead of being our joy, will become our torment and our destruction.

WHEN WE LOVE GOD'S WILL we find Him and own His joy in all things. But when we are against God, that is, when we love ourselves more than Him, all things become our enemies. They cannot help refusing us the lawless satisfaction our selfishness demands of them because the infinite unselfishness of God is the law of every created essence and is printed in everything that He has made. His creatures can only be friends with His unselfishness. If, in men, they find selfishness, then they hate, fear and resist it—until they are tamed and reduced to passivity by it. But the Desert Fathers believed one of the marks of the saint was that he could live at peace with lions and serpents, with nothing to fear from them.

THERE IS NOTHING interesting about sin, or about evil as evil.

Evil is not a positive entity but the absence of a perfection that ought to be there. Sin as such is essentially boring because it is the lack of something that could appeal to our wills and our minds.

What attracts men to evil acts is not the evil in them but the good that is there, seen under a false aspect and with a distorted perspective. The good seen from that angle is only the bait in a trap. When you reach out to take it, the trap is sprung and you are left with disgust, boredom—and hatred. Sinners are people who hate everything, because their world is necessarily full of betrayal, full of illusion, full of deception. And the greatest sinners are the most boring people in the world because they are also the most bored and the ones who find life most tedious.

When they try to cover the tedium of life by noise, excitement and violence—the inevitable fruits of a life devoted to the love of values that do not exist—they become something more than boring: they are scourges of the world and of society. And being scourged is not merely something dull or tedious.

Yet when it is all over and they are dead, the record of their sins in history becomes exceedingly uninteresting and is inflicted on school children as a penance which is all the more bitter because even an eight-year-old can readily see the uselessness of learning about people like Hitler, Stalin, and Napoleon.

NEW SEEDS OF CONTEMPLATION

Eight: IN THE FACE OF DEATH

THE DENTIST tapped at the tooth, and looked serious.

"It will have to come out," he said.

I was not sorry. The thing was hurting me, and I wanted to get rid of it as soon as possible.

But Dr. McTaggart said: "I can't give you anything to deaden the pain, you know."

"Why not?"

"There is a great deal of infection, and the matter has spread far beyond the roots of the tooth."

I accepted his reasoning on trust and said: "Well, go ahead."

And I sat back in the chair, mute with misgivings, while he happily trotted over to his toolbox singing "It won't be a stylish marriage" and pulled out an ugly-looking forceps.

"All ready?" he said, jacking back the chair, and brandishing the instrument of torture. I nodded, feeling as if I had gone pale to the roots of my hair.

But the tooth came out fast, in one big, vivid flash of pain and left me spitting a lot of green and red business into the little blue whispering whirlpool by the side of the dentist's chair.

"Oh, goodness," said Dr. McTaggart, "I don't like that very much, I must say."

I walked wearily back to school, reflecting that it was not really so terrible after all to have a tooth pulled out without novocain. However, instead of getting better, I got worse. By evening, I was really ill, and that night—that sleepless night—was spent in a fog of sick confusedness and general pain. The next morning they took my temperature and put me to bed in the sickroom, where I eventually got to sleep.

That did not make me any better. And I soon gathered in a vague way that our matron, Miss Harrison, was worried about me, and communicated her worries to the headmaster, in whose own house this particular sickroom was.

Then the school doctor came around. And he went away again, returning with Dr. McTaggart who, this time, did not sing.

And I heard them agreeing that I was getting to be too full of gangrene for my own good. They decided to lance a big hole in my gum, and see if they could not drain the pocket of infection there and so, having given me a little ether, they went ahead. I awoke with my mouth full of filth, both doctors urging me to hurry up and get rid of it.

When they had gone, I lay back in bed and closed my eyes and thought: "I have blood poisoning."

And then my mind went back to the sore foot I had developed in Germany. Well, I would tell them about it when they came back the next time.

Sick, weary, half asleep, I felt the throbbing of the wound in my mouth. Blood poisoning.

The room was very quiet. It was rather dark, too. And as I lay in bed, in my weariness and pain and disgust, I felt for a moment the shadow of another visitor pass into the room.

It was death, that came to stand by my bed.

I kept my eyes closed, more out of apathy than anything else. But anyway, there was no need to open one's eyes to see the visitor, to see death. Death is someone you see very clearly with eyes in the center of your heart: eyes that see not by reacting to light, but by reacting to a kind of a chill from within the marrow of your own life.

And, with those eyes, those interior eyes, open upon that coldness, I lay half asleep and looked at the visitor, death.

What did I think? All I remember was that I was filled with a deep and tremendous apathy. I felt so sick and disgusted that I did not very much care whether I died or lived. Perhaps death did not come very close to me, or give me a good look at the nearness of his coldness and darkness, or I would have been more afraid.

But at any rate, I lay there in a kind of torpor and said: "Come on, I don't care." And then I fell asleep.

What a tremendous mercy it was that death did not take me at my word, that day, when I was still only seventeen years old. What a thing it would have been if the trapdoors that were prepared for me had yawned and opened their blackness and swallowed me down in the middle of that sleep! Oh, I tell you, it is a blessing beyond calculation that I woke up again, that day, or the following night, or in the week or two that came after.

And I lay there with nothing in my heart but apathy—there was a kind of pride and spite in it: as if it was life's fault that I had to suffer a little discomfort, and for that I would show my scorn and hatred of life, and die, as if that were a revenge of some sort. Revenge upon what? What was life? Something existing apart from me, and separate from myself? Don't worry, I did not enter into any speculations. I only thought: "If I have to die—what of it. What do I care? Let me die, then, and I'm finished."

Religious people, those who have faith and love God and realize what life is and what death means, and know what it is to have an immortal soul, do not understand how it is with the ones who have no faith, and who have already thrown away their souls. They find it hard to conceive that anyone could enter into the presence of death without some kind of compunction. But they should realize that millions of men die the way I was then prepared to die, the way I then might have died.

They might say to me: "Surely you thought of God, and you wanted to pray to Him for mercy."

No. As far as I remember, the thought of God, the thought of prayer did not even enter my mind, either that day, or all the rest of the time that I was ill, or that whole year, for that matter. Or if the thought did come to me, it was only as an occasion for its denial and rejection. I remember that in that year, when we stood in the chapel and recited the Apostles' Creed, I used to keep my lips tight shut, with full deliberation and of set purpose, by way of declaring my own creed which was: "I believe in nothing." Or at least I thought I believed in nothing. Actually, I had only exchanged a certain faith, faith in God, Who is Truth, for a vague uncertain faith in the opinions and authority of men and pamphlets and newspapers—wavering and varying and contradictory opinions which I did not even clearly understand.

THE SEVEN STOREY MOUNTAIN

Nine: REVIEWS OF NABOKOV AND RANSOM

❖ LAUGHTER IN THE DARK[1]

Laughter in the Dark, written by a Russian *émigré* living in Paris, has already enjoyed some acclaim in Europe under the title of *Camera Obscura* and, indeed, it is a strange, exciting, and unusual book. It does not lack vitality, but, as the story closes, its vitality simply resolves itself into a kind of crazy hectic movement across a plane surface—like oil burning on the face of a pond.

Stated baldly, the plot is both tragic and familiar. It is the story of a man, Albinus is his name, who was "rich, respectable, happy; one day he abandoned his wife for the sake of a youthful mistress; he loved, was not loved, and his life ended in disaster." The author, however, treats his theme more and more in the comic manner as his story goes on.

The book begins well, and holds us as long as the author does not commit himself to either a tragic or a comic tone of voice. Hence we watch the pathetic, rich little puritan Albinus being drawn out of his respectable orbit by the girl, Margot. We can understand how it happens. We are aware of her fascination, and are not unable to appreciate Albinus' discontent with his comfortable life when this is pointed out to us. And as we follow the rapid movements of these two about the windy, rainy Berlin streets, we are never sure if we love or hate the lovers, or admire or despise them. Far from being a fault, it is this ambiguity which keeps the book alive, and once the author resolves it, he robs his book of most of its reality. At the climax of the story the least convincing of the major characters is introduced: one worldly cynical fellow by the name of Rex. Here the author comes out openly for comedy. Albinus goes into decline and takes the whole book with him. From now on we are sure he is too much of a fool to be pitied, and that Margot is far too sluttish to remain even a little bit fascinating.

Uncompromising comedy has thrown too strong a light on them, and their transparencies become too obvious.

However, it is amusing enough to watch Rex, who is a very unpleasant character, use Horner's trick from Wycherly's comedy *The Country Wife* to replace Albinus in Margot's affection while Albinus continues to support him. But Albinus finds out: Margot talks him out of shooting her, for the moment. Before much else can happen he gets a broken head in an automobile accident and goes blind.

She bundles him off to the Swiss Alps. Rex, who has announced he is going to America, follows them to Switzerland, where he continues to live with Margot in the same chalet with Albinus, without the blind man finding out. And, as if the dexterity required for this were not enough to keep Rex amused, he has to invent a lot of practical jokes to play on the poor fellow.

It is here that the author has outdone himself, for Rex's jokes are at the same time stupid and frightening. But we are neither amused nor horrified, because they carry little conviction. Rex is too artificial a character for his actions and ideas to have much force; they are uninteresting, and so is he. Mr. Nabokov lacks the finesse of a Gide or a Huxley in describing an intellectual cad. Rex is little more than a storybook cynic.

However, a word about the style. This is a rapid, colorful, lively, and frequently witty book. The author has a keen eye for movement and outline. In two words he can create the image of a girl getting out of a wet coat or a goalkeeper in a hockey game. The economy and justness of his observation of externals are as striking as the speed and facility with which he tells his story.

[1] *Laughter in the Dark,* by Vladimir Nabokov, Bobbs-Merrill Company, New York, 1938.

New York *Herald Tribune Books*
May 15, 1938

❖ *THE WORLD'S BODY* [2]

MR. RANSOM HAS WRITTEN a distinguished book about poetry—a volume of essays that consider the subject from various standpoints, dealing now with the aesthetics of poetry, now the theory of criticism, as well as with poetry itself. He has chosen examples for discussion from Milton, Shakespeare, and Donne, as well as from different levels of contemporary poetry represented by T. S. Eliot and Edna St. Vincent Millay.

Turning to aesthetic theory, he examines Plato and Aristotle, and finds occasion to disagree with two significant moderns, I. A. Richards and George Santayana. But he has not attempted to give us any systematic theory of literary criticism. The book is simply intended as a collection of ideas that may serve as a basis for some such system.

His ideas are characterized by the word "reactionary," in a technical, not political, sense. Where poetry is concerned—and that is all that concerns us here—the word implies stress on form and technique and a distaste for homiletics in poetry. Mr. Ransom dislikes, for instance, the poetry of vague moods that associates romantic landscapes with man's fate and ends on a moral text.

One of his best arguments against the romantics develops out of his examination of Milton's "Lycidas," which is, of course, a pastoral poem. The pastoral type, with its rigid conventions, forced the poet to step out of his own personality and to put on a mask for poetic purposes. Mr. Ransom points out what a valuable technical resource this "anonymity" was: and this was one of the first things the romantics threw away. Expanding this idea into that of "aesthetic distance," the author describes it as a process in which the poet inhibits direct response to the object, in order to approach it in a roundabout way through convention and form. The advantages of this "technique of restraint" must be obvious: detachment, objectivity, control of the material, and so on.

Going deeper into the subject, he attempts a definition of poetry in terms of cognition: It is a kind of knowledge that cannot be gained by any other means, for the poet is concerned with the aspects of experience that can never be well described, but only reproduced or imitated.

However, for long periods of time men have attempted to repeat, in poetry, the conclusions of science or philosophy, with the result that a great number of poems are badly disguised sermons and not much more. This Mr. Ransom calls the "poetry of ideas," or "platonic poetry," and it forms a category large enough to hold the traditional enemies, Pope and Wordsworth, at the same time.

Besides this, there is pure, or "physical," poetry, of which imagism is one type, but the works he finds most significant are those he classifies as metaphysical. He has stretched this term considerably in order to include Milton and some of Shakespeare. This is, architecturally, the finest and soundest poetry.

This brings the reviewer to the essay "Shakespeare at Sonnets," which will certainly make many of Mr. Ransom's readers angry. It is one of the most stimulating essays in the book, not only because it is a bit startling, but because it is one in which Mr. Ransom examines specific poems instead of poetry in the abstract. Recognizing that Shakespeare's greatness can withstand any attack, he sets upon the sonnets with all his force. He begins bluntly by showing that they are badly constructed, which may be true enough. And then, they are diffuse, self-indulgent pieces of emotionalism: not only that, but he blames Shakespeare for most of the bad romantic poetry that has been written since his time. Naturally Shakespeare cannot too seriously be held responsible for his bad imitators. But there is more: as soon as he has finished Shakespeare off as a romantic, he sets him up as a metaphysical, in order to demolish him all over again for not being as good as Donne. This attack is unfortunate in its unnecessary and disproportionate violence, but that does not mean that it is uninteresting, or, especially, false. It is simply unnecessary; Mr. Ransom is only saying, after all, that Donne is a better lyric poet than Shakespeare, and he will easily find many who will agree with him on that. It is not necessary to try to demolish the sonnets in order to prove it; and besides, he has pitted Shakespeare against Donne in the latter's own well-fortified territory.

It is clear that the further Mr. Ransom gets from poetry, the less sure he is of himself. The closer he is to actual works of art, the more are his statements clear, succinct, and provocative.

ª *The World's Body*, by John Crowe Ransom, Charles Scribner's Sons, New York, 1938.

New York *Herald Tribune Books*
May 8, 1938

Ten: THE PROBLEM OF UNBELIEF

It is absolutely impossible for a man to live without some kind of faith. Faith, in the broadest sense, is the acceptance of truth on the evidence of another. The essence of all faith is the submission of our judgment to the assertion of someone else, on whose word we accept a truth that is not intrinsically evident to our own minds. Human or *natural faith* is the acceptance of truths on the authority of other men. *Supernatural faith* is the belief in truths revealed by God, on the testimony of God, and because of the authority of God Who reveals these truths to us.

One of the paradoxes of our age, which has so far not distinguished itself as an Age of Faith, is that millions of men who have found it impossible to believe in God have blindly submitted themselves in human faith to every charlatan who has access to a printing press, a movie screen, or a microphone. Men who cannot believe in the revealed word of God swallow everything they read in the newspapers. Men who think it absurd that the Church should be able, by virtue of the guidance and protection of the Holy Ghost, to make infallible pronouncements as to what has or has not been revealed by God concerning doctrine or morality, will believe the most fantastic claims of political propaganda, even though the dishonesty of propagandists has become, by now, proverbial.

The final irony of the situation is this: that most men have no intellectual right to their theological unbelief. Strictly speaking, of course, no man has an intellectual right to unbelief because theological faith is eminently reasonable. The intelligence has no right to be consciously unintelligent. But there do nevertheless exist a few men who, in all sincerity, have arrived by their own research at the error that theological faith is unacceptable. We cannot accept their error, but at least we have to admit that they worked hard to reach it. Their ignorance is invincible. They are in "good faith" in having no faith, because they think they have evidence against the validity of faith as such. This supposes (at least in theory) that if they saw the evidence in favor of faith, they would instantly change their view.

But no, the paradox is this. While a few men hold, as a result of reasoning, that theological faith is unacceptable, millions of others reject the notion of faith by an act not of reason but of blind faith. Here is evidence of the supreme intellectual indigence of our civilization: our very refusal to believe is based on faith.

There is still a greater enormity in our unbelief. We disbelieve God on the testimony of man. We reject the word of God because we are told to do so by men who, in their turn, were told to do so by men. The only real reason why most unbelievers cannot accept the word of God is that they have already submitted to the fallible authority of men.

Now, reason shows that the only one who can tell us anything about God is God Himself. Men know nothing of His inner life or of His plans for them. Men can only command belief in their statements about Him when it is reasonable to hold that their statements are not theirs but His—when they speak as His representatives. "The things that are of God no man knoweth, but the Spirit of God" (I Cor. 2:4).

God, being Pure Actuality, Pure Intelligence, not only sees all truth but is all Truth. Every truth, every being, is simply a reflection of Him. Truths are only true in Him, and because of Him. The light of reason is a natural participation in His Truth. Reason itself draws its authority from Him. That is why reason, if it be allowed to light our way, will bring us, without prejudice, to faith.

But men without theological faith, reasoning from false premises which they receive, on faith, from the fallible authority of other men, use the God-given light of reason to argue against God, against faith and even against reason itself.

This issue is generally misunderstood, because faith has so often been proposed as alien to reason and even as contrary to it. According to this view, faith is an entirely subjective experience which can neither be communicated nor explained. It is something emotional. It either happens to you or it does not. If it happens, you "have faith." The fact that you "have faith" does not necessarily have any effect on your reasoning, because your "faith" is an emotional thing beyond the pale of reason. You cannot explain it to yourself or to anybody else. But if faith has no intellectual reference whatever, it is hardly possible to see how "having faith" can contribute much to your outlook on life or to your behavior. It does not seem to be much more important than having red hair or a wooden leg. It is just something that happened to you, but did not happen to your next-door neighbor.

This false idea of faith is the last refuge of religious compromise with rationalism. Fearing that domestic peace is no longer possible, faith barricades itself in the attic, and leaves the rest of the house to reason. Actually, faith and reason are meant to get along happily together. They were not meant to live alone, in divorce or in separation.

II

THE "PROBLEM OF UNBELIEF" in modern times is clearly not a problem of faithlessness but of irrationality. Most men of our time do not have enough brains or training to be capable of a formal sin against the theological virtue of faith. The faithlessness that is so prevalent in a country like America is not formal unbelief but crass ignorance. It is the confusion of well-meaning people who are lost in a fog, who do not know their left hands from their right. The agnosticism and atheism which benight the spirits of men in our time spring less from a formal, deliberate, and studied rejection of revealed truth than from an inability to think.

It is because men are not able to think for themselves that they are so often incapable either of belief or of unbelief. They are lucky if they rise high enough to be able to rehearse clearly in their minds the propositions that have been fed to them by the mass media. No one can expect them to have any means of judging the truth or falsity of the things they read in the papers when their best efforts are devoted to spelling out the words. If they cannot keep pace with the thought of another, how can they think for themselves?

The first step in bringing men to faith is taken on the level not of theology but of philosophy. It is not a matter of faith but of reason. It is impossible to ask anyone to believe in truths revealed by God unless he first understand that there is a God and that He can reveal Truth.

Even in the case of intellectuals who really have some claim to that title, the inability to accept the existence of God springs from powerlessness to think. Not that they do not have brilliant or well-trained minds, but in their approach to ultimate metaphysical problems their minds are all but paralyzed by a philosophical equipment that is worse than ineffectual: it leaves them in doubt as to the nature of being, of truth, and even sometimes of their own existence. It is not for these that we raise the question of unbelief. Even our intellectuals are not sufficiently implemented to sin against faith!

That is why it is a mistake to situate the problem of unbelief on the mere level of proofs for God's existence. On that level we are not dealing with faith, but with the rational preambles to faith. Pascal saw this clearly. He also saw the paradox that philosophers like Descartes, who had in fact reduced theology to the level of philosophy and tended to shift the problem of belief into the area of his "clear ideas" of God, had obscured and falsified the whole issue. Pascal predicted correctly that the influence of Descartes on theology would be a watering down of faith by specious philosophizing.

The problem of unbelief cannot arise until a man has found his way to God. True, since the existence of God is an article of faith as well as a truth accessible to reason, any denial of His existence is materially a sin against faith. But there is so much invincible ignorance of the rational preambles to faith that it would be misleading to suppose that the godlessness of most men presents a real problem of unbelief.

III

IT HAS BEEN SAID that the multitudes are faithless because of their faith in a few. With the unbelief of these few we touch upon the real problem.

The real problem of unbelief is, to my mind, centered in those who to some extent *know* God but cannot *believe in* Him. They are often involved in the most acute spiritual anguish because of this ambivalence. They recognize the existence and the value of faith. They often wish they had some of it. They sincerely envy those who can believe, who can accept the teaching authority of the Church and enter fully into Catholic life, with all its privileges and obligations. They are able to appreciate the happiness of truly religious men. They find the claims of Catholicism entirely reasonable. They are not in the least perplexed at the thought that God speaks to men through Christ and that Christ has handed on His ruling, teaching, and sanctifying power to His Mystical Body, which prolongs His Incarnation and keeps Him visibly present in the world of men. And yet they cannot *believe.*

If we sometimes fail to meet this problem of unbelief in those who would "like to believe but cannot," it is generally because we are merely apologists when we ought to be Apostles. We have been trained to feed men not with Christ, the Bread of Life, but rather with apologetic ar-

guments. The reason for this is, perhaps, that we have been brought up
on the technique of grappling with the Church's strongest and most
vocal opponents: the atheists and skeptics. We imagine that our task
is not to announce the word of God but "to convert atheists," by main
force of argument. Even when someone with a genuine desire to believe comes to a priest with difficulties and with questions drawn from
the enemies of the Church, the chances are that these questions are not
really his difficulties at all. He thinks he needs them as a pretext for
talking—or he hopes to use them as an excuse for not committing himself to any moral action!

To be unable to *understand* the mysteries of faith is by no means to
be unable to *believe* them. And yet, as I have said, faith is in no way
the blind acceptance of a truth which we have no hope of understanding. Although we can never comprehend the full meaning of these
mysteries, yet faith is the key to a relative understanding of them. It
is after the initial act of belief that the believer begins to see. Only then
can the intellectual difficulties presented by these mysteries be dealt
with in a way that is in some sense satisfactory.

IV

THE MOTIVES of credibility always need to be made clear. But their
clarification alone will do nothing to solve a problem that is essentially
concerned not with credibility but with *faith*. Information, reasoning,
sympathetic explanation of truths usually do not suffice. There is a
subtle distinction between merely "making converts" and preaching the
word of God. Saint Paul has already anticipated the complaints of those
who, when they have dealt out all the arguments in the textbook of
fundamental theology, find themselves in a blind alley and attribute
their lack of success to the fact that perhaps God has somehow failed
to give the prospective "convert" enough grace to believe. The man has
accepted all their arguments. He knows that revelation is credible. He
wants to believe in God, in Christ, in the Church. He even sees that he
ought to believe in them. He has a fair idea of all there is to believe, and
it all sounds rational. But after that—he is inarticulate. He cannot go
one step further and formally accept the faith. He cannot "believe."

What shall he do? Fold his hands and wait for grace to descend on
him from heaven? Saint Paul says:

The justice which is of faith, speaketh thus: Say not in thy heart, who
shall ascend into heaven? that is, to bring Christ down. Or who shall descend into the deep, that is to bring up Christ again from the dead. But

what saith the Scripture? The word is nigh thee, even in thy mouth and in thy heart. This is the word of faith, which we preach. (Rom. 10:6-8)

For Saint Paul, the problem of justification is not a matter of proving the truth of this or that doctrine, but of making Christ live in our hearts by faith (Eph. 3:17). An Apostle is one who engenders "new beings" in Christ, by the word of God. "For," says Paul to the Corinthians, "if you have ten thousand instructors in Christ, yet not many fathers. For in Christ Jesus, by the gospel, I have begotten you" (I Cor. 4:15).

The word of faith is what begets spiritual life in the believer. The word, says Saint Paul, is very near to us, once it has been "planted" like the mustard seed in our heart. This planting starts an interior activity which results in a "new birth," or the fundamental spiritual transformation from which emerges a new interior self, a "new creature," united with Christ by faith. This supernatural transformation is precipitated by the "word of faith." Our spiritual generation as "new men in Christ" depends entirely on our reaction to this "word." The problem of the catechumen who wants to believe and cannot do so will be resolved as soon as he finds out what to make of the "word" that has been planted in him. Saint Paul sums up his solution in two statements:

With the heart we believe unto justice: with the mouth confession is made unto salvation. (Rom. 10:10)

Saint Thomas Aquinas, commenting on the words "with the heart we believe unto justice," says:

This means that it is with the *will* that we believe. For other things, which pertain to the exterior worship of God, can be done by a man unwillingly. But no one can believe unless he wills to do so (*Nemo credere potest nisi volens*). For the intellect of the believer is not determined to assent to truth by the force of argument (*ex necessitate rationis*) as is the mind of one who knows. That is why justification [i.e. supernatural life] is *not a matter of knowing but of believing, since justification takes place in the will.*[1]

This movement of the will, by which the intellect accepts the truth of God on faith, is inevitably conditioned by the further action of the will which will be demanded as a consequence of faith. Faith will sooner or later have to be "confessed unto salvation." This means that the truth which we believe must take possession of our entire being, in such a way that faith will "work by charity" and our words and actions will outwardly express the change of life that has taken place within us. If necessary, we must even speak loud our faith into the face of death.

The man who has no real intellectual difficulties about faith and yet "cannot believe" is sometimes one who cannot face the prospect of this interior revolution. He earnestly desires peace: but not at the price of battle. He wants Christ to be a sign for the salvation of his spirit without being a sign of contradiction. Convinced of the credibility of revelation, hungry for a life of faith, he needs only to make an act of will. But that act of will is so tremendous, so sweeping in its consequences! No wonder the poor man is paralyzed.

This moral paralysis often obscures the intellectual issue. A person who has no real difficulties with Catholic truth can suddenly find himself beset with "problems" which are nothing but the transference of his moral impotence into an intellectual sphere. A week ago, a month ago, he was able to grasp quite clearly the outlines of Catholic doctrine: but now, under "instruction" he becomes bewildered, he can no longer see. His mind has been darkened by the hesitation of his will. He is subconsciously diverting himself from the truth which he is afraid to embrace in its entirety.

V

IT IS NOT FOR ANYONE TO SAY how or when God is to dispense His gifts of grace. But it seems to me probable that anyone who sees the credibility of the Catholic faith and feels at some time or other a definite desire to embrace it, has already received sufficient grace to do so. There is no need to wait about for a star to appear in the heavens or for an angel to tell him to get baptized or for him to see Our Lord surrounded by a great light.

If he does not know for sure whether he has the grace to accept the faith, let him start accepting it anyway, and he will soon find out that he has been given not only sufficient but efficacious grace to do so. Let him make the act of will which he thinks is impossible: he will find out, after he has done it, that it was possible. In so doing he will commit himself to embrace all the apparently severe moral consequences of Christian faith. But he can be morally certain that, if he has enough grace to start the journey, he will also receive all the grace he needs to continue it and to reach the end.

It is only when faith, by the action of the will in charity, takes full possession of our being that the so-called "light of faith" becomes what one might classify as an "experience." In the order of faith, light is only procured by the mediation of the will. The intellect cannot find the way alone because in this particular case it is determined by the will.

Only after it has been led over the path by the will can it reflect back on its experience and realize what has happened.

This same law applies all the way from the first act of faith to the highest degree of mystical contemplation. The whole road is ordinarily traveled in darkness. We receive enlightenment only in proportion as we give ourselves more and more completely to God by humble submission and love. We do not first see, then act: we act, then see. It is only by the free submission of our judgment in dark faith that we can advance to the light of understanding: *credo ut intelligam*. And that is why the man who wants to see clearly, before he will believe, never starts on the journey.

[1] *Commentarium in Epistolam ad Romanos*, cap. 10, lectio ii.

THE ASCENT TO TRUTH

Eleven: OUR LADY OF COBRE

I TOLD MYSELF that the reason why I had come to Cuba was to make a pilgrimage to Our Lady of Cobre. And I did, in fact, make a kind of a pilgrimage. But it was one of those medieval pilgrimages that was nine-tenths vacation and one-tenth pilgrimage. God tolerated all this and accepted the pilgrimage on the best terms in which it could be interpreted, because He certainly beset me with graces all the way around Cuba: graces of the kind that even a person without deep spirituality can appreciate as graces, and that is the kind of person I was then and still am.

Every step I took opened up a new world of joys, spiritual joys, and joys of the mind and imagination and senses in the natural order, but on the plane of innocence, and under the direction of grace.

There was a partial natural explanation for this. I was learning a thing that could not be completely learned except in a culture that is at least outwardly Catholic. One needs the atmosphere of French or Spanish or Italian Catholicism before there is any possibility of a complete and total experience of all the natural and sensible joys that overflow from the Sacramental life.

But here, at every turn, I found my way into great, cool, dark churches, some of them with splendid altars shining with carven retables or rich with mahogany and silver, and wonderful red gardens of flame flowered before the saints or the Blessed Sacrament.

Here in niches were those lovely, dressed-up images, those little carved Virgins full of miracle and pathos and clad in silks and black velvet, throned above the high altars. Here, in side chapels, were those *pietàs* fraught with fierce, Spanish drama, with thorns and nails whose very sight pierced the mind and heart, and all around the church were many altars to white and black saints; and everywhere were Cubans in prayer, for it is not true that the Cubans neglect their religion—or not as true as Americans complacently think, basing their judgments on the lives of the rich, sallow young men who come north from the island and spend their days in arduous gambling in the dormitories of Jesuit colleges.

But I was living like a prince in that island, like a spiritual millionaire. Every morning, getting up about seven or half past, and walking out into the warm sunny street, I could find my way quickly to any one of a dozen churches, new churches or as old as the seventeenth century. Almost as soon as I went in the door I could receive Communion, if I wished, for the priest came out with a ciborium loaded with Hosts before Mass and during it and after it—and every fifteen or twenty minutes a new Mass was starting at a different altar. These were the churches of the religious orders—Carmelites, Franciscans, the American Augustinians at El Santo Cristo, or the Fathers of Mercy—everywhere I turned, there was someone ready to feed me with the infinite strength of the Christ Who loved me, and Who was beginning to show me with an immense and subtle and generous lavishness how much He loved me.

And there were a thousand things to do, a thousand ways of easily making a thanksgiving; everything lent itself to Communion: I could hear another Mass, I could say the Rosary, do the Stations of the Cross, or if I just knelt where I was, everywhere I turned my eyes I saw saints in wood or plaster or those who seemed to be saints in flesh and blood —and even those who were probably not saints were new enough and picturesque enough to stimulate my mind with many meanings and my heart with prayers. And as I left the church there was no lack of beggars to give me the opportunity of almsgiving, which is an easy and simple way of wiping out sins.

Often I left one church and went to hear another Mass in another church, especially if the day happened to be Sunday, and I would listen to the harmonious sermons of the Spanish priests, the very grammar of which was full of dignity and mysticism and courtesy. After Latin, it seems to me there is no language so fitted for prayer and for talk about God as Spanish: for it is a language at once strong and supple, it has its sharpness, it has the quality of steel in it, which gives it the accuracy that true mysticism needs, and yet it is soft, too, and gentle and pliant, which devotion needs, and it is courteous and suppliant and courtly, and it lends itself surprisingly little to sentimentality. It has some of the intellectuality of French but not the coldness that intellectuality gets in French; and it never overflows into the feminine melodies of Italian. Spanish is never a weak language, never sloppy, even on the lips of a woman.

The fact that while all this was going on in the pulpit, there would be Cubans ringing bells and yelling lottery numbers outside in the street seemed to make no difference. For a people that is supposed to be excitable, the Cubans have a phenomenal amount of patience with all the things that get on American nerves and drive people crazy, like persistent and strident noise. But for my own part, I did not mind any of that any more than the natives did.

When I was sated with prayers, I could go back into the streets, walking among the lights and shadows, stopping to drink huge glasses of iced fruit juices in the little bars, until I came home again and read Maritain or St. Teresa until it was time for lunch.

And so I made my way to Matanzas and Camagüey and Santiago— riding in a wild bus through the olive-gray Cuban countryside, full of sugar-cane fields. All the way I said rosaries and looked out into the great solitary ceiba trees, half expecting that the Mother of God would appear to me in one of them. There seemed to be no reason why she should not, for all things in heaven were just a little out of reach. So I kept looking, looking, and half expecting. But I did not see Our Lady appear, beautiful, in any of the ceiba trees.

At Matanzas I got mixed up in the *paseo* where the whole town walks around and around the square in the evening coolness, the men in one direction and the girls in the other direction, and immediately I made friends with about fifty-one different people of all ages. The evening ended up with me making a big speech in broken Spanish, surrounded by men and boys in a motley crowd that included the town Reds and the town intellectuals and the graduates of the Marist Fathers' school and some law students from the University of Havana. It was all about faith and morals and made a big impression and, in return, their accept-ance of it made a big impression on me, too, for many of them were glad that someone, a foreigner, should come and talk about these things, and I heard someone who had just arrived in the crowd say:

"Es católico, ese Americano?"

"Man," said the other, "he is a Catholic and a very good Catholic," and the tone in which he said this made me so happy that, when I went to bed, I could not sleep. I lay in the bed and looked up through the mosquito netting at the bright stars that shone in upon me through the wide-open window that had no glass and no frame, but only a heavy wooden shutter against the rain.

In Camagüey I found a Church to La Soledad, Our Lady of Solitude, a little dressed-up image up in a shadowy niche; you could hardly see her. La Soledad! One of my big devotions, and you never find her, never hear anything about her in this country, except that one of the old California missions was dedicated to her.

Finally my bus went roaring across the dry plain towards the blue wall of mountains: Oriente, the end of my pilgrimage.

When we had crossed over the divide and were going down through the green valleys towards the Caribbean Sea, I saw the yellow Basilica of Our Lady of Cobre, standing on a rising above the tin roofs of the mining village in the depths of a deep bowl of green, backed by cliffs and sheer slopes robed in jungle.

"There you are, Caridad del Cobre! It is you that I have come to see; you will ask Christ to make me His priest, and I will give you my heart, Lady. And if you will obtain for me this priesthood, I will remember you at my first Mass in such a way that the Mass will be for you and offered through your hands in gratitude to the Holy Trinity, Who has used your love to win me this great grace."

The bus tore down the mountainside to Santiago. The mining engineer who had got on at the top of the divide was talking all the way down in English he had learned in New York, telling me of the graft that had enriched the politicians of Cuba and of Oriente.

In Santiago I ate dinner on the terrace of a big hotel in front of the cathedral. Across the square was the shell of a five-story building that looked as if it had been gutted by a bomb: but the ruin had happened in an earthquake not so very long before. It was long enough ago so that the posters on the fence that had been put up in front of it had time to get tattered, and I was thinking: perhaps it is now getting to be time for another earthquake. And I looked up at the two towers of the cathedral, ready to sway and come booming down on my head.

The bus that took me to Cobre the next morning was the most dangerous of all the furious buses that are the terror of Cuba. I think it made most of the journey at eighty miles an hour on two wheels, and several times I thought it was going to explode. I said rosaries all the way up to the shrine, while the trees went by in a big greenish-yellow blur. If Our Lady had tried to appear to me, I probably would never even have got a glimpse of her.

I walked up the path that wound around the mound on which the

Basilica stands. Entering the door, I was surprised that the floor was so
shiny and the place was so clean. I was in the back of the church, up
in the apse, in a kind of oratory behind the high altar, and there, facing
me, in a little shrine, was La Caridad, the little, cheerful, black Virgin,
crowned with a crown and dressed in royal robes, who is the Queen of
Cuba.

There was nobody else in the place but a pious middle-aged lady attendant in a black dress who was eager to sell me a lot of medals, and
so I knelt before La Caridad and made my prayer and made my promise. I sneaked down into the Basilica after that, and knelt where I could
see La Caridad and where I could really be alone and pray, but the
pious lady, impatient to make her deal, or perhaps afraid that I might
get up to some mischief in the Basilica, came down and peeked through
the door.

So, disappointed and resigned, I got up and came out and bought a
medal and got some change for the beggars and went away, without
having a chance to say all that I wanted to say to La Caridad or to hear
much from her.

Down in the village I bought a bottle of some kind of *gaseosa* and
stood under the tin roof of the porch of the village store. Somewhere
in one of the shacks, on a harmonium, was played: *"Kyrie Eleison,
Kyrie Eleison, Kyrie Eleison."*

And I went back to Santiago.

But while I was sitting on the terrace of the hotel, eating lunch, La
Caridad del Cobre had a word to say to me. She handed me an idea
for a poem that formed so easily and smoothly and spontaneously in
my mind that all I had to do was finish eating and go up to my room
and type it out, almost without a correction.

So the poem turned out to be both what she had to say to me and
what I had to say to her. It was a song for La Caridad del Cobre, and
it was, as far as I was concerned, something new, and the first real poem
I had ever written, or anyway the one I liked best. It pointed the way
to many other poems; it opened the gate, and set me traveling on a certain and direct track that was to last me several years.

The poem said:

> The white girls lift their heads like trees,
> The black girls go
> Reflected like flamingoes in the street.
>
> The white girls sing as shrill as water,
> The black girls talk as quiet as clay.

> The white girls open their arms like clouds,
> The black girls close their eyes like wings:
> Angels bow down like bells,
> Angels look up like toys,
>
> Because the heavenly stars
> Stand in a ring:
> And all the pieces of the mosaic, earth,
> Get up and fly away like birds.

When I went back to Havana, I found out something else, too, and something vastly more important. It was something that made me realize, all of a sudden, not merely intellectually, but experimentally, the real uselessness of what I had been half deliberately looking for: the visions in the ceiba trees. And this experience opened another door, not a way to a kind of writing but a way into a world infinitely new, a world that was out of this world of ours entirely and which transcended it infinitely, and which was not a world, but which was God Himself.

I was in the Church of St. Francis at Havana. It was a Sunday. I had been to Communion at some other church, I think at El Cristo, and now I had come here to hear another Mass. The building was crowded. Up in front, before the altar, there were rows and rows of children, crowded together. I forget whether they were First Communicants or not: but they were children around that age. I was far in the back of the church, but I could see the heads of all those children.

It came time for the Consecration. The priest raised the Host, then he raised the chalice. When he put the chalice down on the altar, suddenly a Friar in his brown robe and white cord stood up in front of the children, and all at once the voices of the children burst out:

"*Creo en Diós. . . .*"

"I believe in God the Father Almighty, the creator of heaven and earth. . . ."

The Creed. But that cry, "*Creo en Diós!*" It was loud, and bright, and sudden and glad and triumphant; it was a good big shout, that came from all those Cuban children, a joyous affirmation of faith.

Then, as sudden as the shout and as definite, and a thousand times more bright, there formed in my mind an awareness, an understanding, a realization of what had just taken place on the altar, at the Consecration: a realization of God made present by the words of Consecration in a way that made Him belong to me.

But what a thing it was, this awareness: it was so intangible, and yet it struck me like a thunderclap. It was a light that was so bright that it had no relation to any visible light and so profound and so intimate that it seemed like a neutralization of every lesser experience.

And yet the thing that struck me most of all was that this light was in a certain sense "ordinary"—it was a light (and this most of all was what took my breath away) that was offered to all, to everybody, and there was nothing fancy or strange about it. It was the light of faith deepened and reduced to an extreme and sudden obviousness.

It was as if I had been suddenly illuminated by being blinded by the manifestation of God's presence.

The reason why this light was blinding and neutralizing was that there was and could be simply nothing in it of sense or imagination. When I call it a light that is a metaphor which I am using, long after the fact. But at the moment, another overwhelming thing about this awareness was that it disarmed all images, all metaphors, and cut through the whole skein of species and phantasms with which we naturally do our thinking. It ignored all sense experience in order to strike directly at the heart of truth, as if a sudden and immediate contact had been established between my intellect and the Truth Who was now physically really and substantially before me on the altar. But this contact was not something speculative and abstract: it was concrete and experimental and belonged to the order of knowledge, yes, but more still to the order of love.

Another thing about it was that this light was something far above and beyond the level of any desire or any appetite I had ever yet been aware of. It was purified of all emotion and cleansed of everything that savored of sensible yearnings. It was love as clean and direct as vision: and it flew straight to the possession of the Truth it loved.

And the first articulate thought that came to my mind was:

"Heaven is right here in front of me: Heaven, Heaven!"

It lasted only a moment, but it left a breathless joy and a clean peace and happiness that stayed for hours and it was something I have never forgotten.

The strange thing about this light was that although it seemed so "ordinary" in the sense I have mentioned, and so accessible, there was no way of recapturing it. In fact, I did not even know how to start trying to reconstruct the experience or bring it back if I wanted to, except to make acts of faith and love. But it was easy to see that there was nothing I could do to give any act of faith that peculiar quality of sudden obviousness: that was a gift and had to come from somewhere else, beyond and above myself.

However, let no one think that just because of this light that came to me one day, at Mass, in the Church of St. Francis at Havana, I was in the habit of understanding things that clearly, or that I was far advanced in prayer. No, my prayer continued to be largely vocal. And the mental prayer I made was not systematic, but the more or less spontaneous meditating and affective prayer that came and went, according to my reading, here and there. And most of the time my prayer was not so much prayer as a matter of anticipating, with hope and desire, my entrance into the Franciscan novitiate, and a certain amount of imagining as to what it was going to be like, so that often I was not praying at all but only daydreaming.

THE SEVEN STOREY MOUNTAIN

Epilogue

Most of the world is either asleep or dead. The religious people are, for the most part, asleep. The irreligious are dead. Those who are asleep are divided into two classes, like the Virgins in the parable, waiting for the Bridegroom's coming. The wise have oil in their lamps. That is to say they are detached from themselves and from the cares of the world, and they are full of charity. They are indeed waiting for the Bridegroom, and they desire nothing else but His coming, even though they may fall asleep while waiting for Him to appear. But the others are not only asleep, they are full of other dreams and other desires. Their lamps are empty because they have burned themselves out in the wisdom of the flesh and in their own vanity. When He comes, it is too late for them to buy oil. They light their lamps only after He has gone. So they fall asleep again, with useless lamps, and when they wake up they trim them to investigate, once again, the matters of a dying world.

NO MAN IS AN ISLAND

PART TWO

Magnetic North

After we had reached the upper edge
  of the high cliff, on the open hillside,
    "Master," I said, "which way shall we take?"
And he to me, "Let none of your steps fall back;
  make your way behind me up the mount
    until some guide appears to us."

One: WITH A GREAT PRICE

So now is the time to tell a thing that I could not realize then, but which has become very clear to me: that God brought me and a half a dozen others together at Columbia, and made us friends, in such a way that our friendship would work powerfully to rescue us from the confusion and the misery in which we had come to find ourselves, partly through our own fault, and partly through a complex set of circumstances which might be grouped together under the heading of the "modern world," "modern society." But the qualification "modern" is unnecessary and perhaps unfair. The traditional Gospel term, "the world," will do well enough.

All our salvation begins on the level of common and natural and ordinary things. (That is why the whole economy of the Sacraments, for instance, rests, in its material element, upon plain and ordinary things like bread and wine and water and salt and oil.) And so it was with me. Books and ideas and poems and stories, pictures and music, buildings, cities, places, philosophies were to be the materials on which grace would work. But these things are themselves not enough. The more fundamental instinct of fear for my own preservation came in, in a minor sort of a way, in this strange, half-imaginary sickness which nobody could diagnose completely.

The coming war, and all the uncertainties and confusions and fears that followed necessarily from that, and all the rest of the violence and injustice that were in the world, had a very important part to play. All these things were bound together and fused and vitalized and prepared for the action of grace, both in my own soul and in the souls of at least one or two of my friends, merely by our friendship and association together. And it fermented in our sharing of our own ideas and miseries and headaches and perplexities and fears and difficulties and desires and hangovers and all the rest.

✧ DOUBT AND ASCETICISM

SEYMOUR AND LAX were rooming together in one of the dormitories, for Bob Gibney, with whom Lax had roomed the year before, had now graduated and was sitting in Port Washington with much the same dispositions with which I had been sitting in Douglaston, facing a not-too-dissimilar blank wall, the end of his own blind alley. He occasionally came in to town to see Dona Eaton who had a place on 112th Street, but no job, and was more cheerful about her own quandary than the rest of us, because the worst that could happen to her was that she would at last run completely out of money and have to go home to Panama.

Gibney was not what you would call pious. In fact, he had an attitude that would be commonly called impious, only I believe God understood well enough that his violence and sarcasms covered a sense of deep metaphysical dismay—an anguish that was real, though not humble enough to be of much use to his soul. What was materially impiety in him was directed more against common ideas and notions which he saw or considered to be totally inadequate, and maybe it subjectively represented a kind of oblique zeal for the purity of God, this rebellion against the commonplace and trite, against mediocrity, religiosity.

During the year that had passed, I suppose it must have been in the spring of 1937, both Gibney and Lax and Bob Gerdy had all been talking about becoming Catholics. Bob Gerdy was a very smart sophomore with the face of a child and a lot of curly hair on top of it, who took life seriously, and had discovered courses on scholastic philosophy in the graduate school, and had taken one of them.

Gibney was interested in scholastic philosophy in much the same way as James Joyce was—he respected its intellectuality, particularly that of the Thomists, but there was not enough that was affective about his interest to bring about any kind of a conversion.

For the three or four years that I knew Gibney, he was always holding out for some kind of a "sign," some kind of a sensible and tangible interior jolt from God, to get him started, some mystical experience or other. And while he waited and waited for this to come along, he did all the things that normally exclude and nullify the action of grace. So in those days, none of them became Catholics.

The most serious of them all, in this matter, was Lax: he was the one that had been born with the deepest sense of Who God was. But he would not make a move without the others.

And then there was myself. Having read *The Spirit of Medieval Philosophy* and having discovered that the Catholic conception of God was something tremendously solid, I had not progressed one step beyond this recognition, except that one day I had gone and looked up St. Bernard's *De Diligendo Deo* in the catalogue of the University Library. It was one of the books Gilson had frequently mentioned; but when I found that there was no good copy of it, except in Latin, I did not take it out.

Now it was November 1937. One day, Lax and I were riding downtown on one of those buses you caught at the corner of 110th Street and Broadway. We had skirted the southern edge of Harlem, passing along the top of Central Park, and the dirty lake full of rowboats. Now we were going down Fifth Avenue, under the trees. Lax was telling me about a book he had been reading, which was Aldous Huxley's *Ends and Means*. He told me about it in a way that made me want to read it too.

So I went to Scribner's bookstore and bought it, and read it, and wrote an article about it, and gave the article to Barry Ulanov who was editor of *Review* by that time. He accepted the article with a big Greek smile and printed it. The smile was on account of the conversion it represented, I mean the conversion in me, as well as in Huxley, although one of the points I tried to make was that perhaps Huxley's conversion should not have been taken as so much of a surprise.

Huxley had been one of my favorite novelists in the days when I had been sixteen and seventeen and had built up a strange, ignorant philosophy of pleasure based on all the stories I was reading. And now everybody was talking about the way Huxley had changed. The chatter was all the more pleasant because of Huxley's agnostic old grandfather—and his biologist brother. Now the man was preaching mysticism.

Not only was there such a thing as a supernatural order, but as a matter of concrete experience, it was accessible, very close at hand, an extremely near, an immediate and most necessary source of moral vitality, and one which could be reached most simply, most readily by prayer, faith, detachment, love.

The point of his title was this: we cannot use evil means to attain a good end. Huxley's chief argument was that we were using the means that precisely made good ends impossible to attain: war, violence, reprisals, rapacity. And he traced our impossibility to use the proper means to the fact that men were immersed in the material and animal urges of an element in their nature which was blind and crude and unspiritual.

The main problem is to fight our way free from subjection to this more or less inferior element, and to reassert the dominance of our mind and will: to vindicate for these faculties, for the spirit as a whole, the freedom of action which it must necessarily have if we are to live like anything but wild beasts, tearing each other to pieces. And the big conclusion from all this was: we must practice prayer and asceticism.

❖ IN A NEW WORLD

BROADWAY WAS EMPTY. A solitary trolley came speeding down in front of Barnard College and past the School of Journalism. Then, from the high, gray, expensive tower of the Rockefeller Church, huge bells began to boom. It served very well for the eleven o'clock Mass at the little brick Church of Corpus Christi, hidden behind Teachers College on 121st Street.

How bright the little building seemed. Indeed, it was quite new. The sun shone on the clean bricks. People were going in the wide open door, into the cool darkness and, all at once, all the churches of Italy and France came back to me. The richness and fullness of the atmosphere of Catholicism that I had not been able to avoid apprehending and loving as a child, came back to me with a rush; but now I was to enter into it fully for the first time. So far, I had known nothing but the outward surface.

It was a gay, clean church, with big plain windows and white columns and pilasters and a well-lighted, simple sanctuary. Its style was a trifle eclectic, but much less perverted with incongruities than the average Catholic church in America. It had a kind of a seventeenth-century, oratorian character about it, though with a sort of American colonial tinge of simplicity. The blend was effective and original; but although all this affected me, without my thinking about it, the thing that impressed me most was that the place was full, absolutely full. It was full not only of old ladies and broken-down gentlemen with one foot in the grave, but of men and women and children young and old—especially young: people of all classes, and all ranks, on a solid foundation of workingmen and women and their families.

I found a place that I hoped would be obscure, over on one side, in the back, and went to it without genuflecting, and knelt down. As I knelt, the first thing I noticed was a young girl, very pretty too, perhaps fifteen or sixteen, kneeling straight up and praying quite seriously. I was very much impressed to see that someone who was young and beautiful could with such simplicity make prayer the real and serious and principal reason for going to church. She was clearly kneeling that way because she meant it, not in order to show off, and she was praying with an absorption which, though not the deep recollection of a saint, was serious enough to show that she was not thinking at all about the other people who were there.

What a revelation it was to discover so many ordinary people in a place together, more conscious of God than of one another; not there to show off their hats or their clothes, but to pray, or at least to fulfill a religious obligation, not a human one. For even those who might have been there for no better motive than that they were obliged to be, were at least free from any of the self-conscious and human constraint which is never absent from a Protestant church, where people are definitely gathered together as people, as neighbors, and always have at least half an eye for one another, if not all of both eyes.

Since it was summertime, the eleven o'clock Mass was a Low Mass; but I had not come expecting to hear music. Before I knew it, the priest was in the sanctuary with the two altar boys, and was busy at the altar with something or other which I could not see very well, but the people were praying by themselves, and I was engrossed and absorbed in the thing as a whole: the business at the altar and the presence of the people. And still I had not got rid of my fear. Seeing the latecomers hastily genuflecting before entering the pew, I realized my omission, and got the idea that people had spotted me for a pagan and were just waiting for me to miss a few more genuflections before throwing me out or, at least, giving me looks of reproof.

Soon we all stood up. I did not know what for. The priest was at the other end of the altar, and, as I afterwards learned, he was reading the Gospel. And then the next thing I knew there was someone in the pulpit.

It was a young priest, perhaps not much over thirty-three or thirty-four years old. His face was rather ascetic and thin, and its asceticism was heightened with a note of intellectuality by his horn-rimmed glasses, although he was only one of the assistants, and he did not consider himself an intellectual, nor did anyone else apparently consider him so. But anyway, that was the impression he made on me; and his sermon, which was simple enough, did not belie it.

It was not long, but to me it was very interesting to hear this young man quietly telling the people in language that was plain, yet tinged with scholastic terminology, about a point in Catholic doctrine. How clear and solid the doctrine was: for behind those words you felt the full force not only of Scripture but of centuries of a unified and continuous and consistent tradition. And above all, it was a vital tradition: there was nothing studied or antique about it. These words, this terminology, this doctrine, and these convictions fell from the lips of the young priest as something that were most intimately part of his own life. What was more, I sensed that the people were familiar with it all, and that it was also, in due proportion, part of their life also: it was just as much integrated into their spiritual organism as the air they breathed or the food they ate worked in to their blood and flesh.

What was he saying? That Christ was the Son of God. That, in Him, the Second Person of the Holy Trinity, God, had assumed a human nature, a human body and soul, and had taken Flesh and dwelt amongst us, full of grace and truth; and that this Man, Whom men called the Christ, was God. He was both Man and God: two natures hypostatically united in one Person or suppositum, one individual Who was a Divine Person, having assumed to Himself a human nature. And His works were the works of God: His acts were the acts of God. He loved us: God, and walked among us: God, and died for us on the Cross, God of God, Light of Light, True God of True God.

Jesus Christ was not simply a man, a good man, a great man, the greatest prophet, a wonderful healer, a saint: He was something that made all such trivial words pale into irrelevance. He was God. But nevertheless He was not merely a spirit without a true body, God hiding under a visionary body: He was also truly a Man, born of the Flesh of the Most Pure Virgin, formed of her Flesh by the Holy Spirit. And what He did, in that Flesh, on earth, He did not only as Man but as God. He loved us as God, He suffered and died for us, God.

And how did we know? Because it was revealed to us in the Scriptures and confirmed by the teaching of the Church and of the powerful unanimity of Catholic tradition from the First Apostles, from the first

Popes and the early Fathers, on down through the Doctors of the Church and the great scholastics, to our own day. *De Fide Divina.* If you believed it, you would receive light to grasp it, to understand it in some measure. If you did not believe it, you would never understand; it would never be anything but scandal or folly.

And no one can believe these things merely by wanting to, of his own volition. Unless he receive grace, an actual light and impulsion of the mind and will from God, he cannot even make an act of living faith. It is God Who gives us faith, and no one cometh to Christ unless the Father draweth him.

The sermon was what I most needed to hear that day. When the Mass of the Catechumens was over, I, who was not even a catechumen, but only a blind and deaf and dumb pagan as weak and dirty as anything that ever came out of the darkness of Imperial Rome or Corinth or Ephesus, was not able to understand anything else.

It all became completely mysterious when the attention was refocused on the altar. When the silence grew more and more profound, and little bells began to ring, I got scared again and, finally, genuflecting hastily on my left knee, I hurried out of the church in the middle of the most important part of the Mass. But it was just as well. In a way, I suppose I was responding to a kind of liturgical instinct that told me I did not belong there for the celebration of the Mysteries as such. I had no idea what took place in them, but the fact was that Christ, God, would be visibly present on the altar in the Sacred Species. And although He was there, yes, for love of me, yet He was there in His power and His might, and what was I? What was on my soul? What was I in His sight?

It was liturgically fitting that I should kick myself out at the end of the Mass of the Catechumens, when the ordained *ostiarii* should have been there to do it. Anyway, it was done.

Now I walked leisurely down Broadway in the sun, and my eyes looked about me at a new world. I could not understand what it was that had happened to make me so happy, why I was so much at peace, so content with life for I was not yet used to the clean savor that comes with an actual grace—indeed, there was no impossibility in a person's hearing and believing such a sermon and being justified, that is, receiving sanctifying grace in his soul as a habit, and beginning, from that moment, to live the divine and supernatural life for good and all. But that is something I will not speculate about.

All I know is that I walked in a new world. Even the ugly buildings of Columbia were transfigured in it, and everywhere was peace in these streets designed for violence and noise. Sitting outside the gloomy little Childs restaurant at 111th Street, behind the dirty, boxed bushes, and eating breakfast, was like sitting in the Elysian fields.

THE SEVEN STOREY MOUNTAIN

Two: FREEDOM

To CONSIDER PERSONS and events and situations only in the light of their effect upon myself is to live on the doorstep of hell. Selfishness is doomed to frustration, centered as it is upon a lie. To live exclusively for myself, I must make all things bend themselves to my will as if I were a god. But this is impossible. Is there any more cogent indication of my creaturehood than the insufficiency of my own will? For I cannot make the universe obey me. I cannot make other people conform to my own whims and fancies. I cannot make even my own body obey me. When I give it pleasure, it deceives my expectation and makes me suffer pain. When I give myself what I conceive to be freedom, I deceive myself and find that I am the prisoner of my own blindness and selfishness and insufficiency.

It is true, the freedom of my will is a great thing. But this freedom is not absolute self-sufficiency. If the essence of freedom were merely the act of choice, then the mere fact of making choices would perfect our freedom. But there are two difficulties here. First of all, our choices must really be free—that is to say, they must perfect us in our own being. They must perfect us in our relation to other free beings. We must make the choices that enable us to fulfill the deepest capacities of our real selves. From this flows the second difficulty: we too easily assume that we *are* our real selves, and that our choices are really the ones we want to make when, in fact, our acts of free choice are (though morally imputable, no doubt) largely dictated by psychological compulsions, flowing from our inordinate ideas of our own importance. Our choices are too often dictated by our false selves.

Hence I do not find in myself the power to be happy merely by doing what I like. On the contrary, if I do nothing except what pleases my own fancy I will be miserable almost all the time. This would never be so if my will had not been created to use its own freedom in the love of others.

My free will consolidates and perfects its own autonomy by freely co-ordinating its action with the will of another. There is something in the very nature of my freedom that inclines me to love, to do good, to dedicate myself to others. I have an instinct that tells me that I am less free when I am living for myself alone. The reason for this is that I cannot be completely independent. Since I am not self-sufficient I depend on someone else for my fulfillment. My freedom is not fully free when left to itself. It becomes so when it is brought into the right relation with the freedom of another.

At the same time, my instinct to be independent is by no means evil. My freedom is not perfected by subjection to a tyrant. Subjection is not an end in itself. It is right that my nature should rebel against subjection. Why should my will have been created free, if I were never to use my freedom?

If my will is meant to perfect its freedom in serving another will, that does not mean it will find its perfection in serving *every* other will. In fact, there is only one will in whose service I can find perfection and freedom. To give my freedom blindly to a being equal to or inferior to myself is to degrade myself and throw away my freedom. I can only become perfectly free by serving the will of God. If I do, in fact, obey other men and serve them it is not for their sake alone that I will do so, but because their will is the sacrament of the will of God. Obedience to man has no meaning unless it is primarily obedience to God. From this flow many consequences. Where there is no faith in God there can be no real order; therefore, where there is no faith obedience is without any sense. It can only be imposed on others as a matter of expediency. If there is no God, no government is logical except tyranny. And in actual fact, states that reject the idea of God tend either to tyranny or to moral chaos. In either case, the end is disorder, because tyranny is itself a disorder.

THE IMMATURE CONSCIENCE is not its own master. It is merely the delegate of the conscience of another person, or of a group, or of a party, or of a social class, or of a nation, or of a race. Therefore, it does not make real moral decisions of its own, it simply parrots the decisions of others. It does not make judgments of its own, it merely "conforms" to the party line. It does not really have motives or intentions of its own.

Or if it does, it wrecks them by twisting and rationalizing them to fit the intentions of another. That is not moral freedom. It makes true love impossible. For if I am to love truly and freely, I must be able to give something that is truly my own to another. If my heart does not first belong to me, how can I give it to another? It is not mine to give!

FREE WILL is not given to us merely as a firework to be shot off into the air. There are some men who seem to think their acts are freer in proportion as they are without purpose, as if a rational purpose imposed some kind of limitation upon our liberty. That is like saying that one is richer if he throws money out the window than if he spends it.

Since money is what it is, I do not deny that you may be worthy of all praise if you light your cigarettes with it. That would show you had a deep, pure sense of the ontological value of the dollar. Nevertheless, if that is all you can think of doing with money you will not long enjoy the advantages that it can still obtain.

It may be true that a rich man can better afford to throw money out the window than a poor man, but neither the spending nor the waste of money is what makes a man rich. He is rich by virtue of what he has, and his riches are valuable to him for what he can do with them.

As for freedom, according to this analogy, it grows no greater by being wasted, or spent, but it is given to us as a talent to be traded with until the coming of Christ. In this trading we part with what is ours only to recover it with interest. We do not destroy it or throw it away. We dedicate it to some purpose, and this dedication makes us freer than we were before.

NO MAN IS AN ISLAND

Three: PRAYER AND THE SUBCONSCIOUS

It would be a great mistake to turn the interior life into a psychological experiment and make our prayer the object of psychoanalysis. If it is true and valid prayer, it needs no such analysis. But note that I have said *if*: for if it is not true prayer, it might very well benefit from analysis. The disheartening prevalence of false mysticism, the deadening grip that false asceticism sometimes gets on religious souls, and the common substitution of sentimentality for true religious feeling—all these things seem to warrant a little investigation of the subconscious substrate of what passes for "religion."

The subconscious mind plays a very important part in the interior life, even though it remains behind the scenes. Just as a good play depends on the scene, the lighting, and all the rest, so too our interior life owes much of its character to the setting and lighting and background and atmosphere which are provided, without any deliberate action of our own, by our subconscious mind.

In fact, it sometimes happens that the whole tone and atmosphere of a person's life of prayer—a certain emphasis on solitude or on sacrifice or on asceticism or on apostolic radiation—is provided by elements in the subconscious mind. For the subconscious mind is a storehouse of images and symbols, I might almost say of "experiences" which provides us with more than half the material of what we actually experience as "life." Without our knowing it, we see reality through glasses colored by the subconscious memory of previous experiences.

It is, therefore, important that our subconscious mind should enable us to live as our true selves. Indeed, it often happens that a man's true self is literally buried in the subconscious, and never has a chance to express itself except in symbolic protest against the tyranny of a mal-formed conscience that insists on remaining immature.

I do not say that we should try, without training or experience, to explore our own subconscious depths. But we ought at least to admit that they exist, and that they are important, and we ought to have the humility to admit we do not know all about ourselves, that we are not experts at running our own lives. We ought to stop taking our conscious plans and decisions with such infinite seriousness. It may well be that we are *not* the martyrs or the mystics or the apostles or the leaders or the lovers of God that we imagine ourselves to be. Our subconscious mind may be trying to tell us this in many ways—and we have trained ourselves, with the most egregious self-righteousness to turn a deaf ear.

NO MAN IS AN ISLAND

Four: "AS A MAN IS, SO HE PRAYS. . . ."

As a man is, so he prays. We make ourselves what we are by the way we address God. The man who never prays is one who has tried to run away from himself because he has run away from God. But unreal though he be, he is more real than the man who prays to God with a false and lying heart.

The sinner who is afraid to pray to God, who tries to deny God in his heart, is, perhaps, closer to confessing God than the sinner who stands before God, proud of his sin because he thinks it is a virtue. The former is more honest than he thinks, for he acknowledges the truth of his own state, confesses that he and God are not at peace with one another. The latter is not only a liar himself, but tries to make God a liar also, by calling upon Him to approve of his own lie. Such was the Pharisee in the parable, the holy man who practiced many virtues, but who lied before God because he thought his piety made him better than other men. He despised sinners, and worshiped a false god who despised them like himself.

PRAYER IS INSPIRED BY GOD in the depth of our own nothingness. It is the movement of trust, of gratitude, of adoration, or of sorrow that places us before God, seeing both Him and ourselves in the light of His infinite truth, and moves us to ask Him for the mercy, the spiritual strength, the material help that we all need. The man whose prayer is so pure that he never asks God for anything does not know who God is, and does not know who he is himself: for he does not know his own need of God.

All true prayer somehow confesses our absolute dependence on the Lord of life and death. It is, therefore, a deep and vital contact with Him Whom we know not only as Lord but as Father. It is when we pray truly that we really *are*. Our being is brought to a high perfection by this, which is one of its most perfect activities. When we cease to pray, we tend to fall back into nothingness. True, we continue to exist. But since the main reason for our existence is the knowledge and love of God, when our conscious contact with Him is severed we sleep or we die.

NO MAN IS AN ISLAND

Five: MAGNETIC NORTH

ONCE AGAIN, classes were beginning at the university. The pleasant fall winds played in the yellowing leaves of the poplars in front of the college dormitories and many young men came out of the subways and walked earnestly and rapidly about the campus with little blue catalogues of courses under their arms, and their hearts warm with the desire to buy books. But now, in this season of new beginnings, I really had something new to begin.

A year ago the conviction had developed in my mind that the one who was going to give me the best advice about where and how to become a priest was Dan Walsh. I had come to this conclusion before I had ever met him, or sat and listened to his happy and ingenuous lectures on St. Thomas. So on this September day, in 1939, the conviction was to bear its fruit.

Dan was not on the Columbia campus that day. I went into one of the phone booths at Livingston Hall and called him up.

He was a man with rich friends, and that night he had been invited to dinner with some people on Park Avenue, although there was certainly nothing of Park Avenue about him and his simplicity. But we arranged to meet downtown, and at about ten o'clock that evening I was standing in the lobby of one of those big, shiny, stuffy apartments, waiting for him to come down out of the elevator.

As soon as we walked out into the cool night, Dan turned to me and said: "You know, the first time I met you I thought you had a vocation to the priesthood."

I was astonished and ashamed. Did I really give that impression? It made me feel like a whited sepulcher, considering what I knew was

inside me. On the whole, perhaps it would have been more reassuring if
he had been surprised.

He was not surprised, he was very pleased. And he was glad to talk
about my vocation, and about the priesthood and about religious orders.
They were things to which he had given a certain amount of thought,
and on the whole I think that my selection of an adviser was a very
happy one. It was a good inspiration and, in fact, it was to turn out much
better than I realized at first.

The quietest place we could think of in that neighborhood was the
men's bar at the Biltmore, a big room full of comfortable chairs, hushed
and paneled and half empty. We sat down in one of the far corners, and
it was there, two being gathered together in His Name and in His
charity, that Christ impressed the first definite form and direction upon
my vocation.

It was very simply done. We just talked about several different religious orders, and Dan suggested various priests I might consult and
finally promised to give me a note of introduction to one of them.

I spoke to Dan Walsh about the Jesuits, but he said he did not know
any Jesuits, and for my own part, the mere fact that he did not seem to
have any particular reaction, positive or negative, to that order, did away
with the weak and vague preference which I had hitherto given it in my
own mind. I had instinctively turned that way first of all, because I had
read the life of Gerard Manley Hopkins and studied his poems, but
there had never been any real attraction calling me to that kind of a life.
It was geared to a pitch of active intensity and military routine which
were alien to my own needs. I doubt if they would have kept me in their
novitiate—but if they had, they would probably have found me a great
misfit. What I needed was the solitude to expand in breadth and depth
and to be simplified out under the gaze of God more or less the way a
plant spreads out its leaves in the sun. That meant that I needed a Rule
that was almost entirely aimed at detaching me from the world and
uniting me with God, not a Rule made to fit me to fight for God in the
world. But I did not find out all that in one day.

Dan spoke of the Benedictines. In itself, the vocation attracted me: a
liturgical life in some big abbey in the depths of the country. But in
actual fact it might just mean being nailed down to a desk in an expensive prep school for the rest of my life—or, worse still, being a parish
priest remotely attached to such a prep school, and living in more or less
permanent separation from the claustral and liturgical center which had
first attracted me.

"What do you think of the Franciscans?" said Dan.

As soon as I mentioned St. Bonaventure's, it turned out that he had many friends there and knew the place fairly well; in fact they had given him some sort of an honorary degree there that summer. Yes, I liked the Franciscans. Their life was very simple and informal and the atmosphere of St. Bonaventure's was pleasant and happy and peaceful. One thing that attracted me to them was a sort of freedom from spiritual restraint, from systems and routine. No matter how much the original Rule of St. Francis has changed, I think his spirit and his inspiration are still the fundamental thing in Franciscan life. And it is an inspiration rooted in joy, because it is guided by the prudence and wisdom which are revealed only to the little ones—the glad wisdom of those who have had the grace and the madness to throw away everything in one uncompromising rush, and to walk around barefooted in the simple confidence that if they get into trouble, God will come and get them out of it again.

This is not something that is confined to the Franciscans: it is at the heart of every religious vocation, and if it is not, the vocation does not mean much. But the Franciscans, or at least St. Francis, reduced it to its logical limits, and at the same time invested it with a kind of simple thirteenth-century lyricism which made it doubly attractive to me.

However, the lyricism must be carefully distinguished from the real substance of the Franciscan vocation, which is that tremendous and heroic poverty, poverty of body and spirit which makes the Friar literally a tramp. For, after all, "mendicant" is only a fancy word for tramp, and if a Franciscan cannot be a tramp in this full and complete and total mystical sense, he is bound to be a little unhappy and dissatisfied. As soon as he acquires a lot of special articles for his use and comfort and becomes sedate and respectable and spiritually sedentary he will, no doubt, have an easy and pleasant time, but there will be always gnawing in his heart the nostalgia for that uncompromising destitution which alone can give him joy because it flings him headlong into the arms of God.

Without poverty, Franciscan lyricism sounds tinny and sentimental and raw and false. Its tone is sour, and all its harmonies are somewhat strained.

I am afraid that at that time, it was the lyricism that attracted me more than the poverty, but really I don't think I was in a position to know any better. It was too soon for me to be able to make the distinction. However, I remember admitting that one of the advantages of their Rule, as far as I was concerned, was that it was easy.

After all, I was really rather frightened of all religious rules as a whole, and this new step, into the monastery, was not something that presented itself to me, all at once, as something that I would just take in my stride. On the contrary, my mind was full of misgivings about fasting and enclosure and all the long prayers and community life and monastic obedience and poverty, and there were plenty of strange specters dancing about in the doors of my imagination, all ready to come in, if I would let them in. And if I did, they would show me how I would go insane in a monastery, and how my health would crack up, and my heart would give out, and I would collapse and go to pieces and be cast back into the world a hopeless moral and physical wreck.

All this, of course, was based on the assumption that I was in weak health, for that was something I still believed. Perhaps it was to some extent true, I don't know. But the fear of collapse had done nothing, in the past years, to prevent me from staying up all night and wandering around the city in search of very unhealthy entertainments. Nevertheless, as soon as there was question of a little fasting or going without meat or living within the walls of a monastery, I instantly began to fear death.

What I eventually found out was that as soon as I started to fast and deny myself pleasures and devote time to prayer and meditation and to the various exercises that belong to the religious life, I quickly got over all my bad health, and became sound and strong and immensely happy.

That particular night I was convinced that I could not follow anything but the easiest of religious rules.

When Dan began to talk about the one religious order that filled him with the most enthusiasm, I was able to share his admiration but I had no desire to join it. It was the Order of Cistercians, the Cistercians of the Strict Observance. The very title made me shiver, and so did their commoner name: The Trappists.

Once, six years before—and it seemed much longer than that—when I had barely glanced at the walls of the Trappist monastery of Tre Fontane, outside Rome, the fancy of becoming a Trappist had entered my adolescent mind: but if it had been anything but a pure daydream, it would not have got inside my head at all. Now, when I was actually and seriously thinking of entering a monastery, the very idea of Trappists almost reduced me to a jelly.

"Last summer," said Dan, "I made a retreat at a Trappist monastery in Kentucky. It is called Our Lady of Gethsemani. Did you ever hear of it?"

And he began to tell me about the place—how he had been staying with some friends, and they had driven him over to the monastery. It was the first time they had ever been there. Although they lived in Kentucky, they hardly knew the Trappists existed. His hostess had been very piqued at the signs about women keeping out of the enclosure under pain of excommunication, and she had watched with awe as the heavy door closed upon him, engulfing him in that terrible, silent building.

(From where I sit and write at this moment, I look out the window, across the quiet guesthouse garden, with the four banana trees and the big red and yellow flowers around Our Lady's statue. I can see the door where Dan entered and where I entered. Beyond the Porter's Lodge is a low green hill where there was wheat this summer. And out there, yonder, I can hear the racket of the diesel tractor: I don't know what they are plowing.)

Dan had stayed in the Trappist monastery a week. He told me of the life of the monks. He told me of their silence. He said they never conversed, and the impression I got was that they never spoke at all, to anybody.

"Don't they even go to confession?" I asked.

"Of course. And they can talk to the abbot. The retreat master talked to the guests. He was Father James. He said that it was a good thing the monks didn't have to talk—with all the mixture of men they have there, they get along better without it: lawyers and farmers and soldiers and schoolboys, they all live together, and go everywhere together and do everything together. They stand in choir together, and go out to work together and sit together in the same place when they read and study. It's a good thing they don't talk."

"Oh, so they sing in choir?"

"Sure," said Dan, "they sing the Canonical hours and High Mass. They are in choir several hours a day."

I was relieved to think that the monks got to choir and exercised their vocal cords. I was afraid that so much silence would wither them up altogether.

"And they work in the fields," said Dan. "They have to make their own living by farming and raising stock. They grow most of what they eat, and bake their own bread, and make their own shoes. . . ."

"I suppose they fast a lot," I said.

"Oh, yes, they fast more than half the year, and they never eat meat or fish, unless they get sick. They don't even have eggs. They just live on vegetables and cheese and things like that. They gave me a cheese when I was there, and I took it back to my friends' house. When we got there, they handed it to the colored butler. They said to him, 'Do you know what that is? That's monks' cheese.' He couldn't figure it out, and he looked at it for a while, and then he got an idea. So he looked up with a big smile and said: 'Oh, I know what you all mean: *monks!* Them's like goats.' "

But I was thinking about all that fasting. The life took my breath away, but it did not attract me. It sounded cold and terrible. The monastery now existed in my mind as a big gray prison with barred windows, filled with dour and emaciated characters with their hoods pulled down over their faces.

"They are very healthy," said Dan, "and they are big strong men. Some of them are giants."

(Since I came to the monastery I have tried to pick out Dan's "giants." I can account for one or two easily enough. But I think he must have seen the rest of them in the dark—or perhaps they are to be explained by the fact that Dan himself is not very tall.)

I sat in silence. In my heart, there was a kind of mixture of exhilaration and dejection, exhilaration at the thought of such generosity, and depression because it seemed such a drastic and cruel and excessive rejection of the rights of nature.

Dan said: "Do you think you would like that kind of a life?"

"Oh, no," I said, "not a chance! That's not for me! I'd never be able to stand it. It would kill me in a week. Besides, I have to have meat. I can't get along without meat, I need it for my health."

"Well," said Dan, "it's a good thing you know yourself so well."

For a moment it occurred to me that he was being ironical, but there was not a shadow of irony in his voice, and there never was. He was far too good and too kind and too simple for irony. He thought I knew what I was talking about, and took my word for it.

THE SEVEN STOREY MOUNTAIN

Six: THE BARONESS

THE BARONESS was born a Russian. She had been a young girl at the time of the October Revolution. She had seen half her family shot, she had seen priests fall under the bullets of the Reds, and she had had to escape from Russia the way it is done in the movies, but with all the misery and hardship which the movies do not show, and none of the glamour which is their specialty.

She had ended up in New York, without a cent, working in a laundry. She had been brought up a Roman Catholic, and the experiences she had gone through, instead of destroying her faith, intensified and deepened it until the Holy Ghost planted fortitude in the midst of her soul like an unshakable rock. I never saw anyone so calm, so certain, so peaceful in her absolute confidence in God.

Catherine de Hueck is a person in every way big, and the bigness is not merely physical: it comes from the Holy Ghost dwelling constantly within her, and moving her in all that she does.

When she was working in that laundry, down somewhere near Fourteenth Street, and sitting on the curbstone eating her lunch with the other girls who worked there, the sense of her own particular vocation dawned upon her. It was the call to an apostolate, not new, but so old that it is as traditional as that of the first Christians: an apostolate of a laywoman in the world, among workers, herself a worker, and poor; an apostolate of personal contacts, of word and above all of example. There was to be nothing special about it, nothing that savored of a religious order, no special rule, no distinctive habit. She, and those who joined her, would simply be poor—there was no choice on that score, for they were that already—but they would embrace their poverty, and the life of the proletariat in all its misery and insecurity and dead, drab monotony. They would live and work in the slums, lose themselves, in the huge anonymous mass of the forgotten and the derelict, for the only purpose of living the complete, integral Christian life in that environment—loving those around them, sacrificing themselves for those around them, and spreading the Gospel and the truth of Christ most of all by being saints, by living in union with Him, by being full of His Holy Ghost, His charity.

As she spoke of these things, in that hall, and to all these nuns and clerics, she could not help but move them all deeply, because what they were hearing—it was too patent to be missed—was nothing but the pure Franciscan ideal, the pure essence of the Franciscan apostolate of poverty, without the vows taken by the Friars Minor. And, for the honor of those who heard her, most of them had the sense and the courage to recognize this fact, and to see that she was, in a sense, a much better Franciscan than they were. She was, as a matter of fact, in the Third Order, and that made me feel quite proud of my own scapular, which was hiding under my shirt; it reminded me that the thing was not altogether without meaning or without possibilities!

So the Baroness had gone to Harlem. She stepped out of the subway with a typewriter and a few dollars and some clothes in a bag. When she went to one of the tenements, and asked to look at a room, the man said to her:

"Ma'am, you all don't want to live here!"

"Yes, I do," she said, and added, by way of explanation: "I'm Russian."

"Russian!" said the man. "That's different. Walk right in."

In other words, he thought she was a Communist. . . .

That was the way Friendship House had begun. Now they were occupying four or five stores on both sides of 135th Street, and maintained a library and recreation rooms and a clothing room. The Baroness had an apartment of her own, and those of her helpers who lived there all the time also had a place on 135th Street. There were more girls than men staying with her in Harlem.

THE SEVEN STOREY MOUNTAIN

Seven: THE SLEEPING VOLCANO

It was a hot day, a rainy day, in the middle of August when I came out of the subway into the heat of Harlem. There were not many people on the streets that afternoon. I walked along the street until I came to the middle of the block, and saw one or two stores marked "Friendship House" and "Bl. Martin de Porres Center" or some such title in big blue letters. There did not seem to be anyone around.

The biggest of the stores was the library, and there I found half a dozen young Negroes, boys and girls, high school students, sitting at a table. Some of them wore glasses, and it seemed they were having some kind of an organized intellectual discussion, because when I came in they got a little embarrassed about it. I asked them if the Baroness was there, and they said no, she had gone downtown because it was her birthday, and I asked who I should see, so they told me Mary Jerdo. She was around somewhere. If I waited she would probably show up in a few minutes.

So I stood there, and took down off the shelf Father Bruno's *Life of St. John of the Cross* and looked at the pictures.

The young Negroes tried to pick up their discussion where they had left off, but they did not succeed. The stranger made them nervous. One of the girls opened her mouth and pronounced three or four abstract words, and then broke off into a giggle. Then another one opened her mouth and said: "Yes, but don't you think . . . ?" And this solemn question also collapsed in embarrassed tittering. One of the young men got off a whole paragraph or so, full of big words, and everybody roared with laughter. So I turned around and started to laugh too, and immediately the whole thing became a game.

They began saying big words just because it was funny. They uttered the most profoundly dull and ponderous statements, and laughed at them, and at the fact that such strange things had come out of their mouths. But soon they calmed down, and then Mary Jerdo came along, and showed me the different departments of Friendship House, and explained what they were.

The embarrassment of those young Negroes was something that gave me a picture of Harlem: the details of the picture were to be filled in later, but the essentials were already there.

Here in this huge, dark, steaming slum, hundreds of thousands of Negroes are herded together like cattle, most of them with nothing to eat and nothing to do. All the senses and imagination and sensibilities and emotions and sorrows and desires and hopes and ideas of a race with vivid feelings and deep emotional reactions are forced in upon themselves, bound inward by an iron ring of frustration: the prejudice that hems them in with its four insurmountable walls. In this huge cauldron, inestimable natural gifts, wisdom, love, music, science, poetry are stamped down and left to boil with the dregs of an elementally corrupted nature, and thousands upon thousands of souls are destroyed by vice and misery and degradation, obliterated, wiped out, washed from the register of the living, dehumanized.

What has not been devoured, in your dark furnace, Harlem, by marihuana, by gin, by insanity, hysteria, syphilis?

Those who manage somehow to swim to the top of the seething cauldron, and remain on its surface, through some special spiritual quality or other, or because they have been able to get away from Harlem, and go to some college or school, these are not all at once annihilated: but they are left with the dubious privilege of living out the only thing Harlem possesses in the way of an ideal. They are left with the sorry task of contemplating and imitating what passes for culture in the world of the white people.

Now the terrifying paradox of the whole thing is this: Harlem itself, and every individual Negro in it, is a living condemnation of our so-called "culture." Harlem is there by way of a divine indictment against New York City and the people who live downtown and make their money downtown. The brothels of Harlem, and all its prostitution, and its dope rings, and all the rest are the mirror of the polite divorces and the manifold cultured adulteries of Park Avenue: they are God's commentary on the whole of our society.

Harlem is, in a sense, what God thinks of Hollywood. And Hollywood is all Harlem has, in its despair, to grasp at, by way of a surrogate for heaven.

The most terrible thing about it all is that there is not a Negro in the whole place who does not realize, somewhere in the depths of his nature, that the culture of the white men is not worth the dirt in Harlem's gutters. They sense that the whole thing is rotten, that it is a fake, that it is spurious, empty, a shadow of nothingness. And yet they are condemned to reach out for it, and to seem to desire it, and to pretend they like it, as if the whole thing were some kind of bitter cosmic conspiracy: as if they were thus being forced to work out, in their own lives, a clear representation of the misery which has corrupted the ontological roots of the white man's own existence.

The little children of Harlem are growing up, crowded together like sardines in the rooms of tenements full of vice, where evil takes place hourly and inescapably before their eyes, so that there is not an excess of passion, not a perversion of natural appetite with which they are not familiar before the age of six or seven: and this by way of an accusation of the polite and expensive and furtive sensualities and lusts of the rich whose sins have bred this abominable slum. The effect resembles and even magnifies the cause, and Harlem is the portrait of those through whose fault such things come into existence. What was heard in secret in the bedrooms and apartments of the rich and of the cultured and the educated and the white is preached from the housetops of Harlem and there declared, for what it is, in all its horror, somewhat as it is seen in the eyes of God, naked and frightful.

No, there is not a Negro in the whole place who can fail to know, in the marrow of his own bones, that the white man's culture is not worth the jetsam in the Harlem River.

THE SEVEN STOREY MOUNTAIN

Eight: POEMS

AUBADE—HARLEM

(For Baroness C. de Hueck)

Across the cages of the keyless aviaries,
The lines and wires, the gallows of the broken kites,
Crucify; against the fearful light,
The ragged dresses of the little children.
Soon, in the sterile jungles of the waterpipes and ladders,
The bleeding sun, a bird of prey, will terrify the poor,
Who will forget the unbelievable moon.

But in the cells and wards of whiter buildings,
Where the glass dawn is brighter than the knives of surgeons,
Paler than alcohol or ether,
Grayer than guns and shinier than money,
The white men's wives, like Pilate's,
Cry in the peril of their frozen dreams:

"Daylight has driven iron spikes,
Into the flesh of Jesus' hands and feet:
Four flowers of blood have nailed Him to the walls of Harlem."

Along the white walls of the clinics and the hospitals
Pilate vanishes with a cry:
They have cut down two hundred Judases,
Hanged by the neck in the opera houses and museums.
Across the cages of the keyless aviaries,
The lines and wires, the gallows of the broken kites,
Crucify, against the fearful light,
The ragged dresses of the little children.

A MAN IN THE DIVIDED SEA

DIRGE FOR THE PROUD WORLD

Where is the marvelous thief
Who stole whole harvests from the angry sun
And sacked, with his bright sight, the land?

Where he lies dead, the quiet earth unpacks him
And wind is waving in the earth's revenge:
Fields of barley, oats, and rye.

Where is the millionaire
Who squandered the bright spring?
Whose lies played in the summer evening sky
Like cheap guitars?
Who spent the golden fortunes of the fall
And died as bare as a tree?

His heart lies open like a treasury,
Filled up with grass, and generous flowers.

Where is the crazy gambler
Amid the nickels of whose blood have fallen
Heavy half dollars of his last of life?
Where is he gone?

The burning bees come walk, as bright as jewels
Upon that flowering, dark sun:
The bullet wound in his unmoving lung.

Oh you who hate the gambler or his enemy,
Remember how the bees
Pay visits to the patient dead
And borrow honey from their charitable blood.

You who have judged the gambler or his enemy
Remember this, before the proud world's funeral.

                                    A MAN IN THE DIVIDED SEA

AN ARGUMENT—OF THE PASSION OF CHRIST

And what one of you, by taking thought, can add to his stature one cubit?
ST. MATTHEW, VI. 27

I

The furious prisoner of the womb,
Rebellious, in the jaws of life,
Learns, from the mother's conscious flesh,
The secret laws of blood and strife.

The demon raging at the breast,
Arrayed in cries, and crowned with tears,
Has sucked the magics of the east,
The doubts of the philosophers.

In the red straits of his arteries,
Love runs, lost and ravening;
Nothingness feeds upon itself
And swells up to a mighty king!

Wit walks out, in envy's mask;
Love will hide, and be a lecher.
Adultery, by taking thought,
Adds a cubit to his stature,

Until we scan the wastes of death,
And wind blows through our cage of bones;
Sight leaves the sockets of the skull,
And love runs mad among the stones!

II

The worm that watched within the womb
Was standing guard at Jesus' tomb,
And my first angry, infant breath
Stood wakeful, lest He rise from death.
My adolescence, like the wolf,
Fled to the edges of the gulf
And searched the ruins of the night
To hide from Calvary's iron light:

But in the burning jaws of day
I saw the barren Judas Tree;
For, to the caverns of my pride
Judas had come, and there was paid!

III

Seeds of the three hours' agony
Fell on good earth, and grew from me,
And, cherished by my sleepless cares
Flowered with God's Blood, and Mary's tears.
My curious love found its reward
When Love was scourged in Pilate's yard:
Here was the work my hands had made:
A thorny crown, to cut His head.
The growth of thoughts that made me great
Lay on His cross, and were its weight;
And my desires lay, turned to stones,
And where He fell, cut to the bone.
The sharpnesses of my delight
Were spikes run through His hands and feet,
And from the sweetness of my will
Their sponge drew vinegar and gall.

A MAN IN THE DIVIDED SEA

CRUSOE

Sometimes the sun beats up the rocks of capes
And robs the green world with a clangor of banks.

Then the citizens
Come out to stone the sky; and with their guns
Mean to shoot the highpowered spheres to pieces:
At dawn, the laws, in the yards of all the prisons,
Propose to hang the robber, the breeder of life.

What if no more men will learn to turn again
And run to the rainy world's boundaries?

What if no more men will learn to atone
By hard, horseplay of shipwreck in the drench of Magellan,
And still steer by the stars' unending Lent?

What if the last man
Will no more learn, and run
The stern, foundering ocean, north of the line,
Where crew and cargo drown in the thrash of the wreck,
The day he's driven to his Penal Island,
His own rich acre of island, like the wiseguy Crusoe!

A MAN IN THE DIVIDED SEA

THE BOMBARDED CITY

Now let no man abide
In the lunar wood
The place of blood.
Let no man abide here,
Not even in a dream,
Not in the lunar forest of this undersea.

Oh you who can a living shadow show
Grieving in the broken street,
Fear, fear the drowners,
Fear the dead!
But if you swagger like the warring Leader
Fear far more
What curse rides down the starlit air,
Curse of the little children killed!
Curse of the little children killed!

Then let no living man, or dead, abide
In this lunar wood,
No, not even in a dream.

For when the houses lean along the night
Like broken tombs,
And shout, with silent windows,
Naked and windy as the mouths of masks,
They still pour down

(As conch shells, from their curling sleep, the sea)
The air raid's perished roar.

But do not look aside at what you hear.
Fear where you tread,
And be aware of danger growing like a nightshade
Through the openings of the stone.
But mostly fear the forum,
Where, in the midst, an arch and pediment,
Space out, in honor of the guilty Warlord,
A starlit area
Much like the white geometry of peace:

O dread that silent place!
For even when field flowers shall spring
Out of the Leader's lips, and open eyes,
And even while the quiet root
Shall ravel his murdering brain,
Let no one, even on that holiday,
Forget the never-sleeping curse.
And even when the grass grows in his groin,
And goldenrod works in his rib,
And in his teeth the ragweed grins,
As furious as ambition's diligence:
And when, in wind,
His greedy belly waves, kneedeep in weeds,
O dread the childish voices even then,
Still scratching near him like a leaf,
And fear the following feet
That are laid down like little blades,
Nor face the curses of the innocent
That mew behind you like a silver hinge.

For even in the dream of peace
All men will flee the weedy street,
The forum fallen down,
The cursed arenas full of blood,
Hearing the wind creep in the crannied stone:
Oh, no man can remain,
Hearing those souls weep in the hollow ruin.

For there no life is possible,
Because the eyes of soldiers, blind, destroyed,
Lurk like Medusas of despair,
Lay for the living in the lunar door,
Ready to stare outside
And freeze the little leaping nerves
Behind the emperor's sight.

And there no life is possible
Because a weeping childvoice, thin
Unbodied as the sky,
Rings like an echo in the empty window:
And thence its sound
Flies out to feel, with fingers sharp as scalpels,
The little bones inside the politician's ear.

Oh let no man abide
In the lunar wood,
The place of blood.
Let no man abide there, no,
Not even in a dream.

A MAN IN THE DIVIDED SEA

SONG

Come where the grieving rivers of the night
Copy the speeches of the sea:
And hear how this devouring weather
Steals our music.

Under a tent of branches
Let grow our harps in windy trees.

But, in the flowering of our windless morning
We should be slow-paced watchmen,
Crossing, on our ecliptics, with a cry of planets,
Homesick, at the sharp rim
Of our Jerusalem, the day.

Then weep where the splendid armies of the sky
Copy the prisoner's visions:
Yet keep the arrows of your eyes unquivered.
Light more watch fires:

Because the thieving stars may come
And steal our lives.

A MAN IN THE DIVIDED SEA

Nine: EVERYTHING THAT IS, IS HOLY

DETACHMENT FROM THINGS does not mean setting up a contradiction between "things" and "God" as if God were another "thing" and as if His creatures were His rivals. We do not detach ourselves from things in order to attach ourselves to God, but rather we become detached *from ourselves* in order to see and use all things in and for God. This is an entirely new perspective which many sincerely moral and ascetic minds fail utterly to see. There is no evil in anything created by God, nor can anything of His become an obstacle to our union with Him. The obstacle is in our "self," that is to say in the tenacious need to maintain our separate, external, egotistic will. It is when we refer all things to this outward and false "self" that we alienate ourselves from reality and from God. It is then the false self that is our god, and we love everything for the sake of this self. We use all things, so to speak, for the worship of this idol which is our imaginary self. In so doing we pervert and corrupt things, or rather we turn our relationship to them into a corrupt and sinful relationship. We do not thereby make them evil, but we use them to increase our attachment to our illusory self.

Those who try to escape from this situation by treating the good things of God as if they were evils are only confirming themselves in a terrible illusion. They are like Adam blaming Eve and Eve blaming the serpent in Eden. "Woman has tempted me. Wine has tempted me. Food has tempted me. Woman is pernicious, wine is poison, food is death. I must hate and revile them. By hating them I will please God. . . ." These are the thoughts and attitudes of a baby, of a savage, and of an idolater who seeks by magic incantations and spells to protect his egotistic self and placate the insatiable little god in his own heart. To take such an idol for God is the worst kind of self-deception. It turns a man into a fanatic, no longer capable of sustained contact with the truth, no longer capable of genuine love.

In trying to believe in their ego as something "holy" these fanatics look upon everything else as unholy.

IT IS NOT TRUE that the saints and the great contemplatives never loved created things, and had no understanding or appreciation of the world, with its sights and sounds and the people living in it. They loved everything and everyone.

Do you think that their love of God was compatible with a hatred for things that reflected Him and spoke of Him on every side?

You will say that they were supposed to be absorbed in God and they had no eyes to see anything but Him. Do you think they walked around with faces like stones and did not listen to the voices of men speaking to them or understand the joys and sorrows of those who were around them?

It was because the saints were absorbed in God that they were truly capable of seeing and appreciating created things and it was because they loved Him alone that they alone loved everybody.

SOME MEN seem to think that a saint cannot possibly take a natural interest in anything created. They imagine that any form of spontaneity or enjoyment is a sinful gratification of "fallen nature." That to be "supernatural" means obstructing all spontaneity with clichés and arbitrary references to God. The purpose of these clichés is, so to speak, to hold everything at arm's length, to frustrate spontaneous reactions, to exorcise feelings of guilt. Or perhaps to cultivate such feelings! One wonders sometimes if such morality is not after all a love of guilt! They suppose that the life of a saint can never be anything but a perpetual duel with guilt, and that a saint cannot even drink a glass of cold water without making an act of contrition for slaking his thirst, as if that were a mortal sin. As if for the saints every response to beauty, to goodness, to the pleasant, were an offense. As if the saint could never allow himself to be pleased with anything but his prayers and his interior acts of piety.

A saint is capable of loving created things and enjoying the use of them and dealing with them in a perfectly simple, natural manner, making no formal references to God, drawing no attention to his own piety, and acting without any artificial rigidity at all. His gentleness and his sweetness are not pressed through his pores by the crushing restraint of a spiritual straitjacket. They come from his direct docility to the light of truth and to the will of God. Hence a saint is capable of talking about the world without any explicit reference to God, in such a way that his statement gives greater glory to God and arouses a greater love of God than the observations of someone less holy, who has to strain himself to make an arbitrary connection between creatures and God through the medium of hackneyed analogies and metaphors that are so feeble that they make you think there is something the matter with religion.

The saint knows that the world and everything made by God is good, while those who are not saints either think that created things are unholy, or else they don't bother about the question one way or another because they are only interested in themselves.

The eyes of the saint make all beauty holy and the hands of the saint consecrate everything they touch to the glory of God, and the saint is never offended by anything and judges no man's sin because he does not know sin. He knows the mercy of God. He knows that his own mission on earth is to bring that mercy to all men.

WHEN WE ARE ONE with God's love, we own all things in Him. They are ours to offer Him in Christ His Son. For all things belong to the sons of God and we are Christ's and Christ is God's. Resting in His glory above all pleasure and pain, joy or sorrow, and every other good or evil, we love in all things His will rather than the things themselves, and that is the way we make creation a sacrifice in praise of God.

This is the end for which all things were made by God.

THE ONLY TRUE JOY on earth is to escape from the prison of our own false self, and enter by love into union with the Life Who dwells and sings within the essence of every creature and in the core of our own souls. In His love we possess all things and enjoy fruition of them, finding Him in them all. And thus as we go about the world, everything we meet and everything we see and hear and touch, far from defiling, purifies us and plants in us something more of contemplation and of heaven.

Short of this perfection, created things do not bring us joy but pain. Until we love God perfectly, everything in the world will be able to hurt us. And the greatest misfortune is to be dead to the pain they inflict on us, and not to realize what it is.

For until we love God perfectly His world is full of contradiction. The things He has created attract us to Him and yet keep us away from Him. They draw us on and they stop us dead. We find Him in them to some extent and then we don't find Him in them at all.

Just when we think we have discovered some joy in them, the joy turns into sorrow; and just when they are beginning to please us the pleasure turns into pain.

In all created things we, who do not yet perfectly love God, can find something that reflects the fulfillment of heaven and something that reflects the anguish of hell. We find something of the joy of blessedness and something of the pain of loss, which is damnation.

The fulfillment we find in creatures belongs to the reality of the created being, a reality that is from God and belongs to God and reflects God. The anguish we find in them belongs to the disorder of our desire which looks for a greater reality in the object of our desire than is actually there: a greater fulfillment than any created thing is capable of giving. Instead of worshiping God through His creation we are always trying to worship ourselves by means of creatures.

But to worship our false selves is to worship nothing. And the worship of nothing is hell.

THE "FALSE SELF" must not be identified with the body. The body is neither evil nor unreal. It has a reality that is given it by God, and this reality is therefore holy. Hence we say rightly, though symbolically, that the body is the "temple of God," meaning that His truth, His perfect reality, is enshrined there in the mystery of our own being. Let no one, then, dare to hate or to despise the body that has been entrusted to him by God, and let no one dare to misuse this body. Let him not desecrate his own natural unity by dividing himself, soul against body, as if the soul were good and the body evil. Soul and body together subsist in the reality of the hidden, inner person. If the two are separated from one another, there is no longer a person, there is no longer a living, subsisting reality made in the image and likeness of God. The "marriage" of body and soul in one person is one of the things that makes man the image of God; and what God has joined no man can separate without danger to his sanity.

It is equally false to treat the soul as if it were the "whole self" and the body as if it were the "whole self." Those who make the first mistake fall into the sin of angelism. Those who make the second live below the level assigned by God to human nature. (It would be an easy cliché to say they live like beasts: but this is not always true, by any means.) There are many respectable and even conventionally moral people for whom there is no other reality in life than their body and its relationship with "things." They have reduced themselves to a life lived within the limits of their five senses. Their self is consequently an illusion based on sense experience and nothing else. For these the body becomes a source of falsity and deception, but that is not the body's fault. It is the fault of the person himself, who consents to the illusion, who finds security in self-deception and will not answer the secret voice of God calling him to take a risk and venture by faith outside the reassuring and protective limits of his five senses.

NEW SEEDS OF CONTEMPLATION

Ten: NO MAN IS AN ISLAND

ALTHOUGH ALL MEN have a common goal, each individual also has to work out his own personal salvation for himself in fear and trembling. We can help one another to find out the meaning of life, no doubt. But in the last analysis the individual person is responsible for living his own life and for "finding himself." If he persists in shifting this responsibility to somebody else, he fails to find out the meaning of his own existence. You cannot tell me who I am, and I cannot tell you who you are. If you do not know your own identity, who is going to identify you? Others can give you a name or a number, but they can never tell you who you really are. That is something you yourself can only discover from within.

That brings us to a second problem. Although in the end we alone are capable of experiencing who we are, we are instinctively gifted in watching how others experience themselves. We learn to live by living together with others, and by living like them—a process which has disadvantages as well as blessings.

The greatest of disadvantages is that we are too prone to welcome everybody else's wrong solution to the problems of life. There is a natural laziness that moves us to accept the easiest solutions—the ones that have common currency among our friends. That is why an optimistic view of life is not necessarily always a virtuous thing. In a time like ours, only the coarse grained still have enough resistance to preserve their fair-weather principles unclouded by anxiety. Such optimism may be comfortable: but is it safe? In a world where every lie has currency, is not anxiety the more real and the more human reaction?

Now anxiety is the mark of spiritual insecurity. It is the fruit of unanswered questions. But questions cannot go unanswered unless they first be asked. And there is a far worse anxiety, a far worse insecurity, which comes from being afraid to ask the right questions—because they might turn out to have no answer. One of the moral diseases we communicate to one another in society comes from huddling together in the pale light of an insufficient and purely evasive answer to a question we are afraid to ask.

But there are other diseases also. There is the laziness that pretends to dignify itself by the name of despair, and that teaches us to ignore both the question and the answer. And there is the despair which dresses itself up as science or philosophy and amuses itself with clever answers to clever questions—none of which have anything to do with the problems of life. Finally there is the worst and most insidious despair, which can mask as mysticism or prophecy, and which intones a prophetic answer to a prophetic question. That, I think, is likely to be a monk's professional hazard, so I purify myself of it at the beginning, like Amos who complained, "I am not a prophet, nor am I the son of a prophet, but I am a herdsman, plucking wild figs" (Amos, 7:14).

The prophetic illusion—which is quite common in our time—is at the opposite extreme from the gregarious illusion, which is more common still in every time. The false prophet will accept any answer, provided that it is his own, provided it is *not* the answer of the herd. The sheep mentality, on the other hand, accepts any answer that circulates in its own flock, provided only that it is *not* the answer of a prophet who has not been dead for at least five hundred years.

What every man looks for in life is his own salvation and the salvation of the men he lives with. By salvation I mean first of all the full discovery of who he himself really is. Then I mean something of the fulfillment of his own God-given powers, in the love of others and of God. I mean also the discovery that he cannot find himself in himself alone, but that he must find himself in and through others. Ultimately, these propositions are summed up in two lines of the Gospel: "If any man would save his life, he must lose it," and, "Love one another as I have loved you." It is also contained in another saying from St. Paul: "We are all members one of another."

The salvation I speak of is not merely a subjective, psychological thing —a self-realization in the order of nature. It is an objective and mystical reality—the finding of ourselves in Christ, in the Spirit, or, if you prefer, in the supernatural order. This includes and sublimates and perfects the natural self-realization which it to some extent presupposes, and usually effects, and always transcends. Therefore this discovery of ourselves is always a losing of ourselves—a death and a resurrection. "Your life is hidden with Christ in God." The discovery of ourselves in God, and of God in ourselves, by a charity that also finds all other men in God with ourselves is, therefore, not the discovery of ourselves but of Christ. First of all, it is the realization that "I live now not I but Christ liveth in me," and secondly it is the penetration of that tremendous mystery which St. Paul sketched out boldly—and darkly—in his great Epistles: the mystery of the recapitulation, the summing up of all in Christ. It is to see the world in Christ, its beginning and its end. To see all things coming forth from God in the *Logos* Who becomes incarnate and descends into the lowest depths of His own creation and gathers all to Himself in order to restore it finally to the Father at the end of time. To find "ourselves" then is to find not only our poor, limited, perplexed souls, but to find the power of God that raised Christ from the dead and "built us together in Him unto a habitation of God in the Spirit" (Eph. 2:22).

This discovery of Christ is never genuine if it is nothing but a flight from ourselves. On the contrary, it cannot be an escape. It must be a fulfillment. I cannot discover God in myself and myself in Him unless I have the courage to face myself exactly as I am, with all my limitations, and to accept others as they are, with all *their* limitations. The religious answer is not religious if it is not fully real. Evasion is the answer of superstition.

This matter of "salvation" is, when seen intuitively, a very simple thing. But when we analyze it, it turns into a complex tangle of paradoxes. We become ourselves by dying to ourselves. We gain only what we give up, and if we give up everything we gain everything. We cannot find ourselves within ourselves, but only in others, yet at the same time before we can go out to others we must first find ourselves. We must forget ourselves in order to become truly conscious of who we are.

But the truth of who we are will never become clear as long as we assume that each one of us, individually, is the center of the universe. We do not exist for ourselves alone, and it is only when we are fully convinced of this fact that we begin to love ourselves properly and thus also love others. What do I mean by loving ourselves properly? I mean, first of all, desiring to live, accepting life as a very great gift and a great good, not because of what it gives us, but because of what it enables us to give to others. The modern world is beginning to discover, more and more, that the quality and vitality of a man's life depend on his own secret will to go on living. There is a dark force for destruction within us, which someone has called the "death instinct." It is a terribly powerful thing, this force generated by our own frustrated self-love battling with itself. It is the power of a self-love that has turned into self-hatred and which, in adoring itself, adores the monster by which it is consumed.

It is therefore of supreme importance that we consent to live not for ourselves but for others. When we do this we will be able first of all to face and accept our own limitations. As long as we secretly adore ourselves, our own deficiencies will remain to torture us with an apparent defilement. But if we live for others, we will gradually discover that no one expects us to be "as gods." We will see that we are human, like everyone else, that we all have weaknesses and deficiencies, and that these limitations of ours play a most important part in all our lives. It is because of them that we need others and others need us. We are not all weak in the same spots, and so we supplement and complete one another, each one making up in himself for the lack in another.

Only when we see ourselves in our true human context, as members of a race which is intended to be one organism and "one body," will we begin to understand the positive importance not only of the successes but of the failures and accidents in our lives. My successes are not my own. The way to them was prepared by others. The fruit of my labors is not my own: for I am preparing the way for the achievements of another. Nor are my failures my own. They may spring from the failure of another, but they are also compensated for by another's achievement. Therefore the meaning of my life is not to be looked for merely in the sum total of my own achievements. It is seen only in the complete integration of my achievements and failures with the achievements and failures of my own generation, and society, and time. It is seen, above all, in my integration in the mystery of Christ.

NO MAN IS AN ISLAND

Eleven: SENTENCES ON HOPE

W<small>E ARE NOT PERFECTLY FREE</small> until we live in pure hope. For when our hope is pure, it no longer trusts exclusively in human and visible means, nor rests in any visible end. He who hopes in God trusts God, Whom he never sees, to bring him to the possession of things that are beyond imagination.

When we do not desire the things of this world for their own sake, we become able to see them as they are. We see at once their goodness and their purpose, and we become able to appreciate them as we never have before. As soon as we are free of them, they begin to please us. As soon as we cease to rely on them alone, they are able to serve us. Since we depend neither on the pleasure nor on the assistance we get from them, they offer us both pleasure and assistance, at the command of God. For Jesus has said: "Seek first the kingdom of God, and His justice and all these things [that is all that you need for your life on earth] will be given to you besides" (Matt. 6:33).

Supernatural hope is the virtue that strips us of all things in order to give us possession of all things. We do not hope for what we have. Therefore, to live in hope is to live in poverty, having nothing. And yet, if we abandon ourselves to economy of Divine Providence, we have everything we hope for. By faith we know God without seeing Him. By hope we possess God without feeling His presence. If we hope in God, by hope we already possess Him, since hope is a confidence which He creates in our souls as secret evidence that He has taken possession of us. So the soul that hopes in God already belongs to Him, and to belong to Him is the same as to possess Him, since He gives Himself completely to those who give themselves to Him. The only thing faith and hope do not give us is the clear vision of Him Whom we possess. We are united to Him in darkness, because we have to hope. *Spes quae videtur non est spes.*[1]

Hope deprives us of everything that is not God, in order that all things may serve their true purpose as means to bring us to God.

Hope is proportionate to detachment. It brings our souls into the state of the most perfect detachment. In doing so, it restores all values by setting them in their right order. Hope empties our hands in order that we may work with them. It shows us that we have something to work for, and teaches us how to work for it.

Without hope, our faith gives us only an acquaintance with God. Without love and hope, faith only knows Him as a stranger. For hope casts us into the arms of His mercy and of His providence. If we hope in Him, we will not only come to know that He is merciful but we will experience His mercy in our own lives.

HOPE IS THE LIVING HEART of asceticism. It teaches us to deny ourselves and leave the world not because either we or the world are evil, but because unless a supernatural hope raises us above the things of time, we are in no condition to make a perfect use either of our own or of the world's true goodness. But we possess ourselves and all things in hope, for in hope we have them not as they are in themselves but as they are in Christ: full of promise. All things are at once good and imperfect. The goodness bears witness to the goodness of God. But the imperfection of all things reminds us to leave them in order to live in hope. They are themselves insufficient. We must go beyond them to Him in Whom they have their true being.

We leave the good things of this world not because they are not good, but because they are only good for us insofar as they form part of a promise. They, in turn, depend on our hope and on our detachment for the fulfillment of their own destiny. If we misuse them, we ruin ourselves together with them. If we use them as children of God's promises, we bring them, together with ourselves, to God.

"For the expectation of the creature waiteth for the revelation of the sons of God. . . . Because the creature also itself shall be delivered from the servitude of corruption into the liberty of the glory of the children of God" (Rom. 8:19-21).

Upon our hope, therefore, depends the liberty of the whole universe. Because our hope is the pledge of a new heaven and a new earth, in which all things will be what they were meant to be. They will rise, together with us, in Christ. The beasts and the trees will one day share

with us a new creation and we will see them as God sees them and
know that they are very good.

Meanwhile, if we embrace them for themselves, we discover both
them and ourselves as evil. This is the fruit of the tree of the knowledge
of good and evil—disgust with the things we have misused and hatred
of ourselves for misusing them.

But the goodness of creation enters into the framework of holy hope.
All created things proclaim God's fidelity to His promises, and urge us,
for our sake and for their own, to deny ourselves and to live in hope
and to look for the judgment and the general resurrection.

An asceticism that is not entirely suspended from this divine promise
is something less than Christian.

THOSE WHO ABANDON everything in order to seek God know well that
He is the God of the poor. It is the same thing to say that He is the God
of the poor and that He is a jealous God—to say that He is a jealous
God and a God of infinite mercy. There are not two Gods, one jealous,
Whom we must fear, and one merciful, in Whom we must place our
hope. Our hope does not consist in pitting one of these gods against the
other, bribing one to pacify the other. The Lord of all justice is jealous
of His prerogative as the Father of mercy, and the supreme expression
of His justice is to forgive those whom no one else would ever have forgiven.

That is why He is, above all, the God of those who can hope where
there is no hope. The penitent thief who died with Christ was able to
see God where the doctors of the law had just proved impossible Jesus'
claim to divinity.

ONLY THE MAN who has had to face despair is really convinced that he
needs mercy. Those who do not want mercy never seek it. It is better to
find God on the threshold of despair than to risk our lives in a complacency that has never felt the need of forgiveness. A life that is without problems may literally be more hopeless than one that always verges
on despair.

[1] "For we are saved by hope. But hope that is seen, is not hope. For what a man
seeth, why doth he hope for?" (Rom. 8:24)

                                        NO MAN IS AN ISLAND

Twelve: SINCERITY

W<small>E MAKE OURSELVES REAL</small> by telling the truth. Man can hardly forget that he needs to know the truth, for the instinct to know is too strong in us to be destroyed. But he can forget how badly he also needs to tell the truth. We cannot know truth unless we ourselves are conformed to it.

We must be true inside, true to ourselves, before we can know a truth that is outside us. But we make ourselves true inside by manifesting the truth as we see it.

I<small>F MEN STILL ADMIRE SINCERITY</small> today, they admire it, perhaps, not for the sake of the truth that it protects, but simply because it is an attractive quality for a person to have. They like to be sincere not because they love the truth, but because, if they are thought to be sincere, people will love them.

W<small>E ARE TOO MUCH</small> like Pilate. We are always asking, "What is truth?" and then crucifying the truth that stands before our eyes.

But since we have asked the question, let us answer it.

If I ask, "What is truth?" I either expect an answer or I do not. Pilate did not. Yet his belief that the question did not require an answer was itself his answer. He thought the question could not be answered. In other words, he thought it was true to say that the question "What is truth?" had no satisfactory answer. If, in thinking that, he thought there was no truth, he clearly disproved his own proposition by his very thought of it. So, even in his denial, Pilate confessed his need for the truth. No man can avoid doing the same in one way or another, because our need for truth is inescapable.

What, then, is truth?

Truth, in things, is their reality. In our minds, it is the conformity of our knowledge with the things known. In our words, it is the conformity of our words to what we think. In our conduct, it is the conformity of our acts to what we are supposed to be.

IT IS CURIOUS that our whole world is consumed with the desire to know what things are, and actually does find out a tremendous amount about their physical constitution, and verifies its findings—and still does not know whether or not there is such a thing as truth!

Objective truth is a reality that is found both within and outside ourselves, to which our minds can be conformed. We must know this truth, and we must manifest it by our words and acts.

We are not required to manifest everything we know, for there are some things we are obliged to keep hidden from men. But there are other things that we must make known, even though others may already know them.

We owe a definite homage to the reality around us, and we are obliged, at certain times, to say what things are and to give them their right names and to lay open our thought about them to the men we live with.

The fact that men are constantly talking shows that they need the truth, and that they depend on their mutual witness in order to get the truth formed and confirmed in their own minds.

But the fact that men spend so much time talking about nothing or telling each other the lies that they have heard from one another or wasting their time in scandal and detraction and calumny and scurrility and ridicule shows that our minds are deformed with a kind of contempt for reality. Instead of conforming ourselves to what is, we twist everything around, in our words and thoughts, to fit our own deformity.

The seat of this deformity is in the will. Although we still may speak the truth, we are more and more losing our desire to live according to the truth. Our wills are not true, because they refuse to accept the laws of our own being: they fail to work along the lines demanded by our own reality. Our wills are plunged in false values, and they have dragged our minds along with them, and our restless tongues bear constant witness to the disorganization inside our souls—"the tongue no man can tame, an unquiet evil, full of deadly poison. By it we bless God and the Father, and we curse men who are made in the likeness of God. . . . Doth a fountain send forth out of the same hole sweet and bitter water?" (James 3:8-11).

Sincerity in the fullest sense must be more than a temperamental disposition to be frank. It is a simplicity of spirit which is preserved by the *will* to be true. It implies an obligation to manifest the truth and to defend it. And this in turn recognizes that we are free to respect the truth or not to respect it, and that the truth is to some extent at our own mercy. But this is a terrible responsibility, since in defiling the truth we defile our own souls.

Sincerity in the fullest sense is a divine gift, a clarity of spirit that comes only with grace. Unless we are made "new men," created according to God "in justice and the holiness of truth," we cannot avoid some of the lying and double-dealing which have become instinctive in our natures, corrupted, as St. Paul says, "according to the desire of error" (Eph. 4:22).

The sincere man, therefore, is one who has the grace to know that he may be instinctively insincere, and that even his natural sincerity may become a camouflage for irresponsibility and moral cowardice: as if it were enough to recognize the truth, and do nothing about it!

HOW IS IT that our comfortable society has lost its sense of the value of truthfulness? Life has become so easy that we think we can get along without telling the truth. A liar no longer needs to feel that his lies may involve him in starvation. If living were a little more precarious, and if a person who could not be trusted found it more difficult to get along with other men, we would not deceive ourselves and one another so carelessly.

But the whole world has learned to deride veracity or to ignore it. Half the civilized world makes a living by telling lies. Advertising, propaganda, and all the other forms of publicity that have taken the place of truth have taught men to take it for granted that they can tell other people whatever they like provided that it sounds plausible and evokes some kind of shallow emotional response.

Americans have always felt that they were protected against the advertising business by their own sophistication. If we only knew how naïve our sophistication really is! It protects us against nothing. We love the things we pretend to laugh at. We would rather buy a bad toothpaste that is well advertised than a good one that is not advertised at all. Most Americans wouldn't be seen dead in a car their neighbors had never heard of.

Sincerity becomes impossible in a world that is ruled by a falsity that it thinks it is clever enough to detect. Propaganda is constantly held up to contempt, but in contemning it we come to love it after all. In the end we will not be able to get along without it.

This duplicity is one of the great characteristics of a state of sin, in which a person is held captive by the love for what he knows he ought to hate.

YOUR IDEA OF ME is fabricated with materials you have borrowed from other people and from yourself. What you think of me depends on what you think of yourself. Perhaps you create your idea of me out of material that you would like to eliminate from your own idea of yourself. Perhaps your idea of me is a reflection of what other people think of you. Or perhaps what you think of me is simply what you think I think of you.

IT TAKES MORE COURAGE than we imagine to be perfectly simple with other men. Our frankness is often spoiled by a hidden barbarity, born of fear.

False sincerity has much to say, because it is afraid. True candor can afford to be silent. It does not need to face an anticipated attack. Anything it may have to defend can be defended with perfect simplicity.

The arguments of religious men are so often insincere, and their insincerity is proportionate to their anger. Why do we get angry about what we believe? Because we do not really believe it. Or else what we pretend to be defending as the "truth" is really our own self-esteem. A man of sincerity is less interested in defending the truth than in stating it clearly, for he thinks that if the truth be clearly seen it can very well take care of itself.

FEAR is perhaps the greatest enemy of candor. How many men fear to follow their conscience because they would rather conform to the opinion of other men than to the truth they know in their hearts! How can I be sincere if I am constantly changing my mind to conform with the shadow of what I think others expect of me? Others have no right to demand that I be anything else than what I ought to be in the sight of God. No greater thing could possibly be asked of a man than this! This one just expectation, which I am bound to fulfill, is precisely the one they usually do not expect me to fulfill. They want me to be what I am in their sight: that is, an extension of themselves. They do not realize that if I am fully myself, my life will become the completion and the fulfillment of their own, but that if I merely live as their shadow, I will serve only to remind them of their own unfulfillment.

If I allow myself to degenerate into the being I am imagined to be by other men, God will have to say to me, "I know you not!"

THE DELICATE SINCERITY of grace is never safe in a soul given to human violence. Passion always troubles the clear depths of sincerity, except when it is perfectly in order. And passion is almost never perfectly in order, even in the souls of the saints.

But the clean waters of a lake are not made dirty by the wind that ruffles their surface. Sincerity can suffer something of the violence of passion without too much harm, as long as the violence is suffered and not accepted.

Violence is fatal to sincerity when we yield it our consent, and it is completely fatal when we find peace in passion rather than in tranquillity and calm.

Spiritual violence is most dangerous when it is most spiritual—that is, when it is least felt in the emotions. It seizes the depths of the will without any surface upheaval and carries the whole soul into captivity without a struggle. The emotions may remain at peace, may even taste a delight of their own in this base rapture. But the deep peace of the soul is destroyed, because the image of truth has been shattered by rebellion. Such is the violence, for example, of unresisted pride.

There is only one kind of violence that captures the Kingdom of Heaven. It is the seeming violence of grace, which is really order and peace. It establishes peace in the soul's depth even in the midst of passion. It is called "violent" by reason of the energy with which it resists passion and sets order in the house of the soul. This violence is the voice and the power of God Himself, speaking in our soul. It is the authority of the God of peace, speaking within us, in the sanctuary, in His holy place.

The God of peace is never glorified by human violence.

IN THE END, the problem of sincerity is a problem of love. A sincere man is not so much one who sees the truth and manifests it as he sees it, but one who loves the truth with a pure love. But truth is more than an abstraction. It lives and is embodied in men and things that are real. And the secret of sincerity is, therefore, not to be sought in a philosophical love for abstract truth but in a love for real people and real things—a love for God apprehended in the reality around us.

The saint must see the truth as something to serve, not as something to own and manipulate according to his own good pleasure. The selfishness of an age that has devoted itself to the mere cult of pleasure has tainted the whole human race with an error that makes all our acts more or less lies against God. An age like ours cannot be sincere.

OUR ABILITY to be sincere with ourselves, with God, and with other men is really proportionate to our capacity for sincere love. And the sincerity of our love depends in large measure upon our capacity to believe ourselves loved. Most of the moral and mental and even religious complexities of our time go back to our desperate fear that we are not and can never be really loved by anyone.

When we consider that most men want to be loved as if they were gods, it is hardly surprising that they should despair of receiving the love they think they deserve. Even the biggest of fools must be dimly aware that he is not worthy of adoration, and no matter what he may believe about his right to be adored, he will not be long in finding out that he can never fool anyone enough to make her adore him. And yet our idea of ourselves is so fantastically unreal that we rebel against this lack of "love" as though we were the victims of an injustice. Our whole life is then constructed on a basis of duplicity. We assume that others are receiving the kind of appreciation we want for ourselves, and we proceed on the assumption that since we are not lovable as we are, we must become lovable under false pretenses, making ourselves appear something better than we are.

Perhaps the reason why so few men believe in God is that they have ceased to believe that even a God can love them. The man who is not afraid to admit everything that he sees to be wrong with himself, and yet recognizes that he may be the object of God's love precisely because of his shortcomings, can begin to be sincere. His sincerity is based on confidence, not in his illusions about himself, but in the endless, unfailing mercy of God.

NO MAN IS AN ISLAND

Thirteen: THE GROVE AND BEYOND

I⊤ was the end of November. All the days were short and dark. Finally, on the Thursday of that week, in the evening, I suddenly found myself filled with a vivid conviction:

"The time has come for me to go and be a Trappist."

Where had the thought come from? All I knew was that it was suddenly there. And it was something powerful, irresistible, clear.

I picked up a little book called *The Cistercian Life*, which I had bought at Gethsemani, and turned over the pages, as if they had something more to tell me. They seemed to me to be all written in words of flame and fire.

I went to supper, and came back and looked at the book again. My mind was literally full of this conviction. And yet, in the way, stood hesitation: that old business. But now there could be no delaying. I must finish with that, once and for all, and get an answer. I must talk to somebody who would settle it. It could be done in five minutes. And now was the time. Now.

Whom should I ask? Father Philotheus was probably in his room downstairs. I went downstairs, and out into the court. Yes, there was a light in Father Philotheus' room. All right. Go in and see what he has to say.

But instead of that, I bolted out into the darkness and made for the grove.

It was a Thursday night. The Alumni Hall was beginning to fill. They were going to have a movie. But I hardly noticed it: it did not occur to me that perhaps Father Philotheus might go to the movie with the rest. In the silence of the grove my feet were loud on the gravel. I walked and prayed. It was very, very dark by the shrine of the Little Flower. "For Heaven's sake, help me!" I said.

I started back toward the buildings. "All right. Now I am really going to go in there and ask him. Here's the situation, Father. What do you think? Should I go and be a Trappist?"

There was still a light in Father Philotheus' room. I walked bravely into the hall, but when I got within about six feet of his door it was almost as if someone had stopped me and held me where I was with physical hands. Something jammed in my will. I couldn't walk a step further, even though I wanted to. I made a kind of a push at the obstacle, which was perhaps a devil, and then turned around and ran out of the place once more.

And again I headed for the grove. The Alumni Hall was nearly full. My feet were loud on the gravel. I was in the silence of the grove, among wet trees.

I don't think there was ever a moment in my life when my soul felt so urgent and so special an anguish. I had been praying all the time, so I cannot say that I began to pray when I arrived there where the shrine was: but things became more definite.

"Please help me. What am I going to do? I can't go on like this. You can see that! Look at the state I am in. What ought I to do? Show me the way." As if I needed more information or some kind of a sign!

But I said this time to the Little Flower: "You show me what to do." And I added, "If I get into the monastery, I will be your monk. Now show me what to do."

It was getting to be precariously near the wrong way to pray—making indefinite promises that I did not quite understand and asking for some sort of a sign.

Suddenly, as soon as I had made that prayer, I became aware of the wood, the trees, the dark hills, the wet night wind, and then, clearer than any of these obvious realities, in my imagination, I started to hear the the great bell of Gethsemani ringing in the night—the bell in the big gray tower, ringing and ringing, as if it were just behind the first hill. The impression made me breathless, and I had to think twice to realize that it was only in my imagination that I was hearing the bell of the Trappist Abbey ringing in the dark. Yet, as I afterwards calculated, it was just about that time that the bell is rung every night for the *Salve Regina*, toward the end of Compline.

The bell seemed to be telling me where I belonged—as if it were calling me home.

This fancy put such determination into me that I immediately started back for the monastery—going the long way around, past the shrine of Our Lady of Lourdes and the far end of the football field. And with every step I took my mind became more and more firmly made up that now I would have done with all these doubts and hesitations and questions and all the rest, and get this thing settled, and go to the Trappists where I belonged.

When I came into the courtyard, I saw that the light in Father Philotheus' room was out. In fact, practically all the lights were out. Everybody had gone to the movies. My heart sank.

Yet there was one hope. I went right on through the door and into the corridor, and turned to the Friars' common room. I had never even gone near that door before. I had never dared. But now I went up and knocked on the glass panel and opened the door and looked inside.

There was nobody there except one Friar alone, Father Philotheus. I asked if I could speak with him and we went to his room.

That was the end of all my anxiety, all my hesitation.

As soon as I proposed all my hesitations and questions to him, Father Philotheus said that he could see no reason why I shouldn't want to enter a monastery and become a priest.

It may seem irrational, but at that moment, it was as if scales fell off my own eyes, and looking back on all my worries and questions, I could see clearly how empty and futile they had been. Yes, it was obvious that I was called to the monastic life: and all my doubts about it had been mostly shadows. Where had they gained such a deceptive appearance of substance and reality? Accident and circumstances had all contributed to exaggerate and distort things in my mind. But now everything was straight again. And already I was full of peace and assurance —the consciousness that everything was right, and that a straight road had opened out, clear and smooth, ahead of me.

Father Philotheus had only one question:

"Are you sure you want to be a *Trappist?*" he asked me.

"Father," I answered, "I want to give God everything."

I could see by the expression on his face that he was satisfied.

I went upstairs like somebody who had been called back from the dead. Never had I experienced the calm, untroubled peace and certainty that now filled my heart. There was only one more question: would the Trappists agree with Father Philotheus, and accept my application?

Without any delay, I wrote to the abbot of Gethsemani, asking permission to come and make a retreat at Christmastime. I tried to frame my request in words that hinted I was coming as a postulant, without giving them an opportunity to refuse me before I had at least put one foot inside the door. I sealed the envelope and took it downstairs and dropped it in the mailbox, and walked outside, once more, into the darkness, towards the grove.

II

SUNDAY, December the seventh, was the second Sunday in Advent. During High Mass the Seminarians were singing the *Rorate Coeli*, and I came out into the unusually warm sun with the beautiful Gregorian plaint in my ears. I went over to the kitchen, and got one of the Sisters to make me some cheese sandwiches and put them in a shoebox, and started out for Two Mile Valley.

I climbed up the hillside, on the eastern slope of the valley, and reached the rim of the thick woods, and sat down in a windless, sunny place where there were a lot of brown dried ferns. Down the hill by the road was a little country schoolhouse. Further out, at the mouth of the little valley, near the Alleghany, were a couple of small farms. The air was warm and quiet, you could hear nothing but the pounding and coughing of a distant oil pump, back in the woods.

Who would think there was a war anywhere in the world? It was so peaceful here, and undisturbed. I watched some rabbits come out and begin to play among the ferns.

This was probably the last time I would see this place. Where would I be in a week from that day? It was in the hands of God. There was nothing I could do but leave myself to His mercy. But surely, by this time, I should have been able to realize that He is much more anxious to take care of us, and capable of doing so, than we could be ourselves. It is only when we refuse His help, resist His will, that we have conflict, trouble, disorder, unhappiness, ruin.

I started back in the afternoon towards the College. It was two or two and a half miles to the railway trestle over the river, then a half a mile home. I walked slowly along the tracks towards the red brick buildings of the College. The sky was getting cloudy, and it was not long before sunset. When I got to the campus, and was walking down the cement path towards the dormitory, I met two of the other lay professors. They were talking animatedly about something or other, and as I approached they cried:

"Did you hear what happened? Did you hear the radio?"

America was in the war.

III

MY TRAIN was in the evening. It was already dark when the taxi called for me at the College.

"Where you going, Prof?" said somebody, as I passed out of the building with my suitcase.

The cab door slammed on my big general good-by, and we drove away. I did not turn to see the collection of heads that watched the parting cab from the shelter of the arched door.

When we got to town, there was still time for me to go to the church of Our Lady of the Angels, where I used to go to confession and where I often made the Stations of the Cross, when I was in Olean. The place was empty. There were one or two little candles burning out in front of the statue of St. Joseph, and the red sancturary light flickered in the quiet shadows. I knelt there for ten or twelve minutes in the silence without even attempting to grasp or comprehend the immense, deep sense of peace and gratitude that filled my heart and went out from there to Christ in His Tabernacle.

At the station, the Buffalo train came in through the freezing, sleety rain, and I got on, and my last tie with the world I had known snapped and broke.

It was nothing less than a civil, moral death.

IV

THIS JOURNEY, this transition from the world to a new life, was like flying through some strange new element—as if I were in the stratosphere. And yet I was on the familiar earth, and the cold winter rain streaked the windows of the train as we traveled through the dark hills.

And now the sun was up. It was shining on bare, rocky valleys, poor farm land, thin, spare fields, with brush and a few trees and willows growing along the creeks, and gray cabins, from time to time, along the line. Outside one of the cabins a man was splitting a log with an axe and I thought: that is what I will be doing, if God wills it, pretty soon.

It was a strange thing. Mile after mile my desire to be in the monastery increased beyond belief. I was altogether absorbed in that one idea. And yet, paradoxically, mile after mile my indifference increased, and my interior peace. What if they did not receive me? Then I would go to the army. But surely that would be a disaster? Not at all. If, after all this, I was rejected by the monastery and had to be drafted, it would be quite clear that it was God's will. I had done everything that was in my power; the rest was in His hands. And for all the tremendous and increasing intensity of my desire to be in the cloister, the thought that I might find myself, instead, in an army camp no longer troubled me in the least.

I was free. I had recovered my liberty. I belonged to God, not to myself: and to belong to Him is to be free, free of all the anxieties and worries and sorrows that belong to this earth, and the love of the things that are in it. What was the difference between one place and another, one habit and another, if your life belonged to God, and if you placed yourself completely in His hands? The only thing that mattered was the fact of the sacrifice, the essential dedication of one's self, one's will. The rest was only accidental.

V

I STEPPED on to the platform of Louisville station in the glory of that freedom, and walked out into the streets with a sense of triumph, remembering the time I had come this way before, the previous Easter. I was so happy and exultant that I didn't look where I was going and walked into the Jim Crow waiting room: whose shadows, full of Negroes, became somewhat tense with resentment. I hastened out again apologetically.

The Bardstown bus was half full, and I found a somewhat dilapidated seat, and we rode out into the wintry country, the last lap of my journey into the desert.

THE SEVEN STOREY MOUNTAIN

Epilogue: "MY SOUL REMEMBERED GOD"

I̲ₙ ₜₕₑ ᴅᴀʏ of my trouble I sought God with my hands lifted up to Him in the night, and I was not deceived. My soul remembered God, and was delighted, and was exercised, and my spirit swooned away. . . . And I said, Now I have begun: this is the change of the right hand of the Most High" (Psalm 76:3, 4, 11).

We could not seek God unless He were seeking us. We may begin to seek Him in desolation, feeling nothing but His absence. But the mere fact that we seek Him proves that we have already found Him. For if we continue in our prayer, we "remember" Him, that is to say, we become conscious, once again, of Who He really is. And we see that He has found us. When this consciousness is the work of grace, it is always fresh and new. It is more than the recovery of a past experience. It is a new experience, and it makes us new men.

This newness is the "delight" and the "exercise" which are the living evidence of contact with the Spirit of the Lord. It makes us "swoon" in our spirit in a passage from death to life. Thus our eyes are opened. We see all things in a new light. And we realize that this is a new beginning, a change that could only be brought about by the intervention of His Spirit in our lives—the "change of the right hand of the Most High."

ᴛʜᴇ ʟᴏʀᴅ is my rock and my fortress and He dwells in the midst of His people.

Come, let us enter the House of the Almighty and stand to praise Him.

Let us sleep like eagles in the cliff, let us rest in the power of the Lord our God!

Let us hide ourselves in the great mountain of His might, Who dwells concealed in the midst of a forsaken people.

Even His thunder is the refuge of the poor!

NO MAN IS AN ISLAND

PART THREE

The
Monastery

He began, "The holy rule of the mountain
  permits nothing that is disorderly
  or that is contrary to custom.
This place is free from variations;
  only what heaven takes into itself
  can cause change, nothing else. . . ."

Prologue

THE AVERAGE CISTERCIAN MONASTERY is a quiet, out-of-the-way place—usually somewhere in France—occupied by a community of seventy or eighty men who lead a silent energetic life consecrated entirely to God. It is a life of prayer and of penance, of liturgy, study, and manual labor. The monks are supposed to exercise no exterior ministry—no preaching, teaching, or the rest. The only teaching done by the monks is confined to classes of theology and philosophy within the monastery itself—classes attended by the young monks preparing for the priesthood.

The life is physically hard, but the compensation for this hardship is interior peace. In any case, one soon becomes used to the hardships and finds that they are not so hard after all. Seven hours of sleep are normally enough. The monks' diet is extremely plain, but is ordinarily enough to keep a man healthy for long years, and monks traditionally die of old age. One soon gets used to sleeping on straw and boards. Most monks would find it difficult to sleep on a soft mattress after their simple pallets.

The life is usually quiet. There is no conversation. The monks talk to their superiors or spiritual directors when necessary. In the average monastery, Cistercian silence is an all-pervading thing that seeps into the very stones of the place and saturates the men who live there.

Farm labor is the monks' support, and the ordinary thing is for all the monks to work outdoors for five or six hours a day. When they are not working, or praying in choir, the monks devote their time to reading, meditation, contemplative prayer. The whole day is supposed eventually to become a prolonged prayer in which the monk remains united with God through all his occupations. This is the real purpose of the monastic life: a more or less habitual state of simple prayer and union with God which varies in intensity at different times of the day, which finds a particular and proper rhythm in the life of each individual, and which brings the soul of the monk at all times under the direct and intimate influence of God's action.

But now, let us suppose that within four or five years, several hundred men decide that they want lives of silence, prayer, labor, penance, and constant union with God in solitude. And suppose they all decide to enter the same monastery. Although they do not all enter exactly at the same moment, they come in great numbers, continually, and the monastery of seventy grows to a hundred and seventy and then to two hundred and seventy.

Thus two hundred and seventy lovers of silence and solitude are all packed into a building that was built for seventy. Priests are needed to give them their formation and spiritual direction. It takes at least eight years to train a man for the priesthood, unless he has been in a seminary before coming to the monastery. Meanwhile, to relieve the pressure, four foundations—that is, new monasteries—are made. But these new monasteries are staffed with the most capable of the priests in the Mother Community. Consequently there are very few priests left at the Mother House to shoulder the burden of governing and caring for a community of two hundred and seventy. Hence they have a lot of extra work to do!

Meanwhile, new buildings have to be put up, and the farm has to be completely reorganized and expanded, so that all these new arrivals may be fed and housed. Since all this work has to be done in a hurry, many machines are needed. When you have a great crowd of postulants, much work, new buildings, and a small mechanized army of builders all working at high pressure, the silence is not always absolutely perfect.

The young monk who makes his vows at Gethsemani in this unusual moment of crisis and transition is therefore exposing himself to something far more than the ordinary vicissitudes of a Trappist monastery. He is walking into a furnace of ambivalence which nobody in the monastery can fully account for and which is designed, I think, to serve as a sign and a portent to modern America.

The phenomenon which has suddenly happened at Gethsemani came about without anybody's foreseeing it and without anyone making any logical attempt to control it. It was apparently beyond foreseeing and beyond control, and there is no one in the monastery who does not sometimes find himself fearful when he considers its possible issue.

One: TO THE MONASTERY

Wᴴᴇɴ ɪ ꜰɪɴᴀʟʟʏ got off in Bardstown, I was standing across the road from a gas station. The street appeared to be empty, as if the town were asleep. But presently I saw a man in the gas station. I went over and asked where I could get someone to drive me to Gethsemani. So he put on his hat and started his car and we left town on a straight road through level country, full of empty fields. It was not the kind of landscape that belonged to Gethsemani, and I could not get my bearings until some low, jagged, wooded hills appeared ahead of us, to the left of the road, and we made a turn that took us into rolling, wooded land.

Then I saw that high familiar spire.

I rang the bell at the gate. It let fall a dull, unresonant note inside the empty court. My man got in his car and went away. Nobody came. I could hear somebody moving around inside the Gatehouse. I did not ring again. Presently, the window opened, and Brother Matthew looked out between the bars, with his clear eyes and graying beard.

"Hullo, Brother," I said.

He recognized me, glanced at the suitcase, and said: "This time have you come to stay?"

"Yes, Brother, if you'll pray for me," I said.

Brother nodded, and raised his hand to close the window.

"That's what I've been doing," he said, "praying for you."

II

ꜱᴏ ʙʀᴏᴛʜᴇʀ ᴍᴀᴛᴛʜᴇᴡ locked the gate behind me and I was enclosed in the four walls of my new freedom.

And it was appropriate that the beginning of freedom should be as it was. For I entered a garden that was dead and stripped and bare.

The flowers that had been there last April were all gone. The sun was hidden behind low clouds and an icy wind was blowing over the gray grass and the concrete walks.

In a sense my freedom had already begun, for I minded none of these things. I did not come to Gethsemani for the flowers, or for the climate —although I admit that the Kentucky winters were a disappointment. Still, I had not had time to plan on any kind of a climate. I had been too busy with the crucially important problem of finding out God's will. And that problem was still not entirely settled.

There still remained the final answer: would I be accepted into this monastery? Would they take me into the novitiate, to become a Cistercian?

Father Joachim, the guest master, came out the door of the monastery and crossed the garden with his hands under his scapular and his eyes fixed on the cement walk. He only raised them when he was near me, and then he grinned.

"Oh, it's you," he said.

I did not give him a chance to ask if I had come to stay. I said: "Yes, Father, this time I want to be a novice—if I can."

He just smiled. We went into the house. The place seemed very empty. I put the suitcase down in the room that had been assigned to me, and hastened to the church.

If I expected any grand welcome from Christ and His angels, I did not get it—not in the sensible order. The huge nave was like a tomb, and the building was as cold as ice. However, I did not mind. Nor was I upset by the fact that nothing special came into my head in the way of a prayer. I just knelt there more or less dumb, and listened to the saw down at the sawmill fill the air with long strident complaints and the sound of labor.

That evening at supper I found that there was another postulant— an ancient, toothless, gray-haired man hunched up in a huge sweater. He was a farmer from the neighborhood who had lived in the shadow of the abbey for years and had finally made up his mind to enter it as a lay brother. However, he did not stay.

The next day I found out there was still a third postulant. He arrived that morning. He was a fat bewildered youth from Buffalo. Like myself, he was applying for the choir. Father Joachim put the two of us to work together washing dishes and waxing floors, in silence. We were both absorbed in our own many thoughts, and I dare say he was no more tempted to start a conversation than I was.

In fact every minute of the day I was secretly congratulating myself that conversations were over and done with—provided always I was accepted.

I could not be quite sure whether someone would call me and tell me to go down for an interview with the Father Abbot, or whether I was expected to go down to him on my own initiative, but that part of the problem was settled for me toward the end of the morning work.

I went back to my room and started puzzling my head over the copy of the *Spiritual Directory* that Father Joachim had brought me. Instead of settling down quietly and reading the chapter that directly concerned me, the one that said what postulants were supposed to do while they were waiting in the Guesthouse, I started leafing through the two thin volumes to see if I could not discover something absolutely clear and definite as to what the Cistercian vocation was all about.

It is easy enough to say, "Trappists are called to lead lives of prayer and penance," because after all there is a sense in which everybody is called to lead that kind of a life. It is also easy enough to say that Cistercians are called to devote themselves entirely to contemplation without any regard for the works of the active life: but that does not say anything precise about the object of our life and it certainly does not distinguish the Trappists from any of the other so-called "contemplative orders." Then the question always arises: "What do you mean by contemplation, anyway?"

From the *Spiritual Directory* I learned that "the Holy Mass, the Divine Office, Prayer and pious reading which form the exercises of the contemplative life occupy the major part of our day."

It was a frigid and unsatisfying sentence. The phrase "pious reading" was a gloomy one, and somehow the thought that the contemplative life was something that was divided up into "exercises" was of a sort that would have ordinarily depressed me. But I think I had come to the monastery fully resigned to the prospect of meeting that kind of language for the rest of my life. In fact, it is a good thing that I was resigned to it, for it is one of the tiresome minor details of all religious life today that one must receive a large proportion of spiritual nourishment dished up in the unseasoned jargon of transliterated French.

I had no way of saying what the contemplative life meant to me then. But it seemed to me that it should mean something more than spending so many hours a day in a church and so many more hours somewhere else, without having to go to the bother of preaching sermons or teaching school or writing books or visiting the sick.

A few lines further on in the *Directory* there were some cautious words about mystical contemplation which, I was told, was "not required" but which God sometimes "vouchsafed." That word "vouchsafe"! It almost sounded as if the grace came to you dressed up in a crinoline. In fact, to my way of interpreting it, when a spiritual book tells you that "infused contemplation is sometimes vouchsafed" the idea you are supposed to get is this: "infused contemplation is all right for the saints, but as for *you*: hands off!"

III

DOM FREDERIC was deep in a pile of letters which covered the desk before him, along with a mountain of other papers and documents. Yet you could see that this tremendous volume of work did not succeed in submerging him. He had it all under control. Since I have been in the monastery I have often had occasion to wonder by what miracle he manages to *keep* all that under control. But he does.

In any case, that day Father Abbot turned to us with just as much ease and facility as if he had nothing else whatever to do but to give the first words of advice to two postulants leaving the world to become Trappists.

"Each one of you," he said, "will make the community either better or worse. Everything you do will have an influence upon others. It can be a good influence or a bad one. It all depends on you. Our Lord will never refuse you grace. . . ."

I forget whether he quoted Father Faber. Reverend Father likes to quote Father Faber, and after all it would be extraordinary if he failed to do so on that day. But I have forgotten.

We kissed his ring as he blessed us both, and went out again. His parting shaft had been that we should be joyful but not dissipated, and that the Names of Jesus and Mary should always be on our lips.

At the other end of the long dark hall we went into a room where three monks were sitting at typewriters, and we handed over our fountain pens and wrist watches and our loose cash to the Treasurer, and signed documents promising that if we left the monastery we would not sue the monks for back wages for our hours of manual labor.

And then we passed through the door into the cloister.

THE SEVEN STOREY MOUNTAIN

Two: IN THE MONASTIC COMMUNITY

ONE OR TWO of the novices came up and smiled and clasped their hands together and made the kind of a sign a prize fighter makes when he has just won a bout, to acknowledge the applause of his fans. It is the unofficial sign used at Gethsemani for "Congratulations" and you won't find it in the List of Signs in the Book of Usages. So I smiled, and made one of the only signs I had found out how to make, which was "Thank you." It is easy to make and remember. You just kiss your hand. It goes back to the days when people used to kiss one another's hands out of politeness, and we make the same sign when we want to say "Please."

And so I too sank into the obscurity, the anonymity of this big Trappist family, hidden behind the walls of a monastery of which, until a couple of years before, I had never even heard.

With the white woollen habit on me, I had ceased to be a stranger—or at least a complete stranger. And that is the first thing you have to cease to be when you enter a Cistercian community. For there is no cohesion more close and more intense than that of a house full of Trappists. A Cistercian monastery is, in a very real sense, a family. And to live in it according to the Cistercian Rule and vocation, that is, according to God's will, you simply have to become one flesh, one undivided organism with all the rest of the people there.

There is no escaping the fact that monks have to live together as brothers. It is forced upon them by the rule. It is one of the most essential elements in Benedictine asceticism, and the Cistercian Fathers of the twelfth century, especially St. Bernard and St. Ailred of Rievaulx, seized upon it and emphasized it still more. In fact, so marked is the importance given to brotherly love in our monastic ideal that it occupies a crucial position in the structure of Cistercian mystical theology. The ascent of the individual soul to personal mystical union with God is made to depend, in our life, upon our ability to love one another.

We get up at two o'clock in the morning, and jostle one another in the dark trying to get a little water on our faces to wake ourselves up, and we hasten to choir bumping into one another all down the dark cloister. Then for the next two hours we have to stand next to someone who sings faster, or slower, or lower than we do. Or perhaps he has a cold, and we begin to catch it.

We kneel down, all together, to make our mental prayer. Just as you are getting settled, and beginning to get some fruit out of your prayer, your neighbor nudges you and you have to stand up and turn on the light for him so that he can consult a book.

In the canonical office you have someone next to you who turns the pages of the book too fast, and you miss half a line, and have to bend down and make the little satisfaction.

In the Scriptorium, you find a book in the Common Box that begins to interest you intensely: and then someone else gets interested in it too, and every time you want it, you find he has got there first. Out at work you may be put to saw a log with someone who just puts his head down and closes his eyes in prayer and doesn't care how he pulls his end of the saw, so that it continually jams in the log and you have to do five times as much work as usual, with practically no result. Then you go to the refectory, and your bowl of potatoes is missing, and your neighbors do not notice it. The Usages forbid you to ask for it yourself, and so you go hungry.

All this becomes far more interesting when it happens that the same person is the one who coughs down your neck in choir, and takes the book you want in the Scriptorium, and fails to get your portion for you at table: he may even make matters worse by proclaiming you in chapter for not turning on the light promptly when it is needed at meditation.

And yet it is precisely all this that is given us by God to make us solitaries, hermits, living at peace with Him within ourselves, even though we are constantly surrounded by all the others in the community.

BUT CISTERCIAN LIFE brings with it more than this negative peace. It is not merely a question of being able to live in the same house with people who might be naturally quite uncongenial to us: the fact is that the monks really do love one another. They really do enter into a kind of close and intimate cohesion that binds them together as true brothers. In fact, although many of them do not actually realize it explicitly, most Cistercians derive a profound consolation from the mere fact of being with the other monks. They seem not to pay any attention to one another, and yet there is a profound happiness in just being there together, sitting in the same room and reading or writing, in the presence of God Who is the only possible reason for their unity.

In a way, even the weaknesses and imperfections which we all have manage to fit in harmoniously to this picture, so that one even comes to like the habits of others that first appeared to be annoying and strange.

THE CISTERCIANS HAVE CARRIED communism to its ultimate limit. They not only hold their farm and monastery and all the things in it as common property, no one having a legitimate personal claim to anything so small as a handkerchief or a pin or a piece of paper, but they share all their failings and all their weaknesses and all their sicknesses of soul and body. *Alter alterius onera portate:* there are no people in the world who get to be such experts at bearing one another's burdens as Cistercian monks. Watch a group of monks at work together and see with what efficiency they take care of one another's blunders; if they are good monks, they will do so without a sign, without a change of expression, and so expeditiously that you will ask yourself if the mistake really happened after all.

The beauty of the process is in the lack of wasted motion and the absence of fake politeness. They are kind, indulgent, and gentle about it, but it is rare that you will see anybody make a big artificial fuss over the troubles of others. Those who like to have a great deal of attention paid to their woes are out of luck if they come looking for it in a Cistercian monastery. They must learn to be content with unfailing but unobtrusive assistance, kind, generous and complete, but totally unadorned by flattery or any of the artificialities of the world.

II

NOW THAT I had become a child of this Trappist family, I looked around the room to see my home, and my brothers sitting in it. It was a fairly large room, with six large windows opening out in three directions. On one side was a three-sided court dominated by the apse of the church and the steeple and some tall cedar trees. From this side the sun slanted into the novices' Scriptorium, bathing the two big tables with warmth and light. The novices in their white cloaks sat mostly along the walls,

on the low seats under which were their private boxes. A few were at
the tables, writing diligent and mysterious notes on bits of scrap paper
—on dissected pieces of used envelopes and the blank backs of written
pages, letters they had received, and so on.

They were a varied assortment, these novices. Some were young and
tall and thin, others were middle-aged. Most of them were young. All
of them looked intensely happy, although their noses were red with
colds, and the knuckles of the fingers which held their books were
cracked wide open and bleeding with the cold.

It was wonderful, the silence, and peace, and happiness that pervaded
this sunny room, where so many men were together without speaking.
Far from there being any sense of restraint, of awkwardness, of strain,
you felt flooded with a deep sense of ease and quiet and restful well-
being. There was absolutely no kind of tension between those who sat
together in silence: they were all absorbed in their books or their
thoughts or their writing. And their very activities were marked by a
kind of restful quality: they were not imprisoned by any fierce concentration, not driven before the face of some storm of hurry and anxiety. Their eyes rested on the page with a quiet, detached attention; or
else they looked away from the book, in thought; or they entered into
themselves, or wrote something down.

They were diligent, yet peaceful: busy, yet at ease, at rest. They were
together, yet they were alone. They were silent, yet full of occupation:
occupied, but without a trace of confusion. They were recollected, without any evidence of special concentration or of strain—or at least that
was the norm.

THERE MIGHT BE two anomalies, in the midst of such peace and mod-
esty and unaffected recollection: on the one hand, your attention might
be struck by someone who appeared to be working too hard to be a
saint—as if it all depended on him. On the other hand, there might
be one or two who were perhaps not working hard enough, as if nothing
depended on them. The former would hide himself in a corner in such
a way that it made him completely obvious. And the others would have
a way of standing around and making signs that still smacked of "the
world"—a way of holding their head up, and staring around with their
mouth open, and perhaps laughing out loud.

But most of these faces had lost all the toughness and tenseness and
bitterness of the world, as well as the world's flabbiness and sensuality
and conceit. The corners of these mouths were not drawn down by

sarcasm or obscure, nervous antagonisms and fears. These brows were not plowed with angry or anxious lines. These eyes were perfectly clear. They did not evade your gaze, or reply to it with anything but the candor of skies, of lakes: they were unfathomable in their simplicity, and flickered with none of those lights that make men unhappy and afraid.

And yet these were perfectly ordinary men—all the usual types you would find on the street of any American town. You could pick out the ones who had probably been high school football players, those who had worked delivering groceries, or perhaps had worked in garages or soda fountains. One of them, I knew, had come to the monastery out of the Marines—he was my "guardian angel," appointed to teach me how to work the big choirbooks, and to keep me from wandering into parts of the monastery where novices were not allowed to go. One or two others had been soldiers. Some of them had been to colleges and universities. Some had come from the secular priesthood, but now the accidents of their past were being effectively ironed out of them, and they were becoming simple Cistercians, dwelling in the ample folds of their white and hooded cloaks.

Yet nothing was lost that was of any value. No natural gift was lost, no natural quality was destroyed, nothing they had brought with them that could count as a talent would have to be buried here. No, everything they had was sublimated and fused into the big, vital unity of a life concentrated on the highest, the only good, in Whom all other goods are eminently contained and ultimately perfected.

I REALIZED all this in my own case, with a kind of surprise—realized that all the things I might have given up I had really retained, in so far as they were implicit in a higher good: and the wonder of it was, that in this form they continued to give me a joy that I could no longer get out of them in the world.

I could no longer travel around in the countries of the world as I pleased; but a far vaster supernatural geography was to be opened up to me, in not so many days, that would make the whole world look cheap and small. I had left all my friends and the ruins that remained of my family; but I already knew that in Christ I had them all, and loved them all far more perfectly and effectively than I could by any human affection. And the point is: human affection was not destroyed, not rooted out of me, and it did not have to be, except in a metaphorical sense. My human affection for all the people I ever loved has lost none of its reality in the monastery, but it is submerged in a higher and more vital reality, in the unity of a vaster and deeper and more incomprehensible love, the love of God, in Whom I love them, and in Whom, paradoxically, I am much more closely united to them than I could be if I had stayed in the world, preferring their company to His.

And I had given up writing.

Or had I? That was the question. Everything else I had given up I retained, implicit in the higher good for which I had renounced it. Was one thing going to follow me in its proper form, or would this also follow the same way as the rest? Would I give up writing and find again all the joy of the work which, all in all, was probably the greatest joy I had ever had short of prayer and serving God directly?

As far as I was concerned, that was my intention.

But I was still wondering if God had asked it of me. I would see.

Unpublished, from the Original Manuscript of
THE SEVEN STOREY MOUNTAIN

Three: TO BECOME A MONK

LITURGICALLY SPEAKING, you could hardly find a better time to become a monk than Advent. You begin a new life, you enter into a new world at the beginning of a new liturgical year. And everything that the Church gives you to sing, every prayer that you say in and with Christ in His Mystical Body is a cry of ardent desire for grace, for help, for the coming of the Messiah, the Redeemer.

It is a desire all the more powerful, in the spiritual order, because the world around you is dead. Life has ebbed to its dregs. The trees are stripped bare. The birds forget to sing. The grass is brown and gray. You go out to the fields with mattocks to dig up the briars. The sun gives its light, as it were, in faint intermittent explosions, "squibs," not rays, according to John Donne's conceit in his Nocturnal on St. Lucy's Day. . . .

But the cold stones of the abbey church ring with a chant that glows with living flame, with clean, profound desire. It is an austere warmth, the warmth of Gregorian chant. It is deep beyond ordinary emotion, and that is one reason why you never get tired of it. It never wears you out by making a lot of cheap demands on your sensibilities. Instead of drawing you out into the open field of feelings where your enemies, the devil, and your own imagination and the inherent vulgarity of your own corrupted nature can get at you with their blades and cut you to pieces, it draws you within, where you are lulled in peace and recollection and where you find God.

Every day, from now on, the office would ring with the deep impassioned cries of the old prophets calling out to God to send the Redeemer. *Veni, Domine, noli tardare: relaxa facinora plebis tuae.* And the monks took up the cry with the same strong voices, and armed with the con-

fidence of grace and God's own presence within them, they argued with
Him and chided Him as His old prophets had done before. What is
the matter with You, *Domine?* Where is our Redeemer? Where is the
Christ You have promised us? Are You sleeping? Have You forgotten
us, that we should still be buried in our miseries and in the shadow of
war and sorrow?

Now I saw the monastery from within, from the church floor, so to
speak, not from the visitor's gallery. I saw it from the novitiate wing,
not from the shiny and well-heated Guesthouse. Now I was face to face
with monks that belonged not to some dream, not to some medieval
novel, but to cold and inescapable reality. The community which I had
seen functioning as a unity, in all the power of that impressive and
formal liturgical anonymity which clothes a body of men obscurely in
the very personality of Christ Himself, now appeared to me broken up
into its constituent parts, and all the details, good and bad, pleasant and
unpleasant, were there for me to observe at close range.

By this time God had given me enough sense to realize at least obscurely that this is one of the most important aspects of any religious
vocation: the first and most elementary test of one's call to the religious
life—whether as a Jesuit, Franciscan, Cistercian, or Carthusian—is the
willingness to accept life in a community in which everybody is more
or less imperfect.

The imperfections are much smaller and more trivial than the defects and vices of people outside in the world: and yet somehow you
tend to notice them more and feel them more, because they get to be
so greatly magnified by the responsibilities and ideals of the religious
state, through which you cannot help looking at them.

People even lose their vocations because they find out that a man
can spend forty or fifty or sixty years in a monastery and still have a
bad temper. Anyway, now that I was a part of Gethsemani I looked
about me to see what it was really like.

What was important was not the thick, unheated walls, but the things
that went on within them.

The house was full of people, men hidden in white cowls and brown
capes, some with beards, the lay brothers, others with no beards but
monastic crowns. There were young men and old men, and the old ones
were in the minority. At a rough guess, with all the novices we have
in the house now I think the average age of the community cannot be
much over thirty.

There was, I could see, something of a difference between the community proper and the novices. The monks and the professed brothers were more deeply absorbed in things that the novices had not yet discovered. And yet looking around at the novices there was a greater outward appearance of piety in them—but you could sense that it was nearer the surface.

It can be said, as a general rule, that the greatest saints are seldom the ones whose piety is most evident in their expression when they are kneeling at prayer, and the holiest men in a monastery are almost never the ones who get that exalted look, on feast days, in the choir. The people who gaze up at Our Lady's statue with glistening eyes are very often the ones with the worst tempers.

With the novices, their sensible piety was innocent and spontaneous, and it was perfectly proper to their state. As a matter of fact I liked the novitiate at once. It was pervaded with enthusiasm and vitality and good humor.

I liked the way they kidded one another in sign language, and I liked the quiet storms of amusement that suddenly blew up from nowhere and rocked the whole Scriptorium from time to time. Practically all the novices seemed to be very enlightened and sincere about their duties in the religious life; they had been quick in catching on to the rules and were keeping them with spontaneous ease rather than hair-splitting exactitude. And the ingenuous good humor that welled up from time to time in the middle of all this made their faces all shine like the faces of children—even though some of them were no longer young.

THE SEVEN STOREY MOUNTAIN

Four: CHRISTMAS NIGHT

CHRIST ALWAYS SEEKS the straw of the most desolate cribs to make his Bethlehem. In all the other Christmases of my life, I had got a lot of presents and a big dinner. This Christmas I was to get no presents, and not much of a dinner: but I would have, indeed, Christ Himself, God, the Savior of the world.

You who live in the world: let me tell you that there is no comparing these two kinds of Christmas.

What an atmosphere of expectation and joy there is in a Cistercian monastery when the monks get up, not at two in the morning, but at nine in the evening. They have gone to bed at five. Now, at this unaccustomed hour, when the winter night has not yet begun to get that paralyzing desolate coldness of the small hours, the church is full of unaccustomed lights. There is the crib, all lit up with a soft glow, and in the high darkness of the sanctuary the forest of cedar branches that has grown up around the altar sparkles with tinsel here and there.

It is then that the night office begins, begins at once with a solemn and stately invitatory that nevertheless rocks the church with cadences of superlative joy; from then on it is as though the angels themselves were singing their *Gloria in Excelsis* and showering upon the earth from the near stars, the stars that seem to have become close and warm, their messages and promises of peace, peace! Peace on earth to men of good will. As the Midnight Mass begins, the whole place glows with happiness, and after that it is indescribable, building up to the climax of unworldly interior peace at Communion.

It is good that somewhere in the world there are men who realize that Christ is born. There were only a few shepherds at the first Bethle-

158

hem, and it is the same now. The ox and the ass understood more of the first Christmas than the high priests in Jerusalem. And it is the same way today.

The emptiness that had opened out within me, that had been prepared during Advent and laid open by my own silence and darkness, now became filled. And suddenly I was in a new world.

I seemed to be the same person, and I was the same person, I was still myself, I was more myself than I had ever been, and yet I was nothing. It was as if the floor had fallen out of my soul and I was free to go in and out of infinity. The deeps that were suddenly there could not be measured, and it was useless even to think of fathoming them. And they were not a place, not to an extent, they were a Presence. And in the midst of me they formed a citadel. And I knew at once that there was nothing that could ever penetrate into the heart of that peace, nothing from outside myself could ever get in, and there was a whole sphere of my own activity that was irrevocably excluded from it: the five senses, the imagination, the discoursing mind. I could enter in, I was free to come and go, and yet as soon as I attempted to make words or thoughts about it, I was excluded—or excluded to the extent that I attended to the words and thoughts.

Yet I could rest in this dark unfathomable peace without trouble and without worry even while the imagination and the mind itself were in some way active outside of it. They could stand and chatter at the door, in their idleness, waiting for the return of the will, their queen, upon whose orders they depended. They stood like a couple of chauffeurs at the door of a mansion which it was not their business to enter. And yet the mind was not all excluded, only in certain of its operations. But in so far as it was able to rest serene, in itself, the mind too could enter into the peace and harmony of this infinite simplicity that had come to be born within me.

But what are all these words? Shadows, illusions. The soul has not divisions into parts, into sections, into places. It merely operates this way or that, and the experience of this or that kind of operation can be translated by the imagination into terms of place and space, light and darkness: but as soon as it gets into those terms, the whole thing loses its true meaning.

Within the simplicity of that armed and walled and undivided interior peace was the sweetness of an infinite love. Yet this sweetness, as soon as it was grasped, or held, lost its savor. You must not try to reach out and possess it altogether. You must not touch it, or try to take it. You must not try to make it sweeter, or to keep it from going away. . . .

BUT ALL THIS is abstract. There was a far greater reality in all this, the sense of the presence of a Person; not exteriorized in space, not standing opposite one, or inside one, or outside one, not standing here or there or anywhere, but *living* in the midst. You are aware that you are alive: but where do you feel your life? Is it here? Is it here? It is inside you rather than outside you: but where? I suppose you can get to thinking it is in your heart, but it is all over you.

It is easy to realize the life of one's body, and hard to track it down, to place it. It is even easier to realize the life of your soul when it is made known to you, and even harder to track it down and place it.

And the hardest thing about it is that that life is a Person, Christ. *Vivo, jam non ego, vivit vero in me Christus.*

YOU KNOW that Christ is born within you, infinite liberty: that you are free! That there are enemies which can never touch you, if this liberty loves you, and lives within you! That there are no more limitations! That you can love! That you are standing on the threshold of infinite possibilities! That the way lies open to escape from all these useless words! That the darkness has been washed out of your spiritual eyes and that you can open them and begin to see: but above all, that you can know by more perfect knowledge than vision, by the embrace of this liberty, and by the touch of infinite freedom in the midst of your spirit, and above all by rest, peace! This is the true contemplative vocation, the kernel of it, the innermost meaning of our life: *frui Deo,* heaven on earth, the love, the connatural knowledge of God: God as experience.

Unpublished, from the Original Manuscript of
THE SEVEN STOREY MOUNTAIN

Five: OUR LADY OF SORROWS

Now, at the beginning of July, we were in the midst of the harvest, getting in the wheat. The big threshing machine was drawn up at the east end of the cow barn, and wagons loaded with sheaves were constantly coming in, from all directions, from the various fields. You could see the cellarer standing on top of the threshing machine, outlined against the sky, giving directions, and a group of lay-brother novices were busily filling the sacks and tying them up and loading trucks as fast as the clean new grain poured out of the machine. Some of the choir novices were taking the grain down to the mill and unloading the sacks and spilling the wheat out on the granary floor: but most of us were out in the fields.

That year we had a phenomenal harvest, but it was always threatened with ruin by showers of rain. So practically every day the novices went out to the fields and dismantled the shocks and spread the damp sheaves around on the ground, in the sun, to dry before they began to get full of mildew; then we would put them back together again and go home —and there would be another shower of rain. But in the end it was a good harvest, anyway.

How sweet it is, out in the fields, at the end of the long summer afternoons! The sun is no longer raging at you, and the woods are beginning to throw long blue shadows over the stubble fields where the golden shocks are standing. The sky is cool, and you can see the pale half moon smiling over the monastery in the distance. Perhaps a clean smell of pine comes down to you, out of the woods, on the breeze, and mingles with the richness of the fields and of the harvest. And when the undermaster claps his hands for the end of work, and you drop your arms and take off your hat to wipe the sweat out of your eyes, in the stillness you realize how the whole valley is alive with the singing of crickets, a constant universal treble going up to God out of the fields, rising like the incense of an evening prayer to the pure sky: *laus perennis!*

And you take your rosary out of your pocket, and get in your place in the long file, and start swinging homeward along the road with your boots ringing on the asphalt and deep, deep peace in your heart! And on your lips, silently, over and over again, the name of the Queen of Heaven, the Queen also of this valley: "Hail Mary, full of grace, the Lord is with Thee. . . ." And the Name of her Son, for Whom all this was made in the first place, for Whom all this was planned and intended, for Whom the whole of creation was framed, to be His Kingdom. "Blessed is the fruit of Thy womb, Jesus!"

"Full of grace!" The very thought, over and over, fills our own hearts with more grace, and who knows what grace overflows into the world from that valley, from those rosaries, in the evenings when the monks are swinging home from work!

It was a few days after the Feast of the Visitation, which is, for me, the feast of the beginning of all true poetry, when the Mother of God sang her *Magnificat,* and announced the fulfillment of all prophecies, and proclaimed the Christ in her and became the Queen of Prophets and of poets—a few days after that feast, I got news from John Paul.

For the last few months he had been at a camp in the plains of the Canadian west, in Manitoba. Day after day he had been making long flights and doing bombing practice, and now he had his sergeant's stripes and was ready to be sent overseas.

He wrote that he was coming to Gethsemani before he sailed. But he did not say when.

II

THE Feast of St. Stephen Harding, the founder of the Cistercian Order, went by, and every day I was waiting to be called to Reverend Father's room, and told that John Paul had come.

By now the corn was high, and every afternoon we went out with hoes, to make war against our enemies, the morning glories, in the cornfields. And every afternoon, I would disappear into those rows of green banners, and lose sight of everybody else, wondering how anybody would be able to find me if he were sent out there to bring me in with the news that my brother had come. Often you did not even hear the

signal for the end of work, and frequently one or two of the more recollected novices would get left in the cornfield, hoeing away diligently
in some remote corner, after everybody else had gone home.

But I have discovered from experience that the rule, in these things,
is that what you are expecting always comes when you are not actually
expecting it. So it was one afternoon that we were working close to the
monastery, within the enclosure, weeding a patch of turnips, that someone made me a sign to come into the house. I had so far forgotten the
object of my expectations that it took me a moment or two before I
guessed what it was.

I changed out of workclothes and went straight to Reverend Father's
room and knocked on the door. He flashed the "Please wait" sign that
is worked from a button at his desk, and so there was nothing for it but
to sit down and wait, which I did, for the next half hour.

Finally Reverend Father discovered that I was there, and sent for
my brother, who presently came along the hall with Brother Alexander.
He was looking very well, and standing very straight, and his shoulders,
which were always broad, were now completely square.

As soon as we were alone in his room, I began to ask him if he didn't
want to get baptized.

"I sort of hoped I could be," he said.

"Tell me," I said, "how much instruction have you had, anyway?"

"Not much," he said.

After I had questioned him some more, it turned out that "not much"
was a euphemism for "none at all."

"But you can't be baptized without knowing what it is all about," I
said.

I went back to the novitiate before vespers feeling miserable.

"He hasn't had any instruction," I said gloomily to Father Master.

"But he wants to be baptized, doesn't he?"

"He says he does."

Then I said: "Don't you think I could give him enough instruction
in the next few days to prepare him? And Father James could talk to
him when he gets a chance. And of course he can go to all the conferences of the retreat."

One of the weekend retreats was just beginning.

"Take him some books," said Father Master, "and talk to him, and
tell him everything you can. And I'll go and speak to Reverend Father."

So the next day I hurried up to John Paul's room with a whole arm-
ful of volumes purloined from the Novitiate Common Box—and soon

he had a room full of all kinds of books that different people had selected
for him to read. If he had wanted to read them all, he would have had
to stay in the monastery for six months. There was an orange pamphlet
with an American flag on the cover, called "The Truth About Catholics." There were, of course, *The Imitation of Christ* and a New Testament. Then my contribution was the Catechism of the Council of Trent,
and Father Robert's suggestion was *The Faith of Millions* and Father
James had come through with the *Story of a Soul*, the autobiography
of the Little Flower.

But in any case, John Paul looked them all over. He said: "Who
is this Little Flower, anyway?" And he read the *Story of a Soul* all in
one gulp.

Meanwhile, I spent practically the whole of the morning and afternoon work periods talking my head off about everything I could think
of that had something to do with the faith. It was much harder work
than my fellow novices were doing out there in the cornfield—and much
more exhausting.

You might have expected two brothers, at such a time as this, to be
talking about the "old days." In a sense, we were. Our own lives, our
memories, our family, the house that had served us as a home, the things
we had done in order to have what we thought was a good time—all
this was indeed the background of our conversation, and, in an indirect
sort of way, entered very definitely into the subject matter.

It was so clearly present that there was no necessity to allude to it,
this sorry, complicated past, with all its confusions and misunderstandings and mistakes. It was as real and vivid and present as the memory
of an automobile accident in the casualty ward where the victims are
being brought back to life.

Was there any possibility of happiness without faith? Without some
principle that transcended everything we had ever known? The house
in Douglaston, which my grandparents had built, and which they maintained for twenty-five years with the icebox constantly full and the
carpets all clean and fifteen different magazines on the living-room table
and a Buick in the garage and a parrot on the back porch screaming
against the neighbor's radio, was the symbol of a life that had brought
them nothing but confusions and anxieties and misunderstandings and
fits of irritation. It was a house in which Bonnemaman had sat for hours
every day in front of a mirror, rubbing cold cream into her cheeks as
if she were going to the opera—but she never went to the opera, ex-

cept, perhaps, the ones she saw before her in her dreams as she sat there, in peaceless isolation, among the pots of ointment.

Against all this we had reacted with everything our own generation could give us, and we had ended up doing, in the movies, and in the cheap, amber-lit little bars of Long Island, or the noisier ones, fixed up with chromium, in the city, all that she had been doing at home. We never went to our own particular kind of operas either.

If a man tried to live without grace, not all his works were evil, that was true, certainly. He could do a lot of good things. He could drive a car. That is a good thing. He could read a book. He could swim. He could draw pictures. He could do all the things my brother had done at various times: collect stamps, postcards, butterflies, study chemistry, take photographs, fly a plane, learn Russian. All these things were good in themselves and could be done without grace.

But there was absolutely no need to stop and ask him, now, whether, without the grace of God, any of those pursuits had come anywhere near making him happy.

I spoke about faith. By the gift of faith, you touch God, you enter into contact with His very substance and reality, in darkness: because nothing accessible, nothing comprehensible to our senses and reason can grasp His essence as it is in itself. But faith transcends all these limitations, and does so without labor: for it is God Who reveals Himself to us, and all that is required of us is the humility to accept His revelation, and accept it on the conditions under which it comes to us— from the lips of men.

When that contact is established, God gives us sanctifying grace: His own life, the power to love Him, the power to overcome all the weaknesses and limitations of our blind souls and to serve Him and control our crazy and rebellious flesh.

"Once you have grace," I said to him, "you are free. Without it, you cannot help doing the things you know you should not do, and that you know you don't really want to do. But once you have grace, you are free. When you are baptized, there is no power in existence that can force you to commit a sin—nothing that will be able to drive you to it against your own conscience. And if you merely will it, you will be free forever, because the strength will be given you, as much as you need, and as often as you ask, and as soon as you ask, and generally long before you ask for it, too."

By Saturday afternoon I had told John Paul everything I knew. I had got to the Sacramentals and Indulgences and then gone back and given him an explanation of that notion, so mysterious to some outside the Church: The Sacred Heart. After that I stopped. I was exhausted. I had nothing left to give him.

And he sat calmly in his chair and said: "Go on, tell me some more."

The next day was Sunday, the Feast of St. Anne. After Chapter, in the long interval before High Mass, I asked Father Master if I could go over to the Guesthouse.

"Reverend Father told me your brother might be going over to New Haven to get baptized."

I went to the novitiate chapel and prayed.

But after dinner I found out that it was true. John Paul was sitting in his room, quiet and happy. It was years since I had seen him so completely serene.

Then I realized, obscurely, that in those last four days the work of eighteen or twenty years of my bad example had been washed away and made good by God's love. The evil that had been done by my boasting and showing off and exulting in my own stupidity had been atoned for in my own soul, at the same time as it had been washed out of his, and I was full of peace and gratitude.

I taught him how to use a Missal and how to receive Communion, for it had been arranged that his First Communion would be at Reverend Father's private Mass the following day.

The next morning, all through Chapter, the obscure worry that John Paul would get lost and not be able to find his way down to the chapel of Our Lady of Victories had been haunting me. As soon as Chapter was over I hurried to the church ahead of Reverend Father, and entered the big empty building, and knelt down.

John Paul was nowhere in sight.

I turned around. At the end of the long nave, with its empty choir stalls, high up in the empty Tribune, John Paul was kneeling all alone, in uniform. He seemed to be an immense distance away, and between the secular church where he was, and the choir where I was, was a locked door, and I couldn't call out to him to tell him how to come down the long way around through the Guesthouse. And he didn't understand my sign.

At that moment there flashed into my mind all the scores of times in our forgotten childhood when I had chased John Paul away with stones from the place where my friends and I were building a hut. And now, all of a sudden, here it was all over again, a situation that was externally of the same pattern: John Paul, standing, confused and un-happy, at a distance which he was not able to bridge.

Sometimes the same image haunts me now that he is dead, as though he were standing helpless in Purgatory, depending more or less on me to get him out of there, waiting for my prayers. But I hope he is out of it by now!

Father Master went off to get him, and I started lighting the candles on the altar of Our Lady of Victories and by the time the Mass started I could see, out of the corner of my eye, that he was kneeling there at one of the benches. And so we received Communion together, and the work was done.

The next day, he was gone. I went to see him off at the gate, after Chapter. A visitor gave him a ride to Bardstown. As the car was turning around to start down the avenue John Paul turned around and waved, and it was only then that his expression showed some possibility that he might be realizing, as I did, that we would never see each other on earth again.

The fall came, and the Great Tricenary in September when all the young monks have to recite ten psalters for the dead. It is a season of bright, dry days, with plenty of sun, and cool air, and high cirrus clouds, and the forest is turning rusty and blood color and bronze along the jagged hills. Then, morning and afternoon, we go out to cut corn. St. Joseph's field had long been finished—the green stalks had gone into the silo. Now we were working through the vast, stony fields in the middle and lower bottoms, hacking our way through the dry corn with each blow of the knife cracking like a rifle shot. It was as if those glades had turned into shooting galleries and we were all firing away with twenty-twos.

And behind us, in the wide avenues that opened in our wake, the giant shocks grew up, and the two novices that came last garrotted them with a big rope and tied them secure with twine.

Around November when the cornhusking was nearly finished, and when the fat turkeys were gobbling loudly in their pen, running from one wire fence to the other in dark herds, under the gloomy sky, I got news from John Paul in England. First he had been stationed at Bournemouth, from which he sent me a postcard that showed some boardinghouses I recognized, along the West Cliff. It was only ten years since we had spent a summer there: but the memory of it was like something unbelievable, like another life—as if there were some such thing as the transmigration of souls!

After that he was sent somewhere in Oxfordshire. His letters arrived with little rectangles neatly cut out of them, here and there, but when he wrote: "I enjoy going into —— and seeing the —— and the book-stores," it was easy enough for me to insert "Oxford" in the first hole and "Colleges" in the other, since the postmark read "Banbury." Here he was still in training. I could not tell how soon he would get into the actual fighting over Germany.

Meanwhile, he wrote that he had met a girl, whom he described, and it soon turned out that they were going to get married. I was glad on account of the marriage, but there was something altogether pathetic about the precariousness of it: what chance was there that they would ever be able to have a home and live in it, the way human beings were supposed to do?

And so 1943 began, and the weeks hastened on toward Lent.

Lent means, among other things, no more letters. The monks neither receive mail nor write it in Lent and Advent, and the last news I had, before Ash Wednesday, was that John Paul was planning to get married about the end of February. I would have to wait until Easter to find out whether or not he actually did.

I had fasted a little during my first Lent, the year before, but it had been broken up by nearly two weeks in the infirmary. This was my first chance to go through the whole fast without any mitigation. In those days, since I still had the world's ideas about food and nourishment and health, I thought the fast we have in Trappist monasteries in Lent was severe. We eat nothing until noon, when we get the regular two bowls, one of soup and the other of vegetables, and as much bread as we like, but then in the evening there is a light collation—a piece of bread and a dish of something like applesauce—two ounces of it.

Finally the long liturgy of penance came to its climax in Holy Week, with the terrible cry of the Lamentations once more echoing in the dark choir of the abbey church, followed by the four hours' thunder of the Good Friday Psalter in the Chapter Room, and the hush of the monks going about the cloisters in bare feet, and the long sad chant that accompanies the adoration of the Cross!

What a relief it was to hear the bells once more on Holy Saturday, what relief to wake up from the sleep of death with a triple "alleluia." Easter, that year, was as late as it could possibly be—the twenty-fifth of April—and there were enough flowers to fill the church with the intoxicating smell of the Kentucky spring—a wild and rich and heady smell of flowers, sweet and full. We came from our light, five hours' sleep into a church that was full of warm night air and swimming in this rich luxury of odors, and soon began that Easter invitatory that is nothing short of gorgeous in its exultation.

It was into the midst of all this that news from England came.

There had been a letter from John Paul among the two or three that I found under the napkin in the refectory at noon on Holy Saturday. I read it on Easter Monday, and it said that he had been married more or less according to plan, and had gone with his wife to the English Lakes for a week or so, and that after that he had been stationed at a new base, which put him into the fighting.

He had been once or twice to bomb something somewhere: but he did not even give the censor a chance to cut anything out. You could see at once that there was a tremendous change in his attitude toward the war and his part in it. He did not want to talk about it. He had nothing to say. And from the way he said that he didn't want to talk about it, you could see that the experience was terrific.

John Paul had at last come face to face with the world that he and I had helped to make!

On Easter Monday afternoon I sat down to write him a letter and cheer him up a little, if I could.

The letter was finished, and it was Easter Tuesday, and we were in choir for the Conventual Mass, when Father Master came in and made me the sign for "Abbot."

I went out to Reverend Father's room. There was no difficulty in guessing what it was.

I passed the *pietà* at the corner of the cloister, and buried my will and my natural affections and all the rest in the wounded side of the dead Christ.

Reverend Father flashed the sign to come in, and I knelt by his desk and received his blessing and kissed his ring and he read me the telegram that Sergeant J. P. Merton, my brother, had been reported missing in action on April 17.

I have never understood why it took them so long to get the telegram through. April 17 was already ten days ago—the end of Passion Week. Dom Frederic had perhaps held it up until after Easter.

Some more days went by, letters of confirmation came, and finally, after a few weeks, I learned that John Paul was definitely dead.

The story was simply this. On the night of Friday the sixteenth, which had been the Feast of Our Lady of Sorrows, he and his crew had taken off in their bomber with Mannheim as their objective. I never discovered whether they crashed on the way out or the way home, but the plane came down in the North Sea. John Paul was severely injured in the crash, but he managed to keep himself afloat, and even tried to support the pilot, who was already dead. His companions had managed to float their rubber dinghy and pulled him in.

He was very badly hurt: maybe his neck was broken. He lay in the bottom of the dinghy in delirium.

He was terribly thirsty. He kept asking for water. But they didn't have any. The water tank had broken in the crash, and the water was all gone.

It did not last too long. He had three hours of it, and then he died. Something of the three hours of the thirst of Christ Who loved him, and died for him many centuries ago, and had been offered again that very day, too, on many altars.

His companions had more of it to suffer, but they were finally picked up and brought to safety. But that was some five days later.

On the fourth day they had buried John Paul in the sea.

THE SEVEN STOREY MOUNTAIN

Six: POEMS

FOR MY BROTHER:
REPORTED MISSING IN ACTION, 1943

Sweet brother, if I do not sleep
My eyes are flowers for your tomb;
And if I cannot eat my bread,
My fasts shall live like willows where you died.
If in the heat I find no water for my thirst,
My thirst shall turn to springs for you, poor traveler.

Where, in what desolate and smoky country,
Lies your poor body, lost and dead?
And in what landscape of disaster
Has your unhappy spirit lost its road?

Come, in my labor find a resting place
And in my sorrows lay your head,
Or rather take my life and blood
And buy yourself a better bed—
Or take my breath and take my death
And buy yourself a better rest.

When all the men of war are shot
And flags have fallen into dust,
Your cross and mine shall tell men still
Christ died on each, for both of us.

For in the wreckage of your April Christ lies slain,
And Christ weeps in the ruins of my spring:
The money of Whose tears shall fall
Into your weak and friendless hand,
And buy you back to your own land:

The silence of Whose tears shall fall
Like bells upon your alien tomb.
Hear them and come: they call you home.

THIRTY POEMS

THE TRAPPIST CEMETERY—GETHSEMANI

Brothers, the curving grasses and their daughters
Will never print your praises:
The trees our sisters, in their summer dresses,
Guard your fame in these green cradles:
The simple crosses are content to hide your characters.

Oh do not fear
The birds that bicker in the lonely belfry
Will ever give away your legends.
Yet when the sun, exulting like a dying martyr,
Canonizes, with his splendid fire, the somber hills,
Your graves all smile like little children,
And your wise crosses trust the mothering night
That folds them in the Sanctuary's wings.

You need not hear the momentary rumors of the road
Where cities pass and vanish in a single car
Filling the cut beside the mill
With roar and radio,
Hurling the air into the wayside branches
Leaving the leaves alive with panic.

See, the kind universe,
Wheeling in love about the abbey steeple,
Lights up your sleepy nursery with stars.

*   *   *

God, in your bodily life,
Untied the snares of anger and desire,
Hid your flesh from envy by these country altars,
Beneath these holy eaves where even sparrows have their houses.
But oh, how like the swallows and the chimney swifts
Do your free souls in glory play!

And with a cleaner flight,
Keener, more graceful circles,
Rarer and finer arcs
Than all these innocent attacks that skim our steeple!
How like these children of the summer evening
Do your rejoicing spirits
Deride the dry earth with their aviation!

But now the treble harps of night begin to play in the deep wood,
To praise your holy sleep,
And all the frogs along the creek
Chant in the moony waters to the Queen of Peace.
And we, the mariners, and travelers,
The wide-eyed immigrants,
Praying and sweating in our steerage cabins,
Lie still and count with love the measured bells
That tell the deep-sea leagues until your harbor.

Already on this working earth you knew what nameless love
Adorns the heart with peace by night,
Hearing, adoring all the dark arrivals of eternity.
Oh, here on earth you knew what secret thirst
Arming the mind with instinct,
Answers the challenges of God with garrisons
Of unified desire
And facing Him in His new wars
Is slain at last in an exchange of lives.

Teach us, Cistercian Fathers, how to wear
Silence, our humble armor.
Pray us a torrent of the seven spirits
That are our wine and stamina:
Because your work is not yet done.
But look: the valleys shine with promises,
And every burning morning is a prophecy of Christ
Coming to raise and vindicate
Even our sorry flesh.

Then will your graves, Gethsemani, give up their angels,
Return them to their souls to learn
The songs and attitudes of glory.

Then will creation rise again like gold
Clean, from the furnace of your litanies:
The beasts and trees shall share your resurrection,
And a new world be born from these green tombs.

A MAN IN THE DIVIDED SEA

THE TRAPPIST ABBEY: MATINS

(*Our Lady of Gethsemani, Kentucky*)

When the full fields begin to smell of sunrise
And the valleys sing in their sleep,
The pilgrim moon pours over the solemn darkness
Her waterfalls of silence,
And then departs, up the long avenue of trees.

The stars hide, in the glade, their light, like tears,
And tremble where some train runs, lost,
Baying in eastward mysteries of distance,
Where fire flares, somewhere, over a sink of cities.

Now kindle in the windows of this ladyhouse, my soul,
Your childish, clear awakeness:
Burn in the country night
Your wise and sleepless lamp.
For, from the frowning tower, the windy belfry,
Sudden the bells come, bridegrooms,
And fill the echoing dark with love and fear.

Wake in the windows of Gethsemani, my soul, my sister,
For the past years, with smoky torches, come,
Bringing betrayal from the burning world
And bloodying the glade with pitch flame.

Wake in the cloisters of the lonely night, my soul, my sister,
Where the apostles gather, who were, one time, scattered,
And mourn God's blood in the place of His betrayal,
And weep with Peter at the triple cockcrow.

A MAN IN THE DIVIDED SEA

EVENING: ZERO WEATHER

Now the lone world is streaky as a wall of marble
With veins of clear and frozen snow.
There is no bird song there, no hare's track
No badger working in the russet grass:
All the bare fields are silent as eternity.

And the whole herd is home in the long barn.
The brothers come, with hoods about their faces,
Following their plumes of breath
Lugging the gleaming buckets one by one.

This was a day when shovels would have struck
Full flakes of fire out of the land like rock:
And ground cries out like iron beneath our boots

When all the monks come in with eyes as clean as the cold sky
And axes under their arms,
Still paying out *Ave Marias*
With rosaries between their bleeding fingers.

We shake the chips out of our robes outside the door
And go to hide in cowls as deep as clouds,
Bowing our shoulders in the church's shadow, lean and whipped,
To wait upon your Vespers, Mother of God!

And we have eyes no more for the dark pillars or the freezing windows,
Ears for the rumorous cloister or the chimes of time above our heads:
For we are sunken in the summer of our adoration,
And plunge, down, down into the fathoms of our secret joy
That swims with indefinable fire.

And we will never see the copper sunset
Linger a moment, like an echo, on the frozen hill
Then suddenly die an hour before the Angelus.

For we have found our Christ, our August
Here in the zero days before Lent—
We are already binding up our sheaves of harvest
Beating the lazy liturgy, going up with exultation
Even on the eve of our Ash Wednesday,
And entering our blazing heaven by the doors of the Assumption!

FIGURES FOR AN APOCALYPSE

AFTER THE NIGHT OFFICE—GETHSEMANI ABBEY

It is not yet the gray and frosty time
When barns ride out of the night like ships:
We do not see the Brothers, bearing lanterns,
Sink in the quiet mist,
As various as the spirits who, with lamps, are sent
To search our souls' Jerusalems
Until our houses are at rest
And minds enfold the Word, our Guest.

Praises and canticles anticipate
Each day the singing bells that wake the sun,
But now our psalmody is done.
Our hasting souls outstrip the day:
Now, before dawn, they have their noon.
The Truth that transubstantiates the body's night
Has made our minds His temple tent:
Open the secret eye of faith
And drink these deeps of invisible light.

The weak walls
Of the world fall
And heaven, in floods, comes pouring in:
Sink from your shallows, soul, into eternity,
And slake your wonder at that deep-lake spring.
We touch the rays we cannot see,
We feel the light that seems to sing.

Go back to bed, red sun, you are too late,
And hide behind Mount Olivet—
For like the flying moon, held prisoner,
Within the branches of a juniper,
So in the cages of our consciousness
The Dove of God is prisoner yet:
Unruly sun, go back to bed.

But now the lances of the morning
Fire all their gold against the steeple and the water tower.
Returning to the windows of our deep abode of peace,
Emerging at our conscious doors
We find our souls all soaked in grace, like Gedeon's fleece.

A MAN IN THE DIVIDED SEA

THE READER

Lord, when the clock strikes
Telling the time with cold tin
And I sit hooded in this lectern

Waiting for the monks to come,
I see the red cheeses, and bowls
All smile with milk in ranks upon their tables.

Light fills my proper globe
(I have won light to read by
With a little, tinkling chain)

And the monks come down the cloister
With robes as voluble as water.
I do not see them but I hear their waves.

It is winter, and my hands prepare
To turn the pages of the saints:
And to the trees Thy moon has frozen on the windows
My tongue shall sing Thy Scripture.

Then the monks pause upon the step
(With me here in this lectern
And Thee there on Thy crucifix)
And gather little pearls of water on their fingers' ends
Smaller than this my psalm.

THE TEARS OF THE BLIND LIONS

ST. MALACHY

In November, in the days to remember the dead
When air smells cold as earth,
St. Malachy, who is very old, gets up,
Parts the thin curtains of trees and dawns upon our land.

His coat is filled with drops of rain, and he is bearded
With all the seas of Poseidon.
(Is it a crozier, or a trident in his hand?)
He weeps against the gothic window, and the empty cloister
Mourns like an ocean shell.

Two bells in the steeple
Talk faintly to the old stranger
And the tower considers his waters.
"I have been sent to see my festival," (his cavern speaks!)
"For I am the saint of the day.
Shall I shake the drops from my locks and stand in your transept,
Or, leaving you, rest in the silence of my history?"

So the bells rang and we opened the antiphoners
And the wrens and larks flew up out of the pages.
Our thoughts became lambs. Our hearts swam like seas.
One monk believed that we should sing to him
Some stone-age hymn
Or something in the giant language.
So we played to him in the plainsong of the giant Gregory:
Oceans of Scripture sang upon bony Eire.

Then the last salvage of flowers
(Fostered under glass after the gardens foundered)
Held up their little lamps on Malachy's altar
To peer into his wooden eyes before the Mass began.

Rain sighed down the sides of the stone church.
Storms sailed by all day in battle fleets.
At five o'clock, when we tried to see the sun, the speechless visitor
Sighed and arose and shook the humus from his feet
And with his trident stirred our trees
And left downwood, shaking some drops upon the ground.

Thus copper flames fall, tongues of fire fall
The leaves in hundreds fall upon his passing
While night sends down her dreadnought darkness
Upon this spurious Pentecost.

And the Melchisedec of our year's end
Who came without a parent, leaves without a trace,
And rain comes rattling down upon our forest
Like the doors of a country jail.

                                        THE TEARS OF THE BLIND LIONS

ELEGY FOR THE MONASTERY BARN

As though an aged person were to wear
Too gay a dress
And walk about the neighborhood
Announcing the hour of her death,

So now, one summer day's end,
At suppertime, when wheels are still,
The long barn suddenly puts on the traitor, beauty,
And hails us with a dangerous cry,
For: "Look!" she calls to the country,
"Look how fast I dress myself in fire!"

Had we half guessed how long her spacious shadows
Harbored a woman's vanity
We would be less surprised to see her now
So loved, and so attended, and so feared.
She, in whose airless heart
We burst our veins to fill her full of hay,
Now stands apart.
She will not have us near her. Terribly,
Sweet Christ, how terribly her beauty burns us now!

And yet she has another legacy,
More delicate, to leave us, and more rare.

Who knew her solitude?
Who heard the peace downstairs
While flames ran whispering among the rafters?
Who felt the silence, there,
The long, hushed gallery
Clean and resigned and waiting for the fire?

Look! They have all come back to speak their summary:
Fifty invisible cattle, the past years
Assume their solemn places one by one.
This is the little minute of their destiny.
Here is their meaning found. Here is their end.

Laved in the flame as in a Sacrament
The brilliant walls are holy
In their first-last hour of joy.

Fly from within the barn! Fly from the silence
Of this creature sanctified by fire!
Let no man stay inside to look upon the Lord!
Let no man wait within and see the Holy
One sitting in the presence of disaster
Thinking upon this barn His gentle doom!

THE STRANGE ISLANDS

A PRACTICAL PROGRAM FOR MONKS

1

Each one shall sit at table with his own cup and spoon, and with his
   own repentance. Each one's own business shall be his most im-
   portant affair, and provide his own remedies.
They have neglected bowl and plate.
Have you a wooden fork?
Yes, each monk has a wooden fork as well as a potato.

2

Each one shall wipe away tears with his own saint, when three bells
   hold in store a hot afternoon. Each one is supposed to mind his
   own heart, with its conscience, night and morning.
Another turn on the wheel: ho hum! And observe the Abbot!
Time to go to bed in a straw blanket.

3

Plenty of bread for everyone between prayers and the psalter: will you
   recite another?
Merci, and *Miserere.*
Always mind both the clock and the Abbot until eternity.
Miserere.

4

Details of the Rule are all liquid and solid. What canon was the first to
   announce regimentation before us? Mind the step on the way down!
Yes, I dare say you are right, Father. I believe you; I believe you.
I believe it is easier when they have ice water and even a lemon.
Each one can sit at table with his own lemon, and mind his conscience.

5

Can we agree that the part about the lemon is regular?
In any case, it is better to have sheep than peacocks, and cows rather
than a chained leopard says Modest, in one of his proverbs.
The monastery, being owner of a communal rowboat, is the ante-
chamber of heaven.
Surely that ought to be enough.

6

Each one can have some rain after Vespers on a hot afternoon, but *ne
quid nimis,* or the purpose of the Order will be forgotten.
We shall send you hyacinths and a sweet millennium.
Everything the monastery provides is very pleasant to see and to sell for
nothing.
What is baked smells fine. There is a sign of God on every leaf that
nobody sees in the garden. The fruit trees are there on purpose,
even when no one is looking. Just put the apples in the basket.
In Kentucky there is also room for a little cheese.
Each one shall fold his own napkin, and neglect the others.

7

Rain is always very silent in the night, under such gentle cathedrals.
Yes, I have taken care of the lamp. *Miserere.*
Have you a patron saint, and an angel?
Thank you. Even though the nights are never dangerous, I have one of
everything.

SELECTED POEMS

Seven: "IF EVER THERE WAS A COUNTRY . . ."

Iғ ever there was a country where men loved comfort, pleasure, and material security, good health and conversation about the weather and the World Series and the Rose Bowl; if ever there was a land where silence made men nervous and prayer drove them crazy and penance scared them to death, it is America. Yet, quite suddenly, Americans— the healthiest, most normal, most energetic, and most optimistic of the younger generation of Americans—have taken it into their heads to run off to Trappist monasteries and get their heads shaved and put on robes and scapulars and work in the fields and pray half the night and sleep on straw and, in a word, become monks.

When you ask them why they have done such things, they may give you a very clear answer or, perhaps, only a rather confused answer; but in either case the answer will amount to this: the Trappists are the most austere order they could find, and Trappist life was that which least resembled the life men lead in the towns and cities of our world. And there is something in their hearts that tells them they cannot be happy in an atmosphere where people are looking for nothing but their own pleasure and advantage and comfort and success.

They have not come to the monastery to escape from the realities of life but to find those realities: they have felt the terrible insufficiency of life in a civilization that is entirely dedicated to the pursuit of shadows.

What is the use of living for things that you cannot hold on to, values that crumble in your hands as soon as you possess them, pleasures that turn sour before you have begun to taste them, and a peace that is constantly turning into war? Men have not become Trappists merely out of a hope for peace in the next world: something has told them, with unshakable conviction, that the next world begins in this world and that heaven can be theirs now, very truly, even though imperfectly, if they give their lives to the one activity which is the beatitude of heaven.

That activity is love: the clean, unselfish love that does not live on what it gets but on what it gives; a love that increases by pouring itself out for others, that grows by self-sacrifice and becomes mighty by throwing itself away.

Is it any wonder that Trappist monasteries are places full of peace and contentment and joy? These men, who have none of the pleasures of the world, have all the happiness that the world is unable to find. Their silence is more eloquent than all the speeches of politicians and the noise of all the radios in America. Their smiles have more joy in them than has the laughter of thousands. When they raise their eyes to the hills or to the sky, they see a beauty which other people do not know how to find. When they work in the fields and the forests, they seem to be tired and alone, but their hearts are at rest, and they are absorbed in a companionship that is tremendous, because it is three Persons in one infinite Nature, the One Who spoke the universe and draws it all back into Himself by His love; the One from Whom all things came and to Whom all things return: and in Whom are all the beauty and substance and actuality of everything in the world that is real.

THE WATERS OF SILOE

Eight: THE FOUNDATION OF
GETHSEMANI ABBEY

Aᴏᴏ ᴛʜᴇ ꜰᴀʟʟ of Napoleon it quickly became evident that the austere and restless history of the Val Sainte congregation would soon be a closed chapter in the annals of the Cistercian Order. By a queer paradox, after 1815 France became one of the safest places in Europe for monks, after having been for ten years the most dangerous. As a result, the scattered and more or less flourishing monasteries that had been founded in Belgium, Germany, Spain, and Italy by Dom Augustin de Lestrange closed their doors under stress of persecution, and the monks withdrew once more to their native country.

When Dom Augustin died in 1827, the most prosperous and fervent of the Trappist monasteries was Our Lady of Melleray, near Nantes. Melleray reopened its doors as a monastery to receive the monks that had been forced to leave the monastery of Lulworth in England. They brought to France not only the austerity of the contemplative life and the ancient liturgical chant but also some English methods of farming that started what amounted to an agricultural revolution in the Vendée. The peasants of the region were astonished to find that a system of crop rotation would save them the trouble of leaving land fallow for eight or nine years. They soon bought the improved plows manufactured by the monks on the English pattern, and the first threshing machine ever seen in that part of France attracted a curious crowd of farmers to the monastery.

The community of one hundred and seventy-five was under the direction of an abbot whose wisdom and experience in temporal and spiritual matters were equaled only by his generosity and spirit of faith. Dom Antoine de Beauregard, a gifted and noble cleric who had fled to England to escape the Revolution, had become a monk at Lulworth. Here he had lived through poverty and hardships not altogether unlike those which his Cistercian brothers had had to suffer in Kentucky and Illinois.

After Dom Augustin's death Dom Antoine of Melleray became the Visitor General of the Congregation, and his wisdom has left its stamp upon the order even till today. Dom Augustin himself had foreseen that the excessively strict regulations of La Val Sainte would not long survive his death, and practically all his innovations had been under fire for some time.

Dom Antoine thought there could be nothing better for his monks than to keep the Rule of St. Benedict as it had been written and as it had been interpreted by St. Alberic and St. Stephen Harding at Cîteaux. In that way he steered a middle course between the exaggerations of Dom Augustin and the somewhat abstract and academic reform of De Rancé, for whom work had never been a material necessity but only a penance and a humiliation. In other words, it would seem that this was a solution that came somewhere near the healthy and harmonious and well-balanced ideal of the first Cistercians. For them, the monk was a man who labored because he was poor and was poor because he loved God, and who lived apart from the world to praise God and to contemplate Him and to taste the inexpressible joys of His love in silence and in peace.

At the same time, this solution, which looked so good in theory, did not seem to work out altogether in practice. There were some Trappists who found that even the usages of Cîteaux were too difficult and imposed too severe a burden.

In 1834 the Trappists were divided into two congregations, one keeping the usages of Cîteaux and the other those of De Rancé. Each had its own vicar general, and both were subject to the Abbot General of the Cistercians of the Common Observance—for the Common Observance still survived as an ill-defined conglomeration of fragments. This was not a satisfactory arrangement, and it is quite likely that this division, this unsettled and equivocal state of the reform, inhibited the spontaneous and healthy regrowth of a spirituality that was truly Cistercian and contemplative, and which the strictness and fervor of the monks themselves might have led us to expect.

Meanwhile, things were by no means settled in France. The 1830 revolution had brought trouble to La Trappe and to Melleray, as well as to other houses of the order. Melleray, being a large and prosperous house, was singled out for special attention. Six hundred soldiers camped in the monastery, and only the firmness of Dom Antoine in insisting on the rights guaranteed him by the laws of the time saved the monastery from complete suppression. As it was, however, most of the community was turned out of doors.

The result was not altogether an unhappy one. There had been many English and Irish monks in the house, and these were no sooner deported than they settled in Ireland to build Mount Melleray Abbey in county Waterford, a house which has ever since been renowned for its prosperity and vigor.

When the troubles of 1830 had blown over, Melleray was once again crowded with postulants and novices, and the places that had been left vacant by the deportees were rapidly filled. By the year 1847 the house was full to overflowing.

That gave Dom Maxime, who was then abbot, two good reasons for deciding to make a foundation somewhere outside of France. He wanted to make room for postulants, and he foresaw another revolution.

And so it happened that once again the eyes of a Trappist superior were turned to the shores of America. God's Providence definitely designed that a monastery of Cistercian monks was to be built, first of all, in Kentucky. And it was to Kentucky that the prior of Melleray, Father Paulinus, went looking for land on which to build one.

It is not altogether curious that the monks should have looked first of all to Kentucky in their second attempt to settle in the United States. They knew what a hard time Dom Urban's colony had had, and they had heard of the eccentricities of the climate. But probably the sanctity of the first Bishop of Bardstown, who had recently transferred his cathedral to Louisville, was the real explanation why God brought Trappists to that diocese.

Bishop Flaget had come to America in 1792 as a refugee with Father Badin, the first priest to settle permanently in Kentucky. The bishop was a Sulpician, and he probably saw something of Dom Urban and his Trappists, not in Kentucky but at Baltimore, where they were received by the fathers of Monsignor Flaget's community.

In 1808 Bishop Carroll, finding the burden of the entire United States too heavy for his own shoulders, asked Pope Pius VII to give him some more bishops. Accordingly, four new dioceses were erected that year: Boston, New York, Philadelphia—and Bardstown, Kentucky. And so Monsignor Flaget became Bishop of Bardstown and head of a diocese that included Kentucky, Michigan, Indiana, Illinois, Ohio, Missouri, Tennessee, Wisconsin, Iowa, and about half of Arkansas.

It was a task that called for more than human courage and energy.

The new bishop did not arrive in Kentucky until Dom Urban and his Trappists had already moved west to Illinois. They still were in his diocese, no doubt, when Bishop Flaget came down the Ohio River on a flatboat in 1811, accompanied by the priests who were to form the nucleus of his diocesan seminary. But by the time he had had a chance to visit the western reaches of his territory, the bishop found the Trappists had taken flight and were at home in France.

Yet, the memory of the monks and their holiness and their poverty had not died in Kentucky. There were still a few men who had been to the monks' school, and these were among the most solid and hard-working and intelligent and faithful Christians in the bishop's flock. The echoes of the sweet, solemn cadences of Gregorian chant in the monks' log-cabin chapel, in the woods of Nelson County and Casey Creek, still lived in the memories of Kentucky Catholics.

The arrival of Father Paulinus in Louisville in 1847 was the answer to many prayers.

The eighty-six-year-old bishop, white-haired, leonine, beaming with the simplicity and overflowing benevolence of the saints, received the emissary from the French Trappists with open arms and tears of joy. He sent him at once into the country that had once seen the labors of Dom Urban Guillet's men, and his coadjutor, Monsignor Martin Spalding, became the Trappist's guide and adviser.

It was not long before they found a good-sized farm with some buildings on it and plenty of woodland. It was within sight of Rohan's Knob, in whose shadow the Trappists had first settled thirty-two years before in their temporary home on Pottinger's Creek. Gethsemani, as the farm was called, belonged to some religious of a congregation founded by Father Nerinckx—the Sisters of Loretto. The sisters had opened a small orphan asylum in the middle of a valley in Nelson County. But the enterprise proved inconvenient, and they were looking for a less isolated site.

So, Father Paulinus struck a bargain for the fourteen hundred acres of woodland, with a few cornfields and some log cabins in bad repair, and Gethsemani was sold to the Trappists for five thousand dollars.

It was in October 1848 that the colony was organized to leave the abbey of Melleray. At its head, Dom Maxime placed Father Eutropius Proust, a thirty-nine-year-old priest from the strongly Catholic Vendée district who had not yet been four years in the monastery. He had made profession in 1846, and the next year he had taken over Father Paulinus's office as prior when the latter went on his expedition to Kentucky. He was a thin, wiry, intense little man, this Father Eutropius. He had a

quick intelligence and a vivid, dramatic imagination. He was full of
ideals, his heart burned with faith and zeal. And he had more courage
than physical strength—a common trait among Trappists. He needed
all the faith and ardor and enthusiasm and courage he could muster, to
carry out the difficult and complicated mission that was entrusted to him.
He was to lead forty-four men—monks, brothers, novices, postulants, and
familiars—through a France that was once more simmering to the boiling
point with revolution; he was to put them on a boat and take them to
America—fighting his way step by step through a most intricate network
of obstacles and reverses.

Most of the monks who sailed for the United States under Father
Eutropius were perfectly chosen for the foundation. But for one or two
exceptions—like Father Paulinus, a Basque, and the Italian Father
Benezet—the colonists sent to Gethsemani were Bretons and Vendéens.

That meant, first of all, that they were physically hardy, endowed with
plenty of strength and endurance—racial characteristics of these sturdy
and intrepid farmers and mariners. Of course, they were not prepared
for the Kentucky climate, with its unmitigated summer heat and its sudden temperamental changes of warm and cold in the other seasons of
the year. But on the whole they would be well equipped to stand up
under the vicissitudes of the new foundation. Father Euthymius, who
served many years as subprior, died in 1880 at the age of seventy-two,
and Father Emmanuel, the cellarer, lived until 1885 and the age of
seventy-four. Some of the lay brothers did even better. Brother Charles
Potiron, who reputedly died in an aura of sanctity and mysticism, lived to
be seventy-seven, and Brother Theodoret was buried in January 1893,
two months short of his eightieth birthday. Finally, Brother Antonine,
who was only eighteen when he sailed from France with the rest of the
Trappists as a novice, and who was so tempted against his vocation that
he more than once left the monastery and returned to begin over again,
outlasted them all and saw the golden jubilee of Gethsemani in 1898.
He died in 1902, in his seventy-third year.

On October 26, 1848, the monks of Melleray got up as usual for the
night office, at two o'clock in the morning. It was over at about four, and
those who had been designated for the American foundation went to the
dormitory and changed into secular clothing, afterward putting on their
cowls over the unfamiliar garb. Then they descended to the cloister with
the two blankets that were their individual baggage and bedding for the
long journey.

Dom Maxime addressed them for the last time, in terms of which we may find an echo in the act of foundation of the abbey. "Our dearly beloved brothers," he wrote, "will infallibly succeed if they always keep the spirit of their vocation, which will lead them in particular to the study and practice of the virtues of charity, obedience, poverty, mortification, patience, humility. Let our beloved brothers never forget to apply themselves to prayer . . . let them maintain close union among themselves. . . . Then the world and the devil will be able to do nothing against them, for, let them be fully persuaded of this truth: a house divided against itself will fall into ruins. Let them have a cordial and respectful love for their superior and console him in his cares for them by obedience and fraternal union, and let them never put him into the position where the duty of issuing his commands may become a matter of difficulty and embarrassment for him. Let them, in the consideration of their own frailties, remain humble in spirit and in their hearts. Do this and you shall live, my dearly beloved brothers. Amen! Amen!"

After that, the whole community, those traveling and those staying in France, issued from the monastery gate in procession, chanting the litany of Loretto. It was a bleak autumn morning and rain was falling steadily. Father Eutropius, armed with a wooden cross that was a copy of the one with which Dom Augustin de Lestrange had once led his band of refugees from La Trappe to La Val Sainte, walked forward full of emotion into a gray, wet world of bare trees and stubble fields and puddles and deep mud. The procession continued its solemn progress, chanting in the rain for about a kilometer. At the edge of a wood they came to a small wayside cross. Here they stopped. The monks who were leaving took off their rain-soaked cowls and handed them to the ones who were staying. They all embraced one another in silence, and the two groups parted, one to return to the abbey and the other—a strange band of workingmen with shaven heads and ill-fitting suits—to begin a long day's tramp to the Loire, where they were to take a riverboat from Ancenis to Tours.

The first day's journey ended dramatically at Ancenis, where the news of the monks' embarkation had attracted a large crowd of curious and devout Vendéens. The Trappists chanted Compline and sang their ancient, heartrending *Salve Regina* in the parish church, which was crowded to the doors. But when it came time to find their way through the crowds to the boat, they became separated in the darkness, and their superior had a hard time gathering them together again. When they were all finally safe on board, three real misfortunes were discovered. Their baggage had not been put on board at Nantes, as had been planned; their provisions had been mislaid somewhere between Melleray and the boat landing, and finally, a brother who had been sent to Nantes to borrow eight thousand francs had returned empty-handed.

It was a wild journey from Ancenis to Le Havre. They changed from boat to train at Tours, changed trains at Orléans and again in Paris. Each stage of their journey was marked by excitement and confusion. Whenever this weird group of rough-looking men with shaven heads collected around their emaciated leader in station waiting rooms, crowds of curious people flocked from all sides, full of questions and comment. Since they could not get anything out of the monks, who refused to speak to them, the bystanders made their own peculiar surmises. Usually it ended with Father Eutropius making a little speech. "Messieurs," he would say, "do not be alarmed or surprised. These are men dedicated to God, Trappist monks who have renounced everything to live in poverty and labor and silence and prayer. They are going to a distant land to build a monastery. They are going to carry the Name and the worship of God to the forests of North America, among the tigers[1] and panthers and wolves of Kentucky. . . ."

Invariably the gendarmes were on the scene before he had uttered more than four or five sentences. All France was on the alert for riots in 1848. But the Trappists did not get into any trouble.

What was more important, at each new stage of the journey Father Eutropius, with an untiring persistence born of faith married to natural tenacity, pushed and cajoled his way into the offices of the highest railway officials he could find, in order to beg huge reductions for the traveling monks. Thanks to his efforts, they went most of the way to Le Havre riding second-class and paying only half the third-class fare.

For many of the monks it was the first time they had ever ridden in a train or had, indeed, even seen one. For most of them it was also their last experience of the ferocious *chemin de fer*.

At Le Havre, three days before the departure of the boat, the brothers who had been told to bring the fifteen thousand pounds of baggage from Nantes to the port of embarkation arrived without any of it. They innocently presented to their superior the "written promise" which a nice gentleman at Tours had given them, stating that they would certainly have their baggage with them at Le Havre that same evening. Father Eutropius threw up his hands in a paroxysm of woe and took the first train back to Paris.

He arrived at the capital at five the next morning—little more than forty-eight hours before their ship was due to weigh anchor. He inquired at three stations without finding a trace of the monks' equipment—which included everything from plows and bake ovens to folio graduals and antiphoners and straw mattresses. It was not the kind of consignment that would easily be overlooked.

Finally he found it all safe at the Gare d'Ivry. But his troubles had only begun. He had to move this mountain across Paris to the Gare de Batignolles. This would cost much more than he could afford. Soon Father Eutropius was once again seated in the office of the highest and most influential official he could find.

The Trappist abbot has left us a written account, in English, of all this. He says (with a pardonable disregard for syntax): "On telling him that I was a Trappist he appeared totally surprised, and wished to know the life of a Trappist. I gave him a short résumé of our manner of life. . . . I spoke to him of our spiritual exercises, of our different employments, and the happiness experienced in the quiet of solitude. He listened to me with great attention and when I had finished speaking he cried out: 'Ah, Monsieur! That life is beautiful compared with that of the great part of men in the world where we see only sensuality, pride, and self-love. I assure you that if I were not married I would embrace your kind of life and accompany you to America!' " [2]

Father Eutropius Proust was a good talker!

However, this particular official could do nothing to reduce the cost of transporting the monks' baggage across Paris. He sent Father Eutropius off with a letter to another official who gave him just as little satisfaction. By that time it was getting late. In fact, it would soon be too late to move his baggage from the station where it was languishing. He managed to obtain special permission to do so.

Seven o'clock in the evening found Father Eutropius hard at work with three teamsters, loading up wagons at the Gare d'Ivry.

Then there was the problem of the *octroi*, the city customs. If they went through Paris, they would be stopped and all their baggage held up for examination. It was now past nine.

Father Eutropius promised his teamsters a good tip if they would go around the city walls. They agreed.

For a terrible half hour, however, the Trappist superior was tortured with misgivings about the wisdom of such a course. The teamsters pulled up at the first *bistro* along their way and stopped in for a couple of drinks to give them strength for their journey.

At ten o'clock he was wringing his hands in the street, standing in the lurid glare that issued from the bar and illuminated the heavy wagons and idle horses.

But in the end everything arrived safely at Batignolles and left on the early train for Le Havre.

At one in the afternoon of November 2, 1848, the forty Trappists and their books and plows and supplies for the long Atlantic crossing were safe on board the *Brunswick,* an eight-hundred-ton sailing vessel under the command of Captain Thomas of New Orleans.

The ship was crowded. It was the year of the gold rush, and America was more than ever fabulous in the imagination of immigrants. But on this journey the *Brunswick* was bearing a company unusual even in those years. Besides the Trappists themselves, who barricaded themselves off in the steerage and settled in a provisional shipboard monastery to which nobody else had access without their permission, and besides sixty German immigrants of the ordinary kind, there was a party of eighty men, women, and children destined for one of the strange communist "utopias" that were springing up in such profusion in those years.

1848 was the year when the Oneida community was founded. Seven years before, Brook Farm had entered upon the same path of social experimentation. There were not a few Fourieristic phalanxes in the United States, and it was more than twenty years since the English Socialist, Robert Owen, had inaugurated his community at New Harmony, Indiana—a dream of harmony that had been shipwrecked within two years upon the rocks of the same old discord.

By 1848 there was ample evidence that the only ones among these communist groups that stood a fair chance of survival were those that had some kind of religious basis. The Shakers were still flourishing. The Ephrata community, founded in Pennsylvania by a German Protestant hermit more than a century before, was still thriving and continued to do so for many years to come.

The group that sailed from Le Havre at the end of 1848 with the Trappist founders of Gethsemani was destined to be the longest-lived of the explicitly nonreligious communist "utopias" planted on American soil in those optimistic days.

They were Etienne Cabet's "Icarians." The first thing that Dom Eutropius remarked about them was that they were under the direction of a delegate who took the place of Cabet himself, and "to whom the name of representative was given. He was charged with judging the differences that might arise among them, an office of which there was great need during the voyage." [3] In fact, the Icarians were so divided by quarrels and dissensions arising from petty greeds and jealousies that the monks considered themselves fortunate to be separated, by the improvised enclosure, from all communion with their noise.

One of the many things that distinguished the Trappists from the rest of that ship's strange company was the relative efficiency with which they were prepared to meet the emergencies of the voyage. The other passengers, Icarians included, were fasting on hardtack, while the monks had set up their ovens and were drawing out smoking loaves of fresh bread each morning. Caldrons of soup simmered on the ranges of the monks' kitchen, and under the circumstances the lean Trappist fare began to look like luxury indeed in those days before the phenomenal menus of the modern ocean liner.

In a short time the monks found themselves feeding most of the other passengers—at least, all who were sick or weak or needed some special attention. The chief beneficiaries of this charity were some mothers with infants to nurse and an old immigrant who had been left by his companions to starve when he became too weak to prepare his own meals.

The monks had no trouble with the Icarians, whose only hostile act was a decree of their "assembly" forbidding any of their number to hear Mass in the monks' chapel. The Trappists were glad to do some cooking for them on their range, baking pastry, apples, potatoes, and so on for anyone who brought them to the door of the steerage "monastery."

It would seem that Providence threw these two groups, Trappists and Icarians, together just to invite a comparison between them.

After all, they had not a little in common. The ideal of Cistercian monasticism is a communal ideal which goes back explicitly to the life of the first Christians, who were of "one heart and one mind" and "had all things in common." [4]

As a social and economic unit, the Trappist community bound for Kentucky was just as truly and strictly "communistic" as were the Icarians, who were heading for Texas. The monks owned all their property in common. They were, in fact, vowed to the most uncompromising poverty, forbidden to possess anything whatever as individuals, not even the most insignificant of consumer's goods. Everything they used or consumed came to them from the abbot or through his permission as representative of the Christ, the Life and unifying Principle of the monastic community. But in the moral order the monks were bound to a far stricter and more radical communism than the Icarians had ever dreamed of. The monk's body and his very soul belong to his community, insofar as it is a part of the living, mystical organism Who is Christ on earth—the Church. The monk cannot claim proprietorship over the smallest internal act of judgment or desire that interferes with the life of the community—which is love, the charity of Christ. He does not even claim for himself such acts as do not interfere with the organic functioning of the group; he prefers to consecrate and dedicate them to Christ living in His brethren, Christ living in the abbot, Christ in the monk's own soul, Christ in the Tabernacle, the visible heart of the monastic community.

The Icarians' brand of communism was nothing but a working compromise between conflicting human appetites. Like all other materialistic communists, Cabet's disciples simply accepted human passions and greeds as a matter of course and attempted to neutralize their evil social effects by rationing out satisfactions to each one on a basis of mathematical equality.

But the common life of a Cistercian monk is based on far wiser assumptions, on tenets that reject such absurdities from the very start. There is no such thing as mathematical equality in a Cistercian monastery: each one does not strive to raise himself to the level of everybody else by cutting all the others down to his own level. On the contrary, the monk lives on an ideal of self-sacrifice in which he is the servant of all and gives up everything he has, becoming like Christ, his Master, obedient unto the death of the Cross for the glory of God and for the good of his community. It is, in fact, an ideal of self-immolation which the Dictatorship of the Proletariat, the World Revolution, also demands in practice. But the monk sacrifices himself for eternal values and for a reward which he begins to enjoy in the midst of his very act of sacrifice; his reward consists in the supernatural, divinizing selflessness which liberates him forever from the limitations of a narrow and worldly egoism.

It was this peace and purity of heart which, above all, marked the essential difference between the monks and the communists who were traveling together to their respective promised lands on board the *Brunswick* in 1848. How was it that the monks lived together in such harmony and happiness and peace, while the Icarians were always at one another's throats? There is no explanation to be found in the natural order. After all, the two groups were made up of the same kind of material. Both monks and Cabetians had been recruited from various levels of society, and in about the same proportions. In both groups there was a small percentage of professional men and a larger group of farmers and artisans. Moreover, most of the Icarians had been brought up in the atmosphere of what was still a more or less Catholic culture. The difference, then, was to be found not on this superficial level but deeper down: the monks had Christ living and working in them by faith, by charity. The monks were united by the Holy Spirit in the peace of God, which tames and dominates and sublimates man's nature and ordains it to the highest possible ends. But the Icarians were united only by the frail bonds of an "armed neutrality" of insatiable animal appetites.

Leaning over the rail of the *Brunswick* as she hove to and took the pilot on board in the vast estuary of the Mississippi, Father Eutropius was astonished by the sight of a strange commotion in the waters—a battle of different kinds of fish. Those that belonged to the sea were fighting with those of the river. It was a presage of the violence that was to come.

On reaching New Orleans, the Icarians received bad news. A Cabetian colony that had preceded them to Texas that year had found that the country was not exactly the paradise flowing with milk and honey that they had been led to imagine. In fact, it was a dry and treeless waste, full of bitter hardship, in which many of their number had succumbed to sickness and thirst and hunger. And now there were not a few of them in New Orleans, begging and in rags. The reaction of the group on board ship was characteristic, but it brought with it tragedies that horrified the monks. There was a special meeting of the "assembly." It was decided that they should divide up whatever money they had left, so as to be ready to face emergencies. This was done, but not before one of their number had made a gallant attempt to get away with the whole sum for himself. Another wrote a letter of delirious invective against Cabet and then blew out his brains. A third fell overboard and nearly drowned. He was rescued in time, however, and Father Eutropius had an interview with him afterward. The blood nearly froze in the Trappist's veins as the man calmly related how, feeling himself on the point of drowning, he had already unclasped his knife to plunge it into his own heart, when a sailor jumped into the river and saved him.

The monk was left with plenty of food for thought by this insight into the communist mentality.

One brighter touch was added to the dismal picture when one of the Icarians presented himself before Father Eutropius and asked if he could be admitted to the Trappist community. The young superior was not unfriendly to this request. Unfortunately, it turned out that the disillusioned Icarian had a wife.

Cabet eventually reorganized his utopia at Nauvoo, Illinois, on the site vacated by the Mormons, who had left for Utah in 1847.

The journey was to end as it had begun—in a torrent of rain. The monks, huddled together in three wagons, learned that Kentucky can be very bleak and mournful and cold in December. It was the twentieth day of the last month of the year. They peered through the icy rain at the sycamores and the ruined cornfields. Hour followed hour. They climbed hills, and drove through flooded bottom lands in water up to their axles. They had long since been soaked to the skin. They took their dinner of bread and cheese and fruit in their swamped wagons. That was in the middle of the afternoon. By then they should have been near Bardstown. But there was still a long way to go. Darkness fell. Still no sign of a town.

At eight o'clock one of the wagons broke down. The monks alighted and rearranged themselves. The weakest of their number moved into the two remaining wagons. The rest walked into Bardstown at eleven o'clock that night, up to their knees in mud.

They were to spend the night at St. Joseph's College as guests of the Jesuit fathers. They found the college building in the Stygian darkness of the rainy night. Taking with him Brother Hilarion, a Kilkenny Irishman, Father Eutropius made a tour around the walls of the building trying to find the door. Having found it, they knocked, but received no answer.

The monks were in no mood to waste time. They gathered together and took a deep breath, and forty-three powerful voices roared the one word: "T-r-r-ra-PEEST!"

It seemed as if every window in the building flew open on the instant. The Jesuits and their students and their neighbors and probably the whole of Bardstown besides were now informed that the silent monks had arrived.

The Jesuits soon built a big fire and prepared a hot meal for the travelers, but they had no beds to offer them. The monks were content to roll their blankets around them and sleep on the floor.

The next day—the winter solstice and the feast of St. Thomas the Apostle—they started out in the not-too-early morning, after Mass and Communion, to cover the few miles that remained.

For most of them it was to be the end of all journeys. Within a year one of them would already be buried at Gethsemani. Most of the others would find their rest there also, one by one, in years to come. They were tired of traveling by now!

But if they knew that their journey was ended, they could see by the poverty of the land around them that their labors were just about to begin. The pale winter sun reached its zenith, and shone feebly on the low, wooded hills dominating the brown fields of the plateau. The sight of a forest cheered them after so much relatively bare landscape. Their satisfaction grew to joy when a Negro who was driving one of the wagons told them that the forest belonged to them. That was Gethsemani, their land, their new home.

They slowly advanced, among cedars and hickory trees, oak and maple and walnut, and an occasional sycamore with mottled branches pale as dead men's bones. And now they were among the hills. As the track they followed reached a summit in the undulating land, they perceived that they were entering into a different kind of landscape. Ahead of them was a broad valley, bounded in the distance by another line of blue, wooded hills. The cold air was sweet with the scent of pines.

A sharp descent brought them down to a creek which splashed over brown shelves of shale in a covert of dark cedars. Then they climbed again and came to open fields. They saw ahead of them, on a bare, even knoll, a group of log cabins standing amid cornfields. In one of the fields, the stalks stood brown and dry, the ears still clinging to them. The wind stirred sadly in the dry stalks and dry shucks. A Kentucky mule came up to the fence and semaphored his surprise at them with big brown ears. It was their home, the orphanage of Our Lady of Gethsemani, standing in what the monks now call St. Joseph's field, facing south and west, dominating the wide, blue valley.

It was a beautiful site, vast and silent and full of peace, and the monks let their eyes rove over the undulating woods and fields toward the distant village of New Hope. The view was almost beautiful enough to make them overlook the dilapidated cabins that they would have to live in. But in any case, their long journey was at an end and they were glad and their tired hearts thanked the Living God, Whose inscrutable will had destined them to this place from all eternity.

[1] There were still plenty of wildcats in Kentucky in 1848.
[2] *Gethsemani Abbey, a Narrative of the Late Abbot Eutropius,* O.C.R., 1899, p. 34.
[3] *Op. cit.,* p. 41.
[4] Acts ii:44. Cf. Gilson, *Mystical Theology of St. Bernard,* p. 75.

Nine: DAY UNTO DAY

YESTERDAY MORNING I MADE MY WILL. You always make a will before solemn vows, getting rid of everything, as if you were about to die. It sounds more dramatic than it really is. As a matter of fact, as soon as I had renounced all earthly things, I was called into Father Abbot's room and he presented me with a contract with Harcourt, Brace for the publication of *The Seven Storey Mountain.* So after making my will I put my living signature on this contract. The royalties of the dead author will go to the monastery. Meanwhile, I spent the afternoon writing business letters and making all kinds of mistakes.

This morning, before the Blessed Sacrament, it seemed to me that these vows will mean the renunciation of the pure contemplative life. If Jesus wants me to be here at Gethsemani, as my superiors insist He does (*Qui vos audit me audit*), then perhaps He does not want me to be a pure contemplative after all. I suppose it all depends what you mean by a pure contemplative.

I soon came to the conclusion that I could not think straight about the problem anyway. Perhaps this is not the most perfect vocation in the Church, *per se.* Well, what about it? It seems to be *my* vocation. That is the thing that matters. What is the use of having some other vocation that is better in itself but is not your own vocation? But how can it be my vocation if I have such a strong desire for some other vocation? Don't ask me. Our Lord wants that sacrifice. How do I know? I don't know. That is what I am told. Do I have to believe them? I do not have to, I suppose. But something tells me that there is no other way for me. My conscience is on the side of my superiors and anyway, when I have a moment of lucid thought on the subject, experience reminds me that these feelings will go away just as they have gone away before. No doubt they will come back again and go away again many times before I get used to forgetting them.

I was thurifer at the Solemn Abbatial Mass of reposition. On top of all my other troubles, I could not get a decent fire going. The grains of incense we use are so large and so coarse that as soon as they are put on top of the charcoal they melt into a solid mass that gives off no smoke and only puts out the fire. I was working and blowing on the charcoal all through the Canon and got my hands covered with coal and when it was all over I forgot to empty out the censer and put it away.

IT IS A DAY OF RECOLLECTION. That means we are supposed to be thinking about ourselves. It seems as though a year had passed since my solemn profession. But it is only a month. The more I think of my vows the happier I am. For there is only one thing left to live for: the love of God. There is only one unhappiness: not to love God. That is why I wish I did not find my soul so full of movement, and shadows and crosscurrents of dry wind that stir up the dust of my human desires. Everywhere I turn I find the stuff I write sticking to me like flypaper.

THE CISTERCIAN LIFE IS ENERGETIC. There are tides of vitality running through the whole community that generate energy even in people who are lazy. And here at Gethsemani we are at the same time Cistercians and Americans. It is in some respects a dangerous combination. Our energy runs away with us. We go out to work like a college football team taking the field.

Trappists believe that everything that costs them is God's will. Anything that makes you suffer is God's will. If it makes you sweat, it is God's will. But we have serious doubts about the things which demand no expense of physical energy. Are they really the will of God? Hardly! They require no steam. We seem to think that God will not be satisfied with a monastery that does not behave in every way like a munitions factory under wartime conditions of production.

If we want something, we easily persuade ourselves that what we want is God's will just as long as it turns out to be difficult to obtain. What is easy is my own will: what is hard is God's will. If I happen to desire something hard to get, it means that I want to sacrifice myself to do God's will. No other standard applies. And because we make fetishes out of difficulties we sometimes work ourselves into the most fantastically stupid situations, and use ourselves up not for God but for ourselves. We think we have done great things because we are worn out. If we have rushed into the fields or into the woods and done a great deal of damage, we are satisfied. We do not mind ruining all our machinery, as long as we make a deafening noise and stir up a great cloud of dust. Something has been achieved.

ALL DAY I HAVE BEEN WAITING for You with my faculties bleeding the poison of unsuppressed activity. . . . I have waited for Your silence and Your peace to stanch and cleanse them, O my Lord.

You will heal my soul when it pleases You, because I have trusted in You.

I will no longer wound myself with the thoughts and questions that have surrounded me like thorns: that is a penance You do not ask of me.

You have made my soul for Your peace and Your silence, but it is lacerated by the noise of my activity and my desires. My mind is crucified all day by its own hunger for experience, for ideas, for satisfaction. And I do not possess my house in silence.

But I was created for Your peace and You will not despise my longing for the holiness of Your deep silence. O my Lord, You will not leave me forever in this sorrow, because I have trusted in You and I will wait upon Your good pleasure in peace and without complaining any more. This, for Your glory.

I am content that these pages show me to be what I am—noisy, full of the racket of my imperfections and passions, and the wide open wounds left by my sins. Full of my own emptiness. Yet, ruined as my house is, You live there!

ALL THE HILLS AND WOODS are red and brown and copper, and the sky is clear, with one or two very small clouds. A buzzard comes by and investigates me, but I am not dead yet. This whole landscape of woods and hills is getting to be saturated with my prayers and with the Psalms and with the books I read out here under the trees, looking over the wall, not at the world but at our forest, our solitude. Everything I see has become incomparably rich for me, in the years since I made my simple vows and emerged from the novitiate.

This morning I was out there again reciting the 118th Psalm and the Gradual Psalms by heart, looking at the hills. I am finishing my Psalters for the dead, and this is the last time round for this year. I am finishing early. Five days more to go. We have a month in which to say the Psalter ten times over. And I like it. It means a great deal to me. When I am a priest I will no longer be obliged to say the Psalters, because the priests say some Masses instead. But I sometimes think I would like to go on saying a few Psalters during the Tricenary anyway. But I will probably no longer have the time.

WHAT IS THE USE of my complaining about not being a contemplative, if I do not take the opportunities I get for contemplation? I suppose I take them, but in the wrong way. I spend the time looking for something to read about contemplation—something to satisfy my raffish spiritual appetite—instead of shutting up and emptying my mind and leaving the inner door open for the Holy Spirit to enter from the inside, all the doors being barred and all my blinds down.

I SPEND THE ANNIVERSARY of my solemn profession in the infirmary—a piece of great kindness on the part of Saint Joseph as I am beginning to realize. It has all the earmarks of a plot arranged for no other purpose than to give me a little recollection on this feast and make it a very happy one.

As soon as I get into a cell by myself I am a different person! Prayer becomes what it ought to be. Everything is very quiet. The door is closed but I have the windows open. It is warm—gray clouds fly—all night and all day the frogs sing. Reverend Father sold all the ducks (Father Simon Stylites kept proclaiming the Duck Brothers in the Chapter of faults because the ducks quacked all night) and it is an improvement.

Plenty of time. Plenty of time. No manuscripts, no typewriter, no rushing back and forth to church, no Scriptorium, no breaking your neck to get things done before the next thing happens.

I went down to Chapter because Reverend Father wants you to go to Chapter if your temperature is less than 100. Mine was. Father Apollinaris preached vehemently on the sufferings of Saint Joseph—his mental sufferings when he discovered that Mary was with child. I should not have made funny faces when Fr. Apollinaris said Abraham was born 1959 years after the creation of the world, nor can I figure out why he imagined that this event should be commemorated next year—1949. But he says things like that; they come into his head and he says them.

Then I came back to the cell. On the table were bread and butter and a can of barley coffee, and before I said the *Largitor* Father Gerard came in with the bottle of Mass wine in which much was left because Father Odo could not say Mass. And he said "This is a *feast* day" and poured out half a tumbler of wine. He was not aware of any anniversary of mine, but it was then that I realized what was going on—and that Saint

Joseph had arranged all this as a way of giving me some manifestations of God's love, and that I might have joy.

So I drank the wine and it was good and it gave me back my appetite, for last night butter was hateful and I could not eat it.

Then I moved the table to the window and ate looking out of the window as the Carthusians do. The clouds flew, and the huts of the ducks were empty and the frogs sang in the beautiful green pond.

NOW IT IS EVENING. The frogs still sing. After the showers of rain around dinnertime the sky cleared. All afternoon I sat on the bed rediscovering the meaning of contemplation—rediscovering God, rediscovering myself—and the office, and Scripture and everything.

It has been one of the most wonderful days I have ever known in my life, and yet I am not attached to that part of it either. Any pleasure or the contentment I may have got out of silence and solitude and freedom from all care does not matter. But I know that is the way I ought to be *living:* with my mind and senses silent, contact with the world of business and war and community troubles severed—not solicitous for anything high or low or far or near. Not pushing myself around with my own fancies or desires or projects—and not letting myself get hurried off my feet by the excessive current of natural activity that flows through the universe with full force.

LAST EVENING, on the vigil of the feast, we had an unusually long interval after collation. It was a fast day, and so we weren't long in refectory in the evening and got out early. Since the sun was higher than it usually is in that interval I saw the country in a light that we usually do not see. The low-slanting rays picked out the foliage of the trees and highlighted a new wheatfield against the dark curtain of woods on the knobs, that were in shadow. It was very beautiful. Deep peace. Sheep on the slopes behind the sheep barn. The new trellises in the novitiate garden leaning and sagging under a hill of roses. A cardinal singing suddenly in the walnut tree, and piles of fragrant logs all around the woodshed waiting to be cut in bad weather.

I looked at all this in great tranquillity, with my soul and spirit quiet. For me landscape seems to be important for contemplation; anyway, I have no scruples about loving it.

Didn't Saint John of the Cross hide himself in a room up in a church tower where there was one small window through which he could look out at the country?

THE LAST TWO EMBER DAYS were like great feasts. Friday was in fact a feast—the Stigmatization of Saint Francis, and I sat with my empty stomach and prayed behind the church while the wind moved the trees and nobody in the world was in sight and the clouds crossed the sky with motion that was imperceptible and those red wasps clambered all over one another on the wall of the church. I don't know what this business is that they go in for every autumn up under the eaves of the side chapels, but every once in a while a gust of wind would blow a bunch of them off into the bushes and they would struggle back up the wall and start all over again.

Day and night I think about Saint Francis and about poverty as I reread the seventh chapter of Saint Bonaventure's *Itinerarium.*

The best thing of all is that at last I can get out to work. The Tricenary has begun. Saturday after we got our faces shaved with electric shavers, we went out and picked up apples in the orchard, walking around bent double under the low branches like the woman in the day's Gospel. Today we shoveled dirt into ditches that the rain washed out of the sheep pasture, and out of the corner of my eye I could see there was much corn waiting to be cut in the bottom lands.

I know why I will never really be able to write anything about prayer in a journal—because anything you write, even a journal, is at least implicitly somebody else's business. When I say prayer I mean what happens to me in the first person singular. What really happens to what is really me is nobody else's business.

In the novitiate they practice the Gradual for the Feast of Saint Matthew, very loud.

LOVE SAILS ME AROUND THE HOUSE. I walk two steps on the ground and four steps in the air. It is love. It is consolation. I don't care if it is consolation. I am not attached to consolation. I love God. Love carries me all around. I don't want to *do* anything but love. And when the bell rings it is like pulling teeth to make myself shift because of that love, secret love, hidden love, obscure love, down inside me and outside me where I don't care to talk about it. Anyway I don't have the time or the energy to discuss such matters. I have only time for eternity, which is to say for love, love, love. Maybe Saint Teresa would like to have me snap out of it but it is pure, I tell you; I am not attached to it (I hope) and it is love and it gives me soft punches all the time in the center of my heart. Love is pushing me around the monastery, love is kicking me all around like a gong I tell you, love is the only thing that makes it possible for me to continue to tick.

That was the way it was up in the apple trees yesterday morning with all that blue sky. The bulls in their pens were rumbling like old men and I thought it was Father Subprior starting to sing under his breath—I say that not because Father Subprior is old but because he happened to be working near, hidden in the leaves.

But O love, why can't you leave me alone?—which is a rhetorical question meaning: for heaven's sakes don't.

That was the way it was all week. In choir the less I worried about the singing the more I was possessed by love. There is a lesson in that about being poor. You have got to be all the time cooperating with love in this house, and love sets a fast pace even at the beginning and if you don't keep up you'll get dropped. And yet any speed is too slow for love—and no speed is too fast for you if you will only let love drag you off your feet—after that you will have to sail the whole way. But our instinct is to get off and start walking. . . .

I want to be poor; I want to be solitary; I had a tough time after Communion and I think I was twisting and turning too much, as usual. This business burns me. *Aruit tamquam testa virtus mea.*[1] I am all dried up with desire and I can only think of one thing—staying in the fire that burns me.

SOONER OR LATER THE WORLD MUST BURN, and all things in it—all the books, the cloister together with the brothel, Fra Angelico together with the Lucky Strike ads which I haven't seen for seven years because I don't remember seeing one in Louisville. Sooner or later it will all be consumed by fire and nobody will be left—for by that time the last man in the universe will have discovered the bomb capable of destroying the universe and will have been unable to resist the temptation to throw the thing and get it over with.

And here I sit writing a diary.

But love laughs at the end of the world because love is the door to eternity and he who loves God is playing on the doorstep of eternity, and before anything can happen love will have drawn him over the sill and closed the door and he won't bother about the world burning because he will know nothing but love.

Today for the first time we tried a schola of eight, singing during the whole Mass, and I can see where it would one day help a great deal. That was one of the ideas Reverend Father brought back from Cîteaux.

In Chapter he told us about how it was at Lisieux, and La Grande Trappe, and Port du Salut where they run a power station. At La Trappe our Father Bernard, the sculptor, has discovered a system for making plaques of pious subjects, four at a time, all different sizes, and the notion made me quiver.

But sooner or later the world must burn—and *The Seven Storey Mountain* and *Figures for an Apocalypse*. And I have several times thought how at the Last Day I am likely to be one of the ten most abjectly humiliated sinners in the history of the world, but it will be my joy, and it will fill me with love, and I will fly like an arrow to take a back seat very far in the back where the last shall be first. And perhaps if Saint Francis will pray for me, and Saint John of the Cross, and Saint Mary Magdalen, I'll slide down off my high horse now and begin being the last and the least in everything, but not out of injured vanity as I was this morning in the eight-cylinder schola we had, that sang so fast *vir erat in terra Hus nomine Job*.

Now it is a tossup whether I should ask Reverend Father to give me another and fatter book to fill with *Journal*, for we have been talking about my writing less. In fact, I have begun to tell him all about my temptations to become a Carthusian and he says he doesn't see why things can't be fixed up right here.

But *nos qui vivimus benedicamus Domino* by love, love, love, in the cloister and in the choir and out there in the presence of the forest and the hills where all the colors are changing, and under the steeple whose topmost cross has been painted with yellow traffic paint by Brother Processus who swung up there for days in the sky with his angel holding on to him. (He upset a bucket of paint and I could see it flying upside down on the end of a rope, and the paint turned to spray before it was halfway down, and a drop fell on our Psalter and there were little yellow spots all over the stones and the bushes of the cemetery where today I saw a hawk.)

MY COMPLAINTS ABOUT THE WORLD in the *Mountain* and in some poems are perhaps a weakness. Not that there isn't plenty to complain about, but my reaction is too natural. It is impure. The world I am sore at on paper is perhaps a figment of my own imagination. The business is a psychological game I have been playing since I was ten. And yet there is plenty to be disgusted with in the world.

YESTERDAY AFTERNOON I WENT OUT TO THE WOODS. There was a wall of black sky beyond the knobs, to the west, and you could hear thunder growling all the time in the distance. It was very hot and damp but there was good wind coming from the direction of the storm.

(Before None, during the meridienne in the dormitory, I dreamed of going out: and in the dream I crossed the field where the platform still remains, from the centenary, and walked up toward Aidan Nally's. Before I got to Nally's, in the dream, the wagon road developed sidewalks and I came not to solitude but to Jamaica High School, which we used to pass going up a hill on the way to the movies at Loew's Valencia in the old days.) But when I woke up and really went out it was nothing at all like the dream.

First I stopped under an oak tree on top of the hill behind Nally's and sat there looking out at the wide sweep of the valley and the miles of flat woods over toward the straight line of the horizon where Rohan's knob is.

The wind ran over the bent, brown grasses and moved the shoulders of all the green trees, and I looked at the dark mass of woods beyond the distillery, on those hills down to the south of us and realized that it is when I am with people that I am lonely, and when I am alone I am no longer lonely.

Gethsemani looked beautiful from the hill. It made much more sense in its surroundings. We do not realize our own setting as we ought to: it is important to know where you are put, on the face of the earth. Physically, the monastery is in a great solitude. There is nothing to complain about from the point of view of geography. One or two houses a mile and a half away and then woods and pastures and bottoms and cornfields and hills for miles and miles.

I had a vague idea there was a nice place beyond the field we call Hick's House although there has been no house there for years. I went to the calf pasture beyond St. Malachy's field at the foot of the knob where the real woods begin. It is a sort of *cova* where Our Lady might appear. From there we started walking to get to the forest fire we went out to fight on All Saints Day two and a half years ago.

It was quiet as the Garden of Eden. I sat on a high bank, under young pines, and looked out over this glen. Right under me was a dry creek, with clean pools lying like glass between the shale pavement of the stream, and the shale was as white and crumpled as sea biscuit. Down in the glen were the songs of marvelous birds. I saw the gold-orange flame of an oriole in a tree. Orioles are too shy to come near the monastery. There was a cardinal whistling somewhere, but the best song was that of two birds that sounded as wonderful as nightingales and their song echoed through the wood. I could not tell what they were. I had never heard such birds before. The echo made the place sound more remote, and self-contained, more perfectly enclosed, and more like Eden.

HERE I SIT SURROUNDED BY BEES. The bees are happy and therefore they are silent. They are working in the delicate white flowers of the weeds among which I sit. I am on the east side of the house where I am not as cool as I thought I was going to be, and I sit on top of the bank that looks down over the beehives and the pond where the ducks used to be and Rohan's knob in the distance. And that big wobbly stepladder I nearly fell off, cleaning the church once, stands abandoned out there next to one of the cherry trees, and the branches of a little plum tree before me, right by the road, sag with blue plums.

IN THE CHAPTER ROOM they are finishing *Seeds of Contemplation*, reading a couple of pages each evening before Compline. It began when I was on retreat for ordination. I do not know what the general feeling about it has been in the house—as far as I know it is not unfavorable. Father Macarius told me: "Those who think they are intellectuals, like it." Once or twice I felt as if everyone were a bit exasperated—at passages that were at the same time excessively negative and subtle and obscure.

I am glad the book has been written and read. Surely I have said enough about the business of darkness and about the "experimental contact with God in obscurity" to be able to shut up about it and go on to something else for a change. Otherwise it will just get to be mechanical —grinding out the same old song over and over again. But if it had not been read aloud at me I might have forgotten how often I had said all those things, and gone on saying them again as if they were discoveries. For I am aware that this often happens in our life. Keeping a journal has taught me that there is not so much new in your life as you sometimes think. When you reread your journal you find out that your latest discovery is something you already found out five years ago. Still, it is true that one penetrates deeper and deeper into the same ideas and the same experiences.

WE HAVE A NEW MECHANICAL MONSTER on the place called a D-4 Traxcavator which is enormous and rushes at the earth with a wide-open maw and devours everything in sight. It roars terribly, especially when it is hungry. It has been given to the lay-brother novices. They feed it every day and you can't hear yourself think in the monastery while the brute is at table. It is yellow and has a face like a drawbridge and is marked all over with signs saying it comes from the Whayne supply company in Louisville, but really, as I know from secret information, it was born on a raft in Memphis, Tennessee. There, the hippopotamus abounds: which this instrument greatly resembles.

Also we have bought fans. They are exhaust fans. You make a hole in the building and put the fans there and they draw all the hot air out of the dormitory. Nobody knows what happens after that. My guess is that the hot air that went out through the fan is then replaced by the hot air that comes in through the windows. The fans are not yet running because the lay-brother novices have not yet made the holes in the building. However, they have begun. They have a scaffold up on the roof of the infirmary and they have been blasting at the gable of that wing with jackhammers, and two frail novices who are very young were posted down on the ground floor near the doorways with artistic signs which read "Falling Bricks." At first one of them was standing at the precise spot where all the falling bricks would land on his head. He was saying the rosary in an attitude of perfect abandonment. Afterwards he got a stool and moved inside the cloister and propped up the sign in his lap and took to reading the immortal masterpiece of Father Garrigou-Lagrange, *Christian Perfection and Contemplation.*

THIS MORNING, UNDER A COBALT BLUE SKY, summer having abruptly ended, I am beginning the Book of Job. It is not warm enough to sit for long in the shade of the cedars. The woods are crisply outlined in the sun and the clamor of distant crows is sharp in the air that no longer sizzles with locusts.

And Job moves me deeply. This year more than ever it has a special poignancy.

I now know that all my own poems about the world's suffering have been inadequate: they have not solved anything, they have only camouflaged the problem. And it seems to me that the urge to write a real poem about suffering and sin is only another temptation because, after all, I do not really understand.

Sometimes I feel that I would like to stop writing, precisely as a gesture of defiance. In any case, I hope to stop publishing for a time, for I believe it has now become impossible for me to stop writing altogether. Perhaps I shall continue writing on my deathbed, and even take some asbestos paper with me in order to go on writing in purgatory.

Except that I hope Our Lady will arrange some miraculous victory over my sins that will make purgatory unnecessary.

And yet it seems to me that writing, far from being an obstacle to spiritual perfection in my own life, has become one of the conditions on which my perfection will depend. If I am to be a saint—and there is nothing else that I can think of desiring to be—it seems that I must get there by writing books in a Trappist monastery. If I am to be a saint, I have not only to be a monk, which is what all monks must do to become saints, but I must also put down on paper what I have become. It may sound simple, but it is not an easy vocation.

To be as good a monk as I can, and to remain myself, and to write about it: to put myself down on paper, in such a situation, with the most complete simplicity and integrity, masking nothing, confusing no issues: this is very hard, because I am all mixed up in illusions and attachments. These, too, will have to be put down. But without exaggeration, repetition, useless emphasis. No need for breast beating and lamentation before the eyes of anyone but You, O God, who see the depths of my fatuity. To be frank without being boring. It is a kind of crucifixion. Not a very dramatic or painful one. But it requires so much honesty that it is beyond my nature. It must come somehow from the Holy Ghost.

One of the results of all this could well be a complete and holy transparency: living, praying, and writing in the light of the Holy Spirit, losing myself entirely by becoming public property just as Jesus is public property in the Mass. Perhaps this is an important aspect of my priesthood—my living of my Mass: to become as plain as a Host in the hands of everybody. Perhaps it is this, after all, that is to be my way into solitude. One of the strangest ways so far devised, but it is the way of the Word of God.

Yet after all, this only teaches me that nothing vital about myself can ever be public property!

THERE HAS BEEN A LEGAL CHANGE OF SEASONS, and the monastic fast has begun today. It is cool again, and the leaves of the sycamores are already beginning to turn yellow and brown. We brought down our mattresses and blankets from our dormitory cells and spread them out in the bright September sun. My mind is full of Saint Francis on Mount Alvernia.

A moment ago, someone was playing the harmonium in the novitiate. Our psalms sound very wistful and strange on a harmonium: plaintive, sentimental, and thin, as if they were filled with an immense nostalgia

for the heaven of the books of meditations. It reminded me of the night
Father Alberic died, three years ago. I watched by the body in the middle of the night, and then went back to the dormitory and could not
get to sleep, even when I stayed to catch up my two hours while the
others went down to church for the Night Office. Finally they sang
Matins and Lauds of the Dead, for Father Alberic, and I could hear the
garbled music coming into the dormitory through the back of the organ
pipes—that great, big, dusty closet full of muffled chords! The poignancy of that music was very affecting. It seemed to sum up all the sufferings of the long life that was now over. Poor little gray Father Alberic,
writing the history of the order on scraps of paper up in the infirmary!
All the relief, all the mystery, all the unexpected joy of his meeting with
God could be guessed at in those strange harmonies. And so, this morning, the sound of this harmonium in the novitiate (it has begun to play
again) chimes in with the last days of a two weeks' battle, and I feel a
wistful and chastened sobriety filling my heart, as if I were one of the
eight human survivors of the deluge, watching the world come back to
view from the summit of Mount Ararat!

In the tempest, I have discovered once again, but this time with a
peculiarly piercing sharpness, that I cannot possess created things, I cannot touch them, I cannot get into them. They are not my end, I cannot
find any rest in them. We who are supposed to be Christians know that
well enough, abstractly. Or rather, we say we believe it. Actually we
have to discover it over and over again. We have to experience this
truth, with deeper and deeper intensity, as we go on in life. We renounce the pursuit of creatures as ends on certain sacramental occasions.
And we return, bit by bit, to our familiarity with them, living as if we
had in this world a lasting city. . . .

But creatures remain untouchable, inviolable. If God wants you to
suffer a little, He allows you to learn just how inviolable they are. As
soon as you try to possess their goodness for its own sake, all that is
sweet in them becomes bitter to you, all that is beautiful, ugly. Everything you love sickens you. And at the same time your need to love
something, somebody, increases a hundred times over. And God, Who
is the only one who can be loved for His own sake alone, remains invisible and unimaginable and untouchable, beyond everything else that
exists.

You flowers and trees, you hills and streams, you fields, flocks, and
wild birds, you books, you poems, and you people, I am unutterably
alone in the midst of you. The irrational hunger that sometimes gets

into the depths of my will, tries to swing my deepest self away from God and direct it to your love. I try to touch you with the deep fire that is in the center of my heart, but I cannot touch you without defiling both you and myself, and I am abashed, solitary and helpless, surrounded by a beauty that can never belong to me.

But this sadness generates within me an unspeakable reverence for the holiness of created things, for they are pure and perfect and they belong to God and they are mirrors of His beauty. He is mirrored in all things like sunlight in clean water: but if I try to drink the light that is in the water I only shatter the reflection.

And so I live alone and chaste in the midst of the holy beauty of all created things, knowing that nothing I can see or hear or touch will ever belong to me, ashamed of my absurd need to give myself away to any one of them or to all of them. The silly, hopeless passion to give myself away to any beauty eats out my heart. It is an unworthy desire, but I cannot avoid it. It is in the hearts of us all, and we have to bear with it, suffer its demands with patience, until we die and go to heaven where all things will belong to us in their highest causes.

ONE OF THE MANY NICE THINGS about being hebdomadary is that you get the Scriptorium all to yourself during a good part of the wonderful interval after the Night Office. All the other priests are saying Mass and the young professed are going to Communion. I listen to the clock tick. Downstairs the thermostat has just stopped humming. God is in this room. So much so that it is difficult to read or write. Nevertheless I'll get busy on Isaias which is Your word, O my God, and may Your fire grow in me and may I find You in Your beautiful fire. It is very quiet, O my God, Your moon shines on our hills. Your moonlight shines in my wide open soul when everything is silent. *Adolezco peno y muero.*

WALKING BACK FROM THE BARNS in the warm sun on the muddy road between the orchard and the vegetable garden with the *Spiritual Canticle* under my arm, and saying those wonderful words! I found a fine place to read and pray, on the top floor of that barn building where the rabbits used to be. Up under the roof is a place reached by various ladders. Some stovepipes and old buckets are there and many of the little boxes in which the novices gather strawberries in the early summertime. There is a chair and there is a beautiful small rectangular window which faces south over the valley—the outside orchard, Saint Joseph's field, the distant line of hills. It is the quietest and most hidden and most isolated place I have found in the whole enclosure—but not necessarily the warmest. However, it was good yesterday with the sun coming in the window: *Vacio, hambriento, solo, llagado y doliente de amor, suspenso en el aire.* Almost all activity makes me ill, but as soon as I am alone and silent again I sink into deep peace, recollection, and happiness.

RILKE'S NOTEBOOKS have so much power in them that they make me wonder why no one writes like that in monasteries. Not that there have not been better books written in monasteries, and books more serene. But monks do not seem to be able to write so well—and it is as if our professional spirituality sometimes veiled our contact with the naked realities inside us. It is a common failing of monks to lose themselves in a collective, professional personality—to let themselves be cast in a mold. Yet this mold does not seem to do away with what is useless or even unpleasant about some personalities. We cling to our eccentricities and our selfishness, but we do so in a way that is no longer interesting because it is after all mechanical and vulgar.

I HAVE FALLEN into the great indignity I have written against—I am a contemplative who is ready to collapse from overwork. This, I think, is a sin and the punishment of sin but now I have got to turn it to good use and be a saint by it, somehow.

Teaching wears me out. Like Ezechias I am in a big hurry to show all my treasures to the Babylonians. Not that the novices and the young monks are Babylonians in their own right—but relatively to me and my treasures they might just as well be. And yet what can I show them, or what can I share with them? There is so little one can communicate. I talk my head off and they seem to be listening to somebody who wasn't there, to stories I never told them. They have received messages I never intended them to hear. While I talk they sit there—perhaps imagining they like what I say—and all the while they are building up myths of their own upon a few fragments of words that came out of me. I am astonished at their constructions. But in the end I think I am astonished that I am able to say anything at all that passes from me to some other mind except God's.

The terrible thing is the indignity of thinking such an endeavor is really important. The other day while the new high altar was being consecrated I found myself being stripped of one illusion after another. There I stood and sat with my eyes closed and wondered why I read so much, why I write so much, why I talk so much, and why I get so excited about the things that only affect the surface of my life—I came here eight years ago and already knew better when I arrived. But for eight years I have obeyed the other law in my members and so I am worn out with activity—exhausting myself with proclaiming that the thing to do is rest. *In omnibus requiem quaesivi . . .*

YESTERDAY, THE FEAST OF SAINT THOMAS, was, as I think, an important day. It was warm and overclouded and windy but tranquil. I had a kind of sense that the day was building up to some kind of deep decision. A wordless decision, a giving of the depths and substance of myself. There is a conversion of the deep will to God that cannot be effected in words —barely in a gesture or ceremony. There is a conversion of the deep will and a gift of my substance that is too mysterious for liturgy, and too private. It is something to be done in a lucid secrecy that implies first of all the denial of communication to others except perhaps as a neutral thing.

I shall remember the time and place of this liberty and this neutrality which cannot be written down. These clouds low on the horizon, the outcrops of hard yellow rock in the road, the open gate, the perspective of fenceposts leading up the rise to the sky, and the big cedars tumbled and tousled by the wind. Standing on rock. Present. The reality of the present and of solitude divorced from past and future. To be collected and gathered up in clarity and silence and to belong to God and to be nobody else's business. I wish I could recover the liberty of that interior decision which was very simple and which seems to me to have been a kind of blank check and a promise.

TO BELONG TO GOD I have to belong to myself. I have to be alone—at least interiorly alone. This means the constant renewal of a decision. I cannot belong to people. None of me belongs to anybody but God. Absolute loneliness of the imagination, the memory, the will. My love for everybody is equal, neutral, and clean. No exclusiveness. Simple and free as the sky because I love everybody and am possessed by nobody, not held, not bound. In order to be not remembered or even wanted I have to be a person that nobody knows. They can have Thomas Merton. He's dead. Father Louis—he's half dead too. For my part my name is that sky, those fenceposts, and those cedar trees. I shall not even reflect on who I am and I shall not say my identity is nobody's business because that implies a truculence I don't intend. It has no meaning.

Now my whole life is this—to keep unencumbered. The wind owns the fields where I walk and I own nothing and am owned by nothing and I shall never even be forgotten because no one will ever discover me. This is to me a source of immense confidence. My Mass this morning was transfigured by this independence.

THEY ARE PULLING DOWN the horsebarn. The Traxcavator was tethered to it, in the rain, after dinner. The barn was already half in ruins. And house upon house shall fall. The roof was down in a hoisted heap spreading its red old wings clumsily over the wreckage of the stables. The other half of the barn was tied to the monster and ready to fall. The stone pillars were already crooked and awry. When I was at work I could hear the engine roar but did not hear the fall of the old building.

I SEE NO FACE, I treasure no experience, no memory. Anything I write down here is only for personal guidance because of my constant gravitation away from solitude. It will remind me how to go home. Not to be like the man who looked in the glass and straightway forgot what manner of man he was: yet I shall not remember myself in such a way that I remember the person I am not.

As I rediscover solitude, prayer in choir becomes difficult again. But the other day—Tuesday at the Night Office—Psalm 54 had tremendous meaning for me. I felt as if I were chanting something I myself had written. It is more my own than any of my own poems:

Cor meum conturbatum est in me, et formido mortis cedidit super me.
Timor et tremor venerunt super me, et contexerunt me tenebrae:
Et dixi: quis dabit mihi pennas sicut columbae et volabo, et requiescam?
Ecce, elongavi fugiens, et mansi in solitudine.
Expectabo eum, qui salvum me fecit a pusillanimitate spiritus, et tempestate.[2]

It is fear that is driving me into solitude. Love has put drops of terror in my veins and they grow cold in me, suddenly, and make me faint with fear because my heart and my imagination wander away from God into their own private idolatry. It is my iniquity that makes me physically faint and turn to jelly because of the contradiction between my nature and my God. I am exhausted by fear. So that yesterday, for example, I thought I would fall with the ciborium, distributing Communion to the brothers. But last night in the middle of the night I was awake for an hour and a half and the last line I have quoted there was verified. All five lines are truer of my life than anything I have ever written, and this gives me great confidence in the liturgy. This is the secret of the psalms. Our identity is hidden in them. In them we find ourselves, and God. In these fragments he has revealed not only Himself to us but ourselves in Him. *Mittit crystallum suum sicut buccellas.*

I WANTED TO WRITE DOWN an incident that happened New Year's Eve, in the afternoon. I was sitting by the ruins of the old horsebarn, looking down at the bleak pasture, the cedars, the enclosure wall, the woods, and then that little heavenly vista of far hills in the southeast. It was gray. Hunters were in the outside orchard. I saw them going into the woods. White pants and brown pants. They were not very serious hunters because they were talking all the time; their talk echoed all through the wood. Their dog was far ahead of them, barking and barking. Soon they just stopped in the middle of the road and talked. But the dog ranged from one end of the wood to the other, barking. It was easy to see that the whole hunt was a lie. The dog was after nothing. Neither were the hunters.

Suddenly White Pants climbed up on the enclosure wall. He stood on top of it, with his gun. It was all an act: "Well, I am standing on the wall. I am preparing to shoot all the rabbits as they go by. My dog will rout them out and they will all come running past this point in the wall in an orderly procession. From my point of vantage I will easily be able to pick them off, one by one." The whole universe knew that as soon as he fired the gun he would fall off the wall backwards inside the enclosure, perhaps into the dirty old bathtub full of rain water and spring water and green weeds which is placed there as a horsetrough. Then he would have to become a monk.

Meanwhile I was in an equivocal position. I began to wonder if perhaps I was expected to resent the presence of White Pants on top of the enclosure wall. Was I supposed to act like a responsible member of society, stand up, wave my arms and shout "Hey!" and make guttural sounds signifying, "Get down off the wall!" Naturally he knew I could not *talk* to him. But we came to an understanding. I allowed him to gather, by my immobility, that I was invisible. I permitted him, however, to deduce from the fact that I looked in his direction, that I entertained toward him and the universe he represented an abstract, disembodied, and purely official good will. So there we stayed. He sat on top of the wall, hunting, and I sat on a board reading, meditating on eternal truths, or what you will. I believe I must have had some book or other with me, just as he quite clearly had a gun. Both were simply factors in a disguise. I don't know who he was. I am not quite sure I knew who I was. In neither case did it matter.

Soon the dog came inside the enclosure, through a hole under the wall, and ran about barking and wagging his tail with mongrel optimism. Then the three colts ran from the other end of the pasture to investigate the dog. White Pants spoke to his companion, "Call that dog." Then he picked himself up and walked off stiffly, eastward, along the top of the wall. I do not know what became of him. If I had watched I might have ascertained.

Not a shot was fired. I did not turn a page of the book I may or may not have had with me. Not a drop of rain fell. Not a bird sang. Ours is a comfortable world, without either science or wisdom.

I WENT TO THE GARDEN-HOUSE ATTIC, as usual, after dinner. Climbed up the ladder, observing all the hoes and shovels lying on the floor. I made my way through the litter of old stovepipes and broken strawberry boxes to the chair by the window. On the chair is a sack, stained with either paint, creosote, or the blood of something slaughtered. I opened the small window (a pane fell out one day when I let it slam; I can still see the fragments of glass on the red roof of the shed below).

Today it was wonderful. Clouds, sky overcast, but tall streamers of sunlight coming down in a fan over the bare hills.

Suddenly I became aware of great excitement. The pasture was full of birds—starlings. There was an eagle flying over the woods. The crows were all frightened, and were soaring, very high, keeping out of the way. Even more distant still were the buzzards, flying and circling, observing everything from a distance. And the starlings filled every large and small tree, and shone in the light and sang. The eagle attacked a tree full of starlings but before he was near them the whole cloud of them left the tree and avoided him and he came nowhere near them. Then he went away and they all alighted on the ground. They were there moving about and singing for about five minutes. Then, like lightning, it happened. I saw a scare go into the cloud of birds, and they opened their wings and began to rise off the ground and, in that split second, from behind the house and from over my roof a hawk came down like a bullet, and shot straight into the middle of the starlings just as they were getting off the ground. They rose into the air and there was a slight scuffle on the ground as the hawk got his talons into the one bird he had nailed.

It was a terrible and yet beautiful thing, that lightning flight, straight as an arrow, that killed the slowest starling.

Then every tree, every field was cleared. I do not know where all the starlings went. Florida, maybe. The crows were still in sight, but over their wood. Their guttural cursing had nothing more to do with this affair. The vultures, lovers of dead things, circled over the bottoms where perhaps there was something dead. The hawk, all alone, in the pasture, possessed his prey. He did not fly away with it like a thief. He stayed in the field like a king with the killed bird, and nothing else came near him. He took his time.

I tried to pray, afterward. But the hawk was eating the bird. And I thought of that flight, coming down like a bullet from the sky behind me and over my roof, the sure aim with which he hit this one bird, as though he had picked it out a mile away. For a moment I envied the lords of the Middle Ages who had their falcons and I thought of the Arabs with their fast horses, hawking on the desert's edge, and I also understood the terrible fact that some men love war. But in the end, I think that hawk is to be studied by saints and contemplatives; because he knows his business. I wish I knew my business as well as he does his.

I wonder if my admiration for you gives me an affinity for you, artist! I wonder if there will ever be something connatural between us, between your flight and my heart stirred in hiding, to serve Christ, as you, soldier, serve your nature. And God's love a thousand times more terrible! Now I am going back to the attic and the shovels and the broken window and the trains in the valley and the prayer of Jesus.

The song of my Beloved beside the stream. The birds descanting in their clerestories. His skies have sanctified my eyes, His woods are clearer than the King's palace. But the air and I will never tell our secret.

THE FIRST SUNDAY OF LENT, as I now know, is a great feast. Christ has sanctified the desert and in the desert I discovered it. The woods have all become young in the discipline of spring: but it is the discipline of expectancy only. Which one cut more keenly? The February sunlight, or the air? There are no buds. Buds are not guessed at or thought of, this early in Lent. But the wilderness shines with promise. The land is dressed in simplicity and strength. Everything foretells the coming of the holy spring. I had never before spoken so freely or so intimately with woods, hills, birds, water, and sky. On this great day, however, they understood their position and they remained mute in the presence of the Beloved. Only His light was obvious and eloquent. My brother and sister, the light and water. The stump and the stone. The tables of rock. The blue, naked sky. Tractor tracks, a little waterfall. And

Mediterranean solitude. I thought of Italy after my Beloved had spoken and was gone.

I WAS IN THE CELLARER'S NEW OFFICES. The little house is very pleasant, with venetian blinds and two small rooms paneled with cedar, which smells overpowering. There is a nook for the cheese salesman, and a door leads into a fair-sized warehouse, then there is a small garage to hide the jeep in, and a larger place where trucks can drive in and unload the riches of Araby and Ophir.

But my chief joy is to escape to the attic of the garden house and the little broken window that looks out over the valley. There in the silence I love the green grass. The tortured gestures of the apple trees have become part of my prayer. I look at the shining water under the willows and listen to the sweet songs of all the living things that are in our woods and fields. So much do I love this solitude that when I walk out along the road to the old barns that stand alone, far from the new buildings, delight begins to overpower me from head to foot and peace smiles even in the marrow of my bones.

1. EXTERIOR SILENCE—its special necessity in our world in which there is so much noise and inane speech. As *protest* and *reparation* against the "sin" of noise.

Babel. Silence not a virtue, noise not a sin. True. But the turmoil and confusion and constant noise of modern society are the expression of the *ambiance* of its greatest sins—its godlessness, its despair. A world of propaganda, of endless argument, vituperation, criticism, or simply of chatter, is a world without anything to live for. Advertising—radio, television, etc.

Catholics who associate themselves with that kind of noise, who enter into the Babel of tongues, become to some extent exiles from the city of God. (Mass becomes racket and confusion. Tension—babble. All prayer becomes exterior and interior noise—soulless and hasty repetition of rosary. . . .)

Hence: though it is true that we must know how to bear with noise, to have interior life, *by exception* here and there in midst of confusion (Saint Thomas's principles for activity), yet to resign oneself to a situation in which a community is *constantly* overwhelmed with activity, noise of machines, etc., is an abuse.

What to do? Those who love God should attempt to preserve or create an atmosphere in which He can be found. Christians should have quiet homes. Throw out television, if necessary—not everybody, but those who take this sort of thing seriously. Radios useless. Stay away from the movies—I was going to say "as a penance" but it would seem to me to be rather a pleasure than a penance, to stay away from the movies. Maybe even form small agrarian communities in the country where there would be *no* radios, etc.

Let those who can stand a little silence find other people who like silence, and create silence and peace for one another. Bring up their kids not to yell so much. Children are naturally quiet—if they are left alone and not given the needle from the cradle upward, in order that they may develop into citizens of a state in which everybody yells and is yelled at.

Provide people with places where they can go to be *quiet*—relax minds and hearts in the presence of God—chapels in the country, or in town also. Reading rooms, hermitages. Retreat houses without a constant ballyhoo of noisy "exercises"—they even yell the stations of the Cross, and not too far from Gethsemani either.

For many it would mean great renunciation and discipline to give up these sources of noise: but they know that is what they need. Afraid to do it because their neighbors would think they were bats.

But at least *monasteries* should be silent!

2. THE END—Interior Silence—of judgments, passions, desires.
                    Saint Gregory the Great
                    Elizabeth of the Trinity
Conclusion: When you gain this interior silence you can carry it around with you in the world, and pray everywhere. But just as interior asceticism cannot be acquired without concrete and exterior mortification, so it is absurd to talk about interior silence where there is no exterior silence.

IT IS NOW SIX MONTHS since I have been Master of the Scholastics and have looked into their hearts and taken up their burdens upon me. I have not always seen clearly and I have not carried their burdens too well and I have stumbled around a lot, and on many days we have gone around in circles and fallen into ditches because the blind was leading the blind.

I do not know if they have discovered anything new, or if they are able to love God more, or if I have helped them in any way to find themselves, which is to say: to lose themselves. But I know what I have discovered: that the kind of work I once feared because I thought it would interfere with "solitude" is, in fact, the only true path to solitude.

One must be in some sense a hermit before the care of souls can serve to lead one further into the desert. But once God has called you to solitude, everything you touch leads you further into solitude. Everything that affects you builds you into a hermit, as long as you do not insist on doing the work yourself and building your own kind of hermitage.

What is my new desert? The name of it is *compassion*. There is no wilderness so terrible, so beautiful, so arid, and so fruitful as the wilderness of compassion. It is the only desert that shall truly flourish like the lily. It shall become a pool, it shall bud forth and blossom and rejoice with joy. It is in the desert of compassion that the thirsty land turns into springs of water, that the poor possess all things. There are no bounds to contain the inhabitants of this solitude in which I live alone, as isolated as the Host on the altar, the food of all men, belonging to all and belonging to none, for God is with me, and He sits in the ruins of my heart, preaching His Gospel to the poor.

THE JOB IN THE WOODS is this: since October I have been the timber marker. I suddenly found out all about the trees. Next spring I shall presumably be in charge of planting ten thousand seedlings to replace what has been cut down. I started out with my pot of paint in October. The work began on the northeast flank of the lake knob, behind Donohue's place. After that we worked north. I am generally a couple of days' work ahead of the brothers who are after me with chainsaws and axes and that orange army truck and the old jeep. The old jeep is distinguished from the flashy red jeep which some brother postulant brought from Kansas but this "new" jeep is reserved for the novices.

Right now we are in a deep valley I never knew about before. It is between two knobs which do not have names, but one of which has become for me Mount Carmel. I have marked the trees in many different colors. Sometimes white, sometimes slate-blue. I began the year nineteen fifty-two with canary yellow. So all the west side of the smallest knob we see at the east end of our line of knobs is splashed with canary yellow, and it was there, too, that I sang the Epiphany Gospel to the silent glens. *Videntes autem stellam gavisi sunt gaudio magno valde!*

On the whole, the best paint was that casein paint I used on the beech trees and the blighted elms and on the twisted tan oaks along that slope outside the valley, where Frater Caleb brought the novices a couple of times. Frater Caleb the undermaster is one of my scholastics. That was also the place where, just after a lot of timber had been cut down and stacked for loading, and a lot of brush was lying around, a forest fire broke out in November, on the feast of the Dedication of the Church. Brother Gelgan got the jeep in the afternoon and I went out with him and three other brothers and we put out the fire with Indian pumps strapped on our backs. These are very effective—much more so than flapping at the flames with a cedar branch, or scuffing them with pitchforks.

On the feast of the Holy Innocents I took four of the scholastics out on this knob which I secretly call Mount Carmel. It is the finest of all the knobs. It runs north and south behind the lake knob and from the top, which is fairly clear of trees, you can see all over this part of Kentucky—miles of woods over to the northwest, and in the direction of Hanekamp's house and New Haven. Out there somewhere, a few miles on, lies the place where Lincoln was born.

So we took a truck as far as Donohue's. After that we got out and walked to the last cornerstone of our property at the end of the valley, and then climbed the knob. There was a high wind blowing and it was cold but wonderful. And I looked down into the big wide bowl of woods which is McGinty's hollow because somebody called McGinty once had a log cabin there or something. But it is all woods now, and I got lost there exactly a year before, on the feast of the Holy Innocents in 1950.

The more I get to know my scholastics the more reverence I have for their individuality and the more I meet them in my own solitude. The best of them, and the ones to whom I feel closest, are also the most solitary and at the same time the most charitable. All this experience replaces my theories of solitude. I do not need a hermitage, because I have found one where I least expected it. It was when I knew my brothers less well that my thoughts were more involved in them. Now that I know them better, I can see something of the depths of solitude which are in every human person, but which most men do not know how to lay open either to themselves or to others or to God.

The young ones, I admit, do not have half the problems I used to have when I was a scholastic. Their calmness will finally silence all that remains of my own turbulence. They come to me with intelligent questions, or sometimes with an even more intelligent absence of questions. They refresh me with their simplicity. Very spontaneously, they come to share my love of anything I may have discovered, around here, that is simple. But they ignore my persistent interest in theological complications. This is to me both a confusion and an education—to see that they can mostly get along quite well without what I used to think I needed, even though, when I was sane, I realized I did not need it at all.

I say theological complications, not theology. For I constantly preach to them from the encyclicals that they must know theology. Myself, in the afternoons after dinner, I read and love Saint Thomas on a pile of logs beyond the horse pasture where the neighbors come on Sunday afternoons to hunt with shotguns. And there I have discovered that after all what the monks most need is not conferences on mysticism but more light about the ordinary virtues, whether they be faith or prudence, charity or temperance, hope or justice or fortitude. And above all what they need and what they desire is to penetrate the Mystery of Christ and to know Him in His Gospels and in the whole Bible (some of them seem to read nothing else but the Bible).

Thus it is that I live in the trees. I mark them with paint, and the woods cultivate me with their silences, and all day long even in choir and at Mass I seem to be in the forest: but my children themselves are like trees, and they flourish all around me like the things that grow in the Bible.

THE BLUE ELM TREE near at hand and the light blue hills in the distance: the red bare clay where I am supposed to plant some shade trees: these are before me as I sit in the sun for a free half hour between direction and work. Tomorrow is Ash Wednesday and today, as I sit in the sun, big blue and purple fish swim past me in the darkness of my empty mind, this sea which opens within me as soon as I close my eyes. Delightful darkness, delightful sun, shining on a world which, for all I care, has already ended.

It does not occur to me to wonder whether we will ever transplant the young maples from the wood, yonder, to this bare leveled patch—the place where the old horsebarn once stood. It does not occur to me to wonder how everything here came to be transformed. I sit on a cedar log half chewed by some novice's blunt ax, and do not reflect on the plans I have made for this place of prayer, because they do not matter. They will happen when they will happen. The hills are as pure as jade in the distance. God is in His transparent world, but He is too sacred to be mentioned, too holy to be observed. I sit in silence. The big deep fish are purple in my sea.

DIFFERENT LEVELS OF DEPTH.

First, there is the slightly troubled surface of the sea. Here there is action. I make plans. They toss in the wake of other men's traffic: passing liners. I speak to the scholastics. I make resolutions to speak less wildly, to say fewer of the things that surprise myself and them. Where do they spring from?

Second, there is the darkness that comes when I close my eyes. Here is where the big blue, purple, green, and gray fish swim by. Most beautiful and peaceful darkness: is it the cave of my own inner being? In this watercavern I easily live, whenever I wish. Dull rumors only of the world reach me. Sometimes a drowned barrel floats into the room. Big gray-green fish, with silver under their purple scales. Are these the things the blind men see all day? I close my eyes to the sun, and live on the second level, a natural prayer, peace. When I am tired it is almost slumber. There is no sound. Soon even the fish are gone. Night, night. Nothing is happening. If you make a theory about it you end up in quietism. All I say about it is that it is comfortable. It is a rest. I half open my eyes to the sun, praising the Lord of glory. Lo, thus I have returned from the blank abyss, re-entering the shale cities of Genesis. Ferns and fish return. Lovely dark green things. In the depth of the waters, peace, peace, peace. Such is the second level of waters under the sun. We pray therein, slightly waving among the fish.

Words, as I think, do not spring from this second level. They are only meant to drown there.

The question of socialization does not concern these waters. They are nobody's property. Animality. Game preserve. Paradise. No questions whatever perturb their holy botany. Neutral territory. No man's sea.

I think God intended me to write about this second level, however, rather than the first. I abandon all problems to their own unsatisfactory solutions: including the problem of "monastic spirituality." I will not even answer, as I answer the scholastics, that the Desert Fathers talked not about monastic spirituality but about purity of heart and obedience and solitude, and about God. And the wiser of them talked very little about anything. But the divine life which is the life of the soul as the soul is the life of the body: this is a pure and concrete thing and not to be measured by somebody else's books. God in me is not measured by your ascetic theory and God in you is not to be weighed in the scales of my doctrine. Indeed, He is not to be weighed at all.

Third level. Here there is positive life swimming in the rich darkness which is no longer thick like water but pure, like air. Starlight, and you do not know where it is coming from. Moonlight is in this prayer, stillness, waiting for the Redeemer. Walls watching horizons in the middle of the night. *In velamento diei et in luce stellarum nocte.* Everything is charged with intelligence, though all is night. There is no speculation here. There is vigilance; life itself has turned to purity in its own refined depths. Everything is spirit. Here God is adored, His coming is recognized, He is received as soon as He is expected and because He is expected He is received, but He has passed by sooner than He arrived, He was gone before He came. He returned forever. He never yet passed by and already He had disappeared for all eternity. He is and He is not. Everything and Nothing. Not light not dark, not high not low, not this side not that side. Forever and forever. In the wind of His passing the angels cry, "The Holy One is gone." Therefore I lie dead in the air of their wings. Life and night, day and darkness, between life and death. This is the holy cellar of my mortal existence, which opens into the sky.

It is a strange awakening to find the sky inside you and beneath you and above you and all around you so that your spirit is one with the sky, and all is positive night.

Here is where love burns with an innocent flame, the clean desire for death: death without sweetness, without sickness, without commentary, without reference, and without shame. Clean death by the sword of the spirit in which is intelligence. And everything in order. Emergence and deliverance. I think this also is the meaning of Ash Wednesday: mourn man because you are not yet dust. Receive your ashes and rejoice.

Receive, O monk, the holy truth concerning this thing called death. Know that there is in each man a deep will, potentially committed to freedom or captivity, ready to consent to life, born consenting to death, turned inside out, swallowed by its own self, prisoner of itself like Jonas in the whale.

This is the truth of death which, printed in the heart of every man, leads him to look for the sign of Jonas the prophet. But many have gone into hell crying out that they had expected the resurrection of the dead. Others, in turn, were baptized and delivered: but their powers remained asleep in the dark and in the bosom of the depths.

Many of the men baptized in Christ have risen from the depths without troubling to find out the difference between Jonas and the whale.

It is the whale we cherish. Jonas swims abandoned in the heart of the sea. But it is the whale that must die. Jonas is immortal. If we do not remember to distinguish between them, and if we prefer the whale and do not take Jonas out of the ocean, the inevitable will come to pass.

The whale and the prophet will soon come around and meet again in their wanderings, and once again the whale will swallow the prophet. Life will be swallowed again in death and its last state will be worse than the first.

We must get Jonas out of the whale and the whale must die at a time when Jonas is in the clear, busy with his orisons, clothed and in his right mind, free, holy, and walking on the shore. Such is the meaning of the desire for death that comes in the sane night, the peace that finds us for a moment in clarity, walking by the light of the stars, raised to God's connatural shore, dryshod in the heavenly country, in a rare moment of intelligence.

But even if we are not always intelligent, we must inevitably die.

I pursue this thought no further. It came to me because Frater John of God got a lot of kids' pictures from a sister in a school somewhere in Milwaukee. The pictures were supposed to be by backward children. Backward nothing. Most of them were of Jonas in or near the whale. They are the only real works of art I have seen in ten years, since entering Gethsemani. But it occurred to me that these wise children were drawing pictures of their own lives. They knew what was in their own depths. They were putting it all down on paper before they had a chance to grow up and forget. They were proving better than any apologist that there is something in the very nature of man that expects a Redeemer and resurrection from the dead. The sign of Jonas is written in our being. No wonder that this should be so when all creation is a vestige of the Creator but also contains, written everywhere, in symbols, the economy of our Redemption.

IT IS JUNE. On Pentecost Sunday it is my turn again to take my week as hebdomadary and sing the Conventual Mass. Then I am deacon the next week, when Corpus Christi comes. Once again, the cloister is paved with flowers, the sanctuary white-hot under the floodlights concealed behind the pillars, high in the ceiling. You look up at the monstrance through a cloud of hot, sweet smoke from the censer, and the sweat runs down into your eyes! I feel as though I had never been anywhere in the world except Gethsemani—as if there were no other place in the world where I had ever really lived. I do not say I love Gethsemani in spite of the heat, or because of the heat. I love Gethsemani: that means burning days and nights in summer, with the sun beating down on the metal roof and the psalms pulsing exultantly through the airless choir, while, row upon row of us, a hundred and forty singers, we sway forward and bow down. And the clouds of smoke go up to God in the sanctuary, and the novices get thin and go home forever.

On two sides of us the new buildings are complete. Half factory and half a Venetian palace, the new "garden house" with the cheese factory in the cellar and the brothers' novitiate on the roof rises enormous over the cabbages in the garden. Then on the other side, half veiled behind the trees, the slick new yellow guesthouse is full of priests from Evansville who have been coming here on retreat, in shifts, week by week all June. I looked at their namecards where they vested in the sacristy and wondered who these Fathers were: old Fathers and young Fathers, Father Hut, Father Mattingly, Father Pfau. And right at the place where our Father Raymond is vesting for the Mass *pro defunctis,* this week, they have a card for a Father Flanagan, of the Evansville retreat. Now this is very funny, but of course you, reader, do not understand why it is funny because you do not know that Father Raymond's last name is also Flanagan.

Meanwhile there is supposed to be *another* new building. This time it will have to be an infirmary. And when Dom Gabriel Sortais (he is our new Abbot General) came back again last month and made another Visitation, he told us to make rooms opening on the infirmary chapel so that the partition can be rolled back and the very sick monks, the dying monks, can hear Mass from their beds. I do not stop to ask myself if I shall die in such a bed, or in any bed at all. It means another year of cement mixers and air compressors in the yard outside this window, where I no longer have time to write books and where my spiritual children come to talk about God. But if the cement mixers mean that someone who is dying can hear Mass in bed it is all right with me.

This week I am the third hebdomadary, which means it is my turn to say the brothers' Communion Mass, Our Lady's Mass. It is always a votive Mass of the Blessed Virgin, always the same. I like it that way. In the summertime, this Mass is said at three o'clock in the morning. So I leave the choir after morning meditation to go and say it while the rest of the monks recite Matins and Lauds. I generally finish the brothers' Communions by the end of the second nocturn, and then go off into the back sacristy and kneel in the dark behind the relic case next to Saint Malachy's altar, while the sky grows pale outside over the forest, and a little cool air seeps in through the slats of the broken shutters. The birds sing, and the crickets sing, and one priest is silent with God.

As soon as the morning angelus rings, I go out into the new day, my own new private dawn, which belongs to me alone. The other priests are now saying their Masses. The novices and scholastics are getting ready for Communion and the brothers are peeling potatoes in the workroom or slinging milkcans around the tile floor of the new dairy.

I walk out and have the dawn to myself. I have almost two hours to pray or read or think by myself and make up the Night Office. I am all alone in the cool world of morning, with the birds and the blue hill and the herd that lows across the fields in our neighbor's pasture, and the rooster that sings *sol-do* in the coop behind the apple trees, and Aidan Nally growling at a team of mules on the side of his hill over yonder.

Already I am hoping that it will be somewhat the same one day next week, on the feast of Saint John the Baptist, when I will say Mass late, and consequently have this same long interval to myself, in the blue, wide-open, lonely morning. On that day Frater Caleb's family are coming from St. Louis and he wants me to say Mass for them, and thus I will give Communion to his little sister Mary Ann who just made her First Communion and who thinks she wants to be either a policewoman or a Carmelite when she grows up.

How lovely are thy tabernacles, O Lord of hosts! The sparrow hath found herself a house and the turtle dove a nest for herself where she may lay her little ones!

This is the land where you have given me roots in eternity, O God of heaven and earth. This is the burning promised land, the house of God, the gate of heaven, the place of peace, the place of silence, the place of wrestling with the angel. Each tomato patch is named after a saint. And the tomatoes called *"St. Benedict, ora pro nobis"* are under the care of Rod Mudge who came down with Dan Walsh to my ordination. A year later he came back as a novice and soon expects to make profession.

Blessed are they who dwell in thy house, O Lord! They shall praise thee for ever and ever.

The roof is peeling off the old garden house, which has become a rejected building. One of the pillars of the old wagon shed has been knocked down by a tractor. There will be a new metal hangar for all the machines. This corner of the farm, where the old horsebarn used to be, is the desert that has been given to me for the planting of shade trees, that it may some day be a place of contemplation. *Altaria tua, Domine virtutum!*

Down there, the young bulls still sleep behind the single strand of their electric fence.

It is four o'clock in the morning.

[1] "My strength has burned up like a potsherd" (Psalm 21:16).

[2] My heart is troubled within me: and the fear of death is fallen upon me.
Fear and trembling are come upon me: and darkness hath covered me.
And I said: who will give me wings like a dove, and I will fly and be at rest?
Lo, I have gone far off, flying away; and I abode in the wilderness.
I waited for Him that hath saved me from pusillanimity of spirit and a storm.

THE SIGN OF JONAS

Epilogue: FIRE WATCH, JULY 4, 1952

Watchman, what of the night?

The night, O My Lord, is a time of freedom. You have seen the morning and the night, and the night was better. In the night all things began, and in the night the end of all things has come before me.

Baptized in the rivers of night, Gethsemani has recovered her innocence. Darkness brings a semblance of order before all things disappear. With the clock slung over my shoulder, in the silence of the Fourth of July, it is my time to be the night watchman, in the house that will one day perish.

Here is the way it is when I go on the fire watch:

Before eight o'clock the monks are packed in the belly of the great heat, singing to the Mother of God like exiles sailing to their slavery, hoping for glory. The night angelus unlocks the church and sets them free. The holy monster which is The Community divides itself into segments and disperses through airless cloisters where yellow lamps do not attract the bugs.

The watchman's clock together with the watchman's sneakers are kept in a box, together with a flashlight and the keys to various places, at the foot of the infirmary stairs.

Rumors behind me and above me and around me signalize the fathers going severally to bed in different dormitories. Where there is cold water some stay to drink from celluloid cups. Thus we fight the heat. I take the heavy clock and sling it on its strap over my shoulder. I walk to the nearest window, on my silent feet. I recite the second nocturn of Saturday, sitting outside the window in the dark garden, and the house begins to be silent.

One late Father, with a change of dry clothes slung over his shoulder, stops to look out the window and pretends to be frightened when he sees me sitting around the corner in the dark, holding the breviary in the yellow light of the window, saying the Psalms of Saturday.

It is ten or fifteen minutes before there are no more feet echoing along the cloisters, shuffling up the stairs. (When you go late to the dormitories you have to take off your shoes and make your way to bed in socks, as if the others were already sleeping in such weather!)

At eight-fifteen I sit in darkness. I sit in human silence. Then I begin to hear the eloquent night, the night of wet trees, with moonlight sliding over the shoulder of the church in a haze of dampness and subsiding heat. The world of this night resounds from heaven to hell with animal eloquence, with the savage innocence of a million unknown creatures. While the earth eases and cools off like a huge wet living thing, the enormous vitality of their music pounds and rings and throbs and echoes until it gets into everything, and swamps the whole world in its neutral madness which never becomes an orgy because all things are innocent, all things are pure. Nor would I have mentioned the possibility of evil, except that I remember how the heat and the wild music of living things can drive people crazy, when they are not in monasteries, and make them do things which the world has forgotten how to lament. That is why some people act as if the night and the forest and the heat and the animals had in them something of contagion, whereas the heat is holy and the animals are the children of God, and the night was never made to hide sin, but only to open infinite distances to charity and send our souls to play beyond the stars.

Eight-thirty. I begin my round, in the cellar of the south wing. The place is full of naked wires, stinks of the hides of slaughtered calves. My feet are walking on a floor of earth, down a long catacomb, at the end of which there is a brand-new locked door into the guest wing that was only finished the other day. So I punch the clock for the first time in the catacomb, I turn my back on the new wing, and the fire watch is on.

Around one corner is a hole in the wall with a vat where they stew fruit. Under this vat Dom Frederic told me to burn all the letters that were in the pigeonholes of the room where he had been Prior. Around another corner is an old furnace where I burned the rest of the papers from the same room. In this musty silence which no longer smells of wine (because the winery is now in another building) the flashlight creates a little alert tennis ball upon the walls and floor. Concrete now begins under the watchman's catfeet and moonlight reaches through the windows into a dark place with jars of prunes and applesauce on all the shelves.

Then suddenly, after the old brooding catacomb, you hit something dizzy and new: the kitchen, painted by the brother novices, each wall in a different color. Some of the monks complained of the different colored walls, but a watchman has no opinions. There is tile under the shining vats and Scripture close to the ceiling: "Little children, love one another!"

There are blue benches in the scullery, and this one room is cool. Sometimes when you go up the stairs making no noise, a brother comes in late from the barns through the kitchen door and runs into you by surprise in the darkness, blinded by the flashlight, and (if a novice) he is probably scared to death.

For a few feet, the way is most familiar. I am in the little cloister which is the monastery's main stem. It goes from the places where the monks live to the places where they pray. But now it is empty, and like everything else it is a lot nicer when there is nobody there. The steps down to the tailor shop have a different sound. They drum under my rubber soles. I run into the smell of duck and cotton, mixed with the smell of bread. There is light in the bakery, and someone is working late, around the corner, behind the oven. I punch the clock by the bakery door: it is the second station.

The third station is the hottest one: the furnace room. This time the stairs don't drum, they ring: they are iron. I fight my way through a jungle of wet clothes, drying in the heat, and go down by the flanks of the boiler to the third station which is there up against the bricks, beneath an engraving of the Holy Face.

After that, I am in the choir novitiate. Here, too, it is hot. The place is swept and recently painted and there are notice boards at every turn in the little crooked passageways where each blue door is named after a saint. Long lists of appointments for the novices' confessions and direction. Sentences from the liturgy. Fragments of severe and necessary information. But the walls of the building have their own stuffy smell and I am suddenly haunted by my first days in religion, the freezing tough winter when I first received the habit and always had a cold, the smell of frozen straw in the dormitory under the chapel, and the deep unexpected ecstasy of Christmas—that first Christmas when you have nothing left in the world but God!

It is when you hit the novitiate that the fire watch begins in earnest. Alone, silent, wandering on your appointed rounds through the corridors of a huge, sleeping monastery, you come around the corner and find yourself face to face with your monastic past and with the mystery of your vocation.

The fire watch is an examination of conscience in which your task as watchman suddenly appears in its true light: a pretext devised by God to isolate you, and to search your soul with lamps and questions, in the heart of darkness.

GOD, MY GOD, God Whom I meet in darkness, with You it is always the same thing! Always the same question that nobody knows how to answer!

I have prayed to You in the daytime with thoughts and reasons, and in the nighttime You have confronted me, scattering thought and reason. I have come to You in the morning with light and with desire, and You have descended upon me, with great gentleness, with most forbearing silence, in this inexplicable night, dispersing light, defeating all desire. I have explained to You a hundred times my motives for entering the monastery and You have listened and said nothing, and I have turned away and wept with shame.

Is it true that all my motives have meant nothing? Is it true that all my desires were an illusion?

While I am asking questions which You do not answer, You ask me a question which is so simple that I cannot answer. I do not even understand the question.

This night, and every night, it is the same question.

There is a special, living resonance in these steep hollow stairs to the novitiate chapel, where You are all alone, the windows closed tight upon You, shutting You up with the heat of the lost afternoon.

Here, when it was winter, I used to come after dinner when I was a novice, heavy with sleep and with potatoes, and kneel all the time because that was the only period in which we were allowed to do what we liked. Nothing ever happened: but that was what I liked.

Here, on Sunday mornings, a crowd of us would try to make the Way of the Cross, jostling one another among the benches, and on days of recollection in summer we would kneel here all afternoon with the sweat running down our ribs, while candles burned all around the tabernacle and the veiled ciborium stood shyly in the doorway, peeping out at us between the curtains.

And here, now, by night, with this huge clock ticking on my right hip and the flashlight in my hand and sneakers on my feet, I feel as if everything had been unreal. It is as if the past had never existed. The things I thought were so important—because of the effort I put into them—have turned out to be of small value. And the things I never thought about, the things I was never able either to measure or to expect, were the things that mattered.

(There used to be a man who walked down the back road singing, on summer mornings, right in the middle of the novices' thanksgiving after Communion: singing his own private song, every day the same. It was the sort of song you would expect to hear out in the country, in the Knobs of Kentucky.)

But in this darkness I would not be able to say, for certain, what it was that mattered. That, perhaps, is part of Your unanswerable question! Only I remember the heat in the beanfield the first June I was here, and I get the same sense of a mysterious, unsuspected value that struck me after Father Alberic's funeral.

AFTER THE NOVITIATE, I come back into the little cloister. Soon I stand at the coolest station: down in the brothers' washroom, at the door of the ceramic studio. Cool winds come in from the forest through the big, wide-open windows.

This is a different city, with a different set of associations. The ceramic studio is something relatively new. Behind the door (where they burnt out one kiln and bought a new one) little Father John of God suddenly made a good crucifix, just a week ago. He is one of my scholastics. And I think of the clay Christ that came out of his heart. I think of the beauty and the simplicity and the pathos that were sleeping there, waiting to become an image. I think of this simple and mysterious child, and of all my other scholastics. What is waiting to be born in all their hearts? Suffering? Deception? Heroism? Defeat? Peace? Betrayal? Sanctity? Death? Glory?

On all sides I am confronted by questions that I cannot answer, because the time for answering them has not yet come. Between the silence of God and the silence of my own soul, stands the silence of the souls entrusted to me. Immersed in these three silences, I realize that the questions I ask myself about them are perhaps no more than a surmise. And perhaps the most urgent and practical renunciation is the renunciation of all questions.

THE MOST POIGNANT THING about the fire watch is that you go through Gethsemani not only in length and height, but also in depth. You hit strange caverns in the monastery's history, layers set down by the years, geological strata: you feel like an archeologist suddenly unearthing ancient civilizations. But the terrible thing is that you yourself have lived through those ancient civilizations. The house has changed so much that ten years have as many different meanings as ten Egyptian dynasties. The meanings are hidden in the walls. They mumble in the floor under the watchman's rubber feet. The lowest layer is at once in the catacomb under the south wing and in the church tower. Every other level of history is found in between.

The church. In spite of the stillness, the huge place seems alive. Shadows move everywhere, around the small uncertain area of light which the sanctuary light casts on the Gospel side of the altar. There are faint sounds in the darkness, the empty choirstalls creak and hidden boards mysteriously sigh.

The silence of the sacristy has its own sound. I shoot the beam of light down to Saint Malachy's altar and the relic cases. Vestments are laid out for my Mass tomorrow, at Our Lady of Victories altar. Keys rattle again in the door and the rattle echoes all over the church. When I was first on for the fire watch I thought the church was full of people praying in the dark. But no. The night is filled with unutterable murmurs, the walls with traveling noises which seem to wake up and come back, hours after something has happened, to gibber at the places where it happened.

This nearness to You in the darkness is too simple and too close for excitement. It is commonplace for all things to live an unexpected life in the nighttime: but their life is illusory and unreal. The illusion of sound only intensifies the infinite substance of Your silence.

Here, in this place where I made my vows, where I had my hands anointed for the Holy Sacrifice, where I have had Your priesthood seal the depth and intimate summit of my being, a word, a thought, would defile the quiet of Your inexplicable love.

Your Reality, O God, speaks to my life as to an intimate, in the midst of a crowd of fictions: I mean these walls, this roof, these arches, this (overhead) ridiculously large and unsubstantial tower.

Lord, God, the whole world tonight seems to be made out of paper. The most substantial things are ready to crumble or tear apart and blow away.

How much more so this monastery which everybody believes in and which has perhaps already ceased to exist!

O God, my God, the night has values that day has never dreamed of. All things stir by night, waking or sleeping, conscious of the nearness of their ruin. Only man makes himself illuminations he conceives to be solid and eternal. But while we ask our questions and come to our decisions, God blows our decisions out, the roofs of our houses cave in upon us, the tall towers are undermined by ants, the walls crack and cave in, and the holiest buildings burn to ashes while the watchman is composing a theory of duration.

NOW IS THE TIME to get up and go to the tower. Now is the time to meet You, God, where the night is wonderful, where the roof is almost without substance under my feet, where all the mysterious junk in the belfry considers the proximate coming of three new bells, where the forest opens out under the moon and the living things sing terribly that only the present is eternal and that all things having a past and a future are doomed to pass away!

This, then, is the way from the floor of the church to the platform on the tower.

First I must make a full round of the house on the second floor. Then I must go to the third-floor dormitories. After that, the tower.

Cloister. Soft feet, total darkness. The brothers have torn up the tent in the cloister garden, where the novices were sleeping two winters ago, and where some of them got pneumonia.

Just yesterday they put a new door on Father Abbot's room, while he was away with Dom Gabriel, visiting the foundations.

I am in the corridor under the old guesthouse. In the middle of the hallway a long table is set with knives and forks and spoons and bowls for the breakfast of the postulants and family brothers. Three times a day they eat in the corridor. For two years there has been no other place to put them.

THE HIGH, LIGHT DOOR into the old guestwing swings back and I am on the stairs.

I had forgotten that the upper floors were empty. The silence astonishes me. The last time I was on the fire watch there was a retreat party of fifty lined up on the second floor, signing their names in the guest register in the middle of the night. They had just arrived in a bus from Notre Dame. Now the place is absolutely empty. All the notices are off the walls. The bookshelf has vanished from the hall. The population of holy statues has been diminished. All the windows are wide open. Moonlight falls on the cool linoleum floor. The doors of some of the rooms are open and I see that they are empty. I can feel the emptiness of all the rest.

I would like to stop and stand here for an hour, just to feel the difference. The house is like a sick person who has recovered. This is the Gethsemani that I entered, and whose existence I had almost forgotten. It was this silence, this darkness, this emptiness that I walked into with Brother Matthew eleven years ago this spring. This is the house that seemed to have been built to be remote from everything, to have forgotten all cities, to be absorbed in the eternal years. But this recovered innocence has nothing reassuring about it. The very silence is a reproach. The emptiness itself is my most terrible question.

If I have broken this silence, and if I have been to blame for talking so much about this emptiness that it came to be filled with people, who am I to praise the silence any more? Who am I to publicize this emptiness? Who am I to remark on the presence of so many visitors, so many retreatants, so many postulants, so many tourists? Or have the men of our age acquired a Midas touch of their own, so that as soon as they succeed, everything they touch becomes crowded with people?

In this age of crowds in which I have determined to be solitary, perhaps the greatest sin would be to lament the presence of people on the threshold of my solitude. Can I be so blind as to ignore that solitude is itself their greatest need? And yet if they rush in upon the desert in thousands, how shall they be alone? What went they out into the desert to see? Whom did I myself come here to find but You, O Christ, Who have compassion on the multitudes?

Nevertheless, Your compassion singles out and separates the one on whom Your mercy falls, and sets him apart from the multitudes even though You leave him in the midst of the multitudes. . . .

With my feet on the floor I waxed when I was a postulant, I ask these useless questions. With my hand on the key by the door to the tribune, where I first heard the monks chanting the psalms, I do not wait for an answer, because I have begun to realize You never answer when I expect.

The third room of the library is called hell. It is divided up by wallboard partitions into four small sections full of condemned books. The partitions are hung with American flags and pictures of Dom Edmond Obrecht. I thread my way through this unbelievable maze to the second room of the library, where the retreatants used to sit and mop their brows and listen to sermons. I do not have to look at the corner where the books about the Carthusians once sang to me their siren song as I sail past with clock ticking and light swinging and keys in my hand to unlock the door into the first room of the library. Here the scholastics have their desks. This is the upper Scriptorium. The theology books are all around the walls. Yonder is the broken cuckoo clock which Father Willibrod winds up each morning with a gesture of defiance, just before he flings open the windows.

Perhaps the dormitory of the choir monks is the longest room in Kentucky. Long lines of cubicles, with thin partitions a little over six feet high, shirts and robes and scapulars hang over the partitions trying to dry in the night air. Extra cells have been jammed along the walls between the windows. In each one lies a monk on a straw mattress. One pale bulb burns in the middle of the room. The ends are shrouded in shadows. I make my way softly past cell after cell. I know which cells have snorers in them. But no one seems to be asleep in this extraordinary tenement. I walk as softly as I can down to the far west end, where Frater Caleb sleeps in the bell-ringer's corner. I find my station inside the door of the organ loft, and punch the clock, and start off again on soft feet along the other side of the dormitory.

There is a door hidden between two cells. It leads into the infirmary annex, where the snoring is already in full swing. Beyond that, steep stairs to the third floor.

One more assignment before I can climb them. The infirmary, with its hot square little chapel, the room that contains the retreats I made before all the dates in my monastic life: clothing, professions, ordinations. I cannot pass it without something unutterable coming up out of the depths of my being. It is the silence which will lift me on to the tower.

Meanwhile I punch the clock at the next station, at the dentist's office, where next week I am to lose another molar.

NOW THE BUSINESS IS DONE. Now I shall ascend to the top of this religious city, leaving its modern history behind. These stairs climb back beyond the civil war. I make no account of the long laybrothers' dormitory where a blue light burns. I hasten to the corridor by the wardrobe. I look out the low windows and know that I am already higher than the trees. Down at the end is the doorway to the attic and the tower.

The padlock always makes a great noise. The door swings back on swearing hinges and the night wind, hot and gusty, comes swirling down out of the loft with a smell of ancient rafters and old, hidden, dusty things. You have to watch the third step or your feet go through the boards. From here on the building has no substance left, but you have to mind your head and bow beneath the beams on which you can see the marks of the axes which our French Fathers used to hew them out a hundred years ago. . . .

And now the hollowness that rings under my feet measures some sixty feet to the floor of the church. I am over the transept crossing. If I climb around the corner of the dome I can find a hole once opened by the photographers and peer down into the abyss, and flash the light far down upon my stall in choir.

I climb the trembling, twisted stair into the belfry. The darkness stirs with a flurry of wings high above me in the gloomy engineering that holds the steeple together. Nearer at hand the old clock ticks in the tower. I flash the light into the mystery which keeps it going, and gaze upon the ancient bells.

I have seen the fuse box. I have looked in the corners where I think there is some wiring. I am satisfied that there is no fire in this tower which would flare like a great torch and take the whole abbey up with it in twenty minutes. . . .

AND NOW MY WHOLE BEING breathes the wind which blows through the belfry, and my hand is on the door through which I see the heavens. The door swings out upon a vast sea of darkness and of prayer. Will it come like this, the moment of my death? Will You open a door upon the great forest and set my feet upon a ladder under the moon, and take me out among the stars?

The roof glistens under my feet, this long metal roof facing the forest and the hills, where I stand higher than the treetops and walk upon shining air.

Mists of damp heat rise up out of the fields around the sleeping abbey. The whole valley is flooded with moonlight and I can count the southern hills beyond the water tank, and almost number the trees of the forest to the north. Now the huge chorus of living beings rises up out of the world beneath my feet: life singing in the watercourses, throbbing in the creeks and the fields and the trees, choirs of millions and millions of jumping and flying and creeping things. And far above me the cool sky opens upon the frozen distance of the stars.

I lay the clock upon the belfry ledge and pray cross-legged with my back against the tower, and face the same unanswered question.

Lord God of this great night: Do You see the woods? Do You hear the rumor of their loneliness? Do You behold their secrecy? Do You remember their solitudes? Do You see that my soul is beginning to dissolve like wax within me?

Clamabo per diem et non exaudies, et nocte et non ad insipientiam mihi!

Do You remember the place by the stream? Do You remember the top of the Vineyard Knob that time in autumn, when the train was in the valley? Do You remember McGinty's hollow? Do You remember the thinly wooded hillside behind Hanekamp's place? Do You remember the time of the forest fire? Do You know what has become of the little poplars we planted in the spring? Do You observe the valley where I marked the trees?

There is no leaf that is not in Your care. There is no cry that was not heard by You before it was uttered. There is no water in the shales that was not hidden there by Your wisdom. There is no concealed spring that was not concealed by You. There is no glen for a lone house that was not planned by You for a lone house. There is no man for that acre of woods that was not made by You for that acre of woods.

But there is greater comfort in the substance of silence than in the answer to a question. Eternity is in the present. Eternity is in the palm of the hand. Eternity is a seed of fire, whose sudden roots break barriers that keep my heart from being an abyss.

The things of Time are in connivance with eternity. The shadows serve You. The beasts sing to You before they pass away. The solid hills shall vanish like a worn-out garment. All things change, and die and disappear. Questions arrive, assume their actuality, and also disappear. In this hour I shall cease to ask them, and silence shall be my answer. The world that Your love created, that the heat has distorted, and that my mind is always misinterpreting, shall cease to interfere with our voices.

Minds which are separated pretend to blend in one another's language. The marriage of souls in concepts is mostly an illusion. Thoughts which travel outward bring back reports of You from outward things: but a dialogue with You, uttered through the world, always ends by being a dialogue with my own reflection in the stream of time. With You there is no dialogue unless You choose a mountain and circle it with cloud and print Your words in fire upon the mind of Moses. What was delivered to Moses on tables of stone, as the fruit of lightning and thunder, is now more thoroughly born in our own souls as quietly as the breath of our own being.

The hand lies open. The heart is dumb. The soul that held my substance together, like a hard gem in the hollow of my own power, will one day totally give in.

Although I see the stars, I no longer pretend to know them. Although I have walked in those woods, how can I claim to love them? One by one I shall forget the names of individual things.

You, Who sleep in my breast, are not met with words, but in the emergence of life within life and of wisdom within wisdom. You are found in communion: Thou in me and I in Thee and Thou in them and they in me: dispossession within dispossession, dispassion within dispassion, emptiness within emptiness, freedom within freedom. I am alone. Thou art alone. The Father and I are One.

THE VOICE OF GOD is heard in Paradise:

"What was vile has become precious. What is now precious was never vile. I have always known the vile as precious: for what is vile I know not at all.

"What was cruel has become merciful. What is now merciful was never cruel. I have always overshadowed Jonas with My mercy, and cruelty I know not at all. Have you had sight of Me, Jonas My child? Mercy within mercy within mercy. I have forgiven the universe without end, because I have never known sin.

"What was poor has become infinite. What is infinite was never poor. I have always known poverty as infinite: riches I love not at all. Prisons within prisons within prisons. Do not lay up for yourselves ecstasies upon earth, where time and space corrupt, where the minutes break in and steal. No more lay hold on time, Jonas, My son, lest the rivers bear you away.

"What was fragile has become powerful. I loved what was most frail. I looked upon what was nothing. I touched what was without substance, and within what was not, I am."

THERE ARE DROPS of dew that show like sapphires in the grass as soon as the great sun appears, and leaves stir behind the hushed flight of an escaping dove.

THE SIGN OF JONAS

PART FOUR

Mentors
and
Doctrines

Now the explanation had been ended
  by the high teacher, and he was observing
  my face, to see if I seemed contented;
and I, who felt still a new thirst's urging,
  was silent outwardly, within me thought:
  "Perhaps too many questions are a burden."

One: WILLIAM BLAKE

ALTHOUGH the *Songs of Innocence* look like children's poems, and almost seem to have been written for children, they are, to most children, incomprehensible. Or at least, they were so to me when I was ten. Perhaps if I had read them when I was four or five, it would have been different. But when I was ten, I knew too much. I knew that tigers did not burn in the forests of the night. Children are very literal-minded.

I was less literal when I was sixteen. I could accept Blake's metaphors and they already began to astound and to move me, although I had no real grasp of their depth and power. I liked Blake immensely. I read him with more patience and attention than any other poet. I thought about him more. And I could not figure him out. I do not mean, I could not figure out the Prophetic Books—nobody can do that! But I could not place him in context, and I did not know how to make his ideas fit together.

One gray Sunday in the spring, I walked alone out of the Brooke Road and up Brooke Hill, where the rifle range was. It was a long, bare hogback of a hill, with a few lone trees along the top, and it commanded a big sweeping view of the Vale of Catmos, with the town of Oakham lying in the midst of it, gathered around the gray, sharp church spire. I sat on a stile on the hilltop, and contemplated the wide vale, from the north, where the kennels of the Cottesmore hounds were, to Lax Hill and Manton in the south. Straight across was Burley House, on top of its hill, massed with woods. At my feet, a few red brick houses straggled out from the town to the bottom of the slope.

I reflected, that afternoon, upon Blake. I remember how I concentrated and applied myself to it. It was rare that I ever really thought about such a thing of my own accord. I was trying to establish what manner of man he was. Where did he stand? What did he believe? What did he preach?

On one hand he spoke of the "priests in black gowns who were going their rounds binding with briars my joys and desires." And yet on the other hand he detested Voltaire, Rousseau, and everybody like them and everything that they stood for, and he abominated all materialistic deism, and all the polite, abstract natural religions of the eighteenth century, the agnosticism of the nineteenth, and, in fact, most of the common attitudes of our day.

> The atoms of Democritus
> And Newton's particles of light
> Are sands upon the Red-Sea shore
> Where Israel's tents do shine so bright. . . .

I was absolutely incapable of reconciling, in my mind, two things that seemed so contrary. Blake was a revolutionary, and yet he detested the most typical revolutionaries of his time, and declared himself opposed without compromise to people who, as I thought, seemed to exemplify some of his own most characteristic ideals.

How incapable I was of understanding anything like the ideals of a William Blake! How could I possibly realize that his rebellion, for all its strange heterodoxies, was fundamentally the rebellion of the saints. It was the rebellion of the lover of the living God, the rebellion of one whose desire of God was so intense and irresistible that it condemned, with all its might, all the hypocrisy and petty sensuality and skepticism and materialism which cold and trivial minds set up as unpassable barriers between God and the souls of men.

The priests that he saw going their rounds in black gowns—he knew no Catholics at the time, and had probably never even seen a Catholic priest—were symbols, in his mind, of the weak, compromising, pharisaic piety of those whose god was nothing but an objectification of their own narrow and conventional desires and hypocritical fears.

He did not distinguish any particular religion or sect as the objects of his disdain: he simply could not stand false piety and religiosity, in which the love of God was stamped out of the souls of men by formalism and conventions, without any charity, without the light and life of a faith that brings man face to face with God. If on one page of Blake these priests in black gowns were frightening and hostile figures, on another, the "Grey Monk of Charlemaine" was a saint and a hero of charity and of faith, fighting for the peace of the true God with all the ardent love that was the only reality Blake lived for. Toward the end of his life, Blake told his friend Samuel Palmer that the Catholic Church was the only one that taught the love of God.

II

PERHAPS ALL THE GREAT ROMANTICS were capable of putting words together more sensibly than Blake, and yet he, with all his mistakes of spelling, turned out the greater poet, because his was the deeper and more solid inspiration. He wrote better poetry when he was twelve than Shelley wrote in his whole life. And it was because at twelve he had already seen, I think, Elias, standing under a tree in the fields south of London.

It was Blake's problem to try and adjust himself to a society that understood neither him nor his kind of faith and love. More than once, smug and inferior minds conceived it to be their duty to take this man Blake in hand and direct and form him, to try and canalize what they recognized as "talent" in some kind of a conventional channel. And always this meant the cold and heartless disparagement of all that was vital and real to him in art and in faith. There were years of all kinds of petty persecution, from many different quarters, until finally Blake parted from his would-be patrons, and gave up all hope of an alliance with a world that thought he was crazy, and went his own way.

It was when he did this, and settled down as an engraver for good, that the Prophetic Books were no longer necessary. In the latter part of his life, having discovered Dante, he came in contact, through him, with Catholicism, which he described as the only religion that really taught the love of God, and his last years were relatively full of peace. He never seems to have felt any desire to hunt out a priest in the England where Catholicism was still practically outlawed: but he died with a blazing face and great songs of joy bursting from his heart.

As Blake worked himself into my system, I became more and more conscious of the necessity of a vital faith, and the total unreality and unsubstantiality of the dead, selfish rationalism which had been freezing my mind and will for the last seven years. By the time the summer was over, I was to become conscious of the fact that the only way to live was to live in a world that was charged with the presence and reality of God.

To say that, is to say a great deal: and I don't want to say it in a way that conveys more than the truth. I will have to limit the statement by saying that it was still, for me, more an intellectual realization than anything else: and it had not yet struck down into the roots of my will. The life of the soul is not knowledge, it is love, since love is the act of the supreme faculty, the will, by which man is formally united to the final end of all his strivings—by which man becomes one with God.

THE SEVEN STOREY MOUNTAIN

Two: BRAMACHARI

On THE DOOR of the room in one of the dormitories, where Lax and Sy Freedgood were living in a state of chaos, was a large gray picture, a lithograph print. Its subject was a man, a Hindu, with wide-open eyes and a rather frightened expression, sitting cross-legged in white garments. I asked about it, and I could not figure out whether the answer was derisive or respectful. Lax said someone had thrown a knife at the picture and the knife had bounced back and nearly cut all their heads off. In other words, he gave me to understand that the picture had something intrinsically holy about it: that accounted for the respect and derision manifested toward it by all my friends. This mixture was their standard acknowledgment of the supernatural, or what was considered to be supernatural. How that picture happened to get on that door in that room is a strange story.

It represented a Hindu messiah, a savior sent to India in our own times, called Jagad-Bondhu. His mission had to do with universal peace and brotherhood. He had died not very long before, and had left a strong following in India. He was, as it were, in the role of a saint who had founded a new religious order, although he was considered more than a saint: he was the latest incarnation of the godhead, according to the Hindu belief in a multiplicity of incarnations.

In 1932 a big official sort of letter was delivered to one of the monasteries of this new "order," outside of Calcutta. The letter came from the Chicago World's Fair, which was to be held in the following year. How they ever heard of this monastery, I cannot imagine. The letter was a formal announcement of a "World Congress of Religions." I am writing this all from memory but that is the substance of the story: they invited the abbot of this monastery to send a representative to the congress.

I get this picture of the monastery: it is called Sri Angan, meaning "the playground." It consists of an enclosure and many huts or "cells," to use an Occidental term. The monks are quiet, simple men. They live what we would call a liturgical life, very closely integrated with the cycle of the seasons and of nature: in fact, the chief characteristic of their worship seems to be this deep, harmonious identification with all living things, in praising God. Their praise itself is expressed in songs, accompanied by drums and primitive instruments, flutes, pipes. There is much ceremonial dancing. In addition to that, there is a profound stress laid on a form of "mental prayer" which is largely contemplative. The monk works himself into it, by softly chanting lyrical aspirations to God and then remains in peaceful absorption in the Absolute.

For the rest, their life is extremely primitive and frugal. It is not so much what we would call austere. I do not think there are any fierce penances or mortifications. But nevertheless, the general level of poverty in Hindu society as a whole imposes on these monks a standard of living which most Occidental religious would probably find unlivable. Their clothes consist of a turban and something thrown around the body and a robe. No shoes. Perhaps the robe is only for traveling. Their food —some rice, a few vegetables, a piece of fruit.

Of all that they do, they attach most importance to prayer, to praising God. They have a well-developed sense of the power and efficacy of prayer, based on a keen realization of the goodness of God. Their whole spirituality is childlike, simple, primitive if you like, close to nature, ingenuous, optimistic, happy. But the point is, although it may be no more than the full flowering of the natural virtue of religion, with the other natural virtues, including a powerful natural charity, still the life of these pagan monks is one of such purity and holiness and peace, in the natural order, that it may put to shame the actual conduct of many Christian religious, in spite of their advantages of constant access to all the means of grace.

So this was the atmosphere into which the letter from Chicago dropped like a heavy stone. The abbot was pleased by the letter. He did not know what the Chicago World's Fair was. He did not understand that all these things were simply schemes for accumulating money. The "World Congress of Religions" appeared to him as something more than the fatuous scheme of a few restless, though probably sincere, minds. He seemed to see in it the first step toward the realization of the hopes of their beloved messiah, Jagad-Bondhu: world peace, universal brotherhood. Perhaps, now, all religions would unite into one great universal religion, and all men would begin to praise God as brothers, instead of tearing each other to pieces.

At any rate, the abbot selected one of his monks and told him that he was to go to Chicago, to the World Congress of Religions.

This was a tremendous assignment. It was something far more terrible than an order given, for instance, to a newly ordained Capuchin to proceed to a mission in India. That would merely be a matter of a trained missionary going off to occupy a place that had been prepared for him. But here was a little man who had been born at the edge of a jungle told to start out from a contemplative monastery and go not only into the world, but into the heart of a civilization the violence and materialism of which he could scarcely evaluate, and which raised goose-flesh on every square inch of his body. What is more, he was told to undertake this journey *without money*. Not that money was prohibited to him, but they simply did not have any. His abbot managed to raise enough to get him a ticket for a little more than half the distance. After that heaven would have to take care of him.

By the time I met this poor little monk who had come to America without money, he had been living in the country for about five years, and had acquired, of all things, the degree of Doctor of Philosophy from the University of Chicago. So that people referred to him as Doctor Bramachari, although I believe that Bramachari is simply a generic Hindu term for monk—and one that might almost be translated: "Little-Brother-Without-the-Degree-of-Doctor."

How he got through all the red tape that stands between America and the penniless traveler is something that I never quite understood. But it seems that officials, after questioning him, being completely over-whelmed by his simplicity, would either do something dishonest in his favor, or else would give him a tip as to how to beat the various tech-nicalities. Some of them even lent him fairly large sums of money. In any case he landed in America.

The only trouble was that he got to Chicago after the World Con-gress of Religions was all over.

By that time, one look at the Fair buildings, which were already being torn down, told him all he needed to know about the World Congress of Religions. But once he was there, he did not have much trouble. People would see him standing around in the middle of railway stations waiting for Providence to do something about his plight. They would be intrigued by his turban and white garments (which were partly con-cealed by a brown overcoat in winter). They observed that he was wearing a pair of sneakers, and perhaps that alone was enough to rouse their curiosity. He was frequently invited to give lectures to religious and social clubs, and to schools and colleges, and he more than once spoke from the pulpits of Protestant churches. In this way he managed to make a living for himself. Besides, he was always being hospitably entertained by people that he met, and he financed the stages of his journey by artlessly leaving his purse lying open on the living room table, at night, before his departure.

The open mouth of the purse spoke eloquently to the hearts of his hosts, saying: "As you see, I am empty," or, perhaps, "As you see, I am down to my last fifteen cents." It was often enough filled up in the morning. He got around.

How did he run into Sy Freedgood? Well Seymour's wife was studying at Chicago, and she met Bramachari there, and then Seymour met Bramachari, and Bramachari came to Long Beach once or twice, and went out in Seymour's sailboat, and wrote a poem which he gave to Seymour and Helen. He was very happy with Seymour, because he did not have to answer so many stupid questions and, after all, a lot of the people who befriended him were cranks and semimaniacs and theosophists who thought they had some kind of a claim on him. They wearied him with their eccentricities, although he was a gentle and patient little man. But at Long Beach he was left in peace, although Seymour's ancient grandmother was not easily convinced that he was not the hereditary enemy of the Jewish people. She moved around in the other room, lighting small religious lamps against the intruder.

It was the end of the school year, June 1938, when Lax and Seymour already had a huge box in the middle of the room, which they were beginning to pack with books, when we heard Bramachari was again coming to New York.

I went down to meet him at Grand Central with Seymour, and it was not without a certain suppressed excitement that I did so, for Seymour had me all primed with a superb selection of lies about Bramachari's ability to float in the air and walk on water. It was a long time before we found him in the crowd, although you would think that a Hindu in a turban and a white robe and a pair of Keds would have been a rather memorable sight. But all the people we asked, concerning such a one, had no idea of having seen him.

We had been looking around for ten or fifteen minutes, when a cat came walking cautiously through the crowd, and passed us by with a kind of a look, and disappeared.

"That's him," said Seymour. "He changed himself into a cat. Doesn't like to attract attention. Looking the place over. Now he knows we're here."

Almost at once, while Seymour was asking a porter if he had seen anything like Bramachari, and the porter was saying no, Bramachari came up behind us.

I saw Seymour swing around and say, in his rare, suave manner:

"Ah, Bramachari, how are you!"

There stood a shy little man, very happy, with a huge smile, all teeth, in the midst of his brown face. And on the top of his head was a yellow turban with Hindu prayers written all over it in red. And, on his feet, sure enough: sneakers.

I shook hands with him, still worrying lest he give me some kind of an electric shock. But he didn't. We rode up to Columbia in the subway, with all the people goggling at us, and I was asking Bramachari about all the colleges he had been visiting. Did he like Smith, did he like Harvard? When we were coming out into the air at 116th Street, I asked him which one he liked best, and he told me that they were all the same to him: it had never occurred to him that one might have any special preference in such things.

I lapsed into a reverent silence and pondered on this thought.

I was now twenty-three years old and, indeed, I was more mature than that in some respects. Surely by now it ought to have dawned on me that places did not especially matter. But no, I was very much attached to places, and had very definite likes and dislikes for localities as such, especially colleges, since I was always thinking of finding one that was altogether pleasant to live and teach in.

After that, I became very fond of Bramachari, and he of me. We got along very well together, especially since he sensed that I was trying to feel my way into a settled religious conviction, and into some kind of a life that was centered, as his was, on God.

The thing that strikes me now is that he never attempted to explain his own religious beliefs to me—except some of the externals of the cult, and that was later on. He would no doubt have told me all I wanted to know, if I had asked him, but I was not curious enough. What was most valuable to me was to hear his evaluation of the society and religious beliefs he had come across in America: and to put all that down on paper would require another book.

He was never sarcastic, never ironical or unkind in his criticisms: in fact he did not make many judgments at all, especially adverse ones. He would simply make statements of fact, and then burst out laughing—his laughter was quiet and ingenuous, and it expressed his complete amazement at the very possibility that people should live the way he saw them living all around him.

He was beyond laughing at the noise and violence of American city life and all the obvious lunacies like radio programs and billboard advertising. It was some of the well-meaning idealisms that he came across that struck him as funny. According to Bramachari, the prevailing impression among the Hindus seems to be that Christians don't know what asceticism means.

For my own part, I see no reason for discouragement. Bramachari was simply saying something that has long since been familiar to readers of the Gospels. Unless the grain of wheat, falling in the ground, die, itself remaineth alone: but if it die, it bringeth forth much fruit. The Hindus are not looking for us to send them men who will build schools and hospitals, although those things are good and useful in themselves—and perhaps very badly needed in India: they want to know if we have any saints to send them.

Bramachari was not the kind of man to be impressed with such statements as: "There's a quarter of a million dollars' worth of stained glass in this church . . . the organ has got six banks of keys and it contains drums, bells and a mechanical nightingale . . . and the retable is a genuine bas-relief by a real live Italian artist."

The people he had the least respect for were all the borderline cases, the strange, eccentric sects, the Christian Scientists, the Oxford Group, and all the rest of them. That was, in a sense, very comforting. Not that I was worried about them: but it confirmed me in my respect for him.

He did not generally put his words in the form of advice: but the one counsel he did give me is something that I will not easily forget: "There are many beautiful mystical books written by the Christians. You should read St. Augustine's *Confessions,* and *The Imitation of Christ.*"

Of course I had heard of both of them: but he was speaking as if he took it for granted that most people in America had no idea that such books ever existed. He seemed to feel as if he were in possession of a truth that would come to most Americans as news—as if there was something in their own cultural heritage that they had long since forgotten: and he could remind them of it. He repeated what he had said, not without a certain earnestness:

"Yes, you must read those books."

It was not often that he spoke with this kind of emphasis.

THE SEVEN STOREY MOUNTAIN

Three: MENTORS

❖ MARK VAN DOREN

I

For a teacher to be absolutely sincere with generation after generation of students requires either supernatural simplicity or, in the natural order, a kind of heroic humility. There was one man at Columbia, or rather one among several, who was most remarkable for this kind of heroism. I mean Mark Van Doren.

The first semester I was at Columbia, just after my twentieth birthday, in the winter of 1935, Mark was giving part of the "English sequence" in one of those rooms in Hamilton Hall with windows looking out between the big columns on to the wired-in track on South Field. There were twelve or fifteen people with more or less unbrushed hair, most of them with glasses, lounging around. One of them was my friend Robert Gibney.

It was a class in English literature, and it had no special bias of any kind. It was simply about what it was supposed to be about: the English literature of the eighteenth century. And in it literature was treated, not as history, not as sociology, not as economics, not as a series of case histories in psychoanalysis but, *mirabile dictu,* simply as literature.

I thought to myself, who is this excellent man Van Doren who being employed to teach literature, teaches just that: talks about writing and about books and poems and plays: does not get off on a tangent about the biographies of the poets or novelists: does not read into their poems a lot of subjective messages which were never there? Who is this man who does not have to fake and cover up a big gulf of ignorance by teaching a lot of opinions and conjectures and useless facts that belong to some other subject? Who is this who really loves what he has to teach, and does not secretly detest all literature, and abhor poetry, while pretending to be a professor of it?

That Columbia should have in it men like this who, instead of subtly destroying all literature by burying and concealing it under a mass of irrelevancies, really purified and educated the perceptions of their students by teaching them how to read a book and how to tell a good book from a bad, genuine writing from falsity and pastiche: all this gave me a deep respect for my new university.

Mark would come into the room and, without any fuss, would start talking about whatever was to be talked about. Most of the time he asked questions. His questions were very good, and if you tried to answer them intelligently, you found yourself saying excellent things that you did not know you knew, and that you had not, in fact, known before. He had "educed" them from you by his question. His classes were literally "education"—they brought things out of you, they made your mind produce its own explicit ideas. Do not think that Mark was simply priming his students with thoughts of his own, and then making the thought stick to their minds by getting them to give it back to him as their own. Far from it. What he did have was the gift of communicating to them something of his own vital interest in things, something of his manner of approach: but the results were sometimes quite unexpected —and by that I mean good in a way that he had not anticipated, casting lights that he had not himself foreseen.

Now a man who can go for year after year—although Mark was young then and is young now—without having any time to waste in flattering and cajoling his students with any kind of a fancy act, or with jokes, or with storms of temperament, or periodic tirades—whole classes spent in threats and imprecations, to disguise the fact that the professor himself has come in unprepared—one who can do without all these nonessentials both honors his vocation and makes it fruitful. Not only that, but his vocation, in return, perfects and ennobles him. And that is the way it should be, even in the natural order: how much more so in the order of grace!

Mark, I know, is no stranger to the order of grace: but considering his work as teacher merely as a mission on the natural level—I can see that Providence was using him as an instrument more directly than he realized. As far as I can see, the influence of Mark's sober and sincere intellect, and his manner of dealing with his subject with perfect honesty and objectivity and without evasions, was remotely preparing my mind to receive the good seed of scholastic philosophy. And there is nothing strange in this, for Mark himself was familiar at least with some of the modern scholastics, like Maritain and Gilson, and he was a friend of the American neo-Thomists, Mortimer Adler, and Richard McKeon, who had started out at Columbia but had had to move to Chicago, because Columbia was not ripe enough to know what to make of them.

The truth is that Mark's temper was profoundly scholastic in the sense that his clear mind looked directly for the quiddities of things, and sought being and substance under the covering of accident and appearances. And for him poetry was, indeed, a virtue of the practical intellect, and not simply a vague spilling of the emotions, wasting the soul and perfecting none of our essential powers.

It was because of this virtual scholasticism of Mark's that he would never permit himself to fall into the naïve errors of those who try to read some favorite private doctrine into every poet they like of every nation or every age. And Mark abhorred the smug assurance with which second-rate left-wing critics find adumbrations of dialectical materialism in everyone who ever wrote from Homer and Shakespeare to whomever they happen to like in recent times. If the poet is to their fancy, then he is clearly seen to be preaching the class struggle. If they do not like him, then they are able to show that he was really a forefather of fascism. And all their literary heroes are revolutionary leaders, and all their favorite villains are capitalists and Nazis.

It was a very good thing for me that I ran into someone like Mark Van Doren at that particular time, because in my new reverence for Communism, I was in danger of docilely accepting any kind of stupidity, provided I thought it was something that paved the way to the Elysian fields of classless society.

II

PERHAPS IT WAS FOR ME, personally, more than for the others, that Mark's course worked in this way. I am thinking of one particular incident.

It was the fall of 1936, just at the beginning of the new school year—on one of those first, bright, crazy days when everybody is full of ambition. It was the beginning of the year in which Pop was going to die and my own resistance would cave in under the load of pleasures and ambitions I was too weak to carry: the year in which I would be all the time getting dizzy, and in which I learned to fear the Long Island railroad as if it were some kind of a monster, and to shrink from New York as if it were the wide-open mouth of some burning Aztec god.

That day, I did not foresee any of this. My veins were still bursting with the materialistic and political enthusiasms with which I had first come to Columbia and, indeed, in line with their general direction, I had signed up for courses that were more or less sociological and economic and historical. In the obscurity of the strange, half-conscious semiconversion that had attended my retreat from Cambridge, I had tended more and more to be suspicious of literature, poetry—the things toward which my nature drew me—on the grounds that they might lead to a sort of futile aestheticism, a philosophy of "escape."

This had not involved me in any depreciation of people like Mark. However, it had just seemed more important to me that I should take some history course, rather than anything that was still left of his for me to take.

So now I was climbing one of the crowded stairways in Hamilton Hall to the room where I thought this history course was to be given. I looked in to the room. The second row was filled with the unbrushed heads of those who every day at noon sat in the *Jester* editorial offices and threw paper airplanes around the room or drew pictures on the walls.

Taller than them all, and more serious, with a long face, like a horse, and a great mane of black hair on top of it, Bob Lax meditated on some incomprehensible woe, and waited for someone to come in and begin to talk to them. It was when I had taken off my coat and put down my load of books that I found out that this was not the class I was supposed to be taking, but Van Doren's course on Shakespeare.

So I got up to go out. But when I got to the door I turned around again and went back and sat down where I had been, and stayed there. Later I went and changed everything with the registrar, so I remained in that class for the rest of the year.

It was the best course I ever had at college. And it did me the most good, in many different ways. It was the only place where I ever heard anything really sensible said about any of the things that were really fundamental—life, death, time, love, sorrow, fear, wisdom, suffering, eternity. A course in literature should never be a course in economics or philosophy or sociology or psychology: and I have explained how it was one of Mark's great virtues that he did not make it so. Nevertheless, the material of literature and especially of drama is chiefly human acts—that is, free acts, moral acts. And, as a matter of fact, literature, drama, poetry, make certain statements about these acts that can be made in no other way. That is precisely why you will miss all the deepest meaning of Shakespeare, Dante, and the rest if you reduce their vital and creative statements about life and men to the dry, matter-of-fact terms of history, or ethics, or some other science. They belong to a different order.

Nevertheless, the great power of something like *Hamlet, Coriolanus,* or the *Purgatorio* or Donne's *Holy Sonnets* lies precisely in the fact that they are a kind of commentary on ethics and psychology and even metaphysics, even theology. Or, sometimes, it is the other way around, and those sciences can serve as a commentary on these other realities, which we call plays, poems.

All that year we were, in fact, talking about the deepest springs of human desire and hope and fear; we were considering all the most important realities, not indeed in terms of something alien to Shakespeare and to poetry, but precisely in his own terms, with occasional intuitions of another order. And, as I have said, Mark's balanced and sensitive and clear way of seeing things, at once simple and yet capable of subtlety, being fundamentally scholastic, though not necessarily and explicitly Christian, presented these things in ways that made them live within us, and with a life that was healthy and permanent and productive. This class was one of the few things that could persuade me to get on the train and go to Columbia at all. It was, that year, my only health, until I came across and read the Gilson book.

✧ ETIENNE GILSON

ONE DAY, in the month of February, 1937, I happened to have five or ten loose dollars burning a hole in my pocket. I was on Fifth Avenue, for some reason or other, and was attracted by the window of Scribner's bookstore, all full of bright new books.

That year I had signed up for a course in French medieval literature. My mind was turning back, in a way, to the things I remembered from the old days in Saint Antonin. The deep, naïve, rich simplicity of the twelfth and thirteenth centuries was beginning to speak to me again. I had written a paper on a legend of a "Jongleur de Notre Dame," compared with a story from the Fathers of the Desert, in Migne's *Latin Patrology*. I was being drawn back into the Catholic atmosphere, and I could feel the health of it, even in the merely natural order, working already within me.

Now, in Scribner's window, I saw a book called *The Spirit of Medieval Philosophy*. I went inside, and took it off the shelf, and looked at the table of contents and at the title page which was deceptive, because it said the book was made up of a series of lectures that had been given at the University of Aberdeen. That was no recommendation, to me especially. But it threw me off the track as to the possible identity and character of Etienne Gilson, who wrote the book.

I bought it, then, together with one other book that I have completely forgotten, and on my way home in the Long Island train, I unwrapped the package to gloat over my acquisitions. It was only then that I saw, on the first page of *The Spirit of Medieval Philosophy,* the small print which said: "Nihil Obstat . . . Imprimatur."

The feeling of disgust and deception struck me like a knife in the pit of the stomach. I felt as if I had been cheated! They should have warned me that it was a Catholic book! Then I would never have bought it. As it was, I was tempted to throw the thing out the window at the houses of Woodside—to get rid of it as something dangerous and unclean. Such is the terror that is aroused in the enlightened modern mind by a little innocent Latin and the signature of a priest. It is impossible to communicate, to a Catholic, the number and complexity of fearful associations that a little thing like this can carry with it. It is in Latin—a difficult, ancient, and obscure tongue. That implies, to the mind that has roots in Protestantism, all kinds of sinister secrets, which the priests are supposed to cherish and to conceal from common men in this unknown language. Then, the mere fact that they should pass judgment on the character of a book, and permit people to read it: that in itself is fraught with terror. It immediately conjures up all the real and imaginary excesses of the Inquisition.

That is something of what I felt when I opened Gilson's book: for you must understand that while I admired Catholic *culture,* I had always been afraid of the Catholic Church. That is a rather common position in the world today. After all, I had not bought a book on medieval philosophy without realizing that it would be Catholic philosophy: but the imprimatur told me that what I read would be in full conformity with that fearsome and mysterious thing, Catholic Dogma, and the fact struck me with an impact against which everything in me reacted with repugnance and fear.

Now in the light of all this, I consider that it was surely a real grace that, instead of getting rid of the book, I actually read it. Not all of it, it is true: but more than I used to read of books that deep. When I think of the numbers of books I had on my shelf in the little room at Douglaston that had once been Pop's "den"—books which I had bought and never even read, I am more astounded than ever at the fact that I actually read this one: and what is more, remembered it.

And the one big concept which I got out of its pages was something that was to revolutionize my whole life. It is all contained in one of those dry, outlandish technical compounds that the scholastic philosophers were so prone to use: the word *aseitas*. In this one word, which can be applied to God alone, and which expresses His most characteristic attribute, I discovered an entirely new concept of God—a concept which showed me at once that the belief of Catholics was by no means the vague and rather superstitious hangover from an unscientific age that I had believed it to be. On the contrary, here was a notion of God that was at the same time deep, precise, simple and accurate and, what is more, charged with implications which I could not even begin to appreciate, but which I could at least dimly estimate, even with my own lack of philosophical training.

Aseitas—the English equivalent is a transliteration: aseity—simply means the power of a being to exist absolutely in virtue of itself, not as caused by itself, but as requiring no cause, no other justification for its existence except that its very nature is to exist. There can be only one such Being: that is God. And to say that God exists *a se,* of and by and by reason of Himself, is merely to say that God is Being Itself. *Ego sum qui sum.* And this means that God must enjoy "complete independence not only as regards everything outside but also as regards everything within Himself."

This notion made such a profound impression on me that I made a pencil note at the top of the page: "Aseity of God—God is being *per se.*" I observe it now on the page, for I brought the book to the monastery with me, and although I was not sure where it had gone, I found it on the shelves in Father Abbot's room the other day, and I have it here before me.

I marked three other passages, so perhaps the best thing would be to copy them down. Better than anything I could say, they will convey the impact of the book on my mind.

When God says that He is being [reads the first sentence so marked] and if what He says is to have any intelligible meaning to our minds, it can only mean this: that He is the pure act of existing.

Pure act: therefore excluding all imperfection in the order of existing. Therefore excluding all change, all "becoming," all beginning or end, all limitation. But from this fullness of existence, if I had been capable of considering it deeply enough, I would soon have found that the fullness of all perfection could easily be argued.

But another thing that struck me was an important qualification the

author made. He distinguished between the concepts of *ens in genere*
—the abstract notion of being in general—and *ens infinitum,* the concrete and real Infinite Being, Who, Himself, transcends all our con-
ceptions. And so I marked the following words, which were to be my
first step toward St. John of the Cross:

> Beyond all sensible images, and all conceptual determinations, God affirms
> Himself as the absolute act of being in its pure actuality. Our concept of
> God, a mere feeble analogue of a reality which overflows it in every direc-
> tion, can be made explicit only in the judgment: Being is Being, an absolute
> positing of that which, lying beyond every object, contains in itself the suffi-
> cient reason of objects. And that is why we can rightly say that the very
> excess of positivity which hides the divine being from our eyes is neverthe-
> less the light which lights up all the rest: *ipsa caligo summa est mentis
> illuminatio.*

His Latin quotation was from St. Bonaventure's *Itinerarium.*

The third sentence of Gilson's that I marked in those few pages read
as follows:

> When St. Jerome says that God is His own origin and the cause of His
> own substance, he does not mean, as Descartes does, that God in a certain
> way posits Himself in being by His almighty power as by a cause, but sim-
> ply that we must not look outside of God for a cause of the existence of God.

I think the reason why these statements, and others like them, made
such a profound impression on me, lay deep in my own soul. And it
was this: I had never had an adequate notion of what Christians meant
by God. I had simply taken it for granted that the God in Whom religious people believed, and to Whom they attributed the creation and
government of all things, was a noisy and dramatic and passionate
character, a vague, jealous, hidden being, the objectification of all their
own desires and strivings and subjective ideals.

The truth is, that the concept of God which I had always entertained,
and which I had accused Christians of teaching to the world, was a
concept of a being who was simply impossible. He was infinite and
yet finite; perfect and imperfect; eternal and yet changing—subject to
all the variations of emotion, love, sorrow, hate, revenge, that men are
prey to. How could this fatuous, emotional thing be without beginning
and without end the creator of all? I had taken the dead letter of Scripture at its very deadest, and it had killed me, according to the saying
of St. Paul: "The letter killeth, but the spirit giveth life."

I think one cause of my profound satisfaction with what I now read was that God had been vindicated in my own mind. There is in every intellect a natural exigency for a true concept of God: we are born with the thirst to know and to see Him, and therefore it cannot be otherwise.

I know that many people are, or call themselves, "atheists" simply because they are repelled and offended by statements about God made in imaginary and metaphorical terms which they are not able to interpret and comprehend. They refuse these concepts of God, not because they despise God, but perhaps because they demand a notion of Him more perfect than they generally find: and because ordinary, figurative concepts of God could not satisfy them, they turn away and think that there are no other: or, worse still, they refuse to listen to philosophy, on the ground that it is nothing but a web of meaningless words spun together for the justification of the same old hopeless falsehoods.

What a relief it was for me, now, to discover not only that no idea of ours, let alone any sensible image, could delimit the being of God, but also that we *should not* allow ourselves to be satisfied with any such knowledge of Him.

The result was that I at once acquired an immense respect for Catholic philosophy and for the Catholic faith. And that last thing was the most important of all. I now at least recognized that faith was something that had a very definite meaning and a most cogent necessity.

If this much was a great thing, it was about all that I could do at the moment. I could recognize that those who thought about God had a good way of considering Him, and that those who believed in Him really believed in someone, and their faith was more than a dream. Further than that it seemed I could not go, for the time being.

How many there are in the same situation! They stand in the stacks of libraries and turn over the pages of St. Thomas' *Summa* with a kind of curious reverence. They talk in their seminars about Thomas and Scotus and Augustine and Bonaventure and they are familiar with Maritain and Gilson, and they have read all the poems of Hopkins— and indeed they know more about what is best in the Catholic literary and philosophical tradition than most Catholics ever do on this earth. They sometimes go to Mass, and wonder at the dignity and restraint of the old liturgy. They are impressed by the organization of a Church in which everywhere the priests, even the most ungifted, are able to preach at least something of a tremendous, profound, unified doctrine, and to dispense mysteriously efficacious help to all who come to them with troubles and needs.

In a certain sense, these people have a better appreciation of the

Church and of Catholicism than many Catholics have: an appreciation which is detached and intellectual and objective. But they never come into the Church. They stand and starve in the doors of the banquet— the banquet to which they surely realize that they are invited—while those more poor, more stupid, less gifted, less educated, sometimes even less virtuous than they, enter in and are filled at those tremendous tables.

When I had put this book down, and had ceased to think explicitly about its arguments, its effect began to show itself in my life. I began to have a desire to go to church—and a desire more sincere and mature and more deep-seated than I had ever had before. After all, I had never before had so great a need.

❖ FATHER MOORE, DAN WALSH, JACQUES MARITAIN

I CAME OUT of the presbytery with three books under my arm. I had hoped that I could begin taking instructions at once, but the pastor had told me to read these books, and pray and think and see how I felt about it in a week or ten days' time. I did not argue with him: but the hesitation that had been in my mind only an hour or so before seemed to have vanished so completely that I was astonished and a little abashed at this delay. So it was arranged that I should come in the evenings, twice a week.

"Father Moore will be your instructor," said the Pastor.

There were four assistants at Corpus Christi, but I guessed that Father Moore was going to be the one whom I had heard preaching the sermon on the divinity of Christ and, as a matter of fact, he was the one who, in the designs of Providence, had been appointed for this work of my salvation.

If people had more appreciation of what it means to be converted from rank, savage paganism, from the spiritual level of a cannibal or of an ancient Roman, to the living faith and to the Church, they would not think of catechism as something trivial or unimportant. Usually the word suggests the matter-of-course instructions that children have to go through before First Communion and Confirmation. Even where it is a matter of course, it is one of the most tremendous things in the world, this planting of the word of God in a soul. It takes a conversion to really bring this home.

I was never bored. I never missed an instruction, even when it cost me the sacrifice of some of my old amusements and attractions, which had such a strong hold over me and, while I had been impatient of delay from the moment I had come to that first sudden decision, I now began to burn with desire for Baptism, and to throw out hints and try to determine when I would be received into the Church.

My desire became much greater still, by the end of October, for I made the Mission with the men of the parish, listening twice a day to sermons by two Paulist Fathers and hearing Mass and kneeling at Benediction before the Christ Who was gradually revealing Himself to me.

When the sermon on hell began, I was naturally making mental comparisons with the one in Joyce's *Portrait of the Artist* and reflecting on it in a kind of detached manner, as if I were a third and separate person watching myself hearing this sermon and seeing how it affected me. As a matter of fact this was the sermon which should have done me the most good and did, in fact, do so.

My opinion is that it is a very extraordinary thing for anyone to be upset by such a topic. Why should anyone be shattered by the thought of hell? It is not compulsory for anyone to go there. Those who do, do so by their own choice, and against the will of God, and they can only get into hell by defying and resisting all the work of Providence and grace. It is their own will that takes them there, not God's. In damning them He is only ratifying their own decision—a decision which He has left entirely to their own choice. Nor will He ever hold our weakness alone responsible for our damnation. Our weakness should not terrify us: it is the source of our strength. *Libenter gloriabor in infirmitatibus meis ut inhabitet in me virtus Christi.* Power is made perfect in infirmity, and our very helplessness is all the more potent a claim on that Divine Mercy Who calls to Himself the poor, the little ones, the heavily burdened.

My reaction to the sermon on hell was, indeed, what spiritual writers call "confusion"—but it was not the hectic, emotional confusion that comes from passion and from self-love. It was a sense of quiet sorrow and patient grief at the thought of these tremendous and terrible sufferings which I deserved and into which I stood a very good chance of entering, in my present condition: but at the same time, the magnitude of the punishment gave me a special and particular understanding of the greatness of the evil of sin. But the final result was a great deepening and awakening of my soul, a real increase in spiritual profundity and an advance in faith and love and confidence in God, to Whom alone I could look for salvation from these things. And therefore I all the more earnestly desired Baptism.

I went to Father Moore after the sermon on hell and said that I hoped he was going to baptize me really soon. He laughed, and said that it would not be much longer. By now, it was the beginning of November.

Meanwhile, there had been another thought, half forming itself in the back of my mind—an obscure desire to become a priest. This was something which I tended to hold separate from the thought of my conversion, and I was doing my best to keep it in the background. I did not mention it either to Father Ford or Father Moore, for the chief reason that in my mind it constituted a kind of admission that I was taking the thought more seriously than I wanted to—it almost amounted to a first step toward application for admission to a seminary.

However, it is a strange thing: there was also in my mind a kind of half-formed conviction that there was one other person I should consult about becoming a priest before I took the matter to the rectory. This man was a layman, and someone I had never yet seen, and it was altogether strange that I should be inclined so spontaneously to put the matter up to him, as if he were the only logical one to give me advice. In the end, he was the one I first consulted—I mean, the one from whom I first seriously asked advice, for I had long been talking about it to my friends, before I came around to him.

This man was Daniel Walsh, about whom I had heard a great deal from Lax and Gerdy. Gerdy had taken his course on St. Thomas Aquinas in the graduate school of philosophy: and now as the new school year began, my attention centered upon this one course. It had nothing directly to do with my preparation for the exams for the M.A. degree in January. By now degrees and everything else to do with a university career had become very unimportant in comparison with the one big thing that occupied my mind and all my desires.

I registered for the course, and Dan Walsh turned out to be another one of those destined in a providential way to shape and direct my vocation. For it was he who pointed out my way to the place where I now am.

When I was writing about Columbia and its professors, I was not thinking of Dan Walsh: and he really did not belong to Columbia at all. He was on the faculty of the Sacred Heart College at Manhattanville, and came to Columbia twice a week to lecture on St. Thomas and Duns Scotus. His class was a small one and was, as far as Columbia was concerned, pretty much of an academic bypath. And that was in a sense an additional recommendation—it was off that broad and noisy highway of pragmatism which leads between its banks of artificial flowers to the gates of despair.

Walsh himself had nothing of the supercilious self-assurance of the ordinary professor: he did not need this frail and artificial armor for his own insufficiency. He did not need to hide behind tricks and vanities any more than Mark Van Doren did; he never even needed to be brilliant. In his smiling simplicity he used to efface himself entirely in the solid and powerful mind of St. Thomas. Whatever brilliance he allowed himself to show forth in his lectures was all thrown back upon its source, the Angel of the Schools.

Dan Walsh had been a student and collaborator of Gilson's and knew Gilson and Maritain well. In fact, later on he introduced me to Maritain at the Catholic Book Club, where this most saintly philosopher had been giving a talk on Catholic Action. I only spoke a few conventional words to Maritain, but the impression you got from this gentle, stooping Frenchman with much gray hair was one of tremendous kindness and simplicity and godliness. And that was enough: you did not need to talk to him. I came away feeling very comforted that there was such a person in the world, and confident that he would include me in some way in his prayers.

But Dan himself had caught a tremendous amount of this simplicity and gentleness and godliness too: and perhaps the impression that he made was all the more forceful because his square jaw had a kind of potential toughness about it. Yet no: there he sat, this little, stocky man, who had something of the appearance of a good-natured prize fighter, smiling and talking with the most childlike delight and cherubic simplicity about the *Summa Theologica*.

His voice was low and, as he spoke, he half apologetically searched the faces of his hearers for signs of understanding and, when he found it, he seemed surprised and delighted.

I very quickly made friends with him, and told him all about my thesis and the ideas I was trying to work with, and he was very pleased. And one of the things he sensed at once was something that I was far from being able to realize: but it was that the bent of my mind was essentially "Augustinian." I had not yet followed Bramachari's advice to read St. Augustine and I did not take Dan's evaluation of my ideas as having all the directive force that was potentially in it—for it did not even come clothed in suggestion or advice.

Of course, to be called "Augustinian" by a Thomist might not in every case be a compliment. But coming from Dan Walsh, who was a true Catholic philosopher, it was a compliment indeed.

For he, like Gilson, had the most rare and admirable virtue of being able to rise above the petty differences of schools and systems, and seeing Catholic philosophy in its wholeness, in its variegated unity, and in its true Catholicity. In other words, he was able to study St. Thomas and St. Bonaventure and Duns Scotus side by side, and to see them as complementing and reinforcing one another, as throwing diverse and individual light on the same truths from different points of view, and thus he avoided the evil of narrowing and restricting Catholic philosophy and theology to a single school, to a single attitude, a single system.

I pray to God that there may be raised up more like him in the Church and in our universities, because there is something stifling and intellectually deadening about textbooks that confine themselves to giving a superficial survey of the field of philosophy according to Thomist principles and then discard all the rest in a few controversial objections. Indeed, I think it a great shame and a danger of no small proportions, that Catholic philosophers should be trained in division against one another, and brought up to the bitterness and smallness of controversy: because this is bound to narrow their views and dry up the unction that should vivify all philosophy in their souls.

Therefore, to be called an "Augustinian" by Dan Walsh was a compliment, in spite of the traditional opposition between the Thomist and Augustinian schools, Augustinian being taken not as confined to the philosophers of that religious order, but as embracing all the intellectual descendants of St. Augustine. It is a great compliment to find oneself numbered as part of the same spiritual heritage as St. Anselm, St. Bernard, St. Bonaventure, Hugh and Richard of St. Victor, and Duns Scotus also. And from the tenor of his course, I realized that he meant that my bent was not so much toward the intellectual, dialectical, speculative character of Thomism, as toward the spiritual, mystical, voluntaristic, and practical way of St. Augustine and his followers.

His course and his friendship were most valuable in preparing me for the step I was about to take. But as time went on, I decided to leave the notion of becoming a priest out of the way for the time being. So I never even mentioned it to Dan in those days.

THE SEVEN STOREY MOUNTAIN

Four: POETS

FOR THE FIRST TIME this year it has been warm enough to sit outside. After dinner I sat in the sun and read T. S. Eliot's "East Coker"
and part of "The Dry Salvages" from *Four Quartets.* Eight years ago
when we were at the cottage at Olean, Nancy Flagg had "East Coker"
in ms., for it was still not published. We all said we didn't like it, but
today I like it quite a lot except that I paused a bit at two or three lines
of archaic English. I was surprised to find him drawing so heavily on
Saint John of the Cross; I do not immediately see how it fits in. And
in the second section I was brought up short by "That was a way of
putting it" and the other self-conscious passage. Maybe I'll see the point
later. But the beginning is fine and the rhymed sections are very beautiful—as beautiful as anything that has been written in English for fifty
years or more.

> Thunder rolled by the rolling stars
> Simulates triumphal cars
> Deployed in constellated wars
> Scorpion fights against the Sun
> Until the Sun and Moon go down
> Comets weep and Leonids fly
> Hunt the heavens and the plains
> Whirled in a vortex that shall bring
> The world to that destructive fire
> Which burns before the ice-cap reigns.

I think this book is the best of Eliot. Also I admire Eliot's literary
chastity. He is not afraid to be prosaic, rather than write bad verse. But
when he is very prosaic he is weak. However, a word like "grimpen"
can liven up the prose. Then when he comes to the part,

> Do not let me hear
> Of the wisdom of old men, but rather of their folly,

it becomes poetry again.

> The wounded surgeon plies the steel
> That questions the distempered part;

is maybe the best of the whole thing, not only beautiful but deep and
precise and poignant. It makes a good contrast with the cosmic bit about
the triumphal cars in heaven—here everything that was then big, vast,
universal, is brought down to the pointed, the moral, and the human.
The heavens are indifferent, but here are real wounds in a real moral
order. A real death.

> The chill ascends from feet to knees,
> The fever sings in mental wires. . . .

(And I think of Dylan Thomas' "The pleasure bird sings in the hot
wires," but it is the same fever.) As a poet, I have got to be sharp and
precise like Eliot—or else quit.

❖ DYLAN THOMAS

DYLAN THOMAS' INTEGRITY as a poet makes me very ashamed of the
verse I have been writing. We who say we love God: why are we not
as anxious to be perfect in our art as we pretend we want to be in our
service of God? If we do not try to be perfect in what we write, perhaps
it is because we are not writing for God after all. In any case it is de-
pressing that those who serve God and love Him sometimes write so
badly, when those who do not believe in Him take pains to write so
well. I am not talking about grammar and syntax, but about having
something to say and saying it in sentences that are not half dead. Saint
Paul and Saint Ignatius Martyr did not bother about grammar but they
certainly knew how to write.

Imperfection is the penalty of rushing into print. And people who
rush into print too often do so not because they really have anything
to say, but because they think it is important for something by them to
be in print. The fact that your subject may be very important in itself
does not necessarily mean that what *you* have written about it is important. A bad book about the love of God remains a bad book, even

though it may be about the love of God. There are many who think that because they have written about God, they have written good books. Then men pick up these books and say: if the ones who say they believe in God cannot find anything better than this to say about it, their religion cannot be worth much.

❖ ROBERT LOWELL

YESTERDAY Robert Lowell's book, *Lord Weary's Castle*, reached me. It is wonderful. Harcourt, Brace made me a present of it after I had gone begging all around the town. Lowell is a poet, and practically the only poet in the country. I wish I could write an article about him. You could compare the "Quaker Graveyard" with Hopkins' "Wreck of the Deutschland," to the great advantage of "Graveyard." Lowell has little of Hopkins' spiritual depth but he is often more of a poet—more fluent and more finished. Hopkins is *too* finished. Lowell can be much more perfect than Hopkins because he leaves you with less sense of technical struggle. All the emotional intensity is there. Hopkins' spiritual struggles fought their way out in problems of rhythm. He made his asceticism bearable by thrusting it over the line into the order of art where he could handle it more objectively. When fortitude became a matter of sprung rhythm, he could keep his sufferings, for the time being, at arm's length.

The poems of Lowell that I like less are those written "After Rilke" and "After Valéry." He has his roots in New England and not in Europe, although I do not mean that he is in any sense provincial. He does not talk the language of Rilke or Valéry merely as a tourist. However, glad as I am to have him write like Valéry, I find him more completely satisfying when he talks about Boston as "my city." No immigrant could write as he writes about Boston. On the other hand there is nothing of the bad New England about him. I do not merely speak of Dutchland Farms, but also of "Lord-Geoffrey-Amherst-was-a-soldier-of-the-King." You would not dream of insulting the man by expecting to find a shadow of that in him, even though he has grown up in the thick of it. Perhaps I have made a *faux pas*. Harvard higher than Amherst.

Lowell makes a little bit go a long way—but he is always licit and healthy about the way he does it. In him, New England avarice is clean economy after all. I am surprised and happy. For instance he returns,

I forget how many times, to the man in Dante who was rolled away
by the torrent while two angels fought with billhooks for his soul.

THE SIGN OF JONAS

✧ JORGE CARRERA ANDRADE

HUMANITY, TENDERNESS, AND WIT in the sense of *esprit* characterize the
innocence and seriousness of Jorge Carrera Andrade. He is one of the
most appealing of the fine Latin American poets of our century. One
is tempted to call him an incarnation of the genius of his humble and
delightful country, Ecuador: a land of green volcanoes, of hot jungles
and cold sierras, of colonial cities set like jewels in lost valleys; a land
of Indians and poverty. The voice of Ecuador (which sings in his verse)
is a soft, humble voice: a voice, oppressed but without rancor, without
unhappiness, like the voice of a child who does not get much to eat but
lives in the sun. Ecuador is a hungry wise child, an ancient child, like
the child in the Biblical proverbs who was always playing in the world
before the face of the Creator. An eternal child, a secret Christ, who
knows how to smile at the folly of the great and to have no hope in any
of the strong countries of the world. Ecuador has always been, and will
always be, betrayed by the strong. It can despair of them without sorrow, because to despair of shadows is no despair at all. It is, in fact, a
pure and sacred hope. This kind of truth, this kind of confidence, strong
nations, preparing ruin, cannot understand. . . .

Some fifty-seven years ago Carrera Andrade was born in Quito and
in the dawn of his life the cobbled streets of the sleepy capital echoed
for him with the rhythms of Verlaine and Gongora. He read the Sym-
bolists under the eucalyptus trees, and meditated baroque conceits in
the green and white presence of the volcano Pichincha. Yet his poetic
sensitivity remained simple and happy, for he walked among the cornfields and Indians of the country, sharing their blood and their silence,
thinking and making their poems in his heart. He has remained pre-
eminently a South American poet.

He had taken an active part in the politics and journalism of his
country. He had already published more than one book of poems when,
in 1928, he boarded a Dutch steamer in Guyaquil and headed for Europe:

> In a ship of twenty bugles
> I took my trunk of parrots
> To the other end of the world.

His bags and his money were stolen in Panama. He wandered through Holland, Germany, France, Spain. He lived as poor people live, traveling third-class, carrying everywhere his light burden of poetry and of Indian blood. More and more alone in the ancient cities, he wrote poems, first one book then another. In the strikes, the riots, the movements of the day, he stood with the poor. He sided with the Left, hoping for a better world. But the ambiguities of power politics making use of the humble and defenseless to increase its own power did not satisfy him. He broke away from Communism. He found himself more alone.

He set up a small publishing house in Paris. He married. He came home to South America. He was sent as Consul of Ecuador to a small city of Peru. He returned to France as Consul in Le Havre. Later he went to Japan, China, and England, in the consular service of his country. In 1941 he came to the United States as Ecuadorian Consul in San Francisco. He found the city exciting, and he responded gladly to the friendship and to the hard-boiled mystery of North America. He wrote a "Song to the Oakland Bridge" which was to him a symbol of strength and peace:

> Thy spans are of peace,
> Thy sea-chains set men free.
> From thy unceasing journey thou returnest,
> Dragging a city and a handful of orchards.

Yet I do not think Carrera Andrade has built his hopes definitely on any earthly or political power. In the cold war between East and West, he, now working at UNESCO, has been of course "for the West." But at the same time he has learned a new geography, the world which has to be discovered sooner or later by those who do not believe in power, violence, coercion, tyranny, war. "I embarked for the secret country, the country that is everywhere, the country that has no map because it is within ourselves."

It is in this secret country that I have met Carrera Andrade and here we have become good friends. Here without noise of words we talk together of the mountains of Ecuador, and of the silent people there who do not always eat every day. The secret country is a country of loneliness and of a kind of hunger, of silence, of perplexity, of waiting, of strange hopes: where men expect the impossible to be born, but do not always dare to speak of their hopes. For all hopes that can be put into words are now used by men of war in favor of death: even the most sacred and living words are sometimes used in favor of death.

During the last war the poet was silent, except for the quiet irony of his poem about the parachute jumper. He looked about him at the desolation of man, at the prison without a key in which man had enclosed himself, or so it seemed, forever. Carrera Andrade has not reproached anyone, has not joined the harsh chorus of the prisoners in despair. He has listened, silently, to other voices and other harmonies. Can prophecy be so humble, so unassuming? Can the voice of a new world be so quiet? Is this the voice of the gray-green Andes, of the long-hidden America, of the dim and cool twilight of the Sierra dawn out of which peace, perhaps, will one day be born?

Who can answer such absurd questions? It is foolish perhaps to ask them outside of the secret country in which, unasked, they retain their meaning and prepare the hearer, quietly, for the answer they already contain.

NEW DIRECTIONS 17

Five: HERAKLEITOS THE OBSCURE

ONE OF the most challenging, inscrutable, and acute of philosophers is Herakleitos of Ephesus, the "dark" *skoteinos, tenebrosus.* He lived in the Ionian Greek city sacred to Artemis, where he flourished at the turn of the fifth century B.C., in the days of the Greek tyrants, and of the Persian wars. He was a contemporary of Pindar and Aeschylus and of the victorious fighters of Marathon, but unlike the poets who wrote and sang in the dawn of the Attic Golden age, Herakleitos was a tight-lipped and cynical pessimist who viewed with sardonic contempt the political fervor of his contemporaries.

He was one of those rare spirits whose prophetic insight enabled them to see far beyond the limited horizons of their society. The Ionian world was the world of Homer and of the Olympian gods. It was a world that believed in static and changeless order, and in the laws of mechanical necessity—basically materialistic. Against this Olympian formalism, against the ritualism and the rigidity of the conventional exterior cult, the static condition of a society that feared all that was not "ordinary," Herakleitos rose up with the protest of the Dionysian mystic. He spoke for the mysterious, the unutterable, and the excellent. He spoke for the logos which was the true law of all being—not a static and rigid form, but a dynamic principle of harmony in conflict. This logos principle was represented by Herakleitos under the symbolic form of fire. However, fire was not only a symbol for Herakleitos. Later philosophers have derided the intuition by which Herakleitos designated fire as the "primary substance" of the cosmos—but perhaps the experience of our time, in which atomic science has revealed the enormous burning energy that can be released from an atom of hydrogen, may prove Herakleitos to have been nearer the truth than was thought by

Plato or Aristotle. However, the "fire" of Herakleitos is something more than material. It is spiritual and "divine." It is the key to the spiritual enigma of man. Our spiritual and mystical destiny is to "awaken" to the fire that is within us, and our happiness depends on the harmony in conflict that results from this awakening. Our vocation is a call to spiritual oneness in and with the logos. But this interior fulfillment is not to be attained by a false peace resulting from artificial compulsion —a static and changeless "state" imposed by force of will upon the dynamic, conflicting forces with us. True peace is the "hidden attunement of opposite tensions"—a paradox and a mystery transcending both sense and will, like the ecstasy of the mystic.

Herakleitos left no writings of his own. Legend says that he composed a book which he presented to Artemis in her temple, but almost all the stories told of his life and exploits are to be mistrusted. It is much more likely that he wrote nothing at all. His sayings, those cryptic fragments which have so tenaciously survived, have come down to us in the writings of others. Herakleitos is quoted first of all by Plato and Aristotle, but also by later writers like Plotinus, Porphyry, Theophrastus, Philo, and several Christian Fathers such as Clement of Alexandria, Origen, and Hyppolitus. Sometimes these philosophers and theologians quote Herakleitos with approval to illustrate a point of their own; more often they bring him up only in order to refute him. But St. Justin Martyr refers to him, along with Socrates, as a "Saint" of pre-Christian paganism. The fact that he is unknown to us except in the context which others have foisted on him makes him even more difficult to understand than he is in himself. Though the fragments which form his whole surviving work can be printed on two or three pages, long and laborious research is needed to untangle their authentic meaning and to liberate the obscure Ionian from the bias imposed on his thought by the interpretation of opponents.

His enigmatic sayings are terse paradoxes, often wearing the sardonic and oracular expression of the Zen *mondo*. The comparison suggests itself quite naturally in our day when Oriental thought has once again found a hearing (perhaps not always an intelligent hearing) in the West. Herakleitos appears at first sight to be more Oriental than Greek, though this appearance can easily be exaggerated, and Herakleitos himself warns us against irresponsible guesses in difficult matters. "Let us not conjecture at random about the greatest things." But it is true that the logos of Herakleitos seems to have much in common with the Tao of Lao-tse as well as with the Word of St. John. His insistence that apparently conflicting opposites are, at bottom, really one is also a familiar theme in Oriental thought. Herakleitos, we must remember, comes *before* Aristotle's principle of identity and contradiction. He does not look at things with the eyes of Aristotelian logic, and consequently he can say that opposites can be, from a certain point of view, the same.

The variations and oppositions between conflicting forces in the world are immediately evident to sense, and are not a complete illusion. But when men become too intent on analyzing and judging these oppositions, and separating them out into good and evil, desirable and undesirable, profitable and useless, they become more and more immersed in illusion and their view of reality is perverted. They can no longer see the deep, underlying connection of opposites, because they are obsessed with their superficial separateness. In reality, the distinction to be made is not between this force which is good and true, as against that force which is evil and false. Rather it is the perception of underlying oneness that is the key to truth and goodness, while the attachment to superficial separateness leads to falsity and moral error. This is why Herakleitos says, "to God all things are good and just and right, but men hold some things wrong and some right." God sees all things as good and right, not in their separateness by which they are in contrast to everything else, but in their inner harmony with their apparent opposites. But men separate what God has united.

Herakleitos looks on the world not as an abstractionist, but from the viewpoint of experience. However, and this is important, experience for Herakleitos is not merely the uninterpreted datum of sense. His philosophical viewpoint is that of a mystic whose intuition cuts through apparent multiplicity to grasp underlying reality as *one*. This vision of unity which Parmenides was to sum up in the universal concept of being was seen by the poet and mystic, Herakleitos, as "Fire."

We must be very careful not to interpret Herakleitos in a material way. Fire for him is a dynamic, spiritual principle. It is a divine energy, the manifestation of God, the power of God. God, indeed, is for Herakleitos "all things." But this is probably a much more subtle statement than we might be inclined to imagine at first sight, for he says that just as fire when it burns different kinds of aromatical spices becomes a variety of perfumes, so God working in the infinite variety of beings manifests Himself in countless appearances. God, strictly speaking, is then not merely "fire" or "earth" or the other elements, or all of them put together. His energy works, shows itself and hides in nature. He Himself is the Logos, the Wisdom, not so much "at work" in nature but

rather "at play" there. In one of the fragments the "dark one" speaks
of the logos in the same terms as the sapiential literature of the Bible
speaks of the divine Wisdom: as a "child playing in the world":

> When he prepared the heavens, I was present: when with a certain
> law and compass he enclosed the depths:
> When he established the sky above, and poised the fountains of wa-
> ters:
> When he compassed the sea with its bounds, and set a law to the
> waters that they should not pass their limits:
> When he balanced the foundations of the earth;
> I was with him forming all things: and was delighted every day, play-
> ing before him at all times;
> Playing in the world: and my delights were to be with the children
> of men.
>
> —PROVERBS 8:27-31

Herakleitos says: "Time is a child playing draughts. The kingly power
is a child's." The reference to the game of draughts is a metaphor for
his basic concept that all cosmic things are in a state of becoming and
change, and this constant interplay of elements in a state of dynamic
flux is the expression of the divine Law, the "justice," "hidden harmony," or "unity" which constantly keeps everything in balance in the
midst of conflict and movement.

Wisdom, for Herakleitos, does not consist in that "polymathy"—the
"learning of many things"—the scientific research which observes and
tabulates an almost infinite number of phenomena. Nor does it consist
in the willful and arbitrary selection of one of many conflicting principles, in order to elevate it above its opposite and to place it in a position of definitive and final superiority. True wisdom must seize upon
the very movement itself, and penetrate to the logos or thought within
that dynamic harmony. "Wisdom is one thing—it is to know the thought
by which all things are steered through all things." We are reminded
of the words of the Old Testament Book of Wisdom—the one most
influenced by Hellenic thought.

> And all such things as are hid and not foreseen, I have learned: for
> wisdom, which is the worker of all things, taught me.
> For in her is the spirit of understanding: holy, one, manifold, subtile,
> eloquent, active, undefiled, sure, sweet, loving that which is good,
> quick, which nothing hindereth, beneficient,
> Gentle, kind, steadfast, assured, secure, having all power, overseeing
> all things, and containing all spirits, intelligible, pure, subtile.

For wisdom is more active than all active things: and reacheth everywhere by reason of her purity.

For she is a vapour of the power of God, and a certain pure emana-
tion of the glory of the almighty God: and therefore no defiled
thing cometh into her.

For she is the brightness of eternal light, and the unspotted mirror
of God's majesty, and the image of his goodness.

—WISDOM 7:21-26

Here in the inspired language of the sacred writer we find the Scriptural development which perfects and completes the fragmentary intuitions of Herakleitos, elevating them to the sublime level of contemplative theology and inserting them in the economy of those great truths
of which Herakleitos could not have dreamt: the Incarnation of the
Logos and man's Redemption and Divinization as the supreme manifestation of wisdom and of the "attunement of conflicting opposites."

The heart of Herakleitean epistemology is an implicit contrast between man's wisdom, which fails to grasp the concrete reality of unity
in multiplicity and harmony in conflict, but which instead seizes upon
one or other of the conflicting elements and tries to build on this a static
and one-sided truth which cannot help but be an artificial fiction. The
wisdom of man cannot follow the divine wisdom "one and manifold"
in its infinitely varied movement. Yet it aspires to a universal grasp of
all reality. In order to "see" our minds seize upon the movement around
them and within them, and reduce it to immobility. If it were possible
for them to fulfill their deepest wish, our minds would in fact impose
on the dynamism of the cosmos a paralysis willed by our own compul-
siveness and prejudice: and this would ruin the world. For if things
were the way we would have them be, in our arbitrary and shortsighted
conception of "order," they would all move in one direction toward
their ruin, which would be the supreme disorder. All order based purely
on man's conception of reality is merely partial—and partial order leads
to chaos. Then all things would be consumed by fire—or by water. The
real order of the cosmos is an apparent disorder, the "conflict" of opposites which is in fact a stable and dynamic harmony. The wisdom
of man is the product of willfulness, blindness, and caprice and is only
the manifestation of his own insensibility to what is right before his
eyes. But the eyes and ears tell us nothing if our minds are not capable
of interpreting their data.

And so Herakleitos, wielding the sharp weapon of paradox without
mercy, seeks to awaken the mind of his disciple to a reality that is right

before his eyes but that he is incapable of seeing. He wants to liberate him from the cult of "vanity" and to draw him forth from the sleep of formalism and subjective prejudices. Hence the paradox that Herakleitos, who is an uncompromising aristocrat and individualist in thought as well as in life, maintains that the truth is what is common to all. It is the "fire" which is the life of the cosmos as well as of each man. It is spirit and logos. It is "what is right before your eyes." But each individual loses contact with the One Fire and falls back into the "coldness" and moisture and "sleep" of his little subjective world. The awakening is then a recall from the sleep of individualism in this narrow, infantile sense, to the "common" vision of what is universally true. Unfortunately, the sleep of the individual spreads through society and is encouraged by social life itself when it is lived at a low level of spiritual intensity. The life and thought of the "many" is a conspiracy of sleep, a refusal to struggle for the excellence of wisdom which is hard to find. The "many" are content with the inertia of what is commonplace, "given," and familiar. They do not want anything new: or if they do, it must be a mere novelty, a diversion that confirms them in their comfortable inertia and keeps them from being bored with themselves, no more.

Hence, the "many" are complacently willing to be deluded by "polymathy"—the "learning of many things"—the constant succession of novel "truths," new opinions, new doctrines and interpretations, fresh observations and tabulations of phenomena. This multiplicity beguiles the popular mind with a vain appearance of wisdom. But in reality it is nothing but intellectual and spiritual "sleep" which deadens all capacity for the flash of mighty intuition by which multiplicity is suddenly comprehended as basically one—penetrated through and through by the logos, the divine fire.

The wise man must make tremendous efforts to grasp "the unexpected": that is to say he must keep himself alert, he must constantly "seek for himself," and he must not fear to strive for the excellence that will make him an object of hatred and mistrust in the eyes of the conventional majority—as did Hermodorus, whom the Ephesians threw out of their city on the ground that if he wanted to excel he had better go and do it somewhere else, for "we will have none who is best among us."

The aristocratic contempt of Herakleitos for the conventional verbalizing of his fellow citizens was something other than a pose, or a mad reflex of wounded sensibility. It was a prophetic manifestation of intransigent honesty. He refused to hold his peace and spoke out with angry concern for truth. He who had seen "the One" was no longer permitted to doubt, to hedge, to compromise, and to flatter. To treat his intuition as one among many opinions would have been inexcusable. False humility was an infidelity to his deepest self and a betrayal of the fundamental insights of his life. It would have been above all a betrayal of those whom he could not effectively contact except by the shock of paradox. Herakleitos took the same stand as Isaias, who was commanded by God to "blind the eyes of this people" by speaking to them in words that were too simple, too direct, too uncompromising to be acceptable. It is not given to men of compromise to understand parables, for as Herakleitos remarked: "When the things that are right in front of them are pointed out to them, they do not pay attention, though they think they do."

This is the tragedy which most concerns Herakleitos—and which should concern us even more than it did him: the fact that the majority of men think they see, and do not. They believe they listen, but they do not hear. They are "absent when present" because in the act of seeing and hearing they substitute the clichés of familiar prejudice for the new and unexpected truth that is being offered to them. They complacently imagine they are receiving a new light, but in the very moment of apprehension they renew their obsession with the old darkness, which is so familiar that it, and it alone, appears to them to be light.

Divinely impatient with the wordplay and imposture of those pseudo-wise men who deceive others by collecting and reshuffling the current opinions, presenting old errors in new disguises, Herakleitos refused to play their pitiable game. Inspired, as Plato said, by the "more severe muses," he sought excellence, in his intuitions, at the cost of verbal clarity. He would go deep, and emerge to express his vision in oracular verses, rather than flatter the crowd by giving it what it demanded and expected of a philosopher, of a professional scholar we would say today. He would be like "the Lord at Delphi who neither utters nor hides his meaning but shows it by a sign." His words would be neither expositions of doctrine nor explanations of mystery, but simply pointers, plunging toward the heart of reality: "fingers pointing at the moon." He knew very well that many would mistake the finger for the moon, but that was inevitable and he did not attempt to do anything about it.

It is interesting to compare Herakleitos with the Prometheus of Aeschylus. In Prometheus, the Firebearer, we see a similar revolt against Olympian formalism. We notice that the Titan, Prometheus, represents the older, more primitive, more "Dionysian" earth gods of archaic Greece, in rebellion against the newly established tyranny of Zeus.

Aeschylus was consciously introducing politics into his tragedy, and as a result it strikes the modern reader with a tremendous force. The play is as actual as *Darkness at Noon* and the pressure to conform, exercised upon the chained Titan by Hermes, the agent of Zeus, has a shockingly totalitarian ring about it. A great crux for all interpreters of the Prometheus of Aeschylus, in this context, is whether his fire symbolizes science or wisdom. One might argue the point at length but in the end the only satisfactory solution is that it symbolizes both. For Prometheus, fire is science perfected by wisdom and integrally united with wisdom in a "hidden harmony." For the Olympians it is perhaps true to say that wisdom is not important, and that what they begrudge men is science, because science means power. Our interpretation of Prometheus will be completely perverse if we believe that what he wants is power. On the contrary, he represents the protest of love (which unites gods and men in a single family) against power (by which the gods oppress men and keep them in subjection). In this way Herakleitos rebelled against the accepted Olympian order of things preached by Homer and Hesiod.

As a result, most people found him terribly disturbing. They were "fools who are fluttered by every word," "dogs barking at everyone they do not know." In the end they had their revenge: the revenge that popular mediocrity takes upon singular excellence. They created a legend about Herakleitos—a legend which they could understand, for it consigned him forever to a familiar category and left them in comfort. They dismissed him as a crank, a misanthrope, an eccentric kind of beat who thought he was too good for them and who, as a result, condemned himself to a miserable isolation. He preferred loneliness to the warm security of their collective illusion. They called him "the weeping philosopher," though there is very little evidence of tears in his philosophy. The story developed that he finally retired from Ephesus in disgust and went to live alone in the mountains, "feeding on grass and plants." A writer referred to him as the "crowing, mob-reviling, riddling Herakleitos."

The implication was of course that Herakleitos was proud, that he despised the mob. Certainly contempt for other men is not compatible with humility in so far as it excludes love and empathy. It is altogether possible that Herakleitos was a proud man. But can we be sure of this? Is pride synonymous with an aristocratic insistence upon excellence? It takes humility to confront the prejudice and the contempt of all, in order to cling to an unpopular truth. In the popular mind, any failure to "conform," any aspiration to be different, is labeled as pride. But was Herakleitos exalting himself, his own opinions, or the common truth which transcends individuals and opinions? If we understand his doctrine we will see that this latter was the case.

A biographer (writing eight hundred years after his death), collected every story that might make Herakleitos look like a proud eccentric. Basing himself on the fact that Herakleitos had apparently been a member of the hereditary ruling family of Ephesus and had renounced his responsibilities, Diogenes Laertius recorded that:

> When he was asked by the Ephesians to establish laws he refused to do so because the city was already in the grip of its evil constitution. He used to retire to the temple of Artemis (outside the city) and play at knuckle bones with the children; when the Ephesians stood around him he said: "Why, villains, do you marvel? Is it not better to do this than join you in politics?"

No doubt this story is all that the popular mind was able to retain of his mysterious *logion* about "time being a child, playing draughts." They had taken the finger for the moon, and wanted history to ratify their error.

This story of Herakleitos playing knuckle bones in the temple is completely misleading. Several of his fragments show that he was deeply concerned with man's political life. But, as usual with him, the concern is far below the surface of trivial demagoguery and charlatanism which sometimes passes for "politics." Political life, for Herakleitos, was based on the common understanding of the wise, that is of those who were awake, who were aware of the logos, who were attuned to the inner harmony underlying conflicting opposites. Such men would not be easily deluded by the political passion excited by violence and partisan interest. They would not be swept away by popular prejudices or fears, for they would be able to see beyond the limited horizons of their own petty group. Political life is, substantially, the union of those minds who stand far above their group and their time, and who have a deeper, more universal view of history and of men. Such men are necessarily a minority. Their union is not achieved merely by a speculative participation in philosophical insights. It demands great moral energy and sacrifice. They must not be content to see the logos, they must cling to their vision, and defend their insight into unity with their very lives. "Those who speak with understanding must hold fast to what is common as a city holds fast to its law, and even more strongly."

Herakleitos is certainly not antisocial, certainly not an anarchist. He does not reject all law. On the contrary, wise and objective laws are the reflection of the hidden logos and accord with the hidden harmony underlying the seemingly confused movement on the surface of political life. Hence the function of law is not to impose an abstract arbitrary justice which is nothing but the willfulness of a tyrant guided only by his own fantasy and ambition. Law is an expression of that "justice" which is the living harmony of opposites. It is not the vindication of one part of reality as "good" in opposition to another part considered as "evil." It is the expression of the true good which is the inner unity of life itself, the logos which is common to all. Hence it defends the good of all against usurpation by particular groups and individuals seeking only their own limited advantage under the guise of universal "good."

Because of his aphoristic statements about "war" being the "father of all," Herakleitos has been referred to as a fascist. The term is ridiculous, since by war he means chiefly the conflict of apparent opposites wherever it may be found, not simply military conflict. One might just as well call him a Marxist because this reconciliation of opposites looks like Hegelian dialectic. In point of fact, Herakleitos holds that political life is both absurd and unjust as long as the more excellent minds are excluded from fruitful participation in political life by the preponderance of mediocrities. Not that the world must be ruled by academic philosophers: but that the leadership must be in the hands of those who, by their well developed political and moral abilities, are able to discern the common justice, the logos, which is the true good of all and which, in fact, is the key to the meaning of life and of history.

Why write of Herakleitos in our day? Not, after twenty-five hundred years, to make him what he cannot be: popular. But he speaks to our age—if only some of us can hear him—he speaks in parables to those who are afraid of excellence in thought, in life, in spirit, and in intellect. His message to us is spiritual, but few will accept it as such: for we have, by now, got far beyond an Ionian pagan. Or have we? Can it be that some of us who are Christians implicitly use our "faith" as an excuse for not going half as far as Herakleitos went? His thought demands effort, integrity, struggle, sacrifice. It is incompatible with the complacent security which can become for us the first essential in thought and life—we call it "peace." But perhaps Herakleitos is closer than we are to the spiritual and intellectual climate of the Gospel in which the Word that enlightens every man coming into the world is made flesh, enters the darkness which receives Him not: where one must be born again without re-entering the womb; where the Spirit is as the wind, blowing where it pleases, while we do not know where it comes from or where it is going. There was another, far greater than Herakleitos, who spoke in parables. He came to cast fire on the earth. Was He perhaps akin to the Fire of which Herakleitos spoke? The easy way to deny it is to dismiss the Ionian as a pantheist. Tag him with a philosophical label and file him away where he won't make anybody uncomfortable!

But not all Christians have done this. Gerard Manley Hopkins, whose vision of the world is Heraklitean as well as Christian, has wrestled with the thought in a poem that is no complacent evasion of the challenge. For Hopkins, the Cosmos is indeed a "Heraklitean fire." His concept of *inscape* is both Heraklitean and Scotistic. It is an intuition of the patterns and harmonies, the "living character" impressed by life itself revealing the wisdom of the Living God in the mystery of interplaying movements and changes. "Million fueléd, nature's bonfire burns on." The most special, "clearest-selvéd" spark of the divine fire is man himself. This spark is put out by death. But is death the end? Does the fire merely burn with another flame? Hopkins reaches further into the mystery, not playing with words but wrestling with the angel of tribulation, to reach the Resurrection when "world's wildfire leaves but ash" and "I am all at once what Christ is . . . immortal diamond."

Herakleitos did not know Christ. He could not know that the logos would be made flesh and dwell amongst us. Yet he had some intimation of immortality and of resurrection. Some of his mysterious sayings suggest New Testament texts about the Risen Life of man in Christ: "Man kindles for himself a light in the night time when he has died but is alive . . . he that is awake lights up from sleeping." True, he is talking only of the spiritual and intellectual awakening which is the experience of the enlightened one, discovering the logos. But the mystical quality of this experience makes it also a figure of resurrection and new life, in which Herakleitos evidently believed.

He spoke, as we saw above, of the wise man clinging with all his strength to the "common" thought which unites him with other enlightened minds. The wise man must cling to the logos and to his unity with those who are aware of the logos. He must bear witness to the "common" thought even at the cost of his own life. To die for the truth is then the "greatest death" and wins a "greater portion." What is this portion? "There awaits men when they die such things as they look not for nor dream of." The death of the wise man is the "death of fire"; a passage from darkness into greater light, from confusion into unity. The death of the fool clinging to subjective opinion and self-interest is the "death of earth or water," a sinking into coldness, darkness, oblivion, and nonentity. Those who die the death of fire—the death which Christianity was to call martyrdom, and which Herakleitos definitely believed was a "witness" to the Fire and the Logos—become superior beings. They live forever. They take their place among the company of those who watch over the destinies of the cosmos and of men, for they have, in their lives, entered into the secret of the logos. "They who die great deaths rise up to become the wakeful guardians of the living and the dead." The aristocracy in which Herakleitos believed was then not an aristocracy of class, of power, of learning (all these are illusory). It is an aristocracy of the spirit, of wisdom: one might almost say of mysticism and of sanctity.

THE BEHAVIOR OF TITANS

Six: LETTER TO SURKOV

October 29, 1958

To Aleksei Surkov
Soviet Writers' Union
Moscow

Dear Sir:

I am writing this letter to you today as a sincere friend of literature, wherever it may be found, including Russia. I write to you assuming that you are, as I am, interested in the future of man. I assume that we both attach supreme importance to basic human values, in spite of the diversity in the means which we take to protect them. I am aware that for you literature and politics are inseparable. For me, however, I can assure you that this letter has nothing political about it. I am a notoriously, and conspicuously, nonpolitical author. It is probably for this reason that you know little or nothing about me. I am counting on this fact, however, to write an objective and unprejudiced letter about a matter of great importance to us both, and to our respective nations.

But lest you assume too readily that I have some unconscious political bias, I can assure you that I do not find it hard to believe that the capitalist system may sometime evolve into something else, and I will not grieve if it does so. I am passionately opposed to every form of violent aggression in war, revolution, or police terrorism, no matter who may exercise this aggression, and no matter for what "good" ends. I am a man dedicated entirely to peace and to justice, and to the rights of man whether as a citizen, a worker, or, in this case, as a *writer*.

I speak to you in the name of those innumerable Western intellectuals who have waited for years with keen hopeful sympathy to read some great work that might come out of Russia. I speak to you as one who has the most sincere admiration for the Russian literary heritage, in all its extreme richness. But I also speak to you as one who has been repeatedly disappointed by the failure of modern Russian writers to fulfill the tremendous expectations aroused by the great writers of the past.

It was therefore with great joy, and deep respect for Russia, that I and so many like me were able to hail the recent work of Boris Pasternak which burst upon us full of turbulent and irrepressible life, giving us a deeply moving image of the heroic sufferings of the Russian nation and its struggles, sacrifices, and achievements. That this work received the Nobel Prize certainly cannot have been a merely political trick. It is the expression of the sincere and unprejudiced admiration of the world for a Russian genius worthy to inherit the pre-eminence of the great Tolstoi.

What makes you think that we in the West are eager to seize upon those scattered passages which show Communism in a not too favorable light? Have we not heard much stronger things than this said by Khrushchev himself about Stalin in the Twentieth Party Congress of 1956? Was it not natural that when Pasternak heard such things said, he felt that it would be permissible to say much less, and in a much more indirect way, himself?

Pasternak indicates in this book that in the early days of the Revolution there was much senseless brutality. But if you silence Pasternak by violence *now*, are you not giving overwhelming evidence that what he attributed to the early days is still there today? I hardly see how you can avoid condemning yourselves in condemning Pasternak, because he obviously wrote his book with the conviction that tyranny and brutality had come to an end. If you condemn him, and prove him wrong, what does that mean?

If your government is strong and prosperous, what does it have to fear from anything said by Pasternak about the early days of the Revolution? If you silence him it will only be interpreted as a sign of insecurity and weakness. In 1956 the whole world hoped that at last freedom and prosperity would come to reward the long hard years of bitter sacrifice made by the supremely generous Russian nation under Stalin. *Dr. Zhivago* was written with nothing else but this hope in mind. That you condemn the book and its author means that this hope has proved to be a tragic illusion, and that the darkness is settling once again deeper than ever. In condemning Pasternak, you are condemning yourselves and are condemning Russia. If Pasternak suffers unjust and violent retribution for his well-intentioned work, the whole world will feel bitter sorrow for Russia. If Pasternak is punished unjustly when, in good faith, he simply followed the lead of the highest officials in the Party, and spoke out as they did, then it will be a proof that the Soviet system cannot survive where free speech is allowed, and consequently that the Soviet system is committed by its very nature to unrelieved despotism for as long as it may exist.

Are you Communists unable to see how this great book has glorified Russia? Can you not understand that this book will make the whole world love and admire the Russian people and nation, and venerate them for the superb heroism with which they have borne the burdens laid upon them by history? If you punish Pasternak it is because you do not love Russia, do not love mankind, but seek only the limited interests of a political minority.

I had asserted that this would not be a political letter, and yet I find that these last statements have a political nature. You will call them lies. *Please believe that I would be the first man in the world to rejoice if it were proven to me that these statements were false.* I beg you to give me some such proof. I will be delighted to embrace it and to proclaim it. But if Boris Pasternak is beaten down and persecuted for his work, I can never accept any "proof" you might wish to offer. The best proof will be if Pasternak is left free!

You may be offended by the things I have felt it necessary to write. And yet I write to you as a friend, not as an enemy, not as one who hates you. For the Russian nation I have the greatest and most sincere love, and an unbounded admiration. For the present Leaders of Russia I feel no hatred, and no fear, but only sorrow.

In closing, I had thought momentarily that I might challenge you to publishing this letter in *Pravda* along with your arguments against it. Would such a thing be possible in Russia? It would be possible here!

Very sincerely yours,
THOMAS MERTON

Unpublished

Seven: RELIGION AND THE BOMB

MAY, 1962

THE DEVELOPMENTS of the last year have brought home to everyone that war will never be prevented by the sheer menace of nuclear weapons. The H-bomb is too powerful to make war a practical, let alone ethical, solution to international problems. An all-out nuclear war is something that simply cannot be "won." And yet even though we must agree with the coy statement of Herman Kahn, "Almost nobody wants to be the first man in history to kill one hundred million people," it turns out that quite a few men, on both sides of the Iron Curtain, are willing to commit themselves to policies and objectives which may make a nuclear war inevitable.

Since the fifth century, Christian theologians and statesmen have accepted the doctrine of the "just war." Theoretically the just war is a *defensive* war in which force is strictly limited and the greatest care is taken to protect the rights and the lives of noncombatants and even of combatants. History teaches us that these requirements were seldom met in practice. Nevertheless, before the invention of gunpowder, the overwhelming advantage in a contest between equally matched forces belonged to the defender in the walled city or castle.

But today the traditional idea of the "just war" is fraught with ambiguities, since nuclear weapons are *purely offensive* weapons. Not only that, they are weapons which cannot help but annihilate noncombatants, open cities, and even neutrals, due to their enormous and uncontrollable destructive power. Finally, these are weapons against which *there is no really effective defense.* Furthermore, it seems that nuclear weapons are very likely to be used in a massive all-out first strike if they are to be used at all. If tactical nuclear weapons are used in a so-called "limited

288

war" there is no guarantee whatever that the loser will not resort to massive and megatonic retaliation. For a belligerent to control himself in this matter he would have to be far more heroically virtuous than if he were to disarm completely and trust in divine providence.

Hence the theologian is faced with a problem of great complexity if he wants to justify nuclear war by traditional Christian standards.

Meanwhile, in the prevailing climate of uneasiness, with the growing realization that huge stockpiles of nuclear weapons and new missiles not only do not deter a nuclear strike but may well invite one, Christians are beginning to see that the first strike does not necessarily have to come from the Communist side. Though it is true that President Kennedy has declared that the United States would "never strike first," it has been known for presidents to change their minds under pressure, and in any case there are many possibilities of accident, miscalculation, misinterpretation, and plain confusion which might lead to a first strike in the name of Democracy, Liberty, and—Christianity!

The mere suggestion of such a possibility still raises furious protest. One is asked immediately to "prove" it. Well, the United States has been doing a great job preparing for nuclear war, and has given special attention to making our nuclear strike capacity fully *credible*.

Our government clearly wants everyone to know that we have the biggest and best supply of nuclear weapons in the world and that we intend to use them whenever we feel sufficiently provoked to do so. The whole concept of deterrence, on which hopes of peace are still being based by "realists," depends on the *credibility* of this threat. The Russians on their own side are uttering even greater threats. When the full force of two huge mass societies and all their propaganda are devoted to putting this idea across, who am I to disbelieve? I find all that they say about their readiness and willingness to wage a nuclear war entirely credible.

In this grave crisis the future of Christianity and of the whole world may hinge on the heroism and integrity of the faithful. In other words, we find ourselves confronting the possibility of nuclear war with more than common and universal urgency, because we Christians are at least dimly aware that this may still be a matter of *choice* for us and that the future of Christianity on earth may depend on the moral quality of the decision we are making.

Although since Hiroshima there has been a semblance of religious and spiritual renewal in the West, and even in some of the Iron Curtain countries, the reality and depth of the renewal can certainly be questioned. It is true that statistics show quantitative growth, but this does not necessarily imply a development in quality.

The Cold War has been playing on rather inadequate religious sensibilities. It has aroused the dread of imminent disaster. It has at the same time awakened deep hatreds and indeed it has revealed the profoundest tendencies to destructiveness and to suicidal despair.

Precisely the greatest danger of "Cold War religion" is that it provides these destructive tendencies with an apparent ethical and religious justification. It makes nuclear war look like spiritual heroism. It justifies global suicide as sacrifice and martyrdom. If we had not almost completely lost our innate Christian and religious sense we would be utterly aghast at the perversion of the deepest and most sacred of realities. We would be able to see the awful truth that in many ways the Cold War is *systematically perverting and eroding the Christian conscience*.

It is doubtful whether for most Christians the real underlying religious issue is clearly visible. On the contrary, at least in America, the average priest and minister seems to react in much the same way as the average agnostic or atheist. The interests of the West, NATO, and the Church are all confused with one another, and the possibility of defending the West with a nuclear first strike on Russia is sometimes accepted without too much hesitation as "necessary" and a "lesser evil." We assume that Western society and Christendom are still identical and that Communism equals Antichrist. And we are ready to declare without hesitation that "no price is too high" to pay for our religious liberty. The cliché sounds noble to those who are not shocked by its sinister ambiguities.

"Paying the price" used to be equated with Christian sacrifice, or at least with some form of suffering or hardship in which one's own interests were set aside in view of a higher good. But now when we say "no price is too high" we are, it turns out, counting not only our own megacorpses but also twenty, fifty, a hundred, two hundred million dead on the enemy side. No price is too high to pay! In an orgy of sacrificial ardor we will not hesitate to sacrifice *their* children. We will not hesitate to contaminate future generations. No price is too high! We will even annihilate neutrals. We will douse the whole hemisphere with lethal fallout. We will go the limit. We will let Europe and the Near East be immolated. We will sacrifice India (whose inhabitants have not, meanwhile, been consulted).

Should it really be necessary to spell out the fact that this slogan—
"No price is too high"—somehow lacks nobility?

Even if it were established beyond doubt that we were really defending religious freedom, this claim (at such cost) would still be absurd
and immoral. But are we so sure that when we speak of defending our
liberty, our rights, our personal integrity, we are not purely and simply
talking about irresponsibility, good times, a comfortable life?

What are we defending? Our religion or our affluence?

Or have we so identified the two that the distinction is no longer
clear?

◇ COLD WAR AND THEOLOGY

THERE CAN BE no question that we have to defend in every way possible
the true religious, political, and cultural values without which our lives
would lack meaning. But these values cannot be defended by capitula-
tion to a war policy that leads to the defeat and destruction of both sides.
The arguments of those who are now trying to prove that an all-out
nuclear war can be "won" lack even the semblance of plausibility. Their
own most optimistic figures, based on extremely bland assumptions
which they have fed into their computers, show that even if America
"survived" a victory over Russia she could easily become a victim of a
determined aggressor like Red China, which in any case will soon have
its own nuclear weapons.

While there can be no religious justification for a policy of all-out
nuclear aggression, there is a strong and articulate body of theological
opinion in favor of nuclear deterrence and an "adequate posture of
defense." Father John Courtney Murray, who holds this view, hastens
to qualify it by saying the following:

1) The uninhibited violence of nuclear war "disqualifies it as an apt
and proportionate means for the resolution of international conflicts and
even for the redress of just grievances."

2) Appeal to the *jus belli* "seriously blocks progress of the international
community toward that mode of political organization which Pius XII
regarded as the single means for the outlawry of all war, even of defensive war." (In both these statements Father Murray is practically
paraphrasing words of Pius XII.)

3) While he quotes Pius XII to support his contention that the stockpiling of atomic weapons for defense is legitimate, he adds "this does

not morally validate everything that goes on at Cape Canaveral or Los Alamos."

However, Father Murray does not offer a pacifist solution. Taking his stand on the natural law and on the traditional just war theory, he believes that defensive wars may be necessary and that they ought to be fought with conventional weapons or with small nuclear bombs. This is all very well on paper, but when we realize that the twenty-kiloton bomb that was dropped on Hiroshima is now regarded as small and is included among the tactical nuclear weapons which Father Murray would call licit, we see that his position is not so simple. Also, his footnotes and other interpolations seem to suggest that he is not only considering the licitness of megatonic nuclear weapons but also that he is apparently working toward the idea that even a pre-emptive strike could be in some sense regarded as "defense." One wonders if this does not after all tend to validate morally "everything that goes on at Cape Canaveral or Los Alamos."

An eminent Catholic theologian in England, Canon L. L. McReavy, declares without equivocation that the policy of nuclear deterrence, in so far as it relies on a *serious threat of massive nuclear retaliation* against the cities of the enemy is *morally unacceptable*. In an article published in the *Clergy Review* two years ago, Canon McReavy stated, "A positive intention to commit an immoral act in certain circumstances, however much one may hope they will never arise, *is itself here and now immoral*." However, he adds that nuclear weapons may be stockpiled for possible use against "legitimate [military] targets." Here again we fall back into the same practical difficulty, for there is no indication whatever that military strategists are going to make the fine distinctions of the moral theologian.

So Canon McReavy himself admits (in a letter to the *Catholic Herald*) it is probable that nuclear weapons "will not in fact be used with the discrimination required by the moral law, and *I regard it as morally certain that if megaton weapons are used at all, even as a last resort and in self-defense, they will be used immorally.*"

Because of these practical ambiguities there is a strong argument in favor of "relative" or "nuclear" pacifism.

A RECENT COLLECTION of essays by Catholics, *Nuclear Weapons and Christian Conscience* (Merlin Press, London, 1961), frankly takes the stand that the hypotheses of "realists" who seek to justify nuclear war are "doing more from within to undermine Western civilization than the enemy can do from the outside." These Catholic intellectuals protest with all their strength against the "habitual moral squalor" now prevailing, and remind the Christian who may have forgotten the Cross that in a situation like ours we may be forced to choose "the ultimate weapon of meaningful suffering" or deny the Christian faith itself. It is absurd and immoral to pretend that Christendom can be defended by the H-bomb.

As St. Augustine would say, the weapon with which we would attempt to destroy the enemy would pass through our own heart to reach him. We would be annihilated morally and no doubt physically as well. The H-bomb may possibly wipe out Western society if it is used by Communists, but it will destroy Christendom spiritually if it is used as a weapon of aggression by Christians.

It must be noted that these Catholic writers are not formal pacifists. They admit the traditional theory of the "just war" but feel that this concept is no longer viable. At the same time they attack the extreme argument that Christianity must be by its very nature pacifist. One of the writers blames this idealistic view for encouraging the opposite cynical extreme, "doublethink about double effect." The book questions the moral honesty of manufacturing and stockpiling nuclear weapons while "suspending the decision to use them."

Another problem raised by this book: to what extent can the individual claim to remain uncommitted when his government pursues a policy that leads directly to all-out nuclear war? One of the writers answers: "In modern warfare, responsibility for all that is not antecedently, clearly and publicly ruled out must be accepted by anyone who in any way participates in waging the war."

❖ THE FIGHT FOR PEACE

YET IT REMAINS TRUE that there is still a general apathy and passivity among the faithful and the clergy. Perhaps it is exact to say that they are afflicted with a kind of moral paralysis. Hypnotized by the mass media, which tend to be bellicose, baffled and intimidated by the general atmosphere of suspicion, bewildered by the silence or by the ambiguity of their pastors and religious leaders, and remembering the failure of the peace movements that preceded World War II, people tend to withdraw into a state of passive and fatalistic desperation. There they have been literally run to earth by the shelter salesmen, and have set themselves despondently to digging holes in their backyards against the day when the missiles begin to fly.

What are the chances of a religious peace movement in such a grim situation? They would seem to be very slight. On one hand, the astute and tireless propaganda of the Soviets has succeeded without too much difficulty in giving disarmament a bad name by associating it entirely with Communist cold-war pressures. Anyone in the West who speaks up for disarmament, by that very fact automatically runs the risk of being called a Communist agent or a fellow traveler.

Pacifism has a noxious reputation. It is not properly understood. Distinctions between nuclear pacifism and absolute pacifism are not made. The pacifist is automatically categorized as a kind of pathetic idiot, a coward trying to salvage his self-respect by an appeal to confused and sentimental ideals. He can do no good. He only plays into the hands of the enemy.

It is true that pacifist movements tend to attract a certain number of professional oddballs. It is also perfectly true that peace movements in democratic countries run the risk of being exploited by Communist elements, whether secret or overt. But it should not be necessary to state that one can favor a policy of nuclear disarmament, even unilateral, without being a Red, a beatnik, or a "pacifist."

Someone will ask: is it after all permissible for a Catholic to be a limited pacifist? Is not even relative pacifism an expression of radicalism and disobedience, which would be unthinkable in a true Catholic? If the Church has not formally and expressly condemned nuclear war, is not the Catholic who claims to be a nuclear pacifist, by that fact pretending to be "more Catholic than the Church?"

Here we must quite frankly face the ambiguous statement that the Church has "never condemned nuclear weapons." Is this really exact?

Certainly the Pope has never uttered a formal *ex cathedra* condemnation that would outlaw nuclear war. But is it necessary for him to do this? Is it not sufficient that the principles be clarified by the teaching authority of the Church and left to the faithful to apply for themselves?

There exist more than a score of clear statements by Pius XII and John XXIII which deplore, in the strongest terms, all recourse to war and violence in the settlement of international disputes. These statements are not something new. They were not made necessary by the atomic bomb. Even before World War II, Pope Pius XII warned that war with conventional methods could be criminal. In 1939, after the *Blitzkrieg* in Poland, Pope Pius declared that the unlawful use of *conventional* weapons against civilians and refugees "cried out to Heaven for vengeance."

He also said, in October 1953, that "all glorification of war is to be condemned as a deviation of the mind and heart." In his 1944 Christmas Message, before Hiroshima, he had asserted that "the theory of war as an apt and proportionate means of solving international conflicts is now out of date," and he declared that the duty of banning all wars of aggression was *"binding on all."* This duty, he said, *"brooks no delay, no procrastination, no hesitation, no subterfuge."* Pope Pius XII denounced nuclear annihilation bombing very clearly and without any possibility of being mistaken. In an address to the World Medical Association in 1954, he declared that from the moment a weapon was so destructive that its effects could not be controlled and limited to military objectives, it became immoral. Here are his words:

"Should the evil consequences of adopting this method of warfare ever become so extensive as to pass utterly beyond the control of man, then indeed its use must be rejected as immoral. In that event it would no longer be a question of defense against injustice and necessary protection of legitimate possessions, but of the annihilation pure and simple of all human life within the affected area. This is not lawful on any title."

We must note that this applies equally to offensive and defensive war. While it is obligatory to defend one's nation against unjust aggression, only legitimate means can be used. And if the destructive effect of war is far greater than the political injustice suffered, war is not legitimate. "If the damage caused by the war is disproportionate to the injustice suffered, it may well be a matter of obligation to suffer the injustice," Pope Pius XII said to army doctors on October 19, 1953.

Unfortunately, statements like this one, though dutifully reported in the press and respectfully noted by the faithful are seldom really assimilated by them. That is why the serious moral implications of the measured papal denunciations of nuclear war appear overlooked.

The popes have not merely been trying to say that nuclear war is not nice, but that it radically affects traditional Catholic norms of the morality of war. This is an essentially new kind of war and one in which the necessary conditions for "a just" war are extremely difficult to maintain. A war of total annihilation simply cannot be considered a "just war," no matter how good the cause for which it is undertaken.

Such is the view taken by no less authoritative a theologian than Cardinal Ottaviani, Secretary of the Holy Office. Writing before the development of the H-bomb, the Cardinal (then Monsignor) said without ambiguity:

"The war of their treatises is not the war of our experience. Principles

derive from the very nature of things: the difference between war as it
was and as we know it is *precisely one of nature*. . . . Modern wars can
never fulfill the conditions which govern, theoretically, a just and lawful
war. Moreover, no conceivable cause could ever be sufficient justification for the evils, the slaughter, the moral and religious upheavals which
war today entails."

Such is the thesis in an article by Cardinal Ottaviani entitled "War
Is to Be Forbidden Entirely," published in Latin in his *Public Laws of
the Church* (Rome, 1947). Unfortunately such opinions have not been
widely disseminated. It may be said also that statements like this do not
exclude the defensive use of nuclear weapons in tactical warfare, assuming that such warfare can be "kept within limits."

Let us add one more authoritative statement. The French bishops,
when questioned about the lawfulness of nuclear weapons, replied in
June 1950 that such a question *did not even need to be asked,* since
nuclear war was already condemned by the *"elementary sense of humanity."* The bishops nevertheless spelled out the answer quite clearly for
those who no longer knew how to listen to the law of God implanted in
their hearts. They said "we condemn [nuclear weapons] with all our
strength."

After so many statements, made so clearly and with such authority,
can we still assume that a Catholic who protests against nuclear war is
"trying to be more Catholic than the Church?"

How can we go on deceiving ourselves that it is somehow a Christian
duty, prescribed by the Church, for us to collaborate in nuclear mass
murder just because Pope Pius XII also affirmed that the state still retained its legitimate right of self-defense?

Certainly the moral risks of nuclear war do not deprive any nation of
the basic natural right to defend itself by ordinary means. Nor do they
dispense the citizen from helping the nation so to defend itself. The
point at issue is not self-defense, but the *means used* in self-defense. It
is pure sophistry to contend that because Pius XII said that self-defense
by legitimate means was still mandatory, therefore self-defense by *any*
means has now become legitimate.

If the nation prepares to defend itself by methods that will almost
certainly be immoral and illicit, then the Christian has *not only the right
but also the duty* to question the validity of these methods, and to protest against them, even to the point of refusing his cooperation in their
unjust and immoral use.

❖ CONCLUSIONS

THROUGHOUT THIS ARTICLE we have addressed ourselves in a general way to all those who still cling to the Judaeo-Christian traditions of the Western world. In conclusion let us consider our obligation as Catholics. Certainly this obligation cannot and must not be reduced to the choice of one particular political and military policy. But we must recognize the basic moral principle that the *unlimited* and *terroristic* use of nuclear weapons, or for that matter of conventional weapons, is always immoral, always criminal, and therefore always totally unacceptable to the Christian conscience.

This principle having been clarified, we can go on to examine other methods of defending ourselves against the enemies of our nation and of our Christian heritage.

The real problem is not so much the choice of a particular means, the selection of a more or less acceptable policy. The malady lies deeper than that. The present confusion and irresponsibility which lead so many "good Christians" to accept, instinctively and without question, a strategy which has been repeatedly criticized by the popes, must be symptomatic of that "deviation of the mind and heart" deplored by Pius XII. And the fact that they can point to theologians and publicists who encourage them in their aberration makes the problem all the more serious. The truth is that when the popes warn against our grave and imminent danger of being involved in war crimes, we do not hear them, and their message does not register. At best, if we are paying attention at all, we are hunting for the escape clause that enables us to continue in maintaining the more precarious moral position.

If we are going to defend Christianity and save it from the disastrous inroads of materialism and totalitarian autocracy, we must begin by realizing that the struggle necessarily begins within ourselves, both personally and as a group. The problem affects both the individual and the collective conscience of Christians.

If we spontaneously approve of nuclear terrorism, if we become apologists for the uninhibited use of naked power, we are thinking like Communists, we are behaving like Nazis, and we are well on the way to becoming either one or the other. In that event we had better face the fact that we are destroying our own Christian heritage.

Jubilee

Eight: WAR AND THE PRAYER FOR PEACE

AT THE ROOT OF ALL WAR is fear: not so much the fear men have of one another as the fear they have of *everything*. It is not merely that they do not trust one another; they do not even trust themselves. If they are not sure when someone else may turn around and kill them, they are still less sure when they may turn around and kill themselves. They cannot trust anything, because they have ceased to believe in God.

IT IS not only our hatred of others that is dangerous but also and above all our hatred of ourselves: particularly that hatred of ourselves which is too deep and too powerful to be consciously faced. For it is this which makes us see our own evil in others and unable to see it in ourselves.

When we see crime in others, we try to correct it by destroying them or at least putting them out of sight. It is easy to identify the sin with the sinner when he is someone other than our own self. In ourselves, it is the other way round; we see the sin, but we have great difficulty in shouldering responsibility for it. We find it very hard to identify our sin with our own will and our own malice. On the contrary, we naturally tend to interpret our immoral act as an involuntary mistake, or as the malice of a spirit in us that is other than ourself. Yet at the same time we are fully aware that others do not make this convenient distinction for us. The acts that have been done by us are, in their eyes, "our" acts, and they hold us fully responsible.

What is more, we tend unconsciously to ease ourselves still more of the burden of guilt that is in us, by passing it on to somebody else. When I have done wrong, and have excused myself by attributing the wrong to "another" who is unaccountably "in me," my conscience is not yet satisfied. There is still too much left to be explained. The "other in myself"

298

is too close to home. The temptation is, then, to account for my fault by seeing an equivalent amount of evil in someone else. Hence I minimize my own sins and compensate for doing so by exaggerating the faults of others.

As if this were not enough, we make the situation much worse by artifically intensifying our sense of evil, and by increasing our propensity to feel guilt even for things which are not in themselves wrong. In all these ways we build up such an obsession with evil, both in ourselves and in others, that we waste all our mental energy trying to account for this evil, to punish it, to exorcise it, or to get rid of it in any way we can. We drive ourselves mad with our preoccupation and in the end there is no outlet left but violence. We have to destroy something or someone. By that time we have created for ourselves a suitable enemy, a scapegoat in whom we have invested all the evil in the world. He is the cause of every wrong. He is the fomentor of all conflict. If he can only be destroyed, conflict will cease, evil will be done with, there will be no more war.

This kind of fictional thinking is especially dangerous when it is supported by a whole elaborate pseudo-scientific structure of myths, like those which Marxists have adopted as their ersatz for religion. But it is certainly no less dangerous when it operates in the vague, fluid, confused, and unprincipled opportunism which substitutes in the West for religion, for philosophy, and even for mature thought.

❖ MORAL CONFUSION

WHEN THE WHOLE WORLD is in moral confusion, when no one knows any longer what to think, and when, in fact, everybody is running away from the responsibility of thinking, when man makes rational thought about moral issues absurd by exiling himself entirely from realities into the realm of fictions, and when he expends all his efforts in constructing more fictions with which to account for his ethical failures, then it becomes clear that the world cannot be saved from global war and global destruction by the mere efforts and good intentions of peacemakers. In actual fact, everyone is becoming more and more aware of the widening gulf between good purposes and bad results, between efforts to make peace and the growing likelihood of war. It seems that no matter how elaborate and careful the planning all attempts at international dialogue end in more and more ludicrous failures. In the end no one has any more faith in those who even attempt the dialogue. On the contrary, the negotiators, with all their pathetic good will, become the objects of contempt and of hatred. It is the "men of good will," the men who have made their poor efforts to do something about peace, who will in the end be the most mercilessly reviled, crushed, and destroyed as victims of the universal self-hate of man which they have unfortunately only increased by the failure of their good intentions.

Perhaps we still have a basically superstitious tendency to associate failure with dishonesty and guilt—failure being interpreted as "punishment." Even if a man starts out with good intentions, if he fails we tend to think he was somehow "at fault." If he was not guilty, he was at least "wrong." And "being wrong" is something we have not yet learned to face with equanimity and understanding. We either condemn it with godlike disdain or forgive it with godlike condescension. We do not manage to accept it with human compassion, humility, and identification. Thus we never see the one truth that would help us begin to solve our ethical and political problems: that we are *all* more or less wrong, that we are *all* at fault, *all* limited and obstructed by our mixed motives, our self-deception, our greed, our self-righteousness, and our tendency to aggressivity and hypocrisy.

IN OUR REFUSAL to accept the partially good intentions of others and work with them (of course prudently and with resignation to the inevitable imperfection of the result) we are unconsciously proclaiming our own malice, our own intolerance, our own lack of realism, our own ethical and political quackery.

Perhaps in the end the first real step toward peace would be a realistic acceptance of the fact that our political ideals are perhaps to a great extent illusions and fictions to which we cling out of motives that are not always perfectly honest: that because of this we prevent ourselves from seeing any good or any practicability in the political ideals of our enemies—which may, of course, be in many ways even more illusory and dishonest than our own. We will never get anywhere unless we can accept the fact that politics is an inextricable tangle of good and evil motives in which, perhaps, the evil predominate but where one must continue to hope doggedly in what little good can still be found.

But someone will say: "If we once recognize that we are all equally wrong, all political action will instantly be paralyzed. We can only act when we assume that we are in the right." On the contrary, I believe the basis for valid political action can only be the recognition that the true solution to our problems is *not* accessible to any one isolated party or nation but that all must arrive at it by working together.

I DO NOT MEAN to encourage the guilt-ridden thinking that is always too glad to be "wrong" in everything. This too is an evasion of responsibility, because every form of oversimplification tends to make decisions ultimately meaningless. We must try to accept ourselves, whether individually or collectively, not only as perfectly good or perfectly bad, but in our mysterious, unaccountable mixture of good and evil. We have to stand by the modicum of good that is in us without exaggerating it. We have to defend our real rights, because unless we respect our own rights we will certainly not respect the rights of others. But at the same time we have to recognize that we have willfully or otherwise trespassed on the rights of others. We must be able to admit this not only as the result of self-examination, but when it is pointed out unexpectedly, and perhaps not too gently, by somebody else.

These principles which govern personal moral conduct, which make harmony possible in small social units like the family, also apply in the wider area of the state and in the whole community of nations. It is, however, quite absurd, in our present situation or in any other, to expect these principles to be universally accepted as the result of moral exhortations. There is very little hope that the world will be run according to moral principles, all of a sudden, as a result of some hypothetical change of heart on the part of politicians. It is useless and even laughable to base political thought on the faint hope of a purely contingent and subjective moral illumination in the hearts of the world's leaders. Yet outside of political thought and action, in the religious sphere, it is not only permissible to hope for such a mysterious consummation, but it is necessary to pray for it. We can and must believe not so much that the mysterious light of God can "convert" the ones who are mostly responsible for the world's peace, but at least that they may, in spite of their obstinacy and their prejudices, be guarded against fatal error.

✧ ON PRAYING FOR PEACE

WHAT IS THE use of postmarking our mail with exhortations to "pray for peace" and then spending billions of dollars on atomic submarines, thermonuclear weapons, and ballistic missiles? This, I would think, would certainly be what the New Testament calls "mocking God"—and mocking Him far more effectively than the atheists do. The culminating horror of the joke is that we are piling up these weapons to protect ourselves against atheists who, quite frankly, believe there is no God and are convinced that one has to rely on bombs and missiles since nothing else offers any real security. Is it then because we have so much trust in the power of God that we are intent upon utterly destroying these people before they can destroy us? Even at the risk of destroying ourselves at the same time?

I DO NOT MEAN to imply that prayer excludes the simultaneous use of ordinary human means to accomplish a naturally good and justifiable end. One can very well pray for a restoration of physical health and at the same time take medicine prescribed by a doctor. In fact, a believer should normally do both. And there would seem to be a reasonable and right proportion between the use of these two means to the same end.

But consider the utterly fabulous amount of money, planning, energy, anxiety, and care which go into the production of weapons which almost immediately become obsolete and have to be scrapped. Contrast all this with the pitiful little gesture "pray for peace" piously canceling our four-cent stamps! Think, too, of the disproportion between our piety and the enormous act of murderous destruction which we at the same time countenance without compunction and without shame! It does not even seem to enter our minds that there might be some incongruity in praying to the God of peace, the God Who told us to love one another as He had loved us, Who warned us that they who took the sword would perish by it, and at the same time planning to annihilate not thousands but millions of civilians and soldiers, men, women, and children without discrimination, even with the almost infallible certainty of inviting the same annihilation for ourselves!

It may make sense for a sick man to pray for health and then take medicine, but I fail to see any sense at all in his praying for health and then drinking poison.

WHEN I PRAY for peace I pray God to pacify not only the Russians and the Chinese but above all my own nation and myself. When I pray for peace I pray to be protected not only from the Reds but also from the folly and blindness of my own country. When I pray for peace, I pray not only that the enemies of my country may cease to want war, but above all that my own country will cease to do the things that make war inevitable. In other words, when I pray for peace I am not just praying that the Russians will give up without a struggle and let us have our own way. I am praying that both we and the Russians may somehow be restored to sanity and learn how to work out our problems, as best we can, together, instead of preparing for global suicide.

I am fully aware that this sounds utterly sentimental, archaic, and out of tune with an age of science. But I would like to submit that pseudo-scientific thinking in politics and sociology have so far had much less than this to offer. One thing I would like to add in all fairness is that the atomic scientists themselves are quite often the ones most concerned about the ethics of the situation, and that they are among the few who dare to open their mouths from time to time and say something about it.

But who on earth listens?

NEW SEEDS OF CONTEMPLATION

✧ PRAYER FOR PEACE

Almighty and merciful God, Father of all men, Creator and Ruler of the Universe, Lord of History, whose designs are inscrutable, whose glory is without blemish, whose compassion for the errors of men is inexhaustible, in your will is our peace!

Mercifully hear this prayer which rises to you from the tumult and desperation of a world in which you are forgotten, in which your name is not invoked, your laws are derided and your presence is ignored. Because we do not know you, we have no peace.

From the heart of an eternal silence, you have watched the rise of empires and have seen the smoke of their downfall.

You have seen Egypt, Assyria, Babylon, Greece, and Rome, once powerful, carried away like sand in the wind.

You have witnessed the impious fury of ten thousand fratricidal wars, in which great powers have torn whole continents to shreds in the name of peace and justice.

And now our nation itself stands in imminent danger of a war the like of which has never been seen!
This nation dedicated to freedom, not to power,
Has obtained, through freedom, a power it did not desire.

And seeking by that power to defend its freedom, it is enslaved by the processes and policies of power.

Must we wage a war we do not desire, a war that can do us no good,
And which our very hatred of war forces us to prepare?

A day of ominous decision has now dawned on this free nation.
Armed with a titanic weapon, and convinced of our own right
We face a powerful adversary, armed with the same weapon, equally
convinced that he is right.

In this moment of destiny, this moment we never foresaw, we cannot
afford to fail.
Our choice of peace or war may decide our judgment and publish it in
an eternal record.

In this fatal moment of choice in which we might begin the patient
architecture of peace
We may also take the last step across the rim of chaos.

Save us then from our obsessions! Open our eyes, dissipate our confusions, teach us to understand ourselves and our adversary!
Let us never forget that sins against the law of love are punished by loss
of faith,
And those without faith stop at no crime to achieve their ends!

Help us to be masters of the weapons that threaten to master us.
Help us to use our science for peace and plenty, not for war and destruction.
Show us how to use atomic power to bless our children's children, not
to blight them.

Save us from the compulsion to follow our adversaries in all that we
most hate
Confirming them in their hatred and suspicion of us.

Resolve our inner contradictions, which now grow beyond belief and
beyond bearing.
They are at once a torment and a blessing: for if you had not left us
the light of conscience, we would not have to endure them.

Teach us to be long-suffering in anguish and insecurity.

Teach us to wait and trust.
Grant light, grant strength and patience to all who work for peace
To this Congress, our President, our military forces, and our adversaries.

Grant us prudence in proportion to our power,
Wisdom in proportion to our science,
Humaneness in proportion to our wealth and might,
And bless our earnest will to help all races and peoples to travel, in friendship with us,
Along the road to justice, liberty, and lasting peace:
But grant us above all to see that our ways are not necessarily your ways,
That we cannot fully penetrate the mystery of your designs
And that the very storm of power now raging on this earth
Reveals your hidden will and your inscrutable decision.
Grant us to see your face in the lightning of this cosmic storm,
O God of holiness, merciful to men:
Grant us to seek peace where it is truly found!

In your will, O God, is our peace!

AMEN

Unpublished

Nine: ST. JOHN OF THE CROSS

I F YOU HAVE NEVER seen El Greco's view of Toledo, you might take a look at it. It will tell you something about St. John of the Cross. I say it will tell you something—not very much. St. John of the Cross and El Greco were contemporaries, they lived in the same country, they were mystics, though by no means in the same degree. In other ways they were quite different. Father Bruno, in the best life of St. John of the Cross so far written, reminds his reader several times not to go imagining that St. John of the Cross looked like an El Greco painting. He was more like one of Zurbaran's Carthusians. Even that comparison is not altogether exact. The original and authentic portrait of the saint shows him to have an innocent and rather expressionless face. He does not look in any way ascetic. In fact you would think you were looking at the portrait of a Madrid shopkeeper or of a cook.

El Greco's view of Toledo is very dramatic. It is full of spiritual implications. It looks like a portrait of the heavenly Jerusalem wearing an iron mask. Yet there is nothing inert about these buildings. The dark city built on its mountain seems to be entirely alive. It surges with life, coordinated by some mysterious, providential upheaval which drives all these masses of stone upward toward heaven, in the clouds of a blue disaster that foreshadows the end of the world.

Somewhere in the middle of the picture must be the building where St. John of the Cross was kept in prison. Soon after the beginning of St. Theresa's reform he was kidnaped by opponents of the reform, and disappeared. No one had any idea where he had gone and, as St. Theresa lamented, nobody seemed to care. He was locked up in a cell without light or air during the stifling heat of a Toledan summer to await trial and punishment for what his persecutors seriously believed to be a canonical crime. The complex canonical and political implications of the Carmelite reform had involved the saints of that reform in the kind of intrigue for which they alone, of all Spain, had no taste. And even St. Theresa, whose dovelike simplicity was supported by an altogether devastating prudence in these adventures, seems to have rather enjoyed them.

John of the Cross found little that was humanly speaking enjoyable in his Toledo jail. His only excursions from his cell came on the days when he was brought down to the refectory to be publicly scourged by his jailers, who were scandalized at his meek silence, believing it to be the sign of a reprobate conscience, hardened in rebellion. Why didn't the man do something to defend himself?

Here in Toledo, in what he called "the belly of the whale," the saint, wisely more silent than the prophet Jonas, dealt not with men but with God alone, waiting patiently for the divine answer that would end this dark night of his soul. No one knows when or how the answer came, but when St. John made his miraculous escape during the octave of the Assumption, in 1578, he carried in his pocket the manuscript of a poem which respectable critics have declared to be superior to any other in the Spanish language. These critics range from Menendez y Pelayo, who may be deemed to be respectable in a rather stuffy sense, to more recent and more advanced writers. Even the London magazine, *Horizon,* included two very competent articles on St. John of the Cross in a series of "studies of genius." As far as I know, John of the Cross was the only saint in the series.

El Greco was painting in Toledo when St. John of the Cross was in prison there. But the imprisonment of St. John of the Cross, and the *Spiritual Canticle* which bloomed miraculously in the closet where he was jailed, had little to do with the exiled Greek. The color scheme is quite different. The painter's view of the city must be a winter view, black, purple, green, blue, and gray. And the movement is a blind upheaval in which earth and sky run off the top of the canvas like an ebbtide in the arctic ocean. The color scheme of John's imprisonment is black and ocher and brown and red: the red is his own blood running down his back. The movement is centripetal. There is a tremendous stability, not merely in the soul immobilized, entombed in a burning stone wall, but in the depths of that soul, purified by a purgatory that those alone know who have felt it, emerging into the Center of all centers, the Love which moves the heavens and the stars, the Living God.

The last place in the world where one would imagine the *Spiritual Canticle* to have been written is a dungeon!

I will try to translate a little of it:

> My Beloved is like the mountains.
> Like the lonely valleys full of woods
> The strange islands
> The rivers with their sound
> The whisper of the lovely air!
>
> The night, appeased and hushed
> About the rising of the dawn,
> The music stilled
> The sounding solitude
> The supper that rebuilds my life
> And brings me love.
>
> Our bed of flowers
> Surrounded by the lions' dens
> Makes us a purple tent,
> Is built of peace.
> Our bed is crowned with a thousand shields of gold!
>
> Fast-flying birds
> Lions, harts, and leaping does[1]
> Mountains, banks, and vales
> Streams, breezes, heats of day
> And terrors watching in the night:
>
> By the sweet lyres and by the siren's song
> I conjure you: let angers end!
> And do not touch the wall
> But let the bride be safe: let her sleep on!

Only the saint and God can tell what distant echoes of an utterly alien everyday common life penetrated the darkness of the jail cell and the infinitely deep sleep of the peace in which his soul lay hidden in God. *Touch not the wall* . . . but the religious police could not disturb the ecstasy of one who had been carried so far that he was no longer troubled at the thought of being rejected even by the holy!

NO ONE can become a saint without solving the problem of suffering. No one who has ever written anything, outside the pages of Scripture, has

given us such a solution to the problem as St. John of the Cross. I will
not speculate upon his answers. I will merely mention the fact that they
exist and pass on. For those who want to read it, there is the *Dark Night
of the Soul*. But this much must be said: Sanctity can never abide a
merely speculative solution to the problem of suffering. Sanctity solves
the problem not by analyzing but by suffering. It is a living solution,
burned in the flesh and spirit of the saint by fire. Scripture itself tells us
as much. "As silver is tried by fire and gold in the furnace, so the Lord
trieth hearts" (Prov. 17:3). "Son, when thou comest to the service of
God, stand in justice and fear and prepare thy soul for temptation.
Humble thy heart and endure: incline thy ear and receive the words of
understanding and make not haste in the time of clouds. Wait on God
with patience: join thyself to God and endure, that thy life may be
increased in the latter end. Take all that shall be brought upon thee, and
in thy sorrow endure and in thy humiliation keep patience. For gold and
silver are tried in the fire and acceptable men in the furnace of humiliation" (Eccles. 2:1-5).

Sanctity does not consist in suffering. It is not even directly produced
by suffering, for many have suffered and have become devils rather
than saints. What is more, there are some who gloat over the sufferings of the saints and are hideously sentimental about sufferings of
their own, and cap it all by a voracious appetite for inflicting suffering on other people, sometimes in the name of sanctity. Of such were
those who persecuted St. John of the Cross in his last days, and helped
him to enter heaven with greater pain and greater heroism. These
were not the "calced" who caught him at the beginning of his career,
but the champion ascetics of his own reformed family, the men of the
second generation, those who unconsciously did their best to ruin the
work of the founders, and who quite consciously did everything they
could to remove St. John of the Cross from a position in which he
would be able to defend what he knew to be the Theresian ideal.

Sanctity itself is a living solution of the problem of suffering. For
the saint, suffering continues to be suffering, but it ceases to be an
obstacle to his mission, or to his happiness, both of which are found
positively and concretely in the will of God. The will of God is found
by the saint less in *manifestations* of the divine good-pleasure than in
God Himself.

Suffering, on the natural level, is always opposed to natural joy.
There is no opposition between natural suffering and supernatural
joy. Joy, in the supernatural order, is simply an aspect of charity. It

is inseparable from the love that is poured forth in our hearts by the Holy Ghost. But when sanctity is not yet mature, its joy is not always recognizable. It can too easily be buried under pain. But true charity, far from being diminished by suffering, uses suffering as it uses everything else: for the increase of its own immanent vitality. Charity is the expression of a divine life within us, and this life, if we allow it to have its way, will grow and thrive most in the very presence of all that seems to destroy life and to quench its flame. A life that blazes with a hundredfold brilliance in the face of death is therefore invincible. Its joy cannot fail. It conquers everything. It knows no suffering. Like the Risen Christ, Who is its Author and Principle, it knows no death.

THE LIFE OF CHARITY was perfect in the great Carmelite reformer, St. John of the Cross. It was so perfect that it can hardly be said to shine before men. His soul was too pure to attract any attention. Yet precisely because of his purity, he is one of the few saints who can gain a hearing in the most surprising recesses of an impure world. John of the Cross, who seems at first sight to be a saint for the most pure of the Christian elite, may very well prove to be the last hope of harlots and publicans. The wisdom of this extraordinary child "reaches from end to end mightily." Lost in the pure wisdom of God, like God, and in God, he attains to all things. This saint, so often caricatured as an extremist, is actually beyond all extremes. Having annihilated all extremes in the center of his own humility, he remains colorless and neutral. His doctrine, which is considered inhumanly hard, is only hard because it is superhumanly simple. Its simplicity seems to present an obstacle to our nature, which seeks to hide itself from God in a labyrinth of mental complexities, like Adam and Eve amidst the leaves of Paradise.

The hardest thing to accept, in St. John of the Cross, is not the Cross, but the awful neutrality of his interior solitude. After all, as he so reasonably points out, when the soul is detached, by the Cross, from every sensible and spiritual obstacle, its journey to God becomes easy and joyful: "The Cross is the staff whereby one may reach Him, and whereby the road is greatly lightened and made easy. Wherefore Our Lord said through St. Matthew: My yoke is easy and my burden is light, which burden is the Cross. For if a man resolve to submit himself to carrying his cross—that is to say, if he resolve to desire in truth to meet trials and to bear them in all things for God's sake, he will find in them great relief and sweetness wherewith he may travel on this road, detached from all things and desiring nothing." [2]

The two words "desiring nothing" contain all the difficulty and all the simplicity of St. John of the Cross. But no Christian has a right to complain of them. They are simply an echo of two words that sum up the teaching of Jesus Christ in the Gospel: *abneget semetipsum.* "If any man would come after me, let him *deny himself. . . ."*

This total self-denial, which St. John of the Cross pursues into the inmost depths of the human spirit, reduces our interior landscape to a wasteland without special features of any kind whatever. We do not even have the consolation of beholding a personal disaster. A cataclysm of the spirit, if terrible, is also interesting. But the soul of the contemplative is happy to be reduced to a state of complete loneliness and dereliction in which the most significant renouncement is that of self-complacency. Many men are attracted to a solitude in which they believe that they will have the leisure and the opportunity to contemplate themselves. Not so St. John of the Cross: "These times of aridity cause the soul to journey in all purity in the love of God, since it is no longer influenced in its actions by the pleasure and sweetness of the actions themselves . . . but only by a desire to please God. It becomes neither presumptuous nor self-satisfied, as perchance it was wont to become in the time of its prosperity, but fearful and timid with regard to itself, finding in itself no satisfaction whatsoever; and herein consists that holy fear which preserves and increases the virtues. . . . Save for the pleasure indeed which at certain times God infuses into it, it is a wonder if it find pleasure and consolation of sense, through its own diligence, in any spiritual exercise or action. . . . There grows within souls that experience this arid night (of the senses) care for God and yearnings to serve Him, for in proportion as the breasts of sensuality wherewith it sustained and nourished the desires that it pursued, are drying up, there remains nothing in that aridity and detachment save the yearning to serve God, which is a thing very pleasing to God." [3]

The joy of this emptiness, this weird neutrality of spirit which leaves the soul detached from the things of the earth and not yet in possession of those of heaven, suddenly blossoms out into a pure paradise of liberty, of which the saint sings in his *Spiritual Canticle:* it is a solitude full of wild birds and strange trees, rocks, rivers, and desert islands, lions and leaping does. These creatures are images of the joys of the spirit, aspects of interior solitude, fires that flash in the abyss of the pure heart whose loneliness becomes alive with the deep lightnings of God.

IF I SAY that St. John of the Cross seems to me to be the most accessible of the saints, that is only another way of saying that he is my favorite saint—together with three others who also seem to me most approachable: St. Benedict, St. Bernard, and St. Francis of Assisi. After all, the people you make friends with are the ones who welcome you into their company. But besides this, it also seems to me that St. John of the Cross is absolutely and in himself a most accessible saint. This, to those who find him forbidding, will seem an outrageous paradox. Nevertheless it is true, if you consider that few saints, if any, have ever opened up to other men such remote depths in their own soul. St. John of the Cross admits you, in the *Living Flame,* to his soul's "deepest center," to the "deep caverns" in which the lamps of fire, the attributes of God, flash mysteriously in metaphysical shadows; who else has done as much? St. John reveals himself to us not in allegory, as does St. Theresa (in the *Mansions*) but in *symbol.* And symbol is a far more potent and effective medium than allegory. It is truer because it is more direct and more intimate. It does not need to be worked out and applied by the reason. The symbols that spring from the depths of the heart of St. John of the Cross awaken kindred symbols in the depths of the heart that loves him. Their effect, of course, is supported and intensified by grace which, we may believe, the saint himself has begged for the souls of those who have been called to love him in God. Here is a union and a friendship of the soul with God Himself. Earth knows no such intimacies. Those who love St. Peter from the Gospels, and react in vivid sympathy for his all too human experiences, do not come as close to Peter as the one who meets St. John of the Cross in the depths of prayer. We know St. Peter on a more exterior surface of life—the level of passion and emotion. But on that level there is less communion, and less effective communication, than in the depths of the spirit.

And thus St. John of the Cross not only makes himself accessible to us, but does much more: he makes us accessible to ourselves by opening our hearts to God within their own depths.

In the end, however, I may as well have the courtesy to admit one thing: St. John of the Cross is not everybody's food. Even in a contemplative monastery there will be some who will never get along with him—and others who, though they think they know what he is about, would do better to let him alone. He upsets everyone who thinks that his doctrine is supposed to lead one by a way that is exalted. On the contrary, his way is so humble that it ends up by being no way at all, for John of the Cross is unfriendly to systems and a bitter enemy of all exaltation. *Omnis qui se exaltat humiliabitur*. His glory is to do without glory for the love of Christ.

John of the Cross is the patron of those who have a vocation that is thought, by others, to be spectacular, but which, in reality, is lowly, difficult, and obscure. He is the patron and the protector and master of those whom God has led into the uninteresting wilderness of contemplative prayer. His domain is precisely defined. He is the patron of contemplatives in the strict sense, and of their spiritual directors, not of contemplatives in the juridical sense. He is the patron of those who pray in a certain way in which God wants them to pray, whether they happen to be in the cloister, the desert, or the city. Therefore his influence is not limited to one order or to one kind of order. His teaching is not merely a matter of "Carmelite Spirituality," as some seem to think. In fact, I would venture to say that he is the father of all those whose prayer is an undefined isolation outside the boundary of "spirituality." He deals chiefly with those who, in one way or another, have been brought face to face with God in a way that methods cannot account for and books do not explain. He is in Christ the model and the maker of contemplatives wherever they may be found.

When this much has been said, enough has been said. St. John of the Cross was not famous in his own lifetime and will not be famous in our own. There is no need that either he, or contemplation, should be famous. In this world in which all good things are talked about and practically none of them are practiced, it would be unwise to make contemplative prayer a matter for publicity, though perhaps no harm has been done, thus far, by making its name known. God Himself knows well enough how to make the thing known to those who need it, in His designs for them.

Let it suffice to have said that this Spanish saint is one of the greatest and most hidden of the saints, that of all saints he is perhaps the greatest poet as well as the greatest contemplative, and that in his humility he was also most human, although I have not said much to prove it. I know that he will understand that this essay about him was written as a veiled act of homage, as a gesture of love and gratitude, and as a disguised prayer. He knows what the prayer seeks. May he grant it to the writer and to the readers of these words.

[1] I lift this line bodily from the translation of Professor E. Allison Peers.
[2] *The Ascent of Mount Carmel*, ii, 7. *Complete Works of St. John of the Cross*, translated and edited by E. Allison Peers, Westminster, Newman, 1945, Vol. I, p. 91.
[3] *The Dark Night of the Soul*, i, 13. Peers, *op. cit.*, Vol. I, p. 393.

SAINTS FOR NOW

Ten: THE LETTERS OF ST. BERNARD

I<small>T HAS BEEN</small> the ordinary rule of God's dealing with us," says Cardinal Newman, "that personal sanctity should be attendant upon high spiritual dignity of place or work . . . the prophets have ordinarily not only gifts but graces; they are not only inspired to know and teach God's will, but inwardly converted to obey it. For surely those only can preach the truth duly who feel it personally; those only transmit it fully from God to man, who have in the transmission made it their own."

It is this "ordinary rule" that makes God so wonderful in His saints. It is the only explanation of a St. Bernard in whom, as in some of His other great saints, God is not only wonderful but also scandalous. Did not St. Paul warn all generations that the folly of the Cross would always be a scandal?

Bernard of Clairvaux was plunged deep in the mystery of the Cross, which was the mystery of God's will for his world and ours. He who had left the world to become a monk was thrown back into the world to be an apostle, a worker of miracles, a peacemaker and a warmaker, the reformer of abbeys, the monitor of cardinals and popes, a prophet sent to warn kings.

The saint who wrote the *Letters* became the passionate embodiment of the truths in which he believed. The words of God which are purified by fire burned white-hot in a human frame scarcely able to contain them. The zeal for the House of God was devouring a sick man whose continued existence on earth could only be explained by miracle.

Bernard, the contemplative, was a great man of action because he was a great contemplative. And because he was a contemplative he never ceased fearing to be a mere man of action. He knew better than anyone that even the saints cannot touch pitch without being defiled by it. The

315

natural sincerity and the supernatural zeal for divine truth that burned within him could not help showing him the faults of frailty and passion which even a saint could commit in the heat of ruthless and energetic action. Yet he refused to have mercy on his body or on his soul, and threw himself fiercely into the most difficult problems of his age. Most of the letters were hammered out of the white-hot material found in conflict. They show the man as he is, and because he is so much a man, readers who forget that saints must be men may sometimes be inclined to question his sanctity. That would be a great pity in an age which needs saints as badly as ours. Bernard is sent to instruct us how human a saint must be, to forge out the will of God in the heat of the affairs of men. In his *Sermons on the Canticle* he can be as lyrical as St. Francis. In his letters he is too busy upbraiding the bishops to have time for a sermon to the birds.

In the *Letters* we see, more than anything else, the public facets of a many-sided character. Bernard himself would have been ready to admit that he did not appear at his best in some of the petty business which his letters endeavored to settle. How often do we not hear him cry out against the *necessitas,* and the *malitia diei,* the "evils of the day," the trivial and often sordid material questions that inevitably arise in human society to draw men down from God? But Bernard was more humble than his own protestations of humility would lead us to believe. He had the humility to be himself in the thick of a silly argument. He had the good grace to admit that a saint might possibly have to bicker with another saint over their respective rights to a monk who had skipped from one monastery to another without observing the proper formalities. He did not fear to display a bold and grandiose impatience with his correspondents, even were they kings. He could open a letter to the King of England with words like these: "The King of kings has for long chastised your royal majesty, for he is more powerful than you." And he could do so without starting a war, because it was so evident that he knew this King of kings that he spoke of so familiarly: that he was, indeed, His spokesman, and required a respectful hearing.

Father Bruno James suggests that St. Bernard is "at his best when he is angry." I need not defend the righteous anger of St. Bernard, for only God can tell the difference between a holy indignation and the "anger of man which worketh not the justice of God" (James 1:20). But I know that when St. Paul was angry, it was Christ Who spoke in him (II Cor. 13:2-3). I only hope that the angry Bernard, the passionate Bernard, who even in his anger and in his passion was a saint, will not blind everyone to the merciful Bernard, the gentle and long-suffering monk who could be as tender as a mother to anyone who did not give evidence of being a hardened Pharisee, and who had in his heart something of Christ's unending patience with the weak sinner and compassion for the publican.

Some of the letters are curiously amusing, like the one which records a discussion between St. Bernard and St. Norbert, in which St. Norbert expressed his conviction that Antichrist would appear on the scene in their "own generation." St. Bernard "did not feel compelled to agree." Most of the letters contain concise and memorable aphorisms which will bear long meditation. He tells a Cluniac monk, who has just been elected bishop of a wicked city: "You must not only be patient so as not to be overcome by evil, you must also be peaceable so as to overcome evil by good." To another bishop-elect, whose past life offers little to recommend him for such a difficult position, St. Bernard writes dryly: "It is laid down that we should love others as we love ourselves. But if you were to love others as you have hitherto loved yourself, I for one would not wish to be committed to your care." But there are other letters which show St. Bernard as a speculative mystic. The twelfth letter, to the Carthusians, on the subject of "pure love," takes us at once to the heart of St. Bernard's theology. It sets forth the principle that the "immaculate law of God" is charity, and that there is no mystical liberation, no transformation in Christ, for the soul that has not been elevated, by the Spirit of God, above the law of selfishness and cupidity to the realm of divine charity.

Although English can never quite recapture the solidity of Latin, Father Bruno James has preserved most of the vigor and life and rhythm of the original. This is a rare translation, easily the best English version of the saint's *Letters* so far published, which really sounds something like St. Bernard. I think such a success could only have been achieved by someone who had a great love for the saint and for the Cistercians of the twelfth century.

Nothing remains to be said except that whether the reader may like St. Bernard, whether he may understand St. Bernard, he can hardly fail to recognize, in perusing the *Letters*, that he is face to face with an imposing personality. St. Bernard is too important to be overlooked. He belongs on the bookshelves of every educated man, along with St. Augustine and St. Gregory, St. Anselm and St. Thomas Aquinas. The whole Bernard is not to be found in the *Letters* alone: but the whole Bernard can never be known without them.

If we really take the trouble to know him, we will gain more than mere respect for his great gifts. We will come to admire and love him. Admiration and love mean little, however, without imitation. Perhaps our own century needs nothing so much as the combined anger and gentleness of another Bernard.

THE LETTERS OF ST. BERNARD OF CLAIRVAUX

Eleven: CHRISTIAN CULTURE NEEDS
ORIENTAL WISDOM

A HUNDRED YEARS AGO America began to discover the Orient and its philosophical tradition. The discovery was valid, it reached toward the inner truth of Oriental thought. But the intuitions of Emerson and Thoreau were rich in promises that were not fulfilled by their successors. America did not have the patience to continue what was so happily begun. The door that had opened for an instant closed again for a century. Now that the door seems to be opening again (and sometimes one wonders whether it is the door of the same house) we have another chance.

It is imperative for us to find out what is inside this fabulous edifice, for, from where we stand, we can descry the residents dressed in our kind of clothing and engaged in our kind of frantic gesturing. They are tearing the place apart and rebuilding it in the likeness of our own utilitarian dwellings, department stores, and factories. Not that there is anything wrong with industrial production or a higher standard of living. Yet we know, or should know, by this time, that our material riches imply a spiritual, cultural, and moral poverty that is perhaps far greater than we see.

The literal translation of the title *Tao Teh Ching* is *Book of the Way and its (Hidden) Power*. If there is a correct answer to the question, "What is the Tao?" it is: "I don't know."

Tao can be talked about but not the eternal Tao,
Names can be named, but not the Eternal Name.
As the origin of heaven and earth it is nameless:
As "the Mother" of all things it is nameable.

It is like an "empty bowl that can never be filled." It is like the hole in the center of the hub of a wheel, upon which all the spokes converge.

We make doors and windows for a room;
But it is these empty spaces that make the room livable. . . .
Look at it, but you cannot see it!
Its name is *Formless*.
Listen to it, but you cannot hear it!
Its name is *Soundless*.
Grasp at it, but you cannot get it!
Its name is *Incorporeal*.

It is the formless form, the imageless image. It is a "fountain spirit" of inexhaustible life and yet it never draws attention to itself. It does its work without remark and without recognition. It is utterly elusive: if you think you have seen it, what you have seen is not the *Tao*. Yet it is the source of all, and all things return to it "as to their home."

The whole secret of life lies in the discovery of this Tao which can never be discovered. This does not involve an intellectual quest, but rather a spiritual change of one's whole being. One "reaches" the Tao by "becoming like" the Tao, by acting, in some sense, according to the "way" (Tao). For the Tao is at once perfect activity and perfect rest. It is supreme, *actus purissimus*.

Hence human activity, even virtuous activity, is not enough to bring one into line with the Tao. Virtuous activity tends to be busy and showy, and even with the best intentions in the world it cannot avoid sounding the trumpet before itself in the market place.

He who cultivates the Tao is one with the Tao;
He who practices Virtue is one with Virtue;
And he who courts after Loss is one with Loss.

The way of Loss is the way of whirlwind activity, of rash endeavor, of ambition, the accumulation of "extraneous growths." It is the way of aggression, of spectacular success. The way of Virtue is the Confucian way of self-conscious and professional goodness which is in fact a less pure form of virtue. St. Thomas would say it works *humano modo* rather than with the divine and mysterious spontaneity of the Gifts of the Holy Ghost. But the way of Tao is just that: the way of supreme spontaneity which is virtuous in a transcendent sense because it "does not strive."

High virtue is nonvirtuous;
Therefore it has virtue.
Low virtue never frees itself from virtuousness,
Therefore it has no virtue.

The "sage" or the man who has discovered the secret of the Tao has not acquired any special esoteric knowledge that sets him apart from others and makes him smarter than they are. On the contrary, he is, from a certain point of view, more stupid and exteriorly less remarkable. He is "dim" and obscure. While everyone else exults over success as over a sacrificial ox, he alone is silent, "like a babe who has not yet smiled." Though he has in fact "returned to the root," the Tao, he appears to be the "only one who has no home to return to."

He is very much like the One who has nowhere to lay His head; even though the foxes have holes and the birds of the air their nests. He who has found the Tao has no local habitation and no name on the earth. He is "bland like the ocean, aimless as the wafting gale." Again we remember the Gospels: "The wind blows where it will. . . . So is everyone who is born of the spirit" (John 3:8).

The way of the sage is the way of not attacking, not charging at his objective, not busying himself too intently about his goals. The Chinese ideogram for this is unfortunately hardly able to be translated. The "active" symbol in it looks like a charging horse. *Wu Wei* is a Taoist and Zen technical expression, and perhaps it is better left as it stands. Dr. Wu coins an English expression for it: "non-ado"—and one can see what is at the back of his mind. It recalls the Shakespeare title *Much Ado About Nothing*.

The Japanese Zen artist and poet Sengai has left us two Japanese characters, *Bu Ji*, which are a work of art in themselves and eloquent of the spirit of Tao. *Bu Ji* means "nothing doing." I can say that there is more energy, more creativity, more "productiveness" in these two powerful signs created by Sengai than in all the skyscrapers of New York, and yet he dashed them onto paper with four strokes of his brush.

Hence *Wu Wei* is far from being inactive. It is supreme activity because it acts at rest, acts without effort. Its effortlessness is not a matter of inertia, but of harmony with the hidden power that drives the planets and the world.

The sage then accomplishes very much indeed because it is the Tao that acts in him and through him. He does not act of and by himself, still less for himself alone. His action is not a violent manipulation of exterior reality, an "attack" on the outside world bending it to his con-

quering will: on the contrary, he respects external reality by yielding
to it and his yielding is at once an act of worship, a recognition of sa-
credness and a perfect accomplishment of what is demanded by the precise situation.

The world is a sacred vessel which must not be tampered with or grabbed
after.
To tamper with it is to spoil it, and to grasp it is to love it.

   The power of the sage is then the very power which has been revealed
in the Gospels as Pure Love. *Deus caritas est* is the full manifestation
of the truth hidden in the nameless Tao, and yet it still leaves Tao
nameless. For Love is not a name, any more than Tao is. One must
go beyond the word and enter into communion with the reality before
he can know anything about it; and then, more like than not, he will
know "in the cloud of unknowing."

   The sixty-seventh chapter of the *Tao Teh Ching* is one of the most
profound and the most Christian. In the Tao "which is queer like nothing on earth" are found three treasures: mercy, frugality, and not wanting to be first in the world. And the extraordinarily profound statement
is made that

Because I am merciful, therefore I can be brave. . . .
For heaven will come to the rescue of the merciful and protect him with *its*
mercy.

Again one hears echoes of the Gospel: "Blessed are the merciful"; "Perfect love casteth out fear." Comparing Dr. Wu's translation with that of
Lin Yutang in the Modern Library edition of Lao Tzu (another extremely interesting translation, with parallel passages from the poet and
sage Chuang Tzu) we find new perspectives. (It is often necessary to
read a translated Chinese text in two or more versions.)

If one forsakes love and fearlessness,
   forsakes restraint and reserve power,
   forsakes following behind and rushes in front,
He is doomed!

For love is victorious in attack
   And invulnerable in defense,
Heaven arms with love
   Those it would not see destroyed.

The word which Dr. Lin Yutang translates as "love" and Dr. Wu as
"mercy" is in fact the compassionate love of the mother for the child.

Once again, the sage and the wise ruler are men who do not rush forward to aggrandize themselves but cherish, with loving concern, the "sacred" reality of persons and things which have been entrusted to them by the Tao.

It must be remembered that the *Tao Teh Ching* is basically not a manual for hermits but a treatise on government and much is said there on war and peace. It is a classic that our leaders might be expected to read and doubtless some of them might do so with profit. One of its most astute sayings is that in a war the winner is likely to be on the side that enters the war with the most sorrow.

To rejoice over a victory is to rejoice over the slaughter of men!
Hence a man who rejoices over the slaughter of men cannot expect to thrive
   in the world of men.
. . . Even victory is a funeral.

The paradoxical brilliance of the Tao classic contrasts with the simplicity of the *Hsiao Ching,* a primer of Chinese Confucian ethics and one of the first texts formerly studied by Chinese schoolboys. But this makes it even more interesting, in some respects, than the better-known *Tao Teh Ching.* Many who would be secretly irritated by the apparent subtlety of the Tao classic might prefer to meditate on the classic of filial love. It is a revelation of the deepest natural wisdom and its intuitions are surprisingly "modern." In fact we are here on the same ground as Freud and substantially the same conclusions that were reached by Freud more than twenty centuries later are here exposed in all simplicity and without benefit of the Oedipus complex.

One might be tempted to imagine that this treatise is designed merely to keep sons in subjection to their parents and hence to exalt parental authority for its own sake. It is doubtless true that the rigid formalism of Confucian ethics became, after hundreds of years, a somewhat suffocating system. But in its original purity, the Confucian ideal is basically *personalistic.* The fundamental justification for filial piety is that our person is received as a gift from our parents and is to be fully developed out of gratitude toward them. Hence the astounding fact that this filial piety is not simply a cult of the parent as such, but a development of one's own gifts in honor of the parents who gave them to us. Then, when we reach manhood and our parents are old, we make a fitting return to them by loving support. This basic attitude is said to be "the foundation of virtue and the root of civilization."

If a child can enter fruitfully and lovingly into the five basic relationships, he will certainly develop into a good citizen and a worthy leader, supposing that to be his vocation. The five basic relationships are those of father to son, marked by *justice;* mother to son, marked by *compassion,* or merciful love; the son to his parents, marked by *filial love;* the elder brother has *friendship* for his younger brother; the younger, *respect* for his senior.

Thus we see a wonderful organic complex of strength from the father, warmth from the mother, gratitude from the son, and wholesome, respectful friendship between brothers.

He who really loves his parents will not be proud in high station; he will not be insubordinate in an inferior position; among his equals he will not be contentious. To be proud in high station is to be ruined; to be insubordinate in an inferior position is to incur punishment; to be contentious among one's equals leads to physical violence. So long as these three evils are not uprooted a boy cannot be called filial even though he feast his parents daily on the three kinds of choice meat.

On such a ground grows up a love that reaches out through society and makes it the earthly image of the invisible order of heaven.

The *Hsiao Ching* then shows how this love has various ways of coming to fruitful development in all the levels of society from the Son of Heaven down through the princes and scholars to the peasants. "From the Son of Heaven to the commoner, if filial piety is not pursued from beginning to end, disasters are sure to follow." The society of love (compare the works of Pseudo-Dionysius) is hierarchical. The lower depend on the higher in this exercise of love.

The King is at the summit. All depends on him and he should ideally be capable of the widest and most all-embracing love. For he must love all his subjects and care for their needs. In so doing, he embodies the "heavenly principle" on earth and imitates the Son of Heaven who loves all alike. He also has a duty to share with his subjects this knowledge of heavenly love, and this he does by means of *ritual and music.* In other words, the nation which lives by love grows in love by liturgical celebration of the mystery of love: such are the Christian terms in which we would expand this primitive intuition.

It is important to notice that in all this, there is no such thing as blind subservience to age and to authority. On the contrary, one of the basic duties of filial love is to correct the father when he is wrong and one of the basic duties of the minister is to correct his prince when he errs. This of course was the ideal. The pungent humor of Chuang Tzu shows us many occasions when in practice this kind of "filial love" was not appreciated.

Christopher Dawson has remarked on the "religious vacuum" in our education. It is absolutely essential to introduce into our study of the humanities a dimension of *wisdom* oriented to contemplation as well as to wise action. For this it is no longer sufficient merely to go back over the Christian and European cultural traditions. The horizons of the world are no longer confined to Europe. We have to gain new perspectives, and on this our spiritual and even our physical survival may depend.

Does this mean that the suggestion given in our title is strictly true? Does Christian culture *need* Oriental wisdom? It would certainly be rash to state this without further qualification. Yet we may ask ourselves a few pertinent questions on the subject.

First of all, it is quite clear that no non-Christian religion or philosophy has anything that Christianity needs, in so far as it is a supernaturally revealed religion. Yet from the point of view of the "incarnation" of revealed Christian truth in a social and cultural context, in man's actual history, we know how much Greek philosophy and Roman law contributed to the actual formation of Christian culture and even Christian spirituality. We know too with what breadth of view and with what lofty freedom the scholastic doctors of the thirteenth century made use of Aristotle and his Arabian commentators. It can certainly be said that if a similar use had been made of Oriental philosophy and religious thought from the very start, the development of Christianity in Asia would have been a different story. Our Western Christian thought and culture would also have been immeasurably enriched and deepened.

Have we not been too ready to dismiss Oriental philosophy without really attempting to understand it? Do we not still shrug it off with a few easy generalizations? "Oh, that's all pantheism!" "The Buddhists are all quietists!" And so on?

Can we be content to leave the rich Asian heritage of wisdom on the level of "comparative religion," and subject it to a superficial and passing consideration, checking off concepts like "Tao" and "Dharma" and "Dhyana" as a bored tourist might saunter through the Louvre vaguely registering the famous masterpieces as he walked by them? Or can we simply study these Asian religions and philosophies from an apologetic or missiological standpoint, as "rival systems" which are known *a priori* to be "false," but which one must at least know how to refute? One cannot arrive at an understanding of any "wisdom," whether natural

or supernatural, by arguing either for or against it. Wisdom is not penetrated by logical analysis. The values hidden in Oriental thought actually reveal themselves only on the plane of spiritual experience, or
perhaps, if you like, of aesthetic experience. They belong, of course, to
the natural order: but they certainly have deep affinities with supernatural wisdom itself. Surely we cannot doubt that they may be able, if
properly grasped and appreciated, to lead us to a deeper and wiser understanding of our own magnificent mystical tradition, just as Platonism, without actually "influencing" the Greek Fathers, gave them a
language and a sensibility that were equipped to penetrate in a specially
significant way the depths of the revealed mystery of Christ.

At least this much can and must be said: the "universality" and
"catholicity" which are essential to the Church necessarily imply an
ability and a readiness to enter into dialogue with all that is pure, wise,
profound, and humane in every kind of culture. In this one sense at
least a dialogue with Oriental wisdom becomes necessary. A Christian
culture that is not capable of such a dialogue would show, by that very
fact, that it lacked catholicity.

The Catholic World

Twelve: CONQUISTADOR, TOURIST, AND INDIAN

Let me consider the question of the world's future, if it has one. The leaders of the opposed ideologies are persuaded that it has. The masters of Russia think that the self-destruction of our commercial culture will usher in the golden age of peace and love. Our leaders think that if we and they can somehow shoot the rapids of the cold war, waged with the chemically pure threat of nuclear weapons, we will both emerge into a future of happiness, the nature and the possibility of which still remain to be explained.

For my part, I believe in the very serious possibility that both powers may wake up one morning, so to speak, to find that they have burned and blasted each other off the map during the night, and nothing will remain but the spasmodic exercise of automatic weapons still in the throes of what has casually been called "post-mortem retaliation."

In this new situation it is conceivable that Indonesia, Latin America, Southern Africa, and Australia may find themselves heirs to the opportunities and objectives that the U.S.S.R. and the U.S.A. shrugged off with such careless abandon.

The largest, richest, and best-developed single land mass south of the Equator is South America. The vast majority of its population is Indian, or of mixed Indian blood. The white minority in South Africa would quite probably disappear. A relic of European stock might survive in Australia and New Zealand. Let us also hopefully assume the partial survival of India and of some Moslem populations in central and northern Africa.

If this should happen it will be an event fraught with a rather extraordinary spiritual significance. It will mean that the more cerebral and mechanistic cultures, which have tended to live more and more by asbtractions and to isolate themselves more and more from the natural world by rationalization, will be succeeded by the sections of the human race which they oppressed and exploited without the slightest appreciation for, or understanding for, their human reality.

Characteristic of these races is a totally different outlook on life, a spiritual outlook which is not abstract but concrete, not pragmatic but hieratic, intuitive and affective rather than rationalistic and aggressive. The deepest springs of vitality in these races have been sealed up by the Conqueror and Colonizer, where they have not actually been poisoned by him. But if this stone is removed from the spring perhaps its waters will purify themselves by new life and regain their creative, fructifying power.

Let me be quite succinct: the greatest sin of the European-Russian-American complex which we call the West (and this sin has spread its own way to China), is not only greed and cruelty, not only moral dishonesty and infidelity to truth, but above all *its unmitigated arrogance toward the rest of the human race.* Western civilization is now in full decline into barbarism (a barbarism that springs *from within itself*) because it has been guilty of a twofold disloyalty: to God and to Man. To a Christian who believes in the mystery of the Incarnation, and who by that belief means something more than a pious theory without real humanistic implications, this is not two disloyalties but one. Since the Word was made Flesh, God is in man. God is in *all men.* All men are to be seen and treated as Christ. Failure to do this, the Lord tells us, involves condemnation for disloyalty to the most fundamental of revealed truths. "I was thirsty and you gave me not to drink. I was hungry and you gave me not to eat. . . ." This could be extended in every possible sense: and it is meant to be so extended, all over the entire area of human needs, not only for bread, for work, for liberty, for health, but also for truth, for belief, for love, for acceptance, for fellowship and understanding.

One of the great tragedies of the Christian West was the almost complete destruction of the Indian cultures of America by European and Christian conquerors. In the north the Indian was wiped out by Puritans who appealed to the Old Testament example of the conquest of Canaan, and felt themselves exercising a divine mandate to exterminate the godless savage. In South America the appeal was more sophisticated.

In the name of Aristotle and the natural law, as well as of scholastic theology, savagery and treachery in war against the Indian were considered fully justified for several reasons. First, it was just to wipe out a civilization that violated the natural law by its idolatrous worship. Second, it was just to subjugate in warfare an inferior people, destined by its very nature for slavery (Aristotle). Third, it was legitimate to exploit and oppress men who were not fully human, were not really rational animals, and did not really have souls. These ideas were righteously held, with full subjective sincerity, by men who believed themselves to be in possession not only of the full light of divinely revealed truth, but of a social structure that embodied all that was good, noble, and Christian. In imposing their opinions and customs, even in the most violent and unscrupulous ways, they felt that they were acting as the approved agents of the divine will. They could not recognize that *the races they had conquered were essentially equal to themselves and in some ways superior*. Such is the warmaker's thought process in every age, not excluding our own.

It was certainly right that Christian Europe should bring Christ to the Indians of Mexico and the Andes, as well as to the Hindus and the Chinese: but where they failed was in their inability to *encounter Christ* already potentially present in the Indians, the Hindus, and the Chinese.

Christians have too often forgotten the fact that Christianity found its way into Greek and Roman civilization partly by its spontaneous and creative adaptation of the pre-Christian natural values it found in that civilization. The martyrs rejected all the grossness, the cynicism and falsity of the cult of the state gods which was simply a cult of secular power, but Clement of Alexandria, Justin, and Origen believed that Herakleitos and Socrates had been precursors of Christ. They thought that while God had manifested himself to the Jews through the Law and the Prophets he had also spoken to the Gentiles through their philosophers. Christianity made its way in the world of the first century not by imposing Jewish cultural and social standards on the rest of the world, but by abandoning them, getting free of them so as to be "all things to all men." This was the great drama and the supreme lesson of the Apostolic Age. By the end of the Middle Ages that lesson had been *forgotten*. The preachers of the Gospel to newly discovered continents became preachers and disseminators of European culture and power. They did not enter into dialogue with ancient civilizations: they imposed their own monologue and in preaching Christ they also preached themselves. The very ardor of their self-sacrifice and of their humility enabled them to do this with a clean conscience. But they had omitted to listen to the voice of Christ in the unfamiliar accents of the Indian, as Clement had listened for it in the pre-Socratics.

Whatever India may have had to say to the West she was forced to remain silent. Whatever China had to say, though some of the first missionaries heard it and understood it, the message was generally ignored as irrelevant. Did anyone pay attention to the voices of the Maya and the Inca, who had deep things to say? By and large their witness was merely suppressed. No one considered that the children of the Sun might, after all, hold in their hearts a spiritual secret. On the contrary, abstract discussions were engaged in to determine whether, in terms of academic philosophy, the Indian was to be considered a rational animal. One shudders at the voice of cerebral Western arrogance even then eviscerated by the rationalism that is ours today, judging the living spiritual mystery of primitive man and condemning it to exclusion from the category on which love, friendship, respect, and communion were made to depend.

God speaks, and God is to be heard, not only on Sinai, not only in my own heart, but in the *voice of the stranger*. That is why the peoples of the Orient, and all primitive peoples in general, make so much of the mystery of hospitality.

God must be allowed the right to speak unpredictably. The Holy Spirit, the very voice of Divine Liberty, must always be like the wind in "blowing where he pleases" (John 3:8). In the mystery of the Old Testament there was already a tension between the Law and the Prophets. In the New Testament the Spirit himself is Law, and he is everywhere. He certainly inspires and protects the visible Church, but if we cannot see him unexpectedly in the stranger and the alien, we will not understand him even in the Church. We must find him in our enemy, or we may lose him even in our friend. We must find him in the pagan or we will lose him in our own selves, substituting for his living presence an empty abstraction. How can we reveal to others what we cannot discover in them ourselves? We must, then, see the truth in the stranger, and the truth we see must be a newly living truth, not just a projection of a dead conventional idea of our own—a projection of our own self upon the stranger.

There is more than one way of morally liquidating the "stranger" and the "alien." It is sufficient to destroy, in some way, that in him which is different and disconcerting. By pressure, persuasion, or force one can impose on him one's own ideas and attitudes toward life. One can indoctrinate him, brainwash him. He is no longer different. He has been reduced to conformity with one's own outlook. The Communist, who does nothing if not thoroughly, believes in the thorough liquidation of differences, and the reduction of everyone else to a carbon copy of himself. The Capitalist is somewhat more quixotic: the stranger becomes part of his own screen of fantasies, part of the collective dream life which is manufactured for him on Madison Avenue and in Hollywood. For all practical purposes, the stranger no longer exists. He is not even seen. He is replaced by a fantastic image. What is seen and approved, in a vague, superficial way, is the stereotype that has been created by the travel agency.

This accounts for the spurious cosmopolitanism of the naïve tourist and traveling businessman, who wanders everywhere with his camera, his exposure meter, his spectacles, his sunglasses, his binoculars, and though gazing around him in all directions never sees what is there. He is not capable of doing so. He is too docile to his instructors, to those who have told him everything beforehand. He believes the advertisements of the travel agent at whose suggestion he bought the ticket that landed him wherever he may be. He has been told what he was going to see, and he thinks he is seeing it. Under no circumstances does it occur to him to become interested in what is actually there. Still less to enter into a fully human rapport with the human beings who are before him. It just does not occur to him that they might have a life, a spirit, a thought, a culture of their own which has its own peculiar individual character.

He does not know why he is traveling in the first place: indeed he is traveling at somebody else's suggestion. Even at home he is alien from himself. He is doubly alienated when he is out of his own atmosphere. He cannot possibly realize that the stranger has something very valuable, something irreplaceable to give him: something that can never be bought with money, never estimated by publicists, never exploited by political agitators: the spiritual understanding of a friend who belongs to a different culture. The tourist lacks nothing except brothers. For him these do not exist.

The tourist never meets anyone, never encounters anyone, never finds the brother in the stranger. This is his tragedy.

If only North Americans had realized, after a hundred and fifty years, that Latin Americans really existed. That they were really people. That they spoke a different language. That they had a culture. That they had more than something to sell! Money has totally corrupted the brotherhood that should have united all the peoples of America. It has destroyed the sense of relationship, the spiritual community that had already begun to flourish in the years of Bolivar. But no! Most North Americans still don't know, and don't care, that Brazil speaks a language other than Spanish, that all Latin Americans do not live for the siesta, that all do not spend their days and nights playing the guitar and making love. They have never awakened to the fact that Latin America is by and large culturally superior to the United States, not only on the level of the wealthy minority which has absorbed more of the sophistication of Europe, but also among the desperately poor indigenous cultures, some of which are rooted in a past that has never yet been surpassed on this continent.

So the tourist drinks tequila, and thinks it is no good, and waits for the fiesta he has been told to wait for. How should he realize that the Indian who walks down the street with half a house on his head and a hole in his pants, is Christ? All the tourist thinks is that it is odd for so many Indians to be called Jesus.

So much for the modern scene. I am no prophet, no one is, for now we have learned to get along without prophets. But I would say that if Russia and North America are to destroy one another, which they seem quite anxious to do, it would be a great pity if the survivors in the "Third World" attempted to reproduce their collective alienation, horror, and insanity, and thus build up another corrupt world to be destroyed by another war. To the whole third world I would say there is one lesson to be learned from the present situation, one lesson of the greatest urgency: be unlike the two great destroyers. Mark what they do, and act differently. Mark their official pronouncements, their ideologies, and without difficulty you will find them hollow. Mark their behavior: their bluster, their violence, their blandishments, their hypocrisy: by their fruits you shall know them. In all their boastfulness they have become the victims of their own terror, which is nothing but the emptiness of their own hearts. They claim to be humanists, they claim to know and love man. They have come to liberate man, they say. But they do not know what man is. They are themselves less human than their fathers were, less articulate, less sensitive, less profound, less capable of genuine concern. They are turning into giant insects. Their societies are becoming anthills, without purpose, without meaning, without spirit and joy.

What is wrong with their humanism? It is a humanism of termites, because without God man becomes an insect, a worm in the wood, and even if he can fly, so what? There are flying ants. Even if man flies all over the universe, he is still nothing but a flying ant until he recovers a human center and a human spirit in the depth of his own being.

Good Work

PART FIVE

Love

I then: "Master, my sight is made so vivid
in this, your light, that I can see clearly
your meaning, as far as you set its limit;
therefore, dear father, I beg you tenderly
to show me love, to which you have reduced
every good action and its contrary."

Prologue: PURE LOVE

LOVE IS A MOVEMENT of the will toward what the intellect sees to be good. I speak only of spiritual love here. Sensual love is a movement of the will, guided by the senses, seeking their own satisfaction. There is a desire of God that is called charity although it remains a love for God as the highest good I can desire for myself. The desire for my own fulfillment in God, can be charity: but it must be educated and formed. For charity is the love of God, not precisely as my own highest good, but because He is good in Himself.

The highest and most perfect fruition of God is found in a love that rests in Him purely for His own sake alone. This love follows from the vision of Him as He is in Himself. I can and should desire this vision and love as my own highest good. Every Christian must, in fact, have something of the theological virtue of hope, which is explicitly directed toward this end: the fruition of God in heaven.

This is the great paradox of charity: that unless we are selfish enough to desire to become perfectly unselfish, we have not charity. And unless we love ourselves enough to seek perfect happiness in the total forgetfulness of ourselves, we will never find happiness. Charity is a self-interest which seeks fulfillment in the renunciation of all its interests. If I have charity I will seek my highest good in God, but I will find it in Him, not by taking Him to myself but by sacrificing myself for love of Him. And when my charity is thus perfect, I shall find and possess myself in Him.

As long as I am on earth, this paradox can serve as matter for discussion. In heaven, the vision of God disposes of the problem. St. Thomas and Duns Scotus no longer need to argue, there, about the nature of charity and of blessedness. When we see Him, there will be no question

337

of our loving anyone but Him. When we see Him, we will see that
the only way to love any creature is to love God: for all creatures are
meant to be loved in their Creator, and only in Him. We will see that
it is only in Him that we can really love them: and that in thus loving
them we are also loving Him. That is why St. Bernard can say that
we reach the highest degree of pure love when we finally love even
ourselves in God and for His sake.

There too, love has ended in liberation. It has delivered us from com-
plication, problem, and paradox. There at last we arrive at the simplicity
that God created us to have: for, after all, if He loves us, we cannot
say we are not good, or that we are not to be loved. The perfection of
love is a peak of unselfishness so lofty that it is above the stained atmosphere of this earth in which even humility and unselfishness have,
in spite of all our good will, to suffer certain distortions. On that mountaintop we are at last selfless enough to love God in ourselves without
any need for comment or for excuse. For what we thus love is only His
will in us. We love ourselves in the perfection to which He has brought
us, not because we are perfect, not because we are happy, but because
His will is done. And we are at last perfect, at last perfectly happy,
because we no longer care whether or not we are perfect or happy. We
simply find our peace in this: that in our souls, as in all else, His will
is done.[1]

It is clear that this love is the fulfillment of the law because it is the
perfect fulfillment of the will of God. Such love as this, when it is
found on earth, fulfills every smallest detail of the most minute rubric
of the Liturgy, every jot and tittle of its religious rule and its other
obligations, not in a spirit of hair-splitting Pharisaism but with the freedom of a child of God to whom these things are no longer a matter of
compulsion but a source of joy: and that is why the just man needs
no law. This too is the explanation of Christ's words that He came not
to destroy the Law of Moses, but to fulfill it.[2] Only this love can satisfy
Christ's injunction that our justice must abound beyond that of the
Scribes and Pharisees.[3]

St. Bernard knew that such perfection of love was a kind of ecstasy.
And he found it everywhere in the Psalms. This pure and ecstatic love,
this love which is the mystical marriage of the soul with God, is what
is meant by the word "justice" in the line, "Thy justice is as the mountains of God." [4] This love is the *mons coagulatus, mons pinguis* of the
Vulgate version of Psalm 67 (the new translation calls it a "high-ridged
and wooded mountain.") This pure and mystical love, continues St.

Bernard, is the mountain of God in Psalm 23—where the Psalmist asks: "Who can go up to the mountain of the Lord?" It is therefore the term of the ascetic life that is outlined in the middle of the Psalm:

Who can go up to the mountain of the Lord or who shall stand in his holy place?
He that has clean hands and a pure heart, who does not set his mind on vain things, and has not sworn deceitfully to his neighbor.
He shall receive a blessing from the Lord and mercy from God his Saviour.
This is the generation of them that seek him, of them that seek the face of the God of Jacob.[5]

This same Psalm is one of the cornerstones of monastic spirituality, since it has an important place in the Prologue to St. Benedict's Rule. It is therefore interesting to see how much a monastic saint like Bernard of Clairvaux could find in it. A detailed commentary of the apparently prosaic little virtues mentioned in these two or three lines would reveal that the Fathers believed "purity of heart" to be a function of that gift of understanding which is one of the keys to mystical contemplation.[6]

---

[1] "Delectabit sane non tam nostra vel sopita necessitas vel sortita felicitas, quam quod ejus in nobis et de nobis voluntas adimpleta videbitur, quod et quotidie postulamus in oratione cum dicimus fiat voluntas tua sicut in coelo et in terra." —St. Bernard, *De Diligendo Deo*, X, 28.

[2] See Matthew, 5:17-20.

[3] Matthew, 5:20.

[4] Psalm, 35:7. St. John of the Cross gives much the same interpretation of "judicia Domini vera" (Psalm, 18:10-11). *The Ascent to the Cross* II, 26.

[5] Psalm, 23:3-6.

[6] See St. Augustine, *De Sermone Domini in Monte*. St. Thomas Aquinas, II, IIae, Q. 8, a.7.

BREAD IN THE WILDERNESS

One: THE WAYS OF LOVE

WHEN A WOUND is beginning to heal, they strip off the bandages, and the adhesive tape seems to take most of the skin with it. When a man comes into an army, the first thing they do is take away his civilian clothes, and give him a uniform. When a man enters a monastery, the same kind of thing takes place. If it is a good monastery, he will begin right away to be stripped of practically everything. If it is not such a good monastery, he will be left with most of the things he brought with him, and may even acquire a lot more before he is finished.

When a man becomes a Cistercian, he is stripped not only of his clothes, or part of his skin, but of his whole body and most of his spirit as well. And it is not all finished the first day: far from it! The whole Cistercian life is an evisceration, a gutting and scouring of the human soul.

The exchange of secular clothes for a religious habit is symbolic. And it is more than symbolic, because it brings with it the grace of a sacramental: but that very grace is order to the same thing which the symbol represents: the interior stripping and expoliation and exchange.

The reason why we must be emptied of everything that belongs to a man in the world is that God has brought us to the monastery to fill us with something else, and we cannot be filled unless we are first emptied, to make room for what is to come.

WHAT DOES God want to fill us with? His joy, His peace: charity. Therefore we must get rid of all other lesser joys, all false peace, all the loves that are inadequate to satisfy and fulfill the capacities God has given us.

Our happiness consists in the recovery of our true nature: the nature according to which we are made in the image of God, and the fulfillment of our purified natural capacities by supernatural grace and glory. Our happiness consists in being like God, being identified with Him, in Christ.

One of the things rooted in our nature which constitutes us in God's image is our innate liberty. God is infinitely free, because He is infinitely powerful and beyond any other determination except that of His own love; and love is, of its essence, free.

The freedom that is in our nature is our ability to love something, someone besides ourselves, and for the sake, not of ourselves, but of the one we love. There is in the human will an innate tendency, an inborn capacity for disinterested love. This power to love another for his own sake is one of the things that makes us like God, because this power is the one thing in us that is free from all determination. It is a power which transcends and escapes the inevitability of self-love.

For we have also in our nature an inborn tendency to love ourselves. This tendency is good, and a great good: without it we would never be able to survive. But the very fact that it is ordered to our survival means that this good self-love cannot be free. Everything that is, by its very nature, seeks some kind of perfection that is due to that nature, not freely, but by an inner compulsion rooted in the nature itself. So man, as Duns Scotus teaches, together with all the scholastics, is bound necessarily by this inborn self-love, this *affectio commodi,* to seek the highest perfection of his nature, to seek happiness whether he wills it or not. In this respect, then, he is not free. Self-love, even when it is good, is a principle of necessity, of compulsion.

But the inborn principle of disinterested love, which Scotus calls the *affectio justitiae*—meaning that love which we can give things according to what is due to them because of their intrinsic excellence— this disinterested love lifts us above the necessities of our nature, and is destined to control and regulate all the movements of the *affectio commodi* in the interests of freedom and greater perfection of another. A man can love someone else, or God, for that matter, so strongly that he can ignore all the rightful claims of the *affectio commodi* and sacrifice life itself for the object of his love.

However, even if disinterested love delivers us from the limitations of reasonable self-interest, and makes us free of determination as we can be on the natural plane, there is still a far higher freedom than this possible to man. There is another *affectio justitiae,* a higher principle of disinterestedness and liberty, infused into man's soul by God Himself: the virtue of charity, supernatural love, which not only perfects man's inborn tendency to disinterested, free love, but elevates it far above the plane of any created nature to participation in the very perfection of God's own love, God's own liberty. At the same time, of course, since grace perfects all that is worthy to be perfected in nature, even our self-love is sublimated to the supernatural plane by a higher *affectio commodi*, the hope of heaven.

Thus the balance of our nature is never destroyed. These two inseparable tendencies must always remain in our will, whether they be transfigured by the infused virtues, or whether the right order of things is so completely upset and reversed that the *affectio commodi* usurps control over our freedom, and we are no longer capable of loving anything except for our own selfish interests.

The ultimate limit of such a captivity is hell, where, as Scotus says, the damned are completely absorbed in their own frustrated self-love.

I HAVE OUTLINED these principles of Duns Scotus because from them can be drawn a complete understanding of what the contemplative life is all about. Not only that, but their psychological depth is such that when we possess them, we are able to penetrate into the underlying reasons for practically all the things a man has to experience in a Cistercian monastery.

The highest perfection of our nature is in the perfect operation of our highest faculties directed to their most perfect object: in two words, the highest perfection of our nature is *loving God*: loving Him not simply because He is our highest good, but more especially and formally because He is infinitely good in Himself. It is this pure and perfect love that is the glory God asks of us, and it is also our own highest reward, the ultimate in all happiness possible to man.

Accipimus beatitudinem pro summa perfectione beatificabilis naturae ipsam summe suo objecto perfectissimo conjugente. (IV. Ox. xlix q.6, n24).

(*Fruitio beatitudinis*) *est actus amicitiae volendo Deo in se bene esse . . . et iste* (*actus*) *proprie est charitatis.* (I. Ox. i q.5).

Consequently, we can be happy in this world only in so far as we are free to rejoice in the good of another: specifically, in so far as we are free to rejoice in the good which is God's.

If the whole world were only capable of grasping this principle that true happiness consists only in the freedom of disinterested love— the ability to get away from ourselves, and our own limited sphere of interests and appetites and needs, and rejoice in the good that is in others, not because it is also ours, but formally in so far as it is theirs!

Is it not obvious that when we have this freedom, happiness will not only follow as a matter of course: joy would pursue us everywhere and we could not get away from it. Why? Since everything that is, is good, and since the world is full of things that are good in themselves and which all proclaim the infinite goodness and power of God: if we rejoiced in the good that is possessed by others, formally as *possessed by them*, we would not be able to look at a flower or a blade of grass or an insect or a drop of water or a grain of sand or a leaf, let alone a whole tree, or a bird, or a living animal, or a human being, without exploding with exultation.

Now the contemplative life is ordered to one thing above all: the perfecting of this *amor amicitiae*, disinterested love, and the liberation of our wills from the bondage of self-love, and not only of natural self-love, but the unnatural disfigured self-love which is sin, and which goes by the technical name of concupiscence.

Great moments of joy and strength that come to those who have dedicated their lives to God, come when one is able, by a strong and special movement of grace, to perform some act of pure and disinterested love. For the clean fire of that love, flooding the soul with its pure and intense and invisible flame, seems to cleanse the whole man, and leave him filled with an amazing lightness and freedom for action; and a moment of this pure prayer, instantaneously reestablishing the order in the soul, works also on the body, sometimes fortifying one against weariness and infirmity, and bringing a new lease even on physical life.

But one of the bitterest forms that interior suffering can take is a kind of imitation of hell. The closer one comes to God, the more apt a subject will he be for this furious and penetrating pain—until he is purified altogether and is impervious to all pain. The source of this suffering is the realization of the malice there is in the slightest disorder of the *affectio commodi*. The moment we prefer our own satisfaction to the will of the God we love, there is disorder: and God, in His mercy, sometimes leaves us to savor the full bitterness that is in our selfishness and sin. And the better we love Him, the closer we are to Him, the bitterer the experience can become.

For our selfishness, in so far as it implies a rejection of God, Who is our life, casts us into the abyss of a frightful solitude in which we are forced to remain face to face with our own egoism and our own inescapable insufficiency to satisfy ourselves by any means in our

power. God sometimes shows us on earth what has to be suffered by
the souls in hell, and leaves us, for a time, to become the prisoners of
our own tremendous emptiness without Him, and we find ourselves
apparently without power to escape by means of a single unselfish
act. It is a condition in which the very goodness of all that is around
us is a frustration and a crushing reproach, and there seems to be
nothing left but eternal damnation.

The strange thing is that there are people in the world, innocent
men and women, pure of all sin, clean of all selfishness, who have to
suffer these things in expiation for the devouring egoism of a bloodthirsty, cannibal civilization.

And that brings us to the final paradox.

Out of the depths of this, the ultimate trial, can rise the most perfect
charity, like a phoenix, in the flames of that dark hell, singing a song
of triumph so pure and splendid that it comes forth like Christ from
the smashed gates of Limbo, delivering the souls of the just. Crushed
and abandoned in this desolation of our own misery, the *amor amicitiae*
rises from the dead with the blind, unbeatable power of its trust in
the goodness and mercy of God, the Beloved, and with swift and
direct flight, pierces the darkness of the abyss and soars to the height
of heaven to give Him the greatest and purest glory—the glory that
went up to the Father from Christ annihilated in Gethsemani and
crucified on Calvary.

Then even desolation becomes a joy, and one of the greatest joys,
because we find in it a means and instrument to serve the ends of the
one thing that matters, the *affectio justitiae*, the *amicitia*, the pure
charity, the sacrificial love that has given Christ everything, and fills
up what is wanting, of His passion, for His Body, which is the
Church.

Souls that have reached this degree of love on earth will never know
any other purgatory when they come to leave it.

And it is to this that the Cistercian life, and the life of the Carmelite
nun, the Carthusian monk, the Camaldolese hermit are ordered: the
liberation of man's true nature by means of love, by means of sacrifice.

Consequently, every trial, even the smallest, every opportunity to
deny ourselves, whether it be a matter of disordered self-love or the
legitimate *affectio commodi*, does not matter—every chance to offer
some kind of sacrifice is to be regarded as a grace, as a favor, as a
providential opportunity to grasp at freedom.

I thank God that from the first minute I entered the monastery He has given me many such graces, and I am sorry that by my weakness and mistrust and fear I have obliged Him to limit and restrict their number. However, I cannot say that He plunged me into desolation as soon as I came in the front door, nor that He neglected to strengthen my puny nature with consolations, in due time, for which I thank Him: I do not despise them! They have opened the way to new worlds.

Unpublished, from the Original Manuscript of
THE SEVEN STOREY MOUNTAIN

Two: A BODY OF BROKEN BONES

You AND I and all men were made to find our identity in the One Mystical Christ, in Whom we all complete one another "unto a perfect man, unto the measure of the age of the fulness of Christ."

When we all reach that perfection of love which is the contemplation of God in His glory, our inalienable personalities, while remaining eternally distinct, will nevertheless combine into One so that each one of us will find himself in all the others, and God will be the life and reality of all. *Omnia in omnibus Deus.*

God is a consuming Fire. He alone can refine us like gold, and separate us from the slag and dross of our selfish individualities to fuse us into this wholeness of perfect unity that will reflect His own Triune Life forever.

As long as we do not permit His love to consume us entirely and to unite us in Himself, the gold that is in us will be hidden by the rock and dirt which keep us separate from one another.

As long as we are not purified by the love of God and transformed into Him in the union of pure sanctity, we will remain apart from one another, opposed to one another, and union among us will be a precarious and painful thing, full of labor and sorrow and without lasting cohesion.

IN THE WHOLE WORLD, throughout the whole of history, even among religious men and among saints, Christ suffers dismemberment.

His physical Body was crucified by Pilate and the Pharisees; His mystical Body is drawn and quartered from age to age by the devils in the agony of that disunion which is bred and vegetates in our souls, prone to selfishness and to sin.

All over the face of the earth the avarice and lust of men breed unceasing divisions among them, and the wounds that tear men from union with one another widen and open out into huge wars. Murder, massacres, revolution, hatred, the slaughter and torture of the bodies and souls of men, the destruction of cities by fire, the starvation of millions, the annihilation of populations and finally the cosmic inhumanity of nuclear genocide: Christ is massacred in His members, torn limb from limb; God is murdered in men.

The history of the world, with the material destruction of cities and nations and people, expressed the interior division that tyrannizes the souls of all men, and even of the saints.

Even the innocent, even those in whom Christ lives by charity, even those who want with their whole heart to love one another, remain divided and separate. Although they are already one in Him, their union is hidden from them, because it still only possesses the secret substance of their souls.

But their minds and their judgments and their desires, their human characters and faculties, their appetites and their ideals are all imprisoned in the slag of an inescapable egotism which pure love has not yet been able to refine.

As long as we are on earth, the love that unites us will bring us suffering by our very contact with one another, because this love is the resetting of a Body of broken bones. Even saints cannot live with saints on this earth without some anguish, without some pain at the differences that come between them.

There are two things which men can do about the pain of disunion with other men. They can love or they can hate.

Hatred recoils from the sacrifice and the sorrow that are the price of this resetting of bones. It refuses the pain of reunion.

There is in every weak, lost, and isolated member of the human race an agony of hatred born of his own helplessness, his own isolation. Hatred is the sign and the expression of loneliness, of unworthiness, of insufficiency. And in so far as each one of us is lonely, is unworthy, each one hates himself. Some of us are aware of this self-hatred, and because of it we reproach ourselves and punish ourselves needlessly. Punishment cannot cure the feeling that we are unworthy. There is nothing we can do about it as long as we feel that we are isolated, insufficient, helpless, alone. Others, who are less conscious of their own self-hatred, realize it in a different form by projecting it on to others. There is a proud and self-confident hate, strong and cruel, which enjoys the pleasure of hating, for it is directed outward to the unworthiness of another. But this strong and happy hate does not realize that like all hate, it destroys and consumes the self that hates, and not the object that is hated. Hate in any form is self-destructive, and even when it triumphs physically it triumphs in its own spiritual ruin.

Strong hate, the hate that takes joy in hating, is strong because it does not believe itself to be unworthy and alone. It feels the support of a justifying God, of an idol of war, an avenging and destroying spirit. From such blood-drinking gods the human race was once liberated, with great toil and terrible sorrow, by the death of a God Who delivered Himself to the Cross and suffered the pathological cruelty of His own creatures out of pity for them. In conquering death He opened their eyes to the reality of a love which asks no questions about worthiness, a love which overcomes hatred and destroys death. But men have now come to reject this divine revelation of pardon, and they are consequently returning to the old war gods, the gods that insatiably drink blood and eat the flesh of men. It is easier to serve the hate-gods because they thrive on the worship of collective fanaticism. To serve the hate-gods, one has only to be blinded by collective passion. To serve the God of Love one must be free, one must face the terrible responsibility of the decision to love *in spite of all unworthiness* whether in oneself or in one's neighbor.

It is the rankling, tormenting sense of unworthiness that lies at the root of all hate. The man who is able to hate strongly and with a quiet conscience is one who is complacently blind to all unworthiness in himself and serenely capable of seeing all his own wrongs in someone else. But the man who is aware of his own unworthiness and the unworthiness of his brother is tempted with a subtler and more tormenting kind of hate: the general, searing, nauseating hate of everything and everyone, because everything is tainted with unworthiness, everything is unclean, everything is foul with sin. What this weak hate really is, is weak love. He who cannot love feels unworthy, and at the same time feels that somehow *no one* is worthy. Perhaps he cannot feel love because he thinks he is unworthy of love, and because of that he also thinks no one else is worthy.

The beginning of the fight against hatred, the basic Christian answer to hatred, is not the commandment to love, but what must necessarily come before in order to make the commandment bearable and comprehensible. It is a prior commandment, *to believe*. The root of Christian love is not the will to love, but *the faith that one is loved*. The faith that one is loved *by God*. That faith that one is loved by God although unworthy—or, rather, irrespective of one's worth!

In the true Christian vision of God's love, the idea of worthiness loses its significance. Revelation of the mercy of God makes the whole problem of worthiness something almost laughable: the discovery that worthiness is of no special consequence (since no one could ever, by himself, be strictly worthy to be loved with such a love) is a true liberation of the spirit. And until this discovery is made, until this liberation has been brought about by the divine mercy, man is imprisoned in hate.

Humanistic love will not serve. As long as we believe that we hate no one, that we are merciful, that we are kind by our very nature, we deceive ourselves; our hatred is merely smoldering under the gray ashes of complacent optimism. We are apparently at peace with everyone because we think we are worthy. That is to say we have lost the capacity to face the question of unworthiness at all. But when we are delivered by the mercy of God the question no longer has a meaning.

Hatred tries to cure disunion by annihilating those who are not united with us. It seeks peace by the elimination of everybody else but ourselves.

But love, by its acceptance of the pain of reunion, begins to heal all wounds.

IF YOU WANT TO KNOW what is meant by "God's will" in man's life, this is one way to get a good idea of it. "God's will" is certainly found in anything that is required of us in order that we may be united with one another in love. You can call this, if you like, the basic tenet of the Natural Law, which is that we should treat others as we would like them to treat us, that we should not do to another what we would not want another to do to us. In other words, the natural law is simply that we should recognize in every other human being the same nature, the same needs, the same rights, the same destiny as in ourselves. The plainest summary of all the natural law is: to treat other men as if they were men. Not to act as if I alone were a man, and every other human were an animal or a piece of furniture.

Everything that is demanded of me, in order that I may treat every other man effectively as a human being, "is willed for me by God under the natural law." Whether or not I find the formula satisfactory, it is obvious that I cannot live a truly human life if I consistently disobey this fundamental principle.

But I cannot treat other men as men unless I have compassion for them. I must have at least enough compassion to realize that when they suffer they feel somewhat as I do when I suffer. And if for some reason I do not spontaneously feel this kind of sympathy for others, then it is God's will that I do what I can to learn how. I must learn to share with others their joys, their sufferings, their ideas, their needs, their desires. I must learn to do this not only in the cases of those who are of the same class, the same profession, the same race, the same nation as myself, but when men who suffer belong to other groups, even to groups that are regarded as hostile. If I do this, I obey God. If I refuse to do it, I disobey Him. It is not therefore a matter left open to subjective caprice.

Since this is God's will for every man, and since contemplation is a gift not granted to anyone who does not consent to God's will, contemplation is out of the question for anyone who does not try to cultivate compassion for other men.

For Christianity is not merely a doctrine or a system of beliefs, it is Christ living in us and uniting men to one another in His own Life and unity. "I in them, and Thou, Father, in Me, that they may be made perfect in One. . . . And the glory which Thou hast given me I have given them, that they may be One as we also are One." *In hoc cognoscent omnes quia mei estis discipuli, si dilectionem habueritis ad invicem.* "In this shall all men know that you are my disciples— if you have love one for another."

"He that loveth not abideth in death."

IF YOU REGARD contemplation principally as a means to escape from the miseries of human life, as a withdrawal from the anguish and the suffering of this struggle for reunion with other men in the charity of Christ, you do not know what contemplation is and you will never find God in your contemplation. For it is precisely in the recovery of our union with our brothers in Christ that we discover God and know Him, for then His life begins to penetrate our souls and His love possesses our faculties and we are able to find out Who He is from the experience of His mercy, liberating us from the prison of self-concern.

THERE IS ONLY one true flight from the world; it is not an escape from conflict, anguish, and suffering, but the flight from disunity and separation, to unity and peace in the love of other men.

What is the "world" that Christ would not pray for, and of which

He said that His disciples were in it but not of it? The world is the unquiet city of those who live for themselves and are therefore divided against one another in a struggle that cannot end, for it will go on eternally in hell. It is the city of those who are fighting for possession of limited things and for the monopoly of goods and pleasures that cannot be shared by all.

But if you try to escape from this world merely by leaving the city and hiding yourself in solitude, you will only take the city with you into solitude; and yet you can be entirely out of the world while remaining in the midst of it, if you let God set you free from your own selfishness and if you live for love alone.

For the flight from the world is nothing else but the flight from self-concern. And the man who locks himself up in private with his own selfishness has put himself into a position where the evil within him will either possess him like a devil or drive him out of his head.

That is why it is dangerous to go into solitude merely because you like to be alone.

NEW SEEDS OF CONTEMPLATION

Three: THE MORAL THEOLOGY OF THE DEVIL

THE DEVIL has a whole system of theology and philosophy, which will explain, to anyone who will listen, that created things are evil, that men are evil, that God created evil and that He directly wills that men should suffer evil. According to the devil, God rejoices in the suffering of men and, in fact, the whole universe is full of misery because God has willed and planned it that way.

Indeed, says this system of theology, God the Father took real pleasure in delivering His Son to His murderers, and God the Son came to earth because He wanted to be punished by the Father. Both of them together seek nothing more than to punish and persecute their faithful ones. As a matter of fact, in creating the world God had clearly in mind that man would inevitably sin and it was almost as if the world were created in order that man might sin, so that God would have an opportunity to manifest His justice.

So, according to the devil, the first thing created was really hell— as if everything else were, in some sense, for the sake of hell. Therefore the devotional life of those who are "faithful" to this kind of theology consists above all in an obsession with evil. As if there were not already enough evils in the world, they multiply prohibitions and make new rules, binding everything with thorns, so that man may not escape evil and punishment. For they would have him bleed from morning to night, though even with so much blood there is no remission of sin! The Cross, then, is no longer a sign of mercy (for mercy has no place in such a theology), it is the sign that Law and Justice have utterly triumphed, as if Christ had said: "I came not to destroy the Law but to be destroyed by it." For this, according to the devil, is the only way in which the Law could really and truly be "fulfilled."

352

Not love but punishment is the fulfillment of the Law. The Law must devour everything, even God. Such is this theology of punishment, hatred, and revenge. He who would live by such a dogma must rejoice in punishment. He may, indeed, successfully evade punishment himself by "playing ball" with the Law and the Lawgiver. But he must take good care that others do not avoid suffering. He must occupy his mind with their present and future punishment. The Law must triumph. There must be no mercy.

This is the chief mark of the theology of hell, for in hell there is everything but mercy. That is why God Himself is absent from hell. Mercy is the manifestation of His presence.

THE THEOLOGY OF THE DEVIL is for those who, for one reason or another, whether because they are perfect, or because they have come to an agreement with the Law, no longer need any mercy. With them (O grim joy!) God is "satisfied." So too is the devil. It is quite an achievement, to please everybody!

The people who listen to this sort of thing, and absorb it, and enjoy it, develop a notion of the spiritual life which is a kind of hypnosis of evil. The concepts of sin, suffering, damnation, punishment, the justice of God, retribution, the end of the world, and so on, are things over which they smack their lips with unspeakable pleasure. Perhaps this is because they derive a deep, subconscious comfort from the thought that many other people will fall into the hell which they themselves are going to escape. And how do they know they are going to escape it? They cannot give any definite reason except for the fact that they feel a certain sense of relief at the thought that all this punishment is prepared for practically everyone but themselves.

This feeling of complacency is what they refer to as "faith," and it constitutes a kind of conviction that they are "saved."

THE DEVIL makes many disciples by preaching against sin. He convinces them of the great evil of sin, induces a crisis of guilt by which "God is satisfied," and after that he lets them spend the rest of their lives meditating on the intense sinfulness and evident reprobation of other men.

THE MORAL THEOLOGY of the devil starts out with the principle: "Pleasure is sin." Then he goes on to work it the other way: "All sin is pleasure."

After that he points out that pleasure is practically unavoidable and that we have a natural tendency to do things that please us, from which he reasons that all our natural tendencies are evil and that our nature is evil in itself. And he leads us to the conclusion that no one can possibly avoid sin, since pleasure is inescapable.

After that, to make sure that no one will try to escape or avoid sin, he adds that what is unavoidable cannot be a sin. Then the whole concept of sin is thrown out the window as irrelevant, and people decide that there is nothing left except to live for pleasure, and in that way pleasures that are naturally good become evil by deordination and lives are thrown away in unhappiness and sin.

IT SOMETIMES HAPPENS that men who preach most vehemently about evil and the punishment of evil, so that they seem to have practically nothing else on their minds except sin, are really unconscious haters of other men. They think the world does not appreciate them, and this is their way of getting even.

THE DEVIL is not afraid to preach the will of God provided he can preach it in his own way.

The argument goes something like this: "God wills you to do what is right. But you have an interior attraction which tells you, by a nice warm glow of satisfaction, what is right. Therefore, if others try to interfere and make you do something that does not produce this comfortable sense of interior satisfaction, quote Scripture, tell them that you ought to obey God rather than men, and then go ahead and do your own will, do the thing that gives you that nice, warm glow."

THE THEOLOGY of the devil is really not theology but magic. "Faith" in this theology is really not the acceptance of a God Who reveals Himself as mercy. It is a psychological, subjective "force" which applies a kind of violence to reality in order to change it according to one's own whims. Faith is a kind of supereffective wishing: a mastery that comes from a special, mysteriously dynamic will power that is generated by "profound convictions." By virtue of this wonderful energy one can exert a persuasive force even on God Himself and bend His will to one's own will. By this astounding new dynamic soul force of faith (which any quack can develop in you for an appropriate remuneration) you can turn God into a means to your own ends. We become civilized medicine men, and God becomes our servant. Though He is terrible in His own right, He respects our sorcery, He allows Himself to be tamed by it. He will appreciate our dynamism, and will reward it with success in every thing we attempt. We will become popular because we have "faith." We will be rich because we have "faith." All our national enemies will come and lay down their arms at our feet because we have "faith." Business will boom all over the world, and we will be able to make money out of everything and everyone under the sun because of the charmed life we lead. We have faith.

But there is a subtle dialectic in all this, too.

We hear that faith does everything. So we close our eyes and strain a bit, to generate some "soul force." We believe. We believe.

Nothing happens.

We close our eyes again, and generate some more soul force. The devil likes us to generate soul force. He helps us to generate plenty of it. We are just gushing with soul force.

But nothing happens.

So we go on with this until we become disgusted with the whole business. We get tired of "generating soul force." We get tired of this "faith" that does not do anything to change reality. It does not take away our anxieties, our conflicts, it leaves us a prey to uncertainty. It does not lift all responsibilities off our shoulders. Its magic is not so effective after all. It does not thoroughly convince us that God is satisfied with us, or even that we are satisfied with ourselves (though in this, it is true, some people's faith is often quite effective).

Having become disgusted with faith, and therefore with God, we are now ready for the Totalitarian Mass Movement that will pick us up on the rebound and make us happy with war, with the persecution of "inferior races" or of enemy classes, or generally speaking, with actively punishing someone who is different from ourselves.

ANOTHER CHARACTERISTIC of the devil's moral theology is the exaggeration of all distinctions between this and that, good and evil, right and wrong. These distinctions become irreducible divisions. No longer is there any sense that we might perhaps all be more or less at fault, and that we might be expected to take upon our own shoulders the wrongs of others by forgiveness, acceptance, patient understanding and love, and thus help one another to find the truth. On the contrary, in the devil's theology, the important thing is to be absolutely right and to prove that everybody else is absolutely wrong. This does not exactly make for peace and unity among men, because it means that everyone wants to be absolutely right himself or to attach himself to another who is absolutely right. And in order to prove their rightness they have to punish and eliminate those who are wrong. Those who are wrong, in turn, convinced that they are right . . . etc.

Finally, as might be expected, the moral theology of the devil grants an altogether unusual amount of importance to . . . the devil. Indeed one soon comes to find out that he is very center of the whole system. That he is behind everything. That he is moving everybody in the world except ourselves. That he is out to get even us. And that there is every chance of his doing so because, it now appears, his power is equal to that of God, or even perhaps superior to it. . . .

In one word, the theology of the devil is purely and simply that the devil is god.

NEW SEEDS OF CONTEMPLATION

Four: LOVE CAN BE KEPT ONLY BY BEING GIVEN AWAY

A HAPPINESS that is sought for ourselves alone can never be found: for a happiness that is diminished by being shared is not big enough to make us happy.

There is a false and momentary happiness in self-satisfaction, but it always leads to sorrow because it narrows and deadens our spirit. True happiness is found in unselfish love, a love which increases in proportion as it is shared. There is no end to the sharing of love, and, therefore, the potential happiness of such love is without limit. Infinite sharing is the law of God's inner life. He has made the sharing of ourselves the law of our own being, so that it is in loving others that we best love ourselves. In disinterested activity we best fulfill our own capacities to act and to be.

Yet there can never be happiness in compulsion. It is not enough for love to be shared: it must be shared freely. That is to say it must be given, not merely taken. Unselfish love that is poured out upon a selfish object does not bring perfect happiness: not because love requires a return or a reward for loving, but because it rests in the happiness of the beloved. And if the one loved receives love selfishly, the lover is not satisfied. He sees that his love has failed to make the beloved happy. It has not awakened his capacity for unselfish love.

Hence the paradox that unselfish love cannot rest perfectly except in a love that is perfectly reciprocated: because it knows that the only true peace is found in selfless love. Selfless love consents to be loved selflessly for the sake of the beloved. In so doing, it perfects itself.

The gift of love is the gift of the power and the capacity to love, and, therefore, to give love with full effect is also to receive it. So, love

357

can only be kept by being given away, and it can only be given perfectly when it is also received.

LOVE not only prefers the good of another to my own, but it does not
even compare the two. It has only one good: that of the beloved, which
is, at the same time, my own. Love shares the good with another not
by dividing it with him, but by identifying itself with him so that his
good becomes my own. The same good is enjoyed in its wholeness by
two in one spirit, not halved and shared by two souls. Where love is
really disinterested, the lover does not even stop to inquire whether
he can safely appropriate for himself some part of the good which he
wills for his friend. Love seeks its whole good in the good of the
beloved, and to divide that good would be to diminish love. Such a
division would not only weaken the action of love, but in doing so
would also diminish its joy. For love does not seek a joy that follows
from its effect: its joy is in the effect itself, which is the good of the
beloved. Consequently, if my love be pure I do not even have to seek
for myself the satisfaction of loving. Love seeks one thing only: the
good of the one loved. It leaves all the other secondary effects to take
care of themselves. Love, therefore, is its own reward.

TO LOVE ANOTHER is to will what is really good for him. Such love
must be based on truth. A love that sees no distinction between good
and evil, but loves blindly merely for the sake of loving, is hatred,
rather than love. To love blindly is to love selfishly, because the goal
of such love is not the real advantage of the beloved but only the
exercise of love in our own souls. Such love cannot seem to be love
unless it pretends to seek the good of the one loved. But since it
actually cares nothing for the truth, and never considers that it may
go astray, it proves itself to be selfish. It does not seek the true advantage of the beloved or even our own. It is not interested in the truth,
but only in itself. It proclaims itself content with an apparent good:
which is the exercise of love for its own sake, without any consideration
of the good or bad effects of loving.

When such love exists on the level of bodily passion it is easily recognized for what it is. It is selfish, and, therefore, it is not love. Those
whose love does not transcend the desires of their bodies, generally do
not even bother to deceive themselves with good motives. They follow
their passions. Since they do not deceive themselves, they are more
honest, as well as more miserable, than those who pretend to love on a

spiritual plane without realizing that their "unselfishness" is only a deception.

CHARITY is neither weak nor blind. It is essentially prudent, just, temperate, and strong. Unless all the other virtues blend together in charity, our love is not genuine. No one who really wants to love another will consent to love him falsely. If we are going to love others at all, we must make up our minds to love them well. Otherwise our love is a delusion.

The first step to unselfish love is the recognition that our love may be deluded. We must first of all purify our love by renouncing the pleasure of loving as an end in itself. As long as pleasure is our end, we will be dishonest with ourselves and with those we love. We will not seek their good, but our own pleasure.

IT IS CLEAR, then, that to love others well we must first love the truth. And since love is a matter of practical and concrete human relations, the truth we must love when we love our brothers is not mere abstract speculation: it is the moral truth that is to be embodied and given life in our own destiny and theirs. This truth is more than the cold perception of an obligation, flowing from moral precepts. The truth we must love in loving our brothers is the concrete destiny and sanctity that are willed for them by the love of God. One who really loves another is not merely moved by the desire to see him contented and healthy and prosperous in this world. Love cannot be satisfied with anything so incomplete. If I am to love my brother, I must somehow enter deep into the mystery of God's love for him. I must be moved not only by human sympathy but by that divine sympathy which is revealed to us in Jesus and which enriches our own lives by the outpouring of the Holy Spirit in our hearts.

The truth I love in loving my brother cannot be something merely philosophical and abstract. It must be at the same time supernatural and concrete, practical and alive. And I mean these words in no metaphorical sense. The truth I must love in my brother is God Himself, living in him. I must seek the life of the Spirit of God breathing in him. And I can only discern and follow that mysterious life by the action of the same Holy Spirit living and acting in the depths of my own heart.

NO MAN IS AN ISLAND

Five: THE WOMAN CLOTHED WITH THE SUN

ALL THAT HAS BEEN WRITTEN about the Virgin Mother of God proves to me that hers is the most hidden of sanctities. What people find to say about her sometimes tells us more about their own selves than it does about Our Lady. For since God has revealed very little to us about her, men who know nothing of who and what she was tend to reveal themselves when they try to add something to what God has told us about her.

And the things we do know about her only make the true character and quality of her sanctity seem more hidden. We believe that hers was the perfect sanctity outside the sanctity of Christ her Son, Who is God. But the sanctity of God is only darkness to our minds. Yet the sanctity of the Blessed Virgin is in a way more hidden than the sanctity of God: because He has at least told us something about Himself that is objectively valid when it is put into human language. But about Our Lady He has told us only a few important things—and even then we cannot grasp the fullness of what they mean. For all He has told us about her soul amounts to this: that it was absolutely full of the most perfect created holiness. But what that means, in detail, we have no sure way of knowing. Therefore the other certain thing we know about her is that her sanctity is most hidden.

And yet I can find her if I too become hidden in God where she is hidden. To share her humility and hiddenness and poverty, her concealment and solitude is the best way to know her: but to know her thus is to find wisdom. *Qui me inveniet vitam et hauriet salutem a Domino.*

IN THE ACTUAL LIVING, human person who is the Virgin Mother of Christ are all the poverty and all the wisdom of all the saints. It all came to them through her, and is in her. The sanctity of all the saints is a participation in her sanctity, because in the order He has established God wills that all graces come to men through Mary.

That is why to love her and to know her is to discover the true meaning of everything and to have access to all wisdom. Without her, the knowledge of Christ is only speculation. But in her it becomes experience because all the humility and poverty, without which Christ cannot be known, were given to her. Her sanctity is the silence in which alone Christ can be heard, and the voice of God becomes an experience to us through her contemplation.

The emptiness and interior solitude and peace without which we cannot be filled with God were given by Him to Mary in order that she might receive Him into the world by offering Him the hospitality of a being that was perfectly pure, perfectly silent, perfectly at rest, perfectly at peace, and centered in utter humility. If we ever manage to empty ourselves of the noise of the world and of our own passions, it is because she has been sent close to us by God and given us a share in her sanctity and her hiddenness.

MARY ALONE, of all the saints, is, in everything, incomparable. She has the sanctity of them all and yet resembles none of them. And still we can talk of being like her. This likeness to her is not only something to desire—it is one human quality most worthy of our desire: but the reason for that is that she, of all creatures, most perfectly recovered the likeness to God that God willed to find, in varying degrees, in us all.

It is necessary, no doubt, to talk about her privileges as if they were something that could be made comprehensible in human language and could be measured by some human standard. It is most fitting to talk about her as a Queen and to act as if you knew what it meant to say she has a throne above all the angels. But this should not make anyone forget that her highest privilege is her poverty and her greatest glory is that she is most hidden, and the source of all her power is that she is as nothing in the presence of Christ, of God.

This is often forgotten by Catholics themselves, and therefore it is not surprising that those who are not Catholic often have a completely wrong conception of Catholic devotion to the Mother of God. They imagine, and sometimes we can understand their reasons for doing so, that Catholics treat the Blessed Virgin as an almost divine being in her own right, as if she had some glory, some power, some majesty of her own that placed her on a level with Christ Himself. They regard the Assumption of Mary into heaven as a kind of apotheosis and her Queenship as a strict divinization. Hence her place in the Redemption would seem to be equal to that of her Son. But this is all completely contrary to the true mind of the Catholic Church. It forgets that Mary's chief glory is in her nothingness, in the fact of being the "*Handmaid of the Lord,*" as one who in becoming the Mother of God acted simply in loving submission to His command, in the pure obedience of faith. She is blessed not because of some mythical pseudo-divine prerogative, but in all her human and womanly limitations as *one who has believed.* It is the faith and the fidelity of this humble handmaid, "full of grace" that enables her to be the perfect instrument of God, and nothing else but His instrument. The work that was done in her was purely the work of God. "He that is mighty hath done great things in me." The glory of Mary is purely and simply the glory of God in her, and she, like anyone else, can say that she has nothing that she has not received from Him through Christ.

As a matter of fact, this is precisely her greatest glory: that having nothing of her own, retaining nothing of a "self" that could glory in anything for her own sake, she placed no obstacle to the mercy of God and in no way resisted His love and His will. Hence she received *more* from Him than any other saint. He was able to accomplish His will perfectly in her, and His liberty was in no way hindered or turned from its purpose by the presence of an egotistical self in Mary. She was and is in the highest sense a person precisely because, being "immaculate," she was free from every taint of selfishness that might obscure God's light in her being. She was then a freedom that obeyed Him perfectly and in this obedience found the fulfillment of perfect love.

THE GENUINE SIGNIFICANCE of Catholic devotion to Mary is to be seen in the light of the Incarnation itself. The Church cannot separate the Son and the Mother. Because the Church conceives of the Incarnation as God's descent into flesh and into time, and His great gift of Himself to His creatures, she also believes that the one who was closest to Him in this great mystery was the one who participated most perfectly in the gift. When a room is heated by an open fire, surely there is nothing strange in the fact that those who stand closest to the fireplace are the ones who are warmest. And when God comes into the world through the instrumentality of one of His servants, then there is nothing surprising about the fact that His chosen instrument should have the greatest and most intimate share in the divine gift.

Mary, who was empty of all egotism, free from all sin, was as pure as the glass of a very clean window that has no other function than to admit the light of the sun. If we rejoice in that light, we implicitly praise the cleanness of the window. And of course it might be argued that in such a case we might well forget the window altogether. This is true. And yet the Son of God, in emptying Himself of His majestic power, having become a child, abandoning Himself in complete dependence to the loving care of a human Mother, in a certain sense draws our attention once again to her. The Light has wished to remind us of the window, because He is grateful to her and because He has an infinitely tender and personal love for her. If He asks us to share this love, it is certainly a great grace and a privilege, and one of the most important aspects of this privilege is that it enables us to some extent to appreciate the mystery of God's great love and respect for His creatures.

THAT GOD should assume Mary into heaven is not just a glorification of a "Mother Goddess." Quite the contrary, it is the expression of the divine love for humanity, and a very special manifestation of God's respect for His creatures, His desire to do honor to the beings He has made in His own image, and most particularly His respect for the *body* which was destined to be the temple of His glory. If Mary is believed to be assumed into heaven, it is because we too are one day, by the grace of God, to dwell where she is. If human nature is glorified in her, it is because God desires it to be glorified in us too, and it is for this reason that His Son, taking flesh, came into the world.

In all the great mystery of Mary, then, one thing remains most clear: that of herself she is nothing, and that God has for our sakes delighted to manifest His glory and His love in her.

It is because she is, of all the saints, the most perfectly poor and the most perfectly hidden, the one who has absolutely nothing whatever that she attempts to possess as her own, that she can most fully communicate to the rest of us the grace of the infinitely selfless God. And we will most truly possess Him when we have emptied ourselves and become poor and hidden as she is, resembling Him by resembling her.

And all our sanctity depends on her maternal love. The ones she desires to share the joy of her own poverty and simplicity, the ones whom she wills to be hidden as she is hidden, are the ones who share her closeness to God.

IT IS a tremendous grace, then, and a great privilege when a person living in the world we have to live in suddenly loses his interest in the things that absorb that world, and discovers in his own soul an appetite for poverty and solitude. And the most precious of all the gifts of nature or grace is the desire to be hidden and to vanish from the sight of men and be accounted as nothing by the world and to disappear from one's own self-conscious consideration and vanish into nothingness in the immense poverty that is the adoration of God.

This absolute emptiness, this poverty, this obscurity holds within it the secret of all joy because it is full of God. To seek this emptiness is true devotion to the Mother of God. To find it is to find her. And to be hidden in its depths is to be full of God as she is full of Him, and to share her mission of bringing Him to all men.

Yet all generations must call her blessed, because they all receive through her obedience whatever supernatural life and joy is granted to them. And it is necessary that the world should acknowledge her and that the praise of God's great work in her should be sung in poetry and that cathedrals should be built in her name. For unless Our Lady is recognized as the Mother of God and as the Queen of all the saints and angels and as the hope of the world, faith in God will remain incomplete. How can we ask Him for all the things He would have us hope for if we do not know, by contemplating the sanctity of the Immaculate Virgin, what great things He has power to accomplish in the souls of men?

And so, the more we are hidden in the depths where her secret is discovered, the more we will want to praise her name in the world and glorify, in her, the God Who made her His shining tabernacle. Yet we will not altogether trust our own talent to find words in which to praise her: for even if we could sing of her as did Dante or St. Bernard we would still have little to say of her, compared with the Church who alone knows how to praise her adequately and who dares to apply to her the inspired words God uses of His own Wisdom. Thus we find her living in the midst of Scripture, and unless we find her, also, hidden in Scripture wherever and in whatever promises contain her Son, we shall not fully know the life that is in Scripture.

It is she who, in these last days, is destined by the merciful delegation of God to manifest the power He has given to her, because of her poverty, and save the last men living in the ruins of the burnt world. But if the world's last age, by the wickedness of men, is likely to be made the most terrible, yet by the clemency of the Blessed Virgin will it also be, for the poor who have received His mercy, the most victorious and the most joyful.

NEW SEEDS OF CONTEMPLATION

Six: POEMS

FREEDOM AS EXPERIENCE

When, as the captive of Your own invincible consent,
You love the image of Your endless Love,
Three-Personed God, what intellect
Shall take the measure of that liberty?

Compared with Love, Your Triune Law,
All the inexorable stars are anarchists:
Yet they are bound by Love and Love is infinitely free.

Minds cannot understand, nor systems imitate
The scope of such simplicity.
All the desires and hungers that defy Your Law
Wither to fears, and perish in imprisonment:
And all the hopes that seem to founder in the shadows of a cross
Wake from a momentary sepulcher, and they are blinded by their
    freedom!

Because our natures poise and point towards You
Our loves revolve about You as the planets swing upon the sun
And all suns sing together in their gravitational worlds.

And so, some days in prayer Your Love,
Prisoning us in darkness from the values of Your universe,
Delivers us from measure and from time,
Melts all the barriers that stop our passage to eternity
And solves the hours our chains.

And then, as fires like jewels germinate
Deep in the stone heart of a Kaffir mountain,
So now our gravity, our new-created deep desire
Burns in our life's mine like an undiscovered diamond.

Locked in that strength we stay and stay
And cannot go away
For You have given us our liberty.

Imprisoned in the fortunes of Your adamant
We can no longer move, for we are free.

FIGURES FOR AN APOCALYPSE

CANA

"This beginning of miracles did Jesus in Cana of Galilee."

Once when our eyes were clean as noon, our rooms
Filled with the joys of Cana's feast:
For Jesus came, and His disciples, and His Mother,
And after them the singers
And some men with violins.

Once when our minds were Galilees,
And clean as skies our faces,
Our simple rooms were charmed with sun.
Our thoughts went in and out in whiter coats than God's disciples',
In Cana's crowded rooms, at Cana's tables.

Nor did we seem to fear the wine would fail:
For ready, in a row, to fill with water and a miracle,
We saw our earthen vessels, waiting empty.
What wine those humble waterjars foretell!

Wine for the ones who, bended to the dirty earth,
Have feared, since lovely Eden, the sun's fire,
Yet hardly mumble, in their dusty mouths, one prayer.

Wine for old Adam, digging in the briars!

A MAN IN THE DIVIDED SEA

EVENING

Now, in the middle of the limpid evening,
The moon speaks clearly to the hill.
The wheatfields make their simple music,
Praise the quiet sky.

And down the road, the way the stars come home,
The cries of children
Play on the empty air, a mile or more,
And fall on our deserted hearing,
Clear as water.

They say the sky is made of glass,
They say the smiling moon's a bride.
They say they love the orchards and apple trees,
The trees, their innocent sisters, dressed in blossoms,
Still wearing, in the blurring dusk,
White dresses from that morning's first communion.

And, where blue heaven's fading fire last shines
They name the new come planets
With words that flower
On little voices, light as stems of lilies.

And where blue heaven's fading fire last shines,
Reflected in the poplar's ripple,
One little, wakeful bird
Sings like a shower.

A MAN IN THE DIVIDED SEA

THE ANNUNCIATION

Ashes of paper, ashes of a world
Wandering, when fire is done:
We argue with the drops of rain!

Until One comes Who walks unseen
Even in elements we have destroyed.
Deeper than any nerve
He enters flesh and bone.
Planting His truth, He puts our substance on.
Air, earth, and rain
Rework the frame that fire has ruined.
What was dead is waiting for His Flame.
Sparks of His Spirit spend their seeds, and hide
To grow like irises, born before summertime.
These blue things bud in Israel.

The girl prays by the bare wall
Between the lamp and the chair.
(Framed with an angel in our galleries
She has a richer painted room, sometimes a crown.
Yet seven pillars of obscurity
Build her to Wisdom's house, and Ark, and Tower.
She is the Secret of another Testament
She owns their manna in her jar.)

Fifteen years old—
The flowers printed on her dress
Cease moving in the middle of her prayer
When God, Who sends the messenger,
Meets His messenger in her Heart.
Her answer, between breath and breath,
Wrings from her innocence our Sacrament!
In her white body God becomes our Bread.

It is her tenderness
Heats the dead world like David on his bed.
Times that were too soon criminal
And never wanted to be normal
Evade the beast that has pursued
You, me, and Adam out of Eden's wood.
Suddenly we find ourselves assembled
Cured and recollected under several green trees.

Her prudence wrestled with the Dove
To hide us in His cloud of steel and silver:
These are the mysteries of her Son.
And here my heart, a purchased outlaw,
Prays in her possession
Until her Jesus makes my heart
Smile like a flower in her blameless hand.

THE STRANGE ISLANDS

A PSALM

When psalms surprise me with their music
And antiphons turn to rum
The Spirit sings: the bottom drops out of my soul

And from the center of my cellar, Love, louder than thunder
Opens a heaven of naked air.

New eyes awaken.
I send Love's name into the world with wings
And songs grow up around me like a jungle.
Choirs of all creatures sing the tunes
Your Spirit played in Eden.
Zebras and antelopes and birds of paradise
Shine on the face of the abyss
And I am drunk with the great wilderness
Of the sixth day in Genesis.

But sound is never half so fair
As when that music turns to air
And the universe dies of excellence.

Sun, moon, and stars
Fall from their heavenly towers.
Joys walk no longer down the blue world's shore.

Though fires loiter, lights still fly on the air of the gulf,
All fear another wind, another thunder:
Then one more voice
Snuffs all their flares in one gust.

And I go forth with no more wine and no more stars
And no more buds and no more Eden
And no more animals and no more sea:

While God sings by himself in acres of night
And walls fall down, that guarded Paradise.

THE TEARS OF THE BLIND LIONS

THE QUICKENING OF ST. JOHN THE BAPTIST

On the Contemplative Vocation

Why do you fly from the drowned shores of Galilee,
From the sands and the lavender water?
Why do you leave the ordinary world, Virgin of Nazareth,
The yellow fishing boats, the farms,

The winesmelling yards and low cellars
Or the oilpress, and the women by the well?
Why do you fly those markets,
Those suburban gardens,
The trumpets of the jealous lilies,
Leaving them all, lovely among the lemon trees?

You have trusted no town
With the news behind your eyes.
You have drowned Gabriel's word in thoughts like seas
And turned toward the stone mountain
To the treeless places.
Virgin of God, why are your clothes like sails?

The day Our Lady, full of Christ,
Entered the dooryard of her relative
Did not her steps, light steps, lay on the paving leaves like gold?
Did not her eyes as gray as doves
Alight like the peace of a new world upon that house, upon miraculous
    Elizabeth?

Her salutation
Sings in the stone valley like a Charterhouse bell:
And the unborn saint John
Wakes in his mother's body,
Bounds with the echoes of discovery.

Sing in your cell, small anchorite!
How did you see her in the eyeless dark?
What secret syllable
Woke your young faith to the mad truth
That an unborn baby could be washed in the Spirit of God?
Oh burning joy!
What seas of life were planted by that voice!
With what new sense   ,
Did your wise heart receive her Sacrament,
And know her cloistered Christ?

You need no eloquence, wild bairn,
Exulting in your hermitage.
Your ecstasy is your apostolate,
For whom to kick is *contemplata tradere.*
Your joy is the vocation

Of Mother Church's hidden children—
Those who by vow lie buried in the cloister or the hermitage:
The speechless Trappist, or the gray, granite Carthusian,
The quiet Carmelite, the barefoot Clare,
Planted in the night of contemplation,
Sealed in the dark and waiting to be born.

Night is our diocese and silence is our ministry
Poverty our charity and helplessness our tongue-tied sermon.
Beyond the scope of sight or sound we dwell upon the air
Seeking the world's gain in an unthinkable experience.
We are exiles in the far end of solitude, living as listeners
With hearts attending to the skies we cannot understand:
Waiting upon the first far drums of Christ the Conqueror,
Planted like sentinels upon the world's frontier.

But in the days, rare days, when our Theotocos
Flying the prosperous world
Appears upon our mountain with her clothes like sails,
Then, like the wise, wild baby,
The unborn John who could not see a thing
We wake and know the Virgin Presence
Receive her Christ into our night
With stabs of an intelligence as white as lightning.

Cooled in the flame of God's dark fire
Washed in His gladness like a vesture of new flame
We burn like eagles in His invincible awareness
And bound and bounce with happiness,
Leap in the womb, our cloud, our faith, our element,
Our contemplation, our anticipated heaven
Till Mother Church sings like an Evangelist.

THE TEARS OF THE BLIND LIONS

Seven: LOVE IN MEDITATION

THE DISTINCTIVE CHARACTERISTIC of religious meditation is that it is a search for truth which springs from love and which seeks to possess the truth not only by knowledge but also by love. It is, therefore, an intellectual activity which is inseparable from an intense consecration of spirit and application of the will. The presence of *love* in our meditation intensifies and clarifies our thought by giving it a deeply affective quality. Our meditation becomes charged with a loving appreciation of the *value* hidden in the supreme truth which the intelligence is seeking. This affective drive of the will, seeking the truth as the soul's highest good, raises the soul above the level of speculation and makes our quest for truth a prayer full of reverential love and adoration striving to pierce the dark cloud which stands between us and the throne of God. We beat against this cloud with supplication, we lament our poverty, our helplessness, we adore the mercy of God and His supreme perfections, we dedicate ourselves entirely to His worship.

Mental prayer is therefore something like a skyrocket. Kindled by a spark of divine love, the soul streaks heavenward in an act of intelligence as clear and direct as the rocket's trail of fire. Grace has released all the deepest energies of our spirit and assists us to climb to new and unsuspected heights. Nevertheless, our own faculties soon reach their limit. The intelligence can climb no higher into the sky. There is a point where the mind bows down its fiery trajectory as if to acknowledge its limitations and proclaim the infinite supremacy of the unattainable God.

But it is here that our "meditation" reaches its climax. Love again takes the initiative and the rocket "explodes" in a burst of sacrificial praise. Thus love flings out a hundred burning stars, acts of all kinds,

373

expressing everything that is best in man's spirit, and the soul spends
itself in drifting fires that glorify the Name of God while they fall
earthward and die away in the night wind!

That is why St. Albert the Great, the master who gave St. Thomas
Aquinas this theological formation at Paris and Cologne, contrasts the
contemplation of the philosopher and the contemplation of the saints:

> The contemplation of philosophers seeks nothing but the perfection of the
> one contemplating and it goes no further than the intellect. But the con-
> templation of the saints is fired by the love of the one contemplated: that
> is, God. Therefore it does not terminate in an act of the intelligence but
> passes over into the will by love.

St. Thomas Aquinas, his disciple, remarks tersely that for this very
reason the contemplative's knowledge of God is arrived at, on this
earth, by the light of burning love: *per ardorem caritatis datur cognitio
veritatis*. (Commentary on St. John's Gospel, Chapter 5.)

The contemplation of "philosophers," which is merely intellectual
speculation on the divine nature as it is reflected in creatures, would be
therefore like a skyrocket that soared into the sky but never went off.
The beauty of the rocket is in its "death," and the beauty of mental
prayer and of mystical contemplation is in the soul's abandonment and
total surrender of itself in an outburst of praise in which it spends
itself entirely to bear witness to the transcendent goodness of the
infinite God. The rest is silence.

II

ALL COMPARISONS are defective in some respect. Our image of the skyrocket might perhaps mislead imaginative minds. Meditation does not
have to be colorful or spectacular. The effectiveness of our mental
prayer is not to be judged by the interior fireworks that go off inside
us when we pray. On the contrary, although sometimes the fruit of a
good meditation may be an ardent sensible love springing from vivid
insights into the truth, these so-called "consolations of prayer" are not
to be trusted without reserve or sought for their own sake alone. We
should be deeply grateful when our prayer really brings us an increase
of clear understanding and felt generosity, and we should by no means
despise the stimulation of sensible devotion when it helps us to do whatever we have to do, with greater humility, fidelity, and courage.

Nevertheless, since the fruit of mental prayer is harvested in the
depths of the soul, in the will and in the intelligence, and not on the

level of emotion and instinctive reactions, it is quite possible that a meditation that is apparently "cold," because it is without feelings, may be most profitable. It can give us great strength and spiritualize our interior life, lifting it above the level of the senses and teaching us to guide ourselves by reason and the principles of faith.

This is one of the points at which ignorance makes progress in mental prayer difficult or even impossible. Those who think that their meditation must always culminate in a burst of emotion, fall into one of two errors. Either they find that their emotions run dry and that their prayer seems to be "without fruit." Therefore they conclude that they are wasting their time and give up their efforts, in order to satisfy their craving for sensations in some other way.

Or else they belong to the category of those whose emotions are inexhaustible. They can almost always weep at prayer. They can quite easily produce sentiments of fervor, with a little concentration and the right kind of effort, whenever they desire them. But this is a dangerous form of success. Emotional versatility is a help at the beginning of the interior life, but later on it may be an obstacle to progress. At the beginning, when our senses are easily attracted to created pleasures, our emotions will keep us from turning to God unless they themselves can be given some enjoyment and awareness of the value of prayer. Thus the taste for spiritual things has to start out with a humble and earthly beginning, in the senses and in feeling. But if our prayer always ends in sensible pleasure and interior consolation, we will run the risk of resting in these things which are by no means the end of the journey.

III

THE PRECISE WAY in which each individual makes his meditation will depend in large measure upon his temperament and natural gifts. An intellectual and analytic mind will break down a text into its component parts, and follow the thought step by step, pausing in deep reflection upon each new idea, in order to examine it from different points of view and draw forth all its hidden implications, both speculative and practical.

But analysis must not go too far. The mind must ascend, by reasoning, to the threshold of intuition. Meditation enters into its full swing, for an intellectual, when his mind can grasp the whole content of the subject in one deep and penetrating gaze. Then he rests in this intuition, letting the truth sink in and become a part of himself. Above all, intuition, setting the intelligence temporarily at rest, should leave the will free to adapt itself to the practical consequences of the truth thus seen and to direct our whole life in accordance with it.

Such minds as these—which are a minority—can fruitfully meditate on an article of the *Summa Theologica* or on any other theological text. But even they cannot always be contented with an intellectual approach to supernatural things. For a theologian, in practice, mental prayer should become a kind of refuge from his speculative study, an oasis of affectivity to which he can retire to rest after his intellectual labor. In any case, the prayer of love is always higher than mere mental considerations. All mental prayer, whatever may be its beginnings, must terminate in love.

The true end of Christian meditation is therefore practically the same as the end of liturgical prayer and the reception of the sacraments: a deeper union by grace and charity with the Incarnate Word who is the only Mediator between God and man, Jesus Christ.

The peculiar value of mental prayer, however, is that it is completely personal and favors a spiritual development along lines dictated by our own particular needs. The interior life demands of us a heroic struggle to practice virtue and to detach ourselves from inordinate love of temporal, created things. We cannot possibly bring our souls to renounce our most powerful natural desires unless we somehow have a real and conscious appreciation of our contact with something better. The love of God remains a cold and abstract thing unless we can bring ourselves to realize its deeply intimate and personal character. We can never hope, on earth, to achieve anything like a clear realization of what it means to be loved by the three divine Persons in one divine nature. But it is very easy to appreciate the love of God when we see it concretized in the human love of Jesus Christ for us. This is the best and most logical foundation for a life of faith, and therefore this above all should be the primary object of meditation.

SPIRITUAL DIRECTION AND MEDITATION

Eight: PROMETHEUS: A MEDITATION

Eᴿᴬˢᴹᵁˢ once discussed with Colet and other divines the nature
of Cain's sin: not the murder of Abel but his *first* sin. Their conclusions are no longer interesting or important. The only reason I allude
to the discussion is that the Cain of Erasmus turned out to be Prometheus in a fable that tells us much about the mentality of the Renaissance—and about our own.

Cain, says Erasmus, had often heard his parents speak of the wonderful vegetation of Paradise, where the "ears of corn were as high as the
alders," and he persuaded the angel at the gate to bring him a few
seeds from inside the garden. He planted them and succeeded admirably
as a farmer, but this drew down upon him the wrath of the Almighty.
His sacrifices were no longer acceptable.

It is curiously significant that modern and "progressive" man should
consider himself somehow called upon to vindicate Cain, and that in
doing so he should identify Cain with the fire-bearing Titan whom he
has been pleased to make the symbol of his own technological genius
and of his cosmic aspirations.

But what is equally significant is the confusion of the two opposite
interpretations of Prometheus: the version of Hesiod, in which Prometheus is a villain, and the version of Aeschylus in which he is the hero.
The difference between these two versions lies of course in the different
attitude toward the implacable father figure: Zeus.

Hesiod represents and approves the Olympian order, where Zeus
reigns in absolute power over the subversive and dethroned gods of
archaic Greece. Zeus is the god of the invading Achaians who destroyed
the matriarchal and tribal society of primitive Greece, the society of
the Earth Mother, of Demeter, of Hera and Athene. Prometheus, the

son of Earth and of Ocean, is a threat to the static order established by Zeus, the order in which no bird may chirp and no flower may look at the sun without the permission of the jealous Father. Zeus is the master of life rather than its giver. He tolerates man and man's world, but only barely.

According to Hesiod, when Prometheus *stole* the fire for men (there was no other way in which he could get fire away from Zeus) Zeus revenged himself on Prometheus in the way we well know with the added detail that he drives a stake through his heart. But Zeus is also revenged upon mankind: how? By sending woman.

Strange, ponderous fantasy of an aggressively male society! Woman comes from Zeus as a *punishment,* for in her "everything is good but her heart."

Woman, the culminating penance in a life of labor and sorrow!

In the world picture of Hesiod, though it is beautiful, primitive, full of Hellenic clarity, we find this darkness, this oppressive and guilty view that life and love are somehow a punishment. That nothing can ever be really good in it. That life is slavery and sorrow because of Zeus, and because Prometheus has resisted Zeus. That therefore life is nothing but a wheel upon which man is broken like a slave. . . .

Epimetheus, the brother of Prometheus, receives woman as a gift from Zeus and does not wake up to the nature of the gift until it is too late. Then he remembers what Prometheus had told him: *never accept any gift from the gods.*

Hesiod is a great poet and yet to me this view of life is utterly horrible. I hate it and I reject it with everything in my being. All the more because it is, I believe, implicit in the atheism of the world into which I was born and out of which, by Christ's grace and the gift of God, I have been reborn.

The *Prometheus Bound* of Aeschylus is one of the most heartrending, pure, and sacred of tragedies. I know of none that strikes so deep into the roots of man, the root where man is able to live in the mystery of God.

The Prometheus of Aeschylus is the exact opposite of the Prometheus of Hesiod. Between Prometheus and the Earth Mother and Ocean rises the figure of a usurper. For in Aeschylus it is Zeus, not Prometheus, who is the usurper. It is Zeus, not Prometheus, who is sick with *hubris.* True, Prometheus is driven by desperation beyond the wise limits which the Greek mind recognized so well. But his rebellion is the rebellion of life against inertia, of mercy and love against tyranny, of humanity against cruelty and arbitrary violence. And he calls upon the feminine, the wordless, the timelessly moving elements to witness his sufferings. Earth hears him.

In the end of the tragedy (which is only the first of a trilogy, two plays of which have been lost) Earth promises her son a deliverer. Herakles will come and break his brother's chains. Zeus will be mollified. His mind will change, and he will see things in a new light. The struggling gods will be reconciled, and the reconciliation will be the victory of Prometheus but also the victory of Earth, that is to say of mercy, of humanity, of innocence, of trust.

Once more it will be possible for men to receive gifts from heaven. It will be possible and right to wait for gifts, to depend on them. To use them to build, innocently, a better world.

The two faces of Prometheus represent two attitudes toward life, one positive, the other negative. It is significant that the Renaissance, in choosing between the two, selected the negative. It is against this negative choice that my Prometheus is written. My meditation is a rejection of the negative, modern myth of Prometheus. It is a return to the archaic, Aeschylean, and positive aspect of Prometheus, which is, at the same time, to my mind, deeply and implicitly Christian.

The Prometheus of Hesiod is Cain. The Prometheus of Aeschylus is Christ on the Cross.

In my meditation I have started from Hesiod's view in order to argue against it.

❖ PROMETHEUS: A MEDITATION

THE SMALL GODS men have made for themselves are jealous fathers, only a little greater than their sons, only a little stronger, only a little wiser. Immortal fathers, afraid of their mortal children, they are unjustly protected by a too fortunate immortality. To fight with them requires at once heroism and despair. The man who does not know the Living God is condemned, by his own gods, to this despair: because, knowing that he has made his own gods, he cannot help hoping that he will be able to overthrow them. Alas, he realizes too late that he has made them immortal. They must eventually devour him.

THE PROMETHEAN INSTINCT is as deep as man's weakness: that is to say, it is almost infinite. Promethean despair is the cry that rises out of the abyss of man's nothingness—the inarticulate expression of the terror man cannot face, the terror of having to be someone, of having to be himself. That is to say, his terror of facing and fully realizing his divine sonship, in Christ, and in the Spirit of Fire Who is given us from heaven. The fire Prometheus thought he had to steal from the gods is his own identity in God, the affirmation and vindication of his own being as a sanctified creature in the image of God. The fire Prometheus thought he had to steal was his own spiritual freedom. In the eyes of Prometheus to be himself was to be guilty. The exercise of liberty was a crime, an attack upon the gods which he had made (the gods to whom he had given all that was good in himself, so that in order to have all that he had, it was necessary to steal it back from them).

PROMETHEUS KNOWS—for his nature tells him this—that he must become a person. Yet he feels that he can only do this by an exploit, a tour de force. And the exploit itself is doomed to failure. Condemned by his very nature to face this gesture and this crime, he feels drawn, by his very nature itself, to extinction. The fire attracts him more than he can believe possible, because it is in reality his own. But he hates himself for desiring what he has given to his gods, and punishes himself before he can take it back from them. Then he becomes his own vulture, and is satisfied at last. In consuming himself, he finds realization. (Secretly he tells himself: "I have won fire for other men, I have sacrificed myself for others." But in reality he has won nothing for anybody. He has suffered the loss of his own soul, but he has not gained the whole world, or even a small part of it. He has gained nothing.)

GUILTY, frustrated, rebellious, fear-ridden, Prometheus seeks to assert himself and fails. His mysticism enables him to glory in defeat. For since Prometheus cannot conceive of a true victory, his own triumph is to let the vulture devour his liver: he will be a martyr and a victim, because the gods he has created in his own image represent his own tyrannical demands upon himself. There is only one issue in his struggle with them: glorious defiance in a luxury of despair.

To struggle with the gods seems great, indeed, to those who do not know the Living God. They do not know that He is on our side against false gods and defeat is not permissible. One who loves Christ is not allowed to be Prometheus. He is not allowed to fail. He must *keep* the fire that is given him from heaven. And he must assert that the fire is *his*. He must maintain his rights against all the false gods who hold that it was stolen.

GUILT was the precious gift of the false gods to Prometheus, a gift that made all this waste possible. Not knowing that the fire was his for the asking, a gift of the true God, the Living God, not knowing that fire was something God did not need for Himself (since He had made it expressly for man) Prometheus felt he was obliged to steal what he could not do without. And why? Because he knew no god that would be willing to give it to him for nothing. He could not conceive of such a god, because if he himself had been god, he would have needed fire for himself and would never have shared it with another. He knew no god that was not an enemy, because the gods he knew were only a little stronger than himself, and needed fire as badly as he needed it. In order to exist at all, they had to dominate him and feed on him and ruin him (for if he himself had been a god, he knew he would have had to live on what was weaker than himself).

Thus the gods Prometheus knew were weak, because he himself was weak. Yet they were a little stronger than he was, strong enough to chain him to Caucasus. (He had that much strength left in himself, after creating his gods: he was strong enough to consume himself for all eternity in punishment for having desired their fire. In fact, he destroyed himself forever that they might live. For this reason idolatry was, and is, the fundamental sin.)

A MAN must make the best of whatever gods he has. Prometheus had to have weak gods because he was his own god, and no man admits that he is his own god. But he subjects himself to his own weakness, conceived as a god, and prefers it to the strength of the Living God. If Prometheus had known the strong God, and not worshiped weak gods, things would have been different. The guilt Prometheus felt from the beginning was more necessary for his gods than for himself. If he had not been guilty, such gods would not have been able to exist. Without guilt he could not have conceived them, and since they only existed in his own mind he had to be guilty in order to think of them at all. His guilt, then, was a secret expression of love. It was his homage of love and trust. By his guilt he bore witness to his little household gods, his fire hoarders. By stealing their fire he confessed that he loved them and believed in their falsity more than he loved the

Living God and more than he believed in His truth. It was then a supreme act of homage on his part to open his heart to his unreal gods, and steal from them that fire which, in reality, was his own. Surely, he had given them everything, in order to show how much he preferred their nothingness to the Living God and even to himself!

NO ONE was ever less like Prometheus on Caucasus, than Christ on His Cross. For Prometheus thought he had to ascend into heaven to steal what God had already decreed to give him. But Christ, Who had in Himself all the riches of God and all the poverty of Prometheus, came down with the fire Prometheus needed, hidden in His Heart. And He had Himself put to death next to the thief Prometheus in order to show him that in reality God cannot seek to keep anything good to Himself alone.

Far from killing the man who seeks the divine fire, the Living God will Himself pass through death in order that man may have what is destined for him.

If Christ has died and risen from the dead and poured out upon us the fire of His Holy Spirit, why do we imagine that our desire for life is a Promethean desire, doomed to punishment?

Why do we act as if our longing to "see good days" were something God did not desire, when He Himself told us to seek them? Why do we reproach ourselves for desiring victory? Why do we pride ourselves on our defeats, and glory in despair?

Because we think our life is important to ourselves alone, and do not know that our life is more important to the Living God than it is to our own selves.

Because we think our happiness is for ourselves alone, and do not realize that it is also His happiness.

Because we think our sorrows are for ourselves alone, and do not believe that they are much more than that: they are His sorrows.

There is nothing we can steal from Him at all, because before we can think of stealing it, it has already been given.

THE BEHAVIOR OF TITANS

Nine: THE GOOD SAMARITAN

"Who is my neighbor?"

Christ told the parable of the Good Samaritan in answer to that question.

First let us remember that while to us all Samaritans are Good Samaritans, it was not so to those who first heard the parable. In their eyes all Samaritans were, by the very fact, bad. Indeed that was why a Samaritan had to be the subject of the parable: since it was necessary for the hearers to realize that at least one Samaritan could be a good one.

We on the other hand accept Samaritans without difficulty as good, having identified ourselves with them. All Samaritans are good in our eyes because we consider ourselves Samaritans. Since we have come to regard ourselves as good Samaritans, do we not perhaps consider that Jews are less good than ourselves? In that case we will not understand the parable at all, for we shall imagine that the priest and levite passed by the wounded man just because they were Jews. And we shall think that it was because the Samaritan was both "good" and "Samaritan" that he helped him.

But if we interpret the parable in this way we close our minds to its meaning. For neither the Jew nor the Samaritan is our neighbor in any exclusive or comforting sense.

Consider the question that was asked: "Who is my neighbor?" This was, in fact, the second question which a lawyer asked of Christ. His first, intended as a temptation or an embarrassment, was, "How shall I obtain eternal life?" This is an important question, and so important that nobody can be without the answer to it. And note that he asks this question of Him of Whom we read: "This is eternal life: to know

Thee, the One True God, and Jesus Christ Whom Thou hast sent."
Since the answer to the most important of questions is accessible to
everyone, the lawyer should have known it. And he did know it. He
had no need to ask it at all. The Lord made this clear, for He said:
"What is the first commandment?" When the lawyer replied, saying
that the first commandment was the love of God and of our neighbor,
then Christ told him to keep that commandment and he would have
eternal life. In this way it became clear that the question was not
necessary. But in order to prove that he had a real problem, the lawyer
asked again: "Who is my neighbor?"

We can perhaps assume that he meant by this he had no problem
about loving God, since "God is good," but that he was perplexed about
loving his neighbor, since some men are better than others and all are
imperfect. This being the case, in order to protect himself against loving
an unworthy object and thus wasting his love, he wanted to know
where to draw the line. Who is the neighbor to be loved, who is the
alien not to be loved? The question is a matter of classification. Therefore it is a matter of judgment also, for to classify is to judge. How then
does one classify people, and judge them accurately as worthy of love,
or of hatred, or of indifference? This is a pretty question. But to the
Lord it was a question that had no meaning, for He said, "Judge not,
that ye be not judged." Do not classify, and do not be classified.

THE PARABLE seems not to answer this question, or at least not to
answer it directly. For the lawyer is saying, "How shall I identify my
neighbor, in order actively to give him the love that is commanded by
God?" and Christ gives an example of one who needs love, and who
passively receives love from someone who falls outside the category of
"neighbor." And yet the Samaritan is constituted a "neighbor" by the
fact that he gives love. Now what this answer really says is more than
the scribe explicitly asked. For the answer cuts right through the knot
of the question.

Christ does not tell the scribe how to judge and classify but teaches
him that classifications are without significance in this matter of love.
For we do not and cannot love according to classifications. Or if we do,
then we do not love in the full sense of the word. Love is free; it does
not depend on the *desirability* of its object, but loves for love's sake.
But if love submits itself to an object, to a good outside itself, it tends
to its own destruction. If it confers good upon its object, then it thrives
and grows. For the nature of love is to give as well as to receive. It both

gives and receives, but it gives first, and in giving it receives. Therefore if love demands first of all to receive a good from its object, before beginning to love, then it can never begin to love.

If a man has to be pleasing to me, comforting, reassuring, before I can love him, then I cannot truly love him. Not that love cannot console or reassure! But if I demand first to be reassured, I will never dare to love. If a man has to be a Jew or a Christian before I can love him, then I cannot love him. If he has to be black or white before I can love him, then I cannot love him. If he has to belong to my political party or social group before I can love him, if he has to wear my kind of uniform, then my love is no longer love because it is not free: it is dictated by something outside myself. It is dominated by an appetite other than love. I love not the person but his classification, and in that event I love him not as a person but as a thing. I love his label which confirms me in attachment to my own label. But in that case I do not even love myself. I value myself not for what I am, but for my label, my classification. In this way I remain at the mercy of forces outside myself, and those who seem to me to be neighbors are indeed strangers for I am first of all a stranger to myself.

DO YOU THINK perhaps this is the meaning of the parable: that all men are to be loved because they are men? Because they are human, and have the same nature? No, this is not the meaning. This would be simply a matter of extending the classification to its broadest limits, and including all men in one big category, "Man." Christ means more than this however, for He gives a more than philosophical answer. His answer is a divine revelation, not a natural ethical principle. It is a revelation of the mystery of God. Hence in revealing truth it remains mysterious and in some sense hidden. Yet if we get as close as we can to the source of revelation, we can gain deeper insight into the mystery.

The parable of the Good Samaritan is a revelation of God in a word that has great importance through all the Scriptures from the beginning to the end. It is a revelation of what the prophet Hosea says, speaking for the invisible God, "I will have *mercy* and not sacrifices." What is this *mercy* which we find spoken of everywhere in the Scriptures, and especially in the Psalms? The Vulgate rings with *misericordia* as though with a deep church bell. Mercy is the "burden" or the *"bourdon,"* it is the bass bell and undersong of the whole Bible. But the Hebrew word which we render as mercy, *misericordia,* says more still than mercy.

Chesed (mercy) is also fidelity, it is also strength. It is the faithful, the indefectible mercy of God. It is ultimate and unfailing because it is the power that binds one person to another, in a covenant of hearts. It is the power that binds us to God because He has promised us mercy and will never fail in His promise. For He cannot fail. It is the power and the mercy which are most characteristic of Him, which come nearer to the mystery into which we enter when all concepts darken and evade us.

There are other attributes of God which are further from Him and nearer to ourselves. They come and go in the Scriptures. They are flashes and presences, they appear and disappear as if they were in some sense provisional, as if they were approximations: too partial! For all concepts of God have to be corrected and completed in so far as they are analogies. Some however more than others. For example the metaphor that He is angry, when in fact He is not angry. It is true that He manifests His wrath and He judges. He punishes and He strikes. But when we say that He does all these things, He does not do them but something else which we do not understand. And when it has been said that He is angry it has only been said that it seemed to us that He was angry. We are saying that if *we* had been in His place we would have been angry and would have struck. But because "my thoughts are not your thoughts, says the Lord," there is something much nearer the truth which appears on a far more transcendent level when the anger vanishes. This is the sun which does not change, behind the passing clouds which are other aspects of God. This unchanging, fundamental, stable element is the mystery which is revealed in the Hebrew word *chesed*.

For what do we read in Isaiah?

For the Lord hath called thee as a woman forsaken and mourning in spirit, and as a wife cast off from her youth, said thy God. For a small moment have I forsaken thee, but with great mercies will I gather thee.
In a moment of indignation have I hid my face a little from thee, but with everlasting kindness have I had mercy on thee, said the Lord thy Redeemer. (ISA. 54:6-8)

Again Hosea says that the Lord does not want to be called Lord so much as "husband," since to be called Lord is to be worshiped with fear rather than love, as though He were a Baal and not a Savior. For it is characteristic of a Baal to have no *chesed*. The power of the Baal is another power, frightening and capricious, but unable to reach the depths of our own being. *Chesed* can take possession of our hearts and transform them and so it is said

And it shall be in that day, saith the Lord, That she shall call me: My husband, and she shall call me no more Baali.
And I will take away the names of Baalim out of her mouth, and she shall no more remember their name. (HOSEA 2:16-17)

Again *chesed* is something more than mercy. But it contains in itself many varied aspects of God's love which flash forth in mercy and are its fountain and its hidden source. Remember how God revealed Himself to Moses on Sinai. First Moses had begged to see His face, and the Lord had told Moses that no one could see Him and live. Moses had pleaded to see Him, so God showed Himself without showing Himself. That is to say He "passed by" Moses who only "saw Him after He had passed by." That is to say that Moses saw Him by not seeing Him, since He saw Him when He was gone. But He "had been" there (He who is everywhere and nowhere). That is to say that Moses having first known Him in complete darkness without seeing Him, then saw Him in a kind of light-after-darkness without knowing Him. First the dark flash and the passing and the night, then the cries and words drawn out of the depths of the darkness and mystery of that awakening. These great words shot up out of the heart of Moses and exploded in various shapes and tones which all formed the figure of *chesed*:

O the Lord, the Lord God, merciful and gracious, patient and of much compassion and true, who keepest mercy unto thousands: who takest away iniquity and wickedness and sin, and no man of himself is innocent before thee. (EXOD. 34:6-7)

The *chesed* of God is a gratuitous mercy that considers no fitness, no worthiness, and no return. It is the way the Lord looks upon the guilty and with His look makes them at once innocent. This look seems to some to be anger because they fly from it. But if they face it they see that it is love and that they are innocent. (Their flight and the confusion of their own fear make them guilty.) The *chesed* of God is truth. It is infallible strength. It is the love by which He seeks and chooses His chosen, and binds them to Himself. It is the love by which He is married to mankind, so that if humanity is faithless to Him it must still always have a fidelity to which to return: that is His own fidelity. For He has become inseparable from man in the *chesed* which we call Incarnation, and Passion, and Resurrection. He has also given us His *chesed* in the Person of His Spirit. The Paraclete is the full, inexpressible mystery of *chesed*. So that in the depths of our own being there is an inexhaustible spring of mercy and of love. Our own being has become love. Our own self has become God's love for us, and it is full of Christ, of *chesed*. But we must face it and accept it. We must accept ourselves and others as *chesed*. We must be to ourselves and to others signs and sacraments of mercy.

Chesed, MERCY AND POWER, manifests itself visibly in the *chasid*, or the saint. Indeed the saint is one whose whole life is immersed in the *chesed* of God. The saint is the instrument of the divine mercy. Through the *chasid* the love of God reaches into the world in a visible mystery, a mystery of poverty and love, meekness and power. The *chasid* is in many respects a foolish one, who has been made comical by mercy. The apparent tragedy of his nothingness is turned inside out with joy. In his folly the divine wisdom shines forth and his annihilation is a new creation, so that he rejoices in the incongruity of the divine mercies and is everlastingly astonished at the creative love of God. He calls upon all beings to praise this love with him, and most of them do not pay attention. Yet the sun and moon and the sea and the hills and stars join him, nevertheless, in praising *chesed*. The majority of men, perhaps, consider him crazy.

(God, too, is glad to be thought crazy in His *chasid*. For the wisdom of God is folly in the eyes of men.)

The folly of the *chasid* is manifested in his love and concern for his neighbor, the sinner. For the sinner is "next to" the *chasid* or the saint. They are so close to one another, so like one another, that they are sometimes almost indistinguishable. The professionally pious man, on the contrary, makes a whole career out of being evidently distinguishable from sinners. He wants it to be very clear to God and to man that he and the sinner are in different categories. Hence the love of the *chasid* for the sinner (and of the sinner for the *chasid*) is not the patronizing concern of the pious and respectable, but the impractical concern of one who acts as if he thought he were the sinner's mother. Such a one behaves like the Samaritan in the parable, and not like the priest and levite, who were well aware of proprieties, and classifications, and categories. Who knows? Perhaps the priest took a look at the character lying in the ditch and observed that he had blood all over him and that it would never do to contract a ritual impurity. Especially out here in the desert, miles from water. Those who are professionally respectable and whose lives are measured out in long and formal ceremonies, have other and more urgent things to do than to be instruments of *chesed*.

WHO, THEN, is my neighbor? To whom am I bound? Who must I love? These are not intelligent questions, and they do not have clear answers. On the contrary any attempt to answer them involves us in endless subtleties, and vagueness, and ultimate confusion. Love is not limited by classifications. The measure of love that Christ has set for us is beyond measure: we must "be perfect as the heavenly Father is perfect." But what is meant by the "perfection" of the heavenly Father? It is impartiality, not in the sense of justice that measures out equally to all, knowing their merits, but in the sense of *chesed* that knows no classification of good and evil, just or unjust. "For He sends His rain upon the just and the unjust."

We are bound to God in *chesed*. The power of His mercy has taken hold of us and will not let go of us: therefore we have become foolish. And because we have emptied ourselves in this folly which He has sent upon us, we can be moved by His unpredictable wisdom, so that we love whom we love and we help whom we help, not according to plans of our own but according to the measure laid down for us in His hidden will, which knows no measure. In this folly, which is the work of His Spirit, we must love especially those who are helpless and who can do nothing for themselves. We must also receive love from them, realizing our own helplessness, and our own inability to fend for ourselves. *Chesed* has made us as though we were outcasts and sinners. *Chesed* has numbered us among the aliens and strangers: *chesed* has not only robbed us of our reason but declassified us along with everyone else, in the sight of God. Thus we have no home, and no family, and no niche of worthiness in society, and no recognizable function. Nor do we even appear to be especially charitable, and we cannot pride ourselves on virtue. *Chesed* has apparently robbed us of all that, for he who lives by the mercy of God alone shall have nothing else to live by, only that mercy. *Plenitudo legis est charitas.* Mercy fulfills the whole law.

THE MYSTERY of the Good Samaritan, then, is this: the mystery of *chesed*, power and mercy. In the end, it is Christ Himself who lies wounded by the roadside. It is Christ Who comes by in the person of

the Samaritan. And Christ is the bond, the compassion and the understanding between them. This is how the Church is made of living
stones, compacted together in mercy. Where there is on the one hand
a helpless one, beaten and half dead, and on the other an outcast with
no moral standing, and the one leans down in pity to help the other,
then there takes place a divine epiphany and an awakening. There is
"man," there reality is made human, and in answer to this movement
of compassion a Presence is made on the earth, and the bright cloud
of the majesty of God overshadows their poverty and their love. There
may be no consolation in it. There may be nothing humanly charming
about it. It is not necessarily like the movies. Perhaps the encounter is
outwardly sordid and unattractive. But the Presence of God is brought
about on earth there, and Christ is there, and God is in communion
with man.

This is what we are talking about when we speak of "doing the will
of God." Not only fulfilling precepts, and praying, and being holy, but
being instruments of mercy, and fastening ourselves and others to God
in the bonds of *chesed*.

THE TWO QUESTIONS asked by the scribe were, then, useless. Therefore
Christ did not answer them. Yet he did not pass them by without attention. On the contrary, He saw them as indications of the scribe's
plight and of our own. Instead of answering the questions, He poured
oil and wine into the wounds. This He did by His own words, Who is
Himself the answer to all useful questions.

Good Samaritan

Ten: TOWER OF BABEL

Part One   THE LEGEND OF THE TOWER

Scene One   The Building of the Tower

RAPHAEL, THOMAS, FIRST BUILDER, SECOND BUILDER, LEADER, CAPTAIN, CHORUS

[*Musical Prelude—the building of the Tower. Enter* RAPHAEL *and* THOMAS.

THOMAS: Ought we, Raphael, to join
　　　　The builders of this city?
　　　　We can quickly learn
　　　　Their language and their ambition.

RAPHAEL: No, we must stand apart.
　　　　If we learn their language
　　　　We will no longer understand
　　　　What is being said.
　　　　If we imitate their zeal
　　　　We will lose all sense of what is to be done.

THOMAS: They are clear-minded men
　　　　Of one purpose.

RAPHAEL: No. They only appear
　　　　To know what they are building.
　　　　They think it is a tower
　　　　That will reach heaven.
　　　　They think they speak the same
　　　　Language, that they are of one
　　　　Mind.

                                          Presently
                              We shall discover that they are
                              Only of one voice. Many minds,
                              Many thoughts signifying nothing.
                              Many words, many plans
                              Without purpose. Divided hearts,
                              Weak hands. Hearts that will be
                              Closed to one another. Hands
                              Armed against one another.
                              There is no agreement
                              There can be no tower.

FIRST BUILDER: I believe in the tower.
                              Therefore I will work longer hours.

SECOND BUILDER: I believe in the Leader.
                              Therefore I will sacrifice myself
                              To build this tower.

FIRST BUILDER: I believe in our common language,
                              Therefore I will serve the Leader.

SECOND BUILDER: I believe in labor without reward.
                              The tower is reward enough.

FIRST BUILDER: I believe in work without food and sleep
                              Although it is not yet possible.

SECOND BUILDER: The Leader will make it possible.

FIRST BUILDER: Everyone knows that the Leader
                              Will make everything possible.

SECOND BUILDER: It is good that we agree brother.
                              Let us never stop working;
                              Let us build this Tower for the Leader who loves
                                 war.

FIRST BUILDER: Yet, it is good that we agree. Let us
                              Build this Tower for the Leader who loves peace.

CAPTAIN: Silence! Stop work. Listen to the Leader.

LEADER: The Tower is nearly finished.
                              It is the greatest of all Towers, in fact
                              It is the only perfect and eternal Tower. There has
                                 never been
                              And never will be another such Tower.
                              The Tower is inviolable. It will

Be attacked by invisible powers
From above and from below by agents of social
    corruption.
Are you tired of work, my people?
Then, when the Tower is built,
We shall have war. But the Tower is impregnable.
Do your duty. Soon you will
Taste the excitement of war.

CAPTAIN: Back to work. The Tower must be finished by
    nightfall.

CHORUS: Grow Babylon, grow,
    Great Babylon, touch the stars.
    What if the Lord should see you, now?
    Grow, Babylon, grow!

RAPHAEL
[*The dialogue
continues
against the
background of
the* CHORUS]: They suppose that if they build a high tower very quickly, they will be nearly as strong as God, Whom they imagine to be only a little stronger than themselves. And if the highest part of the tower is level with the lowest part of heaven, man and God will have to discuss everything on equal terms.

THOMAS: It is therefore a religious tower, and they are men of faith.

RAPHAEL: No, it is a tower of unbelief.

THOMAS: What have they failed to believe in?

RAPHAEL: Two things: First they do not believe in themselves, and because of this they do not believe in God. Because they do not believe in themselves or in God, they cannot believe in unity. Consequently they cannot be united. Therefore they cannot finish the tower which they imagine they are building.

THOMAS: Nevertheless they are very busy with whatever they think they are doing.

RAPHAEL: That is a pretense. Activity is their substitute for faith. Instead of believing in themselves, they seek to convince themselves, by their activity, that they exist. And their activity pretends to direct itself against God, in order that they may reassure themselves that He does not exist.

THOMAS: Why so?

RAPHAEL: Because if He does not exist, then they do not have to be troubled with the problem of their own existence either. For if they admit they exist they will have to love one another, and this they find insupportable.

THOMAS: But surely they love one another! Otherwise how could they unite in a common endeavor? Surely, they are united, and their union has brought them success.

RAPHAEL: No, they have only united in their common, though hidden, desire to fail. Their ambition is only the occasion for a failure they certainly seek. But they require that this failure come upon them, as it were, out of the stars. They want to blame their ruin on fate, and still have the secret satisfaction of ruining themselves.

THOMAS: Why should they do so much work in order to fail?

RAPHAEL: Their hearts seek disaster as a relief from the tedium of an unsatisfactory existence. Ruin will at least divide them from one another. They will be able to scatter, to run away, to put barricades against one another. Since they cannot stand the pretense of unity, they must seek the open avowal of their enmity.

FIRST BUILDER: What is this thing called war which has been promised us as our reward for finishing the tower?

SECOND BUILDER: It is another work invented by the Leader, more glorious than this one as well as more exhausting.

CAPTAIN: Silence. Stop work! The Leader will ascend to the garden he has planted on the summit of the Tower he has built. He will walk and sing under the exotic trees upon whose branches he will presently hang the heads of our common enemies.

LEADER: Already I see that the skies are as full of words as they are of stars. Each word becomes an instrument of war. Words of the clocks and devils. Words of the wheels and machines. Steel words stronger than flesh or spirit. Secret words which divide the essences of things. Last of all, the one word which strikes at the heart of creation, and dissolves it into its original nothingness. Give me possession of this one word, and I will forget every other.

CHORUS: Fear! Fear!
Fell the business that springs
Out of the dark. Feel fear pass cold
hands (like wind) over your skin!
Fear talks out of the thundercloud.
Ships fold their wings. The almond trees
Grow pale before the storm.
[CHORUS *continues as background to following dialogue.*]

THOMAS: Raphael, I am scared, I see the tower nodding against the moon. I see the great cranes bending under the cloud.

RAPHAEL: Look at the little boats, Thomas, how they fly down the river. See how the carts topple off the side of the road!

THOMAS: O Raphael, that cloud first came up out of the desert no bigger than a man's fist. Then at once it stood over the tower like a man's arm. Then suddenly the burly dark filled the whole sky. Can you still hear me in this wind?

RAPHAEL: Wind with a thousand fingers pulls away the scaffolding. With a thousand invisible fists the wind beats on the battlements of the great Tower.

FIRST WATCHMAN: Blow the trumpets! Blow the storm-warning trumpet!

VOICE: It is too late, the storm is already upon us.

WATCHMAN: Blow the fire trumpet, blow the fire trumpet!

VOICE: It is too late. Fire has sprouted from a hole in the Tower!

CHORUS: Hide us from the fall, hide us from the fall!
Hide us in the catacomb, hide us in the well!
Hide us in the ground, hide us from the sky!
Hide us from the Tower's fall!

WATCHMAN: Blow the poison trumpet, blow the poison trumpet!
VOICE: Too late! The captains have already taken poison.
WATCHMAN: Then blow the trumpet of division.
VOICE: Blow the trumpet of division!
THOMAS: This is Babylon's end!
RAPHAEL: No, it is Babylon's beginning!
CHORUS: Now blow upon this plain you winds of heaven.
Blow, blow, you winds of God, upon the sands.
Scatter the seeds of war to the world's end.

Scene Two   The Trial

RAPHAEL, THOMAS, SOLDIERS, CAPTAIN, LEADER, PROFESSOR, PROPA-
GANDA, FALSEHOOD, LANGUAGE, CHORUS

[SCENE—*Square in a half-ruined city.* RAPHAEL *and* THOMAS.]

RAPHAEL: Everywhere the great machines of war
Stand face to face. The hunters in the sky
Bargain with life and death.
Babylon, like a great star wandering from its orbit,
Unsettles the universe, dragging nations down into
chaos.

THOMAS: Is this the same city? All the cities in the world
Begin to look like the same city.
Wagons come down to the water
Where the crowds stand
After flags have fallen. Angry men
Stand without speech,
Wait for the conquering army.

SOLDIERS [*enter, singing marching song*]:
The bar snake and the zigzag snake
Will bite each other in the head
And drown each other in the river:
Who will reign when both are dead?
The fire bird and the water bird
Have brought good luck to Babylon
But who will reign when both are dead?

CAPTAIN: Gather the citizens in the square
And fill the whole city
With the sound of one voice.
There shall be no other voice. For peace,
Peace is this: only a giant voice.
There shall be one Babylon, fearing the orator.
There shall be one Babylon, hating itself.
[*Enter* LEADER, PROFESSOR, LAWYERS.]

LEADER: Now we must settle the question of guilt.
The Tower fell. Babylon was dishonored.
Our armies, though everywhere victorious,
Are full of traitors. Sabotage
Halts the production of new weapons.
Who is responsible?

CHORUS: Nothing is light, nothing is dark,
Nothing is defined. Sunlight and darkness
Both bring forth new fear.
Things are beginning to lose their names,
Persons their character. All
Wear the look of death, and become terrible.

CAPTAIN: Silence! Traitors. Salute the Leader!
He brings you life, salvation,
Prosperity, peace. Can you not see that despair,
Unhappiness, will presently cease to exist?

LEADER: Who has taught these people the lies they utter?
What enemy has poisoned their minds?

CAPTAIN: We know the traitor's name,
One who was at first our best friend, one who was
Our most capable officer. One we thought
Would not fail us.

LEADER: Who is it then?

CAPTAIN: Language! He and his regiments, the words,
Have sold out to the enemy.

LEADER: Impossible.
Words have always been our best soldiers.
They have defeated meaning in every engagement
And have almost made an end of reality.

CAPTAIN: No, Majesty. They are in league with sense,

Order and even silence. They are in the pay
Of thought and of communication.

LEADER: Then they have betrayed their sacred trust
For theirs is a mission of division and destruction.

CAPTAIN: Our first witness will explain the functions of language.

PROFESSOR: History is a dialogue
Between forward and backward
Going inevitably forward by the abuse of thought
And the gradual destruction of intelligence.
Now the function of the word is
To designate: first the machine,
Then what the machine produces,
And finally what the machine destroys.
Words have no other function.
They belong by right to the political process:
Doing, making, destroying. Or rather
Being done, being made, being destroyed.
Such is history.

CAPTAIN: This witness can prove that language is the enemy
of history and should therefore be abolished.

LEADER: Let him proceed.

PROFESSOR: The word is a means of locomotion
Forward and backward
Along the infinite horizontal plane
Created by the history
Which words themselves destroy
(Substituting what *ought* to have happened
For what actually happened).

LEADER: But if that is the case, Language is the fulfillment
of history. Why then should it be destroyed?

PROFESSOR: The machine must always destroy
The maker of the machine, for this proves
That the machine is greater than the one who made
it
Just as man is more important than God.
Words reflect this principle, in their relation to
history.
Words create history. But they, in turn,

Must be destroyed by the history they have created.
The word supersedes the event, as light emerges from darkness,
Transforming the event into something it was not.
But the event, in turn, supersedes its interpretation as darkness
Replaces light, and in the end it is darkness that wins.
And the Words of the historian are forgotten.

LEADER: Which then is real? The light, or the darkness?

PROFESSOR: Words create reality as fast as they are eaten by it,
And they destroy reality as fast as they themselves
Come back to life, out of the minds of men.
This is the movement of history:
The backward, forward working of the web;
The plunge forward, into the web,
The struggle backward, but not out of the web.

LEADER: Words, then, are the ultimate reality! Let there never again be any silence. Let tongues never be still. For if there be silence, our history will instantly be unmade, and if we stop talking we will cease to exist. Words, therefore, are acquitted. Let Silence be called to the stand.

CAPTAIN: One moment! It is not so simple. There are three kinds of language. There is true language, there is falsehood, and there is propaganda. Let us call all three to the stand, beginning with the most dangerous.

LEADER: Call Truth to the stand!

CLERK: Truth, tell us your name.

TRUTH: My name is Truth.

CLERK: Where do you live?

TRUTH: In things as they are, in minds that see things as they are, in wills that conform to things as they are.

LAWYER: Truth, you are the enemy of the Mammoth State.
You have pretended to serve us, and you have
All the while poisoned the minds of the people
With enemy doctrines. You refuse

To conform your declarations to the pure
Slogans of our Leader. You are therefore
Insubordinate, a saboteur, a spy,
A tool of the enemy.
How many murders, bombings, acts
Of open or hidden violence have you
Not committed against us? You are
The worst of enemies. You are
The destroyer of the Tower.

VOICES: To the salt mines! To the salt mines!

TRUTH: You are your own enemies. You destroyed your own
Tower.

VOICES: Put him to death.
Shoot him! Down with him!
Kill him. He is the People's enemy.

SECOND PHILOSOPHER: I can defend Truth.

CAPTAIN: Shall we hear this witness?

LEADER: Give him one minute, not more.

SECOND PHILOSOPHER: There is no need to put Truth to death.
Truth has never existed, there is no Truth.
Everything is vague. The world, O Leader,
Which only seems to exist,
Needs to be expressed in words which seem to exist.
Actually, nothing has real being.
Seeming is existing. Everything that seems,
Is. It is what it wants to be.
It has no being, only wanting.
Truth, then, may seem to exist.
But what is it? If we look too close
We see right through the seeming.
Leader, there is no Truth.

VOICES: He is right! There is no truth!

OTHER VOICES: He is a liar! Truth exists, but it is not true.

LEADER: Truth or no Truth, words are agents of the traitor:
Meaning. Let them be put to death.

VOICES: Death, death, death,
Let words be put to death!

CAPTAIN: One moment!

Not all words claim to be true.
The pure, holy, divine words of the Leader,
What are they? Are they true?
[*Awkward silence, broken by the* LEADER.]

LEADER: Send this witness to the salt mines.
I have words of my own. Call Propaganda to the stand!

CLERK: Do you swear to conceal the truth, the whole truth, and to confuse nothing but the issue?

PROPAGANDA: I do.

LEADER: What is your name?

PROPAGANDA: Legion.

LEADER: Where do you live?

PROPAGANDA: In the heads of the people.

LEADER: What do the people look like?

PROPAGANDA: Zombies.

LEADER: How long have they looked like zombies?

PROPAGANDA: Since we got inside.

LEADER: How did you get inside?

PROPAGANDA: By shots in the arm, by beatings over the head, noises in the ear, and all the right kind of medicines.

LEADER: Who destroyed the Tower?

PROPAGANDA: The religious warmongers, the clergy, the freemasons, the Pope, the millionaires, the Elders of Zion, the Young Men's Christian Association, the Jesuits, and the Legion of Mary.

LEADER: You are a faithful guardian of the Mammoth Democracy, you shall be decorated with the order of the Tower and you shall possess exclusive freedom of speech and worship in every part of the world. Go forth and form the minds of the young. [*Turning to* CLERK] Call Falsehood to the stand.
[*Solemn music—enter* FALSEHOOD.]

VOICE: This must be one of the gods.

LEADER: Sir, who are you?

FALSEHOOD: Why, I am Truth.

LEADER: Ah, yes. We should have known.

FALSEHOOD: I built the Tower.

VOICES: The builder of the Tower, the builder of the Tower!

LEADER: Your worship, will you be so kind as to tell us the function of language, and indicate whether or not words had anything to do with the ruin of the tower? Are words faithful to our cause, or should they be done away with? Can our empire subsist without language?

FALSEHOOD: I am your strength. Without me you fall. I will give you the only words that will serve your purpose. You should never have listened to anyone but me. Your city is made in my image and likeness. I penetrate reality by destroying it. Those who follow me will be split in half and each one, instead of being one man, will become two angels. If you follow me and listen to my words, you will find this out for yourself.

CAPTAIN: This must be the voice of our creator.

LEADER: Tell us, Majesty, who destroyed the Tower?

FALSEHOOD: The Tower has never been destroyed. Just as I am immortal, the Tower is indestructible. The Tower is a spiritual reality and so am I. The Tower is everywhere. What you call the fall of the Tower was only its beginning, its passage into a new, more active phase of existence. The Tower is not a building but an influence, a mentality, an invisible power. The Tower stands, and I am the King who lives on the summit of the Tower. And because I am everywhere, everywhere is the Tower of Babel.

LEADER: Divine and omnipresent Majesty, forgive us for not having recognized you. What shall we do with the people who resist your authority?

FALSEHOOD: Let all men serve me in chains.

CHORUS: Grow, Babylon, grow,
Serve your Lord in chains.
Chains will be your liberty.

Grow, Babylon, grow!

CLERK: There is one more witness!

LEADER: Who is he?

CAPTAIN: His name is Silence.

LEADER: Useless! Throw him out! Let silence be crucified!
[*Music, an all-out crucifixion of silence.*]

THE STRANGE ISLANDS

Eleven: CHANT TO BE USED IN PROCESSIONS
AROUND A SITE WITH FURNACES

How we made them sleep and purified them
How we perfectly cleaned up the people and worked a big heater
I was the commander I made improvements and installed a guaranteed
system taking account of human weakness I purified and I remained
decent
How I commanded
I made cleaning appointments and then I made the travellers sleep
and after that I made soap
I was born into a Catholic family but as these people were not
going to need a priest I did not become a priest I installed a
perfectly good machine it gave satisfaction to many
When trains arrived the soiled passengers received appointments
for fun in the bathroom they did not guess
It was a very big bathroom for two thousand people it awaited
arrival and they arrived safely
There would be an orchestra of merry widows not all the time much
art
If they arrived at all they would be given a greeting card to send
home taken care of with good jobs wishing you would come to our
joke
Another improvement I made was I built the chambers for two thousand invitations at a time the naked votaries were disinfected with
Zyklon B
Children of tender age were always invited by reason of their youth
they were unable to work they were marked out for play

They were washed like the others and more than the others

Very frequently women would hide their children in the piles of
clothing but of course when we came to find them we would send
the children into the chamber to be bathed

How I often commanded and made improvements and sealed the door
on top there were flowers the men came with crystals I guaranteed
always the crystal parlor

I guaranteed the chamber and it was sealed you could see through
portholes

They waited for the shower it was not hot water that came through
vents though efficient winds gave full satisfaction portholes
showed this

The satisfied all ran together to the doors awaiting arrival it
was guaranteed they made ends meet.

How I could tell by their cries that love came to a full stop I
found the ones I had made clean after about a half hour

Jewish male inmates then worked up nice they had rubber boots
in return for adequate food I could not guess their appetite

Those at the door were taken apart out of a fully stopped love
for rubber male inmates strategic hair and teeth being used later
for defence

Then the males removed all clean love rings and made away with
happy gold

A big new firm promoted steel forks operating on a cylinder they
got the contract and with faultless workmanship delivered very fast
goods

How I commanded and made soap 12 lbs fat 10 quarts water 8 oz to
a lb of caustic soda but it was hard to find any fat

"For transporting the customers we suggest using light carts on
wheels a drawing is submitted"

"We acknowledge four steady furnaces and an emergency guarantee"

"I am a big new commander operating on a cylinder I elevate the
purified materials boil for 2 to 3 hours and then cool"

For putting them into a test fragrance I suggested an express
elevator operated by the latest cylinder it was guaranteed

Their love was fully stopped by our perfected ovens but the love
rings were salvaged

Thanks to the satisfaction of male inmates operating the heaters
without need of compensation our guests were warmed

All the while I had obeyed perfectly

So I was hanged in a commanding position with a full view of
the site plant and grounds

You smile at my career but you would do as I did if you knew
yourself and dared

In my days we worked hard we saw what we did our self sacrifice
was conscientious and complete our work as faultless and detailed

Do not think yourself better because you burn up friends and
enemies with long-range missiles without ever seeing what you
have done

The Catholic Worker

PART SIX

Vision

When I arose the ledges of the holy mountain
were already covered with light,
as we moved on with the sun behind us.

Epigraph

THERE IS INEBRIATION in the waters of contemplation, whose mystery fascinated and delighted the first Cistercians and whose image found its way into the names of so many of those valley monasteries that stood in forests, on the banks of clean streams, among rocks alive with springs.

These are the waters which the world does not know, because it prefers the water of bitterness and contradiction. These are the waters of peace, of which Christ said: *"He that shall drink of the water that I shall give him, shall not thirst for ever. But the water that I shall give him shall become in him a fountain of water, springing up into life everlasting."*

These are the Waters of Siloe, that flow in silence.

THE WATERS OF SILOE

Prologue: MYSTICISM IN THE NUCLEAR AGE

THE HUMAN RACE is facing the greatest crisis in its history, because religion itself is being weighed in the balance. The present unrest in five continents, with everyone fearful of being destroyed, has brought many men to their knees. This should not lead us into the illusion that the world is necessarily about to return to God. Nevertheless, the exposure of the nineteenth-century myths—"unlimited progress" and the "omnipotence" of physical science—has thrown the world into confusion. Many are spontaneously turning to the only evident hope for spiritual and moral integration—an order based on philosophical and theological truth, one which allows free expression to the fundamental religious instinct of man. So vast is this movement that a psychoanalyst as important as Carl Jung can make the following declaration:

I have treated many hundreds of patients, the larger number being Protestants, a smaller number Jews and not more than five or six believing Catholics. Among all my patients in the second half of my life . . . there has not been one whose problem in the last resort was not that of finding a religious outlook on life. It is safe to say that every one of them fell ill because he had lost that which the living religions of every age have given their followers and none of them has really been healed who did not regain his religious outlook.[1]

The big problem that confronts Christianity is not Christ's enemies. Persecution has never done much harm to the inner life of the Church as such. The real religious problem exists in the souls of those of us who in their hearts believe in God, and who recognize their obligation to love Him and serve Him—yet do not!

It would only confuse the issue if we attributed this to perversity and ill-will. This is no time for accusations and for judgments. No one of us can afford to blame others for the progressive decline of the Christian spirit in Christendom, yet it has declined until the world has finally advanced to find itself entering the post-Christian era. We are all to blame, and our fathers were to blame, and perhaps the very concept of "blame" is to blame. When Christian perspectives are warped, Christianity turns from a religion of hope into an obsession with guilt, and in order to evade the pressures of intolerable self-blame, we fling ourselves into activities that are supposed to change the world and ourselves with it. And, effectively, it is from these inner pressures of restless Christendom that they have arisen, the amazing forces that are now indeed changing our world. But the forces thus released are changing the world into one that is no longer Christian.

To keep the world Christian, to halt this terrifying process, there are Christians who are willing to resort to war, and to make full use of the frightful destructive powers that modern man has discovered. This is not only futile but criminal. It is in effect a moral and spiritual apostasy from Christ and from His commandment to love. Can we not see that to risk the destruction of man for the supposed glory of Christ is, in effect, to crucify Christ over again in His members? The great temptation of our time is the temptation of a culminating impiety, a "nuclear crusade." And it is hate that leads us into this temptation. Our constant baiting and condemnation of our enemies is just as bad as their constant blaming and condemnation of us. If we cannot stop judging each other, we run the constant risk of destroying each other. This does not alter the fact that Communism is a false and pernicious doctrine. However, the fact that Communism is wrong does not mean that our politics are infallibly right.

The world we live in is dry ground for the seed of God's Truth. A modern American city is not altogether a propitious place in which to try to love God. You cannot love Him unless you know Him. And you cannot come to know Him unless you have a little time and a little peace in which to pray and think about Him and study His truth. Time and peace are not easily come by in this civilization of ours. And so those who profess to serve God are often forced to get along without either, and to sacrifice their hopes of an interior life. But how far can one go in this sacrifice before it ceases to be a sacrifice and becomes a prevarication? The truth is, we are simply not permitted to devote ourselves to God without at the same time leading an interior life.

The reason for this is plain. Everything we do in the service of God has to be vitalized by the supernatural power of His grace. But grace is granted us in proportion as we dispose ourselves to receive it by the interior activity of the theological virtues: faith, hope, charity. These virtues demand the full and constant exercise of our intelligence and will. But this exercise is frequently obstructed by exterior influences which blind us with passion and draw us away from our supernatural objective. This cannot be avoided, but it must be fought against by a constant discipline of recollection, meditation, prayer, study, mortification of the desires, and at least some measure of solitude and retirement.

It is certainly not possible, or even desirable, that every Christian should leave the world and enter a Trappist monastery. Nevertheless, the sudden interest of Americans in the contemplative life seems to prove one thing quite clearly: that contemplation, asceticism, mental prayer, and unworldliness are elements that most need to be rediscovered by Christians of our time. There is little danger that we will neglect apostolic labor and exterior activity. Pope Pius XII in a recent exhortation drew attention to the fact that external activity had perhaps been overstressed in some quarters, and reminded Catholics that their personal sanctity and union with Christ in a deep interior life were the most important things of all. His Holiness writes:

We cannot abstain from expressing our preoccupation and our anxiety for those who, on account of the special circumstances of the moment, have become so engulfed in the vortex of external activity that they neglect the chief duty [of the Christian]: his own sanctification. We have already stated publicly in writing that those who presume that the world can be saved by what has rightly been called the "heresy of action" must be made to exercise better judgment.[2]

The fact that the Communists used to be in revolt against everything "bourgeois" imposed on every serious Communist the obligation to practice a strict and almost religious asceticism with regard to practically everything that is valued by the society he hates. I say that this *used to be* the case, because it is clear that the Stalinist empire has rapidly reached a cultural level in which everything that was basest in bourgeois materialism has become the Stalinist ideal. If Christianity is to prove itself in open rebellion against the standards of the materialist society in which it is fighting for survival, Christians must show more definite signs of that *agere contra,* that positive "resistance," which is the heart of the Christian ascetic "revolution." The true knowledge of God can be bought only at the price of this resistance.

WE, who live in what we ourselves have called the Atomic Age, have acquired a peculiar facility for standing back and reflecting on our own history as if it were a phenomenon that took place five thousand years ago. We like to talk about our time as if we had no part in it. We view it as objectively as if it existed outside ourselves, in a glass case. If you are looking for the Atomic Age, look inside yourself: because you are it. And so, alas, am I.

The evil that is in the modern world ought to be sufficient indication that we do not know as much as we think we do. It is a strange paradox indeed that modern man should know so much and still know practically nothing. The paradox is most strange because men in other times, who have known less than we know, have in fact known more.

True, in all times there has been wickedness and great blindness in this world of men. There is nothing new under the sun, not even the H-bomb (which was invented by our Father Adam). And it is also true that the ages of greatest despair have sometimes ended up by being ages of triumph and of hope. Now that we have awakened to our fundamental barbarism, it seems to me that there is once again a hope for civilization, because men of good will want more than ever to be civilized. And now that we have our tremendous capacities for evil staring us in the face, there is more incentive than ever for men to become saints. For man is naturally inclined to good, and not to evil. Besides our nature, we have what is infinitely greater—the grace of God, which draws us powerfully upward to the infinite Truth and is refused to no one who desires it.

THE WHOLE HAPPINESS of man and even his sanity depend on his moral condition. And since society does not exist all by itself in a void, but is made up of the individuals who compose it, the problems of society cannot ultimately be solved except in terms of the moral life of individuals. If the citizens are sane, the city will be sane. If the citizens are wild animals, the city will be a jungle.

But morality is not an end in itself. Virtue, for a Christian, is not its own reward. God is our reward. The moral life leads to something beyond itself—to the experience of union with God, and to our transformation in Him. This transformation is perfected in another life, and in the light of glory. Yet even on earth man may be granted a foretaste of heaven in mystical contemplation. And whether he experiences it or not, the man of faith, by virtue of his faith, is already living in heaven. *Conversatio nostra in coelis!*

The fact that contemplation is actually the lot of very few men does not mean that it has no importance for mankind as a whole.

If the salvation of society depends, in the long run, on the moral and spiritual health of individuals, the subject of contemplation becomes a vastly important one, since contemplation is one of the indications of spiritual maturity. It is closely allied to sanctity. You cannot save the world merely with a system. You cannot have peace without charity. You cannot have social order without saints, mystics, and prophets.

II

OUR NATURE imposes on us a certain pattern of development which we must follow if we are to fulfill our best capacities and achieve at least the partial happiness of being human. This pattern must be properly understood and it must be worked out in all its essential elements. Otherwise, we fail. But it can be stated very simply, in a single sentence: *We must know the truth, and we must love the truth we know, and we must act according to the measure of our love.*

What are the elements of this "pattern" I speak of? *First,* and most important of all: I must adapt myself to objective reality. *Second,* this adaptation is achieved by the work of my highest spiritual faculties—intelligence and will. *Third,* it demands expression when my whole being, commanded by my will, produces actions which, by their moral vitality and fruitfulness, show that I am living in harmony with the true order of things.

These are the bare essentials of the pattern. They represent a psychological necessity without which man cannot preserve his mental and spiritual health.

I have only stated these fundamentals of our nature in order to build on them. Contemplation reproduces the same essential outline of this pattern, but on a much higher level. For contemplation is a work of grace. The Truth to which it unites us is not an abstraction but Reality and Life itself. The love by which it unites us to this Truth is a gift of God and can only be produced within us by the direct action of God. The activity which is its final and most perfect fruit is a charity so supreme that it gathers itself into a timeless self-oblation in which there is no motion, for all its perfection is held within the boundless radius of a moment that is eternal.

THESE are difficult matters. To return to our simple sentence: When I say that we must know the truth and love the truth we know, I am not talking primarily about the truth of individual facts and statements but about Truth as such. Truth is reality itself, considered as the object of the intellect. The Truth man needs to know is the transcendent reality, of which particular truths are merely a partial manifestation. Since we ourselves are real, this Truth is not so far distant from us as one might imagine.

Our ordinary waking life is a bare existence in which, most of the time, we seem to be absent from ourselves and from reality because we are involved in the vain preoccupations which dog the steps of every living man. But there are times when we seem suddenly to awake and discover the full meaning of our own present reality. Such discoveries are not capable of being contained in formulas or definitions. They are a matter of personal experience, of uncommunicable intuition. In the light of such an experience it is easy to see the futility of all the trifles that occupy our minds. We recapture something of the calm and the balance that ought always to be ours, and we understand that life is far too great a gift to be squandered on anything less than perfection.

In the lives of those who are cast adrift in the modern world, with nothing to rely on but their own resources, these moments of understanding are short-lived and barren. For, though man may get a glimpse of the natural value of his spirit, nature alone is incapable of fulfilling his spiritual aspirations.

THE TRUTH man needs is not a philosopher's abstraction, but God Himself. The paradox of contemplation is that God is never really known unless He is also loved. And we cannot love Him unless we do His will. This explains why modern man, who knows so much, is nevertheless ignorant. Because he is without love, modern man fails to see the only Truth that matters and on which all else depends.

God becomes present in a very special way and manifests Himself in the world wherever He is known and loved by men. His glory shines in an ineffable manner through those whom He has united to Himself. Those who as yet know nothing of God have a perfect right to expect that we who *do* pretend to know Him should give evidence of the fact, not only by "satisfying every one that asketh us a reason of that hope which is in us," [3] but above all by the testimony of our own lives. For Christ said, in His priestly prayer:

> The glory which thou hast given me I have given them,
> that they may be one as we also are one: I in them
> and thou in me, that they may be made perfect in one:
> and the *world may know that thou hast sent me, and hast*
> *loved them as thou hast also loved me.*[4]

It is useless to study truths about God and lead a life that has nothing in it of the Cross of Christ. No one can do such a thing without, in fact, displaying complete ignorance of the meaning of Christianity. For the Christian economy is by no means a mere philosophy or an ethical system, still less a social theory.

Christ was not a wise man who came to teach a doctrine. He is God, Who became incarnate in order to effect a mystical transformation of mankind. He did, of course, bring with Him a doctrine greater than any that was ever preached before or since. But that doctrine does not end with moral ideas and precepts of asceticism. The teaching of Christ is the seed of a new life. Reception of the word of God by faith initiates man's transformation. It elevates him above this world and above his own nature and transports his acts of thought and of desire to a supernatural level. He becomes a partaker of the divine nature, a Son of God, and Christ is living in him. From that moment forward, the door to eternity stands open in the depths of his soul and he is capable of becoming a contemplative. Then he can watch at the frontier of an abyss of light so bright that it is darkness. Then he will burn with desire to see the fullness of Light and will cry out to God, like Moses in the cloud on Sinai: "Show me Thy face!"

[1] C. G. Jung, *Modern Man in Search of a Soul*, New York, Harcourt, Brace & World, Inc., p. 264.
[2] *Menti Nostrae*, Sept. 23, 1950.
[3] I Pet. 3:15.
[4] John 17:22-23.

THE ASCENT TO TRUTH

One: VISION AND ILLUSION

THE EARTHLY DESIRES men cherish are shadows. There is no true happiness in fulfilling them. Why, then, do we continue to pursue joys without substance? Because *the pursuit itself* has become our only substitute for joy. Unable to rest in anything we achieve, we determine to forget our discontent in a ceaseless quest for new satisfactions. In this pursuit, desire itself becomes our chief satisfaction. The goods that so disappoint us when they are in our grasp can still stimulate our interest when they elude us in the present or in the past.

Few men have so clearly outlined this subtle psychology of illusion as Blaise Pascal, who writes:

A man can pass his whole life without boredom, merely by gambling each day with a modest sum. Give him, each morning, the amount of money he might be able to win in a day, on condition that he must not gamble: you will make him miserable! You may say that what he seeks is the amusement of gaming, not the winnings. All right, let him play for nothing. There will be no excitement. He will be bored to death!

So it is not just amusement that he seeks. An amusement that is tame, without passion, only bores him. He wants to get worked up and to delude himself that he is going to be happy if he wins a sum that he would actually refuse if it were given him on condition that he must not gamble. He needs to create an object for his passions, and to direct upon that object his desire, his anger and his fear—like children who scare themselves with their own painted faces.[1]

A life based on desires is like a spider's web, says Saint Gregory of Nyssa. Woven about us by the father of lies, the Devil, the enemy of our souls, it is a frail tissue of vanities without substance, and yet it can catch us and hold us fast, delivering us up to him as his prisoner.

Nevertheless, the illusion is only an illusion, nothing more. It should be as easy for us to break through this tissue of lies as it is for us to destroy a spider's web with a movement of the hand. Saint Gregory says:

All that man pursues in this life has no existence except in his mind, not in reality: opinion, honor, dignities, glory, fortune: all these are the work of this life's spiders. . . . But those who rise to the heights escape, with the flick of a wing, from the spiders of this world. Only those who, like flies, are heavy and without energy remain caught in the glue of this world and are taken and bound, as though in nets, by honors, pleasures, praise and manifold desires, and thus they become the prey of the beast that seeks to capture them.[2]

The fundamental theme of *Ecclesiastes* is the paradox that, although there is "nothing new under the sun," each new generation of mankind is condemned by nature to wear itself out in the pursuit of "novelties" that do not exist. This concept, tragic as the Oriental notion of *karma* which it resembles so closely, contains in itself the one great enigma of paganism. Only Christ, only the Incarnation, by which God emerged from His eternity to enter into time and consecrate it to Himself, could save time from being an endless circle of frustrations. Only Christianity can, in Saint Paul's phrase, "redeem the times." Other religions can break out of the wheel of time as though from a prison: but they can make nothing of time itself.

Saint Gregory of Nyssa, pursuing his meditations on the psychology of attachment and illusion, vision and detachment, which constitute his commentary on *Ecclesiastes,* observes how time weaves about us this web of illusion. It is not enough to say that the man who is attached to this world has bound himself to it, once and for all, by a wrong choice. No: he spins a whole net of falsities around his spirit by the repeated consecration of his whole self to values that do not exist. He exhausts himself in the pursuit of mirages that ever fade and are renewed as fast as they have faded, drawing him further and further into the wilderness where he must die of thirst. A life immersed in matter and in sense cannot help but reproduce the fancied torments which Greek mythology displays in Hades—Tantalus starving to death with food an inch from his lips, Sysiphus rolling his boulder uphill though he knows it must escape him and roll down to the bottom again, just as he is reaching the summit.

And so, that "vanity of vanities" which so exercised the Ancient Preacher of *Ecclesiastes* and his commentator is a life not merely of deluded thoughts and aspirations, but above all a life of ceaseless and sterile activity. What is more, in such a life the measure of illusion is the very intensity of activity itself. The less you have, the more you do. The final delusion is movement, change, and variety for their own sakes alone.

All the preoccupation of men with the things of this life [writes Saint Gregory], is but the game of children on the sands. For children take delight in the activity of their play and as soon as they have finished building what they build, their pleasure ends. For as soon as their labor is completed, the sand falls down and nothing is left of their buildings.[3]

This profound idea often finds echoes in the pages of Pascal. It might well have provided a foundation for his famous theory of "distraction" —*divertissement*.[4] Pascal knew that the philosophers, who laughed at men for running all day long after a hare that they would probably not have accepted as a present, had not plumbed the full depths of man's inanity. Men who call themselves civilized do not hunt foxes because they want to catch a fox. Neither do they, for that matter, always study philosophy or science because they want to know the truth. No: they are condemned to physical or spiritual movement because it is unbearable for them to sit still. As Pascal says:

We look for rest, and overcome obstacles to obtain it. But if we overcome these obstacles, rest becomes intolerable, for we begin at once to think either of the misfortunes that are ours, or of those that threaten to descend upon us.[5]

Man was made for the highest activity, which is, in fact, his rest. That activity, which is contemplation, is immanent and it transcends the level of sense and of discourse. Man's guilty sense of his incapacity for this one deep activity which is the reason for his very existence, is precisely what drives him to seek oblivion in exterior motion and desire. Incapable of the divine activity which alone can satisfy his soul, fallen man flings himself upon exterior things, not so much for their own sake as for the sake of the agitation which keeps his spirit pleasantly numb. He has but to remain busy with trifles; his preoccupation will serve as a dope. It will not deaden all the pain of thinking; but it will at least do something to blur his sense of who he is and of his utter insufficiency.

Pascal sums up his observations with the remark: "Distraction is the only thing that consoles us for our miseries and yet it is, itself, the greatest of our miseries." [6]

Why? Because it "diverts" us, turns us aside from the one thing that can help us to begin our ascent to truth. That one thing is the sense of our own emptiness, our poverty, our limitations, and of the inability of created things to satisfy our profound need for reality and for truth.

What is the conclusion of all this? We imprison ourselves in falsity by our love for the feeble, flickering light of illusion and desire. We cannot find the true light unless this false light be darkened. We cannot find true happiness unless we deprive ourselves of the *ersatz* happiness of empty diversion. Peace, true peace, is only to be found through suffering, and we must seek the light in darkness.

II

THERE ARE, in Christian tradition, a theology of light and a theology of darkness. On these two lines travel two mystical trends. There are the great theologians of light: Origen, Saint Augustine, Saint Bernard, Saint Thomas Aquinas. And there are the great theologians of darkness: Saint Gregory of Nyssa, Pseudo-Dionysius, Saint John of the Cross. The two lines travel side by side. Modern theologians of genius have found no difficulty in uniting the two, in synthesizing Saint Thomas Aquinas and Saint John of the Cross. Some of the greatest mystics—Ruysbroeck, Saint Theresa of Ávila, and Saint John of the Cross himself—describe both aspects of contemplation, "light" and "darkness."

There are pages in the works of Saint Gregory of Nyssa—as there are also in those of Saint John of the Cross—which might easily fit into a context of Zen Buddhism of Patanjali's Yoga. But we must remember that when a Christian mystic speaks of the created world as an illusion and as "nothingness," he is only using a figure of speech. The words are never to be taken literally and they are not ontological. The world is metaphysically real. Creatures can lead us efficaciously to the knowledge and love of their Creator and ours. But since the created world is present to our senses, and God as He is in Himself is infinitely beyond the reach both of sense and of intelligence, and since the disorder of sin gives us a tendency to prefer sensible goods before all others, we have a way of seeking the good things of this life as if they were our last end.

When Creation appears to us in the false light of concupiscence, it becomes illusion. The supreme value that cupidity seeks in created things does not exist in them. A man who takes a tree for a ghost is in illusion. The tree is objectively real: but in his mind it is something that it is not. A man who takes a cigar coupon for a ten-dollar bill is also in illusion. It is a real cigar coupon, and yet, considered as a ten-dollar bill, it is a pure illusion. When we live as if the multiplicity of the phenomenal universe were the criterion of all truth, and treat the world about us as if its shifting scale of values were the only measure of our ultimate good, the world becomes an illusion. It is real in itself, but it is no longer real to us because it is not what we think it is.

Many Christian mystics look at the world only from the subjective standpoint of fallen man. Do not be surprised, then, if they say that the world is empty, that it is nothingness, and offer no explanation. But Saint Gregory of Nyssa, together with many of the Greek Fathers, not to mention those of the West, sees all sides of the question.

The contemplation of God in nature, which the Greek Fathers called *theoria physica,* has both a positive and a negative aspect. On the one hand, *theoria physica* is a positive recognition of God as He is manifested in the essences (*logoi*) of all things. It is not a speculative science of nature but rather a habit of religious awareness which endows the soul with a kind of intuitive perception of God as He is reflected in His creation. This instinctive religious view of things is not acquired by study so much as by ascetic detachment. And that implies that the positive and negative elements in this "contemplation of nature" are really inseparable. The negative aspect of *theoria physica* is an equally instinctive realization of the vanity and illusion of all things as soon as they are considered apart from their right order and reference to God their Creator. Saint Gregory of Nyssa's commentary on *Ecclesiastes,* from which we have quoted, is a tract on the "contemplation of nature" in its twofold aspect, as vanity and as symbol.

Does all this mean that the *theoria physica* of the Greek Fathers was a kind of perpetual dialectic between the two terms *vision* and *illusion?* No. In the Christian platonism of the Fathers, dialectic is no longer as important as it was in Plato and Plotinus. The Christian contemplation of nature does not consist in an intellectual tennis game between these two contrary aspects of nature. It consists rather in the ascetic gift of a discernment which, in one penetrating glance, apprehends what creatures are, and what they are not. This is the intellectual counterpoise of detachment in the will. Discernment and detachment (*krisis* and *apatheia*) are two characters of the mature Christian soul. They are not yet the mark of a mystic, but they bear witness that one is traveling the right way to mystical contemplation, and that the stage of beginners is passed.

The presence of discernment and detachment is manifested by a spontaneous thirst for what is good—charity, union with the will of God—and an equally spontaneous repugnance for what is evil. The man who has this virtue no longer needs to be exhorted by promises to do what is right, or deterred from evil by threat of punishment.[7]

SO GREAT is the power of man's intelligence that it can start out from the least of all beings and arrive at the greatest. The mind of man is, by its very nature, a participation in the intelligence of God, Whose light illumines the conclusions of rational discourse. Words can be sadly mistreated and misused; but they could not be false unless they could also be true. Language may become a suspicious instrument on the tongues of fools or charlatans, but language as such retains its power to signify and communicate the Truth.

Faith, without depending on reason for the slightest shred of justification, never contradicts reason and remains ever reasonable. Faith does not destroy reason, but fulfills it. Nevertheless, there must always remain a delicate balance between the two. Two extremes are to be avoided: credulity and skepticism, superstition and rationalism. If this balance is upset, if man relies too much on his five senses and on his reason when faith should be his teacher, then he enters into illusion. Or when, in defiance of reason, he gives the assent of his faith to a fallible authority, then too he falls into illusion. Reason is in fact the path to faith, and faith takes over when reason can say no more.

[1] Blaise Pascal, *Les Pensées*, Paris, Ed. Giraud, 1928, p. 66.
[2] Saint Gregory of Nyssa, *Commentary on the Psalms*, P.G. 44:464-465. Cf. Daniélou, *Platonisme et Théologie Mystique*, p. 133.
[3] *Homily 1 on Ecclesiastes*, P.G. 44:628. Cf. Daniélou, *op. cit.*, p. 136.
[4] I am not insisting that Pascal had read Saint Gregory of Nyssa. His thoughts on *divertissement* may have been drawn from a reading of Saint Bernard's *De Gradibus Humilitatis*. It is in any case in the full tradition of Saint Augustine's *De Trinitate*, Bk. xii (on the fall of Adam).
[5] Pascal, *op. cit.*, p. 67.
[6] *Ibid.*, n. 171, p. 75.
[7] Saint Gregory of Nyssa, *Commentary on the Psalms*, C. 5. P.G. 44:450-451.

THE ASCENT TO TRUTH

Two: ASCETICISM AND SACRIFICE

I‍F MY SOUL silences my flesh by an act of violence, my flesh will take revenge on the soul, secretly infecting it with a spirit of revenge. Bitterness and bad temper are the flowers of an asceticism that has punished only the body. For the spirit is above the flesh, but not completely independent of the flesh. It reaps in itself what it sows in its own flesh. If the spirit is weak with the flesh, it will find in the flesh the image and accusation of its own weakness. But if the spirit is violent with the flesh it will suffer, from the flesh, the rebound of its own violence. The false ascetic begins by being cruel to everybody because he is cruel to himself. But he ends by being cruel to everybody but himself.

THERE IS ONLY one true asceticism: that which is guided not by our own spirit but by the spirit of God. The spirit of man must first subject itself to grace and then it can bring the flesh in subjection both to grace and to itself. "If by the Spirit you mortify the deeds of the flesh, you shall live" (Rom. 8:13).

But grace is charitable, merciful, kind, does not seek its own interests. Grace inspires us with no desire except to do the will of God, no matter what His will may be, no matter whether it be pleasing or unpleasant to our own nature.

Those, then, who put their passions to death not with the poison of their own ambition but with the clean blade of the will of God will live in the silence of true interior peace, for their lives are hidden with Christ in God. Such is the meek "violence" of those who take Heaven by storm.

WE CANNOT become saints merely by trying to run away from material things. To have a spiritual life is to have a life that is spiritual in all its wholeness—a life in which the actions of the body are holy because of the soul, and the soul is holy because of God dwelling and acting in it. When we live such a life, the actions of our body are directed to God by God Himself and give Him glory, and at the same time they help to sanctify the soul.

The saint, therefore, is sanctified not only by fasting when he should fast but also by eating when he should eat. He is not only sanctified by his prayers in the darkness of the night, but by the sleep that he takes in obedience to God, Who made us what we are. Not only His solitude contributes to his union with God, but also his supernatural love for his friends and his relatives and those with whom he lives and works.

God, in the same infinite act of will, wills the good of all beings and the good of each individual thing: for all lesser goods coincide in the one perfect good which is His love for them. Consequently it is clear that some men will become saints by a celibate life, but many more will become saints as married men, since it is necessary that there be more married men than celibates in the world. How then can we imagine that the cloister is the only place in which men can become saints? Now the life of the body seems to receive less consideration in the cloister than it does in secular life. But it is clear that married life, for its success, presupposes the capacity for a deeply human love which ought to be spiritual and physical at the same time. The existence of a sacrament of matrimony shows that the Church neither considers the body evil nor repugnant, but that the "flesh" spiritualized by prayer and the Holy Ghost, yet remaining completely physical, can come to play an important part in our sanctification.

IT GIVES GREAT GLORY to God for a person to live in this world using and appreciating the good things of life without care, without anxiety, and without inordinate passion. In order to know and love God through His gifts, we have to use them as if we used them not (I Cor. 7:31)— and yet we have to *use* them. For to use things as if we used them not means to use them without selfishness, without fear, without after-thought, and with perfect gratitude and confidence and love of God. All inordinate concern over the material side of life was reproved by Christ when He said: "What one of you, by taking thought, can add to his stature one cubit?" (Matt. 6:27). But we cannot use created things without anxiety unless we are detached from them. At the same time, we become detached from them by using them sparingly—and yet without anxiety.

The tremulous scrupulosity of those who are obsessed with pleasures they love and fear narrows their souls and makes it impossible for them to get away from their own flesh. They have tried to become spiritual by worrying about the flesh, and as a result they are haunted by it. They have ended in the flesh because they began in it, and the fruit of their anxious asceticism is that they "use things not," but do so as if they used them. In their very self-denial they defile themselves with what they pretend to avoid. They do not have the pleasure they seek, but they taste the bitter discouragement, the feeling of guilt which they would like to escape. This is not the way of the spirit. For when our intention is directed to God, our very use of material things sanctifies both them and us, provided we use them without selfishness and without presumption, glad to receive them from Him Who loves us and Whose love is all we desire.

NO MAN IS AN ISLAND

Three: ART AND SPIRITUALITY

ONE OF THE MOST IMPORTANT—and most neglected—elements in the beginnings of the interior life is the ability to respond to reality, to see the value and the beauty in ordinary things, to come alive to the splendor that is all around us in the creatures of God. We do not see these things because we have withdrawn from them. In a way we have to. In modern life our senses are so constantly bombarded with stimulation from every side that unless we developed a kind of protective insensibility we would go crazy trying to respond to *all* the advertisements at the same time!

The first step in the interior life, nowadays, is not, as some might imagine, learning *not* to see and taste and hear and feel things. On the contrary, what we must do is begin by unlearning our wrong ways of seeing, tasting, feeling, and so forth, and acquire a few of the right ones.

For asceticism is not merely a matter of renouncing television, cigarettes, and gin. Before we can begin to be ascetics, we first have to learn to see life as if it were something more than a hypnotizing telecast. And we must be able to taste something besides tobacco and alcohol: we must perhaps even be able to taste these luxuries themselves as if they too were good.

How can our conscience tell us whether or not we are renouncing things unless it first of all tells us that we know how to use them properly? For renunciation is not an end in itself: it helps us to use things better. It helps us to give them away. If reality revolts us, if we merely turn away from it in disgust, to whom shall we sacrifice it? How shall we consecrate it? How shall we make of it a gift to God and to men?

In an aesthetic experience, in the creation or the contemplation of a work of art, the psychological conscience is able to attain some of its highest and most perfect fulfillments. Art enables us to find ourselves and lose ourselves at the same time. The mind that responds to the intellectual and spiritual values that lie hidden in a poem, a painting, or a piece of music, discovers a spiritual vitality that lifts it above itself, takes it out of itself, and makes it present to itself on a level of being that it did not know it could ever achieve.

THE SOUL that picks and pries at itself in the isolation of its own dull self-analysis arrives at a self-consciousness that is a torment and a disfigurement of our whole personality. But the spirit that finds itself above itself in the intensity and cleanness of its reaction to a work of art is "self-conscious" in a way that is productive as well as sublime. Such a one finds in himself totally new capacities for thought and vision and moral action. Without a moment of self-analysis he has discovered himself in discovering his capacity to respond to a value that lifts him above his normal level. His very response makes him better and different. He is conscious of a new life and new powers, and it is not strange that he should proceed to develop them.

It is important, in the life of prayer, to be able to respond to such flashes of aesthetic intuition. Art and prayer have never been conceived by the Church as enemies, and where the Church has been austere it has only been because she meant to insist on the essential difference between art and entertainment. The austerity, gravity, sobriety, and strength of Gregorian chant, of twelfth-century Cistercian architecture, of Carolingian minuscule script, have much to say about the life of prayer, and they have had much to do, in the past, with forming the prayer and the religious consciousness of saints. They have always done so in proportion as they have freed souls from concentration upon themselves, as well as from mere speculation about technical values in the arts and in asceticism.

NO MAN IS AN ISLAND

❖ POETRY, SYMBOLISM, AND TYPOLOGY

THE PSALMS are poems, and poems have a meaning—although the poet has no obligation to make his meaning immediately clear to anyone who does not want to make an effort to discover it. But to say that poems have meaning is not to say that they must necessarily convey practical information or an explicit message. In poetry, words are charged with meaning in a far different way than are the words in a piece of scientific prose. The words of a poem are not merely the signs of concepts: they are also rich in affective and spiritual associations. The poet uses words not merely to make declarations, statements of fact. That is usually the last thing that concerns him. He seeks above all to put words together in such a way that they exercise a mysterious and vital reactivity among themselves, and so release their secret content of associations to produce in the reader an experience that enriches the depths of his spirit in a manner quite unique. A good poem induces an experience that could not be produced by any other combination of words. It is therefore an entity that stands by itself, graced with an individuality that marks it off from every other work of art. Like all great works of art, true poems seem to live by a life entirely their own. What we must seek in a poem is therefore not an accidental reference to something outside itself: we must seek this inner principle of individuality and of life which is its soul, or "form." What the poem actually "means" can only be summed up in the whole content of poetic experience which it is capable of producing in the reader. This total poetic experience is what the poet is trying to communicate to the rest of the world.

It is supremely important for those who read the Psalms and chant them in the public prayer of the Church to grasp, if they can, the poetic content of these great songs. The poetic gift is not one that has been bestowed on all men with equal lavishness and that gift is unfortunately necessary not only for the writers of poems but also, to some extent, for those who read them. This does not mean that the recitation of the Divine Office is an aesthetic recreation whose full possibilities can only be realized by initiates endowed with refined taste and embellished by a certain artistic cultivation. But it does mean that the type of reader whose poetic appetites are fully satisfied by the Burma Shave rhymes along our American highways may find it rather hard to get anything out of the Psalms.

Since, then, they are poems, the function of the Psalms is to make us share in the poetic experience of the men who wrote them. No matter how carefully and how scientifically we may interpret the words of the Psalms, and study their historical background, if these investigations do not help us to enter into the poetic experience which the

Psalms convey, they are of limited value in showing us what God has revealed in the Psalms, for the revealed content of the Psalter is *poetic*. Let it therefore be clear, that since the inspired writer is an instrument of the Holy Spirit, what is revealed in the Psalter is revealed in the *poetry* of the Psalter and is only fully apprehended in a poetic experience that is analogous to the experience of the inspired writer.

Actually, the simplicity and universality of the Psalms as poetry makes them accessible to every mind, in every age, and in any tongue, and I believe that one's poetic sense must be unusually deadened if one has never at any time understood the Psalms without being in some way moved by their deep and universal religious quality.

The Psalms are more than poems: they are *religious* poems. This means that the experience which they convey, and which the reader must try to share, is not only a poetic but a religious experience. Religious poetry—as distinct from merely devotional verse—is poetry that springs from a true religious experience. I do not necessarily mean a mystical experience. Devotional poetry is verse which manipulates religious themes and which does so, perhaps, even on a truly poetic level. But the experiential content of the poem is at best poetic only. Sometimes it is not even that. Much of what passes for "religious" verse is simply the rearrangement of well-known devotional formulas, without any personal poetic assimilation at all. It is a game, in which souls, no doubt sincere in their piety, play poetic checkers with a certain number of familiar devotional clichés. This activity is prompted by a fundamentally religious intention, if the poem be written for the glory of God or for the salvation of souls. But such poems rarely "save" any souls. They flatter those who are comfortably "saved" but irritate the ones who really need salvation. A truly religious poem is not born merely of a religious purpose. Neither poetry nor contemplation is built out of good intentions. Indeed, a poem that springs from no deeper spiritual need than a devout intention will necessarily appear to be at the same time forced and tame. Art that is simply "willed" is not art, and it tends to have the same disquieting effect upon the reader as forced piety and religious strain in those who are trying hard to be contemplatives, as if infused contemplation were the result of human effort rather than a gift of God. It seems to me that such poetry were better not written. It tends to confirm unbelievers in their suspicion that religion deadens instead of nurtures all that is vital in the spirit of man. The Psalms, on the other hand, are at the same time the simplest and the greatest of all religious poems.

No one will question the truly religious content of the Psalms. They are the songs of men—and David was the greatest of them—for whom God was more than an abstract idea, more than a frozen watchmaker sitting in his tower while his universe goes ticking away into space without him. Nor is the God of the Psalms simply an absolute, immanent Being spinning forth from some deep metaphysical womb an endless pageantry of phenomena. The Psalms are not incantations to lull us to sleep in such a one.

The human symbolism of the Psalter, primitive and simple as it is, should not deceive us into thinking that David had an "anthropomorphic" God. Such a mistake could only be made by materialists who had lost all sense of poetic form and who, moreover, had forgotten the violent insistence of the great Jewish prophets on the transcendence, the infinite spirituality of Jaweh, Who was so far above all things imaginable that He did not even have an utterable name. The God of the Psalter is "above all gods," that is to say, above anything that could possibly be represented and adored in an image. To one who can penetrate the poetic content of the Psalter, it is clear that David's concept of God was utterly pure. And yet this God, Who is "above all the heavens" is "near to those who call upon Him." He Who is above all things is also in all things, and He is capable of manifesting Himself through them all.[1]

The men who wrote the Psalms were carried away in an ecstasy of joy when they saw God in the cosmic symbolism of His created universe.

The heavens declare the glory of God, and the firmament proclaims the work of his hands.
Day unto day heralds the message, and night unto night makes it known.
There is no speech nor words, whose voice is not heard:
Their sound goes forth unto all the earth, and their strains unto the farthest bounds of the world.
There he has set his tabernacle for the sun, which like to the bridegroom coming out from the bridal chamber, he exults like a giant to run his course.
His going forth is from one end of the heavens, and his circuit ends at the other. . . .[2]
Praise ye the Lord from the heavens, praise ye him in the high places.
Praise ye him, all his angels, praise ye him, all his hosts.
Praise ye him, O sun and moon, praise him, all ye shining stars.
Praise him, ye heavens of heavens, and ye waters that are above the heavens:

*Let them praise the name of the Lord, for he commanded and they were
created,*
*And he established them for ever and ever: he gave a decree, which shall
not pass away.*
Praise the Lord from the earth, ye sea-monsters and all ye depths of the sea.
Fire and hail, snow and mist, stormy wind, that fulfil his word,
Mountains and all hills, fruitful trees and all cedars,
Beasts and all cattle, serpents and feathered fowls,
Kings of the earth and all people, princes and all judges of the earth,
Young men and even maidens, old men together with children:
Let them praise the name of the Lord, for his name alone is exalted;[3]

Although we tend to look upon the Old Testament as a chronicle of
fear in which men were far from their God, we forget how many of
the patriarchs and prophets seem to have walked with God with some
of the intimate simplicity of Adam in Eden. This is especially evident
in the first days of the Patriarchs, of which the Welsh metaphysical
poet Henry Vaughan, speaks when he says:

> *My God, when I walke in those groves,*
> *And leaves thy spirit doth still fan,*
> *I see in each shade that there growes*
> *An Angell talking with a man*
> *Under a juniper some house,*
> *Or the coole mirtles canopie,*
> *Others beneath an oakes greene boughs,*
> *Or at some fountaines bubling Eye;*
> *Here Jacob dreames, and wrestles; there*
> *Elias by a Raven is fed,*
> *Another time by th' Angell, where*
> *He brings him water with his bread;*
> *In Abr'hams Tent the winged guests*
> *(O how familiar then was heaven!)*
> *Eate, drinke, discourse, sit downe, and rest*
> *Untill the Coole, and shady even . . .*

As age succeeded age the memory of this primitive revelation of God
seems to have withered away, but its leaf is still green in the Psalter.
David is drunk with the love of God and filled with the primitive sense
that man is the *Leitourgos* or the high priest of all creation, born with
the function of uttering in "Liturgy" the whole testimony of praise
which mute creation cannot of itself offer to its God.

The function of cosmic symbols in the Psalter is an important one.
The revelation of God to man through nature is not the exclusive

property of any one religion. It is shared by the whole human race and forms the foundation for all natural religions.[4] At the same time the vision of God in nature is a natural preamble to supernatural faith, which depends upon distinct and supernatural revelation. Hence even those modern readers who may be repelled by the "historical" Psalms, will nevertheless be attracted by those in which the keynote is struck by cosmic symbolism, and by the vision of God in nature.

However, the cosmic symbolism in the Old Testament is something much more than an element which Judaeo-Christian revelation shares with the cults of the Gentiles. The Old Testament writers, and particularly the author of the creation narrative that opens the *Book of Genesis,* were not only dealing with symbolic themes which had made their appearance in other religions of the Near East: they were consciously attempting to purify and elevate the cosmic symbols which were the common heritage of all mankind and restore to them a dignity of which they had been robbed by being degraded from the level of theistic symbols to that of polytheistic myths.

This question is so important that I hope I may be permitted a brief digression in order to touch upon it.[5]

Everyone knows with what enthusiasm the rationalists of the late nineteenth century berated the Judaeo-Christian revelation for being fabricated out of borrowed materials, because the religious themes and symbols of the Old Testament were similar to those of many other Eastern religions, and because the New Testament made use of language and concepts which bore a great resemblance to the formulas of Platonic philosophy, the ritual language of the mystery cults, and the mythological structure of other Oriental beliefs. Even today the world is full of honest persons who suppose that this parallelism somehow weakens the Christian claim to an exclusive divine revelation. The writers of the Old and New Testament were simple men, but St. John the Evangelist was certainly not so simple as to imagine that the Greek word *logos,* which he may well have borrowed from the Platonists, was a personal discovery of his own. The fact that the Biblical writers were inspired did not deliver them from the common necessity which compels writers to clothe their ideas in words taken from the current vocabulary of their culture and of their time. When God inspired the author of *Genesis* with the true account of the creation of the world, the writer might, by some miracle, have set the whole thing down in the vocabulary of a twentieth-century textbook of paleontology. But that would have made *Genesis* quite inaccessible to anyone except a twentieth-century student of paleontology. So instead, the Creation narrative was set down in the form of a poem which made free use of the cosmic symbolism which was common to all primitive mankind.

Light and darkness, sun and moon, stars and planets, trees, beasts, whales, fishes, and birds of the air, all these things in the world around us and the whole natural economy in which they have their place have impressed themselves upon the spirit of man in such a way that they naturally tend to mean to him much more than they mean in themselves. That is why, for example, they enter so mysteriously into the substance of our poetry, of our visions, and of our dreams. That, too, is why an age, like the one we live in, in which cosmic symbolism has been almost forgotten and submerged under a tidal wave of trademarks, political party buttons, advertising and propaganda slogans and all the rest—is necessarily an age of mass psychosis. A world in which the poet can find practically no material in the common substance of every day life, and in which he is driven crazy in his search for the vital symbols that have been buried alive under a mountain of cultural garbage, can only end up, like ours, in self-destruction. And that is why some of the best poets of our time are running wild among the tombs in the moonlit cemeteries of surrealism. Faithful to the instincts of the true poet, they are unable to seek their symbols anywhere save in the depths of the spirit where these symbols are found. These depths have become a ruin and a slum. But poetry must, and does, make good use of whatever it finds there: starvation, madness, frustration, and death.

Now the writers of the Bible were aware that they shared with other religions the cosmic symbols in which God has revealed Himself to all men. But they were also aware that pagan and idolatrous religions had corrupted this symbolism and perverted its original purity.[6] The Gentiles had "detained the truth of God in injustice"[7] and "changed the truth of God into a lie."[8]

Creation had been given to man as a clean window through which the light of God could shine into men's souls. Sun and moon, night and day, rain, the sea, the crops, the flowering tree, all these things were transparent. They spoke to man not of themselves only but of Him who made them. Nature was symbolic. But the progressive degradation of man after the fall led the Gentiles further and further from this truth. Nature became opaque. The nations were no longer able to penetrate the meaning of the world they lived in. Instead of seeing the sun a witness to the power of God, they thought the sun was god. The whole universe became an enclosed system of myths. The meaning and the worth of creatures invested them with an illusory divinity.

Men still sensed that there was something to be venerated in the reality, in the peculiarity of living and growing things but they no longer knew what that reality was. They became incapable of seeing that the goodness of the creature is only a vestige of God. Darkness settled upon the translucent universe. Men became afraid. Beings had a meaning which men could no longer understand. They became afraid of trees, of the sun, of the sea. These things had to be approached with superstitious rites. It began to seem that the mystery of their meaning, which had become hidden, was now a power that had to be placated and, if possible, controlled by magic incantations.

Thus the beautiful living things which were all about us on this earth and which were the windows of heaven to every man, became infected with original sin. The world fell with man, and longs, with man, for regeneration. The symbolic universe, which had now become a labyrinth of myths and magic rites, the dwelling place of a million hostile spirits, ceased altogether to speak to most men of God and told them only of themselves. The *symbols* which would have raised man above himself to God now became *myths* and as such they were simply projections of man's own biological drives. His deepest appetites, now full of shame, became his darkest fears.

The corruption of cosmic symbolism can be understood by a simple comparison. It was like what happens to a window when a room ceases to receive light from the outside. As long as it is daylight, we see through our windowpane. When night comes, we can still see through it, if there is no light inside our room. When our lights go on, then we only see ourselves and our own room reflected in the pane. Adam in Eden could see through creation as through a window. God shone through the windowpane as bright as the light of the sun. Abraham and the patriarchs and David and the holy men of Israel—the chosen race that preserved intact the testimony of God—could still see through the window as one looks out by night from a darkened room and sees the moon and stars. But the Gentiles had begun to forget the sky, and to light lamps of their own, and presently it seemed to them that the reflection of their own room in the window was the "world beyond." They began to worship what they themselves were doing.

So much, then, for cosmic symbols. In the Psalms we find them clean and bright again, where David sings:

O Lord, our Lord, how glorious is thy name in all the earth, thou who
  hast exalted thy majesty above the heavens. . . .
When I gaze at the heavens, the work of thy fingers, the moon and stars,
  which thou hast made:
What is man, that thou are mindful of him? or the son of man,
  that thou hast care of him?
And thou hast made him a little lower than the angels,
  thou hast crowned him with glory and honor;
Thou hast given him dominion over the works of thy hands;
  thou hast put all things under his feet:
Sheep and oxen, all of them, and the beasts of the field, too,
The birds of the heaven and the fishes of the sea:
  and whatever traverses the paths of the seas.
O Lord, our Lord, how wonderful is thy name in all the earth! [9]

But it is not the cosmic symbolism that is the most important symbolism in the Bible. There is another. This is the symbolism we have already referred to as *typology*. The typological symbolism of the Bible is not common to other religions: its content is peculiar to the Judaeo-Christian revelation. It is the vehicle of the special message, the "Gospel" which is the very essence of Christian revelation. And it is typology above all that makes the Psalms a body of religious poems which are, by their own right, altogether unique.

Scriptural typology is a special kind of symbolism. It is something far purer and more efficacious than allegory. I would even add that in the Psalms allegory is altogether negligible. There is almost nothing in the Psalter that reminds us of the tissue of allegorical complexities which goes to make up a poem like Spenser's *Faerie Queene*. It seems to me that the personification of moral abstractions is foreign to the spirit of true contemplation.

The relation of types and antitypes in Scripture is a special manifestation of God: it is the testimony of His continuous providential intervention in human history. Unlike the universal cosmic symbols, which repeat themselves over and over with the seasons, historical and typical symbols are altogether singular. Cosmic symbols reflect the action of God like the light of the sun on the vast sea of creation. Typological symbols are meteors which divide the dark sky of history with a sudden, searing light, appearing and vanishing with a liberty that knows no law of man. Cosmic symbolism is like clouds and rain: but typology is like a storm of lightning wounding the earth unpredictably with fire from heaven.

Consider for a moment the typology of the Deluge. In the Deluge,

God purifies the world, destroying sin. The Deluge is simply a type of the one great redemptive act in which God destroyed sin: Christ's passion and death. But the symbolism of the Deluge goes further: it also manifests to us the activity of God destroying sin in the souls of individuals by the sacraments, for instance Baptism and Penance, in which the merits of Christ's Passion are applied to our souls. This also corresponds to another Old Testament type: the crossing of the Red Sea by the people of Israel. Finally, all these symbols are tied together in one, final climax of significance. All Scriptural types point to the last end, the crowning of Christ's work, the establishment of His Kingdom, His final and manifest triumph in His mystical body: the Last Judgment. There again, the same creative action by which God manifested Himself in the Deluge will once more strike the world of sin. But this time it will have the nature of a final "accounting" in the sense that then all men will come forth to give testimony to their personal response to God's action in the world. Those who have believed, and who have freely accepted the light and the salvation offered to them from heaven, will pass, like the Israelites, through the Red Sea; they will be rescued in Christ as Noah's sons were saved in the Ark; they will have lived out the meaning of their Baptism because they will have died and risen with Christ. Those who were not with Christ—and all who are not with him are against Him—will manifest what they too have chosen. It will be by their own choice that they will drown in the Deluge, and perish with the Chariots of Egypt in the closing waters of that last sea.

Not only do many of the Psalms literally foretell the suffering and glory of Christ, but David is a "type" of Christ. The Psalter as a whole is "typical" of the New Testament as a whole and often the particular sentiments of the Psalmist are, at least in a broad sense, "typical" of the sentiments in the Heart of the Divine Redeemer. Even the sins of David belong to Christ, in the sense that "God hath laid upon Him the iniquity of us all." [10]

[1] Cf. *The Roman Missal:* Collect for the Mass of the Dedication of a Church.
[2] Psalm 18, 2-7.
[3] Psalm 148, 1-13.
[4] Cf. Romans, 1:18 and Acts, 14:15.
[5] I am especially indebted to the article of Père Jean Daniélou, S.J.: "The Problem of Symbolism" in *Thought,* September 1950. See also his book *Sacramentum Futuri,* Paris, 1950.
[6] The classical passage in this connection is the first chapter of St. Paul's *Epistle to the Romans.*

[7] Romans, 1:18.
[8] Romans, 1:25.
[9] Psalm 8:2, 4-10. Every line of this Psalm has antipolytheistic repercussions. Man, who can see God *through* His creation is in possession of the truth which makes him free. (John, 8:32.) Thus he leads a spiritualized existence "a little less than the angels" and stands in his rightful place in the order of creation, above the irrational animals. The Gentiles, on the other hand, have descended lower than the animals since they have lost the knowledge of God though God remains evident in His creation. For by their ignorance of God, they have doomed themselves to the worship of beasts. (Romans, 1:23.) Compare also: St. Bernard; *De Diligendo Deo*, Chapter II, n. 4; *Patrologia Latina*, Volume 182, Column 970.
[10] Isaias, 53:6.

BREAD IN THE WILDERNESS

❖ POETRY AND CONTEMPLATION:
A REAPPRAISAL

AUTHOR'S NOTE: Ten years ago I wrote an article called "Poetry and the Contemplative Life" which was published first in *The Commonweal* and then appeared in a volume of verse, *Figures for an Apocalypse*.

In its original form, this article stated a "problem" and tried to apply a rather crude "solution" which, at the time, was rather widely discussed by people interested in religious verse and, at least by implication, in religious experience. Many of them were inclined to accept the "solution" that was proposed. Others wisely rejected it because of its somewhat puritanical implications.

As time passed I have found that the confident pronouncements made in my early writing lay more and more heavily on my conscience as a writer and as a priest, and while it is evidently impossible to correct and amend all my wrong-headed propositions, at least I would like to revise the essay of 1948. The revision is unfortunately not fully satisfactory precisely because it is no more than a revision. But I do not want to write a whole new article, approaching the subject from an entirely different angle. I believe it is necessary to revise the earlier article and to restate the case in the same context, arriving at a different conclusion.

One of the unavoidable defects of this kind of revision is that it retains an altogether misleading insistence on the terms "contemplation" and "contemplative life" as something apart from the rest of man's existence. This involves a rather naïve presupposition that "contemplation" is a kind of objectivized entity which gets "interfered with" by such things as aesthetic reflection. There is a certain amount of truth behind this supposed conflict, but to state it thus crudely is to invite all sorts of misunderstanding. In actual fact, neither religious nor artistic contemplation should be regarded as "things" which happen or "objects" which one can "have." They belong to the much more mysterious realm of what one "is"—or rather "who" one is. Aesthetic intuition is not merely the act of a faculty, it is also a heightening and intensification of our personal identity and being by the perception of our connatural affinity with "Being" in the beauty contemplated.

But also, and at the same time, the implied conflict between "contemplation" as rest and poetic creation as activity is even more misleading. It is all wrong to imagine that in order to "contemplate" divine things or what you will, it is necessary to abstain from every kind of action and enter into a kind of spiritual stillness where one waits for "something to happen." In actual fact, true contemplation is inseparable from life and from the dynamism of life—which includes work, creation, production, fruitfulness, and above all *love*. Contemplation is not to be thought of as a separate department of life, cut off from all man's other interests and superseding them. It is the very fullness of a fully integrated life. It is the crown of life and of all life's activities.

Therefore the earlier problem was, largely, an illusion, created by this division of life into formally separate compartments, of "action" and "contemplation." But because this crude division was stated so forcefully and so frequently in my earlier writings, I feel that it is most necessary now to try to do something to heal this wound and draw together the two sides of this unfortunate fissure.

In this present article, the wound is still evident, and it is meant to be so. I am attempting to patch it up, and probably do not fully succeed. If this is true, I do not care so much, as long as it is clear that I am stitching and drawing the wound together, pouring in the disinfectant, and putting on a bandage.

I

IN AN AGE OF SCIENCE and technology, in which man finds himself bewildered and disoriented by the fabulous versatility of the machines he has created, we live precipitated outside ourselves at every moment, interiorly empty, spiritually lost, seeking at all costs to forget our own emptiness, and ready to alienate ourselves completely in the name of any "cause" that comes along. At such a time as this, it seems absurd to talk of contemplation: and indeed a great deal of the talk that has been bandied about timidly enough on this subject, is ludicrous and inadequate. Contemplation itself takes on the appearance of a safe and rather bourgeois "cause"—the refuge of a few well-meaning Christians who are willing to acquaint themselves with St. Thomas and St. John of the Cross, and to disport themselves thereafter in such Edens of passivity and fervor as cannot be disapproved by the so-called "Masters of the Spiritual Life." For others, safer still, contemplation means nothing more than a life of leisure and of study: in many cases more a fond hope than an accomplished fact.

The relative timidity of these adventures, and the harebrained chase after more exotic forms of spirituality, should not make us too prone to laugh at every symptom of man's acute need for an interior life. For one of the most important and most hopeful signs of the times is in the turbulent, anarchic, but fully determined efforts of a small minority of men to recover some kind of contact with their own inner depths, to recapture the freshness and truth of their own subjectivity, and to go on from there not only to an experience of God, but to a dialogue with the spirit of other men. In the face of our own almost hopeless alienation, we are trying to get back to ourselves before it is too late. One of the most outstanding examples of this struggle is seen in the almost symbolic career of Boris Pasternak, whose more recent poetry and prose can most certainly qualify in a broad and basic sense as *contemplative*.

The contemplative is not just a man who sits under a tree with his legs crossed, or one who edifies himself with the answer to ultimate and spiritual problems. He is one who seeks to know the meaning of life not only with his head but with his whole being, by living it in depth and in purity and thus uniting himself to the very Source of Life—a Source which is infinitely actual and therefore too real to be contained satisfactorily inside any word or concept or name assigned by man: for the words of man tend to limit the realities which they express, in order to express them. And anything that can be limited cannot be the infinite actuality known to the contemplative without words and without the mediation of precise analytical thought. We can say, then, that contemplation is the intuitive perception of life in its Source: that Source Who revealed Himself as the unnamable "I Am" and then again made Himself known to us as Man in Christ. Contemplation is experience of God in Man, God in the world, God in Christ: it is an obscure intuition of God Himself, and this intuition is a gift of God Who reveals Himself in His very hiddenness as One unknown.

Contemplation is related to art, to worship, to charity: all these reach out by intuition and self-dedication into the realms that transcend the material conduct of everyday life. Or rather, in the midst of ordinary life itself they seek and find a new and transcendent meaning. And by this meaning they transfigure the whole of life. Art, worship, and love penetrate into the spring of living waters that flows from the depths where man's spirit is united to God, and draw from those depths power to create a new world and a new life. Contemplation goes deeper than all three, and unites them, and plunges man's whole soul into the supernal waters, in the baptism of wordless understanding and ecstatic prayer.

There can be various levels of contemplation. There is contemplation in a broad and improper sense—the religious intuition of the artist, the lover, or the worshiper. In these intuitions, art, love, or worship remain in the foreground: they modify the experience of ultimate reality, and present that reality to us as the "object" of aesthetic vision, or adoration, or love. In an even less proper sense, "contemplation" loses sight of ultimates and becomes preoccupied with a beautiful thing, or a meaningful liturgy, or a loved person.

But in its proper meaning, contemplation transcends all "objects," all "things," and goes beyond all "ideas" of beauty or goodness or truth, passes beyond all speculation, all creative fervor, all charitable action, and "rests" in the inexpressible. It lets go of everything and finds All in Nothing—the *todo y nada* of St. John of the Cross.

On a dark night, kindled in love with yearnings—O happy chance—
I went forth without being observed, my house being now at rest.

In darkness and secure, by the secret ladder, disguised—O happy chance—
In darkness and concealment, my house being now at rest.

In the happy night, in secret when none saw me
Nor I beheld aught, without light or guide save that which burned in my
  heart

This light guided me more surely than the light of noonday
To the place where He (well I knew who!) was awaiting me
A place where none appeared.

Now when we speak of a possible conflict between poetry and contemplation, it is clearly only contemplation in the last, most perfect sense that is intended. For when we speak of contemplation in the more broad and improper sense, we find it uniting itself with art, with worship, and with love. It is not only compatible with poetic creation, but is stimulated by it, and in its turn inspires poetry. And in the realm of worship, contemplation in this broad sense is stimulated by meditation, by prayer, by liturgy, and arises out of these religious activities. Above all, in the sacramental life of the Church, we find contemplation in this broad sense should normally be the fruit of fervent reception of the sacraments, at least sometimes. That is to say that the reception of the sacraments should produce, once in a while, not only interior and unfelt grace but also a certain dim awareness of the presence and the action of God in the soul, though this awareness may be very fleeting, tenuous, and almost impossible to assess. Nor should people trouble their heads about whether or not they feel it, because some are not supposed to feel it: feelings are not important, and what they will experience, without realizing it too clearly, is the fervor of love and the desire to dedicate themselves more perfectly to God. Such things we can call in a broad and improper sense "contemplative" experiences.

This is *active* contemplation, in which grace indeed is the principle of all the supernatural value and ordination of our acts, but in which much of the initiative belongs to our own powers, prompted and sustained by grace. This form of the contemplative life prepares us for contemplation properly so called: the life of *infused* or *passive* or *mystical* contemplation.

Contemplation is the fullness of the Christian vocation—the full flowering of baptismal grace and of the Christ-life in our souls.

Christian contemplation is not something esoteric and dangerous. It is simply the experience of God that is given to a soul purified by humility and faith. It is the "knowledge" of God in the darkness of infused love. "This is eternal life, that they should know Thee, the One True God, and Jesus Christ Whom Thou hast sent" (John 17:3) or "But we all, beholding the glory of the Lord with open face, are transformed into the same image from glory to glory, as by the Spirit of the Lord." (II Cor. 3:18.) St. Paul, in his Epistle to the Hebrews, rebuked those who clung to the "first elements of the words of God" when they should have been "Masters," and he urged them to relinquish the "milk" of beginners and to desire the "strong meat" of the perfect, which is the contemplation of Christ in the great Mystery in which He renews on earth the redemptive sacrifice of the Cross. "For every one that is a partaker of milk is unskillful in the word of justice:

for he is a little child. But strong meat is for the perfect: for them who by custom have their senses exercised to the discerning of good and evil" (Heb. 5:13-14). *Omnis qui ad Dominum convertitur contemplativam vitam desiderat,* said St. Gregory the Great, and he was using contemplation in our sense: to live on the desire of God alone; to have one's mind divested of all earthly things and united, in so far as human weakness permits, with Christ. And he adds that the contemplative life begins on earth in order to continue, more perfectly, in heaven. St. Thomas echoed him with his famous phrase: *quaedam inchoatio beatitudinis* (Contemplation is a beginning of eternal blessedness). St. Bonaventure goes further than any of the other Doctors of the Church in his insistence that all Christians should desire union with God in loving contemplation. And in his second conference on the Hexaemeron, applying Christ's words in Matthew 12:42, he says that the Queen of the South who left her own land and traveled far to hear the wisdom of Solomon will rise up in judgment against our generation which refuses the treasure of divine wisdom, perferring the far lesser riches of worldly wisdom and philosophy.

Infused contemplation is a quasi-experimental knowledge of God's goodness "tasted" and "possessed" by a vital contact in the depths of the soul. By infused love, we are given an immediate grasp of God's own substance, and rest in the obscure and profound sense of His presence and transcendent actions within our inmost selves, yielding ourselves altogether to the work of His transforming Spirit.

By the light of infused wisdom we enter deeply into the Mystery of Christ Who is Himself the light of men. We participate, as it were, in the glory that is radiated mystically by His risen and transfigured Humanity. Our eyes are opened to understand the Scriptures and the mystery of God's intervention in man's history. We become aware of the way in which the infinite mercy and wisdom of God are revealed to men and angels in the Mystery of the Church, which is the Body of Christ. The contemplative life is the lot of those who have entered most fully into the life and spirit of the Church, so that the contemplatives are at the very heart of the Mystery which they have begun really to understand and to "see" with the eyes of their soul. To desire the contemplative life and its gifts is therefore to desire to become in the highest sense a fruitful and strong member of Christ. But it means also, by that very fact, to desire and accept a share in His sufferings and death, that we may rise with Him in the participation of His glory.

Now whether we speak of contemplation as active or passive, one thing is evident: it brings us into the closest contact with the one subject that is truly worthy of a Christian poet: the great Mystery of God, revealing His mercy to us in Christ. The Christian poet should be one who has been granted a deep understanding of the ways of God and of the Mystery of Christ. Deeply rooted in the spiritual consciousness of the whole Church, steeped in the Liturgy and the Scriptures, fully possessed by the "mind of the Church," he becomes as it were a voice of the Church and of the Holy Spirit, and sings again the *magnalia Dei,* praising God and pointing out the wonder of His ways. The Christian poet is therefore the successor to David and the Prophets, he contemplates what was announced by the poets of the Old Testament: he should be, as they were, full of divine fire. He should be one who, like the prophet Isaias, has seen the living God and has lamented the fact that he was a man of impure lips, until God Himself sent Seraph, with a live coal from the altar of the heavenly temple, to burn his lips with prophetic inspiration.

In the true Christian poet—in Dante, St. John of the Cross, St. Francis, Jacopone da Todi, Hopkins, Paul Claudel—we find it hard to distinguish between the inspiration of the prophet and mystic, and the purely poetic enthusiasm of great artistic genius.

II

CHRIST IS THE INSPIRATION of Christian poetry, and Christ is at the center of the contemplative life. Therefore, it would seem fairly evident that the one thing that will most contribute to the perfection of Catholic literature in general and poetry in particular will be for our writers and poets to live more as "contemplatives" than as citizens of a materialistic world. This means first of all leading the full Christian sacramental and liturgical life in so far as they can in their state. This also means a solid integration of one's work, thought, religion, and family life and recreations in one vital harmonious unity with Christ at its center. The liturgical life is the most obvious example of "active contemplation."

A sincere and efficacious desire to enter more deeply into the beauty of the Christian mystery implies a willingness to sacrifice the things which are called "beautiful" by the decadent standards of a materialistic world. Yet the Christian contemplative need not confine himself to religious, still less to professionally "pious" models. He will, of course, read Scripture and above all the contemplative saints: John of the Cross, Theresa of Ávila, John Ruysbroeck, Bonaventure, Bernard. But no one can be a poet without reading the good poets of his own time—T. S. Eliot, Auden, Spender, Rilke, Pasternak, Dylan Thomas, Garcia Lorca. One might add that a fully integrated vision of our time and of its spirit presupposes some contact with the genius of Baudelaire and Rimbaud, who are Christians turned inside out.

Contemplation has much to offer poetry. And poetry, in its turn, has something to offer contemplation. How is this so? In understanding the relation of poetry to contemplation the first thing that needs to be stressed is the essential dignity of aesthetic experience. It is, in itself, a very high gift, though only in the natural order. It is a gift which very many people have never received, and which others, having received, have allowed to spoil or become atrophied within them through neglect and misuse.

To many people, the enjoyment of art is nothing more than a sensible and emotional thrill. They look at a picture, and if it stimulates one or another of their sense appetites they are pleased. On a hot day they like to look at a picture of mountains or the sea because it makes them feel cool. They like paintings of dogs that you could almost pat. But naturally they soon tire of art, under those circumstances. They turn aside to pat a real dog, or they go down the street to an air-conditioned movie, to give their senses another series of jolts. This is not what one can legitimately call the "enjoyment of Art."

A GENUINE AESTHETIC experience is something which transcends not only the sensible order (in which, however, it has its beginning) but also that of reason itself. It is a suprarational intuition of the latent perfection of things. Its immediacy outruns the speed of reasoning and leaves all analysis far behind. In the natural order, as Jacques Maritain has often insisted, it is an analogue of the mystical experience which it resembles and imitates from afar. Its mode of apprehension is that of "connaturality"—it reaches out to grasp the inner reality, the vital substance of its object, by a kind of affective identification of itself with it. It rests in the perfection of things by a kind of union which sometimes resembles the quiescence of the soul in its immediate affective contact with God in the obscurity of mystical prayer. So close is the resemblance between these two experiences that a poet like Blake could almost confuse the two and make them merge into one another as if they belonged to the same order of things.

This resemblance between the experiences of the artist and of the mystic has been extensively discussed in the long and important article on "Art and Spirituality," by Fr. M. Leonard, S.J., in the *Dictionnaire de Spiritualité*.

This theologian pushes the dignity of the aesthetic institution practically to its limit. He gives it everything that it is ontologically able to stand. He insists that the highest experience of the artist penetrates no only beyond the sensible surface of things into their inmost reality, but even beyond that to God Himself. More than that, the analogy with mystical experience is deeper and closer still because, he says, the intuition of the artist sets in motion the very same psychological processes which accompany infused contemplation. This fits in with the psychology of St. Augustine and St. Bonaventure and the latter's notion of contemplation *per speculum,* passing through the mirror of created things to God, even if that mirror may happen to be our own soul. It also fits in with the ideas of the Greek Fathers about *theoria physica* or "natural contemplation" which arrives at God through the inner spiritual reality (the *logos*) of the created thing.

The Augustinian psychology, which forms the traditional substratum of Christian mystical theology in the Western Church, distinguishes between an *inferior* and *superior* soul. Of course, this is only a manner of speaking. There is only one soul, a simple spiritual substance, undivided and indivisible. And yet the soul in so far as it acts through its faculties, making decisions and practical judgments concerning temporal external things, is called "inferior." The "superior" soul is the same soul, but now considered as the principle or *actus primus* of these other diverse and multiple acts of the faculties which as it were flow from this inner principle. Only the superior soul is strictly the image of God within us. And if we are to contemplate God at all, this internal image must be re-formed by grace, and then we must enter into this inner sanctuary which is the substance of the soul itself. This passage from the exterior to the interior has nothing to do with concentration or introspection. It is a transit from objectivization to knowledge by intuition and connaturality. The majority of people never enter into this inward self, which is an abode of silence and peace and where the diversified activities of the intellect and will are collected, so to speak, into one intense and smooth and spiritualized activity which far exceeds in its fruitfulness the plodding efforts of reason working on external reality with its analyses and syllogisms.

IT IS HERE that mystical contemplation begins. It is into this substance or "center" of the soul, when it has transcended its dependence on sensations and images and concepts, that the obscure light of infused contemplation will be poured by God, giving us experimental contact with Himself without the medium of sense species. And in this contact, we are no longer facing God as an "object" of experience or as a concept which we apprehend. We are united to Him in the mystery of love and its transcendent subjectivity, and see Him in ourselves by losing ourselves in Him.

Yet even in the natural order, without attaining to God in us, and without perceiving this "inner spiritual light," the aesthetic experience introduces us into the interior sanctuary of the soul and to its inexpressible simplicity. For the aesthetic intuition is also beyond objectivity—it "sees" by identifying itself spiritually with what it contemplates.

Obviously, then, when the natural contemplation of the artist or the metaphysician has already given a man a taste of the peaceful intoxication which is experienced in the suprarational intuitions of this interior self, the way is already well prepared for infused contemplation. If God should grant that grace, the person so favored will be much better prepared to recognize it, and to cooperate with God's action within him. The mere fact of the artist's or poet's good taste, which should belong to him by virtue of his art, will help him to avoid some of the evils that tend to corrupt religious experience before it has a chance to take root and grow in the soul.

III

MYSTICAL CONTEMPLATION is absolutely beyond the reach of man's natural activity. There is nothing he can do to obtain it by himself. It is a pure gift of God. God gives it to whom He wills, and in the way and degree in which He wills. By cooperating with the work of ordinary grace we can—and, if we really mean to love God, we must—seek Him and even find Him obscurely by a love that gropes humbly for truth in the darkness of this life. But no amount of generosity on our part, no amount of effort, no amount of sacrifice will make us into mystics. That is a work that must be done by God acting as the "principal agent" (the term is that of St. John of the Cross). If He is the principal agent, there is another agent: ourselves. But our part is simply to consent, to listen, and to follow without knowing where we are going. All the rest that we can do amounts to the more or less negative task of avoiding obstacles and keeping our own prejudiced judgments and self-will out of His way. St. Bonaventure tells us in many places that prayer and ardent desire can persuade God to give us this gift, and that *industria* on our part can open the way for His action. The term *industria* stands for active purification, the active emptying of the soul, clearing it of all images, all likenesses of and attachments to created things so that it may be clean and pure to receive the obscure light of God's own presence.

It is the common doctrine of Christian mystical theologians that a great obstacle to "unitive" or "connatural" or "affective" knowledge of God by infused contemplation (the terms are those of St. Thomas and his followers) is attachment to objectivized human reasoning and analysis and discourse that proceeds by abstraction from sense images, and by syllogizing, to conclusions. In other words, a man cannot at the same time fly in an airplane and walk along the ground. He must do one or the other. And if he insists on walking along the ground— all right, it is no sin. But it will take him much longer and cost him much more effort to get to his destination, and he will have a much more limited view of things along his way. What the Holy Spirit demands of the mystic is peaceful consent, and a blind trust in Him: for all this time, since the soul does not act of itself, it remains blind and in darkness, having no idea where it is going or what is being done, and tasting satisfaction that is, at first, extremely tenuous and ineffable and obscure. The reason is, of course, that the soul is not yet sufficiently spiritualized to be able to grasp and appreciate what is going on within it. It remains with nothing but the vaguest and most general sense that God is really and truly present and working there— a sense which is fraught with a greater certitude than anything it has ever experienced before. And yet if one stops to analyze the experience, or if one makes a move to increase its intensity by a natural act, the whole thing will evade his grasp and he will lose it altogether.

Now it is precisely here that the aesthetic instinct changes its colors and, from being a precious gift, becomes a real danger. If the intuition of the poet naturally leads him into the inner sanctuary of his soul, it is for a special purpose in the natural order: when the poet enters into himself, it is in order to reflect upon his inspiration and to clothe it with a special and splendid form and then return to *display it to those outside.* And here the radical difference between the artist and the mystic begins to be seen. The artist enters into himself in order to *work.* For him, the "superior" soul is a forge where inspiration kindles a fire of white heat, a crucible for the transformation of natural images into new, created forms. But the mystic enters into himself, not in order to work but to pass through the center of his own soul and lose himself in the mystery and secrecy and infinite, transcendent reality of God living and working within him.

Consequently, if the mystic happens to be, at the same time, an artist, when prayer calls him within himself to the secrecy of God's presence, his art will be tempted to start working and producing and studying the "creative" possibilities of this experience. And therefore immediately the whole thing runs the risk of being frustrated and destroyed. The artist will run the risk of losing a gift of tremendous supernatural worth, in order to perform a work of far less value. He will let go of the deep, spiritual grace which has been granted him, in order to return to the reflection of that grace within his own soul. He will withdraw from the mystery of identification with Reality beyond forms and objectivized concepts, and will return to the realm of subject and object. He will objectivize his own experience and seek to exploit and employ it for its own sake. He will leave God and return to himself, and in so doing, though he follows his natural instinct to "create" he will, in fact, be less creative. For the creative work done directly in the soul and on the soul by God Himself, the infinite *Creator Spiritus,* is beyond all comparison with the work which the soul of man itself accomplishes in imitation of the divine Creator.

Unable fully to lose himself in God, doomed by the restlessness of talent to seek himself in the highest natural gift that God has given him, the artist falls from contemplation and returns to himself as artist. Instead of passing through his own soul into the abyss of the infinite actuality of God Himself, he will remain there a moment, only to emerge again into the exterior world of multiple created things whose variety once more dissipates his energies until they are lost in perplexity and dissatisfaction.

There is, therefore, a likelihood that one who has the natural gift of artistic intuition and creation may be unable to pass on to the superior and most spiritual kind of contemplation, in which the soul rests in God without images, without concepts, without any intermediary. The artist may be like the hare in the fable, who far outstrips the tortoise without talent in the beginnings of the contemplative life, but who, in the end, is left behind. In a word, natural gifts and talents may be of great value in the beginning, but contemplation can never depend on them.

IV

WHAT, then, is the conclusion? That poetry can, indeed, help to bring us rapidly through that early part of the journey to contemplation that is called active: but when we are entering the realm of true contemplation, where eternal happiness is tasted in anticipation, poetic intuition may ruin our rest in God "beyond all images."

In such an event, one might at first be tempted to say that there is only one course for the poet to take, if he wants to be a mystic or a saint: he must consent to the *ruthless and complete sacrifice of his art.* Such a conclusion would seem to be dictated by logic. If there is an infinite distance between the gifts of nature and those of grace, between the natural and the supernatural order, man and God, then should not one always reject the natural for the supernatural, the temporal for the eternal, the human for the divine? It seems to be so simple as to defy contradiction. And yet, when one has experience in the strange vicissitudes of the inner life, and when one has seen something of the ways of God, one remembers that there is a vast difference between the logic of men and the logic of God. There is indeed no human logic in the ways of interior prayer, only Divine paradox. Our God is not a Platonist. Our Christian spirituality is not the intellectualism of Plotinus or the asceticism of the stoics. We must therefore be very careful of oversimplifications. The Christian is sanctified not merely by always making the choice of "the most perfect thing." Indeed, experience teaches us that the most perfect choice is not always that which is most perfect in itself. The most perfect choice is *the choice of what God has willed for us,* even though it may be, in itself, less perfect, and indeed less "spiritual."

It is quite true that aesthetic experience is only a temporal thing, and like all other temporal things it passes away. It is true that mystical prayer enriches man a hundredfold in time and in eternity. It purifies the soul and loads it with supernatural merits, enlarging man's powers and capacities to absorb the infinite rivers of divine light which will one day be his beatitude. The sacrifice of art would seem to be a small enough price to lay down for this "pearl of great price."

But let us consider for a moment whether the Christian contemplative poet is necessarily confronted with an absolute clean-cut "either/or" choice between "art" and "mystical prayer."

It can of course happen that a contemplative and artist finds himself in a situation in which he is morally certain that God demands of him the sacrifice of his art, in order that he may enter more deeply into the contemplative life. In such a case, the sacrifice must be made, not because this is a general law binding all artist-contemplatives, but because it is the will of God in this particular, concrete case.

But it may equally well happen that an artist who imagines himself to be called to the higher reaches of mystical prayer is not called to them at all. It becomes evidence, to him, that the simplest and most obvious thing for him is to be an artist, and that he should sacrifice his aspirations for a deep mystical life and be content with the lesser gifts with which he has been endowed by God. For such a one, to insist on spending long hours in prayer frustrating his creative instinct would, in fact, lead to illusion. His efforts to be a contemplative would be fruitless. Indeed, he would find that by being an artist—and at the same time living fully all the implications of art for a Christian and for a contemplative in the broad sense of the word—he would enjoy a far deeper and more vital interior life, with a much richer appreciation of the mysteries of God, than if he just tried to bury his artistic talent and be a professional "saint." If he is called to be an artist, then his art will lead him to sanctity, if he uses it as a Christian should.

To take yet another case: it might conceivably be the will of God— as it certainly was in the case of the Old Testament Prophets and in that of St. John of the Cross—that a man should remain *at the same time a mystic and a poet* and ascend to the greatest heights of poetic creation and of mystical prayer without any evident contradiction between them. Here again, the problem is solved not by the application of some abstract, *a priori* principle, but purely by a practically practical appeal to the will of God in this particular case. We are dealing with gifts of God, which God can give as He pleases, when He pleases, to whom He pleases. It is futile for us to lay down laws which say when or how God's gifts must be given, to whom they can be given, to whom they must be refused. It remains true that at a certain point in the interior life, the instinct to create and communicate enters into conflict with the call to mystical union with God. But God Himself can resolve the conflict. And He does. Nor does He need any advice from us in order to do so.

If the Christian poet is truly a Christian poet, if he has a vocation to make known to other men the unsearchable mystery of the love of Christ, then he must do so in the Spirit of Christ. And his "manifestation of the Spirit" not only springs from a kind of contemplative intuition of the mystery of Christ, but is "given to him for his profit" and will therefore deepen and perfect his union with Christ. The Christian poet and artist is one who grows not only by his contemplation but also by his open declaration of the mercy of God. If it is clear that he is called to give this witness to God, then he can say with St. Paul: "Woe to me if I preach not the Gospel."

SELECTED POEMS

Four: POEMS

THE LANDFALL

We are beyond the ways of the far ships
Here in this coral port,
Farther than the ways of fliers,
Because our destinies have suddenly transported us
Beyond the brim of the enamel world.

O Mariner, what is the name of this uncharted Land?
On these clean shores shall stand what sinless voyager,
What angel breathe the music of this atmosphere?

Look where the thin flamingoes
Burning upon the purple shallows with their rare, pale flames,
Stand silent as our thought, although the birds in the high rock
Rinse our new senses with no mortal note,
What are these wings whose silks amaze the traveler?

The flowering palms charm all the strand
With their supernal scent.
The oleander and the wild hibiscus paint
The land with blood, and unknown blooms
Open to us the Gospel of their five wild wounds.

And the deep ferns sing this epithalame:
"Go up, go up! this desert is the door of heaven!
And it shall prove your frail soul's miracle!
Climb the safe mountain,
Disarm your labored flesh, and taste the treasure of these silences
In the high coral hermitage,

While the clean winds bemuse you in the clefted rock;
Or find you there some leafy Crusoe-castle: dwell in trees!

Take down the flagons of the blue and crimson fruits
And reap the everlasting wheat that no man's hand has sown,
And strike the rock that runs with waters strong as wine
To fill you with their fortitude:
Because this island is your Christ, your might, your fort, your paradise.

And lo! dumb time's gray, smoky argosies
Will never anchor in this emerald harbor
Or find this world of amber,
Spoil the fair music of the silver sea
Or foul these chiming amethysts:
Nor comes there any serpent near this isle trenched in deep ocean
And walled with innocent, flowering vines.

But from beyond the cotton clouds,
Between those lovely, white cathedrals full of sun,
The angels study beauty with their steps
And tread like notes of music down the beamy air
To gain this new world's virgin shore:
While from the ocean's jeweled floor
The long-lost divers, rising one by one,
Smile and throw down their dripping fortunes on the sand,

And sing us the strange tale
Of the drowned king (our nature), his return!

                              FIGURES FOR AN APOCALYPSE

THE SOWING OF MEANINGS

See the high birds! Is theirs the song
That flies among the wood-light
Wounding the listener with such bright arrows?
Or do they play in wheeling silences
Defining in the perfect sky
The bounds of (here below) our solitude,

Where spring has generated lights of green
To glow in clouds upon the somber branches?

Ponds full of sky and stillnesses
What heavy summer songs still sleep
Under the tawny rushes at your brim?

More than a season will be born here, nature,
In your world of gravid mirrors!
The quiet air awaits one note,
One light, one ray, and it will be the angels' spring:
One flash, one glance upon the shiny pond, and then
Asperges me! sweet wilderness, and lo! we are redeemed!

For, like a grain of fire
Smoldering in the heart of every living essence
God plants His undivided power—
Buries His thought too vast for worlds
In seed and root and blade and flower,

Until, in the amazing light of April,
Surcharging the religious silence of the spring,
Creation finds the pressure of His everlasting secret
Too terrible to bear.
Than every way we look, lo! rocks and trees
Pastures and hills and streams and birds and firmament
And our own souls within us flash, and shower us with light,
While the wild countryside, unknown, unvisited of men,
Bears sheaves of clean, transforming fire.

And then, oh then the written image, schooled in sacrifice.
The deep united threeness printed in our being,
Shot by the brilliant syllable of such an intuition, turns within,
And plants that light far down into the heart of darkness and oblivion,
Dives after, and discovers flame.

FIGURES FOR AN APOCALYPSE

STRANGER

When no one listens
To the quiet trees
When no one notices
The sun in the pool

Where no one feels
The first drop of rain
Or sees the last star

Or hails the first morning
Of a giant world
Where peace begins
And rages end:

One bird sits still
Watching the work of God:
One turning leaf,
Two falling blossoms,
Ten circles upon the pond.

One cloud upon the hillside,
Two shadows in the valley
And the light strikes home.
Now dawn commands the capture
Of the tallest fortune,
The surrender
Of no less marvelous prize!

Closer and clearer
Than any wordy master,
Thou inward Stranger
Whom I have never seen,

Deeper and cleaner
Than the clamorous ocean,
Seize up my silence
Hold me in Thy Hand!

Now act is waste
And suffering undone
Laws become prodigals
Limits are torn down
For envy has no property
And passion is none.

Look, the vast Light stands still
Our cleanest Light is One!

THE STRANGE ISLANDS

A PRELUDE: FOR THE FEAST OF ST. AGNES

O small St. Agnes, dressed in gold
With fire and rainbows round about your face:
Sing with the martyrs in my Mass's Canon!

Come home, come home, old centuries
Whose soundless islands ring me from within,
Whose saints walk down a winter morning's iris,
Wait upon this altar stone
(Some of them holding palms
But others hyacinths!).

I speak your name with wine upon my lips
Drowned in the singing of the quiet catacomb.
My feet upon forget-me-nots
I sink this little frigate in the Blood of silence
And put my pall upon the cup
Working the mystery of peace, whose mercies must
Run down and find us, Saint, by Saint John's stairs.

No lines, no globes,
No compasses, no staring fires
No candle's cup to swing upon
My night's dark ocean.

There the pretended horns of time grow dim.
No tunes, no signals claim us any more.
The cities cry, perhaps, like peacocks.
But the cloud has come.
I kneel in this stone corner having blood upon my wrist
And blood upon my breast,
O small St. Agnes, dressed in martyrdom
With fire and water waving in your hair.

THE STRANGE ISLANDS

A RESPONSORY, 1948

Suppose the dead could crown their wit
With some intemperate exercise,
Spring wine from their ivory
Or roses from their eyes?

Or if the wise could understand
And the world without heart
That the dead are not yet dead
And that the living live apart

And the wounded are healing,
Though in a place of flame.
The sick in a great ship
Are riding. They are riding home.

Suppose the dead could crown their wit
With some intemperate exercise,
Spring wine from their ivory
Or roses from their eyes?

Two cities sailed together
For many thousand years.
And now they drift asunder.
The tides of new wars

Sweep the sad heavens,
Divide the massed stars,
The black and white universe
The booming spheres.

Down, down, down
The white armies fall
Moving their ordered snows
Toward the jaws of hell.

Suppose the dead could crown their wit
With some intemperate exercise,
Spring wine from their ivory
Or roses from their eyes?

THE TEARS OF THE BLIND LIONS

THE CAPTIVES—A PSALM

Quomodo cantabimus canticum Domini in terra aliena?

Somewhere a king walks in his gallery
Owning the gorges of a fiery city.
Brass traffic shakes the walls. The windows shiver with business.
It is the bulls' day. The citizens
Build themselves each hour another god
And fry a fatter idol out of mud.

They cut themselves a crooked idiom
To the winged animals, upon their houses.
Prayers are made of money, songs of numbers,
Hymns of the blood of the killed.

Old ladies are treasured in sugar.
Young ones rot in wine.
The flesh of the fat organizers smiles with oil.

Blessed is the army that will one day crush you, city,
Like a golden spider.
Blest are they that hate you. Blest are they
That dash your brats against the stones.
The children of God have died, O Babylon,
Of thy wild algebra.

Days, days are the journey
From wall to wall. And miles
Miles of houses shelter terror.
And we lie chained to their dry roots, O Israel!

Our bodies are grayer than mud.
There, butterflies are born to be dancers
And fly in black and blue along the drunken river
Where, in the willow trees, Assyria lynched our song!

May my bones burn and ravens eat my flesh
If I forget thee, contemplation!
May language perish from my tongue
If I do not remember thee, O Sion, city of vision,
Whose heights have windows finer than the firmament
When night pours down her canticles
And peace sings on thy watchtowers like the stars of Job.

THE TEARS OF THE BLIND LIONS

SENESCENTE MUNDO

Senescente mundo, when the hot globe
Shrivels and cracks
And uninhibited atoms resolve
Earth and water, fruit and flower, body and animal soul,
All the blue stars come tumbling down.
Beauty and ugliness and love and hate
Wisdom and politics are all alike undone.

Toward that fiery day we run like crabs
With our bad-tempered armor on.
"With blood and carpets, oranges and ashes,
Rubber and limes and bones,"
(So sing the children on the Avenue)
"With cardboard and dirty water and a few flames for the Peacelover's
      ghost,
We know where the dead bodies are
Studying the ceiling from the floors of their homes,
With smoke and roses, slate and wire
And crushed fruit and much fire."

Yet in the middle of this murderous season
Great Christ, my fingers touch Thy wheat
And hold Thee hidden in the compass of Thy paper sun.
There is no war will not obey this cup of Blood,
This wine in which I sink Thy words, in the anonymous dawn!
I hear a Sovereign talking in my arteries
Reversing, with His Promises, all things
That now go on with fire and thunder.
His Truth is greater than disaster.
His Peace imposes silence on the evidence against us.

And though the world, at last, has swallowed her own solemn laughter
And has condemned herself to hell:
Suppose a whole new universe, a great clean Kingdom
Were to rise up like an Atlantis in the East,
Surprise this earth, this cinder, with new holiness!

Here in my hands I hold that secret Easter.
Tomorrow, this will be my Mass's answer,
Because of my companions whom the wilderness has eaten,
Crying like Jonas in the belly of our whale.

THE TEARS OF THE BLIND LIONS

Five: SEEDS OF CONTEMPLATION

Every moment and every event of every man's life on earth plants something in his soul. For just as the wind carries thousands of winged seeds, so each moment brings with it germs of spiritual vitality that come to rest imperceptibly in the minds and wills of men. Most of these unnumbered seeds perish and are lost, because men are not prepared to receive them: for such seeds as these cannot spring up anywhere except in the good soil of freedom, spontaneity, and love.

This is no new idea. Christ in the parable of the sower long ago told us that "The seed is the word of God." We often think this applies only to the word of the Gospel as formally preached in churches on Sundays (if indeed it is preached in churches any more!). But every expression of the will of God is in some sense a "word" of God and therefore a "seed" of new life. The ever-changing reality in the midst of which we live should awaken us to the possibility of an uninterrupted dialogue with God. By this I do not mean continuous "talk," or a frivolously conversational form of affective prayer which is sometimes cultivated in convents, but a dialogue of love and of choice. A dialogue of deep wills.

In all the situations of life the "will of God" comes to us not merely as an external dictate of impersonal law but above all as an interior invitation of personal love. Too often the conventional conception of "God's will" as a sphinx-like and arbitrary force bearing down upon us with implacable hostility, leads men to lose faith in a God they cannot find it possible to love. Such a view of the divine will drives human weakness to despair and one wonders if it is not, itself, often the expression of a despair too intolerable to be admitted to conscious consideration. These arbitrary "dictates" of a domineering and insensible Father

459

are more often seeds of hatred than of love. If that is our concept of the will of God, we cannot possibly seek the obscure and intimate mystery of the encounter that takes place in contemplation. We will desire only to fly as far as possible from Him and hide from His Face forever. So much depends on our idea of God! Yet no idea of Him, however pure and perfect, is adequate to express Him as He really is. Our idea of God tells us more about ourselves than about Him.

We must learn to realize that the love of God seeks us in every situation, and seeks our good. His inscrutable love seeks our awakening. True, since this awakening implies a kind of death to our exterior self, we will dread His coming in proportion as we are identified with this exterior self and attached to it. But when we understand the dialectic of life and death we will learn to take the risks implied by faith, to make the choices that deliver us from our routine self and open to us the door of a new being, a new reality.

The mind that is the prisoner of conventional ideas, and the will that is the captive of its own desire cannot accept the seeds of an unfamiliar truth and a supernatural desire. For how can I receive the seeds of freedom if I am in love with slavery and how can I cherish the desire of God if I am filled with another and an opposite desire? God cannot plant His liberty in me because I am a prisoner and I do not even desire to be free. I love my captivity and I imprison myself in the desire for the things that I hate, and I have hardened my heart against true love. I must learn therefore to let go of the familiar and the usual and consent to what is new and unknown to me. I must learn to "leave myself" in order to find myself by yielding to the love of God. If I were looking for God, every event and every moment would sow, in my will, grains of His life that would spring up one day in a tremendous harvest.

For it is God's love that warms me in the sun and God's love that sends the cold rain. It is God's love that feeds me in the bread I eat and God that feeds me also by hunger and fasting. It is the love of God that sends the winter days when I am cold and sick, and the hot summer when I labor and my clothes are full of sweat: but it is God Who breathes on me with light winds off the river and in the breezes out of the wood. His love spreads the shade of the sycamore over my head and sends the waterboy along the edge of the wheatfield with a bucket from the spring, while the laborers are resting and the mules stand under the tree.

It is God's love that speaks to me in the birds and streams; but also behind the clamor of the city God speaks to me in His judgments, and all these things are seeds sent to me from His will.

If these seeds would take root in my liberty, and if His will would grow from my freedom, I would become the love that He is, and my harvest would be His glory and my own joy.

And I would grow together with thousands and millions of other freedoms into the gold of one huge field praising God, loaded with increase, loaded with wheat. If in all things I consider only the heat and the cold, the food or the hunger, the sickness or labor, the beauty or pleasure, the success and failure or the material good or evil my works have won for my own will, I will find only emptiness and not happiness. I shall not be fed, I shall not be full. For my food is the will of Him Who made me and Who made all things in order to give Himself to me through them.

My chief care should not be to find pleasure or success, health or life or money or rest or even things like virtue and wisdom—still less their opposites, pain, failure, sickness, death. But in all that happens, my one desire and my one joy should be to know: "Here is the thing that God has willed for me. In this His love is found, and in accepting this I can give back His love to Him and give myself with it to Him. For in giving myself I shall find Him and He is life everlasting."

By consenting to His will with joy and doing it with gladness I have His love in my heart, because my will is now the same as His love and I am on the way to becoming what He is, Who is Love. And by accepting all things from Him I receive His joy into my soul, not because things are what they are but because God is Who He is, and His love has willed my joy in them all.

HOW AM I to know the will of God? Even where there is no other more explicit claim on my obedience, such as a legitimate command, the very nature of each situation usually bears written into itself some indication of God's will. For whatever is demanded by truth, by justice, by mercy, or by love must surely be taken to be willed by God. To consent to His will is, then, to consent to be true, or to speak truth, or at least to seek it. To obey Him is to respond to His will expressed in the need of another person, or at least to respect the rights of others. For the right of another man is the expression of God's love and God's will. In demanding that I respect the rights of another God is not merely asking me to conform to some abstract, arbitrary law: He is enabling me to share, as His son, in His own care for my brother. No man who ignores the rights and needs of others can hope to walk in the light of contemplation, because his way has turned aside from truth, from compassion, and therefore from God.

The requirements of a work to be done can be understood as the will of God. If I am supposed to hoe a garden or make a table, then I will be obeying God if I am true to the task I am performing. To do the work carefully and well, with love and respect for the nature of my task and with due attention to its purpose, is to unite myself to God's will in my work. In this way I become His instrument. He works through me. When I act as His instrument my labor cannot become an obstacle to contemplation, even though it may temporarily so occupy my mind that I cannot engage in it while I am actually doing my job. Yet my work itself will purify and pacify my mind and dispose me for contemplation.

Unnatural, frantic, anxious work, work done under pressure of greed or fear or any other inordinate passion, cannot properly speaking be dedicated to God, because God never wills such work directly. He may permit that through no fault of our own we may have to work madly and distractedly, due to our sins, and to the sins of the society in which we live. In that case we must tolerate it and make the best of what we cannot avoid. But let us not be blind to the distinction between sound, healthy work and unnatural toil.

In any case, we should always seek to conform to the *logos* or truth of the duty before us, the work to be done, or our own God-given nature. Contemplative obedience and abandonment to the will of God can never mean a cultivated indifference to the natural values implanted by Him in human life and work. Insensitivity must not be confused with detachment. The contemplative must certainly be detached, but he can never allow himself to become insensible to true human values, whether in society, in other men or in himself. If he does so, then his contemplation stands condemned as vitiated in its very root.

NEW SEEDS OF CONTEMPLATION

Six: THE WIND BLOWS WHERE IT PLEASES

G<small>OD</small>, Who is everywhere, never leaves us. Yet He seems sometimes to be present, sometimes absent. If we do not know Him well, we do not realize that He may be more present to us when He is absent than when He is present.

There are two absences of God. One is an absence that condemns us, the other an absence that sanctifies us.

In the absence that is condemnation, God "knows us not" because we have put some other god in His place, and refuse to be known by Him. In the absence that sanctifies, God empties the soul of every image that might become an idol and of every concern that might stand between our face and His Face.

In the first absence, He is present, but His presence is denied by the presence of an idol. God is present to the enemy we have placed between ourselves and Him in mortal sin.

In the second absence He is present, and His presence is affirmed and adored by the absence of everything else. He is closer to us than we are to ourselves, although we do not see him.

Whoever seeks to catch Him and hold Him loses Him. He is like the wind that blows where it pleases. You who love Him must love Him as arriving from where you do not know and as going where you do not know. Your spirit must seek to be as clean and as free as His own Spirit, in order to follow Him wherever He goes. Who are we to call ourselves either clean or free, unless He makes us so?

If He should teach us how to follow Him into the wilderness of His own freedom, we will no longer know where we are, because we are with Him Who is everywhere and nowhere at the same time.

Those who love only His apparent presence cannot follow the Lord wherever He goes. They do not love Him perfectly if they do not allow Him to be absent. They do not respect His liberty to do as He pleases. They think their prayers have made them able to command Him, and to subject His will to their own. They live on the level of magic rather than on the level of religion.

Only those men are never separated from the Lord who never question His right to separate Himself from them. They never lose Him because they always realize they never deserve to find Him, and that in spite of their unworthiness they have already found Him.

For He has first found them, and will not let them go.

GOD APPROACHES our minds by receding from them.

We can never fully know Him if we think of Him as an object of capture, to be fenced in by the enclosure of our own ideas.

We know Him better after our minds have let Him go.

The Lord travels in all directions at once.

The Lord arrives from all directions at once.

Wherever we are, we find that He has just departed.

Wherever we go, we discover that He has just arrived before us.

Our rest can be neither in the beginning of this pursuit, nor in the pursuit itself, nor in its apparent end. For the true end, which is Heaven, is an end without end. It is a totally new dimension, in which we come to rest in the secret that He must arrive at the moment of His departure; His arrival is at every moment and His departure is not fixed in time.

EVERY MAN becomes the image of the God he adores.

He whose worship is directed to a dead thing becomes a dead thing.

He who loves corruption rots.

He who loves a shadow becomes, himself, a shadow.

He who loves things that must perish lives in dread of their perishing.

The contemplative also, who seeks to keep God prisoner in his heart, becomes a prisoner within the narrow limits of his own heart, so that the Lord evades him and leaves him in his imprisonment, his confinement, and his dead recollection.

The man who leaves the Lord the freedom of the Lord adores the Lord in His freedom and receives the liberty of the sons of God.

This man loves like God and is carried away, the captive of the Lord's invisible freedom.

A god who remains immobile within the focus of my own vision is hardly even a trace of the True God's passing.

II

EACH TRUE CHILD of God is mild, perfect, docile, and alone. His consciousness springs up, in the Spirit of the Lord, at the precise point where he feels himself to be held in being by a pure gift, an act of love, a divine command. The freedom of God's gift of life calls for the response of our own freedom—an act of obedience, hidden in the secrecy of our deepest being. We find the Lord when we find His gift of life in the depths of ourselves. We are fully alive in Him when the deepest roots of life become conscious that they live in Him. From this consent to exist in dependence upon His gift and upon His freedom springs the interior life.

LET THE COMMAND of His love be felt at the roots of my existence. Let these roots themselves consent to His creative and redemptive will.

Then let me understand that I do not consent in order to exist, but that I exist in order to consent.

This is the living source of virtuous action: for all our good acts are acts of consent to the indications of His mercy and the movements of His grace.

From this we can come to perfection: to the love which consents in all things, seeks nothing but to respond, by goodness, to Goodness, and by love, to Love. Such love suffers all things and is equally happy in action and inaction, in existence and in dissolution.

Let us not only exist, but *obey* in our existing.

From this fundamental obedience, which is a fundamental gift, and the fit return of His gift, all other acts of obedience spring up into life everlasting.

For the full fruitfulness of spiritual life begins in gratitude for life, in the consent to live, and in the greater gratitude that seeks to be dissolved and to be with Christ.

NO MAN IS AN ISLAND

Seven: FALSE MYSTICISM

Tʜᴇ "ignorance" of the true mystic is not unintelligence but superintelligence. Though contemplation sometimes seems to be a denial of speculative thought it is really its fulfillment. All philosophy, all theology that is vitally aware of its place in the true order of things, aspires to enter the cloud around the mountaintop where man may hope to meet the Living God. All true learning should therefore be alive with the sense of its own limitations and with the instinct for a vital experience of reality which speculation alone cannot provide.

Just as there is a Pharisaism of knowledge, so also there is a Pharisaism of studied ignorance, for one perverse instinct can feed on everything under the sun. The man who is proud of an abstruse and technical doctrine, difficult to acquire and acquired by few, may be proud in the same way as another man who is pleased with a sweet religious ignorance that makes him feel complacently superior to all learning. Each of these two men is proud of the same thing. Each thinks he has reached a peak of secret wisdom which is closed to all but a few. But the ignorant Pharisee is perhaps more obnoxious than the other, since he is proud of what he conceives to be his humility, and this is a great perversion.

We are living in a time when false mysticism is a much greater danger than rationalism. It has now perhaps become easier to play on men's emotions with a political terminology that sounds religious than with one that sounds scientific. This is all the more true in an age in which the religious instincts of millions of men have never received their proper fulfillment. A nation that is starved with the need to worship something will turn to the first false god that is presented to it.

Hitler showed the world what could be done with an ersatz mysticism of "race" and "blood." The mythology of Communism, while pretending to be objective and unemotional, is no less romantic in its broad outlines. Marx's vision of a dialectic between economic forces that was to end in the emergence of the proletariat and the establishment of a classless society was a nineteenth-century adaptation of Old Testament themes—the Promised Land, the Chosen People, the Messiah. *Das Kapital* owed much to the subconscious heritage of the Jew. Stalinist imperialism is a new expression of an old Tsarist ideal—the "salvation" of the world by Holy Russia.

There is always a danger that the darkness of faith, which is meant to perfect man's intelligence on a level that transcends man's nature, may be exploited—as it has been exploited for instance by Fascists—to bring man's intelligence into subjection to powers below his nature. There are many Dark Nights of the soul, only one of which is a purification. All the others are a defilement of man's spirit. And their impurity is all the greater when they seem to be the real thing.

False mysticism is often viciously anti-intellectual. It promises man a fierce joy in the immolation of his intelligence. It calls him to throw his spirit into the hands of some blind life force, considered sometimes as beyond man, sometimes as within himself. Sometimes this mysticism is political, sometimes religious. It almost always exalts emotion above thought, and its reply to intellectual argument is sometimes a program of systematic violence—the suppression of schools, the destruction of books, and the imprisonment of learned men. Why all this? Because the intelligence itself is regarded with suspicion.

II

AND THIS brings us to the problem that is our main concern: false mystical experiences in a truly religious soul. False mysticism is most dangerous when it is a deviation of grace. And, since grace is given us by God to bring us to the high supernatural perfection which He has planned to bestow upon our nature, false mysticism ends also in a perversion even of nature.

By nature we seek truth. God's grace can give us an intimate experience of Him Who is infinite Truth. False mysticism turns us aside from the true path to that end. It leads us away after a mirage and leaves us to die in the desert, locked in the embrace of an illusion. This can happen in many different ways, but they all follow a few characteristic patterns. That is why it is quite easy to talk about false mysticism in the abstract. And yet, in concrete cases, the discovery of illusion is sometimes extremely difficult, often impossible.

In the abstract, false mysticism can fall under two characteristic headings. Both of these situate the private mystical experience in an incorrect relation to the Truth which God has revealed publicly to the Church. One of these incorrect definitions says that the mystic has no need whatever of any conceptual knowledge of God, revealed or otherwise. In order to enter into "contemplative union" with God the "spiritual man" must cease from every form of spiritual activity, empty his soul of all thought and affection. As soon as the soul is empty, it automatically and naturally becomes filled with "acquired" contemplation, in which it "knows" God without experiencing the fact that it knows anything at all. Since this is supposed to be the nature of true contemplation, it follows that theological knowledge of God is by its very nature an obstacle to contemplation and that the theologian is professionally ill-equipped to become a mystic, while an ignorant man is naturally best disposed for contemplation. Such were the errors of Quietism condemned by the Church in the seventeenth century. The danger of these errors is speculative rather than practical, because in actual fact it is very laborious to empty your mind of all thought, and few there are who will be disposed to attempt it. However, this is the error that most concerns us here because it resembles, in some superficial respects, the true doctrine which we are going to draw from the pages of Saint John of the Cross.

I should like to point out, parenthetically, that Oriental mysticism at large has no more in common with the Quietism of Molinos than does the mysticism of Saint John of the Cross. It is a very great mistake to think that Yoga seeks absorption in the Absolute by a mere relaxation of the mind and stoppage of activity. The techniques and disciplines of meditation practiced in the Orient are far more laborious and exacting than anything known in the West. The Oriental contemplative is no more indifferent to conceptual knowledge than his Christian counterpart. Divine "revelation" plays a part in Oriental mysticism, and "knowledge" is one of the foundation stones of Yoga. Oriental mysticism is far more intellectual and speculative than the mysticism of the West, and this is, in fact, one of its deficiencies. It is *too* intellectual. It tends to depend too exclusively on the work of man's own intelligence and on human techniques.

I said that false mysticism came under two headings. I have described the first kind of false mysticism, which literally substitutes ignorance for knowledge. The second kind of false mysticism is much more common: it claims to arrive at special supernatural knowledge by means other than those normally ordained by God. The most common illusion of well-meaning religious souls is to imagine that they hear heavenly voices, see visions, fall into ecstasies, and swoon away with rapture when in actual fact they are fabricating these experiences by the work of their own imagination. However, a distinction must be made. Locutions, visions, ecstasies, and other extraordinary experiences can quite easily be supernatural. Such things can and do come from God, although not every vision is from heaven. The important thing to remember is that even when they are supernatural, these experiences are not of the essence of true mysticism. They are only accidental to it. This means that mystical contemplation in the strict sense is an experience of God which is directly achieved, under the inspiration of grace, without the medium of anything that is seen or heard or "understood." In mystical contemplation God is known to the soul without the medium of any species or image, whether of the mind or of the senses. And therefore it follows that all visions and locutions are in a certain sense opposed to true contemplation, at least in so far as they diminish its purity and its perfection. According to the language of the Christian apophatic theologians, in the tradition of Saint Gregory of Nyssa and the Pseudo-Dionysius, if you have a vision in which you think you see God clearly, you have not seen God. Saint John of the Cross devotes a large part of *The Ascent of Mount Carmel* to proving the thesis that visions and locutions and other experiences which purport to give us a precise supernatural knowledge of the divinity should never be either sought after or positively accepted, since no created and visible thing, no clear idea, can convey to us the full reality of God as He is in Himself.

III

TRUE CONTEMPLATION is not produced by images or ideas formed in the soul. It is the experience of an immediate spiritual union with God, a union which can only be effected by God and which is essentially a union of supernatural charity. Needless to say, no spirit other than God Himself can unite himself immediately to the soul, and no one but God can infuse supernatural charity into the soul. True contemplation is, then, the experience of a union that is so purely and perfectly supernatural that no created nature could possibly bring it about. Indeed, no spirit less than the Spirit of God can possibly produce even a plausible imitation of true mystical union. Imitations are of course foisted upon souls, and sometimes with great success. But, as Saint Theresa somewhere says, anyone who has experienced true mystical union can see at once the infinite distance that lies between it and the false article produced by the Devil or by our own imagination.

No such clear division between truth and error exists in the case of imaginary visions, locutions, and other such "distinct" experiences of the supernatural. That is why Saint John of the Cross advises contemplatives to remain negative toward them all, without even bothering to discover whether they come from God or from the Devil. They are all, indiscriminately, to be refused.

It is significant that the opinion of Saint John of the Cross, is far more cautious than that of most authorities. Catholic theologians commonly agree that no contemplative soul should ordinarily be allowed, still less encouraged, to seek after visions, locutions, and other such experiences. Incidentally, they also agree that one who shows signs of sufficient spiritual advancement and of proper dispositions should normally be allowed to aspire to true contemplation and to mystical union, and even encouraged to do so, if mystical union be understood first of all as a union with God in perfect charity. However, many theologians are much more tolerant than Saint John of the Cross in allowing souls to *accept* visions, locutions, and the rest, once they are given.

What are we to conclude? Visions, apparitions, locutions, prophetic inspirations may be, in particular cases, true or false, supernatural, preternatural, or natural. Each case must be judged on its own merits. Such experiences cannot be classified, in general, as being essentially true or essentially false. It is not false mysticism to have visions, but it *is* false to make mysticism consist essentially in visions. It is certainly false mysticism to follow a road that leads to spectacular experiences rather than to obscure union with God, as if spiritual perfection consisted in having such experiences and as if no one could become a saint without them.

All false mysticism misconceives the proper roles of knowledge and love in contemplation, as well as the essence of contemplation itself. It either discards all knowledge of God or else aspires to a "marvelous" knowledge of Him which falls outside the orbit of faith and is actually no knowledge of Him at all. False mysticism tends to treat contemplation either as if it were all love and no knowledge, or all knowledge and no love. Finally, false mysticism turns us away from our true end and seeks the enjoyment of flattering and glorious experiences rather than the perfect gift of our whole being to God alone.

THE ASCENT TO TRUTH

Eight: THE SHADOW OF THY WINGS

I⟨T⟩ CAN SOMETIMES HAPPEN that we are brought down by Christ's love into the dust of death. Then we know, somewhat as He knew, what it is to be "poured out like water." It is the terrible experience of seeing oneself slowly turned inside out. It is the frightful taste of a humility that is not merely a virtue but the very agony of truth. This ghastly emptying, this inexorable gutting of our own appalling nonentity, takes place under the piercing light of the revealed word, the light of infinite Truth. But it is something far more terrible still: we find ourselves eviscerated by our own ingratitude, under the eyes of Mercy.

This is the experience that will come to one who once thought he had virtue, who once thought he had a "degree of prayer," who once thought, perhaps, that he loved God indeed, and was God's good friend and who then, one day, is brought up for judgment, to be purified of all that is too human in his dream. For he has been cornered and accused, pierced and emptied by the shame of remembering who he really is. God seems to turn away His face. God seems to withdraw His protecting hand, and all the things he treasured, that were not God, have wasted away like shadows with the loss of His presence. This emptiness, this sense of spiritual annihilation which is due to us all as men born in sin and grown old in sin, Christ took upon Himself when it was not due to Him at all and He emptied Himself of all His power and glory in order to descend into the freezing depths of darkness where we had crawled to hide ourselves, cowering in blind despair.

But because Christ came down into this no man's land of sin, to find us and bring us back to His Kingdom, we are able to discover the living God in the very darkness of what seems to be His utter absence. And what is more, it may be that we find Him there more truly than when we thought we saw Him in the light of our own dim day.

So it can happen that a soul enters upon the recital of a Psalm applicable to Christ's Passion—let us say Psalm 87. It is a day on which we seem to be buried alive under an inhuman burden of temptation. Perhaps we may also suffer sickness, physical as well as moral desolation. But the worst thing of all remains the inescapable vision of our own almost infinite capacity for pettiness and degradation. "O Lord my God, I cry by day, in the night I weep before thee. Let my prayer come before thee, incline thy ear to my cry. For my soul is full of evils and my life is on the verge of the grave. . . . Thou hast laid me in a deep pit, in darkness, in the abyss. Thine indignation weighs upon me and with all thy waves thou dost overwhelm me. Thou hast taken away my friends from me; thou hast made me abominable to them; I am shut up, I can no longer go forth." [1] This is practically the only Psalm that ends on a note of complete dejection. There is a faint flame of hopeful prayer, but it is beaten down by the cold darkness of apparent refusal, and here is how the Psalm ends: "Thy wrath has swept over me and thy terrors have destroyed me. They surround me like water all the time: they assail me all together. Thou hast taken from me friend and companion; The darkness is my intimate." And that is all.

Yet at such a moment, and in such a Psalm, the soul, catching and comprehending in its own black mirror the fearful darkness of revelation, is confronted in its own depths with the countenance of the murdered Christ. This is more than a meeting. It is an identification. We have entered into a Baptism of darkness in which we are one with His death. But to die with Christ is to rise with Him, for we cannot be dead with Him without our life being hidden with Him in God.[2] Although there remains a formal difference between the grace of the Passion of Christ by which we are delivered from sin, and the grace of His Resurrection in which supernatural life is communicated to us, nevertheless in fact both are poured out in the wonderful night of which the Liturgy sings in the *Exultet*.[3] This night of Mystery in which we rise from death with the hidden Christ is the spiritual Red Sea of which the Psalms have sung to us all along. Now we have entered into it in truth and have passed through it to be nourished by God with His Body in the wilderness.

This is a death in which we have found Him Who is the way, the truth, and the life. We now know that this darkness, which seems to annihilate us, is not the darkness of death but, if such an expression can be understood, the darkness of life. The tides of light that pour down upon the whole Church from the mountaintop which is the soul of the Risen Saviour, blind us by their intense purity and drown us in darkness although they are essential Light, and so the Night of the Spirit is already a sharing of the Resurrection. If the paradox may be allowed, this frightful death is our first taste of glory.

Then we begin to discover that the night in which we seem to be lost is the protection of the shadow of God's wings.[4] If God has brought us into this darkness it is because He wishes to guard us with extreme care and tenderness, or, in the words of the Psalm, "like the apple of His eye."[5] The new life of the soul united Christ in His Mystery is something too delicate and tender to be let loose in a crowd that may contain hidden enemies, and therefore God has isolated the soul in a soundless and vast interior solitude, the solitude of His own Heart where there is no human spectator and where the soul can no longer even see itself. True, the depths of that solitude open and close in a flash: but the soul remains enveloped and penetrated with divine emptiness, saturated with the vastness of God, charged with the living voice of silence in which His Word is eternally uttered.

The protection of darkness and silence is extremely necessary for the soul that begins to burn with these touches of the Spirit of God. If it should come close to Him Who is Life without being enclosed and hidden in His life, it will find itself charged with more power than it can stand and it will burn itself out with an ardor that it cannot control. For when the soul has thus known God divinely, the memory of the encounter is sometimes stirred up by the lines of Psalms, to a blaze that unnerves it beyond its capacity to bear. In this degree of prayer there may arise high seas of inspiration that destroy the mind with the weight of a superhuman demand. But we have no help from God to tackle this demand. It is not the wave of His present power, but an undertow that follows after His passing. Caught in the clenched fist of this bullying sea of love that is neither human nor divine and which seems to be something elemental in its brutality, we are drawn under and seem to drown until God catches us again and holds us under, not under the sea but under the Mystery of His eternity, where alone there is breathing.

This undertow, too, flows through the Psalms. It tends to attack us most where there are appeals made to our mind and will by the word of God, by ceremony and liturgy and chant. These aids to prayer which were a help to us at the very beginning and which went unnoticed as we advanced in living faith and in the prayer of quiet, which were sources of light and brought us into intimate union with Christ in His Mysteries, now turn against us like Goliath and we have no stones and sling with which to fight back. This is the time when every line of the Psalms bursts forth with lights that we no longer need, spurious and tremendous inspirations that exhaust the soul and contribute nothing to its peace. And the soul seems to find no refuge where it may flee them. They come upon it like an army from every side and there is no resistance. The only safety is in darkness, the protection that can only be extended over us by the outstretched hand of God. We need that protection, and more and more we sense our need. For the devils, too, understand our position. They stand to profit if they can destroy and exhaust us with false lights and raptures of their own devising. This is the stage when the soul that is too tough for its own good, too well able to stand the overpowering sweetness of half-natural ecstasies, will be in danger of entering the ways of false mysticism. Prayer will become debauchery, the Liturgy a riot of prophecy and carnal exaltation. The mark of all this falsity is violence. It is sealed with the seal of contention and brutality and strain. These are the spiritual footprints of the devil who, if he cannot deceive the soul with false raptures, soon tears off his mask and lets loose against us a jungle full of terrors and we live in nightmare on the threshold of the deepest darkness that alone can save us.

In this tribulation the Lord God is ever with us, no matter how much we fear. *Cum ipso sum in tribulatione.* These are words from Psalm 90 which are chanted every night in the monastic Compline when the shadows fall upon the cloister and the monks are ending their day of prayer. "I will be with him in trouble, I will rescue him and honor him." [6] The angels are at our side, holding us up lest we should dash our foot against a stone. We could not travel through the forest that the spiritual life has now become unless His power carried us onward, where we tread upon the asp and basilisk and never feel their sting, and never suffer harm! *Altissimum posuisti refugium tuum.* We have made the Most High God our refuge. The scourge will never touch us.

[1] Psalm 87: 1-4, 7-9.
[2] Colossians 3:3.
[3] *The Roman Missal,* Blessing of the Paschal Candle, Holy Saturday.
[4] Psalm 16:8.
[5] Psalm 16:8. Compare also: *The Cistercian Breviary*: Versicle for Compline.
[6] Psalm 90:15.

Nine: SHARING THE FRUITS OF CONTEMPLATION

W<small>E DO NOT SEE</small> God in contemplation—we know Him by love: for He is pure Love and when we taste the experience of loving God for His own sake alone, we know by experience Who and what He is.

True mystical experience of God and supreme renunciation of everything outside of God coincide. They are two aspects of the same thing. For when our minds and will are perfectly free from every created attachment, they are immediately filled with the gift of God's love: not because things necessarily have to happen that way, but because this is His will, the gift of His love to us. "Everyone who has left his home or his father, or his mother, or his wife for my sake shall receive a hundredfold and shall possess eternal life."

We experience God in proportion as we are stripped and emptied of attachment to His creatures. And when we have been delivered from every other desire we shall taste the perfection of an incorruptible joy.

God does not give His joy to us for ourselves alone, and if we could possess Him for ourselves alone we would not possess Him at all. Any joy that does not overflow from our soul and help other men to rejoice in God does not come to us from God. (But do not think that you have to see how it overflows into the souls of others. In the economy of His grace, you may be sharing His gifts with someone you will never know until you get to heaven.)

IF WE EXPERIENCE God in contemplation, we experience Him not for ourselves alone but also for others.

Yet if your experience of God comes from God, one of the signs may be a great diffidence in telling others about it. To speak about the gift He has given us would seem to dissipate it and leave a stain on the pure emptiness where God's light shone. No one is more shy than a con-

476

templative about his contemplation. Sometimes it gives him almost physical pain to speak to anyone of what he has seen of God. Or at least it is intolerable for him to speak about it as his own experience.

At the same time he most earnestly wants everybody else to share his peace and his joy. His contemplation gives him a new outlook on the world of men. He looks about him with a secret and tranquil surmise which he perhaps admits to no one, hoping to find in the faces of other men or to hear in their voices some sign of vocation and potentiality for the same deep happiness and wisdom.

He finds himself speaking of God to the men in whom he hopes he has recognized the light of his own peace, the awakening of his own secret: or if he cannot speak to them, he writes for them, and his contemplative life is still imperfect without sharing, without companionship, without communion.

AT NO TIME in the spiritual life is it more necessary to be completely docile and subject to the most delicate movements of God's will and His grace than when you try to share the knowledge of His love with other men. It is much better to be so diffident that you risk not sharing it with them at all, than to throw it all away by trying to give it to other people before you have received it yourself. The contemplative who tries to preach contemplation before he himself really knows what it is, will prevent both himself and others from finding the true path to God's peace.

In the first place he will substitute his own natural enthusiasm and imagination and poetry for the reality of the light that is in him, and he will become absorbed in the business of communicating something that is practically incommunicable: and although there is some benefit in this even for his own soul (for it is a kind of meditation on the interior life and on God) still he runs the risk of being drawn away from the simple light and silence in which God is known without words and concepts, and losing himself in reasoning and language and metaphor.

The highest vocation in the Kingdom of God is that of sharing one's contemplation with others and bringing other men to the experimental knowledge of God that is given to those who love Him perfectly. But the possibility of mistake and error is just as great as the vocation itself.

In the first place the mere fact that you have discovered something of contemplation does not yet mean that you are supposed to pass it on to somebody else. The sharing of contemplation with others implies two vocations: one to be a contemplative, and another still to teach contemplation. Both of them have to be verified.

But then, as soon as you think of yourself as teaching contemplation to others, you make another mistake. No one teaches contemplation except God, Who gives it. The best you can do is write something or say something that will serve as an occasion for someone else to realize what God wants of him.

II

ONE of the worst things about an ill-timed effort to share the knowledge of contemplation with other people is that you assume that everybody else will want to see things from your own point of view when, as a matter of fact, they will not. They will raise objections to everything that you say, and you will find yourself in a theological controversy—or worse, a pseudo-scientific one—and nothing is more useless for a contemplative than controversy. There is no point whatever in trying to make people with a different vocation get excited about the kind of interior life that means so much to you. And if they are called to contemplation, a long, involved argument full of technicalities and abstract principles is not the thing that will help them to get there.

Those who are too quick to think they must go out and share their contemplation with other men tend to ruin their own contemplation and give false notions of it to others, by trusting too much in words and language and discourse to do the work that can only be accomplished in the depths of man's soul by the infused light of God.

Often we will do much more to make men contemplatives by leaving them alone and minding our own business—which is contemplation itself—than by breaking in on them with what we think we know about the interior life. For when we are united with God in silence and darkness and when our faculties are raised above the level of their own natural activity, and rest in the pure, tranquil, incomprehensible cloud that surrounds the presence of God, our prayer and the grace that is given to us tend of their very nature to overflow invisibly through the Mystical Body of Christ, and we who dwell together invisibly in the bond of the One Spirit of God affect one another more than we can ever realize by our own union with God, by our spiritual vitality in Him.

One who has a very little of this prayer, the mere beginning of contemplation, and who scarcely even realizes anything of what he has, can do immense things for the souls of other men simply by keeping himself quietly attentive to the obscure presence of God, about which he could not possibly hope to formulate an intelligible sentence. And if he did try to start talking about it and reasoning about it, he would at once lose the little that he had of it and would help no one, least of all himself.

Therefore the best way to prepare ourselves for the possible vocation of sharing contemplation with other men is not to study how to talk and reason about contemplation, but withdraw ourselves as much as we can from talk and argument and retire into the silence and humility of heart in which God will purify our love of all its human imperfections. Then in His own time He will set our hand to the work He wants us to do, and we will find ourselves doing it without being quite able to realize how we got there, or how it all started. And by that time the work will not absorb us in a way that will disturb our minds. We will be able to keep our tranquillity and our freedom, and above all we will learn to leave the results to God, and not indulge our own vanity by insisting on quick and visible conversions in everyone we talk to.

Perhaps it looks easy on paper, and perhaps it would really be easy if we were altogether simple and made no difficulties about letting God work in us and through us. But in actual practice one of the last barricades of egoism, and one which many saints have refused to give up entirely, is this insistence on doing the work and getting the results and enjoying them *ourselves*. We are the ones who want to carry off the glory for the work done. And perhaps that was why some saints did not get to the highest contemplation: they wanted to *do* too much for themselves. And God let them get away with it.

And therefore although contemplation like all good things demands to be shared and will only be perfectly enjoyed and possessed by each one of us when it is possessed in common by all who are called to it, we must not forget that this perfect communion belongs only to heaven.

Be careful, then, of assuming that because you like certain people and are naturally inclined to chose them for your friends and share with them your natural interests, that they are also called to be contemplatives and that you must teach them all how to become so. The aptitude may or may not be there. Perhaps there is a strong likelihood that it *is* there: but if it is, be content to let God take care of its development in them. Be glad if He uses you as an occasion or as an instrument, but be careful not to get in His way with your own innate instinct for companionship. For in this world it is not good to be too eager for the achievement of any, even of the best of ends; and one who knows by experience that God is always present everywhere and always ready to make Himself known to those who love Him, will not quickly prefer the uncertain value of human activity to the tranquillity and certitude of this infinite and all-important possession.

III

SUPPOSE A MAN were once in his life to vanish into God for the space of a minute.

All the rest of his life has been spent in sins and virtues, in good and evil, in labor and struggle, in sickness and health, in gifts, in sorrows, in achieving and regretting, in planning and hoping, in love and fear. He has seen things, considered them, known them; made judgments; spoken; acted wisely or not. He has blundered in and out of the contemplation of beginners. He has found the cloud, the obscure sweetness of God. He has known rest in prayer.

In all these things his life has been a welter of uncertainties. In the best of them he may have sinned. In his imperfect contemplation he may have found sin.

But in the moment of time, the minute, the little minute in which he was delivered into God (if he truly was so delivered) there is no question that then his life was pure; that then he gave glory to God; that then he did not sin; that in that moment of pure love he could not sin.

Can such union with God be the object of inordinate desire? Not if you understand it. Because you cannot inordinately desire God to be God. You cannot inordinately desire that God's will be done for His own sake. But it is in these two desires perfectly conceived and fulfilled that we are emptied into Him and transformed into His joy and it is in these that we cannot sin.

It is in this ecstasy of pure love that we arrive at a true fulfillment of the First Commandment, loving God with our whole heart and our whole mind and all our strength. Therefore it is something that all men who desire to please God ought to desire—not for a minute, nor for half an hour, but forever. It is in these souls that peace is established in the world.

They are the strength of the world, because they are the tabernacles of God in the world. They are the ones who keep the universe from being destroyed. They are the little ones. They do not know themselves. The whole earth depends on them. Nobody seems to realize it. These are the ones for whom it was all created in the first place. They shall inherit the land.

They are the only ones who will ever be able to enjoy life altogether.

They have renounced the whole world and it has been given into their possession. They alone appreciate the world and the things that are in it. They are the only ones capable of understanding joy. Everybody else is too weak for joy. Joy would kill anybody but these meek. They are the clean of heart. They see God. He does their will, because His will is their own. He does all that they want, because He is the One Who desires all their desires. They are the only ones who have everything that they can desire. Their freedom is without limit. They reach out for us to comprehend our misery and drown it in the tremendous expansion of their own innocence, that washes the world with its light.

Come, let us go into the body of that light. Let us live in the cleanliness of that song. Let us throw off the pieces of the world like clothing and enter naked into wisdom. For this is what all hearts pray for when they cry: "Thy will be done."

NEW SEEDS OF CONTEMPLATION

Epilogue

Aᴛ ᴛʜᴇ ᴄʟɪᴍᴀx of mystical perfection, which is the consummation of perfect charity in so far as it can be attained on this earth, love cries out with a more and more ardent hunger and sweetly demands the satiation of perfect vision. Here there is no darkness. The dawn has come. The first rays of the morning sun, the Divine Word, have penetrated the pure depths of the soul transformed in His Light.

The soul stands on the bank of another Jordan—the bright calm river of death. It looks across the river and sees clear light upon the mountains of the true promised land. It begins to be ravished to the depths of its being by the clean scent of forests full of spice and balsam. It stands upon the riverbank with the wonderful soft wind of the New World playing upon its cheeks and upon its eyelids and in its hair. And now it knows that the country it once took to be Canaan, the poor indigent earth of early contemplation, was nothing more than a desert—a waste of dry rock to which it had escaped, at great cost, from the vain wisdom that is Egypt.

But here is God. He is the Promised Land. Nothing is lost in Him. The whole world shines in His bosom. Creatures of all kinds spring forth without end from the bright abyss of His Wisdom. The soul itself sees itself in Him, and Him in itself, and in them both, the whole world. It sees all things, all men living and dead, the great souls and the little souls, the saints, the glorious Mother of God, and it is one with them all for they are all One, and Christ, God, is this One. He is the Promised Land, He is the Word, He is the Beloved.

Here, in Him, all the articles of faith have converged their rays and have burst open and showered the mind with fire. From Him they came, through Him they came, to Him they return, bringing with them the minds they have raised up in radiance from the sepulcher of vain learning. In Him the articles of faith have disappeared. He is their substance. There is no further need for them to prophesy in part, for when that which is perfect is come, that which is in part shall be done away.

And so the soul, transformed in God and waiting at the threshold of heaven, sings its desire for His theology.

THE ASCENT TO TRUTH

PART SEVEN

The
Sacred
Land

And you must know that the sacred land
where you are is full of every seed
and has fruit not plucked in your world.

Epigraph

WHAT ARE THE HORIZONS that lie ahead, in the ascent to the City of God in heaven? There are high peaks before us now, serene with snow and light, above the level of tempest. They are far away. We almost never see them, they are so high. But we lift up our eyes toward them, for there the saints dwell: and these are the mountains of holiness whence cometh our help.

BREAD IN THE WILDERNESS

One: SILENCE

THE RAIN CEASES, and a bird's clear song suddenly announces the difference between Heaven and hell.

GOD OUR CREATOR and Savior has given us a language in which He can be talked about, since faith cometh by hearing and our tongues are the keys that open Heaven to others.

But when the Lord comes as a Bridegroom there remains nothing to be said except that He is coming, and that we must go out to meet Him. *Ecce Sponsus venit! Exite obviam ei!* [1]

After that we go forth to find Him in solitude. There we communicate with Him alone, without words, without discursive thoughts, in the silence of our whole being.

When what we say is meant for no one else but Him, it can hardly be said in language. What is not meant to be related is not even experienced on a level that can be clearly analyzed. We know that it must not be told, because it cannot.

But before we come to that which is unspeakable and unthinkable, the spirit hovers on the frontiers of language, wondering whether or not to stay on its own side of the border, in order to have something to bring back to other men. This is the test of those who wish to cross the frontier. If they are not ready to leave their own ideas and their own words behind them, they cannot travel further.

IF YOU GO into solitude with a silent tongue, the silence of mute beings will share with you their rest.

But if you go into solitude with a silent heart, the silence of creation will speak louder than the tongues of men or angels.

THE SILENCE of the tongue and of the imagination dissolves the barrier between ourselves and the peace of things that exist only for God and not for themselves. But the silence of all inordinate desire dissolves the barrier between ourselves and God. Then we come to live in Him alone.

Then mute beings no longer speak to us merely with their own silence. It is the Lord Who speaks to us, with a far deeper silence, hidden in the midst of our own selves.

THOSE WHO LOVE their own noise are impatient of everything else. They constantly defile the silence of the forests and the mountains and the sea. They bore through silent nature in every direction with their machines, for fear that the calm world might accuse them of their own emptiness. The urgency of their swift movement seems to ignore the tranquillity of nature by pretending to have a purpose. The loud plane seems for a moment to deny the reality of the clouds and of the sky, by its direction, its noise, and its pretended strength. The silence of the sky remains when the plane has gone. The tranquillity of the clouds will remain when the plane has fallen apart. It is the silence of the world that is real. Our noise, our business, our purposes, and all our fatuous statements about our purposes, or business, and our noise: these are the illusion.

God is present, and His thought is alive and awake in the fullness and depth and breadth of all the silences of the world. The Lord is watching in the almond trees, over the fulfillment of His words (Jer. 1:11).

Whether the plane pass by tonight or tomorrow, whether there be cars on the winding road or no cars, whether men speak in the field, whether there be a radio in the house or not, the tree brings forth her blossoms in silence.

Whether the house be empty or full of children, whether the men go off to town or work with tractors in the fields, whether the liner enters the harbor full of tourists or full of soldiers, the almond tree brings forth her fruit in silence.

THERE ARE SOME MEN for whom a tree has no reality until they think of cutting it down, for whom an animal has no value until it enters the slaughterhouse, men who never look at anything until they decide to abuse it and who never even notice what they do not want to destroy. These men can hardly know the silence of love: for their love is the absorption of another person's silence into their own noise. And because they do not know the silence of love, they cannot know the silence of God, Who is Charity, Who cannot destroy what He loves, Who is bound, by His own law of Charity, to give life to all those whom He draws into His own silence.

SILENCE DOES NOT EXIST in our lives merely for its own sake. It is ordered to something else. Silence is the mother of speech. A lifetime of silence is ordered to an ultimate declaration, which can be put into words, a declaration of all we have lived for.

Life and death, words and silence, are given us because of Christ. In Christ we die to the flesh and live to the spirit. In Him we die to illusion and live to truth. We speak to confess Him, and we are silent in order to meditate on Him and enter deeper into His silence, which is at once the silence of death and of eternal life—the silence of Good Friday night and the peace of Easter morning.

WE RECEIVE Christ's silence into our hearts when first we speak from our heart the word of faith. We work out our salvation in silence and in hope. Silence is the strength of our interior life. Silence enters into the very core of our moral being, so that if we have no silence we have no morality. Silence enters mysteriously into the composition of all the virtues, and silence preserves them from corruption.

IF WE FILL OUR LIVES with silence, then we live in hope, and Christ lives in us and gives our virtues much substance. Then, when the time comes, we confess Him openly before men, and our confession has much meaning because it is rooted in deep silence. It awakens the silence of Christ in the hearts of those who hear us, so that they themselves fall silent and begin to wonder and to listen. For they have begun to discover their true selves.

If our life is poured out in useless words we will never hear anything in the depths of our hearts, where Christ lives and speaks in silence. We will never be anything, and in the end, when the time comes for us to declare who and what we are, we shall be found speechless at the moment of the crucial decision: for we shall have said everything and exhausted ourselves in speech before we had anything to say.

THERE MUST BE a time of day when the man who makes plans forgets his plans, and acts as if he had no plans at all.

There must be a time of day when the man who has to speak falls very silent. And his mind forms no more propositions, and he asks himself: Did they have a meaning?

There must be a time when the man of prayer goes to pray as if it were the first time in his life he had ever prayed; when the man of resolutions puts his resolutions aside as if they had all been broken, and he learns a different wisdom: distinguishing the sun from the moon, the stars from the darkness, the sea from the dry land, and the night sky from the shoulder of a hill.

IN SILENCE, we learn to make distinctions. Those who fly silence, fly also from distinctions. They do not want to see too clearly. They prefer confusion.

A man who loves God necessarily loves silence also, because he fears to lose his sense of discernment. He fears the noise that takes the sharp edge off every experience of reality. He avoids the unending movement that blurs all beings together into a crowd of undistinguishable things.

The saint is indifferent in his desires, but by no means indifferent in his attitudes toward different aspects of reality.

HERE LIES a dead man who made an idol of indifference.

His prayer did not enkindle, it extinguished his flame.

His silence listened to nothing and, therefore, heard nothing, and had nothing to say.

Let the swallows come and build their nests in his history and teach their young to fly about in the desert which he made of his soul, and thus he will not remain unprofitable forever.

LIFE IS NOT to be regarded as an uninterrupted flow of words which is finally silenced by death. Its rhythm develops in silence, comes to the surface in movements of necessary expression, returns to deeper silence, culminates in a final declaration, then ascends quietly into the silence of Heaven which resounds with unending praise.

Those who do not know there is another life after this one, or who cannot bring themselves to live in time as if they were meant to spend their eternity in God, resist the fruitful silence of their own being by continual noise. Even when their own tongues are still, their minds chatter without end and without meaning, or they plunge themselves into the protective noise of machines, traffic, or radios. When their own noise is momentarily exhausted, they rest in the noise of other men.

How tragic it is that they who have nothing to express are continually expressing themselves, like nervous gunners, firing burst after burst of ammunition into the dark, where there is no enemy. The reason for their talk is: death. Death is the enemy who seems to confront them at every moment in the deep darkness and silence of their own being. So they keep shouting at death. They confound their lives with noise. They stun their own ears with meaningless words, never discovering that their hearts are rooted in a silence that is not death but life. They chatter themselves to death, fearing life as if it were death.

OUR WHOLE LIFE should be a meditation of our last and most important decision: the choice between life and death.

We must all die. But the dispositions with which we face death make of our death a choice either of death or of life.

If, during our life we have chosen life, then in death we will pass from death to life. Life is a spiritual thing, and spiritual things are silent. If the spirit that kept the flame of physical life burning in our bodies took care to nourish itself with the oil that is found only in the silence of God's charity, then when the body dies, the spirit itself goes on burning the same oil, with its own flame. But if the spirit has burned all along with the base oils of passion or egoism or pride, then when death comes the flame of the spirit goes out with the light of the body because there is no more oil in the lamp.

We must learn during our lifetime to trim our lamps and fill them with charity in silence, sometimes speaking and confessing the glory of God in order to increase our charity by increasing the charity of others, and teaching them also the ways of peace and of silence.

IF, AT THE MOMENT of our death, death comes to us as an unwelcome stranger, it will be because Christ also has always been to us an unwelcome stranger. For when death comes, Christ comes also, bringing us the everlasting life which He has bought for us by His own death. Those who love true life, therefore, frequently think about their death. Their life is full of a silence that is an anticipated victory over death. Silence, indeed, makes death our servant and even our friend. Thoughts and prayers that grow up out of the silent thought of death are like trees growing where there is water. They are strong thoughts, that overcome the fear of misfortune because they have overcome passion and desire. They turn the face of our soul, in constant desire, toward the face of Christ.

IF I SAY that a whole lifetime of silence is ordered to a final utterance, I do not mean that we must all contrive to die with pious speeches on our lips. It is not necessary that our last words should have some special or dramatic significance worthy of being written down. Every good death, every death that hands us over from the uncertainties of this world to the unfailing peace and silence of the love of Christ, is itself an utterance and a conclusion. It says, either in words or without them, that it is good for life to come to its appointed end, for the body to return to dust and for the spirit to ascend to the Father, through the mercy of Our Lord Jesus Christ.

A silent death may speak with more eloquent peace than a death punctuated by vivid expressions. A lonely death, a tragic death, may yet have more to say of the peace and mercy of Christ than many another comfortable death.

For the eloquence of death is the eloquence of human poverty coming face to face with the riches of divine mercy. The more we are aware that our poverty is supremely great, the greater will be the meaning of our death: and the greater its poverty. For the saints are those who wanted to be poorest in life, and who, above all else, exulted in the supreme poverty of death.

[1] "Behold the Bridegroom cometh, go yet forth to meet Him" (Matt. 25:6).

NO MAN IS AN ISLAND

Two: ATLAS AND THE FAT MAN

ON THE LAST DAY of a rough but fortunate voyage, near the farthest end of the known world, I found my way to the shores of a sentient mountain.

There stood the high African rock in the shadow of lucky rain: a serious black crag, at the tip of the land mass, with a cloud balanced on its shoulder.

O high silent man of lava, with feet in the green surf, watching the stream of days and years!

We saw the clouds drift by the face of that tame god, and held our peace. We placed our feet on the hot sands as the ship was beached on the edge of night and of summer.

This was Atlas at his lonely work! I never thought I would have seen his face!

His head was hidden in sky. His eyes were staring darkness. His thoughts were full of inscrutable waters. His heart was safe at the bottom of the green ocean. His spirit stood silent and awake in the center of the world.

He held everything in massive silence. In one deep thought without words he kept the continents from drifting apart. The seas obeyed not his eyes, not his words, but the beating of his heart.

His only utterance was one weak light in a lighthouse. Small sharp words, no commentary on the pure mystery of night, they left the mystery alone: touched it and left it alone.

From time to time he spoke (but only to the distance) with the short bass clangor of a bell. The neutral note was uttered, and said nothing.

Yet it was this dim bell in the heavens that moved the weather and changed the seasons. A new summer grew upon the ocean, before our eyes, closely followed by autumn, then winter.

The waves moved by with white hair. Time rode the secret waves, commanded only by Atlas and by his bell. There were ages passing by as we watched. Birds skimmed the white-haired ages. Young birds kept the morning young. The silence of this unvisited shore embraced the beginning of history and its end.

We made believe that it was five o'clock.

We made believe that it was six o'clock. We made believe that it was midnight. Atlas must have deigned to smile on our efforts, since it was now dark. His eyes gave hope to the tumbling ocean. Once again, rain began to fall.

WHEN IT IS EVENING, when night begins to darken, when rain is warm in the summer darkness and rumors come up from the woods and from the banks of rivers, then shores and forests sound around you with a wordless solicitude of mothers. It is then that flowering palms enchant the night with their sweet smell. Flowers sleep. Thoughts become simple. Words cease. The hollows of the mind fill with dreams as with water.

In the sacred moment between sleeping and staying awake, Atlas speaks to the night as to a woman. He speaks freely to the night he loves, thinking no one is at hand.

He speaks of his heart at the bottom of the ocean. He speaks of his spirit at the center of the world. He speaks of fires that night and woman do not understand. Green fires that are extinguished by intelligence, that night and woman possess. Golden fires of spirit that are in the damp warm rocky roots of the earth. White fires that are clear outside of earth and sky which night and woman cannot reach. And waters that are common to night and to woman and to Atlas, ruled by a bell in the moon and by a bell in the sun. Atlas puts out all those fires with his one bell, and looks at nothing. This is the work that supports the activity of seasons: Atlas looking at nothing.

"How lonely is my life as a mountain on the shore of ocean with my heart at the bottom of the sea and my spirit at the center of the earth where no one can speak to me. I ring my bell and nobody listens. All I do is look at nothing and change the seasons and hold up the sky and save the world.

"No one will come near to one so tall, no one will befriend one so strong as I, and I am forgotten forever. It is right that I be forgotten, for if I were not forgotten where would be my vigilance, and if I were not vigilant where would be the world? And if night and woman could understand my thoughts, where would be my strength? My thoughts would draw up my spirit from the center of the earth and the whole world would fall into emptiness.

"My stability is without fault because I have no connections. I have not viewed mankind for ages. Yet I have not slept, thinking of man and his troubles, which are not alleviated by the change of seasons. I wish well to mankind. I give man more seasons and pray that he be not left to himself. I want him not to see my far lights upon the ocean (this is impossible) or hear my dim bell in the heavens (this is not expedient). But I want him to rest at peace under a safe sky knowing that I am here with my lights and my bell and that the ends of the world are watched by an overseer and the seas taken care of.

"I do not tire easily, for this is the work I am used to. Though it is child's play, sometimes I hate it. I bear with loneliness for the sake of man. Yet to be constantly forgotten is more than I can abide.

"Thus I intend not only to watch, but to move watching, and I shall begin by moving the theaters."

At this there was a stir in all the distant cities of the world and the continents heaved up and down like the trays of a scale, as all the great countries were suddenly weighed by Atlas in the middle of the night: the lands of Europe and the lands of Asia were weighed in the hands of a tall hidden power, and knew nothing of it. The shores of America waited in the mist to be weighed in the same balance. It was Atlas, the guardian of nights and seas moving and watching.

We expected movement only after it had already begun and we looked for power when the strong were already overthrown. We saw the dance begin secretly in genteel houses, under the kitchen oilcloth and leap to the tops of the most public monuments. Some buildings woke and walked downhill and would not stop until they came to water. Churches and banks begged pardon as they slipped and fell. People in the unsafe doors set out for earth that escaped them, and trod too late on streets that hurried away. It was more than most men could afford but far more than they could avoid. It was a lame evening. No taxi would take any man to the right place.

This was what happened everywhere when the movement began. The title of the earthquake was "Atlas watches every evening."

THEN UP JUMPED a great fatman in one of the stadiums. He thought that he was god and that he could stop everything from moving. He thought that since he could, he had to. He cried out loud. He swore at the top of his voice. He fired off a gun and made the people listen. He roared and he boasted and made himself known. He blew back into the wind and stamped on the rolling earth and swore up and down he could make it all stop with his invention. He got up in the teeth of the storm and made a loud speech which everybody heard. And the first thing he said was this:

"If anything moves, I am the one to move it: and if anything stops, I am the one to stop it. If anything shakes I am the one to shake it, and not one thing is going to budge unless pushed."

At that moment everything stopped. No one had heard the dim bell at the edge of the sea (which Atlas had struck, in his dream, at this very moment). No one saw the lights in the dark at the edge of the ocean (which had gone on and off with a passing memory in that far place). No one thought of anything, the fatman had all their attention.

NOW THIS FATMAN had been brought up on oats and meat and his name was secret. His father was a grocer and his mother was a butcher. His father was a tailor and his mother ran a train. His father was a brewer and his mother was a general in the army. He had been born with leather hands and a clockwork mind in order to make a lot of money. He hated the country and loved stadiums: a perfect, civilized man! His number was six hundred and sixty-six and he worked hard building up the stadium Atlas had destroyed.

All the people brought him money and played music to him because he was rich. And the music was so loud no one heard the bell ring again. Once again the houses began to tremble.

No one looked at anything, but fixed their eyes only on the fatman in his rage. No one heard Atlas far off thinking in the smoke. All they knew was that the city began to fall again and the fatman roared in the tumbledown theaters: "If I had my way there would be RAIN." He held up his hands and had his way. Rain came down as sudden as a black mountain. The clock struck ten. The world stopped moving. Everyone attributed this to the fatman whose name was secret.

Then in the holes of the broken city the sergeants smiled safe and guns became a thing of the present. Gas was mercy then to many a Jew mother and a quick end came to more than a few as a gift of the popular state. "Here comes a chemical death, with the smile of the public Father. You shall be cheaply made extinct as a present from economy, and we will save your hair and teeth. Cyanide hopes are the face of a popular tomorrow, with ever more fun in the underwears. Everybody has dollars in the home of well-run Demos, and more for cars than for Sunday. But Sunday is public also where Fatman has his office. Only a different name, that's all.

"*Here comes chemical Sunday, with a smile of the Fatman's ghost father. They take the girth of the Fat Father's own gas, on top of the ancient marsh, in the name of a new culture. Toy thugs jump out of every cradle with weapons in their hands. They swing by hard and mean in the name of popularity and boy, that popularity is going to make you jump. It is already famous what they can do with guns, and more so with a piece of small invented pipe, all for the fame and benefit of the new police. Fatman, Fatman, blow us a gassy kiss from the four chimneys of your new heaven!*"

From the four sides of the wind there came together in trolleys a set of delegations in the name of Dad. "Not forgetting Mom" they blowed, "we come to hail the Fatman in the name of Dad." And old Dad sat up high in the memories of the police, a nineteenth-century legend, a corncob angle measuring the west. A piece of trueblue old gold faked-up fortune. True Dad is all fixed up in the mind like a piece of Real Estate, but Mom (cries the Fatman) Mom is real heart and all soft in the easies. Mom is fat from toe to toe, and slimmer than an ankle. Good old American Maw is Father's boast on wedding-cake afternoon, in the days of Coca-Cola. Maw is safe in the new car and Paw cares for corners. The eyes of the innocent sergeant salute Maw with pride as they draw Jewish blood. And we will have a clean America for our boys, clean as the toy toughs punished in rugged Lux. Tomboy Maw is the magic of Fatman's perpetual boast.

Then the fatman moved by intuition placed his feet in the water and established contact with the spirit of night and the waves thrashed about his knees. All at once he began to grow. He gave up meat to become an ascetic. He drank only the most inexpensive mouthwash. He dealt with woman only by mail. He tried out his hands on the sky and began to hold up the firmament. He would hold up the sky and preach at the same time, for he was suddenly religious. He began to list all the dates of history and to tell men another word for love and another word for death. He said he himself was the eldest child of love and death, but principally of death. At this he returned to his meat and dropped his letters and dealt with woman once again directly. He said he could also tell them another name for woman. The people took down notes of what he said next, and he told them his own real name was god.

WE WHO STOOD far off amid the tears of the African night, we who stood with our feet on a hot land, we knew who had rung the bell and changed the weather. We knew who had sent rain. We knew which was power and which was image, which was light and which was legend. And we knew which of the two had his heart at the bottom of the ocean. We knew who watched and who moved under the theaters every time the bell rang. We listened intently to the cloud and the darkness. We lived upon distance, and leaned upon emptiness until we heard our mountain think plain in his own cloud.

"Smoke is not measured by clocks" said Atlas. "Time is not told by disasters. Years are not numbered by the wars that are in them, days are not marked on the calendar for the murders that take place on them. What is it that you are measuring, fatman? What is it that you are interpreting with your machine, meatman? What is it that you are counting, you square, serious stepson of death?

"I take my own time," said Atlas, "which is the time of the sea. The sea tells its own long time, not by the moon or by the sun or by any clock. The time of the sea is infinitely various, and out of it comes all life: but only when the time of the sea is the time of the sun. Not the time of rising and setting, but the time of light itself, which has no hours.

"The sea's time is the time of long life. The jungle's time is the time of many rains. The spirit of the trees takes time out of the slow earth and the leaves are made of this earthtime turning into light. Longer life still undersea, for invisible Tritons. The long life of the earth. The life of spinning suns.

"The gods of the sea tell no time. They are busy with their own music. I Atlas improve the world with mists, evenings, and colors. I have my own music of clouds, skies, and centuries. I strike music from far continents. Others do not hear. They have heard nothing of this a long time. They have heard clock and cannon, not my music. They have eaten smoke and gone down by train to the last mute home of welfare, which is the end.

"Sad is the city of the fatman, for all his industry. Snow cannot make softer the city of the fatman, which is always black in its own breath. Rain cannot wash clean the city of the mercenary, which is always gray with his own despair. Light cannot make fair their houses or wine their faces, though they swim in millions they have won. The fatman with his inventions is propping up a fallen heaven."

Shall we forget the periods of his earthly mischief, not with regret? Shall we forget the fatman and his false rain? The people in that city shuddered and the rain ran down their necks and the fatman struggled with his stadium.

"Fatman" said Atlas, "you are a faithless mad son of clocks and buzzers. I do not know what apparatus was your sire, you bastard of two machines, born with another million. Your mother is not the ocean, your father has not the sun in his heart, you do not know the smell of the earth, your blood is not your own, it is taken from armies. A red flash goes on and off for every thought in your head and a buzzer announces your latest word. I abhor the traffic that comes from such a mad, convulsive mouth. It is the mouth of a horde, the mouth of a system, the mouth of a garage, the mouth of a commission."

Atlas stopped speaking and the rain ended. The fatman raged in his place and all the people sweated under attack. Crowds expected the fatman to stand up for his honor and for the first time to move the world with his invention. Instead he only argued with himself and though he bragged he instantly called himself a liar. But in the same breath he accused Atlas of the most shameful infamies. "Atlas is responsible," he said, "for doors and windows, stairs, chimneys, and every other form of evil." In attacking Atlas he ended by moving no one but himself, and this was the burden of his display:

"Thirteen is an unlucky number and there are *thirteen in this theater.*" (This was his first bravery and very nearly his last, the heart of his argument. For though he said much more, he barely moved beyond this point: oh lucky thirteen!)

"Do you see," he cried, "do you see around me the thirteen beards of Victor Hugo and Karl Marx? Do you see around me the spectacles of Edison, Rockefeller, and behind me the comforting pokerfaces of Stakhanov and Patton? Do you see above my head the thirteen mustaches of Hitler and of Stalin? You who see these thirteen see me and my fathers. . . .

"Now I have fought the elements for thirteen days and nights with my invention. The elements will never be the same again. There were thirteen floods when the world was destroyed for the first time and thirteen sat together at supper in one room when very big business was done by my cousin Judas. (My cousins all prosper in business. We are not lucky in love.)

"Now that the fates are measuring more fires for the cities of men, and I myself am inventing more of them, and walls begin to shake at the work of the atheist Atlas, I stand here to defy walls, fires, earthquake and enemy. I stand here to defy Atlas. Yes I stand here in the name of clean government to defy this upsquirt downpush four-five-six confusion of aliens. Yes I maintain this Atlas is no longer public, and never was mechanical. Is he insured? Has he a license? Ask him for his card, his thumbprint, and his serial number. Has he been registered? Has he been certified? I have been all these things not once but thirteen times, which is fourteen stars on my best stripe. I am the auspicious beginning and the prosperous end, the lucky winner and the marvelous defeat. I am alone in the public eye on thirteen counts. Mine is the middle of the stadium.

"I alone shall shake walls in the future. I alone shall light thirteen fires, or more, or less. I alone shall determine right and wrong; establish time and season; plan day and night as I please, and the sex and the future of children. I alone shall spite or command sea, wind and element. And now by God I hear thirteen allegedly just men walking under the oilcloth and if they don't stop I'LL FIRE!"

WELL, AS YOU MIGHT EXPECT, the citizens came out with bands to hail the fatman, since this had been arranged. But the fatman by now was lost in his own smoke. The strength ebbed out of his invention, and his hands fell slack; his eyes popped out and his fat began to get away from him in all the heat he had caused with his speech. The men in the bands continued to perspire and blow. Their horns would shiver till the drums fell in. There was no rain and the fatman was smaller than a baby. Winds were still as death; buildings swayed for the last fall. Everyone knew the fatman would not get out of the way in time. Generals cried to the fatman as they left by all windows, telling him to jump, but nobody heard his answer.

Then Atlas stood over the world holding up the sky like a great wall of clear ice and the fatman saw Atlas was not his friend. The fatman was blinded by the glare of the ice and closed his eyes upon a world that had been made hateful by his own folly.

So winter comes to the ocean and the quiet city wears plumes of smoke upon helmets of ice. It is a time of golden windows and of a steel sun, a time of more bitter cruelty than before, though the fatman is gone. For even the just man now kills without compunction, because it is duty to be hard and to destroy is mercy. Justice is a myth made of numbers. Mercy is love of system. Christmas goes by without a sound because there are no sinners any more, every one is just.

NO NEED of feast days when everyone is just: no one needs to be saved. No one needs to think. No one needs to confess.

The cold saints of the new age count with their machine the bitter, methodical sacrifices they are making in the fatman's memory, and stand in line before his tomb. Sacrifice is counted in drops of blood (where blood is still left, for many can do without it).

Minutes are counted like Aztecs walking a man to his death with his heart out on top of a bad pyramid: such is order and justice. Such is the beauty of system.

So the children of scandal sit all day in the icy windows and try in vain to shed one tear: but in a time of justice tears are of no avail.

For the just man there is no consolation.

For the good there is no pardon.

For the holy there is no absolution.

Let no man speak of anything but Law, and let no work support anyone but the police.

These are the saints the fatman has left us in the kingdom of his order. . . .

Yet Titans under the sea must once again move. When warmth comes again to the sea, the Titans of spring shall wake. Life shall wake underground and under sea. The fields will laugh, the woods will be drunk with flowers of rebellion, the night will make every fool sing in his sleep and the morning will make them stand up in the sun and cover themselves with water and with light. There is another kind of justice than the justice of number, which can neither forgive nor be forgiven. There is another kind of mercy than the mercy of Law which knows no absolution. There is a justice of newborn worlds which cannot be counted. There is a mercy of individual things that spring into being without reason. They are just without reason, and their mercy is without explanation. They have received rewards beyond description because they themselves refuse to be described. They are virtuous in the sight of God because their names do not identify them. Every plant that stands in the light of the sun is a saint and an outlaw. Every tree that brings forth blossoms without the command of man is powerful in the sight of God. Every star that man has not counted is a world of sanity and perfection. Every blade of grass is an angel singing in a shower of glory.

These are worlds of themselves. No man can use or destroy them. Theirs is the life that moves without being seen and cannot be understood. It is useless to look for what is everywhere. It is hopeless to hope for what cannot be gained because you already have it. The fire of a wild white sun has eaten up the distance between hope and despair. Dance in this sun you tepid idiot. Wake up and dance in the clarity of perfect contradiction.

You fool, it is life that makes you dance: have you forgotten? Come out of the smoke, the world is tossing in its sleep, the sun is up, the land is bursting in the silence of dawn. The clear bell of Atlas rings once again over the sea and the animals come to the shore at his feet. The gentle earth relaxes and spreads out to embrace the strong sun. The grasses and flowers speak their own secret names. With his great gentle hands, Atlas opens the clouds and birds spill back onto the land out of Paradise.

You fool, the prisons are open. The fatman is forgotten. The fatman was only his own nightmare. Atlas never knew him. Atlas never knew anything but the ways of the stars, of the earth and of the ocean. Atlas is a friendly mountain, with a cloud on his shoulder, watching the rising sun.

THE BEHAVIOR OF TITANS

I<small>N</small> <small>THE</small> <small>FOURTH</small> <small>CENTURY</small> <small>A.D.</small> the deserts of Egypt, Palestine, Arabia, and Persia were peopled by a race of men who have left behind them a strange reputation. They were the first Christian hermits, who abandoned the cities of the pagan world to live in solitude. Why did they do this? The reasons were many and various, but they can all be summed up in one word as the quest for "salvation." And what was salvation? Certainly it was not something they sought in mere exterior conformity to the customs and dictates of any social group. In those days men had become keenly conscious of the strictly individual character of "salvation." Society—which meant pagan society, limited by the horizons and prospects of life "in this world"—was regarded by them as a shipwreck from which each single individual man had to swim for his life. We need not stop here to discuss the fairness of this view: what matters is to remember that it was a fact. These were men who believed that to let oneself drift along, passively accepting the tenets and values of what they knew as society, was purely and simply a disaster. The fact that the Emperor was now Christian and that the "world" was coming to know the Cross as a sign of temporal power only strengthened them in their resolve.

It should seem to us much stranger than it does, this paradoxical flight from the world that attained its greatest dimensions (I almost said frenzy) when the "world" became officially Christian. These men seem to have thought, as a few rare modern thinkers like Berdyaev have thought, that there is really no such thing as a "Christian state." They seem to have doubted that Christianity and politics could ever be mixed to such an extent as to produce a fully Christian society. In other words, for them the only Christian society was spiritual and extramundane: the Mystical Body of Christ. These were surely extreme views, and it is almost scandalous to recall them in a time like ours when Christianity is accused on all sides of preaching negativism and withdrawal—of having no effective way of meeting the problems of the age. But let us not be too superficial. The Desert Fathers did, in fact, meet the "problems of their time" in the sense that *they* were among the few who were ahead of their time, and opened the way for the development of a new man and a new society. They represent what modern social philosophers (Jaspers, Mumford) call the emergence of the "axial man," the forerunner of the modern personalist man. The eighteenth and nineteenth centuries with their pragmatic individualism degraded and corrupted the psychological heritage of axial man with its debt to the Desert Fathers and other contemplatives, and prepared the way for the great regression to the herd mentality that is taking place now.

The flight of these men to the desert was neither purely negative nor purely individualistic. They were not rebels against society. The Desert Fathers declined to be ruled by men, but had no desire to rule over others themselves. Nor did they fly from human fellowship—the very fact that they uttered these "words" of advice to one another is proof that they were eminently social. The society they sought was one where all men were truly equal, where the only authority under God was the charismatic authority of wisdom, experience, and love. Of course, they acknowledged the benevolent, hierarchical authority of their bishops: but the bishops were far away and said little about what went on in the desert until the great Origenist conflict at the end of the fourth century.

What the Fathers sought most of all was their own true self, in Christ. And in order to do this, they had to reject completely the false, formal self, fabricated under social compulsion in "the world." They sought a way to God that was uncharted and freely chosen, not inherited from others who had mapped it out beforehand. They sought a God whom they alone could find, not one who was "given" in a set, stereotyped form by somebody else. Not that they rejected any of the dogmatic formulas of the Christian faith: they accepted and clung to them in their simplest and most elementary shape. But they were slow (at least in the beginning, in the time of their primitive wisdom) to get involved in theological controversy. Their flight to the arid horizons of the desert meant also a refusal to be content with arguments, concepts, and technical verbiage.

Obviously such a path could only be traveled by one who was very alert and very sensitive to the landmarks of a trackless wilderness. The hermit had to be a man mature in faith, humble and detached from himself to a degree that is altogether terrible. The spiritual cataclysms that sometimes overtook some of the presumptuous visionaries of the desert are there to show the dangers of the lonely life—like bones whitening in the sand. The Desert Father could not afford to be an illuminist. He could not dare risk attachment to his own ego, or the dangerous ecstasy of self-will. He could not retain the slightest identification with his superficial, transient, self-constructed self. He had to lose himself in the inner, hidden reality of a self that was transcendent, mysterious, half known, and lost in Christ. He had to die to the values of transient existence as Christ had died to them on the Cross, and rise from the dead with Him in the light of an entirely new wisdom. Hence the life of sacrifice, which started out from a clean break, separating the monk from the world. A life continued in "compunction" which taught him to lament the madness of attachment to unreal values. A life of solitude and labor, poverty and fasting, charity and prayer which enabled the old superficial self to be purged away and permitted the gradual emergence of the true, secret self in which the Believer and Christ were "one Spirit."

Finally, the proximate end of all this striving was "purity of heart" —a clear unobstructed vision of the true state of affairs, an intuitive grasp of one's own inner reality as anchored, or rather lost, in God through Christ. The fruit of this was *quies*: "rest." Not rest of the body, nor even fixation of the exalted spirit upon some point or summit of light. The Desert Fathers were not, for the most part, ecstatics. Those who were have left some strange and misleading stories behind them to confuse the true issue. The "rest" which these men sought was simply the sanity and poise of a being that no longer has to look at itself because it is carried away by the perfection of freedom that is in it. And carried where? Wherever Love itself, or the Divine Spirit, sees fit to go. Rest, then, was a kind of simple no-whereness and no-mindedness that had lost all preoccupation with a false or limited "self." At peace in the possession of a sublime "Nothing" the spirit laid hold, in secret, upon the "All"—without trying to know what is possessed.

In many respects, therefore, these Desert Fathers had much in common with Indian Yogis and with Zen Buddhist monks of China and Japan. If we were to seek their like in twentieth-century America, we would have to look in strange, out-of-the-way places. Such beings are tragically rare. They obviously do not flourish on the sidewalk at

Forty-second Street and Broadway. We might perhaps find someone like this among the Pueblo Indians or the Navahos: but there the case would be entirely different. You would have simplicity, primitive wisdom: but rooted in a primitive society. With the Desert Fathers, you have the characteristic of a clean break with a conventional, accepted social context in order to swim for one's life into an apparently irrational void.

Though I might be expected to claim that men like this could be found in some of our monasteries of contemplatives, I will not be so bold. With us it is often rather a case of men leaving the society of the "world" in order to fit themselves into another kind of society, that of the religious family which they enter. They exchange the values, concepts, and rites of the one for those of the other. And since we now have centuries of monasticism behind us, this puts the whole thing in a different light. The social "norms" of a monastic family are also apt to be conventional, and to live by them does not involve a leap into the void—only a radical change of customs and standards. The words and examples of the Desert Fathers have been so much a part of monastic tradition that time has turned them into stereotypes for us, and we are no longer able to notice their fabulous originality. We have buried them, so to speak, in our own routines, and thus securely insulated ourselves against any form of spiritual shock from their lack of conventionality.

The Desert Fathers were pioneers, with nothing to go on but the example of some of the prophets, like St. John the Baptist, Elias, Eliseus, and the Apostles, who also served them as models. For the rest, the life they embraced was "angelic" and they walked the untrodden paths of invisible spirits. Their cells were the furnace of Babylon in which, in the midst of flames, they found themselves with Christ.

They neither courted the approval of their contemporaries nor sought to provoke their disapproval, because the opinions of others had ceased, for them, to be matters of importance. They had no set doctrine about freedom, but they had in fact become free by paying the price of freedom.

In any case these Fathers distilled for themselves a very practical and unassuming wisdom that is at once primitive and timeless, and which enables us to reopen the sources that have been polluted or blocked up altogether by the accumulated mental and spiritual refuse of our technological barbarism. Our time is in desperate need of this kind of simplicity.

What can we gain by sailing to the moon if we are not able to cross the abyss that separates us from ourselves? This is the most important of all voyages of discovery, and without it all the rest are not only useless but disastrous. Proof: the great travelers and colonizers of the Renaissance were, for the most part, men who perhaps were capable of the things they did precisely because they were alienated from themselves. In subjugating primitive worlds they only imposed on them, with the force of cannons, their own confusion and their own alienation. Superb exceptions like Fray Bartolome de las Casas, St. Francis Xavier, or Father Matthew Ricci, only prove the rule.

THE DESERT FATHERS insisted on remaining human and "ordinary." This may seem to be a paradox, but it is very important. If we reflect a moment, we will see that to fly into the desert in order to be extraordinary is only to carry the world with you as an implicit standard of comparison. The result would be nothing but self-contemplation, and self-comparison with the negative standard of the world one had abandoned. Some of the monks of the Desert did this, as a matter of fact: and the only fruit of their trouble was that they went out of their heads. The simple men who lived their lives out to a good old age among the rocks and sands only did so because they had come into the desert to be themselves, their *ordinary* selves, and to forget a world that divided them from themselves. There can be no other valid reason for seeking solitude or for leaving the world. And thus to leave the world, is, in fact, to help save it in saving oneself. This is the final point, and it is an important one. The Coptic hermits who left the world as though escaping from a wreck, did not merely intend to save themselves. They knew that they were helpless to do any good for others as long as they floundered about in the wreckage. But once they got a foothold on solid ground, things were different. Then they had not only the power but even the obligation to pull the whole world to safety after them.

This is their paradoxical lesson for our time. It would perhaps be too much to say that the world needs another movement such as that which drew these men into the deserts of Egypt and Palestine. Ours is certainly a time for solitaries and for hermits. But merely to reproduce the simplicity, austerity, and prayer of these primitive souls is not a complete or satisfactory answer. We must transcend them, and transcend all those who, since their time, have gone beyond the limits which they set. We must liberate ourselves, in our own way, from involvement in a world that is plunging to disaster. But our world is different from theirs. Our involvement in it is more complete. Our danger is far more desperate. Our time, perhaps, is shorter than we think.

We cannot do exactly what they did. But we must be as thorough and as ruthless in our determination to break all spiritual chains, and cast off the domination of alien compulsions, to find our true selves, to discover and develop our inalienable spiritual liberty and use it to build, on earth, the Kingdom of God. This is not the place in which to speculate what our great and mysterious vocation might involve. That is still unknown. Let it suffice for me to say that we need to learn from these men of the fourth century how to ignore prejudice, defy compulsion, and strike out fearlessly into the unknown.

THE WISDOM OF THE DESERT

Four: THE RECOVERY OF PARADISE

O<small>NE</small> OF Dostoevski's "saints," the Staretz Zosima who speaks as a typical witness to the tradition of the Greek and Russian Church, makes an astonishing declaration. He says: "We do not understand that life is paradise, for it suffices only to wish to understand it, and at once paradise will appear in front of us in all its beauty." Taken in the context of the *Brothers Karamazov*, against the background of violence, blasphemy, and murder which fill the book, this is indeed an astonishing statement. Was Zosima perfectly serious? Or was he simply a deluded idiot, dreaming the frantic dreams inspired by the "opium of the people"?

Whatever the modern reader may think of this claim, it was certainly something basic to primitive Christianity. Modern studies of the Fathers have revealed beyond question that one of the main motives that impelled men to embrace the "angelic life" (*bios angelikos*) of solitude and poverty in the desert was precisely the hope that by so doing they might return to paradise.

Now this concept must be properly and accurately understood. Paradise is not "heaven." Paradise is a state, or indeed a place, on earth. Paradise belongs more properly to the present than to the future life, In some sense it belongs to both. It is the state in which man was originally created to live on earth. It is also conceived as a kind of antechamber to heaven after death—as for instance at the end of Dante's *Purgatorio*. Christ, dying on the cross, said to the good thief at His side: "This day thou shalt be with me *in Paradise*," and it was clear that this did not mean, and could not have meant, heaven.

We must not imagine Paradise as a place of ease and sensual pleasure. It is a state of peace and rest, by all means. But what the Desert Fathers sought when they believed they could find "paradise" in the desert was the lost innocence, the emptiness and purity of heart which had belonged to Adam and Eve in Eden. Evidently they could not have expected to find beautiful trees and gardens in the waterless desert, burned by the sun. Obviously they did not expect to find a place, among the fiery rocks and caves, where they could recline at ease in shady groves, by cool running water. What they sought was paradise within themselves, or rather above and beyond themselves. They sought paradise in the recovery of that "unity" which had been shattered by the "knowledge of good and evil."

In the beginning, Adam was "one man." The Fall had divided him into "a multitude." Christ had restored man to unity in Himself. The Mystical Christ was the "New Adam" and in Him all men could return to unity, to innocence, to purity, and become "one man." *Omnes in Christo unum.* This meant, of course, living not by one's own will, one's own ego, one's own limited and selfish spirit, but being "one spirit" with Christ. "Those who are united to the Lord," says St. Paul, "are *one spirit.*" Union with Christ means unity in Christ, so that each one who is in Christ can say, with Paul: "It is now not I that live but Christ that lives in me." It is the same Christ who lives in all. The individual has "died" with Christ to his "old man," his exterior, egotistical self, and "risen" in Christ to the new man, a selfless and divine being, who is the one Christ, the same who is "all in all."

The great difference between Christianity and Buddhism arises at this juncture. From the metaphysical point of view, Buddhism seems to take "emptiness" as a complete negation of all personality, whereas Christianity finds, in purity of heart and "unity of spirit," a supreme and transcendent fulfillment of personality. This is an extremely complex and difficult question which I am not prepared to discuss. But it seems to me that most discussions on the point, up to now, have been completely equivocal. Very often, on the Christian side, we identify "personality" with the illusory and exterior ego-self, which is certainly not the true Christian "person." On the Buddhist side there seems to be no positive idea of personality at all: it is a value which seems to be completely missing from Buddhist thought. Yet it is certainly not absent from Buddhist practice, as is evident from Dr. Suzuki's remark that at the end of Zen training, when one has become "absolutely naked," one finds himself to be the ordinary "Tom, Dick, or Harry" that he has been all along. This seems to me, in practice, to correspond to the idea that a Christian can lose his "old man" and find his true self "in Christ." The main difference is that the language and practice of Zen are much more radical, austere, and ruthless, and that where the Zen-man says "emptiness" he leaves no room for any image or concept to confuse the real issue. The Christian treatment of the subject makes free use of richly metaphorical expressions and of concrete imagery, but we must take care to penetrate beyond the exterior surface and reach the inner depths. In any case the "death of the old man" is not the destruction of personality but the dissipation of an illusion, and the discovery of the new man is the realization of what was there all along, at least as a radical possibility, by reason of the fact that man is the image of God.

These Christian themes of "life in Christ" and "unity in Christ" are familiar enough, but one feels that today they are not understood in all their spiritual depth. Their mystical implications are seldom explored. We dwell rather, with much greater interest, on their social, economic, and ethical implications. I wonder if what Dr. Suzuki has said about "emptiness" ought not to help us to go deeper than we usually do into this doctrine of our mystical unity and purity in Christ. Anyone who has read St. John of the Cross and his doctrine of "night" will be inclined to ask the same question. If we are to die to ourselves and live "in Christ," does that not mean that we must somehow find ourselves "dead" and "empty" with regard to our old self? If we are to be moved in all things by the grace of Christ should we not in some sense realize this as action out-of-emptiness, springing from the mystery of the pure freedom which is "divine love," rather than as something produced in and with our egotistical, exterior self, springing from our desires and referred to our own spiritual interest?

St. John of the Cross compares man to a window through which the light of God is shining. If the windowpane is clean of every stain, it is completely transparent, we do not see it at all: it is "empty" and nothing is seen but the light. But if a man bears in himself the stains of spiritual egotism and preoccupation with his illusory and exterior self, even in "good things," then the windowpane itself is clearly seen by reason of the stains that are on it. Hence if a man can be rid of the stains and dust produced within him by his fixation upon what is good and bad in reference to himself, he will be transformed in God and will be "one with God." In the terms of St. John of the Cross:

In thus allowing God to work in it, the soul (having rid itself of every mist and stain of creatures, which consists in having its will perfectly united with that of God, for to love is to labour to detach and strip itself for God's sake of all that is not God), is at once illumined and transformed in God, and

God communicates to it His supernatural being in such wise that the soul appears to be God Himself, and has all that God Himself has. . . . All the things of God and the soul are one in participant transformation; and the soul seems to be God rather than the soul, and is indeed God by participation.[1]

This, as we shall see, is what the Fathers called "purity of heart," and it corresponds to a recovery of the innocence of Adam in Paradise. The many stories of the Desert Fathers in which they are shown to have exercised an extraordinary control over wild animals were originally undestood as a manifestation of this recovery of paradisiacal innocence. As one of the early writers, Paul the Hermit, declared: "If anyone acquires purity, everything will submit to him as it did to Adam in paradise before the Fall." [2]

If we admit Staretz Zosima's statement that paradise is something attainable because, after all, it is present within us and we have only to discover it there, we may still pause to question one part of his statement: "one has *only to wish to understand it,* and at once paradise will appear before us in all its beauty." That seems to be a little too easy. Much more is required than a simple velleity. Anyone can make a wish. But the kind of "wishing" that Zosima refers to here is something far beyond daydreaming and wishful thinking. It means, of course, a complete upheaval and transformation of one's whole life. One has to "wish" for this one realization alone and give up wishing for anything else. One has to forget the quest of every other "good." One has to devote himself with his whole heart and soul to the recovery of his "innocence." And yet, as Dr. Suzuki has so well pointed out, and as the Christian doctrine of grace teaches us in other terms, this cannot be the work of our own "self." It is useless for the "self" to try to "purify itself," or for the "self" to "make a place in itself" for God. The innocence and purity of heart which belong to paradise are a complete emptiness of self in which all is the work of God, the free and unpredictable expression of His love, the work of grace. In the purity of original innocence, all is done in us but without us, *in nobis et sine nobis.* But before we reach that level, we must also learn to work on the other level of "knowledge"—*scientia*—where grace works in us but "not without us"—*in nobis sed non sine nobis.*

Dr. Suzuki has, in his own terms, very aptly pointed out that it would be a serious error to think that one could hoist himself back by his own bootstraps into the state of innocence and go on blissfully with no further concern about the present life. Innocence does not cast out or destroy knowledge. The two must go together. That, indeed, was where many apparently spiritual men have failed. Some of them were so innocent that they had lost all contact with everyday reality of life in a struggling and complex world of men. But theirs was not true innocence. It was fictitious, a perversion and frustration of the real spiritual life. It was the emptiness of the quietist, an emptiness that was merely blank and silly: an absence of knowledge without the presence of wisdom. It was the narcissistic ignorance of the baby, not the emptiness of the saint who is moved, without reflection or self-consciousness, by the grace of God.

II

ONCE WE FIND OURSELVES in the state of "knowledge of good and evil" we have to accept the fact and understand our position, see it in relation to the innocence for which we were created, which we have lost and which we can regain. But in the meantime it is a question of treating knowledge and innocence as complementary realities. This was the most delicate problem confronting the Desert Fathers, and for many of them it led to disaster. They recognized the difference between "knowledge of good and evil" on the one hand, and innocence or emptiness on the other. But, as Dr. Suzuki has wisely observed, they ran the risk of oversimplified and abstract solutions. Too many of them wanted to get along simply with innocence without knowledge. In our *Sayings,* John the Dwarf is a case in point. He wants to reach a state in which there is no temptation, no further stirring of the slightest passion.[3] All this is nothing but a refinement of "knowledge." Instead of leading to innocence, it leads to the most quintessentially pure love of self. It leads to the creation of a pseudo emptiness, an exquisitely purified self that is so perfect that it can rest in itself without any trace of crude reflection. Yet this is not emptiness: there remains a "self" that is the subject of purity and the possessor of emptiness. And this, as the Desert Fathers saw, is the final triumph of the subtle tempter. It leaves a man rooted and imprisoned in his pure self, a clever discerner of good and evil, of self and nonself, purity and impurity. But he is not innocent. He is a master of spiritual knowledge. And as such, he is still subject to accusation from the devil. Since he is *perfect,* he is subject to the greatest deception of all. If he were *innocent,* he would be free from deception.

The man who has truly found his spiritual nakedness, who has realized he is empty, is not a self that has *acquired* emptiness or *be-*

come empty. He just "is empty from the beginning," as Dr. Suzuki has observed. Or, to put it in the more affective terms of St. Augustine and St. Bernard, he "loves with a pure love." That is to say he loves with a purity and freedom that spring spontaneously and directly from the fact that he has fully recovered the divine likeness, and is now fully his true self because he is lost in God. He is one with God, and identified with God and hence knows nothing of any ego in himself.[4] All he knows is love. As St. Bernard says: "He who loves thus, simply loves, and knows nothing else but love." *Qui amat, amat et aliud novit nihil.*

<h1 style="text-align:center">III</h1>

ONE THING, and this is most important, remains to be said. Purity of heart is not the *ultimate end* of the monk's striving in the desert. It is only a step toward it. We have said above that Paradise is not yet heaven. Paradise is not the final goal of the spiritual life. It is, in fact, only a return to the true beginning. It is a "fresh start." The monk who has realized in himself purity of heart, and has been restored, in some measure, to the innocence lost by Adam, has still not ended his journey. He is only ready to begin. He is ready for a new work "which eye hath not seen, ear hath not heard, nor hath it entered into the heart of man to conceive." Purity of heart, says John Cassian, is the intermediate end of the spiritual life. But the ultimate end is the Kingdom of God. This is a dimension which does not enter into the realm of Zen.

One might argue that this simply overturns all that has been said about emptiness, and brings us back into a state of dualism, and therefore to "knowledge of good and evil," duality between man and God, etc. Such is by no means the case. Purity of heart establishes man in a state of unity and emptiness in which he is one with God. But this is the necessary preparation not for further struggle between good and evil, but for the real work of God which is revealed in the Bible: the work of the *new creation*, the resurrection from the dead, the restoration of all things in Christ. This is the real dimension of Christianity, the eschatalogical dimension which is peculiar to it, and which has no parallel in Buddhism. The world was created without man, but the new creation which is the true Kingdom of God is to be the work of God in and through man. It is to be the great, mysterious, theandric work of the Mystical Christ, the New Adam, in whom all men as "one Person" or one "Son of God" will transfigure the cosmos and offer it resplendent to the Father. Here, in this transfiguration, will take place the apocalyptic marriage between God and His creation, the final and perfect consummation of which no mortal mysticism is able to dream and which is barely foreshadowed in the symbols and images of the last pages of the Apocalypse.

Here, of course, we are back in the realm of concept and image. To think about these things, to speculate on them, is, perhaps, to depart from "emptiness." But it is an activity of faith that belongs to our realm of knowledge, and conditions us for a superior and more vigilant innocence: the innocence of the wise virgins who wait with lighted lamps, with an emptiness that is enkindled by the glory of the Divine Word and enflamed with the presence of the Holy Spirit. That glory and that presence are not objects which "enter into" emptiness to "fill" it. They are nothing else but God's own "suchness."

[1] St. John of the Cross, *Ascent to Mount Carmel,* II, v. Peers trans. vol. i, p. 82.

[2] Quoted in Stolz, Dom Anselm, *Théologie de la Mystique,* Chevetogne, 1947, p. 31.

[3] "Abbot Pastor said that Abbot John the Dwarf had prayed to the Lord and the Lord had taken away all his passions, so that he became impassible. And in this condition he went to one of the elders and said: You see before you a man who is completely at rest and has no more temptations. The elder said: Go and pray to the Lord to command some struggle to be stirred up in you, for the soul is matured only in battles. And when the temptations started up again he did not pray that the struggle be taken away from him, but only said: Lord, give me strength to get through the fight."—*The Wisdom of The Desert,* XCI.

[4] Even when the soul is mystically united with God there remains, according to Christian theology, a distinction between the nature of the soul and the nature of God. Their perfect unity is not then a fusion of natures, but a unity of love and of experience. The distinction between the soul and God is no longer experienced as a separation into subject and object when the soul is united to God.

Five: POEMS

IN THE RAIN AND THE SUN

Watch out for this peeled doorlight!
Here, without rain, without shame
My noonday dusk made spots upon the walk:
Tall drops pelted the concrete with their jewelry
Belonging to the old world's bones.

Owning this view, in the air of a hermit's weather,
I count the fragmentary rain
In drops as blue as coal
Until I plumb the shadows full of thunder.
My prayers supervise the atmosphere
Till storms call all hounds home.

Out of the towers of water
Four or five mountains come walking
To see the little monks' graves.
Flying the neutral stones I dwell between cedars
And see the countries sleeping in their beds:
Lands of the watermen, where poplars bend.
Wild seas amuse the world with water:
No end to all the surfs that charm our shores
Fattening the sands with their old foam and their old roar.

Thus in the boom of waves' advantage
Dogs and lions come to my tame home
Won by the bells of my Cistercian jungle.
O love the livid fringes
In which their robes are drenched!

Songs of the lions and whales!
With my pen between my fingers
Making the waterworld sing!
Sweet Christ, discover diamonds
And sapphires in my verse
While I burn the sap of my pine house
For praise of the ocean sun.

I have walked upon the whole days' surf
Rinsing Thy bays with hymns.
My eyes have swept horizons clean
Of ships and rain.
Upon the lacquered swells my feet no longer run.
Sliding all over the sea I come
To the hap of a slippery harbor.

Dogs have gone back to their ghosts
And the many lions, home.
But words fling wide the windows of their houses—
Adam and Eve walk down my coast
Praising the tears of the treasurer sun:
I hang Thy rubies on these autumn trees,
On the bones of the homegoing thunder.

THE TEARS OF THE BLIND LIONS

WISDOM

I studied it and it taught me nothing.
I learned it and soon forgot everything else:
Having forgotten, I was burdened with knowledge—
The insupportable knowledge of nothing.

How sweet my life would be, if I were wise!
Wisdom is well known
When it is no longer seen or thought of.
Only then is understanding bearable.

THE STRANGE ISLANDS

ELIAS—VARIATIONS ON A THEME

I

Under the blunt pine
In the winter sun
The pathway dies
And the wilds begin.
Here the bird abides
Where the ground is warm
And sings alone.

Listen, Elias,
To the southern wind
Where the grass is brown,
Live beneath this pine
In wind and rain.
Listen to the woods,
Listen to the ground.

O listen, Elias
(Where the bird abides
And sings alone),
The sun grows pale
Where passes One
Who bends no blade, no fern.
Listen to His word.

> *"Where the fields end*
>   *Thou shalt be My friend.*
>   *Where the bird is gone*
>   *Thou shalt be My son."*

How the pine burns
In the furious sun
When the prophets come
To Jerusalem.
(Listen, Elias,
For the fiery wing)
To Jerusalem
Where the knife is drawn.

(Do her children run
To the covering wing?)
Look, look, My son,
At the smashed wood
At the bloody stone.

Where the fields end
And the stars begin
Listen, Elias,
To the winter rain.
For the seed sleeps
By the sleeping stone.
But the seed has life
While the stone has none.

    "Where the fields end
      Thou shalt be My friend.
     Where the bird is gone
     Thou shalt be My son."

II

There were supposed to be
Not birds but spirits of flame
Around the old wagon.
("Bring me my chariot")
There were supposed
To be fiery devices,
Grand machines, all flame,
With supernatural wings
Beyond the full creek.
("Bring me my chariot of fire")
All flame, beyond the rotten tree!
Flame? This old wagon
With the wet, smashed wheels
Is better. ("My chariot")
This derelict is better.
("Of fire.") It abides
(Swifter) in the brown ferns
And burns nothing. Bring me ("Of fire")
Better still the old trailer ("My chariot")
With the dead stove in it, and the rain

Comes down the pipe and covers the floor.
Bring me my chariot of rain. Bring me
My old chariot of broken-down rain.
Bring, bring my old fire, my old storm,
My old trailer; faster and faster it stands still,
Faster and faster it stays where it has always been,
Behind the felled oaks, faster, burning nothing.
Broken and perfect, facing south,
Facing the sound of distant guns,
Facing the wall of distance where blue hills
Hide in the fading rain.

Where the woods are cut down the punished
Trailer stands alone and becomes
(Against all the better intentions of the owners)
The House of God
The Gate of Heaven.
("My chariot of fire")

III

The seed, as I have said,
Hides in the frozen sod.
Stones, shaped by rivers they will
Never care about or feel,
Cover the cultivated soil.

The seed, by nature, waits to grow and bear
Fruit. Therefore it is not alone
As stones, or inanimate things are:
That is to say, alone by nature,
Or alone forever.

Where do so many waters come from on an empty hill?
Rain we had despaired of, rain
Which is sent from somewhere else, descended
To fix an exhausted mountain.
Listen to the waters, if possible,
And discern the words "False prophet"
False prophet! "So much better is the water's message,
So much more confident than our own. It is quite sure
You are a false prophet, so 'Go back'

(You have not had the patience of a rock or tree)
Go back into the cities. They want to receive you
Because you are not sent to them. You are a false prophet."

Go back where everyone, in heavy hours,
Is of a different mind, and each is his own burden,
And each mind is its own division
With sickness for diversion and war for
Business reasons. Go where the divided
Cannot stand to be too well. For then they would be held
Responsible for their own misery.

And I have been a man without silence,
A man without patience, with too many
Questions. I have blamed God
Thinking to blame only men
And defend Him Who does not need to be defended.
I have blamed ("defended") Him for Whom the wise stones
(Stones I lately condemned)
Waited in the patient
Creek that is now wet and clean of all ruins.

So now, if I were to return
To my own city (yes my own city), I would be
Neither accepted nor rejected.
For I have no message,
I would be lost together with the others.

IV

Under the blunt pine
I who am not sent
Remain. The pathway dies,
The journey has begun.
Here the bird abides
And sings on top of the forgotten
Storm. The ground is warm.
He sings no particular message.
His hymn has one pattern, no more planned,
No less perfectly planned
And no more arbitrary

Than the pattern in the seed, the salt,
The snow, the cell, the drop of rain.

   (Snow says: I have my own pattern;
   Rain says: no arbitrary plan!
   River says: I go my own way.
   Bird says: I am the same.
   The pine tree says also:
   Not compulsion plants me in my place,
   No, not compulsion!)

The free man is not alone as busy men are
But as birds are. The free man sings
Alone as universes do. Built
Upon his own inscrutable pattern
Clear, unmistakable, not invented by himself alone
Or for himself, but for the universe also.
Nor does he make it his business to be recognized
Or care to have himself found out
As if some special subterfuge were needed
To get himself known for who he is.

The free man does not float
On the tides of his own expedition
Nor is he sent on ventures as busy men are,
Bound to an inexorable result:
But like the birds or lilies
He seeks first the Kingdom, without care.
Nor need the free man remember
Any street or city, or keep campaigns
In his head, or countries for that matter
Or any other economy.

                Under the blunt pine
Elias becomes his own geography
(Supposing geography to be necessary at all),
Elias becomes his own wild bird, with God in the center,
His own wide field which nobody owns,
His own pattern, surrounding the Spirit
By which he is himself surrounded:

For the free man's road has neither beginning nor end.

                           THE STRANGE ISLANDS

"WHEN IN THE SOUL OF THE SERENE DISCIPLE . . ."

When in the soul of the serene disciple
With no more Fathers to imitate
Poverty is a success,
It is a small thing to say the roof is gone:
He has not even a house.

Stars, as well as friends,
Are angry with the noble ruin.
Saints depart in several directions.

Be still:
There is no longer any need of comment.
It was a lucky wind
That blew away his halo with his cares,
A lucky sea that drowned his reputation.

Here you will find
Neither a proverb nor a memorandum.
There are no ways,
No methods to admire
Where poverty is no achievement.
His God lives in his emptiness like an affliction.

What choice remains?
Well, to be ordinary is not a choice:
It is the usual freedom
Of men without visions.

THE STRANGE ISLANDS

SPRING STORM

When in their ignorance and haste the skies must fall
Upon our white-eyed home, and blindly turn
Feeling the four long limits of the wall,

How unsubstantial is our present state
In the clean blowing of those elements
Whose study is our problem and our fate?

The intellects go mumbling in the snow,
And find the blurred, incredible sun (and moon)
Jammed in the white door, and the troubled straits
The dugout where the fallen sky lies down.
A mess of secret trumpets, with their weight
Of portents, veil the bluntness where we run.

How true a passion has this hour begun!
The sky melts on my patient animal
(My pointless self, the hunter of my home),
My breath burns in the open like a ton
In the blue waking of those elements
Whose study is our quibble and our doom.

O watch the woolen hundreds on the run!

THE STRANGE ISLANDS

DRY PLACES

No cars go by
Where dogs are barking at the desert.
Yet it is not twenty years since many lamps
Shed their juices in this one time town
And stores grew big lights, like oranges and pears.

Now not one lame miner
Sits on the rotten verandah,
Works in the irons where
Judas' shadow dwells.
Yet I could hew a city
From the side of their hill.

O deep stone covert where the dusk
Is full of lighted beasts
And the mad stars preach wars without end:
Whose bushes and grasses live without water,
There the skinny father of hate rolls in his dust
And if the wind should shift one leaf
The dead jump up and bark for their ghosts:
Their dry bones want our penniless souls.

Bones, go back to your baskets.
Get your fingers out of my clean skin.
Rest in your rainless death until your own souls
Come back in the appointed way and sort you out from your remains.

We who are still alive will wring a few green blades
From the floor of this valley
Though plows abhor your metal and your clay.
Rather than starve with you in rocks without oasis,

We will get up and work your loam
Until some prayer or some lean sentence
Bleeds like the quickest root they ever cut.

For we cannot forget the legend of the world's childhood
Or the track to the dogwood valley
And Adam our Father's old grass farm
Wherein they gave the animals names
And knew Christ was promised first without scars
When all God's larks called out to Him
In their wild orchard.

THE TEARS OF THE BLIND LIONS

THE HEAVENLY CITY

City, when we see you coming down,
Coming down from God
To be the new world's crown:
How shall they sing, the fresh, unsalted seas
Hearing your harmonies!

For there is no more death,
No need to cure those waters, now, with any brine;
Their shores give them no dead,
Rivers no blood, no rot to stain them.

Because the cruel algebra of war
Is now no more.
And the steel circle of time, inexorable,
Bites like a padlock shut, forever,
In the smoke of the last bomb:

And in that trap the murderers and sorcerers and crooked leaders
Go rolling home to hell.
And history is done.

Shine with your lamb-light, shine upon the world:
You are the new creation's sun.
And standing on their twelve foundations,
Lo, the twelve gates that are One Christ are wide as canticles:
And Oh! Begin to hear the thunder of the songs within the crystal
    Towers,
While all the saints rise from their earth with feet like light
And fly to tread the quick-gold of those streets,

Oh, City, when we see you sailing down,
Sailing down from God,
Dressed in the glory of the Trinity, and angel-crowned
In nine white diadems of liturgy.

                                        SELECTED POEMS

Six: THEOLOGY OF CREATIVITY

Since there is no genuine creativity apart from God, the man who attempts to be a "creator" outside of God and independent of him is forced to fall back on magic. The sin of the wizard is not so much that he usurps and exercises a real preternatural power, but that his postures travesty the divine by degrading man's freedom in absurd and servile manipulations of reality. The dignity of man is to stand before God on his own feet, alive, conscious, alert to the light that has been placed in him, and perfectly obedient to that light. Wizardry and idolatry obscure the light, dim man's vision, and reduce him to a state of infatuated self-absorption in which he plays at unveiling and displaying powers that were meant to remain secret, not in the sense that they must be concealed from others, but in the sense that the artist ought not to be wasting his own attention upon them or calling the attention of others to them. He should be using them in an "empty" and disinterested manner for the good of others and for the glory of God instead of exploiting them to draw attention to himself. The commandment "to make no graven image" is designed first of all to protect man against his inveterate temptation to make gods in his own image, gods in which he can objectify and venerate the divinely given powers he finds in himself. By this magic man seeks to enjoy in himself those powers that were given him as means to find fulfilment beyond and above himself. This bending back upon self, this fixation upon the exterior self was, for St. Augustine, one of the principal elements in the fall of Adam.[1]

Man's true creativity is lost, then, with his loss of innocence, selflessness, and simplicity. Oblivious of his external self and empty of self, man was originally one with God his creator. So intimate was their union that the creator could live and act with perfect freedom in his created instrument. Having fallen, and been redeemed in Christ, man is once again able to recover this state of innocence and union, in and through Christ. The Spirit of God, the *Creator Spiritus* who brooded over the waters before the world came into being, dwells in man and broods over the abyss of his human spirit, seeking to call forth from it a new world, a new spiritual creation, in union with the liberty of man redeemed in Christ. The theology of creativity will necessarily be the theology of the Holy Spirit re-forming us in the likeness of Christ, raising us from death to life with the very same power which raised Christ from the dead.[2] The theology of creativity will also be a theology of the image and likeness of God in man. The restoration of our creativity is simply one aspect of our recovery of our likeness to God in Christ. The image of God in man is his freedom, say St. Bernard and St. Gregory of Nyssa. The likeness of God in man is fully restored when man's freedom is perfectly united with the divine freedom, and when, consequently man acts in all things as God acts. Or rather when God and man act purely and simply as one. Since "God is love" then for man to be restored to the likeness of God, all his acts must be pure and disinterested love, lacking all taint of that *proprium* which makes him aware of himself as a separate, insecure subject of inordinate needs which he seeks to satisfy at somebody else's expense. Creativity becomes possible in so far as man can forget his limitations and his selfhood and lose himself in abandonment to the immense creative power of a love too great to be seen or comprehended.

A theology of creativity might, then, meditate at some length on the first few chapters of Genesis, the narrative of the creation and the fall. Especially important is Genesis 2:15-24, in which Adam appears as God's collaborator in governing paradise and in which he is given the power to name the animals as he sees fit: "for whatsoever Adam called any living creature, the same is its name." The most significant part of this passage would be sought in the typical sense of verses 21-24, on the creation of Eve. The mystery of Christ and his Church would be the very heart of any fully developed theology of creativity. Patristic works like St. Gregory of Nyssa's *De Hominis Opificio* might furnish a rich variety of intuitions from which to start building a synthesis. We would, of course, have to ransack the works of Origen and St. Augustine. Among the scholastic sources, we ought not to neglect the magnificent *Collationes in Hexaemeron* of St. Bonaventure. Valuable materials for study can only be briefly indicated here.

It would above all be necessary to disentangle the various threads of thought about man's creativity as individual person and man's creativity in society. There can be no doubt that a theology of creativity would give an entirely new perspective to the distorted view produced by undue emphasis on the exceptional personality of the "genius" and his complete independence from all ethical and aesthetic norms by virtue of his talented personality. But the theological view would do nothing to diminish the value of the person: on the contrary, situating the person in his right place in relation to other men and to God, our theology would liberate in him the deepest potentialities of his nature and the highest, most secret endowments of divine grace.

The creativity of the Christian person must be seen in relation to the creative vocation of the new Adam, mystical person of the "whole Christ." The creative will of God has been at work in the cosmos since he said: "Let there be light." This creative *fiat* was not uttered merely at the dawn of time. All time and all history are a continued, uninterrupted creative act, a stupendous, ineffable mystery in which God has signified his will to associate man with himself in his work of creation. The will and power of the Almighty Father were not satisfied simply to make the world and turn it over to man to run it as best he could. The creative love of God was met, at first, by the destructive and self-centered refusal of man: an act of such incalculable consequences that it would have amounted to a destruction of God's plan, if that were possible. But the creative work of God could not be frustrated by man's sin. On the contrary, sin itself entered into that plan. If man was first called to share in the creative work of his heavenly Father, he now became involved in the "new creation," the redemption of his own kind and the restoration of the cosmos, purified and transfigured, into the hands of the Father. God himself became man in order that in this way man could be most perfectly associated with him in this great work, the fullest manifestation of his eternal wisdom and mercy.

The Christian dimensions of creativity are, then, to be meditated in the light of such texts as Ephesians 1:8-10 (the re-establishment of all things in Christ); Colossians 1:9-29 (the work of God building the Church of saints united in Christ, the "firstborn of every creature," and through him reconciling all things to himself). In this text, particularly, we see the creative role of suffering. This is very important. It is the reply to the secular and demonic overemphasis on the individual, his self-fulfillment in art for its own sake. Here, on the contrary, we see that the cross is the center of the new creation: the tree of life, instead of the tree of the knowledge of good and evil. He who has approached the tree of the knowledge of good and evil has tasted the intoxicating fruit of his own special excellence but he dies the death of frustration. He becomes the prisoner of his own gifts and he sticks to his own excellence as if it were flypaper. There is no joy for him because he is alienated from life, love, and communion in creativity by his own demonic self-assertion, which automatically involves a rejection of suffering, of dependence, of charity, and of obedience.

On the contrary, it is the renunciation of our false self, the emptying of self in the likeness of Christ, that brings us to the threshold of that true creativity in which God himself, the creator, works in and through us. The fact that the Christian renounces his own limited ends and satisfactions in order to achieve something greater than he can see or understand means the sacrifice of immediate visible results. But it also means that the efficacy of his action becomes lasting as well as universal. Such creativity does not stop with a little ephemeral success here and there: it reaches out to the ends of time and to the limits of the universe.

[1] *De Trinitate*, xii, ii (PL, XLII, 1007).
[2] Eph. 1:17-21.

Seven: NATIVITY KERYGMA

AUTHOR'S NOTE: Christianity is not so much a body of doctrine as the revelation of a mystery. A mystery is a divine action, something which God does in time in order to introduce men into the sanctuary of eternity. Being a religion of mysteries, Christianity is a religion of facts—divine facts, divine actions.

In celebrating the mysteries of Christ as they recur in time, the Church first of all announces these events: "Christ is born!" "Christ is risen!" She proclaims them, as a herald proclaims the triumphal entrance of a victorious King into a city. Her announcement, her proclamation of the divine event, is a work which she entrusts to her "heralds," her apostles, her preachers. Christianity is thus essentially kerygmatic: the priest is a herald, *kerux*, an angel of the Lord of Hosts, a voice crying out in the desert: "Make straight the ways of the Lord."

The following lines are a proclamation, a *kerygma*, of the nativity of the Son of God, Our Lord and Savior Jesus Christ. They announce the fact of his birth. They proclaim the presence of His mystery among us *now*, this year. They say, as the Church also says in her liturgy, "This day, Christ is born: this day the Savior has appeared: this day the angels sing on earth and the archangels rejoice: this day the just exult, saying: Glory to God in the highest, alleluia."

CHRIST IS BORN. He is born to *us*. And, He is born *today*. For Christmas is not merely a day like every other day. It is a day made holy and special by a sacred mystery. It is not merely another day in the weary round of time. Today, eternity enters into time, and time, sanctified, is caught up into eternity. Today, Christ, the Eternal Word of the Father, Who was in the beginning with the Father, in whom all things were made, by whom all things consist, enters into the world which He created in order to redeem His creatures who were ungrateful for so great a gift. Therefore, Holy Church exults, as the angels come down to announce not merely an old thing which happened long ago, but a new thing which happens today. For, today, God the Father makes all things new, in His Divine Son, our Redeemer, according to His words: *ecce nova facio omnia.*

531

Therefore, the Church on earth joins with the Church in heaven to sing one same song, the new song, the *canticum novum* which the Prophet commanded all to sing after the world should have been redeemed by the Christ, Whose ancestor he knew, by revelation, that he should be. When David cried out: "Sing unto the Lord a new song," he was thinking of the songs the Church would sing on this day in her liturgy, as she proclaims to the whole world the day of salvation and eternal bliss. For, as Saint Leo says: "Today there has shone upon us a day of new redemption, a day restoring that which was long lost, a day of bliss unending."

So, with the *Alleluia* of victory, the triumphant cry of Easter on her lips, the Church renews the mystery in which death is conquered, the power of the devil is broken forever, and sins are forgiven: the mystery of the death and resurrection of the Savior Who is born to us on this day. Today, the Church sings: *Dies sanctificatus illuxit nobis,* which means: A day of salvation, a day sanctified by mystery, a day full of divine and sanctifying power, has shone upon us. And she continues (let us see the whole text): "*Alleluia, Alleluia:* A sanctified day hath shone upon us: come ye gentiles and adore the Lord: for this day a great light hath descended upon the earth." The Church summons all the world to adoration as she prepares with great solemnity to announce the words of the Gospel in her third Mass. This is the Prologue of John, in which with mighty power given him from God, the greatest Evangelist proclaims that the Word, Who was in the beginning with God, is made flesh, and dwells among us full of grace and truth.

At Christmas, more than ever, it is fitting to remember that we have no other light but Christ, Who is born to us today. Let us reflect that He came down from heaven to be our light, and our life. He came, as He Himself assures us, to be our way, by which we may return to the Father, by which we may know Him, in the Father and ourselves in Him, that thus knowing and possessing Christ, we may have life everlasting with Him in the Father. "For this is eternal life, that they may know Thee, Father, the one True God, and Jesus Christ, whom thou has sent" and again "As many as received Him He gave them the power to be made the sons of God."

Having realized, once again, Who it is that comes to us, and having remembered that He alone is our light, let us hasten to receive Him and let us come together to celebrate the great mystery of charity which is the sacrament of our salvation and of our union in Christ. Let us receive Christ that we may in all truth be "light in the Lord" and that Christ may shine not only *to* us, but *through* us, and that we may all burn together in the sweet light of His presence in the world: I mean His presence in us, for we are His Body and His Holy Church.

As Saint Paul says (and we sing this in one or other of the Epistles today): "In these days, God hath spoken to us in His Son, Whom He hath appointed heir of all things, by Whom also He made the world: Who being the brightness of His glory and the figure of His substance, and upholding all things by the word of His power, making purgation of sins, sitteth on the right hand of the majesty." And in another place the same Apostle says: "God who commanded the light to shine out of darkness hath shined in our hearts, to give the light of the glory of God in the face of Christ Jesus."

Christ, light of light, is born today, and since He is born to us, He is born in us, and, therefore, we also are born today. That is to say, our souls are born to new life and new light, by receiving Him Who is the Truth. For Christ, invisible in His own nature, has become visible in our nature. What else can this mean, except that, first, He has become visible as man, and secondly, He has become visible in His Church? In other words, He wills to be visible in us, and to live in us, and work in us, and save us through His secret action in our own hearts and the hearts of our brothers. So, we must receive the light of the newborn Savior by faith, in order to manifest it by our witness and by the works of our charity towards one another.

These two things, this witness and this charity, are united together in the greatest of all our acts of worship in which we celebrate together the divine mysteries, thus proclaiming our faith, and receiving into our midst Him Who is the fountainhead of our faith as well as its object, and giving Him, as it were, to one another, in the fraternal charity which unites us in the bonds of peace. For after Christ has been born in our hearts, He reaches out to Himself in the heart of our brother by the love of His own Spirit, and binding Himself, as He is in us, with Himself, as He is in our brother, He restores us, in that same Holy Spirit, to the embrace of the heavenly Father.

We are born today in Christ, to this embrace and to this peace. Can it be surprising that we feel in our hearts the exultation of the divine light which streams into our spirit from the presence of the newborn Savior and transforms us from glory to glory in His image?

This is the mystery of light which shines upon us today and which the Church everywhere proclaims in her sacred chants and texts. *Tu lumen, tu splendor Patris* she sings at Lauds, not only addressing Him

Who is before her mystically, but also pouring forth the light and
splendor of God that radiates from Him within her own heart. And
notice, this splendor does indeed shine in the heart of every one of us
who has received Baptism, the Sacrament of light. It shines more
brightly in all of us who have come from the altar of God where we
have been inebriated with the fire of the Holy Spirit, filling the sacred
chalice, and blinded by the glorious light from the most blessed Body
of the Savior Whom we have received into our hearts. Indeed, the
chalice of salvation has come to us overflowing with divine fire and the
Body of the Lord has burned away the darkness and impurity of worldliness that kept us from seeing the One Who dwells in the midst of
us, though so often we know Him not. "Our God is a consuming fire."
Therefore, in her various orations, the Church prays in the following
words: "O God, Who hast made this most holy night to shine forth
with the brightness of the true light, grant we beseech thee that we may
enjoy His happiness in heaven, the mystery of whose light we have
known on earth. . . . Grant that we who are bathed in the new light
of Thy Word made flesh, may show forth in our actions that which by
faith shineth in our minds. . . . Grant of thy bountiful grace that
through this sacred communion in mystery (*haec sacrosancta com-
mercia*), we may be found conformed to Him in whom our substance is
united to Thee. . . . May our gifts, we beseech Thee, O Lord, be
agreeable to the mysteries of this day's Nativity, and ever pour down
upon us peace: that even as He Who was born Man shone forth also
as God, so these earthly fruits may bestow upon us that which is
divine."

In all these prayers, the Church plunges us into the Light of God
shining in the darkness of the world, in order that we may be illuminated and transformed in the presence of the newborn Savior, and thus
that He may be born and truly live in us by making all our thoughts
and actions light in Himself. What joy, then, that He who dwells
eternally in the inaccessible light and peace of the Father has left the
throne of His glory and descended to be one of us! Or rather, without
leaving the bosom of the Father, veiling the too brilliant light of His
glory in the cloud of human nature, He who is enthroned above the
cherubim takes up His abode among us in a poor manger. This Child
whom the shepherds, dazzled by the brilliance of the angelic host, can
scarcely see in the darkness of the cave lit by Joseph's lantern, this
Child is (by His divinity) the Ancient of Days, the Creator and Judge
of Heaven and earth, of Whom the prophet Daniel wrote: "I beheld

till thrones were placed and the Ancient of Days sat, His garment was as white as snow, and the hair of His head like clean wool; His throne like flames of fire: the wheels of it like burning fire. A swift stream of fire issued forth before Him: thousands of thousands ministered to Him and ten thousand times a hundred thousand stood before Him." This, indeed, is the vision of the divinity of the Word Who, in His human nature, lies here helpless in the dark. But the Son of Man, who is here born, is Himself the Word, consubstantial with the Father. To this only-begotten Son, Who is equal to the Father in all things as God, but less than the Father in so far as He is man, all power is given by the Father. So, Daniel says again: "I beheld therefore in the vision of the night, and lo one like the Son of Man came with the clouds of heaven, and he came even to the Ancient of Days and they presented Him before Him, and He gave Him power and glory and a kingdom, and all peoples, tribes and tongues shall serve Him, His power is an everlasting power that shall not be taken away and His kingdom that shall not be destroyed." This, then, is the King promised from the beginning of the world and of whose Kingdom there shall be no end.

Do not be afraid of Him. God has emptied Himself and come to us as a child, in order that we who have not been saved by fear, but only destroyed by it, may now take heart and be saved by confidence. In "emptying Himself" and taking the form of a servant that is human nature, the Lord laid aside His majesty and His divine power, in order to dwell among us with all His divine goodness and mercy. Hear what the Fathers say: "The power of God had appeared before in the creation of the world, and His wisdom in the government of that which He had created: but the kindness of His mercy now appears most clearly of all in His humanity. He had made Himself known to the Jews in signs and wonders. . . . But the Jews were crushed by His power and the philosophers who sought impudently to penetrate secrets of His majesty were blinded by His glory." These are the words of Saint Bernard. Neither power nor glory, then, can save us: for if the power and glory of God reveal themselves to our naked eye, we will be blinded by their light and consumed by their fire. What, then, can be done? Saint Bernard cries, as the Church, too, cries out from age to age: "Let Thy goodness then appear, O Lord, that man, who is created in Thy image, may be conformed to it." *Appareat Domine bonitas, cui possit homo qui ad imaginem tuam creatus est, conformari.*

We have seen that God has indeed answered this prayer, for all His goodness and all His love and all His mercy, which we were unable to see in the fearful storm upon Sinai or in the desert whirlwind that punished sinners, in the time of Moses, all the gentleness of the great God has appeared to us in Christ. *Apparuit benignitas et humanitas salvatoris nostri Dei!*

The Child that lies in the manger, helpless and abandoned to the love of His creatures, dependent entirely upon them to be fed and clothed and sustained, remains the Creator and Ruler of the universe. Yet, in this human nature of His, He wills to be helpless, and truly so. For here is no mere matter of appearances. The poverty of the Child and of His mother, their loneliness and dereliction at Bethlehem, their need for food and clothing and support, these are all as real as our own needs and our own limitations. And why? Above all, because of the reality of His love. He has embraced our poverty and our sorrow out of love for us, in order to give us His riches and His joy. And He has become as poor as the poorest of us, that no man may be held back from Him by fear. For, the love with which this divine Child loves us is truly the love of a man-child, but also, and just as truly, the love of our Savior and of our God. The arms with which He embraces us are not strong enough to harm any man, though they are the arms of God. What could be more evident than that God, Who loves us, and Who hates nothing that He has made, does not desire to hurt us? Can God will anything but our good? No, it is we who plunge at our own destruction by flying from His love.

Let us, then, in the words of the Apostle, "deny ungodliness and worldly desires and live soberly, justly and godly in this world, looking for the blessed hope and coming of the great God and our Savior, Jesus Christ: Who gave Himself for us that He might redeem us from all iniquity and might cleanse to Himself a people acceptable, a pursuer of good works." But Saint Paul speaks here of another coming of the Lord, at the Last Judgment: for the Church would have us remember that without the consummation of Christ's work on earth, its beginning would have no meaning. The Sacred Body which the Savior of the world took to Himself in the womb of the Virgin Mother has risen from death and reigns over heaven and earth, enthroned at the right hand of the Father. The Child whom we contemplate in mystery this day lives in fact in the bosom of the Father, where He is ever begotten anew in the "day" of eternity, and where He governs the course of the world and of men's lives with omnipotent mercy. He Who is at once a Child and a King, and an Infant and the Ancient of Days, looks with calm eyes upon the future day in which He shall give our flesh its share in His final victory over death. In that day, He who was once born to earth and time in a mortal Body will clothe our mortality with incorruption. For "the trumpet shall sound and the dead shall rise again incorruptible and we shall be changed." For God became man in order that men might become gods.

If we wish to see Christ in His glory, we must recognize Him now in His humility. If we wish His light to shine on our darkness and His immortality to clothe our mortality, we must suffer with Him on earth in order to be crowned with Him in Paradise. If we desire His love to transform us from glory to glory into His perfect likeness, we must love one another as He has loved us, and we must take our places at that blessed table where He Himself becomes our food, setting before us the Living Bread, the Manna which is sent to us from heaven, this day, to be the Life of the World.

Jesus, Who has come to nourish our spirit with His own Body and Blood, does so not to be transformed into us, but in order to transform us into Himself. He has given Himself to us in order that we may belong to Him. For the center of this great mystery is the Eternal Father's design to re-establish all things in Christ. This, says Saint Paul, is the "Mystery of His will . . . in the dispensation of the fullness of times, to reestablish all things in Christ, that are in heaven and on earth."

This Child and Redeemer Who comes amid the songs of angels to answer the prayers of all the Patriarchs and Prophets, and to satisfy the unrecognized longings of the whole lineage of Adam, exiled from Paradise, comes also to quiet the groanings of all creation. For the whole world has been in labor and in mourning since the fall of man. The whole created universe, with all its manifold beauty and splendor, has travailed in disorder longing for the birth of a Savior. "Every creature groaneth and travaileth in pain even until now . . . for the expectation of the creature waiteth for the revelation of the sons of God."

The Patriarchs and Prophets prayed for the coming of Christ in Bethlehem, and this first coming did not silence the groanings of creation. For, according to the words of the Apostle, which we have just heard, while man waited for the birth of Jesus in Judaea, the rest of the universe still waits for the revelation of Christ in His Church.

The mystery of Christmas, therefore, lays upon us all a debt and an obligation to the rest of men and to the whole created universe. We who have seen the light of Christ are obliged, by the greatness of the grace that has been given us, to make known the presence of the Savior to the ends of the earth. This we will do not only by preaching the glad tidings of His coming, but above all by revealing Him in our lives. Christ is born to us today, O my brothers, in order that He may appear to the gentiles through us. This one day is the day of His birth, but every day of our mortal lives must be His manifestation, His divine Epiphany, in the world which He has created and redeemed.

NATIVITY KERYGMA

Eight: THE WINE OF NEW LIFE

THOSE WHO DWELL in the power of the Communion of Saints are those whom the Lord has "hidden in His tent from the wrangling of tongues." [1] I am not here talking of exterior silence or of a vocation to an enclosed Order, but of the interior silence of the mystic, in no matter what walk of life he may happen to find himself, for it may happen, and it should happen, that even one who has to preach and teach should remain protected from the inanity of vain speech, should keep His heart a sacred sanctuary for the word of God, hidden in the urn of contemplation like manna in the Ark. There is more than meets the eye in this Mystery which the Psalmist speaks of as the "wrangling of tongues."

The "wrangling of tongues" symbolizes the confusion that was sent down by God upon the builders of Babel, who, seeking to scale heaven with a structure of their own devising, were darkened and scattered in a division of tongues. [2] Babylon, the city of division, the city of those who "love themselves unto the hatred of God," [3] was born in a curse of tongues; and the Church, the City of union, the City of those who love God unto hatred of themselves was born of the gift of tongues. The Holy Ghost was poured out at Pentecost in tongues of flame, and made the Apostles speak in all languages in order that men might be drawn back into union and that the division, laid open at Babel, might be closed again and healed in Christ and in His peace. For there is only one language spoken in the City of God. That language is charity. Those who speak it best, speak it in silence. For the eternal Word of Truth is uttered in silence. If He is uttered in silence, He must be heard in deepest silence. And His Spirit, the Spirit of Love, is also poured out into our hearts, proceeding from the Father and the Son, in an everlasting silence.

The Psalms are more than language. They contain within themselves the silence of high mountains and the silence of heaven. It is only when we stand at the bottom of the mountain that it is hard for us to distinguish the language of the Psalter from the tongues of this earth: for Christ must still perforce travel among us as a pilgrim disguised in our own tattered garments. The Psalter only truly begins to speak and sing within us when we have been led by God and lifted up by Him, and have ascended into its silences. When this is done, the Psalms themselves become the Tabernacle of God in which we are protected forever from the rage of the city of business, from the racket of human opinions, from the wild carnival we carry in our hearts and which the ancient saints called "Babylon."

The Liturgy of Heaven is a most perfect harmony which, like the music of the spheres, sees song transfigured into silence. The Psalter is the prelude to that Liturgy. A prelude is a real beginning. We who chant the Psalms are standing in the courts of Heaven. That, indeed, is our chosen testimony. It is the Christian vocation: to begin on earth the life and Liturgy of Heaven. St. John in his Apocalypse describes the songs of the four-and-twenty elders and of the blessed spirits. Their Liturgy is full of echoes of the Psalter. Theirs are the same themes for theirs is the perfect liberty which the Psalms foreshadow. They sing of the great mercy of God their liberator, and in doing so they burn with glory because they see and love Him as He really is. We have already entered with them, but obscurely, into this Mystery. We have tasted the wine of their wedding feast paid out to us in droplets in moments of our own earthly Liturgy.

The wine of the Psalter and the wine of Heaven are the same, and they are ours, because whether in Heaven or on earth there is only one chalice, and that chalice itself is Heaven. It is the cup Jesus gave to His Disciples on the night when He said to them: "With desire have I desired to eat this Pasch with you." [4] There is one Mystery in the Kingdom of heaven, which is the light of the Kingdom, replacing the sun, moon and stars. It is the light also of the Psalter and of the Church on earth, though it shine in darkness. Its light is wine. It was of this wine that Jesus said: "I shall not drink the fruit of this vine again until I drink it with you now in the Kingdom of my Father." [5] He had just chanted the Psalms of the *Hallel* with His Apostles. He knew His Blood would flow like silence through our Psalter.

THE SPIRIT OF GOD, pouring out the charity of God in our hearts, makes us love the sanctity of God. He makes us reach out to receive the gift of holiness which is offered to us in Christ by The Father's infinite mercy. The deep fire of prayer which burns in the heart of the Psalter is therefore a fire of sacrifice, the same fire which consumed the Heart of Jesus Himself and brought Him to the Cross for us, and brings us gladly and triumphantly down into the gates of death for love of Him. This love, this chaste and selfless passion that drives us out into the desert, seeking holiness in the renunciation of all things, this is the key to the understanding of the Psalter because it is itself the fulfillment of the Psalter.

St. Paul says that love is the fulfillment of the Law. Now the Old Law as a whole is a type or figure of the New. The "spiritual meaning" of the Old Law is therefore to be sought in the charity which is the very substance of the New Testament. St. Thomas points out that the New Law is something more than a written document. It is grace itself living and acting in the hearts of the faithful. It is the Holy Spirit, present in the souls of those who have died together with Christ and have risen with Him from the dead. The Angelic Doctor quotes St. Augustine, who says: "The Laws of God, written in our hearts, are nothing else but the presence of the Holy Spirit in us." [6]

Hence we may dare to say that charity, not as a pale abstraction but as the flame breathed through our being by the presence and action of the Holy Spirit, alone enables us to plumb the depths of the "spiritual sense" of Scripture. What is hidden beneath the literal meaning is not merely another and more hidden *meaning*, it is also a new and totally different *reality*: it is the divine life itself. This "meaning" of Scripture is never grasped if it is merely "known." It must be possessed and lived. God is not fully known when He is only "known" by the understanding. He is best known by us when He takes possession of our whole being and unites us to Himself. Then we know Him not in an idea but beyond ideas, in a contact of love, in an experience of Who He is, in a realization that He and He alone is our life and that without Him we are nothing. It is our joy to be nothing, and to know that He is all.

St. Augustine long ago brought out this aspect of the distinction between "letter and spirit." He knew that Paul's phrase: "the letter killeth but the spirit giveth life," was intended to tell us more than the obvious truth that some passages of Scripture had a figurative or typical sense. The "letter" kills us not only by tempting us to miss a meaning. Even when the meaning (whether literal or spiritual) is abundantly clear, even when we fully grasp its implications, it "kills" us if we get no further than *knowledge* of what it means.

The Law tells us: "thou shalt not covet." No hidden sense here. The literal meaning is plain enough. Selfish desires are the root of all evil. But, says St. Augustine: to know this truth without conforming our lives to the commandments not to covet, is to be *killed*, by that commandment. If we had never known our responsibility we could not have been held guilty for not living up to it. In order to fulfill the law, we must be dead to the kind of life which the law intends to kill, and live by the new life which the law sets before us. This is a matter not of knowledge but of love. Everyone knows the ten commandments. Few keep them, because few love them. Men do not love the law of God because they cherish a contrary love, a contrary law, in their flesh, which defeats and denies the law of God. Knowing His law, they still fall short of knowing it, because they only possess the wisdom of the flesh, which cannot be subject to the law of God. It is foredoomed to rebel against Him because it has refused, in advance, to love Him.

The law was given by God to manifest the living death of sin, not to cure it. St. Augustine's tract *"De Spiritu et Littera"* is therefore not a treatise on the senses of the Scripture but on the law and on Grace. Yet it has most interesting implications for the meaning of Scripture, because charity is the fulfillment of the Law. The Law can only be understood when it is kept. It cannot be kept unless God drives out the contrary law, the law of selfishness, of cupidity, and infuses into our hearts His selfless charity. Without grace, the "letter" of the Law, the truth of the Law, serves only to condemn us, because even though we understand it we do not keep it. But the "spirit," grace, fills us with charity, gives us the power to love what the Law tells us. Loving the truth, we are able to live by the truth. When we live by the truth our lives themselves become true. We become what we ought to be. We not only exist, we *live*. We not only hear the word, we keep it, and therefore we *fulfill* it. We live in God. God lives in us. His will is done in us. He is manifested in us. He is glorified in us. This was not possible until He sent His Son to be a propitiation for our sins. St. Augustine says:

Where the Holy Spirit does not help us, inspiring us with good desires to replace evil desires, that is to say pouring out Charity in our hearts, it is evident that the Law, good as it may be, by its very prohibition only intensifies our evil desires.[7]

Without the Holy Spirit we can admire the goodness of God and

His truth. We can even attempt to see Him. But a love that is not inspired and directed by His Spirit misses its aim, even though it be aimed at Him: for only God can reach God. That is why He sent us His Son, to be the "way." We must then receive His Holy Spirit, the Spirit of Jesus, Who will lead us to God by the power of a secret and spiritual delight in the things of God, by a taste for the hidden truth of God, by love that finds Him in the mystery of a presence that is only secret because it is too blinding in its obviousness to be seen by us. *Accipiat homo Spiritum sanctum quo fiat in animo ejus delectatio dilectioque summi atque incommutabilis boni quod Deus est.*[8]

The outpouring of the Spirit is the fulfillment of the Law the Psalms and the Prophets. When Jesus appeared to His disciples in the cenacle after His resurrection, He told them that it was "necessary for all things to be fulfilled which are written in the Law of Moses and in the Prophets and in the Psalms concerning me." [9] Then he "opened their understanding" and showed them the "spiritual meaning" of the Scriptures—as well as the letter. What was this fulfillment? Not only the death and Resurrection of Jesus—these were ordered to something else, to His life in us. It was therefore written not only that Christ should "suffer and rise again from the dead the third day" but also that great effects should follow from these things: "that penance and remission of sins should be preached in His name unto all nations beginning at Jerusalem." The charity of the Saints is the fulfillment of the Scriptures. The outpouring of the Holy Spirit makes this a fact, and enables those in whom He acts to understand what has happened. "And you are witnesses of these things. And I send the promise of my Father (the Holy Spirit) upon you: stay you in the city until you be endued with power from on high." [10]

We who chant the Psalms, hope to praise God. We praise Him best if we understand the things we sing. We understand them if we, too, are "endued with power from on high." When the Spirit of Divine Love sets our souls on fire with charity we realize, at last, that it is not necessary for us to scale heaven to bring down Christ to us by some mysterious technique of contemplation. The Liturgy does not have to bring Christ from heaven. It is the manifestation of His presence and His power on earth. It does not have to prepare our hearts for a future Kingdom. It tells us that His Kingdom has already come. *Regnum Dei intra vos est.* It is established in full power in the midst of a godless humanity. Heaven is within us and all around us, even though we seem to be living in hell.

The Psalms are the language of His Kingdom. They were spoken by prophets to those who were able to understand them centuries before the Kingdom was established. They were sung as they were fulfilled by the Saviour as He hung on the Cross, so that the voice of the Psalms is the voice of Christ Himself. He lives in us, being both the Kingdom and its King. And we, when we take His words upon our lips, speak not our thoughts but His, provided that the Spirt of His promise lives in our own spirit and is the inspiration of our own song.

Therefore, when a Christian chants the Office, if he is fully a Christian, that is to say if he is one who has attained to the knowledge of Christ, who has experienced what it means to live in the great mystery of Christ, who longs to see all things restored in Christ, then he not only understands the Psalms, but he *fulfills* them. The deep contemplative penetration of the Psalms is only achieved by their fulfillment. It is the realization of their fulfillment in us. It shows us our own place in the Mystery of Christ, and our own vocation, to make up what is wanting to His sufferings in our own moment of history. But the Psalms are the songs of eternity since His Kingdom is the Kingdom that will never end. In the simultaneous totality of possession, which is what eternity means, the Psalms reach out to possess the reward together with the suffering, the victory in the midst of the battle. We have only begun to fight, and yet if we believe in Him Who overcomes the world, we have already won. "For whatsoever is born of God overcomes the world: and this is the victory which overcomes the world, our faith." [11]

Laws, rules, and methods are for those who seek to get something for themselves. They therefore savor of this earth and of its slavery, although they are necessary even for those who would begin to be children of the kingdom. But after all, it is not by seeking to "get something out of the Psalms" that we will finally arrive at an understanding of the Psalter or of our Canonical Office. Although the Psalms are given us for our benefit it is not enough to think only of our own benefit: they are first of all for the glory of God. God is glorified most in those who have given up everything for Him and have found everything in Him. The Psalms profit us most when they give God most Glory. This they do when we realize that the Liturgy is not a search for something we have not, but the celebration of what we already have.

The Psalms are the new song, the *canticum novum*, the song of those who have been reborn in a new creation, the song of those for whom there is no law, because in them Christ has fulfilled the Law.

How, then, should the Psalms offer them a method, a technique, that is to say a "law" of contemplation? The true meaning of the Psalms is most fully apprehended by those who have been swept, by an experience of God's mercy, beyond the reach of any rule or any method. The new song of the Psalms is the song of God's children who live by no other rule than God their Father, Who is His own Rule. He is also therefore theirs. His love is their Law. They always do what is pleasing Him. Thus for them there is no law, not because the law has been abrogated but because it has been perfectly fulfilled.

[1] Psalm, 30:21.
[2] Genesis, 11:7.
[3] St. Augustine: *De Civitate Dei*, XIV, 28.
[4] Luke, 22:15.
[5] Matthew, 26:29.
[6] I IIae. Q.106. A.1. and St. Augustine, *De Spiritu et Littera*, 26.
[7] *De Spiritu et Littera*, Chapter iv.
[8] *Ibid.*, Chapter iii.
[9] Luke, 24:44.
[10] Luke, 24:48-49.
[11] I John, 5:4.

BREAD IN THE WILDERNESS

Nine: THE GENERAL DANCE

THE Lord made His world not in order to judge it, not in order merely to dominate it, to make it obey the dictates of an inscrutable and all-powerful will, not in order to find pleasure or displeasure in the way it worked; such was not the reason for creation either of the world or of man.

The Lord made the world and made man in order that He Himself might descend into the world, that He Himself might become Man. When He regarded the world He was about to make He saw His wisdom, as a man-child, "playing in the world, playing before Him at all times." And He reflected, "my delights are to be with the children of men."

The world was not made as a prison for fallen spirits who were rejected by God: this is the gnostic error. The world was made a temple, a paradise, into which God Himself would descend to dwell familiarly with the spirits He had placed there to tend it for Him.

The early chapters of Genesis (far from being a pseudo-scientific account of the way the world was supposed to have come into being) are precisely a poetic and symbolic revelation, a completely *true,* though not literal, revelation of God's view of the universe and of His intentions for man. The point of these beautiful chapters is that God made the world as a garden in which He himself took delight. He made man and gave to man the task of sharing in His own divine care for created things. He made man in His own image and likeness, as an artist, a worker, *homo faber,* as the gardener of paradise. He let man decide for himself how created things were to be interpreted, understood, and used: for Adam gave the animals their names (God gave them no names at all) and what names Adam gave them, that they were. Thus in his intelligence man, by the act of knowing, imitated something of the creative love of God for creatures. While the love of God, looking upon things, brought them into being, the love of man, looking upon things, reproduced the divine idea, the divine truth, in man's own spirit.

As God creates things by seeing them in His own Logos, man brings truth to life in his mind by the marriage of the divine light, in the being of the object, with the divine light in his own reason. The meeting of these two lights in one mind is truth.

But there is a higher light still, not the light by which man "gives names" and forms concepts, with the aid of the active intelligence, but the dark light in which no names are given, in which God confronts man not through the medium of things, but in His own simplicity. The union of the simple light of God with the simple light of man's spirit, in love, is contemplation. The two simplicities are one. They form, as it were, an emptiness in which there is no addition but rather the taking away of names, of forms, of content, of subject matter, of identities. In this meeting there is not so much a fusion of identities as a disappearance of identities. The Bible speaks of this very simply: "In the breeze after noon God came to walk with Adam in paradise." It is after noon, in the declining light of created day. In the free emptiness of the breeze that blows from where it pleases and goes where no one can estimate, God and man are together, not speaking in words, or syllables or forms. And that was the meaning of creation and of Paradise. But there was more.

The Word of God Himself was the "firstborn of every creature." He "in Whom all things consist" was not only to walk with man in the breeze after noon, but would also become Man, and dwell with man as a brother.

The Lord would not only love His creation as a Father, but He would enter into His creation, emptying Himself, hiding Himself, as if He were not God but a creature. Why should He do this? Because He loved His creatures, and because He could not bear that His creatures should merely adore Him as distant, remote, transcendent, and all powerful. This was not the glory that He sought, for if He were merely adored as great, His creatures would in their turn make themselves great and lord it over one another. For where there is a great God, then there are also godlike men, who make themselves kings and masters. And if God were merely a great artist who took pride in His creation, then men too would build cities and palaces and exploit other men for their own glory. This is the meaning of the myth of Babel, and of the tower builders who would be "as Gods" with their hanging gardens, and with the heads of their enemies hanging in the gardens. For they would point to God and say: "He too is a great builder, and has destroyed all His enemies."

(God said: I do not laugh at my enemies, because I wish to make it impossible for anyone to be my enemy. Therefore I identify myself with my enemy's own secret self.)

So God became man. He took on the weakness and ordinariness of man, and He hid Himself, becoming an anonymous and unimportant man in a very unimportant place. And He refused at any time to Lord it over men, or to be a King, or to be a Leader, or to be a Reformer, or to be in any way Superior to His own creatures. He would be nothing else but their brother, and their counselor, and their servant, and their friend. He was in no accepted human sense an important person, though since that time we have made Him The Most Important Person. That is another matter: for though it is quite true that He is the King and Lord of all, the conqueror of death, the judge of the living and of the dead, the *Pantokrator*, yet He is also still the Son of Man, the hidden one, unknown, unremarkable, vulnerable. He can be killed. And when the Son of Man was put to death, He rose again from the dead, and was again with us, for He said: "Kill me, it does not matter."

Having died, He dies no more in His own Person. But because He became man and united man's nature to Himself, and died for man, and rose as man from the dead, He brought it about that the sufferings of all men became His own sufferings; their weakness and defenselessness became His weakness and defenselessness; their insignificance became His. But at the same time His own power, immortality, glory, and happiness were given to them and could become theirs. So if the God-Man is still great, it is rather for our sakes than for His own that He wishes to be great and strong. For to Him, strength and weakness, life and death are dualities with which He is not concerned, being above them in His transcendent unity. Yet He would raise us also above these dualities by making us one with Him. For though evil and death can touch the evanescent, outer self in which we dwell estranged from Him, in which we are alienated and exiled in unreality, it can never touch the real inner self in which we have been made one with Him. For in becoming man, God became not only Jesus Christ but also potentially every man and woman that ever existed. In Christ, God became not only "this" man, but also, in a broader and more mystical sense, yet no less truly, "every man."

THE PRESENCE of God in His world as its Creator depends on no one but Him. His presence in the world as Man depends, in some measure, upon men. Not that we can do anything to change the mystery of the Incarnation in itself: but we are able to decide whether we ourselves, and that portion of the world which is ours, shall become *aware* of His presence, consecrated by it, and transfigured in its light.

We have the choice of two identities: the external mask which seems to be real and which lives by a shadowy autonomy for the brief moment of earthly existence, and the hidden, inner person who seems to us to be nothing, but who can give himself eternally to the truth in whom he subsists. It is this inner self that is taken up into the mystery of Christ, by His love, by the Holy Spirit, so that in secret we live "in Christ."

YET we must not deal in too negative a fashion even with the "external self." This self is not by nature evil, and the fact that it is unsubstantial is not to be imputed to it as some kind of crime. It is afflicted with metaphysical poverty: but all that is poor deserves mercy. So too our outward self: as long as it does not isolate itself in a lie, it is blessed by the mercy and the love of Christ. Appearances are to be accepted for what they are. The accidents of a poor and transient existence have, nevertheless, an ineffable value. They can be transparent media in which we apprehend the presence of God in the world. It is possible to speak of the exterior self as a mask: to do so is not necessarily to reprove it. The mask that each man wears may well be a disguise not only for that man's inner self but for God, wandering as a pilgrim and exile in His own creation.

And indeed, if Christ became Man, it is because He wanted to be any man and every man. If we believe in the Incarnation of the Son of God, there should be no one on earth in whom we are not prepared to see, in mystery, the presence of Christ.

WHAT IS SERIOUS to men is often very trivial in the sight of God. What in God might appear to us as "play" is perhaps what He Himself takes most seriously. At any rate the Lord plays and diverts Himself in the garden of His creation, and if we could let go of our own obsession with what we think is the meaning of it all, we might be able to hear His call and follow Him in His mysterious, cosmic dance. We do not have to go very far to catch echoes of that game, and of that dancing. When we are alone on a starlit night; when by chance we see the migrating birds in autumn descending on a grove of junipers to rest and eat; when we see children in a moment when they are really children; when we know love in our own hearts; or when, like the Japanese poet Bashō we hear an old frog land in a quiet pond with a solitary splash—at such times the awakening, the turning inside out of all values, the "newness," the emptiness and the purity of vision that make themselves evident, provide a glimpse of the cosmic dance.

For the world and time are the dance of the Lord in emptiness. The silence of the spheres is the music of a wedding feast. The more we persist in misunderstanding the phenomena of life, the more we analyze them out into strange finalities and complex purposes of our own, the more we involve ourselves in sadness, absurdity, and despair. But it does not matter much, because no despair of ours can alter the reality of things, or stain the joy of the cosmic dance which is always there. Indeed, we are in the midst of it, and it is in the midst of us, for it beats in our very blood, whether we want it to or not.

Yet the fact remains that we are invited to forget ourselves on purpose, cast our awful solemnity to the winds, and join in the general dance.

NEW SEEDS OF CONTEMPLATION

Epilogue: MEDITATIO PAUPERIS IN SOLITUDINE

Day unto day uttereth speech. The clouds change. The seasons pass over our woods and fields in their slow and regular procession, and time is gone before you are aware of it.

Before we were born, God knew us. He knew that some of us would rebel against His love and His mercy, and that others would love Him from the moment that they could love anything, and never change that love. He knew that there would be joy in heaven among the angels of His house for the conversion of some of us, and He knew that He would bring us all here to Gethsemani together, one day, for His own purpose, for the praise of His love.

The life of each one in this abbey is part of a mystery. We all add up to something far beyond ourselves. We cannot yet realize what it is. But we know, in the language of our theology, that we are all members of the Mystical Christ, and that we all grow together in Him for Whom all things were created.

In one sense we are always traveling, and traveling as if we did not know where we were going.

In another sense we have already arrived.

We cannot arrive at the perfect possession of God in this life, and that is why we are traveling and in darkness. But we already possess Him by grace, and therefore in that sense we have arrived and are dwelling in the light.

But oh! How far have I to go to find You in Whom I have already arrived!

For now, oh my God, it is to You alone that I can talk, because nobody else will understand. I cannot bring any other man on this earth into the cloud where I dwell in Your light, that is, Your darkness, where I am lost and abashed. I cannot explain to any other man the anguish which is Your joy nor the loss which is the Possession of You, nor the distance from all things which is the arrival in You, nor the death which is the birth in You because I do not know anything about it myself and all I know is that I wish it were over—I wish it were begun.

You have contradicted everything. You have left me in no man's land.

You have called me here not to wear a label by which I can recognize myself and place myself in some kind of a category. You do not want me to be thinking about what I am, but about what You are. Or rather, You do not even want me to be thinking about anything much: for You would raise me above the level of thought. And if I am always trying to figure out what I am and where I am and why I am, how will that work be done?

I do not make a big drama of this business. I do not say: "You have asked me for everything, and I have renounced all." Because I no longer desire to see anything that implies a distance between You and me: and if I stand back and consider myself and You as if something had passed between us, from me to You, I will inevitably see the gap between us and remember the distance between us.

My God, it is that gap and that distance which kill me.

That is the only reason why I desire solitude—to be lost to all created things, to die to them and to the knowledge of them, for they remind me of my distance from You. They tell me something about You: that You are far from them, even though You are in them. You have made them and Your presence sustains their being, and they hide You from me. And I would live alone, and out of them. O *beata solitudo!*

For I knew that it was only by leaving them that I could come to You: and that is why I have been so unhappy when You seemed to be condemning me to remain in them. Now my sorrow is over, and my joy is about to begin: the joy that rejoices in the deepest sorrows. For I am beginning to understand. You have taught me, and have consoled me, and I have begun again to hope and learn.

I hear You saying to me:

"*I will give you what you desire. I will lead you into solitude. I will lead you by the way that you cannot possibly understand, because I want it to be the quickest way.*

"*Therefore all the things around you will be armed against you, to deny you, to hurt you, to give you pain, and therefore to reduce you to solitude.*

"*Because of their enmity, you will soon be left alone. They will cast you out and forsake you and reject you and you will be alone.*

"*Everything that touches you shall burn you, and you will draw your hand away in pain, until you have withdrawn yourself from all things. Then you will be alone.*

"*Everything that can be desired will sear you, and brand you with a cautery, and you will fly from it in pain, to be alone. Every created joy will only come to you as pain, and you will die to all joy and be left alone. All the good things that other people love and desire and seek will come to you, but only as murderers to cut you off from the world and its occupations.*

"*You will be praised, and it will be like burning at the stake. You will be loved, and it will murder your heart and drive you into the desert.*

"*You will have gifts, and they will break you with their burden. You will have pleasures of prayer, and they will sicken you and you will fly from them.*

"*And when you have been praised a little and loved a little I will take away all your gifts and all your love and all your praise and you will be utterly forgotten and abandoned and you will be nothing, a dead thing, a rejection. And in that day you shall begin to possess the solitude you have so long desired. And your solitude will bear immense fruit in the souls of men you will never see on earth.*

"*Do not ask when it will be or where it will be or how it will be: On a mountain or in a prison, in a desert or in a concentration camp or in a hospital or at Gethsemani. It does not matter. So do not ask me, because I am not going to tell you. You will not know until you are in it.*

"*But you shall taste the true solitude of my anguish and my poverty and I shall lead you into the high places of my joy and you shall die in Me and find all things in My mercy which has created you for this end and brought you from Prades to Bermuda to St. Antonin to Oakham to London to Cambridge to Rome to New York to Columbia to Corpus Christi to St. Bonaventure to the Cistercian Abbey of the poor men who labor in Gethsemani:*

"*That you may become the brother of God and learn to know the Christ of the burnt men.*"

SIT FINIS LIBRI, NON FINIS QUAERENDI

THE SEVEN STOREY MOUNTAIN